ANXIETY AND RELATED DISORDERS

Recent titles in the

Wiley Series on Personality Processes

Irving B. Weiner, *Editor*
University of South Florida

Anxiety and Related Disorders

A Handbook

Benjamin B. Wolman, Editor
George Stricker, Co-Editor

A WILEY-INTERSCIENCE PUBLICATION

JOHN WILEY & SONS, INC.

New York • Chichester • Brisbane • Toronto • Singapore

Library of Congress Cataloging in Publication Data:

Anxiety and related disorders : a handbook / Benjamin B. Wolman,
    editor ; George Stricker, co-editor.
        p.   cm.—(Wiley series on personality processes)
    Includes index
    ISBN 0-471-54773-5 (cloth : alk. paper)
    1. Anxiety. I. Wolman, Benjamin B.   II. Stricker, George.
III. Series.
    [DNLM: 1. Anxiety. 2. Anxiety Disorders.   WM 172 A63617 1994]
RC531.A573   1994
616.85'223—dc20
DNLM/DLC
for Library of Congress   93-925

Contributors

Dianne L. Chambless, PhD
Professor of Psychology and Director
Agoraphobia and Anxiety Program
The American University
Washington, DC

Roger D. Davis, MS
University Fellow
Department of Psychology
University of Miami
Miami, FL

Robert A. DiTomasso, PhD
Associate Director
Behavioral Medicine
West Jersey Health System
Tatem Brown Family Practice Center
Voorhees, NJ

Paul M.G. Emmelkamp, PhD
Professor of Clinical Psychology &
  Psychotherapy
Head, Department of Clinical
  Psychology
University of Groningen
Groningen, The Netherlands

Edna B. Foa, PhD
Professor of Psychiatry and Director
Center for Treatment and Study of
  Anxiety
Eastern Pennsylvania Psychiatric
  Institute
The Medical College of Pennsylvania
Philadelphia, PA

Arthur Freeman, EdD
Associate Professor of Psychology
University of Pennsylvania
Philadelphia, PA

Lawrence S. Gross, MD
Associate Professor of Clinical
  Psychiatry
University of Southern California
  School of Medicine
Los Angeles, CA

Elizabeth A. Hembree, PhD
Instructor, Department of
  Psychiatry
Eastern Pennsylvania Psychiatric
  Institute
Medical College of Pennsylvania
Philadelphia, PA

Jonathan M. Jackson, PhD
Director, Center for Psychological
  Services
The Gordon Derner Institute of
  Advanced Psychological Studies
Adelphi University
Garden City, NY

Lawrence Josephs, PhD
Associate Professor of Psychology
The Gordon Derner Institute of
  Advanced Psychological Studies
Adelphi University
Garden City, NY

Robert J. Kastenbaum, PhD
Professor of Communication
Arizona State University
Tempe, AZ

Michael J. Kozak, PhD
Associate Professor of Psychiatry
Eastern Pennsylvania Psychiatric
  Institute
Medical College of Pennsylvania
Philadelphia, PA

Beatrice J. Krauss, PhD
Senior Project Director
National Development and Research
  Institutes, Inc.
New York, NY

Herbert H. Krauss, PhD
Professor of Psychology and Chair
Hunter College of the City University
  of New York
Director of Research
International Center for the Disabled
New York, NY

Jeremy Leeds, PhD
Assistant Professor
Department of Applied Psychology
School of Education
New York University
New York, NY

Carol Lindemann, PhD
Private Practice
New York, NY

Karen L. Lombardi, PhD
Associate Professor of Psychology
The Gordon Derner Institute of
  Advanced Psychological Studies
Adelphi University
Garden City, NY

Alison M. Macdonald, BSc
Research Worker
Genetics Section
Institute of Psychiatry
University of London
London, England

Theodore Millon, PhD
Editor, *Journal of Personality
  Disorders*
Professor of Psychology
University of Miami
Coral Gables, FL

**Robin M. Murray, MD, DSC,
  FRCP, FRCPsych**
Professor and Chairman
Department of Psychological
  Medicine
King's College Hospital & Institute
  of Psychiatry
London, England

Robert M. Nagy, MD
Assistant Professor of Clinical
  Psychiatry
University of Southern California
  School of Medicine
Los Angeles, CA

Cory F. Newman, PhD
Clinical Director, Center for
  Cognitive Therapy
Department of Psychiatry, and
Assistant Professor of Psychology in
  Psychiatry
School of Medicine, University of
  Pennsylvania
Philadelphia, PA

Erwin Randolph Parson, PhD
Editor-in-Chief, *Journal of
  Contemporary Psychotherapy*
Perry Point, MD

Edmond H. Pi, MD
Professor of Clinical Psychiatry
University of Southern
    California
School of Medicine
Los Angeles, CA

Max Rosenbaum, PhD
Adjunct Professor
Nova University
Ft. Lauderdale, FL

Agnes Scholing, PhD
Assistant Professor
Department of Clinical Psychology
University of Groningen
Groningen, The Netherlands

Edward K. Silberman, MD
Clinical Professor of Psychiatry
Jefferson Medical College
Philadelphia, PA

K. Elaine Williams, PhD
Psychotherapist
Department of Psychology
Agoraphobia and Anxiety Program
The American University
Washington, DC

Benjamin B. Wolman, PhD
Editor-in-Chief, *International*
    Encyclopedia of Psychiatry,
    Psychology, Psychoanalysis and
    Neurology
Professor Emeritus of Psychology
Long Island University
Brooklyn, NY

Michael D. Zentman, PhD
Adjunct Assistant Clinical Professor
The Gordon Derner Institute of
    Advanced Psychological Studies
Adelphi University
Garden City, NY

Series Preface

This series of books is addressed to behavioral scientists interested in the nature of human personality. Its scope should prove pertinent to personality theorists and researchers as well as to clinicians concerned with applying an understanding of personality processes to the amelioration of emotional difficulties in living. To this end, the series provides a scholarly integration of theoretical formulations, empirical data, and practical recommendations.

Six major aspects of studying and learning about human personality can be designated: personality theory, personality structure and dynamics, personality development, personality assessment, personality change, and personality adjustment. In exploring these aspects of personality, the books in the series discuss a number of distinct but related subject areas: the nature and implications of various theories of personality; personality characteristics that account for consistencies and variations in human behavior; the emergence of personality processes in children and adolescents; the use of interviewing and testing procedures to evaluate individual differences in personality; efforts to modify personality styles through psychotherapy, counseling, behavior therapy, and other methods of influence; and patterns of abnormal personality functioning that impair individual competence.

IRVING B. WEINER

University of South Florida
Tampa, Florida

Preface

Fear is an alarm signal that motivates the organism either to fight against threats or to escape them by flight. Fears can be rational, when they are a reaction to a real danger, but often fears are irrational reactions to nonexisting dangers. Usually fears have a time limit; when help comes or the danger is over, the fear subsides.

Anxiety is not a reaction to any particular danger. *It is an endogenous feeling of helplessness and inadequacy.* Anxiety-ridden people expect horrible things to happen and doubt their ability to cope with them. Anxiety is a state of apprehension and worry, often associated with inability to cope with true or imaginary hardships.

Anxiety is one of the three major mental disturbances; the others are depression and stress. Almost all mental disorders are accompanied by anxiety symptoms.

Anxiety and Related Disorders: A Handbook offers a wealth of objective, thorough, and up-to-date knowledge. All major viewpoints are covered in the 21 chapters of the *Handbook*.

The *Handbook* is comprised of three parts. Part One describes theories and research, Part Two describes symptomatology, and Part Three deals with diagnostic and treatment methods. The *Handbook* is written on the highest scholarly level by leading experts. The *Handbook* will become a must for psychiatrists, psychologists, social workers, and libraries associated with universities, medical schools, and training centers for mental health professionals.

I am happy to express profound gratitude to my Co-Editor, Dr. George Stricker, and to Herb Reich, Senior Editor of John Wiley & Sons, for his unswerving, cordial, and most helpful guidance. I am very grateful to my research assistant Debra Duchin, for her loyal and efficient help and I am indebted to everyone who took part in working on this *Handbook*.

BENJAMIN B. WOLMAN

New York, New York
September 1993

Contents

PART TWO: SYMPTOMATOLOGY

PART THREE: DIAGNOSTIC AND TREATMENT METHODS

ANXIETY AND RELATED DISORDERS

PART ONE

Theories and Research

CHAPTER 1

Defining Anxiety

BENJAMIN B. WOLMAN, PhD

The issue of anxiety is analyzed in this chapter in the framework of *power and acceptance theory.* Power is defined as the ability to satisfy needs, and survival is the fundamental need. Acceptance is defined as the willingness to satisfy needs or prevent their satisfaction. Accordingly, people perceive themselves and others as *strong or weak* (power) and *friendly or hostile* (acceptance). The power and acceptance theory was developed in experimental research with small groups (London, 1977; Wolman, 1974). The theory of personality applied in this chapter is based on a psychoanalytic frame of reference with considerable modifications, somewhat related to the modifications of Hartmann, Kardiner, and Erikson.

Freud's concept of death instinct (Thanatos) was substituted by the concept of aggressiveness (Ares), and the concept of cathexis was modified to include interindividual cathexis. This part of Wolman's theory and its psychopathological corollaries have been developed in clinical settings (Wolman, 1992).

Depression and elation have been redefined in terms of one's evaluation of own power. Group morale has been redefined as a shared high estimate of the group's power. The responses to external and internal threats have been reexamined in terms of fear and anxiety, respectively. Fear was related to a (realistic or unrealistic) high estimate of the external threat, and the resulting overt behavior was necessarily an object-directed hostility (Wolman, 1978).

ANGER AND FEAR

Fight or flight are the most common reactions to a threat from without, but what kind of reaction to a threat will take place greatly depends on an estimate of one's own power in comparison to the power of the threatening person, animal, or inanimate nature.

Reaction to a threat involves several cognitive and emotional elements, among them anger and fear. Anger mobilizes the individual's resources against threatening forces. Anger expresses hostile feelings toward the source of threat and activates the wish to annihilate it.

The less chances one has for winning the fight against one's enemies, the more one hates them. The awareness of one's own weakness increases hatred. Anger increases the level of activity, and makes one feel stronger and more hopeful of overcoming the threat. If the enemy seems to be overpowering, the reaction to a threat is anger combined with fear.

Fear may produce two severe maladjustive behavioral patterns, both of a regressive nature:

1. *Mental paralysis.* Refraining from defensive or offensive goal-directed actions, daydreaming, and infantile hopes of help coming from benevolent powers. Passivity in the face of danger increases one's feeling of guilt.

2. *Disinhibition.* A state of emergency requires the mobilization of one's resources; such a mobilization enables one to cope with exogenous dangers. Disinhibition permits the id to take over and makes one act in an irresponsible way. Severe stress and emergency can and have led to sexual license, alcohol and drug abuse. In cases when the threat seems to be less powerful or less threatening than the powers at the disposal of the individual, the reaction is not fear but *anger.*

The relationship between these two emotions is important for our deliberations. Whenever an individual faces the threat of annihilation or damage or hurt and the threat is not too great to cope with, his or her reaction will be to fight, hoping that the outcome of the fight will be the destruction, or at least the disarming, of the threatening force. Fear proportionate to real danger leads to avoidance of danger by an appropriate behavior. Exaggerated irrational fear may lead to morbid, counterproductive states of panic.

The ideas of birth trauma and interrupted coitus as sources of anxiety were predominant in Freud's theory for a long time. When Freud revised his theories, these two concepts were not abandoned in their entirety, but assigned a lesser role in the new theoretical framework.

The monograph *Inhibitions, Symptoms and Anxiety* was published in 1926 after Rank published his *Birth Trauma* and after Freud had introduced his structural theory in 1923 in *The Ego and the Id.*

Main changes in Freud's theory revolved around his theory of motivation. Freud abandoned in 1914 the ego versus libido theory and merged these two concepts in the theory of narcissism, and later added the Eros versus Thanatos dualism in 1920. In this new framework, anxiety could no longer be related to frustration of the sexual drive. In 1926 Freud introduced a new theory of anxiety: Anxiety originates from the infant's inability to master excitations; the neonate is exposed to more stimulation than he can possibly master. The abundant stimulation is traumatic and creates the painful feeling of primary anxiety.

Birth trauma is the prototype of all future anxiety states. Separation from mother is another anxiety-producing experience. Castration fears, guilt feelings, fear of abandonment, and rejection are the most frequently experienced anxiety-producing situations. The feeling of being helpless is one of the most frequent symptoms of neurotic disturbances; it is especially typical of traumatic neuroses. Also, the inability to control one's own excitation (whether aggressive or sexual) may create a state of anxiety (Freud, 1926).

According to Freud, infants are exposed to powerful stimulations that are beyond their coping ability. These traumatic experiences create in the child the feeling of desperate helplessness, which is the feeling of *primary anxiety*. The first experience of this kind is the birth trauma, in which the main characteristics of anxiety, such as the accelerated action of the heart and lungs, plays a decisive role in the child's survival. Later, separation from the mother is the anxiety-producing factor.

This state of helplessness or anxiety may come back in later life. The feeling of being helpless is one of the main symptoms in practically all neuroses, and especially in a traumatic neurosis. The inability to control excitation, whether stemming from sexual or aggressive impulses, creates the state of anxiety. By this interpretation, the early theory of anxiety becomes a part of the later and more broadly conceived theory, which states that any anxiety can be traced back to situations of external danger. Sooner or later, the ego realized that the satisfaction of some instinctual demands may create one of the well-remembered danger situations. The ego must then inhibit the instinctual wishes. A strong ego accomplishes this task easily, but a weak ego has to invest more energies in a countercathectic effort to ward off the repressed impulse.

FEAR AND ANXIETY

People exposed to danger, whether real or imaginary, experience fear. Fear is an emotional and perceptual reaction to viewing the threatening factor as capable of causing pain, harm, or death. Fear is related to a low estimate of one's power to resist the threat.

Whereas fear is a momentary reaction to a threat, *anxiety is a lasting feeling of unavoidable doom.* Anxiety is a state of tension and expectation of disaster. Anxiety-ridden individuals are *continuously* unhappy, worrisome and pessimistic, irrespective of existing or nonexisting dangers.

The presence of a friendly and protective individual reduces fear, but it has no effect on anxiety. Anxiety-ridden persons do not believe that anyone can save them. Fear is a reaction to danger; anxiety is not always related to danger (Beck & Emery, 1985).

Fear usually leads to the action of fight or flight, depending on one's evaluation of one's own power and the power of the threatening situation. Anxiety reduces one's ability to act. An anxious person doubts that any action could produce results. Anxiety is tantamount to a lasting and profound low self-esteem and feeling of one's weakness, inferiority, and helplessness. Anxiety makes people withdraw from other people, and temporarily affects one's intellectual function, especially memory and ability to express oneself. Anxiety often produces feelings of inferiority, irritability, anger, and hatred directed against others, but mostly against oneself.

Anxiety can be caused by physical ailments and can cause psychosomatic symptoms. In some cardiovascular diseases, physical symptoms are associated with hypochondriacal depression and anxiety (Dohrenwend & Dohrenwend, 1981). Anxiety can cause coronary arrhythmia and a host of psychosomatic symptoms, such as nausea, loss of appetite, headaches, and sleep disturbances (Wolman, 1988).

Acute Anxiety

The history of humanity is full of moments where human lives have been jeopardized by war, revolution, earthquakes, or other upheavals. Fear of death is a universal phenomenon shared by all living beings, but for some people, anticipating future dangers tends to produce more fear of present and future threats.

In cases of *acute anxiety,* two psychological phenomena can take place: a reduction in motor activity and/or an increase in uncontrolled activity. The first could be a sort of psychological paralysis; the latter is disinhibition (Beck & Emery, 1985). In situations of grave and continuous stress and strain, some individuals regress to infantile passivity, as if unconsciously hoping that the threat will be reduced. They regress to the role of infant on the unconscious assumption that infancy was the most safe period of life. How far people regress varies from case to case; sometimes the regression is to a stage of infancy, sometimes it goes to a neonate state or prenatal condition (Wolman, 1978).

During the Second World War and the Israel War of Independence, I saw some adult men, soldiers, developing incontinence, disturbed speech, and exhibiting many other symptoms resembling infantile behavior. The infantile regression served the unconscious purpose of taking the individual out of touch with the dangerous reality and bringing him back to the imaginary world of childhood.

In some cases, certain psychological defense mechanisms take place, such as rationalization. Rationalization leads to the belief that there are divine supernatural forces that can protect the individual and take him out of the danger zone. There have been several reported cases of people who in time of danger suddenly became extremely religious. Some of my patients in times of danger have talked to God; they have made all sorts of promises in order to secure God's graces and intervention in their troubles. This kind of daydreaming and parareligious feelings is quite common (Wolman & Ullman, 1986).

These phenomena sometimes take on mass dimensions. In times of war, threat, and danger, many people regress waiting for messiahs, practicing astrology, joining groups for meditation and believing in the supernatural powers of a guru. The fear of overwhelming external danger facilitates regression into infantile passivity, daydreaming, and hopes of supraparental intervention. Passivity deepens one's feeling of helplessness and invokes a greater feeling of guilt. Feeling helpless and guilty makes one further regress, and the whole process can continue as a progressive demoralization of the individual or the group, which further decreases the ability to face assaults coming from without. Assaults from within decrease one's powers and therefore reduce one's ability to face external dangers (Kaplan & Sadock, 1985; Spielberger, 1966). Blaming others decreases one's feeling of guilt, but it does not increase one's feeling of power; it creates more dissension and dissatisfaction, and the hostility is directed not against the true enemy but against allies, friends, and leaders who are accused of not doing enough.

Social Anxiety

Quite often in order to attain one's goals one plans to act in a manner that will create a good impression and could bring social approval. In social anxiety, one doubts whether his or her communication will be accepted the way one wishes to be accepted. One doubts whether one's words or behavior will be perceived the way one would like to be. It is a state of anxiety caused by a wish to impress others and a fear that this will not be accomplished (Leary & Kowalski, 1990; Schlenker & Leary, 1982). Social anxiety can also affect the efficiency of behavior and cause withdrawal symptoms.

Performance Anxiety

Fight for survival is the basic drive of all humans, and craving for success is the normal corollary of this drive. Human beings try hard to attain success and to avoid failure, and achievement motivation is one of the chief driving forces in human behavior.

People tend to mobilize their mental resources whenever they have to face a challenge. However, even well-balanced individuals may fail on a test or on a job interview or on performance.

The wish to succeed and the fear of failure are normal feelings, but sometimes people do not perform at their best, or they fail because they overestimate the importance of the task or underestimate their own resources. Quite often students fail in mathematics, for they seem to believe that no error is allowed, while in other subjects there might be some leeway. Sometimes people fail on a job interview when they overestimate the importance of the interview or doubt their own abilities. Sometimes a young actor or other performer forgets his or her lines, especially when there is an unconscious fear that this is the last chance. Some people fail because they overestimate the danger or because they demand too much from themselves and are disappointed with their own performance (Foole, 1979; Spielberger, 1966, 1972; Tuma & Maser, 1985).

SISYPHUS COMPLEX

There are people whose main aim in life seems to be failure. They manage to mismanage their lives, and although they give the impression of forging ahead, they act against their own best interests. Quite often they wholeheartedly pursue their goals and make significant progress, but when they are close to achieving their goal, they defeat themselves.

The ancient Greek mythology tells the story of Sisyphus' punishment in Hades' Kingdom of Hereafter. Sisyphus was ordered by the gods to roll a heavy rock up a steep hill. When, after prolonged and strenuous efforts, the rock was just about to reach the top of the hill, the rock rolled all the way down.

I have had several opportunities to watch Sisyphus' complex in my patients. When a young and gifted pianist was invited to give a concert in Carnegie Hall, he suddenly lost control of his fingers. When a brilliant mathematician was appointed by a leading university to teach advanced courses, he confused elementary mathematical equations on the blackboard on the first day of classes. An actress who successfully performed in regional theaters, forgot her lines during an audition for a major role on Broadway; and so on.

ETIOLOGIC REMARKS

Human life starts in a state of helplessness and dependence on parental protection, support, and approval. Little children do not know whether they are pretty or ugly, smart or stupid, good or bad. It is the responsibility of parents or parental substitutes to build the child's self-confidence and self-esteem.

Children rejected by their parents tend to become highly critical of themselves. They are unable to accept themselves; some of them make considerable strides toward scholarly success and defeat themselves on a test. They often work very hard as if trying "to prove" something; actually they strive to overcome their feeling of inadequacy by frantic efforts, and end up in unconsciously motivated self-defeat on a final exam, job interview, or any other significant performance later in life (Achenbach, 1982; Beck & Emery, 1985; Wolman, 1978).

Zinbarg, Barlow, Brown, and Hertz (1992) maintain that animal models have made important contributions to recent theories about the etiology of anxiety disorders. However, I believe that whereas fear is a universal phenomenon, anxiety is limited to human beings and to their ability to experience a continuously pessimistic view of themselves and expect unavoidable doom. Nothing of that kind can be ascribed to animals.

REFERENCES

Achenbach, I. M. (1982). *Developmental psychopathology* (2nd ed.). New York: Wiley.

Beck, A. T., & Emery, G. (1985). *Anxiety disorders and phobias*. New York: Basic Books.

Dohrenwend, B. S., & Dohrenwend, B. P. (Eds.). (1981). *Stressful life events and their contexts*. New York: Watson.

Foole, D. S. (1979). Profaning students for the worse: The power of negative thinking. *Personnel and Guidance Journal, 33,* 615–623.

Freud, S. (1926). Inhibitions, symptoms and anxiety. *Standard Edition, 20,* 74–175.

Kaplan, H. I., & Sadock, B. J. (Eds.). (1985). *Comprehensive handbook of psychiatry* (5th ed.). Baltimore: Williams-Wilkins.

Leary, M. R., & Kowalski, R. M. (1990). Impression management: A literature review and two component model. *Psychological Bulletin, 104,* 34–47.

London, H. (1977). Power and acceptance theory. In B. B. Wolman (Ed.), *International encyclopaedia of psychiatry, psychology, psychoanalysis and neurology, 9,* 11–13. New York: Van Nostrand Reinhold.

Schlenker, B. R., & Leary, M. R. (1982). Social anxiety and self-presentation: A conceptualization and model. *Psychological Bulletin, 92,* 641–649.

Spielberger, C. D. (Ed.). (1966). *Anxiety and behavior.* New York: Academy Press.

Spielberger, C. D. (Ed.). (1972). *Anxiety: Current trends in theory and research* (Vols. 1–2). New York: Academy Press.

Tuma, H., & Maser, J. D. (Eds.). (1985). *Anxiety and the anxiety disorders.* Hillsdale, NJ: Erlbaum.

Wolman, B. B. (1974). Power and acceptance as determinants of social relations. *International Journal of Group Tensions, 4,* 151–183.

Wolman, B. B. (1978). *Childrens fears.* New York: Grosset and Dunlop.

Wolman, B. B. (1988). *Psychosomatic disorders.* New York: Plenum.

Wolman, B. B. (1992). *Personality dynamics.* New York: Plenum.

Wolman, B. B., & Ullman, M. (Eds.). (1986). *Handbook of States of Consciousness.* New York: Van Nostrand Reinhold.

Zinbarg, R. E., Barlow, D. H., Brown, T. A., & Hertz, R. M. (1992). Cognitive-behavioral approaches to the nature and treatment of anxiety disorders. *Annual Review of Psychology, 43,* 234–267.

CHAPTER 2

Psychoanalytic and Related Interpretations

LAWRENCE JOSEPHS, PhD

Anxiety has been a central construct in psychoanalytic theory. Despite its centrality, the concept of anxiety has not been utilized in a consistent manner. Anxiety has been understood as a *cause* of psychic events, as in the idea that anxiety serves as a trigger of defensive operations; and anxiety has been understood as a *result* of psychic events, as in the idea that inhibited affective expression results in a buildup of anxiety. Anxiety has been understood as a symptom of psychological distress, as in an anxiety attack; and anxiety has been understood as a cause of distressing symptoms, as in the idea that sexual impotence is derivative of unconscious castration anxiety.

Anxiety has been explored as an *experiential content of consciousness*—as an intense affective experience of endangerment—and anxiety has been explored as a *hypothetical unconscious mechanism*—as in the idea that anxiety is a product of unconscious conflict resulting in compromise formations. Anxiety has been understood as a psychic *content* (conscious or unconscious) such as castration anxiety, separation anxiety, persecutory anxiety, disintegration anxiety, and so on; and anxiety has been understood as a psychic *function* (conscious or unconscious) such as anxiety serving as an appraisal that signals a situation of danger to be avoided. Anxiety has been understood as an *affect* with an underlying physiological substrate reflecting a high state of arousal, if not stimulus overload; and anxiety has been understood as a *cognition* reflecting an appraisal and anticipation of situations in which there are reasons to be insecure. Thus anxiety is both cause and effect, symptom in and of itself as well as unseen cause of other symptoms, lived experience and mental mechanism, psychic content and psychic function, and an affect as well as a cognition.

Anxiety as a construct in psychoanalytic theory has been utilized in a variety of ways, depending upon the purpose it is designed to serve in the particular theory. For Freud, anxiety was originally a distressing symptom to be explained as a result of intrapsychic processes such as instinctual discharge, conflict, and defense. Yet over time, anxiety became a pivotal theoretical construct, so that by the end of Freud's career castration anxiety could be seen as the originating cause of most psychopathology. For interpersonalists such as Sullivan, anxiety is an interpersonal event reflecting the level of security of one's relationships with others; anxiety in relation to others constituting both a cause and an effect of failures of interpersonal integration. For object relations theorists such as Melanie Klein, interpersonal insecurity is a result of the projection of anxiety, arousing unconscious fantasies onto the interpersonal surround, resulting in psychotic anxiety as the boundary between reality and fantasy (i.e., inner objects and external objects) becomes blurred and confused. Kohut, though, would understand psychotic anxiety not so much as a fear of losing touch with reality but a fear of completely losing one's sense of self as a consequence of the loss of confirmatory feedback from others. For Kohut, all anxiety is at bottom fragmentation anxiety, reflecting a loss of self-cohesiveness.

Given the diversity and richness of psychoanalytic theories of anxiety, it is unfortunate that these theories have been treated as competing rather than complementary. If anxiety can be understood as a multifaceted and multidimensional phenomenon, then different theories can be understood as reflecting different dimensions or facets of the same phenomenon rather than as competing explanations for the same phenomenon. In general, psychoanalytic theory advances as a science not so much through later theories disproving and replacing earlier theories as through later theories enlarging the scope of earlier theories through encompassing neglected dimensions of a phenomenon. Earlier theories are not proven false but are rather shown to be true but within a limited scope, a limitation that heretofore had not been fully appreciated. This chapter will review psychoanalytic theories of anxiety with an eye toward integration of multiple perspectives. Five psychoanalytic theories of anxiety will be discussed; two Freudian, an interpersonal, an object relational, and a self psychological.

FREUD'S TOXIC THEORY OF ANXIETY

Freud's first theory of anxiety has traditionally been referred to as his *toxic theory* of anxiety. In examining Freudian theory, it can be useful to differentiate Freud's *metapsychological theory* from his *clinical theory*. Klein (1976) suggested that whereas Freud's metapsychology may be unsupportable, as its scaffold is often based on anachronistic nineteenth-century biology, Freud's clinical theory—based as it is on insights deriving from the psychoanalytic situation—may remain relevant to the contemporary practitioner. Freud's first metapsychological explanation of anxiety is that dammed-up libido (i.e., libido that is nondischarged, warded-off, or repressed) leads to anxiety. Repressed libido is transformed into a distressing symptom, such as some sort of anxiety disorder. Initially, for Freud, anxiety was not a central theoretical construct but rather a distressing psychiatric symptom to be explained by reference to other theoretical constructs. In 1905, Freud published his theory of infantile sexuality codifying his libidinal drive theory so that from then on instinctual drives became the fuel that drove the mind—a mind conceived as operating analogously to a machine (i.e., mind as mental apparatus).

The empirical basis for the dammed-up libido theory of anxiety was the presumption that people who were sexually frustrated developed nervous anxiety. Freud (1898) differentiated the *actual neuroses* from the *neuropsychoses of defense*. The actual neuroses derive from sexual frustration such as may accrue from *coitus interruptus.* Sexual frustration presumably results in some sort of biochemical imbalance or build-up of noxious or toxic substances that leads to anxiety. In contrast to the actual neuroses, the neuropsychoses of defense lead to sexual frustration more indirectly through repression. Sexual wishes are defended against and, as a consequence of their inhibition, are frustrated, resulting in nondischarged libido which in some sort of biochemical manner is transformed into anxiety.

The empirical basis of the dammed-up libido theory is weak. No one has yet to find a biochemical correlate of Freud's libido, and therefore no one has yet to document the biochemical process through which undischarged libido is transformed into anxiety. On psychological grounds, the theory is weak as well, since many sexually abstinent people do not become anxious or symptomatic in ways that reflect a build-up of anxiety. Many sexually active and presumably sexually gratified people are quite anxious and display symptoms suggestive of being quite anxious. Many people who are sexually frustrated may seem angry or depressed but not particularly anxious. Although in Freud's writings it is difficult to surmise when the concept of undischarged libido is simply a euphemism for the experience of sexual excitement without orgasm or when it refers to a broader sense of disappointment in love; it is clear that although sexual excitement without orgasm may be a source of anxiety for some people it seems insufficient as an all-purpose universal explanation of the cause of anxiety. The broader conception of undischarged libido as frustration of one's desire to love, love encompassing erotic as well as affectionate elements, also seems an overly narrow definition of the source of anxiety, that lacks an empirical base. People in love may or may not be anxious and people out of love may or may not be anxious. People who are loved may or may not be anxious about that circumstance and people who are not loved may or may not be anxious. The presence or absence of anxiety appears to be considerably more complex than whether one is sexually fulfilled or frustrated, in love or out of love, or that one's love is returned or unrequited. Greenberg (1991) noted how drive theory became a procrustean bed for Freudian theorists who were then forced to reduce all psychic phenomena to derivatives of instinctual drives.

If we are able to see past Freud's metapsychological commitment to drive theory to his clinical theory, a more experience-near and empirically justifiable theory of the source of anxiety may be discovered. It has been often noted that Freudian psychoanalysis has been weak on a theory of affects. Since at a theoretical level affect was conceptualized as a derivative of libidinal gratification or frustration, affect has been poorly conceptualized as a phenomenon in its own right. Nevertheless, just because Freud did not develop a specific theory of affects does not mean that as a clinician he neglected affects. Psychoanalysis has always been considered a treatment of emotional disorders rather than as exclusively a treatment of libidinal disorders.

It might be more experience-near to say that Freud treated *strangulated affect* than it would be to say that he treated *dammed-up libido*. Freud's (Breuer & Freud, 1895) first approach to psychotherapy was the *cathartic* or *abreactive* method of treatment. The patient was thought to have repressed the emotions evoked by traumatic events. Treatment involved reliving and re-experiencing the traumatic event, fully experiencing the emotions that the traumatic experience originally evoked but were too painful to endure at the time.

Anxiety is one symptom of unexpressed emotion. Unexpressed sexual feelings or loving feelings could be one source of anxiety, but so could unexpressed anger, sadness, shame, guilt, envy, jealousy, hatred, elation, fear, and so on. Anxiety could then be understood as a fear of one's emotions whatever those emotions may be. The affects evoked by traumatic events due to their overwhelming nature are repressed. As long as repression functions successfully, one remains asymptomatic. Yet as repressed emotions are always seeking expression, repression may prove ineffective and there may be a failure of defense leading to what Freud (1894) referred to as a *return of the repressed*. Failure of defense produces anxiety as a symptom. As repressed emotion threatens to enter conscious awareness, anxiety is aroused as a derivative expression of an unconscious fear of reliving the emotions associated with a traumatic experience.

Secondary defenses re-repress the distressing affects that are threatening to emerge into awareness. Freud (1894) was able to describe the dynamics of a variety of symptoms associated with anxiety by utilizing this model. For example, a phobia such as a fear of heights could be utilized as a defense against underlying depressive affect. Unconsciously, one might be feeling a sense of despair with fantasies of committing suicide. As repression against suicidal despair breaks down, one might become frightened of heights out of a fear of one's unconscious wish to jump from a high place in order to commit suicide. The original traumatic situation in which the suicidal despair was evoked might have been having been fired from one's job. The scene of the trauma is *displaced* from upset over job loss to a fear of heights. Presumably if the depressive reaction to the job loss is abreacted, one will be cured of the acrophobia.

Obsessive worries about forgetting to turn off the stove when leaving for work could be derivative of an unconscious wish to burn one's house down. Perhaps as a consequence of an argument with one's spouse, punitive feelings toward one's spouse are aroused that engender intolerable guilt. As a derivative expression of unconscious guilt, one hates oneself for being irresponsibly forgetful in failing to turn off the stove before leaving for work. In the fantasy of inadvertently burning the house down, both the spouse and the self are unconsciously punished in one fell swoop. Presumably once the anger towards the spouse is abreacted, the obsessive rumination and recrimination about forgetting to turn off the stove will be alleviated.

Paranoia could be linked to intolerance of unconscious shame and guilt. The person *projects* his or her own self-hatred in assuming that others are prejudiced against and persecutory toward the self. The person *repudiates* self-hatred in ascribing intolerant attitudes to others, the idea being that "I am not ashamed or guilty, for it is others who are trying to shame and blame me and I am justified in hating them for that." Intolerable self-hatred is converted into tolerable other-hatred. Presumably, once feelings of shame and guilt are abreacted, one will be able to perceive others in a more realistic and benign light.

When repression fails, secondary defenses such as displacement (in phobias), reversal and reaction-formation (in obsessions), projection (in paranoia), conversion and dissociation (in hysterias), introjection (in depression), overcompensation (in narcissism), denial (in psychoses), and so on come into play to prevent the full experiencing of the affect which threatens to break through the repressive barrier. The secondary defense allows for a compromise solution which entails symptom formation. The symptom partially reveals yet partially conceals the underlying issue. For example, hysterical blindness conceals the true nature of a traumatic event such as an experience of sexual abuse yet the presence of hysterical blindness, a highly distressing symptom that demands public attention, reveals that there is indeed some sort of horrible secret that demands recognition.

The anxiety surrounding the symptom reflects a partial return of the repressed affect evoked by the traumatic event. A tertiary defense may be erected in order to suppress the anxiety reaction. The phobic is not anxious if high places are avoided, the obsessive is not anxious if the stove is compulsively checked and rechecked to see that it is off, the paranoid is not anxious if a hypervigilant attitude is maintained that keeps potential critics at bay, and the hysterically blind expresses "la belle indifference" if the blindness is accepted as an organic deficit for which one need not be held accountable. Failure of tertiary defenses may result in an anxiety attack.

In summary, Freud's first clinical theory of anxiety is that anxiety is a result of repressed affect evoked by traumatic situations. When repression of affect fails due to the fact that affect presses for expression, anxiety is evoked reflecting an unconscious fear of experiencing in consciousness the full intensity of the repressed affect evoked by the traumatic experience. To avoid this eventuality, secondary defenses are brought into play which are only partially effective in that they entail the construction of distressing symptoms as compromise formations, a compromise between rerepressing the warded-off affect and expressing it in a disguised manner. Tertiary defenses may be brought into play in order to suppress the anxiety associated with the symptom. When tertiary defenses are effective the person is anxiety free but when tertiary defenses fail the person may have an anxiety attack.

The empirical evidence that Freud used to support his clinical theory of anxiety is that after the affect associated with the repressed traumatic situation was abreacted, there was symptom remission. The empirical observation that eventually led Freud to revise his first theory of anxiety despite its considerable explanatory power was that abreaction of affect led to only temporary symptom relief. Though emotional ventilation led to temporary anxiety reduction, the effect did not last. Freud (Breuer & Freud, 1895) originally presumed that once a repressed emotion associated with a traumatic memory was abreacted, it would cease to unconsciously build up as a strangulated affect. Whereas unconscious emotions were thought to be timeless, the consciously experienced emotion associated with the memory of a traumatic event was supposed to wear away over time until the memory was eventually recalled as a virtually neutral event. The fact that catharsis brought only temporary relief suggested that some other undiscovered unconscious factors must be at work that result in an eventual return of the anxiety-laden symptomatology.

Despite the limitation of Freud's first theory of anxiety, it remains clinically useful and true in a limited manner. There seems little doubt that one source of anxiety is the unconscious fear of experiencing the emotions associated with the reliving of memories of traumatic events, and that anxiety attacks and distressing symptoms are precipitated when defenses against repressed affect fail. One useful aspect of treatment is abreacting the emotions evoked by traumatic situations. Freud's insight that the repressed affect may be related to intolerable sexual or loving feelings remains useful although it seems reductionistic to see all affective experience as ultimately derivative transformations of libidinal drives.

FREUD'S THEORY OF SIGNAL ANXIETY

In Freud's second theory of anxiety the so-called *signal theory* of anxiety, Freud shifted from looking at anxiety as a *result* to looking at anxiety as a *cause*. Defenses did not so much *cause* anxiety by preventing affective expression as anxiety *caused* defenses to be brought into play. Freud (1926) suggested that anxiety serves as a signal, as an anticipation of danger, which triggers defense mechanisms. Thus anxiety is an unconscious process, a sort of barometer of the intensity of unconscious conflict. The greater the conflict, the greater the anxiety, and therefore the greater the need for defense. In this model, anxiety is understood as a cognition, usually an unconscious one, rather than as an affect. Anxiety reflects an unconscious appraisal by the ego assessing the likelihood that a situation of danger is approaching. Signal anxiety requires such cognitive operations as *anticipation* of a future event, *judgment* as to the likelihood that different actions will lead to different dreaded consequences, and *appraisal* of the dangerousness of an anticipated consequence. Signal anxiety reflects an assessment of cause/effect relationships, especially the relationship between the expression of a wish and its consequence.

The sense of danger for Freud is not so much the accurate assessment of a realistic threat as it is a product of unconscious conflict. A sense of danger arises from the conflict between one's wishes and the forces (internal as well as external) opposing those wishes. To the degree one needs approval, one is vulnerable to the danger of loss of approval. To the degree one is angry, one is vulnerable to the anger of others. To the degree that one is guilty, one is vulnerable to the danger of being blamed. Every unconscious wish, fantasy, or feeling brings with it its own situation of danger. Freud (1926) delineated a number of basic situations of danger. The earliest situation of danger is a sense of helplessness as a result of traumatic overstimulation. Freud believed that the prototype of this situation of danger is the trauma of birth. If the original wish is the desire for a return to the presumed bliss of the intrauterine state, then the original traumatic situation of danger to be avoided is the frustration of this primal wish.

Freud delineated a developmental progression of situations of danger to be avoided. The next situation in this series is the loss of the object. If a basic infantile wish is to be attached to a person who will gratify all one's wishes, then to lose that person is a danger to be avoided. At a somewhat higher level of development, there is a recognition that to lose the love of the object is a danger to be avoided. Not only must the person one needs be physically present in order to meet one's needs, but that person must be loving and approving rather than indifferent or disapproving. Needs for love and approval invariably entail fears of the loss of that love and approval. The development of sexual, especially genital, desires leads to castration anxiety as it is feared that sexual competitors may retaliate. Just as one might like to get rid of the competition, others might like to get rid of oneself. The final situation of danger that Freud delineated was superego anxiety. Once a set of moral values has been internalized, there is a fear of a negative self-evaluation any time one feels tempted to circumvent living by those values.

Situations of danger are essentially fantasy formations that arise out of a fear that one's wishes and desires will be frustrated. Since reality invariably frustrates one's wishes, such fantasies are given an element of reality and conviction. The more frustrating the external reality, the more conviction one holds in the anxiety-laden unconscious fantasy. Thus Freud (1926) conceived of these situations of danger as a "complemental series," a series of fantasies that arise endogenously as maturation progresses but which are given a sense of reality and specificity of historical content through actual experiences that become assimilated into the structure of the fantasy formation. The fantasy maintains a life of its own as an unconscious content that functions as a primary motivational system determining what situations are to be avoided in life.

Signal anxiety in establishing an appraisal of a situation of danger assesses not only the degree of realistic threat in the here-and-now, but the degree to which reality has traumatically frustrated one's wishes in the past and may do so again in the future, the strength of one's wishes in the here-and-now, and the degree to which the superego forbids such wishes. It is the assessment of all these factors in combination that determines the level of signal anxiety. The greater the intensity of the wish and the greater the forces opposing the gratification of the wish, the greater the intrapsychic conflict and therefore the greater the anxiety. Thus anxiety is still a *result* of the intensity of intrapsychic conflict, but now anxiety is also a *cause,* a trigger of defense mechanisms. Defenses prevent the actualization of a situation of danger either by preventing the expression of the wish or by avoiding the life situations in which the wish might be gratified and one would be exposed to the dangerous consequences of having attempted to gratify the wish. For example, if one is afraid of abandonment then one doesn't allow oneself to experience a wish for attachment and one avoids situations in which one's wishes for attachment could be gratified. An anxiety attack could be precipitated by the presence of someone who proffered an opportunity for intimacy. If one is afraid of criticism, then one repudiates one's need for approval and avoids situations in which one might be evaluated. An anxiety attack could be precipitated by the presence of an admiring audience eager to dole out praise and approval.

Anxiety as a lived experience and as part of a symptom disorder arises in the same manner as in the earlier model—as a result of a failure of defense. When defenses fail, a dreaded anticipation is evoked that the situation of danger that one had hoped to avoid might actually occur, leading to a traumatic state. In the second model, it becomes clear that an anxiety attack is traumatic not only because of the dread of repressed affect but because of a dread of the repetition of a situation of danger with which the affect is associated. One is afraid not simply of one's feelings but of the recurrence of the situation in which the feelings were evoked—situations of being helpless, of being abandoned, of being rejected, of being abused, of being blamed, of hating oneself, and so on. Thus, anxiety is comprised of both affective and cognitive elements: the affective element being the dread of being overwhelmed and the cognitive element consisting of the anticipation of the particular situation of danger in which one would feel overwhelmed. The phenomenon of free-floating anxiety reflects a defense operation through which the cognitive content of the situation of danger has been split off and repressed while the affective content is allowed access to consciousness. One feels anxious but the reason why is repressed, creating the illusion of a contentless anxiety state.

Freud's second model makes it clear why abreaction alone is only a partial treatment approach, for it does not address the cognitive element of anxiety. Anxiety is not simply an affect tied to a past traumatic event that has been repressed, but anxiety is more importantly related to the fear of the repetition of the traumatic event in the future. Recognition and catharsis of prior experiences of victimization, abandonment, rejection, failure, and so on do not guarantee that such experiences will not repeat themselves once again in the future. In fact, it may be quite the opposite: Once one has been sensitized to a situation of danger in that one's worst fears seem to have actually come true; one's fears for the future seem that much more realistically based. Permanent anxiety reduction requires decreasing one's anticipation of danger in the future, changing one's unconscious belief system about what the future holds in store.

Decreasing one's anticipation of danger is not achieved through abreaction alone but requires conflict/defense analysis. To the degree anxiety is successfully warded-off through defenses, those defenses must be analyzed, or else the person would never learn that one can function safely in the world without a self-protective, self-defeating, and symptom-generating defensive structure. To the degree anxiety is a product of the intensity of intrapsychic conflict, that conflict must be analyzed to attenuate anxiety. To the degree one's wishes decrease in intensity either through being fulfilled or through being relinquished and to the degree one's wishes are granted greater acceptability, intrapsychic conflict and therefore anxiety is diminished.

In summary of Freud's most mature theory, anxiety is foremost a consequence of unconscious intrapsychic conflict—the greater the inner conflict, the greater the generation of anxiety. Conflict is at bottom a conflict between the desire to fulfill one's wishes and the anticipated dangers that may arise as a consequence of fulfilling one's wishes. Situations of danger constitute fantasy formations that endogenously arise in a developmental sequence, each situation of danger reflecting the traumatic frustration of a vital wish. Real life experiences of frustration and disappointment become woven into the fabric of these anxiety-laden fantasies, forming a complemental series of basic yet personalized anxiety situations that one will spend the rest of one's life unconsciously attempting to avoid. Anxiety then serves as an anticipation of danger that triggers an unconscious defensive operation in the service of avoiding the situation of danger. If defenses fail, one may experience anxiety and develop distressing psychological symptoms as a stop-gap measure. Secondary and tertiary defenses may be employed to rerepress the anxiety state and the distress associated with the emergence of symptoms. If secondary and tertiary defenses fail, one may experience a full-blown anxiety attack. The essential treatment approach warranted by this model is conflict-defense analysis with abreaction of repressed affect as defenses are lifted and unconscious conflict is made conscious.

Though Freud's theory of anxiety is quite impressive in its scope and sophistication, it is nevertheless limited in a number of ways that have been addressed by later theorists. First, the role of external reality is apparently limited in Freudian theory to giving a sense of reality and historical content to endogenously occurring anxiety-laden fantasies. The theory seems to imply that reality in and of itself is never dangerous or traumatic but that it is only the meaning which we ascribe to reality that makes events upsetting. Abandonment, rejection, abuse, and so on are only traumatic to the degree to which we wish for nurturance, love, and respect. Although in some philosophical sense it is certainly true that we are all constructionists who create meaning, we do not create meaning in a vacuum based solely upon innate needs and desires; we create meaning in a sociocultural-historical context that informs our meaning-making activities. Freud—in emphasizing the contribution of endogenously arising fantasies—deemphasized the formative influence of this larger context and its relation to why we behave anxiously in certain situations. Even our most basic needs, desires, and wishes can be understood as social constructions that betray an unwitting assumption of prevailing societal attitudes.

Freud developed a complex theory of the mind in conflict, but in a sense possessed little theory of the person whose mind is conflicted. A theory of a mind in conflict is not identical to a theory of a person in conflict (with others as well as in conflict with him or herself). For Freudians, the self is a content of the mind, a compromise formation, whereas for theorists of the self such as Winnicott or Kohut, the mind is a content of self-experience. To speak of a person whose mind is con-flicted is to speak of a self as an agent who is conflicted between compet-ing priorities and who experiences anxiety about failing to achieve personal goals. There is always a person—not merely a mental appara-tus—who has wishes, who experiences frustration, who anticipates dan-ger, who acts defensively to avoid feeling anxiously, and who fails to effect a stable compromise to conflicting priorities. It is the nature of this person, this agent, which later theorists have addressed.

THE INTERPERSONAL THEORY OF ANXIETY

Sullivan (1953) developed a theory of anxiety in which anxiety was con-strued as an interpersonal rather than an exclusively intrapsychic event. As an interpersonal event, anxiety can be understood as a communica-tion between persons in regard to the state of an interpersonal relation-ship. Sullivan described how an anxious mother communicates that anxiety to her baby, who becomes anxious as a result of registering the communication. Sullivan believes that the baby is capable of a primitive form of empathy with the mother based on emotional contagion so that the baby always knows in some intuitively immediate manner what the mother is feeling. As a communication, anxiety sends the message that the state of the relationship is insecure and precarious so that there is cause for alarm.

Whereas Freud construed affects as discharge phenomena, Sullivan viewed affects as forms of interpersonal communication. Affects serve a communicative function, to tell the other person how one feels about the relationship in which they are engaged. Anxiety communicates the sense of insecurity, that one is feeling unsafe and endangered in relation to the other. Sullivan suggested that the two basic interpersonal needs were the need for security and the need for self-esteem. The need for security reflects the need for relationships in which one feels safe, a sense of be-longing, of fitting in, of being loved, and of being cared for. When such relationships are disrupted, there is a sense of anxiety reflecting the fail-ure of secure interpersonal integration. What Sullivan referred to as *secu-rity operations* are brought into play in order to attentuate anxiety. Security operations are similar to Freudian defense mechanisms in that they serve to reduce anxiety, but security operations function interper-sonally as well as intrapsychically. Security operations entail defensive strategies of interpersonal engagement that promote a sense of security. Since the source of anxiety is interpersonal, the source of anxiety reduc-tion must be some change in a real interpersonal situation.

What Sullivan called the *self-system* develops as a security operation in order to attenuate anxiety. The self develops in response to *reflected self-appraisals.* The self develops through accommodation to social role assignment in order to maintain a sense of security and reduce the sense of anxiety by fitting into the social surround in which one must learn to survive. As a result of reflected self-appraisals, the person develops a sense of *good me or bad me,* and *not me.* When the person acts consistently with the good me, there is a sense of security; but when the person acts consistently with the bad me or the not me, there is a sense of anxiety. Anxiety is triggered whenever there is a sense of failing to fit into the social organization of which one is a member. The self-system then institutes security operations in order to find a manner of fitting in and feeling secure once again.

Psychological symptoms can be understood as security operations designed to attenuate anxiety. For example, the obsessive individual has learned that one will only be accepted if one is compliant, dutiful, conscientious, and obeys the rules with precision. If the obsessive senses disapproval about being careless or irresponsible, in order to regain a sense of security he or she might institute a security operation such as ruminative worry about doing things perfectionistically and dread lest the smallest thing go wrong. The hysteric has learned that one will only be accepted if one is likable, friendly, accommodating, and pleasing. If the hysteric senses disapproval in being seen as unfriendly, as a security operation, the hysteric might begin to demand excessive attention in order to counter feeling unlovable and unattractive. The narcissist has learned that one will only be accepted if one is exceptional, extraordinary, and unique. If the narcissist begins to feel unnoticed and unseen, as a security operation, the narcissist may become arrogant and contemptuous to alleviate a sense of threatened dignity.

Whereas Sullivan focused on how persons need to accommodate to the role expectations of the social surround in order to fit in. Horney (1950) focused on how the social surround needs to accommodate to the needs of the person's *real self.* Horney believes that everyone is born with a real self that seeks self-actualization. *Basic anxiety* arises when others are experienced as inhospitable to the need of the real self to realize its intrinsic program. When the real self is thwarted, the person develops a *comprehensive neurotic solution* as a means of compensation. If the person's natural need for love is thwarted, the person may develop a *self-effacing solution* as a means of staying close to others by submitting to them. If the person's natural need for mastery is thwarted, the person may develop an *expansive solution* as a means of remaining superior to others. If the person's natural need for autonomy is thwarted, the person may develop a *resigned solution* as a means of maintaining a protective distance from others.

Unfortunately, comprehensive neurotic solutions give rise to *neurotic anxiety.* The self-effacing person possesses a neurotic anxiety that if one is not submissive or subordinate in relationships, one will be rejected.

The expansive person possesses a neurotic anxiety that if one is not superior to others, one will be shamed and humiliated. The resigned person possesses a neurotic anxiety that if one does not keep a safe distance from others, one will be smothered and enslaved. For both Sullivan and Horney, anxiety derives from interpersonal assumptions and beliefs about what is acceptable or unacceptable to others. There is anxiety in not being what it is felt that others expect one to be, and there is anxiety in feeling that others do not accept one for whom one actually is.

The treatment approach that is derived from the interpersonal view of anxiety entails examination and testing of one's interpersonal belief system. Security operations and comprehensive neurotic solutions may be based upon maladaptive, self-defeating, and narrowly conceived interpersonal belief systems. These belief systems may once have been truly applicable, given the interpersonal dynamics of the family of origin, but may no longer be relevant to one's current situation.

The innovation of the interpersonal view over the Freudian view of anxiety is in the appreciation of the extent to which familial and sociocultural belief systems shape and inform the growing individual's interpersonal belief systems. Ideas about gender roles, family roles, occupational roles, religious identity, political identity, race, ethnicity, social class, and so on are all shaped by the prevalent assumptions of the society of which one is a member. This is not to say that endogenously arising needs, desires, and wishes do not color one's perception of the social surround, but it does say that the social surround provides the linguistic meaning system through which endogenously arising needs, desires, and wishes will be understood. Freud's basic conflict/defense model remains true, but is limited to the degree that conflict is seen as arising only in relation to endogenously occurring needs, wishes, and desires that have been frustrated. The interpersonal view allows us to see a broader view of conflict as also entailing conflict between conflicting social role assignments and expectations as well as conflict between those social roles and one's innate aims.

THE OBJECT RELATIONS VIEW OF ANXIETY

Whereas interpersonal theory looks at relationships with others from the outside looking in, object relations theory looks at relationships with others from the inside looking out. Object relations theorists such as Klein, Fairbairn, Winnicott, Guntrip, and Bowlby—despite their many differences—all share a common assumption that the basic building blocks of the mind are internalized representations of the self in relation to others. Internalized representations of self in relation to others provide the inner templates or schemas through which real life interpersonal experience is assimilated. Intrapsychic conflict in the object relations view is not so much between wish and defense as it is between contrasting and contradictory representations of self in relation to others. A representation of self in relation to others is not so much a static representation, like a photographic image, but more like a moving image that encodes a storyline in enacting a relational scenario.

Object relations theorists have described two archaic relational scenarios from which they believe all more complex scenarios derive: the nurturant scenario and the antagonistic scenario (Josephs, 1992). In the nurturant scenario, the relationship between self and other is basically caring and harmonious. In the antagonistic scenario, the relationship between self and other is basically conflictual and hostile. These two relational scenarios give rise to two primary anxieties: *depressive anxiety* and *persecutory anxiety*. Depressive anxiety reflects a fear of the loss of the caring other in the nurturant scenario, and persecutory anxiety reflects the fear of being hurt by the hostile other in the antagonistic scenario. Defenses are brought into operation to prevent the materialization of either of these two dreaded scenarios.

Defenses in object relations theory are essentially counter-fantasies. If depressive anxiety reflects a fantasy of losing the nurturant other, then the antidote to that anxiety-laden fantasy must be some sort of counter-fantasy that negates the anxiety-laden one. If one has a fantasy of being self-sufficient (i.e., the manic defense), then one need not fear losing those to whom one is attached. If one has a fantasy of being inseparably merged with those to whom one is attached, then one need not worry about being separated from them. If persecutory anxiety reflects a fantasy of being harmed by an antagonistic other, then the defensive counter-fantasy must be one of neutralizing that threat in some manner or other. If one imagines vanquishing the antagonistic other (i.e., identification with the aggressor), then one need not fear the other. If one imagines maintaining a protective distance from the antagonistic other (i.e., schizoid defense), then one need not fear the other's animosity. Anxiety is precipitated whenever the defensive counter-fantasies are challenged and punctured. In object relations theory, fantasy serves an anxiety attenuating function. Fantasies not only serve to fulfill wishes and anticipate imaginary dangers, as in Freudian theory; but fantasy also serves to construct a safe reality in which those imaginary dangers have been neutralized as a threatening eventuality.

Just as fantasies of the self in relation to others are the building blocks of the mind, the organization of these building blocks determines one's proneness or vulnerability to anxiety. Kernberg (1975) delineated three levels of psychostructural integration associated with three levels of organization of internalized object relations. These three levels of integration are associated with three levels of psychopathology—neurotic, borderline, and psychotic—and therefore three levels of vulnerability to anxiety. Neurotics are able to clearly differentiate representations of self from representations of others and are able to integrate good and bad representations of self and good and bad representations of others, resulting in self and object constancy. Neurotic conflicts as a consequence of being organized on the basis of whole object relations are conflicts of ambivalence. Anxiety arises from hating the people one loves and loving the people one hates.

Borderlines are able to clearly differentiate representations of self from representations of others but are unable to integrate good with bad representations of self and are unable to integrate good with bad representations of others. Borderline conflicts organized on the basis of part object relations result in a fear of persecution from bad objects and in a fear of abandonment from good objects. Psychotics are unable to differentiate representations of self from representations of others and are also unable to integrate good and bad representations of self and others. As a result of a failure to differentiate self from others, anxiety derives from a confusion about what is reality and what is fantasy. Psychotics, like borderlines, experience persecutory and depressive anxieties but in a context in which the capacity for reality-testing is lost. Psychotic anxiety is the fear of losing one's sanity.

The object relations approach suggests that vulnerability to anxiety is dependent upon one's level of psychostructural integration. The more integrated one is, the less vulnerable one is to anxiety. The goal of conflict/defense analysis is not so much to gain insight as it is to achieve an integration between conflicting and disparate aspects of self. It is the achievement of integration that attenuates anxiety and it is the loss of integration that precipitates anxiety. Ironically, *splitting*—a defense through which anxiety is attenuated by maintaining a distance between good and bad representations of self and others—is ultimately self-defeating in preventing integration. In analyzing the defensive use of splitting, one might provoke *integration anxiety,* the fear that the assumption of an integrated state will lead to either loss or persecution. The counter-fantasy to integration anxiety is the fantasy of how blissful it would be to be a whole person.

THE SELF PSYCHOLOGICAL THEORY OF ANXIETY

Self psychology takes as its starting point the quest for an integrated sense of self. For self psychologists, the superordinate motivational principle of human functioning is the effort to maintain what Stolorow and Lachmann (1980) have referred to as the cohesiveness, temporal continuity, and positive affective coloring of the self. Kohut (1977) defined the self as a center of initiative guided by nuclear ideals and ambitions. Anxiety in self psychology is at bottom always fragmentation or disintegration anxiety, reflecting the loss of self-cohesion, self-continuity, and self-esteem. The sense of self, though, cannot be maintained in a vacuum but requires what Kohut (1971) called *selfobjects*. Selfobjects are extensions of the self that function to bolster the sense of self. When selfobjects fail, the sense of self falters.

Kohut (1971) delineated three major selfobject functions. Mirroring selfobjects bolster the self's need for validation and affirmation. The loss of mirroring evokes anxiety about the loss of self-esteem. Idealizing selfobjects bolster the self's sense of safety and belonging in allowing the self to be connected to something greater than itself. The failure of idealizing selfobjects evokes anxiety about being vulnerable to hostile forces. Alter-ego or twinship selfobjects bolster the self's sense of normalcy and of being human in being like someone else. When alter-ego selfobjects fail, anxiety is evoked about being abnormal, alien, and inhuman. Wolf (1988) delineated several other selfobject functions. Efficacy selfobjects bolster the self's sense of mastery. The failure of efficacy selfobjects evokes anxiety about inadequacy and incompetence. Adversarial selfobjects bolster the self's sense of being different from others through defining the self in contradistinction to the adversarial selfobject. The failure of adversarial selfobjects evokes anxiety about the loss of the sense of individuality.

Kohut (1971) noted that selfobject failure, if it is not of traumatic proportions, may be an impetus to growth. Tolerable selfobject failure leads to the establishment of *transmuting internalizations* through which the self assumes the selfobject function and thus develops a measure of functional autonomy. Transmuting internalizations allow for a more autonomously self-regulated and therefore more resiliently integrated sense of self that is less prone to the anxiety provoked by selfobject failure. Yet even highly integrated senses of self are not entirely autonomous but require the bolstering of mature selfobjects which support the sense of autonomy and of integration.

The implication for treatment is that the therapist always serves a selfobject function for the patient. To the extent the therapist is experienced as failing in the execution of this function, the patient's sense of self will be destabilized and anxiety will be evoked. To the extent the therapist is experienced as succeeding in the execution of this function, the patient's sense of self will be stabilized and anxiety will be attenuated. Yet the transformative element of treatment that distinguishes a self psychological approach from supportive psychotherapy is that the pivotal moment in treatment is the moment of selfobject failure. If the therapist can empathize with the patient's sense that the therapist has failed as a selfobject, then the rupture in the therapeutic relationship can be bridged and the patient can effect a transmuting internalization that increases the resilience of the self. Repairing ruptures in the selfobject relationship with the therapist through empathic interpretations is the essential process through which the sense of self is strengthened and the self becomes less vulnerable to anxiety.

INTEGRATIVE OVERVIEW

Freud taught us that anxiety derives from intrapsychic conflict and that anxiety as an anticipation of danger triggers defense mechanisms. When those defenses fail, anxiety becomes manifest and the person may become symptomatic. This basic model remains fundamentally true and remains clinically useful as psychoanalytic treatment invariably entails conflict/defense analysis. Yet the model does not fully address the question of what determines the intensity of conflict and therefore the intensity of anxiety, and what determines the success or failure of defenses against the experience of anxiety. To answer these two questions, one must possess a theory of the formative influence of the social surround that determines which wishes will be frustrated and to what extent, and that determines the extent to which different wishes will be deemed socially acceptable or unacceptable. Thus intrapsychic conflicts and anxieties will invariably mirror interpersonal conflicts and anxieties as they have been experienced in the family and culture of origin.

Yet the amount of conflict one experiences is not simply a product of the challenging conflicts to which one has been subjected in life, but also a product of how successful one has been in resolving conflict and achieving an integrated level of functioning. The more poorly integrated one is, the greater the vulnerability to anxiety; and the more successfully integrated one is, the greater the resilience to anxiety. Anxiety is therefore a barometer of one's level of integrated functioning. Anxiety functions as a homeostat which signals the threat of dis-integration, spurring efforts to re-integrate. Though the need for integration can be appreciated as an endogenously arising human tendency that may be seen as superordinate to other endogenously arising tendencies such as sexual, aggressive, and attachment drives; the drive for self-integration cannot succeed in a vacuum. The social surround must facilitate the person's innate integrative tendencies. Failure of the social surround to succeed in this function thwarts the person's drive to establish an integrated sense of self and leaves the person fragmented, conflicted, and anxious. Anxiety is then a reflection of the failure of the social surround to support an integrated level of functioning. Given the hopelessly pluralistic conditions of modern and postmodern society, it is unclear whether contemporary society is capable of supporting an integrated sense of self within its individual members (Frosch, 1991).

Defenses stabilize the person at a lower level of integration than the person's highest potential level of integrated functioning. Integration anxiety, a fear of relinquishing the stability of a lower level of functioning in trying to achieve a higher level of integrated functioning, may thwart the drive toward self-integration. Analysis still entails conflict/defense analysis, yet it is not so much defenses against forbidden wishes that are analyzed as it is defenses against integrating conflicting and seemingly incompatible aspects of the self. Overall, the analyst functions as a selfobject who promotes the acquisition of higher levels of integrated functioning and as such strengthens the self and in so doing makes the self less vulnerable to anxiety. Anxiety is the signal of a self in distress. That signal is not only a communication to the self to institute defenses, but a signal to the selfobject to execute its function more effectively. To the degree that the analyst can register the patient's anxiety as a communication of interpersonal distress, the analyst may be able to respond with empathy and thereby support the patient's own strivings toward integration.

REFERENCES

Breuer, J., & Freud, S. (1895). *Studies on hysteria. Standard Edition 2*. London: Hogarth Press, 1955.

Freud, S. (1894). *The neuropsychoses of defense. Standard Edition 3*, 43–61. London: Hogarth Press, 1962.

Freud, S. (1898). *Sexuality in the aetiology of the neuroses. Standard Edition 3*, 261–285. London: Hogarth Press, 1962.

Freud, S. (1905). *Three essays on the theory of sexuality. Standard Edition 7*, 125–243. London: Hogarth Press, 1953.

Freud, S. (1926). *Inhibitions, symptoms, and anxiety. Standard Edition 20*, 77–174. London: Hogarth Press, 1959.

Frosch, S. (1991). *Identity crisis: Modernity, psychoanalysis, and the self*. New York: Routledge.

Greenberg, J. (1991). *Oedipus and beyond: A clinical theory*. Cambridge, MA: Harvard University Press.

Horney, K. (1950). *Neurosis and human growth*. New York: Norton.

Josephs, L. (1992). *Character structure and the organization of the self*. New York: Columbia University Press.

Kernberg, O. (1975). *Borderline conditions and pathological narcissism*. New York: Aronson.

Klein, G. (1976). *Psychoanalytic theory: An exploration of essentials*. New York: International Universities Press.

Kohut, H. (1971). *The analysis of the self*. New York: International Universities Press.

Kohut, H. (1977). *The restoration of the self.* New York: International Universities Press.

Stolorow, R., & Lachmann, F. (1980). *Psychoanalysis of developmental arrests.* New York: International Universities Press.

Sullivan, H. S. (1953). *The interpersonal theory of anxiety.* New York: Norton.

Wolf, E. (1988). *Treating the self: Elements of clinical self psychology.* New York: Guilford.

CHAPTER 3

Behavioral Interpretations

PAUL M.G. EMMELKAMP, PhD, and AGNES SCHOLING, PhD

In this chapter an overview is given of behavioral theories with respect to the etiology and maintenance of anxiety disorders. After a discussion of the current status of learning theories in explaining the acquisition and maintenance of fears and phobias, separate sections are devoted to the development of panic disorder, social phobia, generalized anxiety disorder, post-traumatic stress disorder, and obsessive-compulsive disorder.

LEARNING THEORIES

The two-stage theory (Mowrer, 1960) of fear acquisition has been highly influential, and despite some serious criticisms (e.g., Mineka, 1979), it still plays a prominent role in current thinking of the development of phobias. Mowrer explicitly distinguished between a classical conditioning process, responsible for the conditioning of fear, and an operant conditioning or instrumental learning process, responsible for the conditioning of the avoidance response. The model was developed on the basis of animal experiments. In training procedures, animals receive repeated pairings of a warning signal (for example, a tone (CS)) and an aversive stimulus (for example, a shock (UCS)). After some time, the tone will acquire aversive properties and the animal will experience anxiety (CR) on tone presentation when no shock is applied. This phase of the experimental procedure represents the first stage of learning, in which anxiety is attached to previously neutral cues through classical conditioning. In the second stage, the animal learns to terminate the tone by making escape responses, reducing thereby the anxiety. The termination or avoidance of aversive stimuli leads to negative reinforcement (anxiety reduction), thus strengthening the avoidance behavior. This second stage of learning involves operant conditioning. In summary, it is assumed that fear is acquired through a process of classical conditioning and motivates avoidance behavior.

The assumption of the two-stage theory that avoidance is mediated by fear is supported neither by everyday experiences nor by experimental results. There is ample evidence that avoidance behavior can be acquired and maintained in the absence of fear as a mediating factor (Gray, 1975). A more serious difficulty for the theory is the observation that often extinction of avoidance responses does not occur (Mineka, 1979). If the first stage of the theory is correct, it would be expected that rapid extinction of fear, and hence of avoidance behavior, should occur when the UCS is no longer present. However, there is abundant evidence that avoidance behavior, when established, is highly resistant to extinction, despite the fact that, according to the extinction paradigm, conditioned fear itself must start to extinguish as soon as the shocks are no longer given. Modifications of the two-stage theory have been proposed involving the safety-signal theory (Mowrer, 1960) and Herrnstein's (1969) theory of expectancies. In current theorizing, instrumental conditioning is held responsible for maintaining the avoidance behavior for some of the time only.

The safety signal theory assumes that it is not anxiety reduction *per se* but safety signals that positively reinforce avoidance behavior. This version differs from Mowrer's original position in that it includes, in addition to the negative reinforcement (anxiety reduction), the presence of secondary rewarding stimuli (i.e., safety signals) as a potential source of reinforcement for avoidance behavior (Gray, 1975). According to this model, safety signals acquire positive reinforcement properties, so that avoidance behavior is motivated not only by an escape from fear, but also by an approach to safety, and resistance to extinction is explained by the reinforcement of the avoidance behavior through the simultaneous presence of safety signals.

Research by Herrnstein and his colleagues led to another important modification of the two-stage theory (Herrnstein, 1969). In Mowrer's original view, avoidance behavior is maintained by the reinforcing escape from the anxiety-provoking conditioned stimulus. Herrnstein (1969) argued that CS termination is an unnecessary feature of avoidance procedures. In a particularly well-designed study, Herrnstein and Hineline (1966) were able to demonstrate that the classically conditioned fear responses are not a requirement for the instrumental behavior. In their study, rats were offered a choice between two frequencies of being shocked at unpredictable intervals. Lever pressing resulted in the lower shock frequency, but after some time control reverted to the schedule with the higher shock frequency until the animal's next lever press. Thus, animals could learn to choose being shocked at a lower frequency, rather than escape or avoid shock. Most animals learned to respond. Herrnstein (1969) argued that the reinforcement for avoidance behavior is a reduction in time of aversive stimulation. Further experiments suggested that the conditioned stimuli may function as discriminative stimuli for avoidance responses.

As shown in studies by Herrnstein (1969), avoidance behavior can be ruled by preferences rather than by anxiety *per se*. This could explain the persistence of avoidance behavior in the absence of fear, as is often seen in clinical cases.

Theoretical Innovations

Paradigmatic behaviorists (e.g., Eifert & Evans, 1990; Hekmat, 1987) hold that phobias are not acquired exclusively through a first-order conditioning process. In their view, phobic reactions are not only acquired through aversive classical conditioning, but may also be acquired by higher-order semantic conditioning processes. Thus, language conditioning is given an important role in the development of human fear reactions. In this view, a snake phobia does not necessarily develop through classical conditioning or vicarious learning, but "The word 'snake' by virtue of being semantically accrued to negatively valued words such as 'ugly, poison, disgusting, slimy, etc.' may have indirectly acquired negative reactions through higher-order semantic conditioning" (Hekmat, 1987, p. 201).

Other authors have attempted to amplify the conditioning hypotheses with recent insights of cognitive theories (Baeyens, Eeelen, Crombez, & Van den Bergh, 1992; Davey, 1992; Martin & Levey, 1985). Levey and Martin (1983, 1985) distinguished between two ways of learning, the first being a relatively immediate registration of stimuli associated with (positive or negative) events, the second being a more cognitive process, in which experiences of the past are summarized and repeated. They stated that these summaries form the basis of the hypotheses and schemata that are assumed in cognitive theories. In the same way, Baeyens et al. (1992) described signal learning versus evaluative learning, the second being conceived as a kind of referential learning in which the CS activates a (cognitive) UCS-representation. Davey (1992) proposed a model of human conditioning, in which outcome expectancy, expectancy evaluation, cognitive representations of the UCS, and revaluation processes play a major role. According to Davey, this model differs from more traditional conditioning theories in the following aspects: (1) the association between CS and UCS can be influenced by factors other than the experienced contingency, and (2) a performance component is added that suggests that the strength of the CS is determined by nonassociative factors, which influence the evaluation of the UCS. Models assuming cognitive representations may be promising in that they have better explanations for phenomena that could not be explained by the more traditional models, like the absence of clear traumatic experiences at the onset of a fear reaction, the failure to develop a phobia after clear traumatic experiences, and incubation effects.

More recently, Barlow (1988) has formulated a model in which both biological vulnerability and learning factors play a role. In this model, it is assumed that in biologically vulnerable individuals severe stress will lead to alarm reactions (fear or panic attack) that prepare the individual for immediate action (fight or flight). The stressor is experienced as uncontrollable ("I may not be able to deal effectively with it") and unpredictable ("It might happen again"), resulting in a preparatory coping set that is manifested as chronic arousal and anxious apprehension. Apart from the biological vulnerability, which is possibly genetically transmitted, the model also assumes a psychological vulnerability, namely a specific attribution style. This style is characterized by thoughts of uncontrollability and unpredictability and is considered to be a consequence of specific developmental experiences. Thus individuals who were raised by parents who were oversensitive to illnesses are likely to interpret physical sensations as threatening, meaning that something is wrong with their body. Alternatively, individuals raised by parents who were overly concerned with scrutiny of others may focus their anxious apprehension on social evaluation. The focus of anxious apprehension in individuals with post-traumatic stress disorder is on cognitive and physiological cues associated with the original trauma.

Barlow (1988) differentiated three types of alarm: (1) true alarm, (2) false alarm, and (3) learned alarm. Reactions during a real life-threatening event are seen as true alarm, whereas false alarms occur in the absence of real life-threatening events. The association of false alarms with internal or external cues results in the phenomenon of learned alarm. Conditioned responses to either interoceptive or external cues are considered learned alarms. Such learned alarms may be only partial responses, such as cognitive representations without the physiological component of anxiety.

Thus, according to Barlow, anxious apprehension is the result of a complex interaction of biological, psychological, and environmental events. In individuals with a biological and psychological vulnerability, an anxious circle develops: " . . . once this cycle begins, it becomes self-perpetuating: a sense of unpredictability and uncontrollability increases emotionality, which in turn increases the probability of learned alarms . . ." (p. 276).

Classical Conditioning of Fear

What evidence is available that fears and phobias are acquired through a process of classical conditioning? The classical conditioning paradigm states that neutral stimuli, when associated with fear or pain, elicit fear reactions, and that the strength of the fear is determined by (1) the number of repetitions of the association between the stimuli and the emotional reactions, and (2) the intensity of the emotion experienced. Central to the model are one or more traumatic experiences in which the association between stimulus and fear reaction is learned.

A number of studies obtained information about the acquisition of simple phobias and specific fears; and results suggest that classical conditioning may be involved in a number of cases. Research done by Rimm, Janda, Lancaster, Nahl, and Ditmar (1977) showed that 16 out of 45 phobic volunteers reported direct experiences of a more or less traumatic nature. In a study by Fazio (1972), on the genesis of insect phobias, similar results were found. In contrast, Murray and Foote (1979), studying the origins of snake phobia, found very few frightening experiences with snakes in their phobic group. These studies are, however, of questionable relevance, since the subjects consisted of normal subjects with fears, rather than patients with simple phobics.

Lautch (1971) found that patients with dental phobia ($n = 34$) reported having had a traumatic dental experience on at least one occasion in childhood. However, all patients were diagnosed as generally neurotic, whereas 10 control subjects with comparable traumatic experiences showed little sign of dental fear. Goldstein and Chambless (1978) compared 32 agoraphobics with 36 patients with simple phobias and found that only 4 agoraphobics reported conditioning events at the onset of the phobia, in contrast with 17 simple phobics, suggesting that conditioning events are etiologically more important in simple phobias than in agoraphobia. McNally and Steketee (1985) reported data on the etiology of severe animal phobias. All patients ($n = 22$) stated that the phobia had begun in early childhood and had remained stable or worsened with age. The majority of the patients (77%) could not remember the onset of the phobia. Two of them had parents who witnessed the origin of the phobia, which left 68% of the cases unclassifiable. Out of the 7 patients who remembered the onset, 6 patients attributed it to experiences interpretable as conditioning events (which were frightening encounters, no patient reported that the animal had inflicted pain). Only 1 patient reported indirect learning experiences, like watching frightening movies. In a study by DiNardo, Guzy, Jenkins, Bak, Tomasi, et al. (1988) on fear of dogs, conditioning events were reported by 56% of the fearful subjects and 66% of nonfearful subjects. All fearful subjects believed that fear and physical harm were likely consequences of confrontation with a dog, while few nonfearful subjects had such expectations. The study suggested that painful experiences seem to be common in the history of dog fears, in contrast with the results of McNally and Steketee (1985) and results found with snake fears (Murray & Foote, 1979). However, no evidence was found for etiological significance, because those experiences were at least equally common among nonfearful subjects. Exaggerated expectation of harm, a cognitive factor, seemed to play a role in the maintenance of the fear.

Öst and Hugdahl (1981, 1983, 1985) studied how patients with clinical phobias remembered the onset of their fears. Patients rated the way they acquired their fear on a phobic origin questionnaire, based on the three pathways to fear theory that was proposed by Rachman (1978). The first pathway, *conditioning,* includes exposure to traumatic experiences. The second, *vicarious learning,* refers to direct or indirect observations of people displaying fear. The third pathway is by *transmission of fear-inducing information.* The results showed that conditioning experiences were most frequently mentioned in all subgroups of simple phobias studied: claustrophobics (67.7%), dental phobics (65.6%), animal phobics (50.0%), and blood phobics (50.0%). Hekmat (1987) investigated the factors leading to development and maintenance of human fear reactions in animal phobics ($n = 56$) and nonphobic undergraduate controls ($n = 18$). Evidence was found for fear acquisition through conditioning, vicarious processes, and information / instruction pathways. Ollendick and King (1991) obtained data from 556 female and 536 male Australian and American children and adolescents. The majority attributed onset of their fears to vicarious and instructional factors, although these indirect sources of fear were often combined with direct conditioning experiences. The findings suggested that the three pathways to fear are interactive rather than independent.

In sum, although the results suggest that conditioning processes may play a role in the onset of some simple phobias, it is more and more recognized that other factors, like indirect conditioning processes, seem to be important as well.

Several studies have investigated the role of classical conditioning in the etiology of *agoraphobia.* As noted, Goldstein and Chambless (1978) found that the onset of the agoraphobia was marked by a conditioning event in only 4 out of 32 agoraphobics. In the Buglass, Clarke, Henderson, Kreitman, and Presley (1977) study, results showed that in only 7 out of 30 agoraphobics discrete events at the time of the onset of the agoraphobia could be identified. Also, only two of these events were "specific," meaning that the event occurred in the setting in which the patient was subsequently phobic. Similar results were found by Solyom, Beck, Solyom, and Huger (1974) and Bowen and Kohout (1979). In contrast, research by Öst and his colleagues (Öst & Hugdahl, 1983; Öst, 1985, 1987) suggested that conditioning was much more frequently involved in the development of agoraphobia (ranging from 81–89%).

To summarize the studies reviewed so far, there is conflicting evidence that classical conditioning is an important factor to account for development of agoraphobia. There is more evidence provided that classical conditioning of fear is involved in the development of specific phobias. The latter conclusion, however, needs to be qualified by the finding that even with specific phobias in a substantial number of cases no traumatic experiences could be identified in relation with onset of the phobia. A problem in these studies is the definition of a traumatic conditioning event. A minimum requirement of the classical conditioning paradigm is that not only should a traumatic experience be identified, but also that the subject should have experienced pain or anxiety in the situation that subsequently led to the phobia. Unfortunately, most studies we reported on did not provide data with respect to this point. Thus, the occurrence of traumatic incidents in the history of a phobic patient, even when in some way related to the development of the phobia, is by itself insufficient evidence that classical conditioning can be held responsible for the acquisition of the phobia.

Vicarious Learning

In an attempt to explain the development of fears that are not associated with traumatic learning experiences, one might argue that in these cases fears are acquired through vicarious learning (Rachman, 1978). According to this paradigm, observing others experiencing anxiety in specific situations might lead to fear of those situations for the observer.

Indirect evidence in favor of a vicarious learning interpretation for the acquisition of phobias came from studies demonstrating that children often share the fears of their parents. Particularly, mothers may be an important etiological factor in children's fear (Emmelkamp, 1982). Several studies indicated that mother and children are frequently fearful of the same situation, which can be considered to support a vicarious learning interpretation of the etiology of children's fears. On the other hand, it should be noted that a relationship between fears of mother and child can also be the result of processes other than vicarious learning, for example, informational processes, genetic influences, or similar traumatic experiences.

That fears can be acquired through modeling was demonstrated by Mineka and her colleagues. For example, laboratory reared monkeys who initially were not fearful of snakes, developed a snake phobia as a result of observing wild monkeys displaying fear in the presence of a snake (Cook & Mineka, 1991). Other indirect evidence in favor of the vicarious transmission of fear came from retrospective patient reports. Several investigations of war neurosis showed that in certain cases fear of war experiences was caused by observing accidents of other soldiers (e.g., Kipper, 1977). Kipper, in analyzing the circumstances surrounding the development of fears in soldiers in the Yom Kippur War, identified three sets of conditions under which these fears were acquired. The first set of conditions involved a sudden realization of danger. In the second group, fears developed "more or less accidentally." A third group of conditions "involved fears acquired vicariously while observing the unfortunate fate of fellow soldiers" (p. 218).

The studies by Fazio (1972) and Rimm et al. (1977) provided further evidence that vicarious learning might be responsible for the acquisition of fears in only a few cases: 13% of the subjects with an insect phobia (Fazio, 1972) and 7% of the subjects with other specific phobias (Rimm et al., 1977) reported vicarious learning experiences. Further, the Murray and Foote (1979) study presented "only marginal evidence of vicarious experiences in the acquisition of fear of snakes" (p. 491) and, in the studies by Öst and his colleagues discussed above, vicarious learning was less prevalent than conditioning. Finally, results of a study by Merkelbach, de Ruiter, Van den Hout, and Hoekstra (1989) suggested that in most phobic patients both conditioning factors and vicarious learning are involved.

In sum, studies on etiology of phobias have demonstrated that patients attribute onset of the fears to traumatic experiences, vicarious learning, and fearful information or instruction about the feared stimuli. However, studies that compared phobic patients with controls without such fears did not show clear differences in the frequency of one of these factors, pointing to the fact that conditioning experiences, even those of a painful nature, do not automatically lead to phobic reactions. Development of fear seems to be determined by other factors, for example neuroticism (Eysenck & Rachman, 1965; Lautch, 1971) or expectations (DiNardo et al., 1988), interpretations (Rachman, 1991a,b) and, more generally, spoken, cognitive representations of the feared stimulus (Davey, 1992). A major drawback of all studies is their retrospective character. Only prospective studies will be able to give more reliable information on acquisition of phobic reactions.

Preparedness

Some hold that individuals differ in genetically based predispositions to acquire fears to specific situations. From an evolutionary perspective, phobias represent examples of evolutionarily primed predispositions to acquire fears for situations involving danger. What evidence is available that there are predispositions to acquire phobias for specific situations over other situations? According to the classical conditioning theory, any stimulus that is paired with an unconditioned stimulus that invokes pain or anxiety should result in a conditioned emotional reaction after a number of pairings. However, this assumption is no longer adequately defensible. Consider, for example, experiments of the kind in which one has attempted to condition fear in infants. Several such experiments have been reported and they show that the nature of the conditioned stimulus is of paramount importance for conditioning of fear to occur. English (1929) was unable to condition fear to a wooden toy duck, but he succeeded in producing conditioned fear to a stuffed black cat. Bregman (1934) also failed to condition fear in infants. In this study, the conditioned stimuli consisted of shapes and colored clothes. Taken together, the variable results of the studies by Bregman (1934), English (1929), and Watson and Rayner (1920) seem to indicate that fear might be much more easily conditioned to animals and furry objects than to wooden objects, shapes, and clothes. This finding suggests that there might be an innate base for some fear development. Marks (1969) suggested the concept of "prepotency" of certain stimuli to explain the development of some human phobias. Along similar lines, Seligman (1971) viewed phobias as instances of highly "prepared" learning. According to Seligman, the majority of clinical phobias concerns objects of natural importance to the survival of the species. In his view, evolution has preprogrammed the human species to easily acquire phobias to potentially dangerous situations. Such prepared learning is selective, highly resistant to extinction, probably noncognitive, and can be acquired in one trial.

In recent years, Öhman and his colleagues (Öhman, 1987) have tested the preparedness theory experimentally. The studies by Öhman and his associates demonstrated that the stimulus content variable plays a major role with respect to resistance to extinction and far less so with respect to the acquisition phase, thus partially supporting the preparedness theory. As phrased by Öhman (1987):

> Potentially phobic stimuli such as pictures of snakes or angry faces have special effects, compared to those of neutral stimuli, when they are presented in a Pavlovian contingency with electric shock US. The results, therefore, are in accord with the basic premise of the preparedness theory that these types of stimuli have a biologically determined readiness to become easily imbued with fear. (p. 148)

On the theoretical side, Öhman (1987) argued that social fears are associated with a social submissiveness system, whereas animal fears are associated with a predatory defense system. As yet, this differentiation is purely speculative and not substantiated by experimental evidence. Despite some evidence in favor of preparedness provided by Öhman and his colleagues, the results of these studies need to be qualified in several ways (Emmelkamp, 1982; McNally, 1987). Although Öhman provides some evidence in support of the role of preparedness in laboratory fear extinction, it is a very bold claim to generalize these findings to human phobias. All subjects in their experiments were normal nonphobic college students. Further, only psychophysiological data were used as the dependent variable. Phobic anxiety is usually conceptualized as three different systems—subjective, physiological, and behavioral—which do not always covary.

Another line of research was followed by Mineka (1979). She investigated whether fear of snakes in monkeys had a prepared basis. Laboratory-reared animals with no fear of snakes were exposed to a wild-reared animal displaying fear of snakes. As a result of vicarious learning, the laboratory-reared animals developed a phobia for snakes. Related studies on monkeys showed that the fear was conditioned only to snakes and not to flowers, even when the model monkey had displayed fear to both snake and flower. Similar results were found with the acquisition of fear of crocodiles in contrast with the nonacquisition of fear of rabbits.

Although the results of the studies by Öhman and associates and Mineka are intriguing and provided support for the preparedness theory, it is still unclear what the implications are for the development of clinical phobias in humans. To make this theory clinically relevant, it needs to be demonstrated that phobias of phobic patients are of a prepared nature. In retrospective analyses, it was found that most of the phobias of phobic patients could be classified as prepared both in Western (De Silva, Rachman, & Seligman, 1977; Zalfiropoulo & McPherson, 1986) and non-Western cultures (De Silva, 1988). However, results of a study by Merkelbach, Van den Hout, Hoekstra, and Van Oppen (1988) did not corroborate these findings. In their study among Dutch severe phobics, no evidence was found that most of the phobias were of a prepared nature.

PANIC DISORDER

Until the 1980s, panic had not been of central interest to behavioral researchers. In behavioral research, the emphasis was more on the avoidance behavior (agoraphobia) than on the panic associated with it. Klein (1981) argued that panic was mediated by a discrete biological mechanism and that the emphasis in treatment should be on remedying the dysfunctional biological structure, preferably by tricyclic-antidepressants, rather than on dealing with the avoidance behavior.

Behavioral clinicians have been aware for decades that in a number of agoraphobics the development of the agoraphobia was preceded by an episode or a series of episodes of panic attacks, but—forced by the emphasis on panic in the biological psychiatry camp—only recently panic has been studied more directly. This research, more extensively discussed elsewhere (e.g., Ehlers & Margraf, 1989; McNally, 1990), emphasizes psychological factors in the development and course of panic disorder.

Interoceptive Conditioning

Both Van den Hout (1988) and Wolpe and Rowan (1988) suggested that panic may be acquired through interoceptive conditioning. According to Van den Hout (1988), anxiety is the aversive event and the associated bodily sensations act as conditioned stimuli. As a result of repeated pairings between panic and bodily sensations, the latter evoke anxiety as a conditioned response. Similarly, Wolpe and Rowan (1988) hold that "the initial panic is an unconditioned response to a bizarre stimulus complex produced by excessive hyperventilation, and panic disorder is the result of contiguous stimuli, especially endogenous stimuli, being conditioned to the elicited anxiety" (p. 441). The interoceptive conditioning model, however, is not without problems. First, as noted by Van den Hout (1988) the notion that panic patients fear bodily sensations is not unique for interoceptive conditioning but also plays a crucial role in the cognitive explanatory account of panic, a model in which catastrophic misinterpretations of bodily sensations account for the acquisition and maintenance of panic. Further, McNally (1990) has criticized the vagueness of the definition of the CS and UCS in the interoceptive conditioning model. It is indeed difficult to define exactly which interoceptive cue might be regarded as UCS or CS, making it difficult to verify the theory.

Separation Anxiety

It has been suggested that childhood separation from parents and associated anxiety are precursors of panic disorders in adults. The separation anxiety hypothesis has some face validity, given the apparent similarities between the two conditions. A number of studies suggested that panic patients or agoraphobics were in childhood more frequently separated from their parents than patients with other anxiety disorders, like generalized anxiety and social phobia (Persson & Nordlund, 1985; Raskin, Peek, Dickman, & Pinsker, 1982). There is no evidence, however, that actual separation in childhood occurred more often in panic patients or agoraphobics than in simple phobics (Thyer, Himle, & Fischer, 1988) or in patients with other psychiatric disorders (Van der Molen, Van den Hout, Van Dieren, & Griez, 1989). Further, Raskin et al. (1982) did *not* find differences in separation *anxiety* in childhood. Similarly, Thyer, Nesse, Cameron, and Curtis (1985) and Thyer, Nesse, Curtis, and Cameron (1986) found no difference in childhood separation anxiety between panic patients and simple phobics. Finally, Van der Molen et al. (1989) found no more childhood separation anxiety in panic patients than in psychiatric controls and normal controls. In sum, although the results are inconclusive, there is little support yet for the notion that childhood separation and separation anxiety are precursors of panic or agoraphobia in adults.

Life Events

Life events have been hypothesized to be related to the onset of panic. Results of studies in this area are inconclusive: some (e.g., Faravelli, 1985; Hibbert, 1984; Last, Barlow, & O'Brien, 1984; Öst & Hugdahl, 1983; Ottaviani & Beck, 1987; Sheehan, Sheehan, & Minichiellon, 1981) found an excess of life events before the onset of the panic disorders or agoraphobia, but others did not (e.g., Roy-Byrne, Geraci, & Uhole, 1986). Foa, Steketee, and Young (1984), reviewing the literature, found that the most frequent stressors preceding agoraphobia were loss of a significant other and physical threat. Kleiner and Marshall (1987), however, found marital conflict and family conflict as the two most frequent precipitants. Research in this area has a number of problems. Both the onset of the panic disorder and the occurrence of the life events can often not be dated exactly. Further, most studies did not involve a control group, thus it is unclear whether this incidence of life events exceeds that in a normal population. Moreover, even though a number of stressors are involved, they cannot completely account for the development of panic disorders, because (1) such stressors have also been found to be associated with other psychiatric and psychosomatic disorders, and (2) many individuals who experience these stressors do not develop any disorder at all.

How does stress relate to the development of panic disorders in behavioral terms? The most parsimonious explanation is in terms of interceptive conditioning. Anxiety, as a result of such stressors, may result in a panic attack, which may be experienced as coming "out of the blue." As a consequence, persons with such unexpected attacks may develop fear of somatic sensations associated with a panic attack (e.g., heart palpitations, shortness of breath) and become quite sensitive to somatic manifestations, which can result in a vicious circle. They tend to interpret somatic sensations as evidence of a serious medical problem ("catastrophizing"), which will increase the anxiety level and may accumulate into other panic attacks.

Panic and Agoraphobic Avoidance

Theoretically, one would expect that patients who experience panic attacks in a particular situation will try to escape that situation and will avoid that situation subsequently. Indeed, for most patients, panic precedes the development of agoraphobic avoidance behavior (Lelliott, Marks, McNamer, & Tobema, 1989; Rapee & Murrell, 1988; Schneier et al., 1991; Thyer & Himle, 1985). According to the two-stage theory, a linear relationship between severity of the panic attack and severity of the avoidance behavior is expected. Clum and Knowless (1991) reviewed the research in this area and found support neither for the hypothesis that severity of attacks was related to severity of avoidance, nor that more frequent attacks and attacks that persist over a long period of time predicted severity of avoidance behavior. There is, however, some evidence that cognitions are related to avoidance. Anticipation of panic in specific situations leads to avoidance of that situation. As phrased by Rachman (1991b), "They do not engage in avoidance behavior simply because of past panics; rather . . . they avoid because of their current prediction that they are likely to panic in a particular place during a particular period of time" (p. 188). Further, strong expectations of negative (social) consequences were found to be related to avoidance of situations in which these consequences may occur. In this respect, results of a study of Rapee and Murrell (1988) are also of interest. They found that panic disorder patients with extensive avoidance were less assertive, less extravert, and more socially anxious than patients with minimal avoidance. More recently, Robinson and Brichwood (1991) found that panic patients with marked avoidance have significantly stronger social-evaluative concerns. There is some evidence that gender is related to avoidance. The prevalence of female panic patients with avoidance behavior is four times as high as the prevalence of panic disorder with avoidance among males, whereas panic disorder without avoidance behavior is more equally distributed across the sexes. The reasons why more females develop avoidance behavior after a (series of) panic attack(s) are unclear. Chambless (1989) found that severity of avoidance behavior was associated with femininity scores on measures of gender role.

SOCIAL PHOBIA

Few studies have been conducted on the etiology and maintenance of social phobia—an irrational and excessive fear of social evaluation. It has been suggested that this state of affairs is caused by a number of factors, for example, lack of recognition of the disorder and symptom overlap with other anxiety disorders (Bruch, 1989) and problems in distinguishing social phobia from "normal" social anxiety on the one hand (Scholing & Emmelkamp, 1990) and from related disorders like avoidant personality disorder or shyness (Turner, Beidel, Dancu, & Keys, 1986) on the other. Initially, fear of social situations was conceptualized as a conditioned response, acquired by traumatic experiences in social situations (Wolpe, 1958). Another influential paradigm, more exclusive for social phobia, is the skills deficit model, in which a central role is ascribed to inadequate social skills, provoking aversive reactions from other people, which in turn lead to anxiety (Trower, Bryant, & Argyle, 1978). In fact, the models are not mutually exclusive. They both emphasize traumatic or aversive experiences in social contacts, the skills deficit model placing more emphasis on the origin of those experiences. Results from studies that were conducted to test the models are equivocal. Some support for the conditioned response hypothesis was found by Öst and Hugdahl (1981), who found that 58% of social phobics recalled a traumatic social experience before the onset of the complaint. As was noted earlier, results from these studies should be interpreted cautiously, because memories often yield a distorted picture of the past, and because results must be compared with results about childhood memories of normals. In addition, results of such studies are heavily dependent on definitions of what qualifies as a conditioning event. Apart from this, the classical conditioning explanation has other shortcomings. Although this paradigm can explain the development of a phobia after a traumatic experience, the model is inadequate in explaining the gradual development of social phobias that is often reported by social phobic patients (Amies, Gelder, & Shaw, 1983). Evidence for the skills deficit model was partly inferred from the fact that social skills training led to a decrease of fear in social situations (Marzillier, Lambert, & Kellett, 1976). However, the effectiveness of social skills training is on its own not sufficient to conclude that inadequate skills play a role in the etiology of the complaints. Results of studies investigating whether social phobics are less socially competent than normals are inconclusive (Arkowitz, 1977; Beidel, Turner, & Dancu, 1985; Dow, Biglan, & Glaser, 1985), and it has been suggested that social skills deficits are of less importance in the etiology of social anxiety than once thought (Edelmann, 1985; Newton, Kindness, & McFudyen, 1983). As a consequence of the shortcomings of the conditioned anxiety and skills-deficits models in explaining the origin of social phobia, attention shifted to more cognitively oriented models (Hartman, 1983; Leary, 1988; Lucock & Salkovskis, 1988), which will be discussed in Chapter 5 of this volume. However, the recent developments and refinements of the conditioning hypothesis, placing more emphasis on indirect ways of conditioning and cognitive representations of conditioned stimuli, may be especially useful for social phobics. Although onset age of social phobia was found to be early adolescence (Marks & Gelder, 1966; Öst, 1987), it has been suggested that factors predisposing individuals to such fears originate from early socialization processes. The fact that parental attitudes may play a prominent role in these processes has led to family studies and research on child-rearing practices.

Windheuser (1977) found a remarkable similarity between phobias of children and those of their mothers, especially for social phobics. Bruch, Heimberg, Berger, and Collins (1989) also reported that parents of social phobics avoided certain social situations. These results could be interpreted in terms of vicarious learning.

Buss (1980) stated that social anxiety is the result of negative childhood and adolescent experiences in situations in which evaluation by other people plays a major role. He assumed specific parental rearing styles to be responsible for hypersensitivity for social evaluation. As a matter of fact, studies on parental rearing styles have yielded differences in perceived parental behaviors between social phobics and agoraphobics. Parker (1979) found that social phobics (retrospectively) described both of their parents as showing little affection and being overprotective, whereas agoraphobics only reported that their mother had been low on emotional support but not overprotective. This finding led Parker to conclude that " . . . parental overprotection, by restricting the usual developmental processes of independence, autonomy and social competence, might further promote any diathesis to a social phobia . . ." (p. 559). Arrindell, Emmelkamp, Monsma, and Brilman (1983) compared memories of parental rearing styles of social phobics and agoraphobics, and found the same results as Parker did. Bruch et al. (1989) again found differences between social phobics and agoraphobics in that the social phobics reported that their parents had isolated them from social events and often worried about other people's opinions of the family.

GENERALIZED ANXIETY

There is no specific behavioral theory with respect to the development of generalized anxiety disorder (GAD). GAD is often conceptualized as a life-long characteristic, so if learning factors are involved, these have to be located in childhood. Not surprisingly, the few studies into the etiology of GAD are of a retrospective nature (Rapee, 1991) and have no direct bearing on an interpretation of the development of GAD in terms of learning theories. Since GAD does not have a specific focus, but is characterized by free-floating anxiety, it has many similarities with trait anxiety (Eysenck & Mathews, 1987), which is defined as an individual's disposition to perceive a wide range of stimulus situations as dangerous or threatening (Spielberger, 1972). Recent experimental work has considered the information processing of GAD patients. Mathews and his colleagues consistently have shown in a number of laboratory experiments that selective attentional attraction to threat cues is characteristic for generalized anxiety patients (Mathews, 1989). It remains to be shown whether selective emotional processing is cause, consequence, or just one of the cognitive symptoms of GAD. A detailed discussion of these cognitive studies is outside the scope of this chapter.

Another important theoretical development from a behavioral perspective are studies into worrying (Borkovec & Inz, 1990). Worrying is one of the characteristic components of GAD. According to DSM-III-R (APA, 1987), GAD is characterized by unrealistic or excessive anxiety and worry (apprehensive expectation) about two or more life circumstances, for example, worry about possible misfortune to one's child (who is in no danger) and worry about finances (for no good reason), for a period of six months or longer, during which the person has been upset more days than not by these concerns. Worries are characterized by having a continuous stream of thoughts and images with respect to future negative events and the (un)ability to cope with them. The focus of the anxious apprehension is usually rather diffuse and often on "daily hassles." Such persons are oversensitive to relatively minor events. Borkovec and his colleagues found, however, that worriers were unable to solve the problem or come to a definite solution. Worriers are further differentiated from nonworriers in terms of distraction: worriers are unable to stop their ruminations and to engage in distracting thoughts, images, or activities. It is tempting to assume that such worrying increases arousal which in turn increases the worrying so that the individual is no longer able to shut off worry activity. According to Borkovec and Inz (1990), this vicious circle is self-perpetuating. Actually, the worrier may have the illusory feeling that by worrying he or she is doing something to deal with the negative future events (Barlow, 1988). It has further been suggested that worry "may represent an avoidance of affect in general or emotional experience in particular" (Borkovec & Inz, 1990, p. 158). By engaging in worrying, actual exposure to fearful situations is prevented, resulting in maintenance of the anxiety. Thus, worrying is conceptualized as an inadequate coping device (cognitive avoidance), which impedes emotional processing of fear stimuli and actually maintains GAD.

Barlow (1988) has argued that GAD is the end result of a process in which multiple etiological factors are involved. According to Barlow (1988), GAD patients have a biological vulnerability and experience external stressors (life events and daily hassles) as uncontrollable and unpredictable, eventually culminating in a spiral of worrying. Although this model has some appeal, it is far from proven yet.

POST-TRAUMATIC STRESS DISORDER (PTSD)

According to Foa, Steketee, and Olasov Rothbaum (1989), it is tempting to consider PTSD as a prototype for etiology and symptomatology of phobia. " . . . there is a recognizable traumatic stimulus, following which an individual shows fear reactions when confronted with situations associated with or similar to the original trauma" (p. 156). As they themselves note, however, there are many important differences between phobias and PTSD. Anxiety is sufficient for the diagnosis of phobia, whereas in PTSD other emotions as hostility and numbness of feelings are also important. Other characteristic symptoms of PTSD as flashbacks, nightmares, sleep disturbance, startle responses, and feeling of detachment from others are not characteristic of phobias.

Most behavioral researchers use Mowrer's two-stage theory to explain post-traumatic stress disorder (e.g., Kilpatrick, Veronen, and Best (1985) on PTSD in rape victims and Keane, Zimmerling, and Caddell (1985) on PTSD in Vietnam veterans). Two other learning processes are also involved; higher order conditioning and stimulus generalization. In higher order conditioning stimuli that were originally conditioned to the traumatic event are paired with other unconditioned stimuli, which eventually may result in a new conditioned response. Through this process of higher order conditioning, many stimuli, including thoughts and images, may evoke anxiety. Stimulus generalization refers to the tendency of an organism to transfer its acquired response to new stimulus situations as a function of stimulus similarity. Taken together, these two learning processes may explain the gradual worsening of symptoms over time. As a result, often many more cues than actually present at the time of the traumatic event are capable of eliciting traumatic memories and emotions. Further, Keane et al. (1985) stressed the importance of lack of social support in the development of PTSD. They hypothesize that patients who have an adequate social support system are less likely to develop a (severe) PTSD than patients who have less adequate or no social support at all.

The conditioning explanation of PTSD has some appeal, but is not without problems. Why does exposure to traumatic memories as occurs in re-experiencing the original trauma not lead to habituation and extinction of anxiety? It has been suggested by Keane et al. (1985) that such exposure is incomplete because not the whole stimulus complex is included. Indeed, most PTSD sufferers tend to avoid thinking of important aspects of the traumatic situations because of the aversiveness of the situation and the anxiety it evokes. Thus, it does not come as a surprise that such occasional exposure is ineffective. In addition, patients are inclined to shut off memories and re-experiences when these occur, resulting in a too short exposure time to be effective (Emmelkamp, 1982). Further, the hostility, numbness of affect, startle response, and the occurrence of nightmares are not easily explained in conditioning terms. Part of these problems may be solved by taking into account research on experimental neurosis. Mineka and Kihlstrom (1978) interpreted results of studies into experimental neurosis in terms of uncontrollability and unpredictability of the stimuli. Many of the symptoms of laboratory animals who are exposed to a loss of predictability or controllability, symptoms such as agitation, sudden outbursts of aggressive behavior, passivity, and lethargy, resemble characteristics of PTSD (Foa et al., 1989). Foa et al. (1989) suggest that other characteristic phenomena in PTSD as re-experiencing of the trauma via intrusive thoughts, images, flashbacks, and nightmares are better accounted for by information processing theories. Discussion of these theories, however, is outside the scope of this chapter (see Chemtob, Roitblat,

Hamada, Carlson, & Twentyman, 1988; Foa et al., 1989; and Litz & Keane, 1989).

OBSESSIVE-COMPULSIVE DISORDER

In obsessive-compulsives, it is useful to differentiate between active and passive avoidance. With passive avoidance, the individual avoids stimuli, situations, and so on, that might provoke anxiety and discomfort. Active avoidance usually refers to the motor component of obsessive-compulsive behavior, for example, checking and cleaning. Active avoidance can be explained by the escape learning paradigm, whereas passive avoidance fits the avoidance paradigm. Washing, cleaning, and checking can be regarded as escape responses, in the sense that performance of the washing ritual terminates anxiety.

The criticism of the process learning theory of fear acquisition applies equally well in the case of explaining obsessive-compulsive behavior.

As to the classical conditioning component of the two-stage theory, there is little evidence that this type of learning plays a crucial role in the development of obsessive-compulsive behavior. According to a classical conditioning interpretation, a traumatic event should mark the beginning of the obsessive-compulsive disorder. An analysis of the history of our obsessive-compulsive cases revealed that in a significant number of cases the onset of the obsessive-compulsive behavior was gradual. Generally speaking, patients related the onset of their problems to life stress in general rather than to one or more traumatic events (Emmelkamp, 1982). Further, many patients do not mention traumatic experiences associated with the onset of the symptoms. When such traumatic events were reported, they often took place much earlier than the onset of the obsessive-compulsive problems, thus making an explanation in terms of classical conditioning less credible. Finally, clinical observations clearly demonstrate the occurrence of several obsessions together as well as the regular change of obsessions in some patients, unrelated to new traumatic learning experiences. Based on patients' accounts of the course of the problem, it can be assumed that in a stressful period ritualistic activities have powerful anxiety-reducing effects.

Although there is little evidence that classical conditioning plays an important role in the development of obsessive-compulsive behavior, there is some evidence that the rituals may serve to reduce anxiety. Rachman and Hodgson (1980) studied the provocation of compulsive acts and the effects of performance of the rituals under controlled laboratory conditions to test the anxiety-reduction theory of obsessive-compulsive behavior. The design of these studies was usually as follows: Obsessive-compulsive behavior was provoked and measurements of subjective anxiety were taken before and after provocation, and after performance of the (checking or cleaning) ritual. In addition, patients' reactions were tested when the performance of the ritual was interrupted and when it was delayed.

The results of these studies can be summarized as follows. With patients whose primary problem was obsessive-compulsive washing arising out of fears of contamination or dirt, contamination led to an increase of subjective anxiety/discomfort, while the completion of a washing ritual had the opposite effect. Spontaneous decrease in discomfort occurred when the performance of the hand-washing ritual was postponed for half an hour. The interruption of the ritual produced neither an increase nor a decrease in subjective anxiety/discomfort (Rachman & Hodgson, 1980). The results of studies on checkers were along the same line but more variable. Taken together, the findings of these studies support the anxiety-reduction theory, as far as the maintenance of obsessive-compulsive behavior is concerned. With only a few exceptions among checkers, provocation of rituals led to an increase in subjective anxiety/discomfort and performance of rituals reduced discomfort.

Rachman (1976) postulated that differences in ritualistic behavior arise from differences in rearing practices. According to this theory, checking rituals are most likely to arise from families where the parents set high standards and are over-critical. Checking compulsions can therefore be identified with active avoidance behavior in order to avoid errors, motivated by fear of criticism or guilt. On the other hand, cleaning rituals will emerge in families where the parents are over-controlling and overprotective. Cleaning rituals can be considered as passive avoidance behavior, in order to avoid danger or anxiety-provoking situations in which the coping abilities of the patient might not be sufficient. Four studies have been reported to test this theory. Turner, Steketee, and Foa (1979) investigated whether checkers are more sensitive to criticism than washers. No differences in fear of criticism were found between washers and checkers. Using the same checklist, Thyer, Curtis, and Fechner (1984) reported no differences between obsessive-compulsives, agoraphobics, and social phobics; some slight differences appeared between these patient groups and simple phobics. Steketee, Grayson, and Foa (1985) found that checkers more often perceived their mothers as meticulous and demanding than washers did.

In a study by Hoekstra, Visser, and Emmelkamp (1989), Rachman's theory was tested on a large sample of obsessive-compulsives, using a validated questionnaire to assess rearing practices (Perris, Jacobsson, Lindström, Van Knörring, & Perris, 1980). The results partially supported Rachman's theory: Washers reported a more overprotective father than checkers. They also rated their mothers as more rejecting than checkers, which is not in line with the theory. Taking together the four studies discussed, there is insufficient evidence yet to support a rearing practice specificity in the etiology of compulsive rituals.

Emmelkamp and Rabbie (1982) and Hoekstra et al. (1989) postulated that those occupations for which persons hold themselves responsible are crucial for the type of compulsions they might develop. If activities are in the area of hygiene and tidiness (e.g., housekeeping, nursing) those persons are expected to develop cleaning rituals. On the other hand, people who have to be punctual and accurate at work (e.g., administrator) are expected to develop checking rituals. According to this theory, the profession will have a great influence on the type of compulsion that develops. In most Western societies, women are responsible for housekeeping and according to this sex-role pattern one may expect more women to exhibit cleaning rituals than men. Both in the Emmelkamp & Rabbie (1982) study and in the Hoekstra et al. study (1989), clear support was found for this hypothesis. In the Hoekstra et al. (1989) study, for most of the patients the type of compulsion could be predicted by their profession.

CONCLUDING REMARKS

The emphasis in this chapter has been on behavioral factors involved in the etiology and maintenance of anxiety disorders. As discussed, learning theories are inadequate as a uniform theory for the development of anxiety disorders. Even in the case of phobias and post-traumatic stress disorder, centered around clear stimuli that trigger the anxiety, simple learning theories are inadequate in explaining the acquisition and maintenance. In other anxiety disorders like obsessive-compulsive disorder, generalized anxiety, and social phobia, there is even less evidence that conditioning plays a crucial role. Recent developments have stressed cognitive representations and cognitive schemata as important determinants of anxiety disorders. For example, Beck, Emery, and Greenberg (1985) hold that cognitive schemata and automatic thoughts that are typical of anxiety play a central role in the etiology and maintenance of anxiety disorders. Other research has shown that biological factors may be involved in the etiology of anxiety disorders. Although discussion of these developments was outside the scope of this chapter, we wholeheartedly agree with an interactional perspective, in which biological, cognitive, and behavioral factors all play an important role. There are likely to be several factors operating at different levels and influencing each other in the etiology and maintenance of anxiety disorders. A comprehensive account of the acquisition and maintenance of fears and anxiety disorders is much more complex than once thought and needs to integrate biological, behavioral, and cognitive factors.

REFERENCES

American Psychiatric Association (1987). *Diagnostic and statistical manual of mental disorders* (3rd ed. rev.). Washington, DC: Author.

Amies, P. L., Gelder, M. G., & Shaw, P. M. (1983). Social phobia: A comparative clinical study. *British Journal of Psychiatry, 142,* 174–179.

Arkowitz, H. (1977). The measurement and modification of minimal dating behavior. In M. Hersen, R. M. Eisler, & P. M. Miller (Eds.), *Progress in behavior modification, Vol. 5.* New York: Academic Press.

Arrindell, W. A., Emmelkamp, P. M. G., Monsma, A., & Brilman, E. (1983). The role of perceived parental rearing practices in the aetiology of phobic disorders: A controlled study. *British Journal of Psychiatry, 143,* 183–187.

Baeyens, F., Eelen, P., Crombez, G., & Van den Bergh, O. (1992). Human evaluative conditioning: Acquisition trials, presentation schedule, evaluative style and contingency awareness. *Behaviour Research and Therapy, 30,* 133–142.

Barlow, D. H. (1988). *Anxiety and its disorders: The nature and treatment of anxiety and panic.* New York: Guilford.

Beck, A. T., Emery, G., & Greenberg, R. L. (1985). *Anxiety disorders and phobias: A cognitive perspective.* New York: Basic Books.

Beidel, D. C., Turner, S. M., & Dancu, C. V. (1985) Psychological, cognitive and behavioral aspects of social anxiety. *Behaviour Research and Therapy, 23,* 109–117.

Borkovec, T. D., & Inz, J. (1990). The nature of worry in generalized anxiety disorder.: A predominance of thought activity. *Behaviour Research and Therapy, 28,* 153–158.

Bowen, R. C., & Kohout, J. (1979). The relationship between agoraphobia and primary affective disorders. *Canadian Journal of Psychiatry, 24,* 317–322.

Bregman, E. (1934). An attempt to modify the emotional attitudes of infants by the conditioned response technique. *Journal of Genetic Psychology, 45,* 169–196.

Bruch, M. A. (1989) Familial and developmental antecedents of social phobia: Issues and findings. *Clinical Psychology Review, 9,* 1, 37–47.

Bruch, M. A., Heimberg, R. G., Berger, P., & Collins, T. M. (1989). Social phobia and perception of early parental and personal characteristics. *Anxiety Research, 2,* 57–65.

Buglass, D., Clarke, J., Henderson, A. S., Kreitman, N., & Presley, A. S. (1977). A study of agoraphobic housewives. *Psychological Medicine, 7,* 73–86.

Buss, A. H. (1980). *Self-consciousness and social anxiety.* San Francisco: Freeman.

Chambless, D. L. (1989). Gender and phobias. In P. M. G. Emmelkamp, W. T. A. M. Everaerd, F. Kraaimaat, & M. J. M. Van Son (Eds.), *Fresh perspectives on anxiety disorders* (pp. 133–142). Amsterdam/Berwyn: Swets.

Chemtob, C., Roitblat, H. C., Hamada, R. S., Carlson, J. G., & Twentyman, C. T. (1988). A cognitive action theory of post-traumatic stress disorder. *Journal of Anxiety Disorders, 2,* 253–275.

Clum, G. A., & Knowless, S. L. (1991). Why do some people with panic disorders become avoidant? A review. *Clinical Psychology Review, 11,* 295-313.

Cook, M., & Mineka, S. (1991). Selective associations in the origins of phobic fears and their implications for behavior therapy. In P. R. Martin (Ed.), *Handbook of behavior therapy and psychological science: An integrative approach* (pp. 413–434). New York: Pergamon.

Davey, G. C. L. (1992). Classical conditioning and the acquisition of human fears and phobias: A review and synthesis of the literature. *Advances in Behavior Research & Therapy, 14,* 29–66.

De Silva, P. (1988). Phobias and preparedness: Replication and extension. *Behaviour Research and Therapy, 26,* 97–98.

De Silva, P., Rachman, J., & Seligman, M. E. A. (1977). Prepared phobias and obsessions: Therapeutic outcome. *Behaviour Research and Therapy, 15,* 65–77.

DiNardo, P. A., Guzy, L. T., & Bak, R. M. (1988). Anxiety response patterns and etiological factors in dog-fearful and nonfearful subjects. *Behaviour Research & Therapy, 26,* 245–252.

DiNardo, P. A., Guzy, T., Jenkins, J. A., Bak, R. M., Tomasi, S. F., & Copland, M. (1988). Etiology and maintenance of dog fears. *Behaviour Research and Therapy, 26,* 3, 241–244.

Dow, M. G., Biglan, A., & Glaser, S. R. (1985). Multimethod assessment of socially anxious and socially unanxious women. *Behavioral Assessment, 7,* 273–282.

Edelmann, R. J. (1985). Dealing with embarrassing events: Socially anxious and non-socially anxious groups compared. *British Journal of Clinical Psychology, 24,* 281–288.

Ehlers, A., & Margraf, J. (1989). The psychophysiological model of panic attacks. In P. M. G. Emmelkamp, W. T. A. M. Everaerd, F. Kraaimaat, & M. J. M. Van Son (Eds.), *Fresh perspectives on anxiety disorders* (pp. 1–29). Amsterdam/Berwyn: Swets.

Eifert, G. H., & Evans, I. M. (Eds.). (1990). *Unifying behavior therapy: Contributions of paradigmatic behaviorism.* New York: Springer.

Emmelkamp, P. M. G. (1982). *Phobic and obsessive-compulsive disorders: Theory, research and practice.* New York: Plenum.

Emmelkamp, P. M. G., & Rabbie, D. (1982) Parental rearing styles and sex-role differences in obsessive-compulsive disorders. Unpublished manuscript, University of Groningen.

English, H. B. (1929). Three cases of the "conditioned fear response." *Journal of Abnormal and Social Psychology, 34,* 221–225.

Eysenck, H. J., & Rachman, S. (1965). The causes and cures of neurosis. London: Routledge & Kegan Paul.

Eysenck, M. W., & Mathews, A. (1987). Trait anxiety and cognition. In H. J. Eysenck & I. Martin (Eds.), *Theoretical foundations of behavior therapy.* New York: Plenum.

Faravelli, C. (1985). Life events preceding the onset of panic disorder. *Journal of Affective Disorders, 9,* 103–105.

Fazio, F. (1972). Implosive therapy with semiclinical phobias. *Journal of Abnormal Psychology, 50,* 183–188.

Foa, E. B., Steketee, G., & Olasov Rothbaum, B. (1989). Behavioral/cognitive conceptualizations of post-traumatic stress disorder. *Behavior Therapy, 20,* 155–176.

Foa, E. B., Steketee, G., & Young, M. C. (1984). Agoraphobia: Phenomenological aspects, associated characteristics, and theoretical considerations. *Clinical Psychological Review, 4,* 431–457.

Goldstein, A. J., & Chambless, D. L. (1978). A reanalysis of agoraphobia. *Behavior Therapy, 9,* 47–59.

Gray, J. A. (1975). *Elements of a two-process theory of learning.* New York: Academic Press.

Hartman, L. M. (1983). A metacognitive model of social anxiety: Implications for treatment. *Clinical Psychology Review, 3,* 435–456.

Hekmat, H. (1987). Origins and development of human fear reactions. *Journal of Anxiety Disorders, 1,* 197–218.

Herrnstein, R. J. (1969). Method and theory in the study of avoidance. *Psychological Review, 76,* 49–69.

Herrnstein, R. J., & Hineline, P. N. (1966). Negative reinforcement as shock-frequency reduction. *Journal of Experimental Analysis of Behavior, 9,* 421–430.

Hibbert, G. A. (1984). Ideational components of anxiety: Their origin and content. *British Journal of Psychiatry, 144,* 618–624.

Hoekstra, R. J., Visser, S., & Emmelkamp, P. M. G. (1989). Social learning formulation of the etiology of obsessive-compulsive disorders. In P. M. G. Emmelkamp, W. T. A. M. Everaerd, F. Kraaimaat, & M. J. M. Van Son (Eds.), *Fresh perspectives on anxiety disorders* (pp. 115–124). Amsterdam/Berwyn: Swets.

Keane, T. M., Zimmerling, R. T., & Caddell, J. M. (1985). A behavioral formulation of post-traumatic stress disorder in Vietnam veterans. *The Behavior Therapist, 8,* 9–12.

Kilpatrick, D. G., Veronen, L. J., & Best, C. L. (1985). Factors predicting psychological distress among rape victims. In C. R. Figley (Ed.), *Trauma and its wake.* New York: Brunner/Mazel.

Kipper, D. A. (1977). Behavior therapy for fears brought on by war experiences. *Journal of Consulting and Clinical Psychology, 45,* 216–221.

Klein, D. F. (1981). Anxiety reconceptualized. In D. F. Klein, J. G. Rabkin (Eds.), *Anxiety: New research and changing concepts.* New York: Raven Press.

Kleiner, L., & Marshall, W. L. (1987). The role of interpersonal problems in the development of agoraphobia with panic attacks. *Journal of Anxiety Disorders, 1,* 313–323.

Last, C. G., Barlow, D., & O'Brien, G. T. (1984). Precipitants of agoraphobia: Role of stressful life-events. *Psychological Reports, 54,* 567–570.

Lautch, H. (1971). Dental phobia. *British Journal of Psychiatry, 119,* 151–158.

Leary, M. R. (1988). A comprehensive approach to the treatment of social anxieties: The self-presentation model. *Phobia Practice and Research Journal, 1,* 1, 48–57.

Lelliott, P., Marks, I., McNamer, G., & Tobema, A. (1989). Onset of panic disorder with agoraphobica: Toward an integrated model. *Archives of General Psychiatry, 46,* 100–104.

Levey, A. B., & Martin, I. (1983). Cognitions, evaluations and conditioning. Rules of sequence and rules of consequence. *Advances in Behaviour Research & Therapy, 4,* 181–195.

Litz, B. T., & Keane, T. M. (1989). Information processing in anxiety disorders: Application to the understanding of post-traumatic stress disorder. *Clinical Psychological Review, 9,* 243–257.

Lucock, M. P., & Salkovskis, P. M. (1988). Cognitive factors in social anxiety and its treatment. *Behaviour Research and Therapy, 26,* 297–302.

Marks, I. M. (1969). *Fears and phobias.* London: Heinemann.

Marks, I. M., & Gelder, M. G. (1966). Different ages of onset in varieties of phobias. *American Journal of Psychiatry, 123,* 218–221.

Martin, I., & Levey, A. B. (1985). Conditioning, evaluations and cognitions: An axis of integration. *Behaviour Research and Therapy, 23,* 167–175.

Marzillier, J. S., Lambert, C., & Kellett, J. (1976). A controlled evaluation of systematic desensitization and social skills training for socially inadequate psychiatric patients. *Behaviour Research and Therapy, 14,* 225–238.

Mathews, A. (1989). Cognitive aspects of the etiology and phenomenology of anxiety disorders of panic attacks. In P. M. G. Emmelkamp, W. T. A. M. Everaerd, F. Kraaimaat, & M. J. M. Van Son (Eds.), *Fresh perspectives on anxiety disorders* (pp. 1225–1232). Amsterdam/Berwyn: Swets.

McNally, R. J. (1987). Preparedness and phobias: A review. *Psychological Bulletin, 101,* 283–303.

McNally, R. J. (1990). Psychological approaches to panic disorder: A review. *Psychological Bulletin, 108,* 403–419.

McNally, R. J., & Steketee, G. S. (1985). The etiology and maintenance of severe animal phobias. *Behaviour Research and Therapy, 23,* 4, 431–435.

Merkelbach, H., Van den Hout, M. A., Hoekstra, R., & Van Oppen, P. (1988). Are prepared fears less severe, but more resistant to treatment? *Behaviour Research and Therapy, 25,* 527–530.

Merkelbach, H., de Ruiter, C., Van den Hout, M. A., & Hoekstra, R. (1989). Conditioning experiences and phobias. *Behaviour Research and Therapy, 27,* 657–662.

Mineka, S. (1979). The role of fear in theories of avoidance learning, flooding, and extinction. *Psychological Bulletin, 86,* 985–1010.

Mineka, S., & Kihlstrom, J. F. (1978). Unpredictable and uncontrollable events: A new perspective on experimental neurosis. *Journal of Abnormal Psychology, 87,* 256–271.

Mowrer, O. H. (1960). *Learning theory and behavior.* New York: Wiley.

Murray, E. J., & Foote, F. (1979). The origins of fear of snakes. *Behaviour Research and Therapy, 17,* 489–493.

Newton, A., Kindness, K., & McFudyen, M. (1983). Patients and social skills groups: Do they lack social skills? *Behavioural Psychotherapy, 11,* 116–128.

Öhman, A. (1987). Evolution, learning, and phobias: An interactional analysis. In D. Magnusson & A. Öhman (Eds.), *Psychopathology: An interactional perspective* (pp. 143–158). New York: Academic Press.

Ollendick, T. H., & King, N. J. (1991). Origins of childhood fears: An evaluation of Rachman's theory of fear acquisition. *Behaviour Research and Therapy, 29,* 117–123.

Öst, L-G. (1985). Ways of acquiring phobias and outcome of behavioural treatments. *Behaviour Research and Therapy, 23,* 683–689.

Öst, L-G. (1987). Age of onset in different phobias. *Journal of Abnormal Psychology, 96,* 3, 223–229.

Öst, L-G., & Hugdahl, K. (1981). Acquisition of phobias and anxiety response patterns in clinical patients. *Behaviour Research and Therapy, 19,* 439–447.

Öst, L-G., & Hugdahl, K. (1983). Acquisition of agoraphobia, mode of onset and anxiety response patterns. *Behaviour Research and Therapy, 21,* 623–631.

Öst, L-G., & Hugdahl, K. (1985). Acquisition of blood and dental phobia and anxiety response patterns in clinical patients. *Behaviour Research and Therapy, 23,* 27–34.

Ottaviani, R., & Beck, A. T. (1987). Cognitive aspects of panic disorders. *Journal of Anxiety Disorders, 1,* 15–28.

Parker, G. (1979). Reported parental characteristics of agoraphobics and social phobics. *British Journal of Psychiatry, 135,* 555–560.

Perris, C., Jacobsson, L., Lindström, H., Van Knörring, L., & Perris, H. (1980). Development of a new inventory for assessing memories of parental rearing behaviour. *Acta Psychiatrica Scandinavia, 61,* 265–274.

Persson, G., & Nordlund, C. L. (1985). Agoraphobics and social phobics: Difference in background factors, syndrome profiles and therapeutic response. *Acta Psychiatrica Scandinavica, 71,* 148–162.

Rachman, S. (1976). Obsessive-compulsive checking. *Behaviour Research and Therapy, 14,* 269–277.

Rachman, S. (1978). *Fear and courage.* San Francisco: Freeman & Co.

Rachman, S. (1991a). Neo-conditioning and the classical theory of fear acquisition. *Clinical Psychology Review, 11,* 155–173.

Rachman, S. (1991b). The consequences of panic. *Journal of Cognitive Psychotherapy: An International Quarterly, 5,* 187–197.

Rachman, S., & Hodgson, R. J. (1980). *Obsessions and compulsions.* Englewood Cliffs, NJ: Prentice-Hall.

Rapee, R. M. (1991). Generalized anxiety disorder: A review of clinical features and theoretical concepts. *Clinical Psychology Review, 11,* 419–440.

Rapee, R. M., & Murrell, E. (1988). Predictors of agoraphobic avoidance. *Journal of Anxiety Disorders, 2,* 203–218.

Raskin, M., Peek, H. V. S., Dickman, W., & Pinsker, H. (1982). Panic and generalized anxiety disorders: Developmental antecedents and precipitants. *Archives of General Psychiatry, 39,* 687–689.

Rimm, D. C., Janda, L. H., Lancaster, D. W., Nahl, M., & Ditmar, K. (1977). An exploratory investigation of the origin and maintenance of phobias. *Behaviour Research and Therapy, 15,* 231–238.

Robinson, S., & Brichwood, M. (1991). The relationship between catastrophic cognitions and the components of panic disorder. *Journal of Cognitive Psychotherapy: An International Quarterly, 5,* 175–186.

Roy-Byrne, P. P., Geraci, M., & Uhole, T. W. (1986). Life events and the onset of panic disorder. *American Journal of Psychiatry, 143,* 1424–1427.

Schneier, F. R., Fyer, A. J., Martin, L. Y., Ross, D., Manuzza, S., Liebowitz, M. R., Gorman, J. M., & Klein, D. F. (1991). A comparison of phobic subtypes within panic disorder. *Journal of Anxiety Disorders, 5,* 66–75.

Seligman, M. E. P. (1971). Phobias and preparedness. *Behavior Therapy, 2,* 307–320.

Sheehan, D. V., Sheehan, K. E., & Minichiello, W. E. (1981). Age of onset of phobic disorders: A reevaluation. *Comprehensive Psychiatry, 22,* 544–553.

Solyom, L., Beck, P., Solyom, C., & Huger, R. (1974). Some etiological factors in phobic neurosis. *Canadian Psychiatric Association Journal, 19,* 67–68.

Spielberger, C. D. (1972). *Anxiety: Current trends in theory and research.* New York: Academic Press.

Steketee, G. S., Grayson, J. B., & Foa, E. B. (1985). Obsessive-compulsive disorders: Differences between washers and checkers. *Behaviour Research and Therapy, 23,* 197–201.

Thyer, B. A., Curtis, G. C., & Fechner, S. L. (1984). Fear of criticism is not specific to obsessive-compulsive disorder. *Behaviour Research and Therapy, 22,* 77–80.

Thyer, B. A., & Himle, J. (1985). Temporal relationship between panic attack onset and phobic avoidance in agoraphobia. *Behaviour Research and Therapy, 23,* 607–608.

Thyer, B. A., Himle, J., & Fischer, D. (1988). Is parental death a selective precursor to either panic disorder or agoraphobia: A test of the separation anxiety hypothesis. *Journal of Anxiety Disorders, 2,* 333–338.

Thyer, B. A., Nesse, R. M., Cameron, O. G., & Curtis, G. C. (1985). Agoraphobia: A test of the separation anxiety hypothesis. *Behaviour Research and Therapy, 23,* 75–78.

Thyer, B. A., Nesee, R. M., Curtis, G. E., & Cameron, O. G. (1986). Panic disorder: A test of the separation anxiety hypothesis. *Behaviour Research and Therapy, 24,* 209–211.

Trower, P., Bryant, B. M., & Argyle, M. (1978). *Social skills and mental health.* London: Methuen.

Turner, S. M., Beidel, D. C., Dancu, C. V., & Keys, D. J. (1986). Psychopathology of social phobia and comparison to avoidant personality disorder. *Journal of Abnormal Psychology, 95,* 4, 389–394.

Turner, R. M., Steketee, G. S., & Foa, E. B. (1979). Fear of criticism in washers, checkers and phobics. *Behaviour Research and Therapy, 17,* 79–81.

Van den Hout, M. A. (1988). The explanation of experimental panic. In S. Rachman & J. D. Maser (Eds.), *Panic: Psychological perspectives.* Hillsdale, NJ: Erlbaum.

Van der Molen, G. M., Van den Hout, M. A., Van Dieren, A. C., & Griez, E. (1989). Childhood separation anxiety and adult-onset panic disorders. *Journal of Anxiety Disorders, 3,* 97–106.

Watson, J., & Rayner, R. (1920). Conditioned emotional reactions. *Journal of Experimental Psychology, 3,* 1–22.

Windheuser, H. J. (1977). Anxious mothers as models for coping with anxiety. *Behavioural Analysis and Modification, 1,* 39–58.

Wolpe, J. (1958). *Psychotherapy and reciprocal inhibition.* Stanford: Stanford University Press.

Wolpe, J., & Rowan, V. C. (1988). Panic disorder: A product of classical conditioning. *Behaviour Research & Therapy, 26,* 441–450.

Zafiropoulo, M., & McPherson, F. M. (1986). Preparedness and the severity and outcome of clinical phobias. *Behaviour Research and Therapy, 24,* 221–222.

CHAPTER 4

Existential Theories

JEREMY LEEDS, PhD

For existentialism and existential psychotherapy in particular, anxiety is the heart of the matter, the central concern. Whatever the vast differences between existential practitioners and ambiguities or contradictions in each, an understanding that anxiety is central to human existence unites them all.

Goodwin (1986) says in his treatise on anxiety, "This book is based on the premise that *nobody* needs or wants anxiety. . . . It leads to nothing useful because the true source of the distress is unknown" (p. 3). While such a view is in the mainstream of behaviorist and perhaps general psychotherapeutic understanding, it could not be further from an existentialist position. For the existentially oriented psychotherapist, anxiety is the experience that provides the way into our understanding what it is to be human. While generally categorizing experiences of anxiety along the lines of "normal" and "neurotic," and attempting to help the patient overcome the latter, existential psychotherapists view "normal anxiety" as something to be embraced if we are to be truly alive.

This chapter will cover a range of existential and existential-psychotherapeutic perspectives on anxiety. Before we begin, some caveats are in order.

First, we will limit our discussion to those psychotherapists most explicitly and exclusively linked to existentialism. This excludes such "humanist" therapists as Rogers and Perls, as well as psychoanalysts significantly influenced by existentialism such as Fromm. Yalom has developed a typology of existentialist psychotherapists. On the one hand, are the "Existential Analysts," whom he calls the "old country cousins," who are Europeans and express a characteristic interest in issues of limits, and anxiety. On the other hand, are the "Humanistic Psychologists," the "flashy American cousins," who are generally characterized by optimism, pragmatism, and expansiveness (1980, pp. 16–17). While we will discuss the views of Americans such as Yalom and May, the main focus of this chapter will be on the "European" concerns (according to Yalom).

Second, like any other system of psychotherapy, there is a wide variety of opinion and even difference about what is called "existentialist." Unlike other systems, existentialist therapy sprang from and remains closely linked to a philosophical trend. This trend, as Kaufmann (1975, p. 11 passim) and others have pointed out, contains bitter enemies, thinkers who never used the "existentialist" label, and even those who have renounced it. There is also a tendency to use "phenomenological" as a synonym for "existential," and indeed they have been closely linked by many existentialists. While there is truth in such usage, it blurs important distinctions. Given that this is a chapter specifically concerning existential psychotherapy, and anxiety in particular, we will not present an exhaustive survey of existential philosophical ideas and controversies; we will however begin this chapter with a brief overview of the important definitions and concepts in phenomenology and existentialism, and the thinkers with whom they are associated.

PHENOMENOLOGY

Originally developed by Husserl, phenomenology places "emphasis on the theoretically unprejudiced examination of the immediate givens of consciousness" (Izenberg, 1976, p. 21). It is part of a trend of thought that originally developed as a conservative reaction to Enlightenment ideas, which were seen as individualist, atomistic, and rationalist (Izenberg, p. 19; Towse, 1986, p. 149; see also Jay, 1988). Husserl's model of phenomenology involved "bracketing" all beliefs and presuppositions in order to get at the true nature of "essences" (Cooper, 1990, pp. 40, 41). "Essences," whole phenomena, such as physical object, thought, and value, are the objects of study and concern, as opposed to isolated and disjointed facts.

Husserl's phenomenology has been modified (some might say supplanted) by other philosophers who are similarly concerned with the "givens of experience," but who feel that "bracketing" is for various reasons an impossible or undesirable exercise (Cooper, 1990, p. 52). Existentialists are among these.

The motivation for a phenomenological approach to psychotherapy was that other approaches and categorization schemes were not able to express the patient's *experience* of a disorder (Ellenberger, 1958, p. 95). Jaspers applied a phenomenological method to psychopathology in an attempt to "liv[e] into the patients' experiences" (Havens, 1987, p. 130). Ellenberger presents a three-part typology of phenomenologies: descriptive, genetic-structural (the search for a common denominator), and categorical analysis (time, causality, space, materiality) (1958, p. 97). We might call these "lenses" through which the psychotherapist tries to "live into" the experiences of the patient. All of these will have a place in existential psychotherapy.

EXISTENTIALISM

Existentialism is a tradition with many roots. Its key concern, according to one recent interpretation, is to elucidate human existence—meaning, in large part, that which differentiates human existence from any other variety (Cooper, 1990, p. 3).

Most modern existentialist psychotherapy is founded primarily on ideas and themes found in Kierkegaard and Heidegger. Ironically, Kierkegaard is not always regarded as "existentialist" (perhaps he is a precursor to existentialism; see Cooper, 1990, p. 9); and Heidegger denied the label in the context of his differences with the most famous public existentialist, Sartre (p. 1). Sartre, meanwhile, had a lot to say about psychology, much of it trenchant. However, he has, for many reasons beyond the scope of this chapter, not been as influential among existential psychotherapists. May, for example, claims Sartre "represents a nihilistic, subjectivist extreme in existentialism. . . ." (1958a, p. 11).

While not often adopting the entire philosophical systems or specific commitments of Kierkegaard and Heidegger, existential psychotherapists find important perspectives on the experience of human existence in their work.

Kierkegaard

From Kierkegaard, the important concepts that are applied are the struggle for individual existence and the role of commitment in becoming an individual; and "Angst."

According to Rollo May, existential psychotherapists ask Kierkegaard's question: How does one become an individual? (1958a, pp. 24–25) Kierkegaard's answer was, "in passion and commitment," He specifically related this to living the life of a good Christian (Fischer, 1988, p. 85). May has adopted what one writer has termed a "semi-theological view," (Speigelberg, 1972, p. 162). This is a constant tension in existentialism: Is it necessary to embrace religion per se, in order to embrace commitment in general, as central to existence as a person?

In his comments on the importance of existential thinkers, May also sees Kierkegaard, along with Marx and Nietzsche, as someone who opposed the technical world-view of modern Western culture, and saw its alienating consequences for modern men and women (May, 1967, pp. 64–65). A consequence of this characteristic Western-modern preoccupation with technical concerns is a split between reason and emotion.

Kierkegaard tried to heal the split by focusing on immediate experience (p. 67). May and other theorists are aware that the Kierkegaardian project involves some conflict with the dominant culture: "the individual . . . struggl[es] to affirm his experience as his own . . . to resist the pressure of society's demand that he experience something else" (Fischer, 1988, p. 89). For Kierkegaard, the struggle entails religious commitment.

Kierkegaard was also a major and early figure in the conceptualization of anxiety (variously translated as "angst" and "dread"). This anxiety, far from a self-contained emotion, is a defining characteristic of human existence. He differentiates between "fear," which has an object, and "anxiety," which has none (Fischer, 1988, p. 88; Yalom, 1980, p. 43). Kierkegaard uses "dizziness" (others speak of "vertigo") to characterize this basic experience of anxiety:

> Hence anxiety is the dizziness of freedom, which emerges when the spirit wants to posit the synthesis and freedom looks down into its own possibility, laying hold of finiteness to support itself. Freedom succumbs in this dizziness. Further than this, psychology cannot and will not go. In that very moment everything is changed, and freedom, when it again rises, sees that it is guilty. Between these two moments lies the leap, which no science has explained and which no science can explain . . . I will say that this is an adventure that every human being must go through—to learn to be anxious in order that he may not perish either by never having been in anxiety or by succumbing in anxiety. Whoever has learned to be anxious in the right way has learned the ultimate . . . Anxiety is the possibility of freedom. (Kierkegaard in Hoeller, 1990, p. 9)

In Kierkegaard's view, anxiety is the enemy of certainty and "finiteness," to which it must succumb. In doing so, freedom is lost. Note that alongside, and perhaps in contradiction to, the pessimistic note struck at the beginning of this quote, is an optimistic finish, in which one might "learn the ultimate," and through anxiety indeed experience the possibility of freedom. Anxiety is thus a teacher (Yalom, 1980, p. 69).

> He who is educated by dread is educated by possibility, and only the man who is educated by possibility is educated in accordance with his infinity. (Kierkegaard, 1991, pp. 370–371)

For Kierkegaard, "The greater the anxiety, the greater the man" (Fischer, 1988, p. 87).

Developmentally, children have an "awareness that something might happen" (Fischer, 1988, p. 86) which is a predecessor of later anxiety. In the absence of seeing themselves as truly individual, children do not comprehend the aspect of personal responsibility and choice that is so central to adult, individual anxiety, or dizziness before freedom.

Kierkegaard's sense of anxiety, and the tragic nature of human existence that underlies it, is characteristic of May's psychotherapeutic world view (Spiegelberg, 1972, p. 162).

Heidegger

Heidegger, perhaps the central "existentialist" for the existential psychotherapists, saw his work as a species of phenomenology (Cooper, 1990, pp. 5–6). But it was a phenomenology that did not "bracket" and try to step outside of lived experience; on the contrary, it embraced and tried to theorize just this experience. The key concepts adapted from Heidegger by existentialist psychotherapists are *Dasein;* clearing and world design; "thrownness;" the modes of being-in-the-world; and further explication of anxiety.

Dasein is the fundamental concept in the Heidegerrian, and perhaps entire existentialist, world-view. It literally means "the There-being," and has numerous connotations in defining the existentialist stance regarding human existence. The central concept contained herein is that dichotomies of person and world, subject and object, mind and body, are abstractions that obscure the fundamental unity of existence. *Relation* is central to being; we are always being-in-relation (Hoeller, 1990, p. 12). Thus the concept "being-in-the-world." It is the experience of existence as a unity that Heidegger seeks to illuminate.

Key to this endeavor are the Heidegerrian ideas of "clearing" (Dreyfus & Wakefield, 1988, p. 275) or "world design" (Friedman, 1991, p. 512). Both are phenomenological categories through which one looks at how a person experiences the world. Dreyfus and Wakefield explain,

> It [the "clearing"] is a context that both opens up and limits the kinds of objects we can deal with—or, as Heidegger puts it, what things can show up for us *as,* for example, *as* a hammer, or *as* a person. (p. 275)

The "clearing" is like water to the fish; like the light that illuminates a room (Dreyfus & Wakefield 1988, p. 276). Individuals have different illuminated spaces, some very narrow, some very dim. Psychotherapy helps widen or brighten them, leading to more full experience of the world.

Friedman explains the difference between psychoanalytic and existential-phenomenological understandings of the person in the context of the "world design" idea:

> The issue between phenomenology and psychoanalysis essentially is whether actions, dreams, and speech directly reveal a meaning taken in the context of the personality . . . or mask a *hidden* meaning . . . "an unconscious second person." (1991, p. 512)

Clearing and world-design are the rules, the boundaries in which the person lives.

"Throwness" is a central characteristic of *Dasein* and of the clearing. The concept refers to the already-existing, already-interpreted, already-structured nature of the world in which the person finds him or herself, the boundaries and limits on one's choices and existence (Cooper, 1990, p. 153 passim). Binswanger, an existentialist therapist, says:

> as a creature "come into existence," it [*Dasein*] is and remains, *thrown,* determined, i.e., enclosed, possessed and compelled by beings in general. Consequently, it is not "completely free" in its world-design either. (Binswanger, 1991, pp. 414–415)

According to Moss (1989, p. 204), psychotherapy challenges the individual to take "throwness" and make it "my own." Thus one modifies, expands the clearing/world design.

Existential psychotherapists like May and Yalom use the concept "boundary situation" as what seems to be a spin-off of, and related to, "throwness:"

> A *boundary situation* is a type of urgent experience that propels the individual into a confrontation with an existential situation. (May & Yalom, 1989, pp. 386–387)

They consider death to be one of the chief of these. We will see how anxiety plays a major role in this process of confrontation.

The three modes or realms of being-in-the-world are the *Eigenwelt* (one's relation to oneself), the *Mitwelt* (one's relation to others), and the *Umwelt* (one's natural environment) (Friedman, 1991, p. 512). Each of these is a central and indivisible part of Dasein.

Binswanger, an early existentialist analyst, claimed that Freud was a theorist of *Umwelt* but was unable to fully comprehend the *Mitwelt* and the *Eigenwelt* (May, 1958a, p. 34). This led, May says, to an objectivism and technical orientation that fed into social conformism.

Keen takes these three modes as defining criteria of healthy existence:

> Being able to move in space according to the demands of the *Umwelt,* being able to live one's confirmations and confirm others' living, according to the demands of the *Mitwelt,* and being able to sustain one's direction in life through the by-ways of the *Eigenwelt*—these are touchstones of health intuitively given from our analysis. When we see pathology, in ourselves or others, "what" we see are failures to meet these norms. There are so many ways to meet these norms, and to fail to meet them, that they cannot be separately specified." (1978, p. 262)

For Heidegger, anxiety is the unavoidable and essential corollary to *Dasein* and its forms. It springs from our knowledge of our own death as the ultimte limit, one that we do not dwell on normally, but one that anxiety forces us to see. According to Heidegger, anxiety is a dread of nonbeing (Stolorow, 1973, pp. 478–479). It is only through a confrontation with this nonbeing, with death, that we really experience life. Anxiety "may compel us to face the fact that we will die, and that this fact distinguishes us as humans" (Hoeller, 1990, p. 11).

As with Kierkegaard, anxiety is a teacher. It is at first unpleasant and disturbing. Most of the time, people flee from it, into what Sartre would call "bad faith," or what Sullivan might refer to as "security." But Heidegger also speaks of "sober anxiety" accompanied by "unshakable joy" (Cooper, 1990, p. 128).

> The function of this "angst"/anxiety is summed up by Cooper: In the "disengagement" or "detachment" of *Angst,* a person apprehends that exigencies and values—the summons of the alarm-clock, the need to get to work, the imperative to feed a family—only have the force which that person, unconstrained, grants to them. . . . What "sinks away" in *Angst* is the world as interpreted by the "they." (Cooper, 1990, pp. 130–131)

Heidegger's claim is that what we might call the "givenness" of the world, the "thrownness," shows up in the light of *Angst* as actually contingent. *Angst* individualizes (Cooper, 1990, p. 131).

Izenberg believes that this Heideggerian-existentialist perspective provides the answers to the clinical phenomena that Freud ended up biologizing with his "death instinct."

> Heidegger discovered that the deepest meaning of "objectivity" was its meaning as not-self. . . . The conferring of an absolute determinateness on the roles and norms of one's social environment gave one a sense of solidity, of sameness through time and of legitimate belonging. At the same time, it involved a surrender of authenticity, an abnegation of the responsibility for choice that was passed off to the facticity of the environment. . . . (Izenberg, 1976, p. 210)

> The quest for Being as stability of selfhood through stability of meaning structures made Freud's "drive to inorganic stability," as he defined the death instinct, intelligible in human terms as a will to a changeless state of rest that, while decidedly not death in the physical sense, meant an end to uncertainty and open-endedness. . . . (Izenberg, 1976, p. 211)

The "vertigo" of anxiety provides a crack in the solid wall of the given, of thrownness, that allows the person to see existence as individual, as one's own.

Let us now turn more specifically to how existential psychotherapists have used these insights, and specifically the concept of "anxiety," as a framework and guide.

EXISTENTIAL PSYCHOTHERAPY

Just as existential philosophy is difficult, if not impossible, to summarize and systemize, so existential psychotherapy is varied, vague, but often powerfully evocative. In a recent study, Norcross (1987) found that only 4% of therapists today characterize themselves as existentialist (p. 42). He also found that the ideas have wider influence than this number conveys. Part of the difficulty in "pinning down" the influence of existential psychotherapy is that it is itself hard to pin down. Hoeller says,

> existential therapy has been consistently resistant to systematization and the development of one particular set of techniques and applications. (1990, p. 15)

According to Havens,

> it is characteristic of existential writings that technical matters get short shrift beside abstruse, philosophical discussions, despite the great technical problems the existential method generates. (1987, p. 152)

In true existentialist fashion, May sees this as a positive response to our predominantly technical and conformist culture: "It is precisely the movement that protests against the tendency to identify psychotherapy with technical reason" (1958a, p. 35).

It is possible, despite the variety of, or indifference to, technique, to discern a common theme in existential psychotherapy: the quest to more fully experience one's existence as one's own. In this endeavor, the existentialist understanding of anxiety has been given a major role.

"Existentialism" and "psychotherapy" make an interesting mix. On the one hand, the philosophy that puts the analysis of existence as experienced at center stage is perfectly suited to application as a psychotherapeutic intervention. In fact, Heidegger maintained a longstanding personal relationship with Boss and approved of his existential psychotherapy. On the other hand, most psychotherapy has the purging of unpleasant feelings as a central concern. Existentialism not only does not concur; it elevates the experience of anxiety to a central position in living an authentic existence. Hoeller, the editor of *Review of Existential Psychology and Psychiatry,* says,

This flies in the face of all treatment of depression today, but it is one of the major tenets of existential psychology that despair and crisis are not necessarily bad things to be tranquilized and cured as quickly as possible. (1990, pp. 8–9)

We will look at how three existential psychotherapists—Boss, May, and Yalom—have sought to employ the existential (essentially Heidegerrian) concept of anxiety, as they each understand it, to the idea of "therapy."

Boss

Boss, as noted above, was considered by Heidegger to be the authentic adaptor of his ideas to psychotherapy. His "Anxiety, Guilt, and Psychotherapeutic Liberation" (1990) is something of a manifesto of existential psychotherapy. It discusses both the functions and the path to possible transcendence of anxiety.

Boss sees anxiety as the inevitable response to the boredom, ennui, and meaninglessness of modern society. Anxiety eats away at and destroys people's lives. It also leads to the potential for transcendence. It is a primary experience, and one that can be overcome.

Boss traces anxiety, first, to the always-present issue of nonbeing.

Fundamentally *every* anxiety fears the destruction of the capacity to be, fears the possibility, that is, of not being allowed to exist any longer unimpaired. (1990, p. 77)

He also sees anxiety as the response to the historically specific technical/ scientific world view of "modern" society.

It is, in fact, the today all-powerful technical spirit that makes us think of ourselves also as but cogs in the mechanism of a gigantic social organization and makes us treat ourselves accordingly. (p. 72)

At the same time, he notes anxiety's role as teacher and facilitator, in a fashion we have come to expect in our discussion of existential philosophy:

it is precisely anxiety that opens to man that dimension of freedom into which alone the experiences of love and trust can unfold to all. . . . In other words, anxiety confronts man with the Great Nothingness, a Nothingness, though, which is the opposite of any nihilistic emptiness, which is rather the cradle of all that is released into being. (p. 84)

In contrast to Freud, Boss sees adult anxiety as not necessarily derivative of childhood issues and concerns. The Freudian view both contradicts the phenomenological stance and avoids the spiritual/religious bases
both of anxiety and its transcendence.

> Thus it is in the special sphere of human anxiety pure speculation, which
> can find no support in anything perceivable, not to regard the feats aris-
> ing very late in a human life, like those of metaphysical nothingness or of
> the loss of the divine love and eternal life in the hereafter, as authentic
> and primal human phenomena possessing just as much validity as the
> early anxieties at the loss of physical integrity, the loss of personal im-
> portance and material property or as the still earlier infantile anxieties
> about the drives or about the loss of maternal security, or even—should
> anything of the sort exist—the very first anxiety at being born. (p. 76)

Boss thinks anxiety can actually be overcome. The process he outlines
is a spiritual-sensual awakening that allows the patient to accept him or
herself and the world, making it possible for "Being to speak to him in a
way which allows him to respond to it in harmonizing fashion" (Spiegelberg, 1972, p. 342). This corresponds to the discussion of "thrownness,"
the world of the "they," as discussed previously. Acceptance of self and
world, and the abandonment of superego-like social strictures, leads to
the removal of the plague of anxiety:

> The highest aim of all psychotherapy is and remains the opening up of
> our patients to an ability-to-love-and-trust which permits all oppression
> by anxiety and guilt to be surmounted as mere misunderstandings. (Boss,
> 1990, p. 88–89)

Boss applies the psychoanalytic method in psychotherapy. Indeed, he
feels he does so more systematically than Freud. He can do this because,
where Freud views certain impulses as derivative, Boss treats such concerns as religion and spirituality as primary and authentic (p. 91). Thus
he is not concerned with re-interpreting the patients' experiences into
other experiences; he can let them speak for themselves. The goal of the
process is an attitude of *Gelassenheit,* or "letting be-ness" (Moss, 1989,
p. 200).

May

Rollo May is probably the best-known existential psychotherapist, at least
in the United States. He actually prefers the label "humanist" to "existentialist" (Bilmes, 1978, p. 292). Indeed, he says, "I do not believe there
is a special school of therapy to be put in a category of 'existential'"
(May, 1990, p. 49). It was he, however, who is largely responsible for

bringing the existentialist tradition in psychology and psychotherapy to these shores, with the publication of *Existence* in 1958.

May has developed a theory of etiology of modern neurosis. He connects this to a typology of anxiety, differentiating the normal, or self-actualizing, from the neurotic.

May's etiology of neurosis is a reiteration, in "American," of the European existentialist theme of the destructive consequences to the individual of the technical/scientific world view and way of being. In *Psychology and the Human Dilemma* (1967), as well as other works, May traces a historical path from the Enlightenment rationalism, (to which he grants a certain historical legitimacy), to the breakdown of community and the isolation of the individual. He traces his critique of the alienating effects of the technical emphasis in modern life to Marx, Nietzsche, and Kierkegaard (pp. 64–65). He finds that conformism and the "organization man" are the forms that this alienation takes in America (May, 1990, p. 56). People are alienated from each other and from the natural world (May, 1958b, p. 57). Ostracism has replaced castration as the "dominant fear" (May, 1967, p. 56).

> Patient after patient I've seen . . . chooses to be castrated, that is, to give up his power, in order not to be ostracized. (May, 1967, p. 56)

He accuses psychotherapy of participating in this world-view, to the extent that there is no positive definition of health to be strived for. "Health becomes the vacuum which is left when the socalled neurosis is cured . . . ." (May, 1967, p. 53).

For May, existentialism provides an answer to this state of affairs:

> Existentialism, in short, is the endeavor to understand man by cutting below the cleavage between subject and object which has bedeviled Western thought and science since shortly after the Renaissance. (May, 1958a, p. 11)

The key for May is for the person to recognize him or herself as a valuing source, ". . . to affirm personal goals and values, rather than seeking these in external criteria or adjusting to the moral majority" (DeCarvalho, 1992, p. 10).

This idea has been expressed as the "I Am" experience (May & Yalom, 1989, pp. 363–364). The experience of being, the idea that "'I am' the one living, experiencing. I choose my own being" (p. 364), is the precondition for therapeutic progress.

In this context, anxiety is inevitable and indeed often indispensable. As one experiences one's being, one necessarily comes face-to-face with threats to this being, and ultimately nonbeing.

> Anxiety is not an affect among other affects such as pleasure or sadness. It is rather an ontological characteristic of man, rooted in his very existence as such. . . . Anxiety is *the experience of the threat of imminent non-being*. . . . Anxiety is the subjective state of the individual's becoming aware that his existence can become destroyed, that he can lose himself and his world, that he can become "nothing." (May, 1958b, p. 50)

Anxiety is a "core" threat, as opposed to fear, which is peripheral to one's basic values (May, p. 51).

The internal impetus for cultural conformity and adaptation is the avoidance of this anxiety (May, 1958b, p. 87; 1967, p. 68). But this is not the last word. In fact, this is where "neurotic anxiety" becomes the issue. Neurotic anxiety is the consequence of the blocking of normal anxiety (May, 1967, p. 69; 1958b, p. 55). It in turn is itself a block to self-awareness (DeCarvalho, 1992, p. 12).

> what differentiates neurotic from self-actualizing reactions to such threats to being as death, anxiety, and guilt is whether the person represses and cuts himself off from the threatening stimuli or whether he wills to consciously face and assimilate it. (Bilmes, 1978, p. 291)

In neurotic anxiety, the person narrows his or her range of experience in the name of security:

> His symptoms are his way of shrinking the range of his world in order that his centeredness may be protected from threat . . . (May, 1990, p. 54)

In terms of the discussion of these existentialist concepts, the clearing or world design is narrowed.

The goal of therapy, May says, is to free the person from neurotic anxiety so that he or she can confront normal anxiety. "All growth consists of the anxiety-creating surrender of past values as one transforms them into broader ones" (May, 1967, p. 80). The therapist will help the patient experience his or her existence as real, and to experience the value of commitment and decision. This does not necessarily mean making bold decisions or changes, which themselves could be shortcuts; rather, the patient should develop a decisive attitude toward existence itself (May, 1958b, pp. 86–88).

As might be inferred from the foregoing, May has a skeptical attitude towards the use of anxiety-reducing drugs except to head off a more serious breakdown or to relieve the symptom and make psychotherapy possible (1967, pp. 81–82).

While there is no specific technique or set of techniques prescribed for this endeavor, partly intentionally, partly due to the youth of the movement (at least at the time May was writing) (1967, p. 147), the real relationship of the patient and therapist, the "encounter," becomes central (1990, p. 58).

Yalom

Yalom is perhaps the chief systematizer and popularizer of existential psychotherapy today. He has written a widely used text on the subject (Yalom, 1980). He classifies existential psychotherapy as a dynamic therapy, like psychoanalysis. However, it has a different kind of basic conflict at its center: "*a conflict that flows from the individual's confrontation with the givens of existence*" [emphasis in original] (1980, p. 8).

There are four such givens, or "ultimate concerns" of existence that Yalom enumerates. They are, death, freedom, isolation, and meaninglessness (p. 8). Yalom says existential psychotherapists keep Freud's dynamic *structure* but revise its *content*. As opposed to

Drive $\rightarrow$ Anxiety $\rightarrow$ Defense Mechanism

Yalom substitutes

Awareness of Ultimate Concern $\rightarrow$ Anxiety $\rightarrow$ Defense Mechanism

Within this more structured and systematic context, Yalom elucidates some of the specific concerns of existentialism as he understands them.

Fear of death, or "death anxiety," is one of his basic clinical touchstones. A major difference between Yalom and a drive-oriented psychoanalyst is that each listens for a different range of experience and concern in the patient. Yalom refers to Rank, who says the therapist has more leverage when viewing the patient as fearful and suffering, rather than instinctually driven (p. 10). Like Boss, he challenges the Freudian developmental scheme, claiming that fear of death is a more central and intuitively logical fount of anxiety:

> Surely the feces-weaning-castration linkage is not more logically compelling than the concept of an innate, intuitive awareness of death. (Yalom, 1980, p. 65)

Indeed, that there is so little said about death anxiety in traditional psychotherapy is shocking to him:

> The omission of the fear of death in clinical case reports, to take one example, is so blatant that one is tempted to conclude that nothing less than a conspiracy of silence is at work. (Yalom, 1980, p. 55)

The clinician rarely discovers death anxiety directly; it is intuited from derivative case material (p. 45). Yalom discusses several specific defenses against death anxiety. Among these are Specialness, under which comes compulsive heroism, compulsive work, narcissism and aggression and control; and the search for the Ultimate Rescuer, be it the therapist, another person, or an ideology (p. 117 passim).

Yalom gives an example of a patient whose compulsive sexuality is a shield against being alone. He recounts that when the patient was somewhat better able to tolerate the anxiety, he suggests that he spend an evening alone and record his thoughts and feelings.

> Without the protection of sex Bruce encountered massive death anxiety: the images were vivid—a dead woman, a skeleton's hand, a death's head. (Yalom, 1958, p. 192)

Yalom says sex served as a form of death defiance for this patient, and as a reinforcement of "specialness."

> Thus, his search for a woman was not truly a search for sex, nor even a search powered by infantile forces . . . but instead it was a search to enable Bruce to deny and to assuage his fear of death. (Yalom, 1958, p. 193)

Yalom also discusses the fear of death in patients with significant physical illnesses. He says the major goal is to separate out the inevitable feelings of helplessness that arise from such a confrontation with mortality, from "ancillary *feelings* of helplessness" (p. 212).

Yalom treats freedom, isolation, and meaninglessness along these same lines. They overlap in defensive strategies that a patient would use to counteract them; and in the remedies applied by the therapist. Yalom, as a good existentialist, stresses the importance of the *encounter,* or relationship, between patient and therapist (p. 402); and he stresses the curative role of patient engagement, or commitment, especially in response to the concern of meaninglessness (p. 481).

EVALUATION AND CRITIQUE

As noted above, according to a recent study by Norcross (1987), only 4% of all psychotherapists consider themselves existentialist; only 1.5% of clinical psychologists accept this label for themselves, down from 3% 8 years previous to the study (p. 42). The existentialist ideas have been largely eclipsed in philosophy, having come under attack from both the analytic and the postmodern schools or trends. What can we say about the usefulness and applicability to psychotherapy of the existentialist concepts of anxiety?

Let us start with critical comments. There is an unresolved tension, expressed in various ways, between anxiety as a given of existence and anxiety as surmountable. Both ideas are present in existentialism and especially in existential psychotherapy. The former concept does not easily lend itself to psychotherapeutic "cure" in the traditional sense.

The division between "normal" and "neurotic" anxiety is one answer to this and has been adopted by May and Yalom. Such judgments and divisions, however, imply an outside frame of reference and evaluation that contradicts the original goal of phenomenology and existentialism: to understand existence as it is lived by the person. It is in some sense an arbitrary division; one not necessarily "felt" by the patient.

Boss tries to solve this problem with what is essentially a "deus ex machina," a rescue from anxiety by faith, understanding, and spirituality. This again undermines the power of the basic insight of anxiety as central to existence.

The social criticism of Western culture presented by existentialist psychotherapists, much as it may be valid in various points, also contradicts the inevitability of anxiety. Boss and May especially point to the deleterious effects of the scientific/technical world view on "modern" people. But cannot this "historicizing" of anxiety be seen, if we are to be consistently existential, as itself a defense against the "givens of being," which though their forms may change, are always present?

Izenberg both highlights and tries to find a way out of this problem of historical influence versus timelessness of the human situation, in his critique of Binswanger's (and Heidegger's) use of the concept of "thrownness" with his patients:

> This alone ought to have been sufficient to make Binswanger realize that 'thrownness' was not a monolithic concept, that distinctions had to be made between the limitations of human finitude per se and the extra limitations imposed by some individuals on others in different historical and social conditions. (Binswanger, 1976, p. 311)

Again, however, such distinctions as Izenberg advocates, admirable as they are, do not "have to be made" *within* the framework of existentialism in general, and thrownness in particular. They require an extra-existentialist framework, and one which in some way mitigates the force of the existentialist "monolithic concept."

Let us at this point switch to the power and usefulness of the existentialist legacy. To point to unresolved contradictions in their approach to freedom and determinism is in some sense to condemn them for the unresolved and perhaps unresolvable problems of existence itself. It is these that the existentialists tackle in a way that is unique in psychotherapy. However questionable the particular philosophical and historical standpoint, existentialism highlights an "emperor's new clothes" aspect of some current views of anxiety as a needless inconvenience in an otherwise blissful existence. A confrontation with existentialist concepts of anxiety will hopefully be the impetus for the therapist's evaluating, or reevaluating, the values and premises under which he or she is operating: specifically, when a patient presents with anxiety and other uncomfortable feelings.

REFERENCES

Bilmes, M., & May, R. (1978). In R. S. Valle & M. King (Eds.), *Existential-phenomenological alternatives for psychology* (pp. 290–294). New York: Oxford University Press.

Binswanger, L. (1991). Heidegger's analytic of existence and its meaning for psychiatry. In M. Friedman (Ed.), *The worlds of existentialism: A critical reader* (pp. 414–416). New Jersey: Humanities Press International. (Originally published 1963)

Boss, M. (1990). Anxiety, guilt and psychotherapeutic liberation. In K. Hoeller (Ed.), *Readings in existential psychology and psychiatry* (pp. 71–92). Seattle: Review of Existential Psychology and Psychiatry. (Originally published as *Review of existential psychology & psychiatry, 20* (1, 2, 3), 1986–1987)

Cooper, D. E. (1990). *Existentialism.* Cambridge: Basil Blackwell.

DeCarvalho, R. J. (1992). The humanistic ethics of Rollo May. *Journal of Humanistic Psychology, 32*(1), 7–18.

Dreyfus, H. L., & Wakefield, J. (1988). From depth psychology to breadth psychology: a phenomenological approach to psychopathology. In S. B. Messer, L. A. Sass, & R. L. Woolfolk (Eds.), *Hermeneutics and psychological theory* (pp. 272–289). New Jersey: Rutgers University Press.

Ellenberger, H. F. (1958). A clinical introduction to psychiatric phenomenology and existential analysis. In R. May (Ed.), *Existence* (pp. 92–124). New York: Touchstone.

Fischer, W. F. (1988). *Theories of anxiety* (2nd ed.). Washington, DC: University Press of America.

Friedman, M. (1991). Existential psychotherapy and the image of man. In M. Friedman (Ed.), *The worlds of existentialism: a critical reader* (pp. 507–521). New Jersey: Humanities Press International. (Originally published 1962)

Goodwin, D. W. (1986). *Anxiety.* New York: Oxford University Press.

Havens, L. (1987). *Approaches to the mind.* Cambridge: Harvard University Press.

Hoeller, K. (1990). An introduction to existential psychology and psychiatry. In K. Hoeller (Ed.), *Readings in existential psychology and psychiatry* (pp. 3–20). Seattle: Review of Existential Psychology and Psychiatry. (Originally published as *Review of existential psychology & psychiatry, 20* (1, 2, 3), 1986–1987)

Izenberg, G. N. (1976). *The existentialist critique of Freud.* Princeton, NJ: Princeton University Press.

Jay, M. (1988). Should intellectual history take a linguistic turn? Reflections on the Habermas-Gadamer debate. In M. Jay (Ed.), *Fin-de-siecle socialism* (pp. 17–36). New York: Routledge.

Kaufmann, W. (1975). Existentialism from Dostoyevsky to Sartre. In W. Kaufmann (Ed.), *Existentialism from Dostoyevsky to Sartre* (pp. 11–51). New York: New American Library.

Keen, E. (1978). Psychopathology. In R. S. Valle & M. King (Eds.), *Existential-phenomenological alternatives for psychology* (pp. 234–264). New York: Oxford University Press.

Kierkegaard, S. (1991). Excerpts from *The concept of dread.* In M. Friedman (Ed.), *The worlds of existentialism: A critical reader.* New Jersey: Humanities Press International. (Originally published 1944)

May, R. (1958a). The origins and significance of the existential movement in psychology. In R. May (Ed.), *Existence* (pp. 3–36). New York: Touchstone.

May, R. (1958b). Contributions of existential psychotherapy. In R. May (Ed.), *Existence* (pp. 37–91). New York: Touchstone.

May, R. (1967). *Psychology and the human dilemma.* Canada: Van Nostrand Co.

May, R. (1990). On the phenomenological bases of psychotherapy. In K. Hoeller (Ed.), *Readings in existential psychology and psychiatry* (pp. 49–61). Seattle: Review of Existential Psychology and Psychiatry. (Originally published as *Review of existential psychology & Psychiatry, 20* (1, 2, 3), 1986–1987)

May, R., & Yalom, I. (1989). Existential psychotherapy. In R. J. Corsini & D. Wedding (Eds.), *Current Psychotherapies* (pp. 362–402). Illinois: Peacock Publishers.

Moss, D. (1989). Psychotherapy and human experience. In R. S. Valle & S. Halling (Eds.), *Existential-phenomenological perspectives in psychology* (pp. 193–213). New York: Plenum.

Norcross, J. C. (1987). A rational and empirical analysis of existential psychotherapy. *Journal of Humanistic Psychology, 27*(1), 41–68.

Spiegelberg, H. (1972). *Phenomenology in psychology and psychiatry.* Evanston: Northwestern University Press.

Stolorow, R. D. (1973). Perspectives on death anxiety: A review. *Psychiatric Quarterly, 47*(4), 473–486.

Towse, M. S. (1986). "To be or not to be"—anxiety following bereavement. *British Journal of Medical Psychology, 59,* 149–156.

Yalom, I. D. (1980). *Existential psychotherapy.* New York: Basic Books.

CHAPTER 5

The Cognitive Theory of Anxiety

ARTHUR FREEMAN, EdD, and ROBERT A. DiTOMASSO, PhD

Within the past three decades, the field of psychology has witnessed a cognitive revolution (Beck, 1991). Traditional behavioral methods of psychopathology and therapy (Wolpe, 1958; 1973), based upon principles of experimental research derived from the animal research paradigm, naturally favored conditioning explanations and paradigms and consequently excluded consideration of cognitive factors. Zinbarg (1990) has argued that traditional behavior therapists have continued to base their conceptualizations upon outdated models of conditioning and have not kept pace with the most recent developments in the field of conditioning. One of the most significant developments in conditioning theory over the past 20 years has been the blending of conditioning and information processing models; that is, even the basic theories upon which behavior therapy was built have subsumed cognitive variables (Zinbarg, 1990). Thus, it seemed quite natural that the emergence of cognitive and cognitive behavioral approaches (Beck, 1967; Ellis, 1962; Mahoney, 1974; Meichenbaum, 1977) would serve as an extension and expansion of black-box approaches.

The view of patients as beings whose thoughts, images, beliefs, expectancies, and assumptions play an influential role in shaping perceptions, thinking, and feeling is now firmly rooted in the field. While there is still some controversy about whether the addition of cognitive approaches adds anything over and above behavioral approaches for selected problems (Wolpe, 1973), Michaelson (1987) suggests that the use of cognitive techniques within treatment packages may reflect a more state-of-the-art approach to treatment. Others (Simon & Fleming, 1985) have argued for the efficacy of cognitive approaches. At this point while more research is needed to clarify some of these important questions, the cognitive behavioral approach occupies an important position in our understanding of psychopathological states such as anxiety and in the design of clinically useful interventions.

While the earliest roots of the role and importance of cognition in human behavior can be traced to Eastern, Greek, and Roman philosophers (Ellis, 1989), there is little doubt that the theorizing of Aaron T. Beck (1967) has been perhaps the most influential source in guiding and nurturing the cognitive movement. Basing his earliest observations and theorizing on unipolar depression (Beck, 1967), the cognitive model enjoyed wide application to a variety of other disorders (Freeman, 1989).

In this chapter, our goal is to outline and elucidate the cognitive theory and model of anxiety and its disorders. We address the definition of anxiety and anxiety disorders, its epidemiology, basic assumptions of the cognitive theory of anxiety, the role of predisposing and precipitating factors, a cognitive case conceptualization derived from the cognitive model, and common misconceptions about cognitive theory.

Where relevant, we have used clinical research and examples to illustrate our points.

ANXIETY: A DEFINITION

Three cases that exemplify the typical characteristics of the anxious patient highlight the important aspects of the problem.

Case 1

A well-built 30-year-old white male comes to your office complaining of chronic attacks of anxiety during the past year. He is a supervisor of 46 workers in an extremely stressful, high pressure job. Three weeks ago, his wife delivered their first child. His mother-in-law passed away after a long bout with cancer which has precipitated severe depression in his wife. One year ago, his older brother had a heart attack that began with chest pain. His father died suddenly from a heart attack several years earlier. His mother also had recent unsuccessful cardiac bypass surgery. One year ago at the time of his brother's heart attack, his anxiety attacks began with pain in his chest, a warm rush, and a variety of sympathetic symptoms. He has made several visits to the emergency room despite repeated reassurance from his family physician. He continues to worry about having future attacks and to be very frightened.

Case 2

A 26-year-old male supervisor at a gambling casino has recently been informed that he will be presenting an award to one of his supervisees who received an Employee of the Month distinction. The thought of standing in front of 300 people and making this presentation absolutely terrifies him. When the day arrives and he begins to make his presentation, he is unable to express himself, is extremely self-conscious, and notices several people in the front row who are laughing at his fumbling. He concludes that he has made an absolute fool of himself and subsequently develops a fear of answering the phone at home and at work. The patient reports a rather long history of interpersonal anxiety, unassertiveness, and self-consciousness in social situations.

Case 3

The husband of a 68-year-old woman calls the family practice center to make an appointment with the psychologist for his wife because of her intense anxiety about a lesion under her right axilla that has a discharge. The patient is totally convinced that she has a recurrence of cancer and is extremely frightened about being examined by a physician to the point that she has avoided medical care for 35 years. Forty years earlier, she had a double mastectomy and related therapeutic abortion. Since that time, she has extreme anxiety whenever she is in the presence of a physician. The thought of being in a medical setting, talking to a physician, or being examined by a physician who might discover something medically wrong with her creates anxiety of phobic proportions.

COMMON ASPECTS OF ANXIETY

These three cases have commonalities. First, each of these individuals suffered to a significant degree from distressing levels of anxiety. Second, each person's life was compromised in some significant manner by this emotion. Third, in each instance, the individual experienced either a series of life events or some traumatic experience of relevance to their problem. Fourth, there was clear motivation to avoid those situations associated with anxiety or the very symptoms of anxiety itself. Fifth, each individual perceived a great degree of danger or threat in these situations. Finally, those situations that struck at a particular vulnerability of each patient precipitated an anxiety response.

Anxiety may be defined as a tense emotional state characterized by a variety of sympathetic symptoms including, for example, chest discomfort, palpitations, shortness of breath. Under normal circumstances, the human nervous system is designed to prepare and mobilize the individual to fight or flee from an objective and physically dangerous threat. The hallmark of the anxious patient, however, is the presence of perceived threat and the activation of the physiological concomitants in the absence of objective real threat. In other words, the anxious disordered person sees threat and reacts to threat where no real threat exists.

While anxiety is a universal human experience and is undoubtedly a common human emotion, its evocation does not necessarily imply the presence of a clinically significant disorder. The DSMIII-R (American Psychiatric Association, 1987) is quite explicit about the definition of a disorder that "is conceptualized as a clinically significant behavioral or psychological syndrome or pattern that occurs in a person and that is associated with present distress (a painful symptom) or disability (impairment in one or more important areas of functioning) or with a significantly increased risk of suffering death, pain, disability, or an important loss of freedom (p. xxii)." In effect, a disorder implies a duration, frequency, number, and intensity of symptoms that are significant enough to interfere with a person's quality of life. The DSMIII-R delineates the following anxiety disorders: Panic Disorder With or Without Agoraphobia, Agoraphobia Without a History of Panic Disorder, Social Phobia, Simple Phobia, Obsessive Compulsive Disorder, Posttraumatic Stress Disorder, Generalized Anxiety Disorder, and Anxiety Disorder Not Otherwise Specified.

The National Institute of Mental Health Epidemiological Catchment Area Survey (Reiger, Myers, Kramer et al., 1984) revealed that anxiety disorders are the most common mental health problems affecting about 8.3% of the population. These disorders outrank both depression and substance abuse, yet only one of every four patients ever receives treatment.

BASIC ASSUMPTIONS

The cognitive model of anxiety makes several basic assumptions about anxiety, its evocation, its medication, and significance (Beck, Emery, & Greenberg, 1985). These assumptions are crucial in understanding the phenomenon of anxiety and the nature of anxiety disorders.

1. Anxiety, an emotional response, has adaptive significance for humans when evoked in response to objective danger. (Beck, Emery, & Greenberg, 1985; Canon, 1929; Emery & Tracy, 1987; Izard & Blumberg, 1985; Lindsley, 1952; 1957; 1960; Plutchik, 1980)
2. The evocation of anxiety in response to misperceived or exaggerated danger when there is none is maladaptive. (Beck, Emery, & Greenberg, 1985; Beck & Greenberg, 1988; Foa & Kozak, 1986)
3. Anxiety disordered individuals are prone to precipitate false alarms that create a relatively constant state of emotional tension and subjective distress. (Barlow & Cerney, 1988; Beck, Emery, & Greenberg, 1985; Beck & Greenberg, 1988)
4. During episodes of anxiety, an individual's cognitive, physiological, motivational, affective, and behavioral systems are involved. (Persons, 1989; Taylor & Arnow, 1988)

5. The cognitive system plays a vital and essential role in appraising danger and resources and activating the physiological, motivational, affective, and behavior systems, each of which serve important functions. (Beck, Emery, & Greenberg, 1985; Foa & Kozak, 1986; Lazarus, 1991)

6. The cognitive system mediates its influence through repetitive unpremeditated and rapid involuntary thoughts and/or images of which the individual is unaware (unless attention is called to them) and which the individual accepts without question. (Beck, Emery, & Greenberg, 1985; Beck & Greenberg, 1988; Emery & Tracy, 1987)

7. Automatic thoughts are derived from underlying deeper cognitive structures called schemas, also referred to as underlying beliefs or assumptions. (Emery & Tracy, 1987; Foa & Kozak, 1986; Kendall & Ingram, 1987; Persons, 1989)

8. Automatic thoughts and underlying beliefs are disorder specific and, in anxiety disordered individuals, reflect themes of threat and danger as opposed to themes of loss in depressed individuals. (Beck, Emery, & Greenberg, 1985; Beck & Rush, 1975; Beck & Weisher, 1989; Foa & Kozak, 1986; Hilbert, 1984)

9. Anxiety reactions and disorders may be more fully and parsimoniously understood by elucidating the individual's automatic thoughts, cognitive distortions and underlying assumptions. (Beck, 1976; Butler & Matthews, 1983; Deffenbacher, Zwemer, Whisman, Hill, & Sloan, 1986; Freeman, Pretzer, Fleming, & Simon, 1991; Marluzzi & Bollwood, 1989; Zwemer & Deffenbacher, 1984)

10. In trigger situations, anxiety disordered individuals have a tendency to activate danger/threat schemas by which they selectively screen in stimuli that indicate danger and screen out those stimuli that are incompatible with danger. (Beck, 1976; Beck, Emery, & Greenberg, 1985; Freeman, Pretzer, Fleming, & Simon, 1991)

11. Anxiety disordered individuals have impaired objectivity and ability to evaluate their threat bound cognitions in a realistic manner. (Beck, Emery, & Greenberg, 1985)

12. Anxiety disordered individuals exhibit systematic errors in processing information by, for example, catastrophizing, selectively abstracting, thinking dichotomously, and making arbitrary inferences. (Beck, Emery, & Greenberg, 1985)

The cognitive model of anxiety also makes explicit assumptions about the predisposing and precipitating factors that are associated with the onset of anxiety disorders. In the sections that follow, we will discuss several predisposing and precipitating variables related to anxiety disorders. It is important to bear in mind that any combination of these factors may set the stage and provide the impetus for the development, onset, maintenance, and exacerbation of anxiety problems.

PREDISPOSING FACTORS

According to cognitive model (Beck, Emery, & Greenberg, 1985), there are five possible factors that may predispose or make an individual potentially vulnerable and more prone to anxiety and anxiety disorders. These factors are: (1) genetic inheritability, (2) physical disease states, (3) psychological trauma, (4) absence of coping mechanisms, and (5) dysfunctional thoughts, beliefs, assumptions, and cognitive processing. We will discuss each of these factors in detail. As a result of individual differences, an anxiety disorder may result from a unique combination of predisposing and precipitating variables (Beck, Emery, & Greenberg, 1985).

Genetics

Within recent years, the role of possible genetic factors in certain psychopathological disorders have assumed more importance. Anxiety disorders are no exception. Some authors (e.g., Sheenan, 1983) have even gone to the extreme of viewing it as a strictly biological disease necessitating pharmacological therapy.

Cognitive therapists consider hereditary predisposition to anxiety as an important variable. Panic disorder, phobic disorders, and obsessive-compulsive disorder are more common among first-degree biological relatives of patients suffering from these disorders (American Psychiatric Association, 1987). However, the role of genetic factors in generalized anxiety disorder is less clear (Beck, Emery, & Greenberg, 1985). Nonetheless, the question about how heredity exerts an influence in anxiety disorders is important to consider in the cognitive conceptualization of anxiety. Heredity may manifest its influence by the existence of an easily aroused or labile autonomic nervous system (Barlow & Cerney, 1988). In other words, in certain anxiety conditions, a family history of the disorder may make it more likely for a patient to exhibit anxiety symptoms under the right set of conditions. Barlow and Cerney (1988), for example, have thoroughly examined the possible role of genetic factors in panic disorder. Research has supported the aggregation of panic in monozygotic twins (Torgerson, 1983) and families (Crowe, Noyes, Pauls, & Slymen, 1983; Harris, Noyes, Crowe, & Chaudry, 1983; Moran & Andrews, 1985) and is supported by clinical observation. For example, one of us (RDT) treated an elderly woman with a long history of panic disorder whose daughter exhibited an identical problem and was being treated independently. The role of genetic vulnerability cannot be fully appreciated without considering the interactive role of environmental psychological and social factors (Barlow & Cerney, 1988). Genetics may be viewed as transmitting the biological substrate that makes the individual more vulnerable to develop clinical anxiety. As such, the cognitive model appreciates the role of possible genetic influences in anxiety disorders.

Physical Disease

The cognitive model also considers the possible role of physical factors in making an individual vulnerable to an anxiety disorder. There are two issues to consider: First, ruling out possible physical causes that can mimic anxiety is essential in assessing anxiety disorders. In many instances, treating the physical problem may alleviate the symptoms. Second, however, the existence of a physical problem does not necessarily rule out the existence of an anxiety problem. A physical problem can co-exist with an anxiety disorder and treating both problems may be necessary. Barlow and Cerney (1988) provide a list of nine organic conditions that are associated with anxiety symptoms and panic. These physical conditions include hypoglycemia, hyperthyroidism, hypoparathyroidism, Cushing syndrome, pheochromocytoma, temporal lobe epilepsy, hyperventilation syndrome, caffeine intoxication, audiovestibular problems, and mitral valve prolapse.

Mental Trauma

The third possible predisposing factor is a mental trauma during development (Beck, Emery, & Greenberg, 1985) that can render an individual more vulnerable to experience anxiety in situations similar to the experience of the trauma. The cognitive model assumes that developmental traumas occurring in the context of high emotional arousal can result in an individual developing a threat schema. Such schemas would presumably relate to themes of danger in anxious patients and would be expected to become activated in situations that are similar to the circumstances in which the schema was learned. As Foa and Kozak (1986) noted, "A fear memory is accessed when a fearful individual is presented with fear information that matches some of the information structure in memory" (p. 23). According to their emotional processing model, fear is expressed as a memory network that incorporates information about the stimulus situations, responses, and the meaning of the stimuli and responses. Fear structures by definition involve themes of danger. One of us (RDT) treated a woman with a 25-year history of panic disorder with agoraphobia whose anxiety attacks were traced to an experience when she was locked in the trunk of a car by her brother and a friend as a prank, and learned to fear suffocating to death. Subsequently, any situations that resembled enclosed places from which escape might be difficult (e.g., planes, buses, cars, elevators) and stuffy odors were associated with the threat of suffocation which precipitated extreme anxiety.

Another predisposing factor in the development of anxiety disorders is a deficit in coping responses. Anxiety disordered patients often exhibit deficits in adaptive coping strategies. Not only are their primary appraisals of situations more likely to result in perceptions of threat where no threat exists, but their secondary appraisals of their resources to cope with threat more often reveal inability to cope. Anxiety patients may have failed to learn adequate coping strategies or employ responses such as avoidance that strengthen their anxiety and preclude effective coping. As a result, they leave themselves vulnerable to experience anxiety in the presence of life events or other stressors.

Irrational Thoughts, Assumptions and Cognitive Processing Errors

The cognitive model of anxiety places primary emphasis on the role of cognitive factors in predisposing individuals to anxiety disorders. In anxiety disordered individuals, underlying unrealistic beliefs about threat or danger are presumed to be activated by trigger events or situations that are similar to situations during which these schemas are learned. When these schemas are activated, they fuel the patient's thinking, behavior, and emotion, all of which can serve to reciprocally reinforce each other as well as the underlying schema. Persons' (1989) case conceptualization model provides an excellent approach for elucidating the central role of cognitive factors in predisposing individuals to anxiety.

PRECIPITATING FACTORS

The cognitive model of anxiety posits a number of possible factors that may precipitate anxiety: physical disease or toxic substances, severe external stressors, long-term stress, and stressors affecting a specific emotional vulnerability of an individual.

Physical Problems or Toxic Substances

Anxiety can be precipitated by the onset of a physical problem that does or does not mimic anxiety. For example, the development of anxiety after the onset of a physical problem is not an uncommon reaction during an individual's attempt to adjust to illness. Physical problems may cause symptoms such as fatigue or depression that could compromise or overtax the individual's tolerance for handling even normal, every day stressors;

the result may be that previously handled stressors overburden the individual's resources. In addition, it is quite possible that a physical problem may present an individual with an array of symptoms that are viewed as signs of a serious problem when in actuality the problem is relatively benign.

Finally, there are those instances where individuals have ingested a psychoactive substance that produces some physical effect that is interpreted as threatening. In our clinical experience, we have encountered patients who developed anxiety attacks after using marijuana or cocaine, or even after unintentionally inhaling toxic fumes. Perhaps even more interesting is the situation in which an individual consumes large quantities of caffeine. One of us (RDT) recalls the case of a young female paramedic who presented at a medical outpatient center reporting panic-like symptoms. She indicated that she had recently been seen in the emergency room after losing consciousness at home. She also claimed that she required CPR from her paramedic brother after she stopped breathing at home. What made her story even less credible in this litigious age was that she was sent home from the emergency room after spending only a short time there. Her physical and medical history were unremarkable. However, further probing revealed that she was drinking between 12 to 15 cups of caffeinated coffee on a daily basis. Her symptoms subsided with the gradual withdrawal of caffeine over time.

Severe External Stressors

The occurrence of a severe stressor or life event such as loss of a loved one or loss of a job is another possible precipitant of anxiety. The role of life events (Last, Barlow, & O'Brien, 1984) in precipitating anxiety reactions is well known.

Chronic Insidious External Stressors

Stressors may be cumulative over a long period of time and in a sense may piggyback on each other. The result may be a situation in which a person's coping resources are exhausted and overwhelmed. One of us saw a woman who was experiencing profound distress following a series of events including chronic cystitis, two carpal tunnel surgeries, two car accidents, severe neck injury, cancer in her father followed by his eventual death, and home problems.

Vulnerability

Stressors may also strike at an individual's particular emotional vulnerability. What may precipitate anxiety in one person may not do so in another. To partially account for this, we would infer and test whether an individual suffers from a particular vulnerability. For example, consider an individual who believes that to be worthwhile, one must be loved by everyone. As long as this individual receives acceptance from others, we may not expect him to become symptomatic. The rejection by a lover may precipitate an emotional reaction.

THEORY AND CASE CONCEPTUALIZATION

The relationship between cognitive theory and case conceptualization is clearly provided by Persons (1989). Theory should guide clinicians in assessing, planning, implementing, and evaluating treatment. In this section, we use Persons' (1989) model to highlight how the cognitive model and theory of anxiety can be helpful.

One of us (RDT) treated P, an elderly woman with a 15-year history of panic disorder. Following the cognitive model and Persons' formulation model, the following areas were identified: problem list, behavior, cognitive factors, hypothesized mechanism, relationship between mechanism and problem, current precipitants, and predicted obstacles to treatment. This conceptualization emphasizes the interaction between the predisposing and precipitating factors.

Cognitive-Behavioral Case Formulation Example

I.   *Problem List*
     A. *Feelings*
         1. *Panic Attacks:* P. was experiencing the sudden onset of intense fear and accompanying panic attacks several times a week at the beginning of therapy. These attacks were intefering significantly with the quality of life and provoked a great deal of fear.
         2. *Generalized Anxiety:* She also suffered from a chronic sense of generalized anxiety characterized by anticipation of the next attack. She lived in anticipation of experiencing fear provoking thoughts.
         3. *Depression:* P. was experiencing a dysthymia secondary to her panic problems. She was constantly aware of the demoralizing effect that the panic attacks had upon her quality of life. There was also a sense of loss and guilt related to her view that she had changed from the person everybody knew and was now a burden on her family.

B. *Behavior*

1. *Fear-Provoking Situations:* While P. exhibited no avoidance of situations, she was fearful of being alone at times. She was also fearful about the possibility of having an attack in the presence of her family. This created a great deal of anticipatory anxiety.

2. *Difficulties in Relationships with Family:* A significant source of distress is the negative effect that her problems have had on her family. Family members felt that "all she wants is attention" and attributed her problems to the fact that she "doesn't want to live alone." There was also some indication of resentments toward her family that she was unable to verbalize.

3. *Lack of Assertiveness:* P. had assertiveness deficits which seriously undermined her ability to obtain social reinforcement. Her dependent features also interfered with her ability to assert herself for fear of alienating family members on whom she was dependent.

C. *Cognitive*

1. *Cognitive Distortions:* P. exhibited a variety of cognitive distortions, most especially catastrophizing. She tended to misinterpret her symptoms as cause for threat to her mental status. She also exhibited a variety of other distortions such as selective abstraction and jumping to conclusions. These distortions typically escalated her anxiety symptoms to panic proportions and also fueled her dysthymias.

2. *Suicidal Ideation:* P. reported thoughts at times of wishing she were dead and demoralization about her ability to cope with the panic for the rest of her life. She openly reported these thoughts and was willing to discuss them. On several occasions, a thorough suicide assessment was found to be negative.

3. *Decreased Self-Efficacy:* P. had little belief in her ability to do what she could do to resolve her problems. This may have been her reason for choosing medication initially. She had been treated with medication for such a long time that her attributions about improving were externalized.

II. *Hypothesized Mechanisms*

1. *Cognitive:* P. had a variety of underlying schemas that fueled her problematic thoughts, feelings, and behaviors. Some examples of her core schema were as follows:

Vulnerability:

"Something terrible will happen to me at any moment, and I will lose control and go crazy."

"I will forget who I am and forget my family."

"If I experience too much anxiety, I will lose my identity."

Dependence:

"I am unable to cope on my own."

"If I don't please others, they will abandon me."

View of Self, Environment and Future:

"I'll never improve."

"I'm inadequate."

"My problem is so bad that no one can help me."

2. *Social:* Although P. viewed herself as an independent person, it was very clear from her social history that she was extremely dependent on her husband. She apparently never had to rely upon herself as he "did everything for me." She was also socialized in a society that placed women in her ago group in a dependent role.

3. *Biological:* A possible underlying biological mechanism in P. is suggested by the fact that one of her daughters suffered from panic disorder. This finding suggests some possible genetic vulnerability to panic in the face of stressors.

III. *How the Mechanisms Produce the Problem*

P.'s panic attacks were possibly precipitated as a result of a variety of mechanisms including a number of stressful life events, a possible biological vulnerability, and the activation of strongly held beliefs about her vulnerability to threat. She appeared to be a rather dependent woman with low self-efficacy about her ability to cope. Her extreme dependence on her husband buffered her against the effects of stress. Following his death, a major stressor, basic schemas about her vulnerability were probably activated and fueled her negative thoughts, feelings, and behaviors, and increased the likelihood of a panic attack. When she experienced this attack, she was extremely frightened by it and interpreted it as a sign of her vulnerability to losing control and going crazy. Her distorted style of processing information exacerbated her anxiety, fueled her anticipation and generalized anxiety, demoralized her, and precipitated anxiety in certain situations. The patient found herself in a vicious cycle of precipitating the very symptoms she feared. Probably as a result of her low self-efficacy, she sought a "pill" to solve her problems. Her initial physician placed her on a low-potency benzodiazepine of questionable efficacy which may have contributed to her depression. She also exhibited several depressogenic assumptions that fueled her depression, undermined her hopefulness, and precipitated suicidal thinking. P.'s difficulties with her family related to her underlying beliefs about pleasing others and inability to assert herself.

IV. *Current Precipitants:* The original precipitant of P.'s panic related to a situation in which she misinterpreted a benign experience as a sign of an impending catastrophe. One might hypothesize that P. was socialized as a dependent weak person who is unable to cope on her own.

V. *Predicted Obstacles to Treatment:* A number of factors were hypothesized that could interfere with treatment. First, there was evidence that the patient was nonadherent with appointment keeping for her medical visits. Second, her view of medication and externalization of sources of improvement could undermine her participation in therapy.

COMMON MISCONCEPTIONS ABOUT THE COGNITIVE MODEL OF ANXIETY

There are a variety of common misconceptions about the cognitive model of psychopathology (Freeman, Pretzer, Fleming, & Simon, 1990) and anxiety in general. Next we address each of these myths and provide a more accurate description about what the cognitive model implies.

1. *Faulty cognitions cause anxiety disorders.* This misconception is perhaps the most commonly cited unjustified criticism of the cognitive model. The cognitive model does not assume that thoughts cause anxiety disorders. Rather, this model proposes that a variety of predisposing and precipitating factors including cognitive patterns may coexist and relate to the development of anxiety disorders. Cognitions and cognitive processing are not all that are important but do represent a useful focus for intervening.

2. *The cognitive model is simply a variant of the Norman Vincent Peale power of positive thinking approach.* The cognitive model of anxiety assumes that anxiety disordered individuals have a tendency to perceive threat where no danger exists. Anxiety patients exhibit unrealistic thinking and are unlikely to respond to positive reassuring thoughts. Many of these patients have had numerous individuals including family, friends, and even their physician encourage positive

thinking to no avail. The model proposes that patients must learn to evaluate the triggers for anxiety in a realistic valid manner.

3. *The cognitive model denies the importance of behavioral principles such as exposure in overcoming anxiety.* While the cognitive model of anxiety views that there is a basic problem in the cognitive apparatus of the patient, it is simply untrue that the model overlooks the importance of behavioral principles. In fact, Freeman & Simon (1989) have noted that the model might more appropriately be referred to as the cognitive-behavioral-emotive model. It is true that the model places primary emphasis upon the cognitive aspects but most certainly does not ignore the importance and role of behavior and emotion. Cognitive therapists freely use techniques that are designed to modify behavior (e.g., assertiveness training) and emotions (e.g., relaxation therapy).

4. *Applying the cognitive model is simply a matter of talking patients out of their fears and worries.* The cognitive approach actively relies upon the principles of collaborative empiricism and guided discovery. The model assumes that the Socratic approach through which patients are lead through questioning to examine and alter faulty cognitions and underlying beliefs teaches the patient a process that they can take with them. Cognitive therapists do not talk patients out of their problems by persuading or cajoling them to adopt a new perspective. Rather, cognitive therapists talk to patients in ways that assist them in guiding themselves to think, act, and feel more realistically and adaptively.

CONCLUSION

In summary, from our perspective, the cognitive model of anxiety appears to be both a viable and useful vehicle for furthering our understanding of the complex phenomenon of anxiety and the onset development, exacerbation, and treatment of anxiety-related disorders. Continued clinical research designed to further test and refine the hypotheses of the cognitive theory of anxiety is warranted. Likewise, we await further research aimed at more carefully delineating and clarifying the possible role of cognitive factors in the treatment of anxiety disorders.

REFERENCES

American Psychiatric Association. (1987). *Diagnostic and statistical manual of mental disorders (3rd ed., rev.).* Washington, DC: American Psychiatric Association.

Barlow, D. H., & Cerney, J. A. (1988). *Psychological treatment of panic.* New York: Guilford Press.

Beck, A. (1967). *Depression: Causes and treatment.* Philadelphia: University of Pennsylvania Press.

Beck, A. T. (1976). Cognitive therapy and the emotional disorders. New York: International Universities Press.

Beck, A. T. (1991). Cognitive therapy: A 30-year retrospective. *American Psychologist, 46,* 368–375.

Beck, A. T., Emery, G., & Greenberg, R. (1985). *Anxiety disorders and phobias: A cognitive perspective.* New York: Basic Books.

Beck, A. T., & Greenberg, R. L. (1988). Cognitive therapy of panic disorders. In R. E. Hales & A. J. Frances (Eds.), American psychiatric press review of psychiatry (Vol. 7, pp. 571–583). Washington, DC: American Psychiatric Press.

Beck, A. T., & Rush, A. J. (1975). A cognitive model of anxiety formation and anxiety resolution. In J. D. Saranson & C. D. Spielberger (Eds.), *Stress and Anxiety, 2,* 69–80. Washington, DC: Hemisphere Publishing.

Beck, A. T., & Weisher, M. (1989). Cognitive therapy. In A. Freeman, K. M. Simon, L. E. Beutler, & H. Arkowitz (Eds.), *Comprehensive handbook of cognitive therapy.* New York: Plenum Press.

Butler, G., & Matthews, A. (1983). Cognitive processes in anxiety. *Advances in Behavior Research and Therapy, 5,* 51–62.

Cannon, W. B. (1929). *Bodily changes in pain, hunger, fear and rage.* New York: Appleton.

Crowe, R. R., Noyes, R., Pauls, D. L., & Slymen, D. T. (1983). A family study of panic disorder. *Archives of General Psychiatry, 40,* 1065–1069.

Deffenbacher, J. L., Zwemer, W. A., Whisman, M. A., Hill, R. A., & Sloan, R. D. (1986). Irrational beliefs and anxiety. *Cognitive Therapy and Research, 10,* 281–292.

Ellis, A. (1962). Reason and emotion in psychotherapy. New York: Lyle Stuart.

Ellis, A. (1989). The history of cognition in psychotherapy. In A. Freeman, K. Simon, L. Beutler, & H. Arkowitz (Eds.), *Comprehensive handbook of cognitive therapy.* New York: Plenum Press.

Emery, G., & Tracy, N. L. (1987). Theoretical issues in the cognitive-behavioral treatment of anxiety disorders. In L. Michaelson & L. M. Ascher (Eds.), *Anxiety and stress disorders: Cognitive-behavioral assessment and treatment.* New York: Guilford Press.

Foa, E. B., & Kozak, M. J. (1986). Emotional processing of fear: Exposure to corrective information. *Psychological Bulletin, 99,* 20–35.

Freeman, A., Pretzer, J., Fleming, B., & Simon, K. M. (1990). *Clinical applications of cognitive therapy.* New York: Plenum Press.

Freeman, A., & Simon, K. M. (1989). Cognitive therapy of anxiety. In A. Freeman, K. M. Simon, L. E. Beutler, & H. Arkowitz (Eds.), *Comprehensive handbook of cognitive therapy.* New York: Plenum Press.

Harris, E. L., Noyes, R., Crowe, R. R., & Chaudry, D. R. (1983). Family study of agoraphobia. *Archives of General Psychiatry, 40,* 1061–1064.

Hilbert, G. N. (1984). Ideational components of anxiety: Their origin and content. *British Journal of Psychiatry, 144,* 618–624.

Izard, C. E., & Blumberg, S. H. (1985). Emotion theory and the role of emotions in children and adults. In A. H. Tuma & J. D. Maser (Eds.), *Anxiety and the anxiety disorder* (pp. 109–125). Hillsdale, NJ: Erlbaum.

Kendall, P. C., & Ingram, R. (1987). The future for cognitive assessment of anxiety: Let's get specific. In L. Michaelson & L. M. Ascher (Eds.), *Anxiety and stress disorders: Cognitive-behavioral assessment and treatment.* New York: Guilford Press.

Last, C. G., Barlow, D. H., & O'Brien, G. T. (1984). Cognitive change during behavioral and cognitive-behavioral treatment of agoraphobia. *Behavior Modification, 8,* 181–210.

Lazurus, R. L. (1991). Progress on a cognitive-motivational-relational theory of emotion. *American Psychologist, 46,* 819–834.

Lindsley, D. B. (1952). Psychological phenomena and the electroencephalogram. *Electroencephalography and Clinical Neurophysiology, 4,* 443–456.

Lindsley, D. B. (1957). Psychophysiology and motivation. In M. R. Jones (Ed.), *Nebraska symposium on motivation* (pp. 45–105). Lincoln: University of Nebraska Press.

Lindsley, D. B. (1960). Attention, consciousness, sleep, and wakefulness. In J. Freld & H. W. Magoan (Eds.), *Handbook of physiology* (Vol. 3; pp. 1553–1593). Washington, DC: Harper & Row.

Mahoney, M. J. (1974). *Cognition and behavior modification.* Cambridge, MA: Ballinger.

Marluzzi, T. V., & Bollwood, M. D. (1989). Cognitive assessment. In A. Freeman, K. M. Simon, L. E. Beutler, & H. Arkowitz (Eds.), *Comprehensive handbook of cognitive therapy.* New York: Plenum Press.

Meichenbaum, D. (1977). *Cognitive behavior modification: An integrative approach.* New York: Plenum.

Moran, C., & Andrews, G. (1985). The familial occurrence of agoraphobis. *British Journal of Psychiatry, 146,* 262–267.

Persons, J. B. (1989). *Cognitive therapy in practice: A case formulation approach.* New York: Norton.

Plutchik, R. (1980). *Emotion: A psychoevolutionary synthesis.* New York: Harper & Row.

Reiger, D. A., Myers, J. K., Kramer, M., et al. (1984). The NIMH epidemiologic catchment area program: Historical context, major objectives, and study population characteristics. *Archives of General Psychiatry, 41,* 934–941.

Sheehan, D. V. (1983). *The anxiety disease.* New York: Bantam.

Simon, K. M., & Fleming, B. M. (1985). Beck's cognitive therapy of depression, treatment and outcome. In R. M. Turner & L. M. Ascher (Eds.), *Evaluation behavior therapy outcome.* New York: Springer.

Taylor, C. B., & Arnow, B. (1988). *The nature and treatment of anxiety disorders.* New York: Free Press.

Torgerson, S. (1983). Genetic factors in anxiety disorders. *Archives of General Psychiatry, 40,* 1085–1089.

Wolpe, J. (1958). *Psychotherapy by reciprocal inhibition.* Stanford: Stanford University Press.

Wolpe, J. (1973). *The practice of behavior therapy.* New York: Pergamon Press.

Zinbarg, R. E. (1990). Animal research and behavior therapy is not what you think it is. *The Behavior Therapist, 13,* 171–175.

Zwemer, W. A., & Deffenbacher, J. L. (1984). Irrational beliefs, anger, and anxiety. *Journal of Counseling Psychology, 31,* 391–393.

CHAPTER 6

The Genetics of Anxiety Disorders

ALISON M. MACDONALD, BSc, and ROBIN M. MURRAY, MD

There is considerable evidence that fear is partly genetically transmitted in the animal kingdom, as might be expected for an emotion with evolutionary advantages for survival (Marks, 1987). If, as seems likely, the related experience of anxiety in humans is also partly innate, then one way of conceptualizing anxiety disorders is as occurring in vulnerable individuals on the extreme of a continuum of liability distributed normally throughout the population (Falconer, 1965). Such vulnerabilities are generally conferred by a combination of genetic and environmental factors, partly transmitted within families; it is the task of genetic research to identify patterns of familial transmission, to quantify these effects, and to disentangle the relationships of the multiple contributing factors.

The principle tools of psychiatric genetic epidemiology are family, twin, and adoption studies. These rely on the combination of principles derived from Mendelian and quantitative genetics with reliable assessment of psychopathology in relatives of affected individuals. A full discussion of these methods and their current applications to psychiatric disorders may be found in Tsuang, Kendler, and Lyons (1991).

To date there have been no adoption studies of anxiety disorders. Most work has been conducted on families, usually with first degree relatives alone but one or two studies have also examined second degree relatives; comparisons have also been made between identical (monozygotic, MZ) and non-identical (dizygotic, DZ) twins. Families and twins have usually been ascertained through an index case, the proband, diagnosed with the disorder of interest, either through his or her attendance at a clinic, through answering advertisements, or less often, by population screening. There are also a number of genetic studies of nonclinical samples of volunteer twins that provide complementary information about symptoms of anxiety and neurotic personality traits in the "normal" population.

ANXIETY NEUROSIS

Early studies of anxiety disorder before the development of operational diagnostic criteria (Feighner et al., 1972; Spitzer, Endicott, & Robins, 1978) examined relatives of index cases diagnosed variously as anxiety neurosis (Brown, 1942; McInnes, 1937), neurocirculatory asthenia (Cohen, Badal, Kilpatrick, Reed, & White, 1951), irritable heart or Da-Costa's syndrome (Wood, 1941). These studies probably include cases who today would be diagnosed as panic disorder (PD) or generalized anxiety disorder (GAD) in the United States by DSM-III-R (American Psychiatric Association, 1987), or would fall under one of the subcategories of anxiety neurosis covered in the International Classification of Diseases (World Health Organization, 1978) used elsewhere. However, some cases included in these old studies would not meet modern criteria; for example, an individual would have been diagnosed as having neurocirculatory asthenia by Cohen et al. (1951) for reporting headaches and breathlessness (which would not meet modern criteria for PD) or, on the other hand, for suffering anxiety attacks, palpitations, and a range of somatic symptoms (which probably would). This unknown element makes the older reports hard to compare with recent studies. Nevertheless, as seen in Table 6.1, there is considerable agreement among the studies, with the reported rates of disorder in first degree relatives in the range 15% to 16% compared with 1% to 5% in controls.

The early studies relied on the family history (FH) method; that is, the probands were asked about their relatives and judgments were made about the latters' diagnostic status on the basis of such reports. One family history study, conducted using operational criteria (Noyes et al., 1978), produced findings remarkably similar to the earlier studies. However, the FH method is known to underestimate levels of pathology (Andreasen, Endicott, Spitzer, & Winokur, 1977; Andreasen, Rice, Endicott, Reich, & Coryell, 1986) and the preferred method is the family interview (FI); in this, details of the family are obtained from the proband, then as many relatives as possible are directly interviewed about their psychiatric history and current symptoms. The single family interview study predating operational criteria found a 49% rate of anxiety neurosis (neurocirculatory asthenia) among 37 adult offspring versus 5.6% in controls (Wheeler, White, Reed, & Cohen, 1948). This study was reported only as an abstract for a conference presentation, and few details are given, but it seems to be related to that of Cohen et al. (1951).

A more recent interview study by Cloninger, Martin, Clayton, and Guze (1981) reported that 8% of interviewed first degree relatives of 66 anxiety neurotics had a definite anxiety neurosis, using strict criteria (Feighner et al., 1972), rising to 14% when questionable cases were included, a rate comparable with the earlier family history studies. A

TABLE 6.1. Family Studies of Anxiety Neurosis

Study	Relative[1]	Family History (FH) or Family Interview (FI)	Proband Diagnosis[2]	Prevalence in Relatives (%)			In Controls
				Males	Females	Total	
Brown (1942)	2°	FH	AN			3	
Pauls et al. (1979)	2°	FH	AN	5	14	10	4-5
McInnes (1937)	1°	FH	AN			15	0
Brown (1942)	1°	FH	AN			15	0.4
Cohen et al. (1951)	1°	FH	AN	12	20	16	3
Noyes et al. (1978)	1°	FH	AN	13	24	18	
Moran & Andrews (1985)	1°	FH	AG	7	19	13	
Hopper et al. (1987)	1°	FH	PD	9	15	12	
Wheeler et al. (1948)	1°	FI	AN			49	
Crowe et al. (1983)	1°	FI	AN	22	42	31	
Cloninger et al. (1981)	1°	FI	AN (1)[3]	2	13	8	3
			(2)	9	18	14	7

[1]° First degree relative
2° Second degree relative
[2]AN Anxiety neurosis (includes Neurocirculatory asthenia)
PD Panic Disorder
AG Agoraphobia
[3](1) Definite cases
(2) Combined definite and questionable cases

TABLE 6.2. Twin Studies of Anxiety Neurosis

Study	Co-Twin Diagnosis	Zygosity	Number of Pairs (N)	Concordance (%)
Slater & Shields (1969)	Any anxiety disorder	MZ	17	41
		DZ	28	4
	Any diagnosis	MZ	20	47
		DZ	40	18
Torgersen (1978)	Definite & anxiety	MZ	30	31
		DZ	56	9

further feature of the family studies of anxiety neurosis is that about twice as many female relatives are found to be affected compared with male relatives; thus any attempts to fit genetic models to the data must take these sex differences into account (Table 6.1). It is clear from the studies reviewed, for all their faults, that anxiety neurosis is familial, but that does not make it genetic. Twin studies have been used to try and separate genetic and environmental factors.

Two twin studies of anxiety neurosis preceded the development of operationalized criteria. Slater and Shields (1969) studies a series of twins ascertained through the routine registration procedures of the Maudsley Hospital, London, UK. As with the family studies, they found that the proportion of affected co-twins increased as the criteria for concordance were relaxed (Table 6.2). Torgersen (1978) examined twins from the population-based Norwegian twin registry and his lower concordance rates may well reflect the different ascertainment procedures. It can be seen from Table 6.2 that both the London and Norwegian studies reported higher concordance in MZ than in DZ twins, that is, a genetic effect. Torgersen has subsequently shown that concordance rates for neurosis vary according to the "severity" of the treatment center where the proband was ascertained (Torgersen, 1983a), which is assumed to reflect the severity of the disorder. These differing levels of severity will certainly be negatively related to prevalence rates; this may partly explain the changing concordance rates, but these probably also reflect differing levels of genetic influence on mild and severe disorders.

With the introduction of DSM-III (American Psychiatric Association, 1980), subsequent studies have focused on subcategories of anxiety neurosis; panic disorder (PD), agoraphobia (Ag), simple and social phobias (SP), generalized anxiety disorder (GAD), and obsessive-compulsive disorder (OCD). For simplicity, we discuss the genetic research under the diagnostic headings.

TABLE 6.3. Family Studies of DSM-III Categories of Anxiety Disorder: Panic Disorder and Agoraphobia

Study	Relative[1]	Family History (FH) or Family Interview (FI)	Proband Diagnosis[2]	Prevalence in Relatives (%)		
				Males	Females	Total
Moran & Andrews (1985)	1°	FH	AG	7	19	13
Hopper et al. (1987)	1°	FH	PD	9	15	12
Crowe et al. (1983)	1°	FI	PD	17	33	35
Harris et al. (1983)	1°	FI	AG	17	46	32
			PD	18	46	33
Noyes et al. (1986)	1°	FI	AG			AG 11.6
						PD 8.3
			PD			AG 1.9
						PD 17.3

1° First degree relative,
2° Second degree relative
[2]AN Anxiety neurosis (includes Neurocirculatory asthenia)
PD Panic Disorder
AG Agoraphobia

Panic Disorder (PD) and Agoraphobia (Ag)

Most of the recent family interview studies of the DSM-III categories of PD and Ag have been conducted by a group in Iowa (Crowe, Noyes, Pauls, & Slymen, 1983; Harris, Noyes, Crowe, & Chaudhry, 1983; Noyes et al., 1986) using overlapping samples. The results are summarized in Table 6.3.

The final report (Noyes et al., 1986) compared relatives of 40 Ag patients, 40 PD patients, and 20 non-anxious controls, in an attempt to examine whether the separation of Ag from anxiety states (PD) incorporated in DSM-III, could be justified on familial grounds. The morbidity risks for Ag and PD, respectively, among relatives of PD index cases were 1.9% and 17.3%, while among relatives of Ag index cases the corresponding risks were 11.6% and 8.3%; that is, PD occurs in the relatives of both PD and Ag probands, but Ag is largely confined to the relatives of Ag index cases. These findings led the authors to suggest that Ag is a more severe variant of PD, in effect what Hallam (1978) argued. This view has been adopted in DSM-III-R.

Other studies that have focused on agoraphobia have found higher rates of the disorder in relatives of index cases than in controls. Solyom, Beck, Solyom, and Hugel (1974) examined histories of 47 phobic patients, 91% of whom were agoraphobic, and found that in 45% of the cases there was a family history of psychiatric disorder with 30% of the mothers having phobias, as opposed to between 19% to 23% of families of nonphobic controls.

Buglass, Clarke, Henderson, Kreitman, and Presley (1977) noted a positive family history of phobic disorder in 7% of parents and 8% of siblings of 30 agoraphobic women, compared with 2% and 3%, respectively, in families of controls. Moran and Andrews (1985) investigated the family histories of 60 probands who were consecutive attenders at an Ag treatment unit and found a 12.5% estimated lifetime risk of Ag among their 232 parents and siblings.

Noyes et al. (1986) also noted increased risks of alcohol disorders in male relatives of Ag cases (30.8%), though 30% of probands also had secondary alcohol or sedative drug use disorders. However, they found no increase in affective disorders in either group of relatives, in spite of 35% of PD probands and 48% of Ag probands themselves having secondary major affective disorder. This latter finding may be in part a result of the application of a diagnostic hierarchy (Leckman, Weissman, Merikangas, Pauls, & Prusoff, 1984).

Others (Pauls, Crowe, & Noyes, 1979; Pauls, Bucher, Crowe, & Noyes, 1980) have argued that the mode of transmission of PD is that of an autosomal dominant gene with incomplete penetrance, based on the distribution of cases in second degree relatives and on a pedigree analysis of

19 families. Subsequently, Crowe et al. (1983) fitted single major locus models and multifactorial polygenic transmission models with sex dependent thresholds (Reich, James, & Morris, 1972) to family data on PD. However, the results were inconclusive and they were unable to exclude either model.

A more recent study of pure PD cases with and without agoraphobia, albeit using family history data (Hopper, Judd, Derrick, & Burrows, 1987; Hopper, Judd, Derrick, Macaskill, & Burrows, 1990) used modelling techniques to explore the familial pattern of PD. This study found evidence for contributions to familiality from both genetic factors and sibship environment (i.e., the family environmental factors shared by brothers and sisters and contributing to their resemblance) as well as a suggestion of negative assortative mating. The latter finding, that individuals with PD may be less likely to marry a similarly affected spouse, reflects the experience of many clinicians.

Torgersen (1983b) re-analyzed data from his twin study (Torgersen, 1978) in terms of DSM-III criteria. The study included 32 MZ and 53 DZ adult same-sexed twin pairs with a proband with an anxiety disorder. They were selected from a population-based psychiatric twin register, and directly assessed using a structured psychiatric interview. Thirty-one percent of the MZ co-twins of 13 probands with panic disorder and agoraphobia with panic attacks were concordant for anxiety disorder with panic attacks, while there was zero concordance among the 16 DZ twin pairs. It should be noted that none of the 4 concordant MZ pairs had exactly the same diagnostic subtype, and the co-twin concordance was for a looser diagnosis than DSM-III PD, involving less frequent panic attacks.

The results of the recent twin and family studies have been used to support arguments for Panic Disorder (with or without phobic avoidance, i.e., Ag) as a distinct category, distinct that is from other anxiety disorders and from major affective disorder (e.g., Crowe, 1988) in keeping with Klein and Klein (1988) pharmacologically based dissection of the anxiety neurosis category placing primacy upon the panic symptoms. However, family studies of index cases with major depression, with or without secondary anxiety, have found different and apparently conflicting results which are only just beginning to be resolved. The Yale family studies (Leckman, Weissman, Merikangas, Pauls, & Prusoff, 1983; Leckman, Merikangas, Pauls, Prusoff, & Weissman, 1983; Weissman, Leckman, Merikangas, Gammon, & Prusoff, 1984) found that first degree relatives of individuals with both major depressive and anxiety disorders had higher rates of both diagnoses than did relatives of individuals with major depression only. Other studies show that this pattern only seems to occur if the index cases have mixed disorders, and not among relatives of probands with depression secondary to anxiety; in such cases relatives had higher rates of anxiety disorders but not of depression

(Coryell et al., 1988; Van Valkenburg, Akiskal, Puzantian, & Rosenthal, 1984). A recent family study of probands with primary depression and various secondary anxiety syndromes found that only the relatives of cases with secondary panic attacks had higher rates of anxiety disorders than relatives of patients with depression alone. The excess anxiety disorders were obsessional and phobic disorders and not panic disorder (Coryell, Endicott, & Winokur, 1992), a finding which awaits replication, but may reflect a nonspecific vulnerability to neurotic symptoms in these relatives.

A further re-analysis of the Norwegian twin data appears to confirm the family study findings; Torgersen (1990) found that co-twins of MZ twin index cases with major depression or mixed anxiety depression were significantly more likely to have diagnoses of depression or mixed anxiety depression than might be expected by chance. For index twins with "pure" anxiety, however, co-twins were more likely to have a diagnosis of anxiety disorder, but not of depression or a mixed anxiety depression. This relationship became even more marked when the same data were analyzed in terms of depression with and without panic attacks versus anxiety disorder with panic attacks; though the numbers are very small, depression with and without panic attacks seemed to be related while cases of "pure" anxiety with panic showed concordance for anxiety with panic only. Although 4 of 18 MZ co-twins are concordant for anxiety with panic attacks, the specificity of diagnosis only extends as far as the fact that they all have panic attacks; an earlier paper indicates that the co-twins have different subcategories of anxiety disorder from the index twins in each case (Torgersen, 1983b).

To conclude, interpretation of the literature on familiality of panic disorder and agoraphobia is complicated by methodological differences among the studies, particularly in the selection of probands and application of diagnostic hierarchies. There is considerable evidence that the two subcategories are familial, and that they are related, with both family and twin studies supporting the notion that agoraphobia is a more severe variant of panic disorder. Earlier suggestions that PD is a form of anxiety disorder transmitted according to a Mendelian autosomal dominant pattern have not been vindicated, and the transmission pattern remains unclear; both autosomal dominant with incomplete penetrance and polygenic models have been postulated. The contribution of familial environment and negative assortative mating to familial prevalence further complicates interpretation of segregation patterns in relatives.

The relationship of PD, Ag, and affective disorders is complex; it appears that in families ascertained through probands with mixed disorders, there may be a predisposition to both anxiety and affective disorders. For those ascertained through a more "pure" anxiety disorder, and panic disorder in particular, the familial predisposition is more specifically to anxiety disorders, though not perhaps to PD alone but to a broader spectrum of related syndromes of PD, Ag, phobias and OCD.

Generalized Anxiety Disorder (GAD)

Only one study has specifically addressed the familiality of GAD. Noyes, Clarkson, Crowe, Yates, & McChesney, (1987) recruited 20 probands diagnosed GAD, according to DSM-III and DSM-III-R, through newspaper advertisements. The frequency of anxiety disorders in their 123 first degree relatives (of whom two thirds were interviewed) was compared with that in 241 relatives of 20 PD probands, 256 relatives of 40 Ag probands, and 113 relatives of controls who had been involved in an earlier study (Noyes et al., 1986).

Noyes et al. found a higher proportion of relatives of GAD probands with GAD than in the other groups (19.5% versus 3.5–5.4%). However, this must, as the authors recognized, be interpreted with caution; the use of volunteer probands, 14 of whom had additional affective disorder and 37% of whom had axis II personality disorders, as well as the nonblind diagnostic assignment and small number of families studied, preclude specific conclusions about familiality. The lack of evidence for a relationship of GAD and MDD is consistent with earlier family studies of PD and Ag probands (Noyes et al., 1986). The perceived importance of psychological stressors, and the high rates of personality disturbance in relatives of these GAD probands (35% versus 13.7% in controls) is also of interest. It may be that these findings in part reflect ascertainment biases associated with recruiting by advertising, but they also suggest some personality predisposition to GAD; this is of interest to clinicians in the light of other studies finding a relationship between levels of neurotic symptoms and personality disorders (Tyrer et al., 1990).

Phobic Disorders and Fears

Most family studies of phobic disorders deal with agoraphobia, and these have already been discussed. Fyer et al. (1990) conducted a blind family interview study of 49 first degree relatives of 15 simple phobic (SP) probands (without other anxiety disorder) compared with 119 relatives of 38 well controls. Thirty-one percent of 58 relatives versus 16% of control relatives received a lifetime diagnosis of SP and the risk for other psychiatric disorders did not differ. Only 2 of the 15 relatives had the same type of SP as the proband. However, when the simple phobias were subcategorized into animal and situational (non-animal) there was some evidence for specificity of transmission, animal phobias occurring more frequently in relatives of animal phobics than in relatives of either situational phobics or controls, and a similar pattern for situational phobias. The study also collected family history data on non-interviewed relatives, and found a significant, albeit lower, difference in rates of SP in relatives of SP probands and controls (10% versus 2%). The authors conclude that DSM-III-R simple phobia is a "highly functional disorder that breeds true and does not transmit an increased risk for other phobia or anxiety disorders."

Fyer et al. (1990) also investigated ratings for 17 irrational fears in their study and found no evidence for familiality, nor any association with increased risk for SP. This is in marked contrast with studies of fears conducted in normal populations (Philips, Fulker, & Rose, 1987; Rose & Ditto, 1983).

A single family history study (Reich & Yates, 1988) nonblindly compared relatives of 17 probands with social phobias (6 of whom also had MDD), 10 controls, and 88 probands with panic disorder. The SP group were recruited from a treatment study, the other two groups through advertising. While the rates for SP in relatives of SP and PD probands were significantly different (6.6% versus 0.4%, respectively) the finding that 2.2% of control relatives had SP was not significantly different from the rate in SP relatives, probably due to the small sample size.

Fyer et al.'s (1990) family interview study of simple phobias found no excess of social phobia in relatives.

Obsessive-Compulsive Disorder (OCD)

OCD is a relatively rare disorder amongst the categories of anxiety disorder, with a prevalence rate traditionally accepted as being in the region of 0.05% (Raudin, 1953). Recent studies suggest that individual symptoms and more loosely defined forms of OCD may be much more common in the general population than hitherto realized (Karno, Golding, Sorenson, & Burnam, 1988; Sanavio, 1988). This difficulty in defining OCD has made interpretation of family and twin studies difficult, and the methodology and existing literature are examined in detail by Macdonald et al. (1991).

Family studies predating operationalized criteria report rates of OCD between 1% and 10% in first degree relatives (Brown, 1942; Luxenberger, 1930; Rosenberg, 1967; Raudin, 1953), but when criteria are broadened to include obsessional traits in relatives, these rates rise to between 3% and 37% (Kringlen, 1965; Lewis, 1936; Lo, 1967). The levels are even higher when "any abnormality" is included. Such variable rates make familiality difficult to interpret when the population rates needed for comparison are just as variable (Carey, Gottesman, & Robins, 1980), but these older studies suggest that there is at least some familial component to the disorder.

The one family study of OCD using a series of RDC diagnosed hospital patients and diagnoses of relatives based on SADS-L interviews, and a control group (McKeon & Murray, 1987), found only one case of OCD among the 149 relatives of 50 probands (0.7%) and one case among the 151 control relatives (0.7%). However, the relatives of OCD cases were found to have higher rates of other neurotic disorders, rates for "any abnormality" were 27% versus 14% in control relatives. These results suggest a familial liability to a broader spectrum of neuroses, rather than to OCD specifically.

Twin studies of OCD have been primarily case reports, and as such are biased towards being MZ and concordant (Rachman & Hodgson, 1980), apart from Carey and Gottesman's (1981) study of phobic and obsessional twins from the Maudsley Hospital Twin Register. Carey and Gottesman (1981) found that 33% of co-twins in 15 MZ pairs had psychiatric or general practitioner treatment involving obsessional symptoms versus 7% of co-twins in 15 DZ pairs. Obsessional symptoms with or without treatment were noted in 87% of MZ co-twins and 47% of DZ co-twins; in the families of these twins, a history of obsessional traits was reported in between 6% and 27% of first degree relatives (depending on definition) with levels of any psychiatric symptoms up to 48%.

Torgersen (1983b) has also reported 3 MZ and 9 DZ twin pairs, ascertained through the Norwegian population-based twin registry, with a proband with OCD. None of the co-twins were concordant for OCD, but one MZ and one DZ co-twin had other anxiety disorders and three other co-twins had unspecified non-anxiety diagnosis.

The statistical improbability of identifying a pair of MZ twins concordant for OCD by chance (Marks, Crowe, Drewe, Young, & Dewhurst, 1969) has perpetuated the idea that the finding of even one or two such pairs indicates a strong genetic component to the disorder. However, recent indications that obsessional symptoms are more common than previously thought, as well as the well-known biases that nonsystematic ascertainment of affected twins produce (Rachman & Hodgson, 1980), indicate that as in genetic studies of other types of anxiety disorder more weight should be given to studies of systematically ascertained and assessed probands and their relatives, including twins. Such studies (Macdonald, Murray, & Clifford, 1991; Carey & Gottesman, 1981; McKeon & Murray, 1987; Torgersen, 1983b) indicate that while obsessionality is certainly familial, any genetic predisposition to OCD may be a broader spectrum of neurotic complaints, with little specificity.

The higher rates of obsessional symptoms in the general population and availability of questionnaires for dimensional assessment of obsessionality make this a more fruitful field for behavioral geneticists. Clifford, Murray, and Fulker (1984) fitted genetic models to the scores of 419 pairs of volunteer twins on the Leyton Obsessional Inventory (LOI) (Snowdon, 1980) and the neuroticism scale of the Eysenck Personality Questionnaire (EPQ) (Eysenck & Eysenck, 1975). Heritability of the trait and symptom scales of the LOI were 47% and 44%, respectively; there seemed to be a genetic factor influencing general neuroticism and contributing to the correlation of the obsessional and N scores, as well as a separate genetic factor contributing to obsessional traits. These findings await replication, but are in accord with clinical studies suggesting a familial predisposition to a broader neurotic spectrum.

SYMPTOMS OF ANXIETY IN NON-CLINICAL POPULATIONS

A series of papers (Jardine, Martin, & Henderson, 1984; Kendler, Heath, Martin, & Eaves, 1986; Kendler, Heath, Martin, & Eaves, 1987; Martin, Jardine, Andrews, & Heath, 1988) have analyzed data collected on 3,798 pairs of adult twins from the Australian National Health and Medical Research Council twin register, on the 14 item anxiety and depression scales of the DSSI (Bedford, Foulds, & Sheffield, 1976) and the neuroticism scale of the EPQ (Eysenck & Eysenck, 1975). These authors have shown that some 33% to 46% of the variance in total anxiety symptom scores seems to be due to additive genetic factors, with most of the remaining variation due to environmental factors specific to the individual. More complex multivariate analyses of individual symptom scores (Kendler et al., 1987) have shown that genes seem to act in a fairly nonspecific way, influencing the overall level of symptoms on the depression-distress (a mixture of depression/anxiety symptoms), general anxiety, and "insomnia" factors generated from the data, but that apparently there are some minor specific influences of genes on somatic anxiety symptoms. Environmental influences differ across the factors. These results are obtained by fitting various genetic models to the data obtained from twin pairs and testing the fit of these models. Applying rules of parsimony, the model with the smallest number of parameters that provides the best fit to the data is accepted.

Though the specific relevance of these questionnaire assessments of "symptoms" to clinical anxiety and depression is not known, it is interesting that these data coincide with the most recent clinical findings from family studies of depressed and anxious patients (vide supra). That is, there seems to be a mixed anxiety-depression type, with higher levels of familial depression and anxiety symptoms, while if a more "pure" form of anxiety is examined, then relatives have raised rates of anxiety symptoms alone and not of other affective symptoms. This is congruent with the model from Kendler et al. (1987) of an overlapping cluster of symptoms of anxiety and depression which they called "depression-distress" that has nonspecific genetic influences on overall level of symptoms, but with another factor of a more specific type of somatic anxiety that does seem to have some separate heritable influence.

Andrews, Stewart, Allen, and Henderson (1990a) have also reported concordance rates for neurotic disorders in a directly interviewed volunteer twin sample of 446 pairs: 10.2% of MZ pairs were concordant for any lifetime diagnosis of neurotic disorder versus 9.6% of DZ pairs, a nonsignificant difference, and only one DZ female pair and one MZ male pair were concordant for PD/Ag among a total of 34 individual twins receiving these diagnoses. In this twin study, the twins were ascertained through a volunteer sample, not through clinics or by cross-matching population samples with psychiatric registers, and so the twins had not necessarily sought treatment for neurotic disorders. Andrews et al. (1990a) suggest that their findings of no MZ/DZ difference in concordance for neurosis in general or any subtype in particular, the co-occurrence of multiple diagnoses, and the comparable prevalences in this sample with other epidemiological studies may indicate that any underlying genetic vulnerability to neurosis is to trait neuroticism that may itself be sufficiently powerful to lead to severe and chronic symptoms and seeking specialist treatment. This would account for the finding of significant MZ/DZ concordance differences in those twin studies that have ascertained twins through affected probands who had sought treatment (who might be expected to have a higher genetic loading). Such a model would also take account of Torgersen's (1983a) findings of a positive relationship between level of genetic influence and severity of neurotic disorder.

The most recent work on this area addresses the idea of a general neurotic syndrome (Andrews et al., 1990b), an idea popular with some European psychiatrists (Tyrer, 1985), by assessing lifetime prevalence of the various neurotic subcategories in a sample of volunteer twins from the Australian NHMRC register. In all, 27% of the subjects reported symptoms consistent with some diagnosis in their lifetime and the frequencies of co-occurrence of multiple diagnoses was higher than might be expected assuming independent co-occurrence. The twins in this study were not used for a genetic analysis, but new studies from the population-based Virginia twin registry involving direct psychiatric interviews of adult female twins should shed further light on this area (Kendler, Neale, Kessler, Heath, & Eaves, 1992).

MOLECULAR GENETIC AND BIOLOGICAL MARKER STUDIES

In spite of the absence of any convincing pedigree data to suggest that PD could be inherited as a single gene disorder, Crowe, Noyes, Wilson, Elston, and Ward (1987) examined the possibility of linkage between PD and 29 blood type and protein electrophoretic polymorphisms in 198 members (39% affected) of 26 pedigrees. Analysis excluded linkage to 18 of the market loci, but revealed one suggestive of linkage at the alpha-haptoglobin locus on chromosome 16q22 (lod score 2.23). A subsequent study including 10 further pedigrees (Crowe, Noyes, Samuelson, Wesner, & Wilson, 1990) however excluded linkage at this locus.

Other proposed "biological" markers for PD have been of some interest for geneticists. Wooley (1976) suggested an association between mitral valve prolapse syndrome (MVPS) and PD based on the similarity of clinical pictures and the similar epidemiology, both disorders being familial. As MVPS can be diagnosed echocardiographically, it could have proved to be a useful marker for PD for genetic studies, but further studies (Hickey, Andrews, & Wilken, 1983) have not supported the idea that MVPS accounts for a subgroup of PD. Other authors have been interested in the apparent sensitivity to lactate and carbon dioxide of PD sufferers, as markers of biological aetiology, but these associations have also been shown to be nonspecific and complex as well as causing difficulty on theoretical grounds (Margraf, Ehlers, & Roth, 1986).

DISCUSSION AND CONCLUSIONS

Interest in the role of genetic factors in the aetiology of psychiatric disorders has waxed and waned over the course of the last century. The rapid development of recombinant DNA technology in the last decade has led to success in locating the genes that cause a number of single locus mendelian disorders (such as Fragile X mental retardation syndrome, Cystic fibrosis, myotonic dystrophy). This has resulted not only in an upsurge of interest in the genetics of psychiatric disorders but also new challenges for psychiatric geneticists. The identification of phenotypes (the observed symptom patterns) of disorders that are transmitted according to the patterns found in single gene disorders has become a priority for those whose aim is to identify the disease alleles and develop biological treatments.

Distinguishing the transmission patterns of disorders caused by just a few major genes against a background of other genetic and environmental effects from those that are polygenic multifactorial disorders is extremely difficult and requires large studies (Reich et al., 1972). Therefore, much recent work has focused on development of methodology, as well as refinement of diagnostic techniques to separate heterogeneous types of disorder. Single gene disorders tend to be rare, and, because anxiety disorders are relatively common (Robins et al., 1984), it is likely that the long observed familiality is due to the combination of multiple genetic and environmental factors, each of small effect; there may be some subtypes or families in which major genes are transmitted.

Although genetic studies of anxiety disorders have increased in sophistication, there has been little integration of the considerable advances in both psychological theory and treatment using behavioral (Marks, 1987) and cognitive (Beck, Emery, & Greenberg, 1985) techniques with behavior genetics methods; the importance of environmental factors in anxiety disorders has been thoroughly demonstrated in these areas and disentanglement of genetic and environmental factors in aetiology requires reliable and valid assessment of the many putative environmental factors as well as of the diagnostic status of relatives. A recent attempt to combine such approaches (Kendler et al., 1992) led the authors to conclude there would be a "great gain in analytic power . . . as genetic-epidemiological models for psychiatric disorders move from treating the environment as an unmeasured latent 'black box' to considering it as an array of specific measurable environmental variables."

This study demonstrated that while parental loss, a much researched early risk factor for affective disorders, contributed only a modest amount (2%) to total variance in liability, it contributed substantially to aggregation within sibships of generalized anxiety disorder, panic disorder, and phobias.

The race to identify single gene mutations is paradoxically invigorating the genetic epidemiological field; the simple quantification of heritability or h^2 can no longer be justified as an adequate goal, there are far more complex and interesting issues to tackle. Twin and family studies, using large samples and varied methodologies can be used to identify phenotypes of anxiety disorder which may be "more genetic" than others and hence to justify and guide linkage work. Such studies can also investigate the influence of assortative mating, family environment and other specific environmental factors in aetiology. The identification of new types of non-Mendelian inheritance (Flint, 1992) will increase the variety of genetic models available to be tested on family data. We are at the beginning of a period of much more systematic application of genetic methods to anxiety disorders. Hopefully, this will finally bury the destructive "nature v. nurture" quarrels, and bring new understanding of our patients' predicaments.

REFERENCES

American Psychiatric Association. (1980). *Diagnostic and Statistical Manual of Mental Disorders* (3rd ed.), Washington, DC: Author.

American Psychiatric Association. (1987). *Diagnostic and Statistical Manual of Mental Disorders* (3rd. ed., rev.), Washington, DC: Author.

Andreasen, N. C., Endicott, J., Spitzer, R. L., & Winokur, G. (1977). The family history method using diagnostic criteria: Reliability and validity. *Archives of General Psychiatry, 34,* 1229–1235.

Andreasen, N. C., Rice, J., Endicott, J., Reich, T., & Coryell, W. (1986). The family history approach to diagnosis: How useful is it? *Archives of General Psychiatry, 43,* 421–429.

Andrews, G., Stewart, G., Allen, R., & Henderson, A. S. (1990a). The genetics of six neurotic disorders: A twin study. *Journal of Affective Disorders, 19,* 23–29.

Andrews, G., Stewart G., Morris-Yates, A., Holt, P., & Henderson, S. (1990b). Evidence for a general neurotic syndrome. *British Journal of Psychiatry, 157,* 6–12.

Beck, A. T., Emery, G., & Greenberg, R. L. (1985). *Anxiety disorders and phobias: A cognitive perspective.* (New York: Basic Books).

Bedford, A., Foulds, G. A., & Sheffield, B. F. (1976). A new personal disturbance scale (DSSI-sAD). *British Journal of Social Clinical Psychiatry, 15,* 387–394.

Brown, F. W. (1942). Heredity in the psychoneuroses. *Proceedings of the Royal Society of Medicine, 35,* 785–790.

Buglass, D., Clarke, J., Henderson, A. S., Kreitman, N., & Presley, A. S. (1977). A study of agoraphobic housewives. *Psychological Medicine, 7,* 73–86.

Carey, G., Gottesman, I. I., & Robins, E. (1980). Prevalence rates for the neuroses: Pitfalls in the evaluation of familiality. *Psychological Medicine, 10,* 437–443.

Carey, G., & Gottesman, I. I. (1981). Twin and family studies of anxiety, phobic, and obsessive disorders. In *Anxiety: New research and changing concepts,* D. F. Klein & J. G. Rabkin, (Eds.), pp. 117–136 (New York: Raven Press).

Clifford, C. A., Murray, R. M., & Fulker, D. W. (1984). Genetic and environmental influences on obsessional traits and symptoms. *Psychological Medicine, 14,* 791–800.

Cloninger, C. R., Martin, R. L., Clayton, P., & Guze, S. B. (1981). A blind follow-up and family study of anxiety neurosis: Preliminary analysis of the St. Louis

500. In *Anxiety: New research and changing concepts,* D. F. Klein & J. G. Rabkin. (Eds.) (New York: Raven Press).

Cohen, M. E., Badal, D. W., Kilpatrick, A., Reed, E. W., & White, P. D. (1951). The high familial prevalence of neurocirculatory asthenia (anxiety neurosis, effort syndrome). *American Journal of Human Genetics, 3,* 126–158.

Coryell, W., Endicott, J., Andreasen, N. C., Keller, M. B., Clayton, P. J., Hirschfeld, R. M. A., Scheftner, W. A., & Winokur, G. (1988). Depression and panic attacks: The significance of overlap as reflected in follow-up and family study data. *American Journal of Psychiatry, 145,* 293–300.

Coryell, W., Endicott, J., & Winokur, G. (1992). Anxiety syndromes as epiphenomena of primary major depression: Outcome and familial psychopathology. *American Journal of Psychiatry, 149,* 100–107.

Crowe, R. R. (1988). Genetic studies of anxiety disorders. In M. T. Tsuang, K. Kendler, & M. Lyons (Eds.), *Genetic issues in psychosocial epidemiology.* New Brunswick, NJ: Rutgers University Press.

Crowe, R. R., Noyes, R., Jr., Pauls, D. L., & Slymen, D. (1983). A family study of panic disorder. *Archives of General Psychiatry, 40,* 1065–1069.

Crowe, R. R., Noyes, R., Jr., Samuelson, S., Wesner, R., & Wilson, R. (1990). Close linkage between panic disorder and alpha-haptoglobin excluded in 10 families. *Archives of General Psychiatry, 47,* 377–380.

Crowe, R. R., Noyes, R., Jr., Wilson, A. F., Elston, R. C., & Ward, L. J. (1987). A linkage study of panic disorder. *Archives of General Psychiatry, 44,* 933–937.

Eysenck, H. J. & Eysenck, S. B. G. (1975) *Manual of the Eysenck Personality Questionnaire.* London: Hodder & Stoughton.

Falconer, D. S. (1965). The inheritance of liability to certain diseases estimated from the incidence among relatives. *Annals of Human Genetics, 29,* 51–76.

Feighner, J. P., Robins, E., Guze, S. B., Woodruff, R. A., Winokur, G., & Munoz, R. (1972). Diagnostic criteria for use in psychiatric research. *Archives of General Psychiatry, 26,* 57–63.

Flint, J. (1992). Implications of genomic imprinting for psychiatric genetics. *Psychological Medicine, 22,* 5–10.

Fyer, A. J., Mannuzza, S., Gallops, M. S., Martin, L. Y., Aaronson, C., Gorman, J. M., Liebowitz, M. R., & Klein, D. F. (1990). Familial transmission of simple fears and phobias. *Archives of General Psychiatry, 40,* 1061–1064.

Hallam, R. S. (1978). Agoraphobia: A critical review of the concept. *British Journal of Psychiatry, 133,* 314–319.

Harris, E. L., Noyes, R., Crowe, R. R. & Chaudhry, D. R. (1983). Family study of agoraphobia. Report of a pilot study. *Archives of General Psychiatry. 40,* 1061–1064.

Hickey, A., Andrews, G., & Wilken, D. (1983). The independence of mitral valve prolapse and neurosis. *British Heart Journal, 50,* 333–336.

Hopper, J. L., Judd, F. K., Derrick, P. L., & Burrows, G. D. (1987). A family study of panic disorder. *Genetic Epidemiology, 4,* 33–41.

Hopper, J. L., Judd, F. K., Derrick, P. L., Macaskill, G. T., & Burrows, G. D. (1990). A family study of panic disorder: A reanalysis using a regressive logistic model that incorporates a sibship environment. *Genetic Epidemiology, 7,* 151–161.

Jardine, R., Martin, N. G., & Henderson, A. S. (1984). Genetic covariation between neuroticism and the symptoms of anxiety and depression. *Genetic Epidemiology, 1,* 89–107.

Karno, M., Golding, J. M., Sorenson, S. B., & Burnam, M. A. (1988). The epidemiology of obsessive-compulsive disorder in five U.S. communities. *Archives of General Psychiatry, 45,* 1094–1099.

Kendler, K. S., Heath, A., Martin, N. G., & Eaves, L. J. (1986). Symptoms of anxiety and depression in a volunteer twin population. *Archives of General Psychiatry, 42,* 213–221.

Kendler, K. S., Heath, A., Martin, N. G., & Eaves, L. J. (1987). Symptoms of anxiety and symptoms of depression: Same genes, different environments? *Archives of General Psychiatry, 44,* 451–457.

Kendler, K. S., Neale, M. C., Kessler, R. C., Heath, A. C., & Eaves, L. J. (1992). The genetic epidemiology of phobias in women: The inter-relationship of agoraphobia, social phobia, situational phobia and simple phobia. *Archives of General Psychiatry.*

Klein, D. F., & Klein, H. M. (1988). The status of panic disorder. *Current Opinion in Psychiatry, 1,* 177–183.

Kringlen, E. (1965). Obsessional neurotics: A long-term follow-up. *British Journal of Psychiatry, 111,* 709–722.

Leckman, J. F., Merikangas, K. R., Pauls, D. L., Prusoff, B. A., & Weissman, M. M. (1983). Anxiety disorders and depression: Contradictions between family study data and DSM-III conventions. *American Journal of Psychiatry. 140,* 880–882.

Leckman, J. F., Weissman, M. M., Merikangas, K. R., Pauls, D. L., & Prusoff, B. A. (1983). Panic disorder and major depression: Increased risk of depression, alcoholism, panic, and phobic disorders in families of depressed probands with panic disorder. *Archives of General Psychiatry, 40,* 1055–1060.

Leckman, J. F., Weissman, M. M., Merikangas, K. R., Pauls, D. L., & Prusoff, B. A. (1984). Methodologic differences in major depression and panic disorder studies. *Archives of General Psychiatry, 41,* 722–723.

Lewis, A. (1936). Problems of obsessional illness. *Proceedings of the Royal Society of Medicine, 29,* 325–336.

Lo, W. H. (1967). A follow-up study of obsessional neurotics in Hong Kong Chinese. *British Journal of Psychiatry, 113,* 823–832.

Luxenberger, H. (1930). Hereditat und Familientypus der Zwangsneurotiker. V KongreBer.f. Psychotherapie in Baden-Baden 1930. Psychiatr. Erblehre, Munchen-Berlin 1938. In Just, *Hdb. d. Erbbiol. d. Menschen.,* Bd.V,2. Teil 853. Berlin: Springer.

Macdonald, A. M., Murray, R. M., & Clifford, C. A. (1991). The contribution of heredity to obsessive-compulsive neurosis and obsessional personality: A review of family and twin study evidence. In M. T. Tsuang, K. Kendler, M.

Lyons (Eds.), *Genetics issues in psychosocial epidemiology.* New Brunswick, NJ: Rutgers University Press.

Margraf, J., Ehlers, A., & Roth, W. T. (1986). Sodium lactate infusions and panic attacks: A review and critique. *Psychosomatic Medicine, 48,* 25–51.

Marks, I. M. (1987). *Fears, phobias and rituals.* New York, NY: Oxford University Press.

Marks, I. M., Crowe, M., Drewe, E., Young, J., & Dewhurst, W. G. (1969). Obsessive-compulsive disorder in identical twins. *British Journal of Psychiatry, 115,* 991–998.

Martin, N. G., Jardine, R., Andrews, G., & Heath, A. C. (1988). Anxiety disorders and neuroticism: Are there genetic factors specific to panic? *Acta Psychiatrica Scandinavia. 77,* 698–706.

McInnes, R. G. (1937). Observations on heredity in neurosis. *Proceedings of the Royal Society of Medicine, 30,* 23–32.

McKeon, P., & Murray, R. (1987). Familial aspects of obsessive-compulsive neurosis. *British Journal of Psychiatry, 151,* 528–534.

Moran, C., & Andrews, G. (1985). The familial occurrence of agoraphobia. *British Journal of Psychiatry, 146,* 262–267.

Noyes, R., Clancy, J., & Garvey, M. J. (1978). Is agoraphobia a variant of panic disorder or a separate illness? *Journal of Anxiety Disorders, 1,* 3–13.

Noyes, R., Jr., Clarkson, C., Crowe, R. R., Yates, W. R., & McChesney, C. M. (1987). A family study of generalized anxiety disorder. *American Journal of Psychiatry, 144,* 1019–1024.

Noyes, R., Jr., Crowe, R. R., Harris, E. L., Hamra, B. J., McChesney, C. M., & Chaudhry, D. R. (1986). Relationship between panic disorder and agoraphobia: A family study. *Archives of General Psychiatry, 43,* 227–232.

Pauls, D. L., Bucher, K. D., Crowe, R. R., & Noyes, R. (1980). A genetic study of panic disorder pedigrees. *American Journal of Human Genetics, 32,* 639–644.

Pauls, D. L., Crowe, R. R., & Noyes, R. (1979). Distribution of ancestral secondary cases in anxiety neurosis (panic disorder). *Journal of Affective Disorders, 1,* 287–290.

Philips, K., Fulker, D. W., & Rose, R. J. (1987). Path analysis of seven fear factors in adult twin and sibling pairs and their parents. *Genetic Epidemiology, 4,* 345–355.

Rachman, S. J., & Hodgson, R. I. (1980). Obsessions and compulsions. New Jersey: Prentice-Hall, pp. 39–42.

Raudin, E. (1953). Ein Beitrag zur Frage der Zwangskrankheit, insbesondere ihrer hereditaren Beziehungen. *Archiv fur Psychiatrie und Zeitschrift Neurologie, 191,* 14–54.

Reich, T., James, J. W., & Morris, C. A. (1972). The use of multiple thresholds in determining the mode of transmission of semi-continuous traits. *Annals of Human Genetics, 36,* 162–184.

Reich, T., & Yates, W. (1988). Family history of psychiatric disorders in social phobia. *Comprehensive Psychiatry. 29,* 72–75.

Robins, L. N., Helzer, J. E., Weissman, M. M., Orvaschel, H., Gruenberg, E., Burke, J. D., & Register, D. A. (1984). Lifetime prevalences of specific psychiatric disorders in three sites. *Archives of General Psychiatry, 41,* 949–958.

Rose, R. J., & Ditto, W. B. (1983). A developmental genetic analysis of common fears from early adolescence to early adulthood. *Child Development, 54,* 361–368.

Rosenberg, C. M. (1967). Familial aspects of obsessional neurosis. *British Journal of Psychiatry, 113,* 405–413.

Sanavio, E. (1988). Obsessions and Compulsions: The Padua Inventory. *Behaviour Research and Therapy, 26,* 169–177.

Slater, E. & Shields, J. (1969). Genetical aspects of anxiety. *British Journal of Psychiatry, 3,* 62–71.

Snowdon, J. (1980). A comparison of written and postbox forms of the Leyton Obsessional Inventory. *Psychological Medicine, 10,* 165–170.

Solyom, L., Beck, P., Solyom, C., & Hugel, R. (1974). Some etiological factors in phobic neurosis. *Canadian Psychiatric Association Journal, 19,* 69–78.

Spitzer, R. L., Endicott, J., & Robins, E. (1978). Research Diagnostic Criteria (RDC). Rationale and Reliability. *Archives of General Psychiatry, 35,* 773–783.

Torgersen, S. (1983a). Genetics of neurosis. The effects of sampling variation upon the twin concordance ratio. *British Journal of Psychiatry, 142,* 126–132.

Torgersen, S. (1983b). Genetic factors in anxiety disorders. *Archives of General Psychiatry, 40,* 1085–1089.

Torgersen, S. (1990). Comorbidity of major depression and anxiety disorders in twin pair. *American Journal of Psychiatry. 147,* 1199–1202.

Torgersen, T. (1978). Contribution of twin studies to psychiatric nosology. In *Twin research: Psychology and Methodology* (pp. 125–130). New York: Alan R. Less.

Tsuang, M. T., Kendler, K. S., & Lyons, M. (Eds.) (1991). *Genetic issues in psychosocial epidemiology.* New Brunswick, NJ: Rutgers University Press.

Tyrer, P. (1985). Neurosis divisible? *Lancet, i,* 685–688.

Tyrer, P., Sewewright, N., Ferguson, B., Murphy, S., Darling, C., Brothwell, J., Kingdon, D., & Johnson, A. L. (1990). The Nottingham Study of Neurotic Disorder: Relationship between personality status and symptoms. *Psychological Medicine, 20,* 423–431.

Van Valkenburg, C., Akiskal, H. S., Puzantian, V., & Rosenthal, T. (1984). Anxious depressions: Clinical, family history, and naturalistic outcome— comparisons with panic and major depressive disorders. *Journal of Affective Disorders, 6,* 67–82.

Weissman, M. M., Leckman, J. F., Merikangas, K. R., Gammon, G. D., & Prusoff, B. A. (1984). Depression and anxiety disorders in parents and children: Results from the Yale Family Study. *Archives of General Psychiatry, 41,* 845–852.

Wheeler, E. O., White, P. D., Reed, E., & Cohen, M. E. (1948). Familial incidence of neurocirculatory asthenia ("anxiety neurosis," "effort syndrome"). *Journal of Clinical Investigation, 27,* 562.

Wood, P. (1941). Aetiology of DaCosta's syndrome. *British Medical Journal, 1,* 845–851.

Wooley, C. F. (1976). Where are the diseases of yesteryear? DaCosta's syndrome, soldier's heart, the effort syndrome, neurocirculatory asthenia, and the mitral valve prolapse syndrome. *Circulation, 53,* 749–751.

World Health Organization. (1978). Mental disorders: Glossary and guide to their classification in accordance with the ninth revision of the international classification of diseases. Geneva: WHO.

CHAPTER 7

Biochemical Factors in Anxiety and Related Disorders

EDMOND H. PI, MD, LAWRENCE S. GROSS, MD, and
ROBERT M. NAGY, MD

In coping with certain stressful stimuli, a biologic "fight or flight" re-sponse becomes a necessity and would be considered a "normal" anxiety response. However, if such a reaction was excessive in intensity and dura-tion, or occurred without sufficient objective reasons, then it would be considered an "abnormal" anxiety response (Hoehn-Saric, 1979). Differ-entiating "pathological" from "normal" anxiety requires careful clinical assessment, and use of specifically defined diagnostic criteria for anxi-ety disorders such as the Diagnostic and Statistical Manual of Mental Disorders, third edition revised (DSM-III-R) published by the American Psychiatric Association (1987) are essential. According to the most re-cent Epidemiologic Catchment Area (ECA) study, anxiety disorders for persons 18 years and older were the most prevalent of all the major psy-chiatric disorders with a one-month prevalence rate of 7.3% (Regier et al., 1988). For the above reasons, understanding the pathology of anxiety and its treatment is necessary.

Although, psychoanalytic, behavior, and biologic models exist in ex-plaining "pathological" anxiety, this chapter will focus on the recent de-velopments related to the biochemical factors implicated in the genesis of anxiety.

The correlation between central nervous system (CNS) anatomy and anxiety has not been fully elucidated. However, during the last few decades, significant advancements in the neurosciences has led to inves-tigations into the biochemistry of anxiety, the mechanisms of biological treatments for anxiety, and how these are related to each other. Neuro-transmitters mediating anxiety have been discovered and include nore-pinephrine (NE), serotonin (5-HT), and gamma-aminobutyric acid (GABA).

NOREPINEPHRINE

Catecholamines such as norepinephrine mediate a variety of physiologic responses initiated by interactions at specific cellular membrane sites known as adrenergic receptors. The binding of catecholamines or related drugs induces changes in these receptors that lead to cellular events resulting in the characteristic physiologic effect of the neurotransmitter or drug. Agonist drugs are capable of inducing a response, with full agonists producing a maximal response and partial agonists producing a qualitatively similar response, but of lesser magnitude. An antagonist interacts with the receptor and elicits no response on its own but may reduce the effect of an agonist by occupying the receptor (Hoffman & Lefkowitz, 1980).

Norepinephrine is the principal postganglionic sympathetic neurotransmitter. Sympathetic nervous system pathways originate from preganglionic neurons with cell bodies in the thoracolumbar segments of the spinal cord that synapse in the sympathetic ganglia with postganglionic neurons which innervate end-organs, including the heart and vascular, gastrointestinal, and genitourinary smooth muscle. Stimulation of the sympathetic nervous system leads to the classic flight or fight response (Lefkowitz, 1988). Based on the relative potencies of several adrenergic agonists, Ahlquist (1948) classified adrenergic receptors into two distinct types, termed alpha and beta. Alpha-adrenergic receptors recognize epinephrine and norepinephrine with high affinity and isoproterenol with much lower affinity while beta-adrenergic receptors have a higher affinity for the agonist isoproterenol than either epinephine or norepinephrine. The development of highly specific antagonist drugs has led to the identification of two subtypes of both alpha- and beta-adrenergic receptors. Beta receptors are subtyped based on the relative potencies of epinephrine and nonepinephrine. At beta1-receptors, which mediate positive inotropic effects in the heart and lipolysis in adipose tissue, epinephrine and norepinephrine are of similar potency. In contrast, at beta2-receptors, epinephrine is much more potent than norepinephrine; these receptors mediate vascular and bronchial smooth muscle relaxation. Both beta1- and beta2-adrenergic receptors are believed to act by stimulating the plasma membrane-bound enzyme adenylate cyclase, generating cyclic adenosine monophosphate (cAMP) (Lefkowitz, 1988).

Alpha-adrenergic receptor subtypes differ in pharmacologic specificity and in mechanism of action. Alpha1-receptors are found in vascular smooth muscle and mediate the vasoconstrictor effects of sympathetic stimulation. These receptors interact with specific agonists and antagonists and, while their exact mechanism of action is not clearly understood, alpha1-adrenergic effects do not appear to involve changes in activity of adenylate cyclase. On the other hand, stimulation of alpha2-adrenergic receptors mediates platelet aggregation via inhibition of adenylate cyclase activity and reduction in cellular cAMP levels. It is not known whether a similar mechanism accounts for the other known alpha2-adrenergic effects of presynaptic nerve terminal inhibition of norepinephrine release and postsynaptic smooth muscle contraction in some vascular beds (Lefkowitz, 1988).

In addition to the spinal sympathetic pathways, there are central nervous system noradrenergic pathways that originate in the pons and the medulla oblongata. The brain's principal norepinephrine-containing nucleus, the pontine nucleus locus ceruleus, provides noradrenergic innervation to the cerebral and cerebellar cortices, the limbic system, the brain stem, and the spinal cord; it also receives extensive afferent projections. Electrical stimulation of the locus ceruleus in monkeys and drugs, such as the alpha2-adrenergic antagonist yohimbine, which stimulate locus ceruleus activity and norepinephrine release, have been shown to induce anxiety in monkeys and man; drugs that decrease locus ceruleus function, such as the alpha2-agonist clonidine, have anxiety-reducing properties (Hoehn-Saric, 1982; Redmond & Huang, 1979). An exception to this is buspirone, a nonbenzodiazepine anxiolytic that increases locus ceruleus adrenergic activity (Sanghera, McMillen, & German, 1983). Therefore, with its unique anatomic and functional connections, the locus ceruleus is thought to be involved in but not totally responsible for the manifestation of anxiety, which requires numerous CNS systems for full expression. It has been suggested that the locus ceruleus may function as an "alarm system" that modulates emotional and autonomic responses, with clinical anxiety resulting from alterations in the operation of this system (Redmond & Huang, 1979).

Both types of alpha- and beta-adrenergic receptors are present in the brain. Alpha2-autoreceptors present in the locus ceruleus respond to norepinephrine and noradrenergic agonists by inhibiting norepinephrine release in the brain, probably as part of a negative feedback loop that regulates locus ceruleus activity (Hoehn-Saric, 1982). In addition to norepinephrine, other neurotransmitters such as epinephrine, serotonin, Met-enkephalin, GABA, and glycine are reported to influence activity in noradrenergic locus ceruleus neurons. Various psychotherapeutic agents, including amphetamine, morphine, benzodiazepines, and tricyclic antidepressants, also inhibit these cells (Foote, Bloom, & Aston-Jones, 1983). It has been postulated that agents which decrease net noradrenergic function should have anxiolytic properties (Redmond & Huang, 1979). This may account for the antianxiety effects of certain tricyclic antidepressants by increasing norepinephrine levels at alpha2-adrenergic autoreceptors in the locus ceruleus. However, both nonsedating tricyclic and monoamine oxidase inhibitor antidepressants have no immediate anxiolytic effects and usually require several days to several weeks of continuous treatment to be effective. Therefore, the actions of these antidepressants must be ascribed to long-term adjustments rather than short-term changes in neurotransmission (Hoehn-Saric, 1982).

Norepinephrine has long been implicated in physiological and psychological responses to stress, and it has recently been suggested that, in addition to norepinephrine-mediated sympathetic effects, some somatic and psychological symptoms of stress may be attributable to circulating adrenaline (Greenwood, 1990). Patients with flight phobia demonstrated increased heart rate, plasma adrenaline, blood pressure, and perceived anxiety during flight while plasma noradrenaline did not change (Ekeberg, Kjeldsen, Greenwood, & Enger, 1990). Examination stress in medical students has been shown to be associated with reduced platelet alpha2-adrenergic receptor binding affinity and increased levels of plasma norepinephrine and reported anxiety (Freedman et al., 1990).

Noradrenergic Status in Specific Anxiety Disorders

As described above, preclinical and clinical studies have generally supported a role for norepinephrine in stress and anxiety. Recent clinical investigations using the alpha2-adrenergic antagonist yohimbine and alpha2-receptor agonist clonidine have attempted to clarify noradrenergic function in specific anxiety disorders.

Panic Disorder

The effects of yohimbine and clonidine indicate dysregulation of noradrenergic activity in some patients with panic disorder (Charney & Heninger, 1986). More specifically, the ability of yohimbine to preferentially induce panic attacks in patients with panic disorder compared to controls supports the hypothesis that increased noradrenergic neuronal activity is associated with the pathophysiology of panic attacks in a subgroup of panic disorder patients (Charney et al., 1990). Consistent with this theory is clonidine's ability to decrease noradrenergic function and reduce anxiety in panic disorder patients compared to controls. While intravenous clonidine has been demonstrated to have short-term anxiolytic effects in panic disorder patients, the effects reportedly did not persist in most patients with long-term oral administration (Uhde et al., 1989). Regulation of beta-adrenergic receptors may also be abnormal in panic disorder patients. The lack of consistent noradrenergic responses, as well as the ability of drugs such as lactate and caffeine to induce similar panic states, suggests that it is unlikely that panic anxiety is associated with disturbances in a single neurotransmitter system (Charney et al., 1990).

Obsessive-Compulsive Disorder (OCD)

Recent data suggest that abnormal noradrenergic function probably does not play a primary role in the pathogenesis of obsessive-compulsive disorder. Following administration of yohimbine, behavioral responses and plasma levels of the norepinephrine metabolite 3-methoxy-4-hydroxyphenylglycol (MHPG) failed to differentiate OCD patients from healthy controls (Rasmussen, Goodman, Woods, Heninger, & Charney, 1987). Other studies have failed to show differences between OCD patients and controls in pulse, blood pressure, growth hormone, and MHPG responses to clonidine (Hollander et al., 1991; Lee et al., 1990). One report did indicate a transient but significant reduction in obsessions and compulsions correlated with growth hormone response to clonidine, suggesting noradrenergic mediation (Hollander et al., 1991).

Generalized Anxiety Disorder (GAD)

Recent studies have reported conflicting results about noradrenergic activity in generalized anxiety disorder. One report indicated that noradrenergic activity appeared to be increased in patients with GAD compared to normal controls and patients with major depression (Sevy, Papadimitriou, Surmont, Goldman, & Mendlewicz, 1989). Another study found that behavioral, cortisol, and cardiovascular responses to yohimbine did not differ between GAD patients and healthy controls, suggesting that GAD patients do not exhibit noradrenergic hyperactivity (Charney, Woods, & Heninger, 1989).

Other Anxiety Disorders

A recent review of clinical and preclinical studies describes evidence for the involvement of central noradrenergic systems in the pathophysiology of post-traumatic stress disorder (PTSD) (Krystal et al., 1989). Clinical improvement reported in social phobia patients following treatment with beta-adrenergic blocking drugs suggests possible peripheral catecholamine mediation of symptoms, but the pathophysiology of social phobia remains uncertain (Gorman & Gorman, 1987; Liebowitz, Gorman, Fyer, & Klein, 1985).

Implications for Treatment

The effectiveness of some tricyclic and monoamine oxidase inhibitor (MAOI) antidepressants in panic disorder may be related to their inhibitory noradrenergic effects, including reductions in tyrosine hydroxylase activity, locus ceruleus neuronal firing rates, norepinephrine turnover, and postsynaptic beta-adrenergic receptor sensitivity. Interestingly, bupropion and trazodone, two antidepressants without antipanic efficacy, have different effects on noradrenergic function (Charney et al., 1990; Sheehan, Davidson, & Manschrek, 1983).

Clonidine has been shown to have some antianxiety effects independent of sedation in patients with panic disorder and generalized anxiety disorder, although the degree of response was highly variable and less impressive than with other drugs (Hoehn-Saric, 1982). As described, clonidine has been shown in research settings to produce transient improvement in OCD symptoms (Hollander et al., 1991), limiting its clinical usefulness.

Beta-adrenoreceptor blocking drugs have been used in the treatment of a variety of anxiety and stress-related disorders, such as performance anxiety. In general, they are most effective in treating somatic or autonomic symptoms of anxiety, such as tremor and palpitations, and are thought to do so by blocking peripheral beta-adrenergic receptors (Tyrer, 1988). Some improvement in psychic anxiety has also been reported with propranolol treatment at higher doses for longer periods of time. It is postulated that the antianxiety effects of lipophilic beta-adrenergic blockers such as propranolol may be partly due to central mechanisms involving other neurotransmitter systems (Greenwood, 1990).

Summary

There is extensive preclinical and clinical information implicating excessive noradrenergic activity in the etiology of stress and anxiety, and abnormalities in norepinephrine function have been associated with specific anxiety disorders. Antidepressants may exert their antianxiety effects by reduction of overall noradrenergic activity via stimulation of presynaptic alpha2-adrenergic autoreceptors in locus ceruleus neurons as part of a negative feedback (inhibitory) control mechanism. Beta-adrenergic blocking drugs are thought to reduce somatic manifestations of anxiety primarily by blocking peripheral beta-adrenergic receptors, although some central nervous system actions have also been postulated. While norepinephrine apparently plays a role in the pathophysiology of certain types of anxiety, its role certainly does not seem to be an exclusive one as other neurotransmitters are also implicated.

SEROTONIN

When serotonin was initially studied and isolated in the 1930s and 1940s, the primary interest was its vasoconstrictive properties. It is unlikely that anyone at that time could have anticipated the emerging role serotonin would assume as an important neurotransmitter involved in anxiety disorders.

Researchers at the Cleveland Clinic first crystallized this substance and named it serotonin (Rapport, Green, & Page, 1948) because it was found in blood *(sero)* and induced contraction *(tonin)* of the gastrointestinal smooth muscle. Later Rapport determined that the chemical structure for serotonin was 5-Hydroxytryptamine (5-HT). In the mid-1950s, serotonin was demonstrated to be in brain tissue (Amin, Crawford, & Gaddum, 1954).

Serotonin is present throughout the body with 90% in the enterochromaffin cells of the gastrointestinal tract. Most of the rest is found in the central nervous system and in platelets. The function of serotonin in these non-nervous system areas includes regulating gastrointestinal motility, hemostasis involving platelets, and vasospasms associated with certain vascular diseases (Garrison, 1990). In the central nervous system, serotonin's role includes being the precursor for the pineal hormone melatonin as well as a neurotransmitter. As a neurotransmitter, serotonin is noted to mediate pain sensation, itch sensation, appetite regulation, migraines, depression, and anxiety. This extensive and diverse list of functions for serotonin reveals how prophetic Brodie and Shore's words were in 1957 when proposing serotonin as a chemical mediator in the brain, "It is fascinating to learn how the discovery of serotonin, a substance that appears to have no part in the general metabolism of cells, has proved to be of such significance to the pharmacologist, the biochemist, the neurologist, and possibly, to the psychiatrist" (1957).

The investigation of serotonin's role in anxiety has centered on the heterogeneous and complex nature of the various serotonin receptor sites and serotonin re-uptake sites in both normal and abnormal brains as well as the effects of various serotonin agonists and antagonists. There are currently seven different serotonin receptor sites that have been identified and located in a variety of pre- and postsynaptic sites throughout the brain (Gonzalez-Heydrich & Peroutka, 1990). These seven receptors are broken into three classes: $5-HT_1$ class ($5-HT_{1A}$, $5-HT_{1B}$, and $5-HT_{1D}$), 5-HT class ($5-HT_{1C}$, $5-HT_{2A}$, and $5-HT_{2B}$), and the $5-HT_3$ class ($5-HT_3$). $5-HT_{1C}$ is grouped in the $5-HT_2$ family because of its similarities to the $5-HT_{2A}$ and $5-HT_{2B}$ subtypes. It is expected that this list will expand in the future.

To complicate things further, different second messenger systems have been associated with different serotonin receptors (Gonzalez-Heydrich & Peroutka, 1990). All of this helps explain the seemingly conflicting data obtained from various animal and human studies involving serotonin.

Recent studies of the anxiety disorders (obsessive-compulsive disorder, panic disorder, and generalized anxiety disorder), have implicated the involvement of serotonin. This common factor is remarkable when compared to the distinct signs and symptoms of these disorders as categorized in the DSM-III-R. 5-HT selective drugs such as 5-HT releasing agents (e.g., fenfluramine) and 5-HT receptor agonists (e.g., metachlorophenylpiperazine [m-CPP], buspirone) have distinguished anxiety disorders in terms of behavioral and neuroendocrine responses. Fenfluramine by itself had minimal behavioral effects in obsessive-compulsive disorder (OCD) patients but produced panic episodes in panic disorder (PD) patients (Murphy & Pigott, 1990).

m-CPP produced changes in neuroendocrine responses as well as behavioral differences among various psychiatric patient groups as well as when compared to control groups. Some of the anxiety related responses could be differentiated depending on the dosage and route of administration of m-CPP.

When obsessive-compulsive disorder patients were given oral m-CPP, they showed transient exacerbations of their obsessive-compulsive symptoms while normal controls had no response (Zohar, Mueller, Insel, Zohar-Kadouch, & Murphy, 1987). This exacerbation of symptoms occurred in 11 of 12 OCD patients. Also notable is that a number of these affected patients reported the emergence of new symptoms or symptoms that had not been present for many months. A review of a number of studies using m-CPP showed that panic symptoms could be significantly increased in PD patients at oral doses of 0.25 mg/kg and in OCD patients at oral doses of 0.5 mg/kg while in healthy volunteers minimal anxiety symptoms occurred with 0.5 mg/kg (Zuardi, 1990).

Cortisol level responses to intravenous and oral doses of m-CPP are different between PD patients and OCD patients. These in turn are distinct from control group responses (Murphy & Pigott, 1990).

Other evidence for the involvement of serotonin includes the actions of psychopharmacological agents used to treat anxiety disorders. Of the tricyclic antidepressants, clomipramine has shown a significantly greater ability to stop the re-uptake of 5-HT into brain synaptic terminals. In the treatment of OCD, clomipramine has proven superior to other tricyclics and monoamine oxidase inhibitors in numerous studies (Murphy & Pigott, 1990). Another 5-HT re-uptake blocker, fluoxetine, is also very effective in treating OCD.

The mechanism of action of agents like clomipramine and fluoxetine in blocking 5-HT re-uptake is not well understood. It is thought not to be related to the specificity of action of the agent on serotonin transport after acute administration of the agent but rather to adaptive changes in these sites following chronic administration (Leonard, 1988). This stands in contrast to GABA-mediated agents such as benzodiazepines that show reduction in anxiety within hours after intake. 5-HT$_{1A}$ receptor agonists are currently being established as effective tools to treat GAD. Again, the mechanism of action is not clearly identified. Agents such as buspirone act as agonists on presynaptic 5-HT_{1A} receptors but are also partial agonists at the postsynaptic 5-HT_{1A} receptor (Eison, 1990). An important distinction between these 5-HT_{1A} agonists and the previously discussed serotonin re-uptake blockers is that the 5-HT_{1A} agonists act specifically at 5-HT_{1A} while the re-uptake blockers make serotonin available to interact with all subtypes of 5-HT receptors (Eison, 1990).

Buspirone has been shown to be as equally effective in treating generalized anxiety disorder as benzodiazepines (e.g., diazepam). Two significant differences should be noted. First, benzodiazepines work after the first dose while buspirone takes weeks of administration to get a similar result. Two, the side effect profile of buspirone does not include sedation, ataxia, amnesia, and withdrawal problems that can be associated with benzodiazepines (Charney, Krystal, Delgado, & Heninger, 1990). Clinical indications for using buspirone in GAD include patients who are elderly, have concurrent medical problems, show mixed symptoms of depression and anxiety, and those who do not demand immediate gratification or the immediate relief they associate with a benzodiazepine response (Rickels, 1990).

The 5-HT_2 receptor is also being studied because various 5-HT_2 receptor antagonists, such as ritanserin, have been effective in GAD (Charney, Krystal, Delgado, & Heninger, 1990). Early animal studies looking at 5-HT_3 receptor antagonists indicate it may have anxiolytic properties (Jones et al., 1988).

GABA/BENZODIAZEPINE RECEPTOR COMPLEX

Gamma-aminobutyric acid (GABA) is an amino acid neurotransmitter in the CNS which, as the most important inhibitory neurotransmitter, is potent in its ability to affect neuronal discharge. There are two subtypes of GABA receptors: GABA-A receptors where benzodiazepines enhance the binding of GABA, and GABA-B receptors where benzodiazepines do not enhance the binding of GABA (Wojcik & Neff, 1984). Currently, the most predictable anxiolytic effects are associated with the benzodiazepines, which facilitate the activity of GABA. The benzodiazepines diazepam and alprazolam have been widely prescribed for generalized and anticipatory anxiety, and panic disorder (Rickels, Schweizer, Csanalosi, Case, & Chung, 1988; Sheehan, 1987), respectively. Such linkage between the GABA-ergic subsystem and specific benzodiazepine receptors has provided a molecular basis of anxiety and understanding the neurobiology of anxiety. Presently, there are two receptor hypotheses for the genesis of anxiety. The first one is that changes in activity of endogenous ligands for the benzodiazepine receptor (e.g., an excess of anxiogenic) or a deficiency of anxiolytic substances regulates anxiety. The second one is that shifts in the benzodiazepine receptor sensitivity (e.g., increased or decreased receptor sensitivity to agonist drugs) may regulate anxiety (Nutt, Glue, & Lawson, 1990).

In 1977, two independent groups of researchers in Denmark and Switzerland reported the existence of saturable, high affinity, and stereospecific binding sites for benzodiazepines in the CNS of reptiles and mammals (Mohler & Okada, 1977; Squires & Braestrup, 1977). The highest concentrations of benzodiazepine receptors are found in the cerebral cortex, cerebellum, and amygdala, and lesser concentrations in the hippocampus, striatum, and spinal cord (Braestrup, Albrechtsen, & Squires, 1977). Studies exploring the relationship between the GABA-ergic system and benzodiazepines have substantiated the presence of a pharmacologic receptor for benzodiazepines in brain.

Benzodiazepines potentiate the effects of GABA, but do not produce anxiolysis when GABA is absent (Guidotti, 1981). Activation of benzodiazepine binding sites causes an allosteric change in the GABA receptor recognition site, consequently increasing receptor sensitivity to GABA (Enna, 1984; Paul & Skolnick, 1983; Tallman, Thomas, & Gallager, 1978; Tallman, Paul, Skolnick, & Gallager, 1980). Small permeable anions such as chloride also increase the binding of GABA to their receptors (Costa, Rodbard, & Pert, 1979). These two effects combined suggest that GABA inhibits neuronal excitability by opening the chloride channel ionophore directly linked to GABA receptors. Consequently, chloride conductance increases and allows chloride ions to move more readily from the extracellular space to the inside of the neuron (McDonald & Barker, 1979). Therefore, a structural and functional model of the GABA/Benzodiazepine receptor "supramolecular receptor complex" consisting of a chloride ion channel and two binding sites has been formulated. One receptor site binds GABA and the other one binds benzodiazepine (Breier & Paul, 1990). Barbiturates also enhance the GABA receptors by interacting directly with the chloride channel (Enna, 1984).

It has been proposed that hyperexcitability of certain neuropathways is associated with anxiety. In an overactive state, a feedback signal to a GABA neuron is sent and then GABA is released into the synaptic cleft. GABA binds to its receptor to open chloride channels and increase the influx of chloride ions into the neuron. The net effect of enhanced chloride permeability causes hyperpolarization of the nerve membrane. Hyperpolarization makes the neuron less likely to be excitable and this is associated with the alleviation of anxiety. With the administration of a benzodiazepine, GABA-mediated chloride conductance is facilitated and excitability of the neuron is further inhibited (Goldberg, 1984).

Isotope-labeled ligands of benzodiazepine receptors have been used to explore the neurochemical basis of epileptic patients: indirect evidence for the role of the GABA/benzodiazepine receptor in the pathophysiology of anxiety has been found (Savic et al., 1988).

Reduced benzodiazepine sensitivity was reported through a study in response to intravenous administration of diazepam. Saccadic eye movement velocity decreased less in patients with panic disorder than in nonanxious control subjects and suggests that panic disorder is associated with a functional subsensitivity of the GABA/benzodiazepine supramolecular complex in brainstem areas controlling saccadic eye movements (Roy-Byrne, Cowley, Greenblatt, Shader, & Hommer, 1990). The reason for the reduced sensitivity is not clear but may be related to the anxiety disorder or may be related to the effect of benzodiazepine (Hoehn-Saric, 1991).

Under stressful conditions, the secretion of steroid hormones such as progesterone and deoxycorticosterone will increase and significantly affect the CNS function. Their metabolites have potent benzodiazepine-like effects that mediate through recognition sites on the GABA/benzodiazepines receptor (Breier & Paul, 1990).

Data from the use of β-carboline-3-carboxylate ethyl ester (β-CCE) supports the role of the GABA receptor in mediating anxiety. β-CCE, a benzodiazepine receptor antagonist, has been used to probe the neurobiological base of anxiety (Braestrup & Nielsen, 1981). Administration of β-CCE to rhesus monkeys and a β-carboline derivative, FG-7142, to humans induced behaviors similar to the stress-related responses of behavioral "agitation" accompanied by marked physiologic and endocrine changes. Administration of a benzodiazepine then blocks such responses (Dorow, Horowski, Paschelke, Amin, & Braestrup, 1983; Insel et al., 1984).

At present, the activation of a GABA-ergic subsystem has the most predictable anxiolytic effects (Hoehn-Saric, 1982). More sophisticated research in this area has been carried out and will eventually lead to a better biochemically based explanation into the genesis of anxiety disorders in the future.

OTHER BIOCHEMICAL MEASUREMENTS IN ANXIETY

Lactic Acid (Lactate)

Higher blood concentrations of lactate were found in anxiety-prone individuals than in normal individuals after exercise (Linko, 1950). Pitts and McClure (1967) and other researchers (Gorman et al., 1988, 1989) intravenously infused lactate solution, anxiety symptoms were provoked only in susceptible individuals. This precipitation can be successfully inhibited or attenuated by the administration of tricyclic antidepressants (TCAs) or monoamine oxidase inhibitors (MAOIs), but not by benzodiazepine or β-adrenergic antagonists (e.g., propranolol) (Liebowitz et al., 1984). Although the mechanism for lactate's effect is not clearly understood, it may be related to the rise in the lactate-pyruvate ratio, lowering the level of ionized calcium, and the concomitant fall of intraneuronal pH in the chemoreceptor (Carr & Sheehan, 1984). The biochemistry of these chemically induced anxiety symptoms still needs to be studied further (Gaffney, Fenton, Lane, & Lake, 1988; Gorman et al., 1989; Reiman et al., 1989).

Carbon Dioxide

The investigation of carbon dioxide's role in causing anxiety remains confusing and perplexing to researchers. Carbon dioxide levels are adjusted acutely through a person's respiratory rate. Increasing an individual's breathing rate (hyperventilation) leads to hypocapnia (reduced carbon dioxide in the circulating blood) while decreasing the breathing rate (hypoventilation) leads to hypercapnia (elevated carbon dioxide in the circulating blood). Investigators have used this phenomenon as well as exposing patients to predetermined concentrations of carbon dioxide to accurately measure its effect on anxiety, especially panic attacks.

One initial proposal was that alterations in blood carbon dioxide, which can have profound effects on cerebral blood flow, caused anxiety. However, repeated studies have shown that hypercapnia and hypocapnia have opposite actions on blood flow but both are anxiogenic (Nutt, 1990). The possibility that marked hyperventilation seen in compensation to hypercapnia as the cause of panic has also been discredited.

Another hypothesis involves carbon dioxide induced stimulation of noradrenergic neuronal function leading to panic attacks. Although animal studies have shown evidence for this, it has not been replicated in human studies (Woods, Charney, Goodman, & Heninger, 1988). Along these lines, one recent study has implicated hyperventilation to increased vagal tone and subsequent reduced parasympathetic nervous system activity. This would result in a relative increase in sympathetic activity without direct sympathetic excitation (George et al., 1989).

A combination cognitive-physiological model has also been suggested. Hyperventilation or hypoventilation induces body sensations that are perceived as unpleasant and are interpreted in a catastrophic manner. This would account for the paradoxical anxiogenic effect of both hypo- and hyperventilation. Also, this is consistent with studies showing evidence for behavioral hypersensitivity to carbon dioxide and weak or no evidence for physiologic hypersensitivity to carbon dioxide in patients with panic disorders (Woods, Charney, Goodman, & Heninger, 1988).

Caffeine

Because it is thought to have stimulant actions that could elevate mood, decrease fatigue, and increase capacity to work, caffeine is a popular ingredient in a variety of drinks, foods, and medications (Rall, 1990).

Caffeine is found mostly in drinks such as coffee (90 mg to 125 mg/250 ml), tea (40–60 mg/ml), cola drinks (40 mg/330 ml), and hot chocolate (5 mg/225 ml). Foods with coffee or chocolate also contain caffeine. Chocolate bars have about 20 mg per small bar. A significant number of over-the-counter preparations for analgesia, coughs, colds, and asthma also contain caffeine (Bruce, 1990). It is estimated that 80% of the world's population consumes caffeine. The per capita consumption among American adults is about 200 mg per day (Jaffe, 1990).

Caffeine is a methylxanthine and is similar in structure to xanthine, theophylline, and theobromine (Rall, 1990). As a central nervous system stimulant, caffeine's biochemical action is thought to be mediated by blocking receptors for adenosine (Boulenger, Patel, & Marangos, 1982). Caffeine does cause increased cerebrovascular resistance with resultant reduction in cerebral blood flow (Rall, 1990). However, attempts to correlate this specific action to caffeine's anxiogenic properties has been unsuccessful (Mathew & Wilson, 1990).

The clinical presentation of caffeine-induced anxiety can mimic other anxiety disorders such as PD and GAD (Charney, Heninger, & Breier, 1984). The DSM-III-R lists three criteria for the diagnosis of caffeine intoxication. One, the recent consumption of caffeine, usually more than 250 mg. Two, at least five of the following signs: restlessness, nervousness, excitement, insomnia, flushed face, diuresis, gastrointestinal disturbance, muscle twitching, rambling flow of thought and speech, tachycardia or cardiac arrhythmia, periods of inexhaustibility, or psychomotor agitation. Three, that the anxiety is not due to any physical or other mental disorder. Thus caffeine toxicity can be difficult to distinguish from other anxiety disorders unless an accurate history is obtained or toxicology tests are ordered.

In addition to appearing similar to other states, caffeine is known to complicate and worsen the conditions of persons with a pre-existing anxiety disorder. This has been noted in the clinical observation that many panic patients will put themselves on a caffeine-free diet because the subjective effects of caffeine (arousal, insomnia, upset stomach, and tremor) are unpleasant (Nutt, 1990).

In one study, patients with either generalized anxiety or panic disorders who underwent caffeine abstinence showed a significant reduction in long-standing anxiety symptoms as well as reductions in their anxiolytic medications. Some of these patients consumed less than 200 mg of caffeine a day prior to abstaining, thus illustrating the powerful effect of even low doses of caffeine (Bruce & Lader, 1989).

Caffeine is also associated with a withdrawal syndrome. Headache and fatigue are the most frequently listed symptoms along with anxiety, impaired performance, nausea, and vomiting. The onset is 12 to 24 hours with a peak at 20 to 48 hours and lasting up to one week. Thus patients wishing to abstain from caffeine should be advised of the short-term withdrawal symptoms and high users of caffeine should taper their intake over one to two weeks to minimize these symptoms (Bruce, 1990).

Miscellaneous Biochemical Measurements

Other studies suggest certain physiological differences between individuals with and without anxiety. Individuals with anxiety disorders show an increased resting forearm blood flow (Kelly & Walter, 1968), brisker deep tendon reflexes, and an elevated resting pulse-rate (Claycomb, 1983). They can also be more sensitive to various types of painful stimuli, have a low exercise tolerance, and experience spontaneous fluctuations of galvanic skin response (Lader, Gelden, & Marks, 1967).

Brain imaging methods, especially positron emission tomography (PET) and single photon emission computerized tomography (SPECT) have been used to study blood flow, oxygen consumption, and receptors (Sadzot, Frost, & Wgner, 1989; Innis et al., 1989). During an anticipatory anxiety state, activity in the bilateral temporal poles increased. They also occurred in lactate-induced anxiety states. These findings suggest that anxiety state is related to the function of the temporal cortex (Reiman, Fusselman, Fox, & Raichle, 1989; Reiman et al., 1989).

CONCLUSION

The pathophysiology of anxiety most likely involves the interactions between different brain neuronal systems. The GABA-ergic system associated with benzodiazepine receptors, the noradrenergic (NA) systems and the serotonergic systems are definitely involved in the biochemistry of anxiety. An interaction between the NA system and GABA/Benzodiazepine receptor system has been proposed (Redmond & Huang, 1979), and serotonin has been proposed to be involved in the anxiolytic properties of benzodiazepine (Paul, Marangos, & Skolnick, 1981). Insel, et al., (1984) suggested that there are two different neuropharmacological models of anxiety: NA and GABA-ergic pathways. The GABA-ergic system corresponds to "fear or conflict" or "psychic" manifestations of anxiety that often require benzodiazepine treatment. The NA activation corresponds to "alarm" or "autonomic" manifestations of anxiety such as panic attacks and these respond favorably to tricyclic antidepressant therapy. Anxiety induced by yohimbine, a noradrenergic α-2 receptor antagonist, has been successfully attenuated by alprazolam, a triazolo-benzodiazepine. This suggests that a yohimbine-induced anxiety state may be related to both NA and GABA activities (Charney, Breier, Jatlow, & Heninger, 1986). Also, other data suggest that the serotonergic pathway is involved in anxiety. At present, the role of other neurotransmitters such as acetylcholine, dopamine, histamine, adenosine, and neuropeptides, is not well understood; it appears to be minimal (Hoehn-Saric, 1982).

Of all the discussed hypotheses and methods for exploring the biochemistry of anxiety disorders, none is without flaws. As research activities continue, certain subtypes of pathological anxiety will be better understood by applying certain biochemical paradigms. These models can also help clinicians to identify specific biological etiologies for their patients which will promote an accurate diagnosis and effective treatment.

REFERENCES

Ahlquist, R. P. (1948). A study of the adrenotropic receptors. *American Journal of Physiology, 153,* 586–600.

American Psychiatric Association (1987). Diagnostic and Statistical Manual of Mental Disorders. American Psychiatric Association. Washington, DC: Author.

Amin, A. H., Crawford, T. B. B., & Gaddum, J. H. (1954). The distribution of substance P and 5-hydroxytryptamine in the central nervous system. *Journal of Physiology, 126,* 596–618.

Boulenger, J. P., Patel, J., & Marangos, P. J. (1982). Effects of caffeine and theophylline on adenosine and benzodiazepine receptors in human brain. *Neuroscience Letter, 30,* 161–166.

Braestrup, C., Albrechtsen, R., & Squires, R. F. (1977). High densities of benzodiazepine receptors in human cortical areas. *Nature, 269,* 702–704.

Braestrup, C., & Nielsen, M. J. (1981). [3H] propyl β-carboline-3-carbosylate as a selective radioligand for the BZ1 benzodiazepine receptor subclass. *Journal of Neurochemistry, 37,* 333–341.

Breier, A., & Paul, S. M. (1990). The GABA/benzodiazepine receptor: Implications for the molecular basis of anxiety. *Journal of Psychiatric Research, 24,* 91–104.

Brodie, B. B., & Shore, P. A. (1957). A concept for a role of serotonin and norepinephrine as chemical mediators in the brain. *Annals New York Academy of Sciences,* 631–642.

Bruce, M. S. (1990). The anxiogenic effects of caffeine. *Postgraduate Medical Journal, 66 (suppl. 2),* 518–524.

Bruce, M. S., & Lader, M. (1989). Caffeine abstention in the management of anxiety disorders. *Psychological Medicine, 19,* 211–214.

Carr, D. B., & Sheehan, D. V. (1984). Panic anxiety: A new biological model. *Journal of Clinical Psychiatry, 45,* 323–330.

Charney, D. S., Breier, A., Jatlow, P. I., & Heninger, G. R. (1986). Behavioral, biochemical, and blood pressure responses to alprazolam in healthy subjects: Interactions with yohimbine. *Psychopharmacology, 88,* 133–140.

Charney, D. S., & Heninger, G. R. (1986). Abnormal regulation of noradrenergic function in panic disorders. *Archives of General Psychiatry, 43,* 1042–1054.

Charney, D. S., Heninger, G. R., & Breier, A. (1984). Noradrenergic function in panic anxiety: Effects of yohimbine in healthy subjects and patients with agoraphobia and panic disorder. *Archives of General Psychiatry, 41,* 751–763.

Charney, D. S., Krystal, J. H., Delgado, P. L., & Heninger, G. R. (1990). Serontonin-specific drugs for anxiety and depressive disorders. *Annual Review of Medicine, 41,* 437–446.

Charney, D. S., Woods, S. W., & Heninger, G. R. (1989). Noradrenergic function in generalized anxiety disorder: Effects of yohimbine in healthy subjects and patients with generalized anxiety disorder. *Psychiatry Research, 27,* 173–182.

Charney, D. S., Woods, S. W., Nagy, L. M., Southwick, S. M., Krystal, J. H., & Heninger, G. R. (1990). Noradrenergic function in panic disorder. *Journal of Clinical Psychiatry, 51 (12, suppl. A),* 5–11.

Claycomb, J. B. (1983). Endogenous anxiety: Implications for nosology and treatment. *Journal of Clinical Psychiatry, 44 (8 sec. 2),* 19–22.

Costa, T., Rodbard, D., & Pert, C. (1979). Is the benzodiazepine receptor coupled to chloride anion channel? *Nature (London), 277,* 315.

Dorow, R., Horowski, R., Paschelke, G., Amin, M., & Braestrup, C. (1983). Severe anxiety induced by FG 7142, a β-carboline ligand for benzodiazepine receptors. *Lancet, ii,* 98–99.

Eison, M. S. (1990). Serotonin: A common neurobiologic substrate in anxiety and depression. *Journal of Clinical Psychopharmacology, 10 (suppl.),* 265–305.

Ekeberg, O., Kjeldsen, S. E., Greenwood, D. T., & Enger, E. (1990). Correlations between psychological and physiological responses to acute flight phobia stress. *Scandinavian Journal of Clinical and Laboratory Investigation, 50,* 671–677.

Enna, S. J. (1984). Role of γ-aminobutyric acid in anxiety. *Psychopathology, 17 (suppl. 1),* 15–24.

Foote, S. L., Bloom, F. E., & Aston-Jones, G. (1983). Nucleus locus ceruleus: New evidence of anatomical and physiological specificity. *Physiological Reviews, 63,* 844–914.

Freedman, R. R., Embury, J., Migaly, P., Keegan, D., Pandey, G. N., Javaid, J. I., & Davis, J. M. (1990). Stress-induced desensitization of alpha2-adrenergic receptors in human platelets. *Psychosomatic Medicine, 52,* 624–630.

Gaffney, F. A., Fenton, B. J., Lane, L. D., & Lake, C. R., (1988). Hemodynamic, ventilatory, and biochemical responses of panic patients and normal controls with sodium lactate infusion and spontaneous panic attacks. *Archives of General Psychiatry, 45,* 53–60.

Garrison, J. C. (1990). Histamine, bradykinin, 5-hydroxytryptamine, and their antagonists. In A. Goodman et al. (Ed.), *Goodman and Gillman's the pharmacological basis of therapeutics,* 8th ed. (pp. 592–596). New York: Pergamon Press.

George, D. T., Nutt, D. J., Walker, W. V., Porges, S. W., Adinoff, B., & Linnoila, M. (1989). Lactate and hyperventilation substantially attenuate vagal tone in normal volunteers. *Archives of General Psychiatry, 46,* 153–156.

Goldberg, H. L. (1984). Benzodiazepine and nonbenzodiazepine anxiolytics. *Psychopathology, 17 (suppl. 1),* 45–55.

Gonzalez-Heydrich, J. & Peroutka, S. J. (1990). Serotonin receptor and re-uptake sites: Pharmacologic significance. *The Journal of Clinical Psychiatry, 51 (suppl.),* 5–12.

Gorman, H. M., Battista, D., Goetz, R. R., Dillon, D. J., Liebowitz, M. R., Fyer, A. J., Kahn, J. P., Sandberg, D., & Klein, D. F. (1989). A comparison of sodium bicarbonate and sodium lactate infusion in the induction of panic attacks. *Archives of General Psychiatry, 46,* 145–150.

Gorman, H. M., Fyer, M. R., Goetz, R., Askanazi, J., Martinez, J., Leibowitz, M. R., Fyer, A. J., Kinney, J., & Klein, D. F. (1988). Ventilatory physiology of patients with panic disorder. *Archives of General Psychiatry, 45,* 31–39.

Gorman, J. M., & Gorman, L. K. (1987). Drug treatment of social phobia. *Journal of Affective Disorders, 13,* 183–192.

Greenwood, D. T. (1990). Stress, catecholamines, and β-adrenoreceptor blockade. *Postgraduate Medical Journal, 66,* S36–S40.

Guidotti, A. (1981). Interaction between benzodiazepine and GABA receptors: A base for the therapeutic action of benzodiazepines. In E. Usdin, W. E. Bunney, & J. M. Davis (Eds.), *Neuroreceptors-basic and clinical aspects* (pp. 189–197). New York: John Wiley.

Hoehn-Saric, R. (1979). Anxiety-normal and abnormal. *Psychiatric Annals, 9,* 447–455.

Hoehn-Saric, R. (1982). Neurotransmitters in anxiety. *Archives of General Psychiatry, 39,* 735–742.

Hoehn-Saric, R. (1991). Benzodiazepine sensitivity in panic disorder. *Archives of General Psychiatry, 48,* 669–670.

Hoffman, B. B., & Lefkowitz, R. J. (1980). Alpha-adrenergic receptor subtypes. *New England Journal of Medicine, 302,* 1390–1396.

Hollander, E., DeCaria, C., Nitescu, A., Cooper, T., Stover, B., Gully, R., Klein, D. F., & Liebowitz, M. R. (1991). Noradrenergic function in obsessive-compulsive disorder: Behavioral and neuroendocrine responses to clonidine and comparison to healthy controls. *Psychiatry Research, 37,* 161–177.

Innis, R. B., Heninger, G. R., Zoghbi, S., Al-Tikriti, M., Woods, S. W., Johnson, E., Charney, D. S., Koster, K., Zubel, I. G., Smith, E. O., Kung, H. F., Alavi, A., & Hoffer, P. B. (1989). SPECT imagining of dopamine D2 receptors in non-human primate brain. *Society of Neuroscience Abstracts, 15,* Part 1, 171.

Insel, R. R., Ninan, P. T., Aloi, J., Jimerson, D. C., Skolnick, P., & Paul, S. M. (1984). A benzodiazepine receptor-mediated model of anxiety: Studies in non-human primates and clinical implications. *Archives of General Psychiatry, 41,* 741.

Jaffe, J. H. (1990). Drug addiction and drug abuse. In A. Goodman et al. (Ed.), *Goodman and Gillman's the pharmacological basis of therapeutics,* 8th ed. (p. 559). New York: Pergamon.

Jones, B. J., Costall, B., Domeney, A. M., Kelly, M. E., Naylor, R. J., Oakley, N. R., & Tyers, M. B. (1988). The potential anxiolytic activity of GR38032F, a 5-HT3 receptor antagonist. *British Journal of Pharmacology, 93,* 985–993.

Kelly, D. H. W., & Walter, C. J. S. (1968). The relationship between clinical diagnosis and anxiety assessed by forearm blood flow and other measurements. *British Journal of Psychiatry, 114,* 611–626.

Krystal, J. H., Kosten, T. R., Southwick, S., Mason, J. W., Perry, B. D., & Giller, E. L. (1989). Neurobiological aspects of PTSD: Review of clinical and preclinical studies. *Behavior Therapy, 20,* 177–198.

Lader, M. H., Gelder, M. G., & Marks, I. M. (1967). Palmar skin-conductance measures as predictors of response to desensitization. *Journal of Psychosomatic Research, 11,* 283–290.

Lee, M. A., Cameron, O. G., Gurguis, G. N. M., Glitz, D., Smith, C. B., Hariharan, M., Abelson, J. L., & Curtis, G. C. (1990). Alpha2-adrenoreceptor status in obsessive-compulsive disorder. *Biological Psychiatry, 27,* 1083–1093.

Lefkowitz, R. J. (1988). Pharmacologic principles related to the autonomic nervous system. In J. B. Wyngaarden & L. H. Smith, Jr. (Eds.), *Cecil textbook of medicine* (pp. 133–140). Philadelphia: W. B. Saunders.

Leonard, B. E. (1988). Pharmacological effects of serotonin re-uptake inhibitors. *Journal of Clinical Psychiatry, 49,* 8 (suppl.), 12–17.

Liebowitz, M. R., Fyer, A. J., Gorman, J. M., Dillon, D., Appleby, I. L., Levy, G., Anderson, S., Levitee, M., Palij, M., Davies, S. O., & Klein, D. F. (1984). Lactate provocation of panic attacks: I. Clinical and behavioral findings. *Archives of General Psychiatry, 41,* 764–770.

Liebowitz, M. R., Gorman, J. M., Fyer, A. J., & Klein, D. F. (1985). Social phobia: Review of a neglected anxiety disorder. *Archives of General Psychiatry, 42,* 729–736.

Linko, E. (1950). Lactic acid response to muscular exercise in neurocirculatory asthenia. *Annales Medicinae Internae Fenniae, 39,* 161–176.

Mathew, R. J., & Wilson, W. H. (1990). Behavioral and cerebrovascular effects on caffeine in patients with anxiety disorders. *Acta Psychiatrica Scandinavacia, 82,* 17–22.

McDonald, J. R., & Barker, J. (1970). Enhancement of GABA-mediated post-synaptic inhibition in cultured mammalian spinal cord neurons: A common mode of anticonvulsant action. *Brain Research, 167,* 323.

Mohler, H., & Okada, T. (1977). Benzodiazepine receptor: Demonstration in the central nervous system. *Science, 198,* 849–851.

Murphy, D. L., & Pigott, T. A. (1990). A comparative examination of a role for serotonin in obsessive-compulsive disorder, panic disorder, and anxiety. *Journal of Clinical Psychiatry, 52, 4 (suppl.),* 53–58.

Nutt, D. J. (1990). The pharmacology of human anxiety. *Pharmacology and Therapeutics, 47,* 233–266.

Nutt, D. J., Glue, P., & Lawson, C. (1990). The neurochemistry of anxiety: An update. *Progress in Neuro-Psychopharmacology and Biological Psychiatry, 14,* 737–752.

Paul, S. M., Marangos, P. J., & Skolnick, P. (1981). The benzodiazepine-GABA-chloride ionophore receptor complex: Common site of minor tranquilizer action. *Biological Psychiatry, 16,* 213–229.

Paul, S. M., & Skolnick, P. (1983). Comparative neuropharmacology for antianxiety drugs. *Pharmacology, Biochemistry and Behavior, 17,* 37.

Pitts, F. N., & McClure, J. N. (1967). Lactate metabolism in anxiety neurosis. *New England Journal of Medicine, 277,* 1329–1336.

Rall, T. W. (1990). Drugs used in the treatment of asthma. In A. Goodman et al. (Ed.), *Goodman and Gillman's the pharmacological basis of therapeutics,* 8th ed. (pp. 618–630). New York: Pergamon Press.

Rapport, M. M., Green, A. A., & Page, I. H. (1948). Serum vasoconstrictior (serotonin) IV. Isolation and characterization. *Journal of Biological Chemistry, 176,* 1243–1251.

Rasmussen, S. A., Goodman, W. K., Woods, S. W., Heninger, G. R., & Charney, D. S. (1987). Effects of yohimbine in obsessive-compulsive disorder. *Psychopharmacology, 93,* 308–313.

Redmond, D. E., & Huang, Y. H. (1979). New evidence for a locus coeruleus-norepinephrine connection with anxiety. *Life Science, 25,* 2149–2162.

Regier, D. A., Boyd, J. H., Burke, J. D., Rae, D. S., Myers, J. K., Kramer, M., Robins, L. N., George, L. K., Karno, M., & Locke, B. Z. (1988). One-month prevalence of mental disorders in the United States: Based on five epidemiologic catchment area sites. *Archives of General Psychiatry, 45,* 977–986.

Reiman, E. M., Fusselman, M. J., Fox, P. T., & Raichle, M. E. (1989). Neuroanatomical correlates of anticipatory anxiety. *Science, 243,* 1071–1074.

Reiman, E. M., Raichle, M. E., Robins, E., Mintun, M. A., Fusselman, M. J., Fox, P. T., Price, J. L., & Hackman, K. A. (1989). Neuroanatomical correlates of a lactate-induced anxiety attack. *Archives of General Psychiatry, 46,* 493–500.

Rickels, K. (1990). Buspirone in clinical practice. *Journal of Clinical Psychiatry, 51 (suppl.),* 51–54.

Rickels, K., Schweizer, E., Csanalosi, I., Case, G., & Chung, H. (1988). Long-term treatment of anxiety and risk of withdrawal. *Archives of General Psychiatry, 45,* 444–450.

Roy-Byrne, P. P., Cowley, D. S., Greenblatt, D. J., Shader, R. I., & Hommer, D. (1990) Reduced benzodiazepine sensitivity in panic disorders. *Archives of General Psychiatry, 47,* 534–538.

Sadzot, B., Frost, J. J., & Wgner, Jr., H. N. (1989). In vivo labeling of central benzodiazepine receptors with the partial inverse agonist [3H] Ro15-4513. *Brain research, 49,* 128–135.

Sanghera, M. K., McMillen, B. A., & German, D. C. (1983). Buspirone, a non-benzodiazepine anxiolytic, increases locus coeruleus noradrenergic neuronal activity. *European Journal of Pharmacology, 86,* 107–110.

Savic, I., Roland, P., Sedvall, G., Persson, A., Pauli, S., & Widen, L. (1988). In-vivo demonstration of reduced benzodiazepine receptor binding in human epileptic foci. *Lancet, ii,* 863–866.

Sevy, S., Papadimitriou, G. N., Surmont, D. W., Goldman, S., & Mendlewicz, J. (1989). Noradrenergic function in generalized anxiety disorder, major depressive disorder, and healthy subjects. *Biological Psychiatry, 25,* 141–152.

Sheehan, D. V. (1987). Benzodiazepines in panic disorder and agoraphobia. *Journal of Affective Disorders, 13,* 169–181.

Sheehan, D. V., Davidson, J., & Manschrek, T. (1983). Lack of efficacy of a new antidepressant (buproprion) in the treatment of panic disorder with phobias. *Journal of Clinical Psychopharmacology, 3,* 28–31.

Squires, R. F., & Braestrup, C. (1977). Benzodiazepine receptors in rat brain. *Nature (London) 266,* 732.

Tallman, J. D., Paul, S. M., Skolnick, P., & Gallager, D. W. (1980). Receptors for the age of anxiety: Pharmacology of the benzodiazepines. *Science, 207,* 274.

Tallman, J. D., Thomas, J., & Gallager, D. (1978). GABAergic modulation of benzodiazepine site sensitivity. *Nature (London) 274,* 383.

Tyrer, P. (1988). Current status of β-blocking drugs in the treatment of anxiety disorders. *Drugs, 36,* 773–783.

Uhde, T. W., Stein, M. B., Vittone, B. J., Siever, L. J., Boulenger, J. P., Klein, E., & Mellman, T. A. (1989). Behavioral and physiologic effects of short-term and long-term administration of clonidine in panic disorder. *Archives of General Psychiatry, 46,* 170–177.

Wojcik, W. J., & Neff N. H. (1984). γ-Aminobutyric acid β receptors are negatively coupled to adenylate cyclase in brain and in the cerebellum these receptors may be associated with granule cells. *Molecular Pharmacology, 25,* 24–28.

Woods, S. W., Charney, D. S., Goodman, W. K., & Heninger, G. R. (1988). Carbon dioxide-induced anxiety. *Archives of General Psychiatry, 45,* 43–52.

Zohar, J., Mueller, E. A., Insel, T. R., Zohar-Kadouch, R. C. & Murphy, D. L. (1987). Serotonergic responsivity in obsessive-compulsive disorder. *Archives of General Psychiatry, 44,* 946–995.

Zuardi, A. W. (1990). 5-HT related drugs in human experimental anxiety. *Neuroscience & Biobehavioral Reviews, 14,* 507–510.

CHAPTER 8

Anxiety and the Experience of Time

HERBERT H. KRAUSS, PhD, and BEATRICE J. KRAUSS, PhD

*Time is a very strange thing. So long as one takes
it for granted, it is nothing at all. But then, all
of a sudden, one is aware of nothing else.*

—*HUGO VON HOFMANNSTHAL*

Tempora mutantur, nos et mutamur in illis.
The times are changed, and we are changed with them.

—*LATIN PROVERB*

Anxiety is introduced as a common emotion. Anxiety's distressing affectual tone is often accompanied by disturbing thoughts, physical discomforts, and behaviors. Anxiety is considered a normal emotion that, when functioning appropriately, provides necessary information to the individual about the quality and adaptive efficiency of the individual's transactions with the environment. To understand anxiety's role in this process, a neuropsychological information-processing paradigm similar to that which has proven so powerful in explicating visual perception is proposed.

The model provisionally adopted suggests that anxiety normally arises whenever the self *anticipates* a significant threat to its integrity or core, personal, biographical plans. The model recognizes, however, that pathological anxiety may be produced by dysfunctions in any of the self's hierarchical array of components. Such dysfunction may arise at the highest levels, that is, cultural rules affecting the conceptualization of the self, or, at the lowest levels, as a change in bodily processes that force reorganization of self-experience.

Any attempt to understand the self's anticipations leads necessarily to a study of its organization and orientation in time.* An account, albeit an

---

We would like to thank Michael Krauss, The Graduate Center, City University of New York, for his critical reading and substantive comments on this chapter.
*The discerning reader will note that the authors describe no explicit computational model for temporal representations either in the self or any subpart of its hierarchy.

incomplete one, is offered of the formation of the self within social time and the self's continuous interassociation with time in health, emotional dysfunction, and in illness.

PSYCHOLOGY'S UNDERSTANDING OF ANXIETY

The terms "fear" and "anxiety," as Wolman (1992, p. 76) points out, are often used interchangeably. When a distinction between the two is made,

> fear is taken to refer to feelings of apprehension about tangible and pre-dominantly realistic dangers, whereas anxiety is sometimes taken to refer to feelings of apprehension which are difficult to relate to tangible sources of stimulation. (Rachman, 1987, p. 257)

Anxiety is more than simply a distressing emotion. Combined with its unpleasant affectual tone are a complement of cognitive, somatic, and motoric features in complex interaction (e.g., Mandler, 1984; Papillo, Murphy, & Gorman, 1988; Wolman, 1992).

> An anxious person is in suspense, waiting for information to clarify his situation. He is watchful and alert, often excessively alert and over-reacting to noise or other stimuli. He may feel helpless in the face of a danger which, although felt to be imminent, cannot be identified or communicated. (Davis, 1987, p. 30)

Anxiety's manifestations are complex and multifaceted; each aspect has been investigated separately and incompletely giving rise to an over-supply of "explanatory" frameworks or schemata. This reflects the case in psychology generally where no prepotent guiding paradigms are in force, for emotions, cognitions, behaviors, or their interactions. Psychology's variety of efforts to make anxiety intelligible, therefore, are not exceptional. Mandler (1984) indicates,

> There is no single problem of anxiety. Anxiety has variously been con-sidered as a phenomenal state of the human organism, as a physiological

---

While there are many different paradigms of human memory and information process-ing, e.g., Johnson-Laird's mental modeling, Bartlett's schema, Schank and Abelson's scripts (Posner, 1989), there is as yet no one comprehensive and widely accepted theory or paradigm. In addition, none of the more complete models describe temporal organiza-tion in detail. However, several authors have recognized the importance of focusing on how episodes are represented in time (cf. Block, 1990; Diamond, 1990; Gibbon & Alan, 1984). The complexities of any model incorporating temporal information will go far be-yond the difficult problems inherent in adequately representing static information.

syndrome, and as a theoretical construct invoked to account for a defensive behavior, the avoidance of noxious events, and neurotic symptoms. (p. 220)

Whether or not these several constructions of anxiety can be reconciled is unclear. They have some themes in common, however. Again to cite Mandler (1984),

Briefly, the following shared characteristics of contemporary theories of anxiety can be noted. First, an archetypical event or class of events exists that evokes anxiety primitively, innately, or congenitally. For Freud, this original inciter is overstimulation; for Mowrer, it is pain; for Miller the "innate fear reaction"; for Rank the birth trauma; for Selye, stress; for the existentialists, the very fact of being human and alive. The second communality in theories about anxiety is the postulation that, somehow, the response to the archetypical event is transferred to previously innocuous events—events either in the external environment or in the action of the organism. The typical assumption is that this association takes place with the contiguous occurrence of trauma and neutral events . . . . Finally, it is assumed that the events terminating or reducing anxiety are closely related to events that evoke it. Thus, the primitive danger of overstimulation is controlled by a reduction in the level of stimulation. Similarly, the "fear" of electric shock is reduced by moving away from events associated with shock, presumably in inverse analogue to the model of hunger and thirst, in which a deficit of some substance (deprivation) is repaired by replacement (eating or drinking). (p. 230)

The multidimensional nature of anxiety, however, makes it no different than any other "normal" emotion. Modern descriptions of emotion stress the significance of effective conformation of individuals to their life circumstances (e.g., Mandler, 1984). Frijda (1988) has provided one of the most accessible summaries of the function of emotion in adaptation. From his reading of the investigative evidence, he formulated a number of propositions which he unfortunately and too grandly calls "laws of emotion," of which there are 11:

1. Emotions arise in the person's response to meaning structures evoked by different situations; the particular emotions arising being a function of the particular understanding one has of the situation.
2. Meaning structures are predictably connected to potential actions (e.g., moving toward food).
3. Meaning structures are those schemata which hold significance for an individual's goals, motives, and concerns.

4. The intensity of an evoked emotion varies directly with the extent to which a situation is believed "real."

5. Emotions are elicited more as a consequence of expected or perceived changes in the favorability of circumstances than the actual continuous experience of the situation.

6. The intensity of an emotion is a reflection of a relational process in which the consequences of an event are compared to a frame of reference.

7. To a degree, an asymmetry exists between pleasure and pain. Pleasure is contingent upon change to a greater degree than pain and disappears with satisfaction. Pain persists under adverse conditions.

8. Events linked to emotions retain their power to evoke emotions unless exposure to them produces either habituation or extinction.

9. Emotions tend to be closed judgments, tend to control other action systems, and, if intense enough, override other concerns. Emotions are, therefore, phenomenologically decisive; "[c]losure, or control precedence, may well be considered the essential feature of emotion. The notion of control precedence captures in some sense the involuntary nature of emotional impulse or apathy, its characteristic of being an 'urge,' in both experience and in behavior" (Frijda, 1988, p. 355).

10. Every emotional impulse induces internal processes that tend to modify the original emotions and its possible consequences. That is, at some level of place in the action hierarchy, the consequences of an emotion—rage, for example—can be appreciated and procedures activated to modify the emotion.

11. Whenever a situation can be interpreted in alternative ways, the individual has a tendency to select the interpretation that minimizes negative "emotional load" and maximizes emotional gain.

APPLYING INFORMATION PROCESSING MODELS TO EMOTION AND ANXIETY

Recognizable in Frijda's (1988) depiction of emotion is the influence of those model's that have proved enormously successful in illuminating visual perception (e.g., Livingstone & Hubel, 1988; Van Essen, Anderson, & Fellerman, 1992), and to a lesser extent motor coordination (Bizzi, Mussa-Ivaldi, & Giszter, 1991; Kalaska & Grammand, 1992) and memory (e.g., Baddeley, 1992; Cohen, Eichenbaum, Deacedo, & Corkin, 1985; Squire & Zola-Morgan, 1991; Tulving, 1989). They depict the central nervous system as a central information processing system, an enormously complex, hierarchical structure of branched, interacting, information-transforming processing components or modules. An example of this paradigm is Van Essen, Anderson, and Fellerman's (1992) representation of the primate's visual system. The primate visual system, they reason,

> contains dozens of distinct areas in the cerebral cortex and several major subcortical structures. These subdivisions are extensively interconnected in a distributed hierarchical network that contains several intertwined processing streams. A number of strategies are used for efficient information processing within this hierarchy. These include linear and nonlinear filtering passage through informational bottlenecks, and coordinated use of multiple types of information. In addition, dynamic regulation of information flow within and between visual areas may provide the computational flexibility needed for the visual system to perform a broad spectrum of tasks accurately and at high resolution. (p. 419)

The visual system is but one component of the central information processing system; the ability to acquire new memories is a distinct cerebral function, for example, separable from other perceptual and cognitive abilities; and the ability to acquire new memories is not a singular faculty, but is composed, instead, or multiple separable systems that are differentially affected by lesions of the central nervous system (Squire & Zola-Morgan, 1991). The enormous difficulties inherent in appropriately applying these models to personality-environmental transactions may be intuitively estimated. Such complex coordination requires temporal organization of information flow for each module. Consider the simultaneous intellectual, expressive, memory, emotional control, and motor coordination necessary for the concert pianist to perform. Consider also how the pianist works over time to reduce the possibility of potential miscoordination.

The prospect in the foreseeable future of delineating and explicating those central information processing system's configurations that underlie anxiety is even more reduced when one considers that the system patterns which produce anxiety and the disorders in which it is manifest are likely to be multiple and vary from person to person (e.g., Lang, 1977) and situation to situation.

Speculations, however, about the mechanisms of anxiety have not ceased. One promising line of conjecture, and certainly one that reduces the complexity of the problem, is that anxiety in many, if not all, of its forms follows a common path. One indicator of that route may be the linkage between *anxiety* and the sense of *foreboding* that psychologically-minded theorizers, diverse as Bandura (1986), Freud (e.g., 1964),

Geertz (1973), Heidegger (1962), Kelly (1963), Lewin (1943), and Sherover (1971) have uniformly emphasized. Skinner (1969), for example, described the connection in this way:

A *premonition* is a prior warning, and one has *foreboding* only with respect to coming ills. *Anxiety,* in the sense of fear of an impending event, is more than expectancy, and so is *anticipation,* which seems to be as close as the English language comes to an antonym of anxiety. Anxiety involves emotional responses to a conditioned aversive stimulus, anticipation to a conditioned positive reinforcer. (p. 127)

Kelly (1963) expressed the relationship between anxiety and foreboding somewhat differently:

[T]he person is bent on anticipating events . . . . Each person attunes his ear to the replicative themes he hears and each attunes his ear in a somewhat different way . . . . More and more he seeks to anticipate all impending events of whatever nature. This means that he must develop a system in which the most unusual future can be anticipated in terms of a replicated aspect of the familiar past.
   Now it so happens that a person must occasionally decide what to do about remodeling his system . . . . How much can he tear down and still have a roof over his head? How disruptive will a new set of ideas be? Dare he jeopardize the system in order to replace some of its constituent parts? . . . Sometimes his anticipation of events will be more effective if he chooses to conserve the system. (p. 58)

What the client experiences, assuming that the construct [self] fails to work for him is *anxiety.* (p. 118)

Considerable research evidence supports the putative relationship between threat and anxiety (e.g., MacLeod, Mathews, & Tata, 1986; Mathews & MacLeod, 1986; Mogg, Mathews, & Weinman, 1987). Furthermore, although disorders of anxiety frequently co-occur with depressive disorders (e.g., de Ruiter, Ruken, Garssen, van Schaik, & Kraaimaat, 1989; Lesser, et al., 1988; Sanderson, DiNardo, Rapee, & Barlow, 1990) and both have in common general affective distress as well as other common symptoms (e.g., Clark & Watson, 1991), anxiety and depression can still be differentiated because only anxiety is co-joined with anticipated threat (Clark, Beck, & Steward, 1990; Clark & Watson, 1991).
   Gray (1988) has advanced the most cogent argument that a separable subsystem of the brain mediates anxiety. He suggests evidence drawn from three separate sources: (1) the action of drugs known to reduce anxiety, namely barbituates, ethanol, and benzodiazepines; (2) the effects of infantile stress on adult behavior; and (3) selective animal

breeding designed to produce "reactive" and "nonreactive" genotypes—
has converged and supports the hypothesis that a "behavioral inhibition
system," the crucial constituent of the anxiety network, exists. The behavioral inhibition system depends upon neuronal activity in the septal
area, the hippocampal formation, noradrenergic neurons in the locus
coeruleus, serotonergic neurons in the raphe nuclei, and their intercon-
nections. "The primary function of this system," Gray (1988) posits:

> is apparently to suppress behavior that threatens to produce an unwelcome
> outcome (pain, nonreward, etc.). It follows that the system can only use-
> fully be put to work if some other system is producing behavior that needs
> to be suppressed. There are essentially two major motivational systems
> that can do this . . . a 'reward system' . . . mediating approach and ac-
> tive avoidance behavior and in response to stimuli associated with reward
> or the omission of anticipated punishment; and the fight/flight sys-
> tem . . . . To these should be added a number of more specialized mecha-
> nisms that mediate various forms of unconditional appetitive behavior
> (eating, drinking, copulation, etc.). These conditions imply . . . when
> the behavioral inhibition system is active, the total emotional experience
> will be an amalgam of the emotional effects of activity in this system and
> those of the activity in the system whose output is under inhibition . . . .
> [S]uch an amalgam will be maximally negative in affective tone when the
> system inhibited is the fight/flight system. (p. 24)

Normal operation of Gray's "anxiety system" (or any viable alternative) "breaks down" when any significant component at any level functions aberrantly. Just as anemia may be caused by many things—iron
deficiency, defective red blood cells, and so on—so too may anxiety
disorders.

The examples that follow describing how the "anxiety system" might
go "haywire" are based upon extrapolations from Dennett's (1991) summary description of well-regarded models of how the perceptual system
works. Because of their success in explaining visual perception, models
developed from that field are often applied to other systems and problems. Characteristic of these models are rounds of expectation-informed
hypothesis testing.

> It is widely held that human vision, for instance, cannot be explained as
> an *entirely* "data-driven" or "bottom-up" process, but needs, at the
> highest level, a few "expectation-driven" rounds of hypothesis testing.
> Another member of the family is the "analysis-by-synthesis" model of
> perception that also supposes that perceptions are built up in a process
> that weaves back and forth between centrally generated expectations,
> on the one hand, and confirmation (and disconfirmations) arising from
> the periphery on the other hand . . . . The general idea of these theo-
> ries is that after a certain amount of "preprocessing" has occurred in

the early or peripheral layers of the perceptual system, the tasks of perception are completed—objects are identified, recognized, categorized—by generate-and-test cycles. (p. 12)

If similar cycles occur in the "anxiety network" as Gray (1988) sup-
poses, dysfunctional anxiety might be produced when an individual's
hypothesis-generation (i.e., the expectation) side of the "analysis-by-
synthesis" cycle requests information about whether the situation was
threatening, and the data-driven side (the confirmation side) produces a
series of inappropriate confirmations, perhaps attributable to defective
regulation in the arousal system. A different, but equally damaging,
route to dysfunction would be followed if the hypothesis-generating
side of the cycle allowed no other possibility than threat.

The hypothesis that both specialized brain structures and anticipation
play an important role in anxiety is supported by Tulving's (1989) fascinating case history of K.C. Especially interesting is the implication one
can draw from it that episodic memory and the self-system may be intrinsic to the experience of anxiety.

> On 30 October 1980, a 30-year-old man, whom we shall call K.C., had an
> accident that changed his life. Driving his motorcycle home from work in
> a town near Toronto, he went off a curve at high speed. When help ar-
> rived, he was alive but unconscious, and he remained so for three days in
> the hospital. He had suffered a severe closed head injury. Now, nearly
> nine years later, with extensive brain lesions in the left frontal-parietal
> and right parietal-occipital regions and possibly in other parts of the
> brain, he is densely amnesic.
>
> K.C.'s case is remarkable in that he cannot remember, in the sense of
> bringing back to conscious awareness, a single thing that he has ever done
> or experienced in the past. He cannot remember himself experiencing sit-
> uations and participating in life's events. This total absence of personal
> recollections makes K.C.'s case unique: no other reports exist of amnesic
> patients who have been incapable of recollecting *any* personal happen-
> ings. (p. 362)

Tulving (1989) wrote about K.C. to differentiate between episodic
memories (memories of personal experiences), and semantic memories
(memories of impersonal facts). K.C. experienced minor upset in re-
trieval of the latter, and seemingly total loss of the former. For example,
confronted with chess pieces, K.C. "knew" how to play chess, knew fac-
tually that his father had played chess, but could remember no incident
of playing chess with his father nor that he, K.C., had participated in any
other chess games. He remembered that his family owned a summer cot-
tage, but had no recollection of being there or taking part in any of the
activities that occurred there. Tulving generalizes from this case,

[C]ritical features of episodic information have to do with the self in time. The concept of a personal past ties together these two entities. K.C. has no particular difficulty apprehending and discussing himself or physical time. He knows what facts about himself could be said to be true and what facts could not; he also knows what most other people know about physical time, its units, its structure, and its measurement by clocks and calendars. It is his apprehension of objectively experienced time that seems grossly impaired.

The impairment not only encompasses the past, it also extends to the future. Thus, when asked, K.C. cannot tell a questioner what he is going to do later on that day, or the day after, or at any time in the rest of his life . . . . K.C. is destined to spend the remainder of his life in a permanent present. (pp. 363–364)

Concomitant with K.C.'s loss of a "personal" future came a diminished sense of anxiety. When queried about his level of anxiety, Tulving (personal communication, March, 1992) characterized K.C. "as one of the least anxious—under all circumstances—individuals" Tulving has met; Tulving further observed that amnesics, in general, even without the peculiar features of K.C.'s case, seemed to experience less anxiety than either normals or those with other brain syndromes which had not affected their episodic memory (Tulving, personal communication, March 1992).

K.C.'s unique symptoms were driven by a biological event that disrupted his recognition of a past self and projection of a future one. It has been argued (Aaronson, 1972; Fischer, 1970; Krauss, 1967; Lazarus, 1991; Mandler, 1984; May, Angel, & Ellenberger, 1958; Wallis, 1966) that, at the molar and phenomenological level, anxiety is experienced as a threat to self, with the concept of the self and its powers to cope often originating in the past, but aimed toward the future. In such systems, anxiety occurs in response to an event that signals an impending "identity" threat, with anxiety's intensity varying with the self's assessment of the reality of that threat and its "impendingness" (Lewin, 1943).

As Brewer (1991) points out, psychologists have become increasingly "self centered." Too much emphasis on the term *self*, however, masks the extent to which psychologists believe the self is both internally and socially constructed. "Two features characterize the dominant view of 'self' within modern empirical psychology," according to Deci and Ryan (1990, p. 237). "First, the self tends to be conceptualized as a set of cognitive appraisals and schemata; second, the self tends to be understood as a reflection of social evaluations." In addition, however, Deci and Ryan argue the concept of the self broadens with social experience beyond these immediate evaluations.

[T]he self does not simply reflect social forces; rather it represents intrinsic growth processes whose tendency is toward integration of one's own experience and action with one's sense of relatedness to the selves of others. Thus the self is not simply an outcome of social evaluations and pressures but instead is the very process through which a person contacts the social environment and works to integration with respect to it. (p. 238)

It has been debated as to how the self might be schematized to capture both active individual processes and social forces. Currently, distributed models of the central information processing system have been applied to the self (e.g., McClelland, 1985), with centers of control at multiple nodes. One such is Dennett's (1991):

A self, according to my theory, is not any old mathematical point, but an abstraction defined by the myriads of attributions and interpretations (including self-attributions and self-interpretations) that have composed the biography of the living body whose Center of Narrative Gravity it is. As such, it plays a singularly important role in the ongoing cognitive economy of that living body, because of all the things in the environment an active body must make mental models of, none is more crucial than the model the agent has of itself. To begin with, every agent has to know which thing in the world it is. (p. 427)

Because it must act within the circumstances of culture and it is a reflection of culture, self and culture are necessarily interlocked. If the experience of anxiety is to be understood, therefore, not only must the self's teleology be appreciated but the culture's construction of temporality, its timeframe for *foreboding*.

The theme of a teleological identity or teleological self is certainly not new to psychology (Krauss, 1967). It was explored in depth by the Europeans Adler (Ansbacher, 1950; Ansbacher & Ansbacher, 1956) and Jung (e.g., 1934/1965), but comes rather late to American personality theory (e.g., Kelly, 1963). Allport, the dean of American personologists, remarked "People, it seems, are busy leading their lives into the future, whereas psychology, for the most part, is busy tracing them into the past (1955, p. 51).

Although they had different reasons for doing so, both Adler and Jung considered individuals to be goal directed, their actions directed toward the realization or warding off of a future:

Life is teleology par excellence; it is the intrinsic striving towards a goal, and the living organism is a system of directed aims which seek to fulfill themselves. The end of every process is its goal. All energy flow is like a runner who strives with the greatest effort and the utmost expenditure of strength to reach his goal. Youthful longing for the world and for life, for the attainment of high hopes and distant goals, is life's obvious teleological urge which at once changes into fear of life, neurotic resistances, depressions and phobias if at some point it remains caught in the past, or shrinks from risks without which the unseen goal cannot be achieved. (Jung, 1934/1965, p. 5)

Decades after Kelly's brilliant attempt, American psychology and sociological psychology have come to focus on the construction of the self in time. The self, it has been hypothesized, is created through an individual's development of a "narrative" life story or "life script" (e.g., Charmaz, 1991; Dennett, 1991; Mandler, 1984). This life script defines the individual's identity by placing the individual in a setting with other characters and confronting them with an unfolding series of events. The actions of characters and subtexts of assumed motivation, goals and intentions reveal and create "identity." To the extent events create major discontinuities in an evolving life story, "biographical work" or rewriting a life script "to put one's life back together" occurs.

Perhaps the most sophisticated and articulated psychologist-produced elaboration of person-environment transaction across time (and the most relevant to this chapter) is the stress-appraisal-coping model of Lazarus and his colleague (e.g., Folkman, 1984; Lazarus, 1991; Lazarus & Folkman, 1984). According to this model, a dynamic set of "transactions" occurs between an individual and his or her surroundings. Environmental events are appraised as potential sources of benefits, threats, challenges, or harm, in a definitional process labeled *primary appraisal.* The definition of threat, benefit, harm, or challenge is measured against the individual's commitments and meaning structures. A *secondary* appraisal process occurs when the individual judges whether he or she possesses the personal or situational resources to deal with a potential harm or threat from the environment. If sufficient resources are believed to be on hand, a threat may be redefined as a challenge. Primary and secondary appraisal together instigate an important set of psychological behaviors, coping. Coping can be problem-focused, focused on the emotions arising from the situation, or both. Lazarus (1991) suggests fright and anxiety arise from a concentration on the threat of future harm:

A *threatening* encounter makes one feel uneasy (anxious) which is not only unpleasant but is apt to constrict one's ability to think and perform. The constriction is connected with a strong effort to protect oneself from anticipated danger. (p. 18)

The transactional and existential nature of anxiety in Lazarus' mind is, however, clear:

Anxiety arises when existential meaning is disrupted or endangered as a result of physiological deficit, drugs, intrapsychic conflict, and difficult-to-interpret events. The threat involved is symbolic rather than concrete. If the threat is mild, and the structures that are endangered not very central to the person's identity the result is apt to be mild uneasiness. If the threat is severe and the meaning structures central, the result is apt to be a full-grown anxiety attack and a personal crisis of major proportions. (p. 234)

Coping and the engagement of personal resources are particularly difficult when one is anxious, because Lazarus argues, the "hallmark" of anxiety is that it is in response to a situation of ambiguity, and, indeed, the psychological feelings accompanying anxiety are feelings of uncertainty:

The core relational theme of *anxiety* is *uncertain, existential threat.* The uncertainty about what will happen and when obviates any clear idea on the part of the person what to do to prevent or ameliorate it. We are nagged by abstract, ambiguous, and symbolic threats to our ego-identity. (p. 236)

Lazarus locates the threat to meaning that generates anxiety in the future. Melges (1990), more directly than Lazarus, holds that one's sense of identity (that which Lazarus notes is under threat when the individual is anxious) is related to one's ability to maintain a time perspective, especially a vision of one's self in the future.

Melges offers three reasons for this. Each reason can be construed as originating from a different level of the personality, and as being more or less involved in, or originating from socially coordinated activity. That is an individual has a comfortable rate of performance or foresight that partially originates from, and is maintained and validated by social responses, much as, *within* the individual, components are coordinated by a Central Information Processing System.

(a) Because a person becomes familiar with his or her self over time, the disruption of the continuity of temporal perspective impairs this sense of familiarity . . . and thus the self feels strange.

(b) Within the framework of temporal perspective, momentary changes of sequence, rate, and rhythm are evaluated . . . . When this framework becomes blurred, the interpretation of the self (identity) also becomes compromised.

(c) Because human beings are basically goal-correcting organisms, a firm grip on the personal future . . . provides a key anchoring point for the continuity of temporal perspective. Future time perspective, as a means-to-ends process, gives order and direction to temporal perspective. (pp. 256–257)

If Melges is correct, two conclusions may be drawn. Each individual, as the existentialists aver (e.g., Hoffman, 1986; Krauss & Krauss, 1990), fashions a self that is necessarily rooted in time, and one's experience of anxiety is necessarily conditioned by one's temporal perspective.

THE SELF IN SOCIAL TIME

The external flow of time into which we emerge at birth and in interassociation with which we are shaped across our life spans (e.g., Montanegro, 1985; Piaget, 1966; Solomon, Groccia-Ellison, Levine, Blanchard, & Pendlebury, 1991) has been structured differently in different historical eras (e.g., Elias, 1982; Poulet, 1956; Sarap, 1989; Wilcox, 1987; Yaker, 1972) and is culturally distinctive (e.g., Duncan, 1968; Geertz, 1973; Kluckhohn & Strodtbeck, 1961; Levine, 1990; Maxwell, 1972; Triandis, 1989). "Biblical man," according to Yaker (1972, p. 32) "perceived time as a series of linear moments . . . . Each day of life was one day closer to its fulfillment, and one day further from its creation." On the other hand, for the Greeks of the classical age, time was episodic: "The subject matter determined the shape of Greek time. A particular war, polity, people, or religion created its own temporal boundary; a particular lesson, its own time frame" (Wilcox, 1987, p. 81). When a Trobriand Islander wishes to distinguish between different kinds of occasions, Maxwell (1972) notes "he will say, for example, 'Molubabeba-in-childhis,' that is, in the childhood of Molubabeba, not a previous phase of *this* time, but a different kind of time. For him, history is an unordered repository of anecdote, he is not interested in chronological sequence" (p. 46).

Significant aspects of an individual's self derive from and depend upon his or her culture's orientation to time. Selves will differ among cultures which differ in temporal orientation; selves will differ within cultures in the extent to which the temporal perspective predominant in that culture is congenial. From the perspective of twentieth-century America, for example, the Balinese formulation of personhood is "depersonalizing" according to Geertz (1973, p. 390). This he attributes to the "presentness" of their society:

> Consociates, as they meet, confront and grasp one another in an immediate present, a synoptic "now"; and in so doing they experience the elusiveness and ephemerality of such a now as it slips by in the ongoing stream of face-to-face interaction. (p. 390)

Duncan (1968), to select an example closer to home, argues that unlike Europeans whose actions are determined by their past, the behavior of Americans is determined by their sense of the future. "This does not mean that we Americans have no history," he remarks (1968), ". . . we have a great historical tradition in America, but it is the history of the future, not the past, which concerns us" (p. 27).

Both proximal and distal forces produce a culture's temporal orientation and act to induce the self's participation in it. For Lacan (cf. Sarap, 1989; Wilder, 1968) the experience of temporality and the persistence of human identity is an effect of language, and languages do differ in the treatment of time.

> Nearly all languages enable their speakers to discriminate between past, present, and future events, but they do so with varying degrees of difficulty. In English we use three basic tenses, and combinations of these. We cannot speak of an event without using one or another tense, so that the recognition of this tripartite division of time is built into our language. Other languages, however, operate differently . . . . [S]peakers of the Luganda language . . . are compelled by their grammar to note whether an event occurs within or before the twenty-four-hour period immediately preceding the time at which the event is described . . . . Other languages, however, are much more careless in their handling of time and in some cases . . . may not use any tenses at all. (Maxwell, 1972, pp. 44–45)

Language is more than tense structure, it creates meaning. Consider how powerful the metaphor "time is money" has been in defining our own:

> In our culture time is money in many ways; we calculate telephone calls, hourly wages, interest on loans. But not only do we *act* as if time is a valuable commodity, we also *conceive* of time in that way. 'I don't have the time to give you.' 'How do you spend your time these days?' Thus we understand and experience time as the kind of thing that can be spent, wasted, budgeted, invested wisely or foolishly, saved or squandered. (Sarap, 1989, p. 53)

But as important as language is, other cultural configurations also contribute to cultural temporality. Whether culture is individualistic or collectivist also makes a difference in time perspective:

> Interaction is conceived in a longer time perspective by collectivists than it is by individualists. Specifically, goals are closer in time among individualists; one expects tit-for-tat rewards from social interactions. Distant goals are more common among collectivists. One does not expect immediate reciprocity, but long-term reciprocity is most important. . . . For Buddhist collectivists one's acts have consequences for many generations to come and can determine whether one may enter nirvana. (Triandis, 1990, p. 60)

Perhaps the best descriptive summary as to how modern Western culture's temporal orientation is formed has been provided by Elias (1982):

> With Western society as its starting point, a network of interdependence has developed which not only encompasses the oceans further than any other in the past, but extends to the furthest arable corners of vast inland regions. Corresponding to this is the necessity for an attunement of human conduct over wider areas, and foresight over longer chains of actions, than ever before. Corresponding to it, too, is the strength of self-control and the permanence of compulsion, affect inhibition and drive control, which life at the centres of this network imposes. One of the characteristics which make this connection between the size of and pressure within the network of interdependence on the one hand, and the psychological make-up of the individual on the other particularly clear is what we call the 'tempo' of our time. This 'tempo' is in fact nothing other than a manifestation of the multitude of intertwining chains of interdependence which run through every single social function people have to perform, and of the competitive pressure permeating this densely populated network and affecting, directly or indirectly, every single set of individuals. (pp. 247–248)

Implicit in this description are three important points. As has been affirmed since Plato (Krauss, 1990), personality and culture are reciprocal creations; there is a tacit hierarchy of needs and goals, within an individual, within a society, and in an individual's relationship to society, which must be negotiated out in a time-bounded framework (e.g., Durkheim, 1933); and social contexts demand temporary or permanent inhibition of some needs and goals, for others to be fulfilled in a social milieu which more and more is regulated by an objective external tempo. This inhibition or control, the reader will recall, was a central aspect of Gray's (1988) conceptualization of anxiety.

However extensive or necessary an external arbitrary organizer of social life it might be, social time, as William James (1928) has so astutely pointed out, may not necessarily uniformly penetrate into the various components of self-structure:

> That one Time which we all believe in and in which each event has its definite date, that one Space in which each thing has its position, these abstract notions unify the world incomparably; but in their finished shape as concepts how different they are from the loose unordered time and space experiences of natural men! Everything that happens to us brings its own duration and extension, and both are vaguely surrounded by a more meaningful 'more' that runs into the duration and extension of the next thing that comes. But we soon lose our definite bearings; and not only do our children make no distinction between yesterday and the day

before yesterday, the whole past being churned up together, but we adults still do so when the times are large. (p. 178)

This description, however, does not make clear whether James believed individuals participate in two or more time schemes simultaneously, switch from one to another, or interweave these time schemes. We still do not know.

INDIVIDUAL DIFFERENCES IN PHENOMENAL AND SELF-TIME

Time perception varies not only over the life span, and with the smaller or larger impact of events, but is influenced differentially by aspects of the biological and social self. Drug- and disease-induced alterations in time-perception have been noted. Often, they have been attributed to changes in the usual rhythms of the central or the sympathetic nervous system, affecting heart rate, breathing, rate of movement, and other "regularities" of internal pace against which one would almost unconsciously measure the external flow of events (Goldstone, 1967). For example, after taking psilocybin, a subject found his handwriting slow compared to his inner sensations, "A hundred years, so it appeared to me, would not suffice to describe the fullness of experience contained in a single minute." Many psychotomimetic compounds induce a central sympathetic excitation syndrome, characterized by hyperthermia, pilo-erection, hyperglycaemia, tachycardia, and so on (Fischer, 1967). Barbiturates, in contrast, induce a central slowing (Goldstone, 1967). Contractions and expansions of personal time are experienced during the "dreamy state" accompanying temporal lobe seizures (Fischer, 1967), and time speeds for those who have experienced the slowing of bodily processes accompanying hypothermia (Cohen, 1967).

The significance and meaning of these observations are complicated by a more articulated view of internal rhythms which postulate multiple internal clocks, some constantly running (i.e., circadian rhythms), some stopping and starting, that is, interval clocks (e.g., Church, 1984; Kristofferson, 1984; Richter, 1960). Long-term clocks have been hypothesized for cyclic events; sleeping-waking, feeding, menstruating, and processes involved in the hormonal regulation of the body (Friedman, 1990). Interval clocks are necessary for the coordination of the multiple systems required in complex activities, for example, sports, cooking (Michon, 1990), and can be inferred from the time-sense necessary in humans and other animals for conditioning to occur (Friedman, 1990).

Such multiple clocks may be responsible for some of the paradoxical findings in the literature on accuracy of time estimation, a literature that varies between psychophysical scaling of time intervals of minutes and seconds, and perception of biographical time (e.g., Cohen, 1967). These findings suggest time may be differentially *experienced* by components of the self:

> Acute situational anxiety and chronic pathological conditions of depersonalization and derealization influence a person's subjective awareness of time, but leave his objective estimation of time intervals quite intact— a rather unexpected finding. (Lehmann, 1967, p. 801)

Zakay (1990) also notes that generally the literature reports filled or busy time appears to pass more slowly than "empty" time. (Zakay warns these findings must be considered tentative because researchers rarely are aware of subjects' cognitive processes during "empty" time.)

Habitual orientations toward time perception can be *used* to induce motivational states. At least three authors (De Volder & Lens, 1982; Friedman & Rosenman, 1974; Yarnold & Grimm, 1982) suggest an orientation toward the future creates urgency and time pressure in the present, characteristic of high-achieving students and those with Type A personality.

In a series of experiments on hypnotic time distortion, Aaronson (1972) explored subjects' motivational and affective states when their orientation toward time was altered. He reported subjects to whom it was suggested they had no present were immobile; no past were confused and irritable; and no future were euphoric and semi-mystical, a finding which incidentally reinforces the belief that a future orientation is necessary to anxiety.

In the world of the compulsive (in DSM-III-R obsessive-compulsive disorder is considered an anxiety disorder, American Psychiatric Association, 1987), von Gebsattel (1958, p. 185) hypothesizes, the future is seen as negative and frozen. "[A] world without mercy and without grace of Fate . . . opens up or, rather, shuts up." The obsessive-compulsive binds anxiety in the present and wards off the future with a "rule-ridden unchangeability."

ANXIETY AND SOCIAL TIME

Coping with anxiety can be facilitated or inhibited by a synchrony or dissynchrony between an individual's internal pacing for actions and decisions, and the external flow of events (e.g., Freund & McGuire, 1991; Michon, 1990). As Elias (1982) suggested, any dissynchrony challenges individuals' structuring of activities and leads to new attempts to control either themselves or external events. A dissynchrony, indeed, can "erode our sense of coherence"; and our social position can remove us from control over the social resources we need to cope.

> Control over time—our own or other people's—is a form of power. Powerful persons have the ability to regulate other people's time and labor. The ability to manage our own schedule is limited by our position in society . . . *Time is socially organized, and the ability to schedule time and manage it is socially distributed.* (p. 97)

In exploring powerlessness over time, Freund and McGuire (1991) introduce the concepts of environmental overload, produced by an environment that "demands too much, too fast," and underload:

> Overload and underload have been linked to increased excretions of catecholamine, a stress hormone. A study of sawmill workers found that those whose jobs were characterized by a lack of control over their situation were most likely to have increased catecholamine secretions in urine and feel tired, tense, anxious and ill more frequently than other workers. (Frankenhauser & Gardell, cited in Freund & McGuire, 1991, p. 99)

Likewise, underload and lack of control produced stress.

The dissynchrony can be *internally,* as well as externally imposed; self-imposed over-control is characteristic of the "time-sickness" of the Type A personality, these authors argue. In a reworking of Freud, Marcuse (1955) essentially makes the same argument, but in the language of existentialism, that control over time, in its *content,* is aimed for or against an unalienated self:

> Man exists only *part*-time, during the working days, as an instrument of alienated performance; the rest of the time he is free for himself . . . This free time would be potentially available for pleasure. But the pleasure principle which governs the id is "timeless" also in the sense that it militates against the temporal dismemberment of pleasure, against its distribution in small separated doses. A society governed by the performance principle must of necessity impose such distribution because the organism must be trained for its alienation at its very roots—the *pleasure ego.*
>
> The irreconcilable conflict is not between work (reality principle) and Eros (pleasure principle), but between *alienated* labor (performance principle) and Eros. (pp. 42–43)

Elias (1982) sees such conflict unfolding historically in Western culture as the demands of interdependence increasingly structure and delay the inclinations of an individual self:

[I]t makes people accustomed to subordinating momentary inclinations to the overriding necessities of interdependence; it trains them to eliminate all irregularities from behavior and to achieve permanent self-control. This is why tendencies in the individual so often rebel against social time represented by his own super-ego, and why so many people come into conflict with themselves when they wish to be punctual. From the development of chronometric instruments and the consciousness of time—as from that of money and other instruments of social integration—it is possible to read off with considerable accuracy how the division of functions, and with it the self-control imposed on the individual advances. (p. 248)

TIME AND BIOGRAPHICAL WORK

Some of the most dramatic alterations in time perception/orientation occur for individuals to whom "life-changing" events beyond their control have occurred. Such individuals must rework their futures by examining and finding new life stories in their pasts (Wallis, 1966), in a process some authors call "biographical work."

Many researchers have looked at these adaptations in persons with illnesses or accidents that change possible futures. For such persons, biographical work consists of projecting future life scripts that incorporate valued goals independent of illness while accommodating the discontinuities evoked by illness (Corbin & Strauss, 1987). The former identities and future plans of the chronically ill often "become questioned, undermined, altered or negated" (Charmaz, 1987, p. 283) both by the realities of limits imposed by illness and by the danger illness will take on a "master status" (an attribute which serves as a filter through which all other attributes of the person are viewed; Hughes, 1945) either in one's own mind or in others' (Charmaz, 1987; Nerenz & Leventhal, 1983; Schur, 1979). Chronically ill individuals achieve control and purpose by reviewing and reconstructing their biographies (Corbin & Strauss, 1987). Biographical work may, as Brooks and Matson (1982) suggest in their work with multiple sclerosis patients, involve considerable self-redefinition. The biographies look forward not only to how time should be filled in the service of the self, but also to different endpoints, immanent death, permanent "differentness," as in irreversible disability, or recovery (Adams & Lindemann, 1974).

Relatively early in the HIV epidemic, with little hope of cure, HIV seropositive men had to cope with a sense of urgency about the time remaining to them (Siegel & Krauss, 1991). They decided to what extent to invest in their futures. In so doing, many seemed to be expediting a script for a completed life. Career-related concerns were often central to the script—one man, who recently returned to school, remarked he wanted to see Ph.D. on his tombstone. Though many HIV seropositive men had hopes a cure for HIV/AIDS would be found, most accepted their infection as irreversible and life-limiting.

Career choices and achievement frequently reflected key identity issues for these men in their 20s to 50s; similar concerns emerge for cancer patients in this age group (Rowland, 1989) and reordering of priorities is commonly found among cancer patients in general (Siegel & Christ, 1990). The HIV seropositive men's urgency for achievement was quite different from the time-sense of individuals with spinal cord injury (Lilliston, 1985) who, while waiting to find out if functions will recover, may feel anxiously "imprisoned" in the present, or from the experience of an individual with a cancer for which treatments are well-developed. In the latter case, the passage of disease-free time, although characterized by persisting anxieties about recurrence (Siegel & Christ, 1990), signals "cure" and a tentatively grasped, new normalcy.

Studies of those who experience illness or accident make clear that their identity challenges can be "written" toward three futures: I will persist, that is, I will someday be myself again; I will end; I will change.

CONCLUSION

Anxiety is created or moderated at multiple levels. It can be induced or reduced by changes in bodily sensation some of which in turn alter time sense; it is responsive to the fit between a culture's and individual's pace; it is modified by an individual's satisfaction with the projection of his or her future self; it is altered by an individual's sense of control over the possible futures that social contexts and circumstances allow; and it is emphasized or diminished by a socially negotiated temporal perspective.

Common to the experience of anxiety in time is a sense of *foreboding* or threat emanating from the future. We have argued that one central aspect of the phenomenology of this foreboding is perception of threat for key self-identity concerns. If a sense of self is dampened, by biologic (e.g., deficits in episodic memory) or social factors (e.g., a collectivist vs. individualistic orientation that does not also overstructure time), we predict the *probability* of anxiety will change. For the individual, a perception of resources and abilities to control what the future self will be, what the future context of the self will be, or to negotiate the junctions of self and environmental challenge will alleviate anxiety. Part of the task of control is for the individual to construct a life story capable of satisfactorily encompassing probable futures, but based in a real past and enacted in the present. In contrast, where there is harmony, what Ruth Benedict (1934) refers to as *synergy,* between social and individual integrity, both the necessity for control and the experience of anxiety ought be diminished.

REFERENCES

Aaronson, B. S. (1972). Behavior and the place names of time (pp. 405–436). In H. Yaker, H. Osmond, & F. Cheek (Eds.), *The future of time: Man's temporal environment.* Garden City, NY: Anchor Books.

Adams, J. E., & Lindemann, E. (1974). Coping with long-term disability (pp. 127–38). In G. V. Coehlo, D. A. Hamburg, & J. E. Adams (Eds.), *Coping and adaptation.* New York: Basic Books.

Allport, G. S. (1955). *Becoming.* New Haven: Yale University Press.

American Psychiatric Association. (1987). *Diagnostic and statistical manual of mental disorders (DSM-III-R).* Washington, DC: Author.

Ansbacher, H. L. (1950). Causality and indeterminism according to Alfred Adler and some current American personality theories. *Individual Psychology Bulletin, 9,* 96–107.

Ansbacher, H. L., & Ansbacher, R. R. (1956). *The individual psychology of Alfred Adler.* New York: Basic Books.

Baddeley, A. (1992). Working memory. *Science, 255,* 556–559.

Bandura, A. (1986). *Social foundations of thought and action: A social cognitive theory.* Englewood Cliffs, NJ: Prentice-Hall.

Benedict, R. (1934). *Patterns of culture.* New York: New American Library.

Bizzi, E., Mussa-Ivaldi, F. A., & Giszter, S. (1991). Computations underlying the execution of movement: A biological perspective. *Science, 253,* 287–291.

Block, R. (1990). *Cognitive models of psychological time.* Hillsdale, NJ: Lawrence Erlbaum.

Brewer, M. B. (1991). The social self: On being the same and different at the same time. *Personality and Social Psychology Bulletin, 17,* 475–482.

Brooks, N. A., & Matson, R. R. (1982). Social-psychological adjustment to multiple sclerosis. *Social Science and Medicine, 16,* 2129–35.

Charmaz, K. (1987). Struggling for a self: Identity levels of the chronically ill (pp. 283–321). In J. A. Roth & P. Conrad (Eds.), *Research in the sociology of health care,* Vol. 6. Greenwich, CT: JAI Press.

Charmaz, K. (1991). *Good days, bad days: The self in chronic illness and time.* New Brunswick, NJ: Rutgers University Press.

Church, R. M. (1984). Properties of the internal clock. In J. Gibbon & L. Allen (Eds.), *Timing and time perception* (pp. 566–582). New York: New York Academy of Sciences.

Clark, D. A., Beck, A. T., & Steward, B. (1990). Cognitive specificity and positive-negative affectivity: Contemporary or contradictory views of anxiety and depression? *Journal of Abnormal Psychology, 99,* 148–155.

Clark, L. A., & Watson, D. (1991). Tripartite model of anxiety and depression: Psychometric evidence and taxonomic implications. *Journal of Abnormal Psychology, 100,* 316–336.

Cohen, J. (1967). *Psychological time in health and disease.* Springfield, IL: Charles C. Thomas.

Cohen, N. J., Eichenbaum, H., Deacedo, B. S., & Corkin, S. (1985). Different memory systems underlying acquisition of procedural and declarative knowledge (pp. 54–71). In D. S. Olten, E. Gamzu, & S. Corkin (Eds.), *Memory dysfunctions: An integration of animal and human research from preclinical and clinical perspectives.* Vol. 444. New York: Annals of the New York Academy of Science.

Corbin, J. M., & Strauss, A. (1987). Accompaniments of chronic illness: Changes in body, self, biography, and biographical time (pp. 249–81). In J. A. Roth & P. Conrad (Eds.), *Research in the sociology of health care,* Vol. 6, Greenwich, CT: JAI Press.

Davis, D. R. (1987). Anxiety. In R. L. Gregory (Ed.), *The Oxford companion to the mind* (pp. 30–31). New York: Oxford Press.

Deci, E. L., & Ryan, R. M. (1990). A motivational approach to self: Integration in personality (pp. 237–288). In R. A. Dientsbier, (Ed.), *Perspectives on motivation.* Lincoln, NE: University of Nebraska Press.

Dennett, D. C. (1991). *Consciousness explained.* Boston: Little Brown and Company.

de Ruiter, C., Ruken, H., Garssen, B., van Schaik, A., & Kraaimaat, F. (1989). Comorbidity among the anxiety disorders. *Journal of Anxiety Disorders, 3,* 57–68.

De Volder, M. L., & Lens, W. (1982). Academic achievement and future time perspective as a cognitive-motivational concept. *Journal of Social and Personality Psychology, 42,* 566–571.

Diamond, A. (Ed.). (1990). *The development and neural bases of higher cognitive functions.* New York: New York Academy of Sciences.

Duncan, H. D. (1968). *Symbols in society.* New York: Oxford Press.

Durkheim, E. (1933). *The division of labor in society.* New York: Macmillan.

Elias, N. (1982). *Power and civility.* New York: Pantheon.

Fischer, R. (1967). The biological fabric of time (pp. 440–488). In R. Fischer (Ed.), *Interdisciplinary perspectives of time.* New York: New York Academy of Sciences.

Fischer, W. F. (1970). *Theories of anxiety.* Evanston, IL: Harper & Row.

Folkman, S. (1984). Personal control and stress and coping processes: A theoretical analysis. *Journal of Personality and Social Psychology, 4,* 839–852.

Freud, S. (1964). An outline of psychoanalysis. In J. Strachey (Ed. and trans.), *The standard edition of the complete psychological works of Sigmund Freud* (pp. 81–111). Vol. 20. London: Hogarth.

Freund, P. E. S., & McGuire, M. B. (1991). *Health, illness and the social body: A critical sociology.* Englewood Cliffs, NJ: Prentice-Hall.

Friedman, M., & Rosenman, R. H. (1974). *Type A behavior and your heart.* New York: Knopf.

Friedman, W. J. (1990). *About time.* Cambridge, MA: MIT press.

Frijda, N. H. (1988). The laws of emotion. *American Psychologist, 43,* 349–358.

Geertz, C. (1973). *The interpretation of cultures.* New York: Basic Books.

Gibbon, J., & Allan, L. (Eds.). (1984). *Timing and time perception.* New York: New York Academy of Sciences.

Goldstone, S. (1967). The human clock: A framework for the study of healthy and deviant perception (pp. 767–783). In R. Fischer (Ed.), *Interdisciplinary perspectives of time.* New York: New York Academy of Sciences.

Gray, J. A. (1988). The neuropsychological basis of anxiety (pp. 10–37). In C. G. Last & M. Hersen (Eds.), *Handbook of anxiety disorders.* New York: Pergamon.

Heidegger, M. (1962). *Being and time.* J. Macquarrie & E. Robinson (trans.). London: SCM Press.

Hoffman, P. (1986). *Doubt, time, violence.* Chicago: University of Chicago Press.

Hughes, E. (1945). Dilemmas and contradictions of status. *American Journal of Sociology, 1,* 353–359.

James, W. (1928). *Pragmatism.* New York: Longmans, Green.

Jung, C. G. (1934/1965). The soul and death (pp. 3–15). In H. Feifel (Ed.), *The meaning of death.* New York: McGraw-Hill.

Kalaska, J. F., & Grammand, D. C. (1992). Cerebral mechanisms of reaching movements. *Science, 255,* 1517–1522.

Kelly, G. A. (1963). *A theory of personality: The psychology of personal constructs.* New York: Norton.

Kluckhohn, F. R., & Strodtbeck, F. L. (1961). *Variations in value orientations.* New York: Harper & Row.

Krauss, H. H. (1967). Anxiety: The dread of a future event. *Journal of Individual Psychology, 23,* 1, 88–93.

Krauss, H. H. (1990). Intra-psychic conflict: A conceptual review (pp. 19–48). In J. B. Gittler (Ed.), *The Annual Review of Conflict Knowledge and Conflict Resolution.* Vol. 2. New York: Garland Press.

Krauss, H., & Krauss, B. J. (1990). Existential approaches to depression (pp. 38–63). In B. B. Wolman & G. Stricker (Eds.), *Depressive disorders: Facts, theories, and treatment methods.* New York: Wiley.

Kristofferson, A. B. (1984). Quantal and determinate timing in human duration discrimination (pp. 3–15). In J. Gibbon & L. Allen (Eds.), *Timing and time perception.* New York: Annals of the New York Academy of Sciences.

Lang, P. J. (1977). Physiological assessment of anxiety and fear (pp. 178–195). In J. D. Cone & R. P. Hawkins (Eds.), *Behavioral assessment: New directions in clinical psychology.* New York: Brunner/Mazel.

Lazarus, R. S. (1991). *Emotion and adaptation.* New York: Oxford Press.

Lazarus, R. S., & Folkman, S. (1984). *Stress, appraisal and coping.* New York: Springer.

Lehmann, H. (1967). Time and psychopathology (pp. 798–821). In R. Fischer (Ed.), *Interdisciplinary perspectives of time.* New York: New York Academy of Sciences.

Lesser, I. M., Rubin, R. T., Pecknold, J. C., Rifkin, A., Swinson, R. P., Lydiard, R. B., Burrows, G. D., Noyes, R., & Dupont, R. L. (1988). Secondary depression in panic disorder. *Archives of General Psychiatry, 45,* 437–443.

Levine, R. V. (1990). The pace of life. *American Scientist, 78,* 450–459.

Lewin, K. (1943). Defining the field at a given time. *Psychological Review, 50,* 292–310.

Lilliston, B. A. (1985). Psychosocial responses to traumatic physical disability. *Social Work in Health Care, 10,* 4, 1–13.

Livingstone, M., & Hubel, D. (1988). Segregation of form, color, movement, and depth: Anatomy, physiology, and perception. *Science, 240,* 740–749.

MacLeod, C., Mathews, A., & Tata, P. (1986). Attentional biases in emotional disorders. *Journal of Abnormal Psychology, 95,* 15–20.

Mandler, G. (1984). *Mind and body: Psychology of emotion and stress.* New York: Norton.

Marcuse, H. (1955). *Eros and civilization: A philosophical inquiry into Freud.* New York: Vintage.

Mathews, A., & MacLeod, C. (1986). Discrimination of threat cues without awareness in anxiety states. *Journal of Abnormal Psychology, 95,* 131–138.

Maxwell, R. J. (1972). Anthropological perspectives (pp. 36–72). In H. Yaker, H. Osmond & F. Cheek (Eds.), *The future of time: Man's temporal environment.* Garden City, NY: Anchor.

May, R., Angel, E., & Ellenberger, H. F., (Eds.) (1958). *Existence.* New York: Basic Books.

McClelland, J. L. (1985). Distributed models of cognitive processes: Applications to learning and memory (pp. 1–9). In D. S. Olton, E. Gamzu, & S. Corkin (Eds.), *Memory dysfunctions.* New York: Annals of the New York Academy of Sciences.

Melges, F. T. (1990). Identity and temporal perspective (pp. 235–266). In R. A. Block (Ed.), *Cognitive models of psychological time.* Hillsdale, NJ: Lawrence Erlbaum.

Michon, J. A. (1990). Implicit and explicit representations of time (pp. 37–58). In R. A. Block (Ed.), *Cognitive models of psychological time.* Hillsdale, NJ: Lawrence Erlbaum Associates.

Mogg, K., Mathews, A., & Weinman, J. (1987). Memory bias in clinical anxiety. *Journal of Abnormal Psychology, 96,* 94–98.

Montanegro, J. (1985). The development of temporal inferences and meanings in 5- to 8-year-old children (pp. 278–284). In J. A. Michon & J. L. Jackson (Eds.), *Time, mind, and behavior.* New York: Springer-Verlag.

Nerenz, D. R., & Leventhal, H. (1983). Self-regulation theory in chronic illness. In T. G. Burish & L. A. Bradley (Eds.), *Coping with chronic disease: Research and applications.* New York: Academic Press.

Papillo, J. F., Murphy, P. M., & Gorman, J. M. (1988). Psychophysiology (pp. 217–250). In C. G. Last & M. Hersen (Eds.) *Handbook of anxiety disorders.* New York: Pergamon.

Piaget, J. (1966). Time perception in children. In J. Fraser (Ed.), *The voices of time.* New York: George Braziller.

Posner, M. (1989). *Foundations of cognitive science.* Cambridge, MA: MIT Press.

Poulet, G. (1956). *Studies in human time.* New York: Harper.

Rachman, S. (1987). Fear and courage. (pp. 256–258). In R. L. Gregory (Ed.), *The Oxford companion to the mind.* New York: Oxford Press.

Richter, C. P. (1960). Biological clocks in medicine and psychiatry: Shock phase hypothesis. *Proceedings of the National Academy of Sciences, 46,* 1506–1530.

Rowland, J. H. (1989). Developmental stages and adaptation: Adult model (pp. 25–43). In J. Holland & J. H. Rowland (Ed.), *Handbook of psychooncology.* New York: Oxford University Press.

Sanderson, W. C., DiNardo, P. A., Rapee, R. M., & Barlow, D. H. (1990). Syndrome comorbidity in patients diagnosed with DSM-III-R anxiety disorder. *Journal of Abnormal Psychology, 99,* 308–312.

Sarap, M. (1989). *An introductory guide to post-structuralism and postmodernism.* Athens, GA: University of Georgia Press.

Schneider, Joseph W., and Conrad, P. (1983). *Having epilepsy: The experience and control of illness.* Philadelphia: Temple University Press.

Schur, E. (1979). *Interpreting deviance.* New York: Harper & Row.

Sherover, C.H. (1971). *Heidegger, Kant, and time.* Bloomington, IN: Indiana University Press.

Siegel, K., & Christ, G. H. (1990). Hodgkin's disease survivorship: Psychosocial consequences (pp. 383–399). In M. J. Lacher & J. R. Redman (Eds.), *Hodgkin's disease: The consequences of survival.* Philadelphia: Lea and Febiger.

Siegel, K., & Krauss, B. (1991). Living with HIV infection: Adaptive tasks of seropositive gay men. *Journal of Health and Social Behavior, 32,* 1, 17–32.

Skinner, B. F. (1969). *Contingencies of reinforcement: A theoretical analysis.* New York: Appleton-Century-Crofts.

Solomon, P. R., Groccia-Ellison, M., Levine, E., Blanchard, S., & Pendlebury, W. W. (1991). Do temporal relationships in conditioning change across the life span? Perspectives from eyelid conditioning in humans and rabbits (pp. 212–238). In A. Diamond (Ed.), *The development and neural basis of higher cognitive functions.* New York: Annals of the New York Academy of Sciences.

Squire, L. R., & Zola-Morgan, S. (1991). Medial temporal lobe memory system. *Science, 253,* 1380–1386.

Stierlin, H. (1969). *Conflict and reconciliation: A study of human relations and schizophrenia.* New York: Anchor.

Triandis, H. C. (1990). Cross-cultural studies of individualism and collectivism (pp. 41–133). In J. J. Berman (Ed.), *Cross-cultural perspectives.* Lincoln, NE: Nebraska Symposium on Motivation, University of Nebraska Press.

Tulving, E. (1989). Remembering and knowing the past. *American Scientist, 77,* 4, 361–367.

Tulving, E. (1992, March). Personal communication.

Van Essen, D. C., Anderson, C. H., & Fellerman, D. J. (1992). Information processing in the primate visual system: An integrated system perspective. *Science, 255,* 419–423.

von Gebsattel, V. E. (1958). The world of the compulsive (pp. 170–187). In R. May, R. E. Angel, & H. F. Ellenberger (Eds.), *Existence.* New York: Basic Books.

Wallis, R. (1966). *Time: Fourth dimension of the mind.* New York: Harcourt, Brace and World.

Wilcox, D. J. (1987). *The measures of time past: Pre-Newtonian chronologies and the rhetoric of relative time.* Chicago: University of Chicago Press.

Wilder, A. (1968). *The language of the self.* Baltimore: Johns Hopkins University Press.

Wolman, B. B. (1992). *Personality dynamics.* New York: Plenum.

Yaker, H. M. (1972). Time in the Biblical and Greek worlds (pp. 15–35). In H. Yaker, H. Osmond, & F. Cheek (Eds.), *The future of time: Man's temporal environment.* Garden City, NY: Anchor.

Yarnold, P. R., & Grimm, L. G. (1982). Time urgency among coronary prone individuals. *Journal of Abnormal Psychology, 91,* 175–177.

Zakay, D. (1990). The evasive art of subjective time measurement: Some methodological dilemmas (pp. 59–84). In R. A. Block (Ed.), *Cognitive models of psychological time.* Hillsdale, NJ: Lawrence Erlbaum.

PART TWO

Symptomatology

CHAPTER 9

Phobias

CAROL LINDEMANN, PhD

Phobias are the most common emotional disorders known and have been recorded since the earliest writings, from the Old Testament and Hippocrates through the 17th-century diagnostician, Robert Burton, and continuing into current times.

Anxiety disorder is the most prevalent of all the major groups of mental disorders and within this group, phobias are the most common disorder. For phobias, one-month incidence (the likelihood of occurrence in a single individual during one month) is 6.2% and prevalence (the occurrence over the population at any given time) is 12.5%. Anxiety disorders are twice as common in women (9.7%) as in men (4.7%) (Regier et al., 1988). The median age of onset for phobias is 13 years of age (Burke, Burke, Regier, & Roe, 1990). Weissman and Merikangas (1986) found that over 9% of the population has had a least one panic attack, and 3% to 4% have had recurrent panic attacks.

The clinical definition of phobias includes:

1. An intense experience of fear occurring in a situation that is harmless.
2. Recognition that the fear is excessive for the actual threat; that it is irrational.
3. The reaction is automatic and pervasive; the person cannot voluntarily control the fear reaction.
4. The fear reaction includes symptoms such as rapid heart beat, shortness of breath, trembling, and an overwhelming desire to flee the situation.
5. The object or situation is actually avoided.

Not all of these features need be present to diagnose a phobia. For example, while avoidance of the phobic situation or object is a hallmark of phobias, a fearful flier who will still ride in an airplane when necessary, despite severe anxiety, might be classified as phobic. Conversely, a person who always avoids an airplane despite never actually experiencing panic in the phobic situation, or one who is not experiencing panic at the time of diagnosis, might still be phobic because of the prominence of avoidance.

Phobias are so common that often they are trivialized and may become a source of humor. Far from being trivial, this disorder causes significant disability in the population it afflicts. There is often a significant decrease in the quality of life, including an increase in emergency room visits, depression, suicide, and financial difficulties (Weissman & Merikangas, 1986). The risk for drug abuse disorder doubles in young adults who have had an earlier anxiety disorder, and alcoholism similarly increases (Christie et al., 1988; Regier et al., 1990).

The panic attack is often described by patients as "the most horrible feeling I have ever experienced." Unlike the memory of pain, people vividly recall every instant of the feeling of panic and can often reproduce the symptoms of anxiety merely by thinking about it. The intense unpleasantness of the experience is a strong deterrent to putting oneself in the same situation again, and if the likelihood is deemed high that future panics cannot be avoided, the person may become preoccupied with worry and fear. The content of the preoccupations may vary according to the individual's experience of panic; this includes such common examples as concerns about the disintegration of the physical self (dying, having a heart attack), the psychological self (going crazy, losing control), or the social self (humiliation).

The American Psychiatric Association Diagnostic and Statistical Manual (DSM-III-R, 1987) divides the phobias into three categories: agoraphobia, social phobia, and simple phobia. The phobias are categorized according to what triggers the fear, how the person reacts, and the thing feared. In agoraphobia, the panic attack may occur when the person is not in a phobic situation, whereas in social and simple phobias, the panic is specific to the situation. In agoraphobia, the person fears being in a situation in which he or she cannot escape to safety in the event of a panic attack. The agoraphobic thus typically either restricts travel far from home or travels only with a trusted companion. The social phobic fears and avoids situations in which he or she might be exposed to the scrutiny of others, such as public speaking. The simple phobias are specific discrete fears; often more than one fear is present. Common types include animal phobias, acrophobia, and claustrophobia. Despite the variety of triggers, all share the traits of panic or anxiety in the phobic situation; avoidance of the situation; and being unable to control the reaction despite awareness that the fear is excessive, unreasonable, or irrational. Although the validity of separating the phobias into these categories is controversial, the varieties of phobias will be discussed under these headings for convenience.

CLASSIFICATION OF PHOBIAS

Agoraphobia

Westphal is credited with coining the term, agoraphobia, describing in 1871 a symptom syndrome of feelings of impending doom, fear of dying, and anticipatory anxiety when walking in open spaces (Westphal, 1871). The greek word, *agora,* means marketplace, yet this term is misleading since an agoraphobic may be as fearful of a claustrophobic space as of a wide open space. Agoraphobia is, in fact, usually a syndrome of multiple phobias (Marks, 1987).

The concept of panic attack and spontaneous panic attack is crucial to the understanding of this diagnostic category. The panic attack, fully described elsewhere in this volume, is "hardwired" into all people as a survival tactic, and shared by all mammals as well. In phobias, the normal mechanism of panic is triggered at inappropriate times or to inappropriate objects. When the panic is triggered by a specific situation such as being in a high place, or seeing a snake, it is called "situational." In agoraphobia, however, the experience is of panics occurring while not in the presence of a phobic object, "spontaneous" panics. The phrase "spontaneous panic attack" alludes to the lack of an immediate environmental cause; the cause is sought rather in the person's physical and psychological internal environment. It does not mean that there is no cause, but, rather, implies an agnostic position as to the cause of the panic attack. Breier, Charney, and Heninger (1986) found that in 78% of agoraphobics, the first panic was a spontaneous panic attack and in only 22% was it situational. The defining feature of spontaneous panic attack in agoraphobia explains the multiple phobia picture so often seen. The disorder often begins with a single attack. While in other phobias, the attack occurs with an obvious environmental object that can then be avoided, for the agoraphobic, the attack may be unpredictable. Sufferers may then avoid any situation that is not familiar and protected, so that when the panic occurs, they will not be endangered or humiliated. In addition to the terror of the panic attack proper, the dread of future panic, called anticipatory anxiety, can be crippling, thus further inhibiting the person's activity. Since avoidance of phobic objects is insufficient to insure that panic will not occur, a state of generalized anxiety might follow.

Although agoraphobia is not the most common of phobias, it is the phobia for which people most frequently seek treatment. Agras, Sylvester, and Oliveau (1969) report that over half of people seeking treatment for anxiety disorders are agoraphobic. The extreme forms of limitation connected with agoraphobia can develop even if the person is no longer experiencing panic attacks because of the anticipatory dread, therefore a diagnostic distinction is made between agoraphobia with and without panic attacks. Thyer, Nesse, Cameron, and Curtis (1985) found a ratio of 83% agoraphobia with panic attacks and 17% agoraphobia without panic. Unlike social and simple phobias which are equally likely to occur in men as in women, Thorpe and Burns (1983) found that the ratio of women to men with agoraphobia is approximately 4 to 1.

Agoraphobics seem sicker than the general phobic population. Mavissakalian and Hamann (1986) found a personality disorder in over a quarter of agoraphobics, especially the dependent, avoidant, and histrionic personalities, just as might be expected. There is a high co-morbidity rate between the phobias, especially agoraphobia, and the affective disorders (Breier et al., 1986; Weissman & Merikangas, 1986). The relationship between depression and agoraphobia is a complex one since in some cases it seems to be a consequence of the panic attacks, while in some cases, the anxiety seems to be caused by the onset of the depression. Furthermore, some patients reported that they became depressed or "demoralized," only after the phobic restrictions began to curtail their activities. Most outcome studies have found an improvement in depression coinciding with improvement on agoraphobia (Michelson, Mavissakalian, & Marchione, 1985).

Mrs. A. sought treatment at 22 for agoraphobia with symptoms of panic attacks several times a day and an inability to leave home without her parents. She was an exceptionally pretty young woman who paid great attention to details of personal grooming and, due to her considerable charm, she prided herself on being liked by everyone. The content of the sessions was often about clothes and fashion, gossip about her friends, and talk of boyfriends, usually presented in a humorous fashion.

She first started having panic attacks at age 13, at the time of menarche. She avoided going to school, complaining of dizziness and stomachaches. Her family doctor gave her tranquilizers and suggested that she could stay home from school. In retrospect she sees this as a mistake and did not start to feel better until she went to summer camp and was engaged with friends and activities. Although she continued to have occasional panic attacks over the next few years, she was able to attend college, but upon returning home after graduation began to have massive and frequent panic attacks. She refused to leave the house unless accompanied by one of her parents. At this point, she sought treatment. Therapy consisted of behavioral and supportive psychotherapy once a week for a year and a half. After a few months of treatment and despite considerable anxiety, she found a job in the fashion industry. She felt relatively anxiety-free at home with her parents, and at work with her friends and, on a "good day," could walk around within a circumscribed area downtown. She soon met a young man whom she dated and was able to travel everywhere in his company. Although she continued to have occasional panic attacks, she also continued to achieve good symptom remission and we mutually agreed to terminate treatment.

Four years later, soon after her marriage, she returned to treatment for a recurrence of panic attacks and increasing difficulty leaving the house. She was terrified that she was having another "nervous breakdown." She dreaded the social ostracism she imagined if people knew she was "weird." She cried frequently, felt confused and depressed. She decided to try medication, the tricyclic antidepressant, imipramine. The panic attacks abated within a month with the help of medication and psychotherapy. She attributed the relapse to the life change that marriage entailed and fears about the expectation to be both an adult and a woman. Within a year, she started a new career in which she was very successful. Her mood improved as did her self-esteem.

Some 6 years later, she returned to therapy. She had a series of medical problems that required surgery and multiple hospitalizations and she had learned that she would not be able to bear children. Panic attacks had recurred and she had re-instituted a course of the same tricyclic antidepressant with which she had been treated successfully earlier. This time, however, the phobic restriction did not recur. She felt she had learned to control her anxiety experience, understood why it recurred at this point in her life, and would not give in to avoidance. Rather than fearing that she was "having a nervous breakdown," she felt she had a biological disorder that she would have to learn to cope with, if necessary, for life. At the same time, she felt she was psychologically fragile and continued in psychotherapy once weekly for two and a half more years. The psychodynamic issues dealt with were ambivalence concerning her femininity, excessive narcissistic need for admiration and love, and difficulties in expressing aggression.

This case illustrates several features of the course of agoraphobia in therapy. The disorder often begins with a single spontaneous panic attack, then there is a tendency for multiple attacks. During this period, there are increasing restrictions in activities that usually persist well after panic is no longer present. The course is fluctuating, with relative remission and resurgence. The occurrence of panic and possibly a series of multiple panic attacks may recur throughout the person's lifetime, especially at times of crisis, life change, or other sources of fragility (Marks, 1969). With proper treatment, however, the person can learn to handle the recurrent panic without again becoming agoraphobic.

Social Phobia

Social phobics fear being judged or evaluated. This may vary from avoidance of even being seen by others, to anxiety only about performing complicated tasks. Common social phobias are fear of public speaking, performance anxiety, and test anxiety. Other manifestations may include fear of eating or signing one's name in public and difficulty in urinating in a public bathroom.

The experience is of intense self-consciousness and embarrassment about oneself. The paradox facing many social phobics is that because of their intense social anxiety, they often bring upon themselves the kind of humiliation they fear most. The anxious performer is more likely to blush, or forget lines, and the person trembling with anticipatory anxiety is more likely to have shaking hands when he or she lifts a spoon or signs a check (Beck & Emery, 1985).

Although may social phobias are mild, they also can be very disabling, sometimes carrying with them an increased risk of depression, suicide, alcohol or drug abuse, and impaired physical health (Davidson, 1991).

> Mr. B. was a 34-year-old, unmarried Italian-American photographer. He gave the impression of a mild-mannered, unassertive man who was ill at ease with himself and his surroundings. A big grin covered his face regardless of its appropriateness to what was being said. He came to treatment because of a fear of choking that occurred primarily when he tried to swallow food, but which might also occur during anxiety attacks. The fear had started about 10 years before, when he had an anxiety attack accompanied by a tightening of the throat, and the fear that he could not swallow. He became increasingly frightened and ended up in the emergency room. He remembers this incident and the period in which it occurred as the nadir of his life. He had recently returned from living in California and was rejected both in his hunt to find employment and his fiancee. After this anxiety attack, he became increasingly dysfunctional and symptomatic. He rarely ate in restaurants or in front of others for fear of embarrassing himself with a choking attack. This concern led to painful social limitations, and the fear that he would never be able to marry.

The cognitive component of social phobias involves worry both over the public embarrassment and the private shame of not meeting the demands of the situation. Beck and Emery (1985) find cognitive distortions in the global judgments made: First any mis-step, regardless of how slight, proves to them that their entire performance is to be evaluated negatively; and second, a negative evaluation of a performance is generalized to the entire personhood. Turner and Beidel (1985) found that negative thoughts about the self and the performance were the hallmark of the socially anxious, regardless of whether there was a significant physiological arousal, such as trembling hands. As might be expected, those with social anxiety set unrealistically high standards (Alden & Cappe, 1981).

There is considerable overlap between social phobias and agoraphobia: Most agoraphobics have social phobia. However, the autonomic symptoms experienced by social phobic tend to be those that can be observed by others, such as blushing or trembling. Also, the situations feared by the social phobic tend to be interpersonal and the concern is being scrutinized by others. The agoraphobic is more concerned with situations of being alone or in which the retreat to safety is impeded (Amies, Gelder, & Shaw, 1983). The distinction drawn by Beck and Emery (1985) is that agoraphobics fear the internal disaster of a panic attack and social phobics fear embarrassment and shame.

Simple or Single Phobia

Simple phobias are by far the most common form of phobia. They are simple in the sense that they may consist of only a single, discrete feared object or situation, such as a specific animal or fear of flying, although several of such may co-exist. The defining features of a simple phobia are a reaction of anxiety and sometimes panic in the presence of the phobic stimulus, and an attempt to avoid it. The person recognizes that the fear is irrational, but cannot change the distressing reaction. Anticipatory anxiety is usually present, that is, the person becomes extremely anxious, and possibly panicky in anticipation of being unable to avoid the feared object. It is generally the case that the anticipatory anxiety is worse than the anxiety in the phobic situation itself. The diagnosis of simple phobia is made only if the person is not an agoraphobic or social phobic and, in that sense, it is the residual category of all other phobias.

Because the phobia is circumscribed, however, the simple phobic, unlike the agoraphobic, does not usually become preoccupied with the "fear of fear." When not in the presence of the feared object, or actively anticipating it, the simple phobic would not seem more anxious, depressed, or show higher neuroticism than a nonphobic (Agras et al., 1969).

Although the prevalence of simple phobias is 8% in the general population, only a small percentage seek treatment (Agras et al., 1969). The degree of impairment may be mild, especially if the feared situation is not encountered often, such as the form associated with open heights, or can be easily avoided, as is the case with most animal phobias. Very often the simple phobic learns to live with the specific restriction, but on occasion, they do constitute a significant disability and treatment is sought. This most often occurs when there is a change in life style that causes the restriction to become intolerable. For example, a young woman sought treatment for a lifelong fear of cats only after her marriage. She had married a man born on an island in Greece renowned for hundreds of freely roaming cats. A visit to her new husband's homeland was inconceivable to her, causing considerable friction in the relationship, until she had overcome the phobia.

Another common precipitant for seeking treatment is a particularly bad panic attack. For example, a man in his 50s who had a fear of thunderstorms dating back to age 7, sought treatment after he had a severe panic in his home during a thunderstorm.. He felt terrified, was crying and trembling, and tried to seek shelter under a couch. Afterwards, his reaction of humiliation and self-disgust at his performance led him to decide to deal with the phobia. In this case, he had recently suffered the death of a parent which may have precipitated a reaction more severe than usual. As with other forms of phobia, a separation or other stress can initiate or intensify an existing anxiety disorder (Roy-Bryne, Geraci, & Uhde, 1986).

In simple phobias, there is a strong component of maladaptive cognitions that maintain the phobic reaction. Forecasting disastrous consequence when one is in the phobic situation can increase the psychophysiological arousal. This physiological component of fear is a primary source of subjective discomfort, and in turn often causes the person to avoid or flee the phobic situation, even in the absence of panic.

In vivo exposure therapy seems to be the most effective treatment for the simple phobias. Gradual exposure to the feared object reduces the fear reaction.

ETIOLOGY

Despite the distinctions drawn between agoraphobia, social phobia, and simple phobia, the causes and treatment of the phobias can be discussed together.

The origin of phobias is multiply determined. There is considerable evidence of a familial trend in anxiety disorders, indicating both a genetic component and the role of early training (Turner, Beidel, & Costello, 1987). Some physiological disorders may predispose people to panic attacks, such as mitral valve prolapse and thyroid disorders (Lindemann, Zitrin, & Klein, 1984). Marks (1969) proposes a "preparedness theory," that the object or situation feared is one that is in nature dangerous and we are predisposed to a fear reaction, for example, to open places, heights, or snakes, and so on. Learning theory posits that phobias are learned through the highly negative experience of intense anxiety in confrontation with the object or situation. Cognitive theory holds that we are told in childhood that certain things are dangerous and learn to fear them, and further, we develop our own interior fearful dialogue. Traumatic origin (for example, a plane crash) can occasionally account for a phobia. Some of these major theories of origin and causes of phobias will be discussed in depth in other chapters of this volume.

Freud's initial theory of phobias was psychobiological, a result of thwarted libidinal discharge, however, it must be remembered that Freud revised his central theory of anxiety several times. In his 1909 case of Little Hans, he reformulated his position on phobias, and this case serves as a model for the psychoanalytic understanding and treatment of phobias. Little Hans had a fear of horses, and in his effort to avoid them he resisted going out on the street where horses and carriages were encountered. Freud helped Hans' father understand Hans' unconscious Oedipal fears and his defenses of denial of his forbidden wish and projection of the feared retribution for this wish onto the horse. The phobia is thus a symptom of an unconscious conflict. The anxiety of the conflict is experienced, but the source is shifted or displaced onto some harmless object that becomes its symbol. This displacement helps to keep the real source of anxiety from conscious awareness. The treatment implications of this position are that the symptoms of the phobia indicate that there are unresolved unconscious conflicts and the phobia will be given up after the real source of the anxiety is successfully addressed by the analyst and the patient.

The learning theories follow the conditioning model of the origin of phobias. Pavlov's (1927) classical conditioning model is: the dog is given food and salivates, the sound of the bell is presented a few seconds before the food, and the dog therefore becomes conditioned to salivate at the sound of the bell. The application of the classical conditioning model to phobias runs as follows: a panic attack occurs, for reasons unspecified, in the elevator. The person, on the basis of a "one-trial learning," becomes conditioned to have a fear response when in the elevator. Mowrer's (1939) two-factor theory of anxiety adds that leaving the situation is reinforced by the anxiety reduction experienced and thus the tendency to escape the phobic object is perpetuated. Although learning theory is not totally satisfactory in explaining the variety of theoretical issues in the development of phobias (Rachman & Seligman, 1976), nevertheless, the treatment of the disorder based on learning theory is generally rapid and effective.

The cognitive model of the origin of phobias makes significant contributions to the understanding of the catastrophic thoughts and irrational beliefs that occur in phobias. The catastrophic thoughts, for example, "I would die if I were stuck in a crowded elevator," serve to maintain the avoidance (Beck & Emery, 1985). Mis-attribution of common anxiety symptoms of physiological arousal, such as sweaty palms or increased heartbeat, can become erroneously conceived as of warnings of an incipient panic. The person might then avoid the phobic object, retreat from the object, or become so anxiously preoccupied with the physiological arousal that there is a rapid escalation to an actual panic attack (Goldstein & Chambless, 1978). Such patients may seek to avoid any arousal, including even intense pleasurable emotions. They may also develop an obsessional focus on the symptoms of anxiety, constantly checking on their current psychophysiological state for distress. Cognitive theorists also point out a deficit in problem-solving skills, as a result of phobic worry, the common experience of being so anxious you "can't think straight."

TREATMENT

With proper treatment, over 70% of phobia patients improve significantly or completely overcome their fears. Moreover, once a phobia is successfully overcome, over 66% of the patients will be free of symptoms for years if not for life (Zitrin et al., 1975). Conversely, left untreated, 42% of phobics do not improve over a four-year period, and under 10% will be symptom free (Marks, 1971). In 1964 before the new treatment techniques were developed, Roberts found that with standard psychotherapy interventions only 24% recovered.

Psychoanalytic Treatment and Related Schools

The psychoanalytically oriented treatment of phobias is derived from the theory of the origin of phobias just described. The purpose of psychoanalysis and psychoanalytic psychotherapy is not so much symptom relief as it is understanding unconscious meaning and increasing the patient's awareness. Thus, it is not the phobia itself that is directly treated, but the symptom that is seen as a symbol of underlying conflict. Further, the symptoms and anxiety are seen as a motivation for the patient to work in his treatment, and in this sense rapid symptom reduction would be counterproductive. Symptom change is a byproduct rather than a goal.

The current popular direct symptom reduction treatments of phobias differ from previous psychodynamic psychotherapies in several characteristics: The focus is on a particular diagnostic category rather than on a theory or technique, specific empirically developed techniques are used, and the goal is symptom relief rather than broader psychosocial goals.

There are several components to phobic anxiety, all of which must be addressed for effective and stable symptom remission: the avoidance of the phobic object, the panic attack itself, the fear of the symptoms of intense anxiety and their consequences ("fear of fear"), the anticipatory anxiety, and the generalized anxiety or hypervigilence.

Techniques currently accepted as the most effective for rapid symptom relief include exposure therapy, cognitive restructuring, medication, education, and breathe retraining and supportive psychotherapy, all of which will be briefly described.

Exposure Therapy

Current research indicates that the most crucial issue for change in phobias is exposure to the phobic situation, such as an elevator, until the anxiety that might be experienced subsides to tolerable levels. A panic attack is self-limiting, lasting only a few minutes at peak. The anxiety will gradually diminish over time, therefore, if the person stays in the situation long enough.

Exposure therapy is often preceded by *imaginal desensitization.* In this technique introduced by Wolpe (1958), the patient is first given a progressive muscle relaxation exercise (see Wilson, 1989, for a sample relaxation exercise). When the patient is relaxed, images of the things he fears are presented to him on a hierarchial scale, from the least fearsome to the most. If the patient can remain relaxed while contemplating the feared event, the next step of the hierarchy is presented. For maximum effectiveness, this hierarchy is then repeated in the situation itself (*in vivo*) where feasible.

Much of the behavioral research literature is concerned with discovering what elements of exposure are the most important for rapid and complete eradication of the anxiety response. Exposure *in vivo* is more effective than *in imagination,* and exposure with the therapist present is more effective than self-exposure, (although good results can often be obtained with self-exposure). Long periods of exposure are better than shorter ones, but it is of primary importance that the anxiety be allowed to subside before the patient leaves the situation. Returning to the situation several times is better than only one exposure. Periodic re-exposure is necessary; for example, someone who has overcome a fear of flying must continue to fly.

As mentioned, learning theory is not perfect in explaining why exposure therapy works. One unexplained paradox is that if the phobia began with a traumatic exposure to the phobic object, why would repeated exposure be ameliorative. Obviously, some new element must intervene as a corrective experience, and this is the contribution of the cognitive therapists.

Cognitive Restructuring

Cognitive therapy is an *anxiety coping skill,* that is, it helps the patient to control anxiety in the phobic situation. Like relaxation therapy, it can have a direct impact in lowering physiological arousal and thus it facilitates the person's facing the phobic object with reduced anxiety.

The cognitive aspects of the panic attacks are a set of automatic negative thoughts, such as "what if I panic," "I can't do that," "I have to get out of here," "I'm having a heart attack." Taking the example of the elevator phobic, to say, "I will surely panic if I am stuck in an elevator" is more likely to induce anxiety in a person than to say, "I can cope with whatever emerges." The anxiety-provoking thoughts predict catastrophes that are extremely unlikely, and seriously overestimate the probability of panic. The therapist discusses the irrational nature of these thoughts and points out that they actually increase the anxiety rather than protecting the patient from the eventualities they fear.

Psychodynamic therapists see cognitive therapy as the behaviorists way out of the "black box"; it allows behaviorists to deal with mental content as well as observable behavior. The role of irrational thoughts in the development and maintenance of phobias is crucial to psychoanalytic theory as well, since the point of bringing unconscious fantasy to awareness is so that the fantasy can be evaluated as irrational or irrelevant to the current reality. However, the more direct approach of the cognitive therapists is considerably faster. Further, the cognitive therapists have developed a variety of techniques to deter these thoughts, once the patient is convinced they are maladaptive (See for example, Beck & Emery, 1985; Meichenbaum, 1977).

Psychotropic Medication

Panic attacks are a measurable psychophysiological event and the treatment of anxiety disorders is firmly grounded in psychobiology and the use of psychotropic medication. The first major breakthrough in the psychopharmacological treatment of phobias was the effective use of the tricyclic antidepressant imipramine (Tofranil) (Klein & Fink, 1962). Imipramine was found to block panic attacks, facilitating the phobic's confrontation of the phobic object. However, many phobics continue avoidance because of high levels of anticipatory anxiety. The medication most frequently found to be useful for anticipatory anxiety is the benzodiazepine group. A common treatment protocol is to treat the panic attacks with antidepressant medication and to treat any residual avoidance with minor tranquilizers and desensitization (Klein, 1964). The antidepressants (tricyclics, mao inhibitors, tetracyclics, and serotonin reuptake blockers) are more effective in blocking nonsituational panic attacks, than in those panics of the simple phobics, and thus are more commonly used with panic disorder and agoraphobic patients. For social phobics, beta blockers are frequently employed to block the symptoms of tremor, rapid heartbeat, weakness in the knees, and so on, that may cause the social phobic embarrassment and avoidance of the situation.

Alcohol is the most common self-medication, for example, having a drink to ease anxiety in social situations. Thus, it is not surprising that co-morbidity of alcoholism and phobias is high (Regier et al., 1990).

Psychoeducation

Most programs begin with some instructional material. The value is especially great for the confused and frightened patient, who may fear that the phobia is far more serious a disorder than it is ("I am losing my mind"). It is explained to the patient that anxiety and panic are a natural reaction to threat; they are of survival value. They are not inherently dangerous or harmful. It is emphasized that phobias are extremely common and that the prognosis is excellent. Space does not allow a thorough discussion of the subject, but excellent sources are found in Rapee, Craske, and Barlow (1989) for the therapist, and Weekes (1968) for the patient.

Breathe Retraining

It is very common for anxiety disorder patients to hyperventilate when they become anxious, thus exacerbating the problem. If hyperventilation continues, sufficient carbon dioxide may be blown off to bring on alkalosis which in turn can lead to tingling or numbness in the fingers and other extremities, lightheadedness, dizziness, and feelings of unreality. These highly unpleasant sensations in turn increase the patient's experience of anxiety and the interaction continues to spiral toward a panic attack. Readily detectable signs of hyperventilation in the office might be sighing, periodic deep breaths, rapid speech with gasping, and so forth.

Several cases had significant symptom remission attributable solely to changing the breathing pattern, for example:

> Ms. A. came to treatment for performance anxiety which was impairing her ability to work. She was an opera singer, but her primary income was derived from teaching voice. Recently, she started to have anxiety attacks while teaching. She was considering giving up her job which would mean not only a loss of income, but also a loss of considerable satisfaction in her life. As she described her work, and the excitement she experienced in teaching, I could easily discern that she took gasps of breath before running on in long-phrased sentences. I pointed this out to her. She was unaware of the breathing pattern, despite teaching breathing techniques herself in voice class. I suggested to her that she merely pay attention to her breathing while teaching. This led to immediate improvement. I further suggested that when she started to feel dizzy, and the symptoms of impending panic, she try to notice if she was overbreathing, and if so, she take a few deep breaths. This further helped to re-enforce the change in the breathing pattern, and was sufficient for her to continue teaching without further experiences of dizziness, lightheadedness, and anxiety.

This very elementary intervention can be as simple as suggesting the patient take three deep breathes (preferred to breathing into a paper bag), to more extensive retraining techniques (Weiss, 1989).

Supportive Therapy

With the exception of exposure, all of the techniques mentioned above, cognitive therapy, medication, training in anxiety coping skills, and so on, are supportive techniques. Support is needed to bolster ego strength while the patient is exposing himself or herself to phobic objects. Simultaneous focus on painful psychodynamic material, unconscious conflict, and separation from important objects may be counterproductive during this phase, although research to study this effect has not yet been designed. However, after symptom remission, without the debilitating effect of the phobia, a decrease in dysphoria associated with the disorder and an increase in pleasure in everyday activity, in self-confidence and self-esteem, are often seen. The shift may also lead to increase in productive activity, both in terms of fulfilling everyday obligations and in pursuing plans and goals that were impossible to carry out during the period of symptomatic restrictions. The most propitious time to deal with psychodynamic issues and character change may thus be after symptom change rather than at the beginning of treatment. (Lindemann, 1992). Not only is the patient then feeling more confident in his or her own ability to cope and to change, but also more confident in the therapist's ability to be an effective facilitator for change.

SUMMARY

Phobias are a common disorder that can vary from a mild annoyance to a severe disability. They are defined by a severe anxiety reaction that is disproportionate to the actual threat. The phobic avoids the phobic object despite awareness that the reaction is irrational. Phobias are divided into three categories: agoraphobia, social phobia, and simple phobia, according to the situation feared and to the anxiety reaction experienced. The theoretical understanding of the origin and development of the phobia results in treatment techniques that can be effective in over 70% of patients suffering from phobic disorder.

REFERENCES

Agras, W. S., Sylvester, D., & Oliveau, D. C. (1969). The epidemiology of common fears and phobias. *Comprehensive Psychiatry, 10,* 151–156.

Alden, L., & Cappe, R. (1981). Nonassertiveness: Skill deficit or self-evaluation? *Behavior Therapy, 12,* 107–114.

American Psychiatric Association, Committee on Nomenclature and Statistics (1987). *Diagnostic and Statistical Manual of Mental Disorders* (3rd ed. rev.). Washington, DC: Author.

Amies, P. L. Gelder, M. G., & Shaw, P. M. (1983). Social phobia: A comparative clinical study. *British Journal of Psychiatry, 142,* 174–179.

Beck, A. T., & Emery, G. (1985). *Anxiety disorders and phobias: A cognitive perspective.* New York: Basic Books.

Breier, A., Charney, D. S., & Heninger, G. R. (1986). Agoraphobia with panic attacks: Development, diagnostic stability and course of illness. *Archives of General Psychiatry, 43,* 1029–1036.

Burke, Kimberly C., Burke, Jack D., Regier, Darrel A., & Roe, Donald S. (1990). Age of onset of selected mental disorders in five community populations. *Archives of General Psychiatry, 47,* 511–518.

Christie, Kimberly A., Burke, Jack D., Regier, Darrel A., Rae, Donald S., Boyd, Jeffrey H., & Locke, Ben Z. (1988). Epidemiologic evidence for early onset of mental disorders and higher risk of drug abuse in young adults. *American Journal of Psychiatry, 145,* 971–975.

Davidson, Jonathan R. T. (1991). Introduction: Social phobia in review. *Journal of Clinical Psychiatry, 52* (Suppl.), 3–4.

Freud, S. (1909). Analysis of a phobia in a five-year-old boy. In *The standard edition.* Vol. 10 (pp. 5–149). London: Hogarth Press.

Goldstein, Alan J., & Chambless, Dianne L. (1978). A reanalysis of agoraphobia. *Behavior Therapy, 9,* 47–59.

Klein, Donald F. (1964). Delineation of two drug-responsive anxiety syndromes. *Psychoparmacologia, 53,* 397–408.

Klein, D. F., & Fink, M. (1962). Psychiatric reaction patterns to imipramine. *American Journal of Psychiatry, 119,* 432–438.

Lindemann, Carol (1992). Change in the expression of aggression following symptom reduction in phobias. Paper presented at the Anxiety Disorder Association of America National Conference, Houston, Texas.

Lindemann, Carol, Zitrin, C. M., & Klein, D. F. (1984). Thyroid dysfunction in phobia patients. *Psychosomatics, 25,* 603–606.

Marks, I. M. (1969). *Fears and phobias.* New York: Academic Press.

Marks, I. M. (1971). Phobic disorders four years after treatment: A prospective follow-up. *British Journal of Psychiatry, 118,* 683–686.

Marks, I. M. (1987). *Fears, phobias and rituals: Panic anxiety and their disorders.* New York: Oxford University Press, Inc.

Mavissakalian, M., and Hamann, M. S. (1986). DSM-III personality disorder in agoraphobia. *Comprehensive Psychiatry, 27,* 471–479.

Meichenbaum, D. T. (1977). *Cognitive behavior modification.* New York: Plenum Press.

Michelson, L., Mavissakalian, M., & Marchione, K. (1985). Cognitive-behavioral treatments of agoraphobia. Clinical, behavioral and psychophysiological outcome. *Journal of Consulting and Clinical Psychology, 53,* 913–925.

Mowrer, O. H. (1939). Stimulus response theory of anxiety. *Psychological Review, 46,* 553–565.

Pavlov, I. P. (1927). *Conditioned reflexes.* London: Oxford University Press.

Rachman, S., & Seligman, M. (1976). Unprepared phobias: Be prepared. *Behaviour Research and Therapy, 14,* 333–338.

Rapee, Ronald M., Craske, Michelle, & Barlow, David H. (1989). Psychoeducation (pp. 225–236). In C. Lindemann (Ed.), *Handbook of phobia therapy: Rapid symptom relief in anxiety disorders.* Northvale, NJ: Jason Aronson.

Regier, Darrel A., Boyd, Jeffrey H., Burke, Jack D., Rae, Donald S., Myers, Jerome K., Kramer, Morton, Robins, Lee N., George, Linda K., Karno, Marvin, & Locke, Ben, Z. (1988). One month prevalence of mental disorders in the United States: Based on five edidemiologic catchment area sites. *Archives of General Psychiatry, 45,* 977–986.

Regier, Darrel A., Farmer, Mary E., Rae, Donald S., Locke, Ben Z. Keith, Samuel J., Judd, Lewis L., & Goodwin, Fredrick K. (1990). Comorbidity of mental disorders with alcohol and other drug abuse: Results from the epidemiologic catchment area (ECA) study. *JAMA, 264,* 2511–2518.

Roberts, A. H. (1964). Housebound housewives: A follow-up study of phobic anxiety states. *British Journal of Psychiatry, 110,* 191–197.

Roy-Byrne, P. P., Geraci, M., & Uhde, T. W. (1986). Life events and the onset of panic disorder. *American Journal of Psychiatry, 143,* 1424–1427.

Thorpe, G. K., & Burns, L. E. (1983). *The Agoraphobia Syndrome.* New York: Wiley.

Thyer, B. A., Nesse, R. M., Cameron, O. G., & Curtis, G. C. (1985). Agoraphobia: A test of the separation anxiety hypothesis. *Bèhaviour Research and Therapy, 23,* 75–78.

Turner, S. M., & Beidel, D. C. (1985). Empirically derived subtypes of social anxiety. *Behavior Therapy, 16,* 384–392.

Turner, S. M., Beidel, D. C., & Costello, A. (1987). Psychopathology in the offspring of anxiety disorder patients. *Journal of Consulting and Clinical Psychology, 55,* 229–235.

Weekes, Claire (1968). *Hope and help for your nerves.* New York: Hawthorne.

Weiss, J. H. (1989). Breathing control. In C. Lindemann (Ed.), *Handbook of phobia therapy: Rapid symptom relief in anxiety disorders.* Northvale, NJ: Jason Aronson.

Weissman, Myrna M., & Merikangas, Kathleen R. (1986). The epidemiology of anxiety and panic disorders: An update. *Journal of Clinical Psychiatry, 47,* (Suppl.), 11–17.

Westphal, C. (1871). Agraphobia: A Neuropathological description. *Archives of Psychiatry and Neurology, 3,* 384–412.

Wilson, Reid. (1989). Imaginal Desensitization (pp. 271–296). In C. Lindemann (Ed.) *Handbook of phobia therapy: Rapid symptom relief in anxiety disorders.* Northvale, NJ: Jason Aronson.

Wolpe, J. (1958). *Psychotherapy by reciprocal inhibition.* Stanford: Stanford University Press.

Zitrin, C. M., Klein, D. F., Lindemann, C., Rock, M., Tobak, P., Kaplan, J. H., & Ganz, V. H. (1975). Comparison of short-term treatment regimens in phobic patients: A preliminary report. In R. L. Spitzer & D. F. Klein (Eds.), *Evaluation of Psychological Therapies.* Baltimore: The Johns Hopkins Press.

CHAPTER 10

Obsessive-Compulsive Disorder

ELIZABETH A. HEMBREE, PhD, EDNA B. FOA, PhD, and
MICHAEL J. KOZAK, PhD

In this chapter, the DSM-III-R diagnostic criteria for obsessive-compulsive disorder are reviewed, and difficulties that can arise in the application of these criteria are considered. Specifically, we discuss: (1) the functional relationship between obsessions and compulsions, (2) whether neutralizing thoughts are obsessions or compulsions, and (3) the extent to which obsessive-compulsives recognize their obsessive fears as senseless. In addition, issues of comorbidity and differential diagnoses are reviewed. Specifically, we consider the relationship of obsessive-compulsive disorder to depression, simple phobia and generalized anxiety disorder, delusional disorder, hypochondriasis, obsessive-compulsive personality disorder, tic disorder, and impulse control disorders. Three case examples are included to illustrate the symptoms of OCD.

The symptoms that characterize the obsessive-compulsive disorder (OCD) have been described in the psychiatric literature for over a century. This unique condition has been known as religious melancholy (Maudsley, 1895), folie de doute (Janet, 1903), obsessional neurosis (Freud, 1909), and recently, obsessive-compulsive disorder (American Psychiatric Association, 1980). Once considered a rare disorder, the lifetime prevalence of OCD was recently estimated to be as high as 2% to 3% (National Epidemiology Catchment Area Survey; Robins et al., 1984). Even those who speculated that the methodology of the ECA survey led to inflated prevalence rates for some disorders have estimated the prevalence of OCD to be at least 1 to 2% (Rasmussen & Eisen, 1989).

According to the current Diagnostic and Statistical Manual of Mental Disorders (3rd ed.-rev.) (DSM-III-R; APA, 1987), the essential features

---

Although they represent actual cases, certain details and information were modified in the three patient descriptions presented in this chapter in the interests of patient confidentiality.

of OCD are "recurrent obsessions or compulsions sufficiently severe to cause marked distress, be time-consuming, or significantly interfere with the person's normal routine, occupational functioning, or usual social activities or relationships with others" (p. 245). Descriptions of two representative cases follow.

Case 1

Alex is a 26-year-old white, married male with one child. He presented for treatment with extensive checking compulsions which he performed in order to prevent catastrophic events. When driving, he was obsessed with the idea that he might run over a pedestrian. In order to ensure that he had not done so, he constantly checked his rearview mirror so that he was unmindful of the traffic in front of his car, resulting in a car collision. In addition, he frequently retraced his route to further ensure that he had not hit anyone. Other obsessions concerned catastrophes that could befall his family due to his negligence. He repeatedly checked at home that appliances were off and/or unplugged, faucets were turned off firmly, and doors and windows were locked. When a criminal's physical description matched his own appearance, Alex was consumed with obsessive fear that he would be blamed for committing the crime.

Alex recalled performing rituals as early as age 10 or 11 that over the years became increasingly disruptive. At the time of clinical presentation, his checking rituals were taking up to 4 or 5 hours per day. As a result of his checking, Alex was often late, and he avoided many situations that triggered the rituals: unnecessary driving, paying bills, leaving his home, and using the stove or oven. His OC symptoms disrupted his relationship with his wife and severely impaired his performance at work.

Case 2

Cindy is a 30-year-old, white, divorced woman with 3 children. Beginning in her early childhood, she developed obsessive fear of vomiting. She spent several hours each day cleaning herself and objects in her home in order to "kill germs" that might cause illness. In order to decrease exposure to germs, Cindy also avoided crowded places (especially where young children were present), doctors offices, hospitals, and other places she thought there might be sick people. She insisted that her children engage in the same washing and avoidance behavior to prevent them from becoming ill and passing the illness to her. Cindy also attempted to prevent illness and vomiting with "magical" thinking and rituals. For example, in her mind, the particular arrangement of her furniture was associated with good health in the family. Therefore, no one was permitted to move any furniture from its designated place. She also recited ritualistic set prayers each day to ensure her health.

Cindy traced the onset of her obsessive compulsive symptoms to age 5, after she had witnessed her sister vomit a large quantity of blood. Her concerns about illness and germs began shortly afterwards, and led to excessive handwashing as well as frequent refusal to attend school.

CURRENT CRITERIA FOR OBSESSIVE-COMPULSIVE DISORDER (OCD): A CRITICAL VIEW

Obsessions are defined in the DSM-III-R (APA, 1987) as repeated ideas, thoughts, impulses, or images that the person experiences as intrusive and senseless, and attempts to ignore, suppress, or neutralize with some other thought or action. Rasmussen and Tsuang (1986) and Rasmussen and Eisen (1989) reported that the most common obsessions, in descending order of prevalence, were contamination (e.g., becoming infected or spreading infection by shaking hands); aggression (e.g., having an impulse to attack or kill another person); pathologic doubt (e.g., repeatedly wondering whether one has performed some act such as turning off appliances or having left the door unlocked); somatic (e.g., worrying about the possibility of having a disease such as AIDs); need for having things in a particular order or arrangement (e.g., intense distress when objects are disordered or asymmetrical); and sexual (e.g., having an unwanted impulse to sexually assault another person).

Compulsions are defined as repetitive, purposeful, and intentional behaviors that the person feels driven to perform. They are usually carried out in response to an obsession or according to idiosyncratic rules and are intended to reduce or avert discomfort or some terrible event or predicament. However, either the behavior is not realistically related to its aim or the frequency of the behavior is excessive.

For example, individuals with obsessions about being contaminated by urine or feces often feel driven to wash their hands and shower excessively; individuals with obsessions about doubting their performance as in locking doors or windows may be driven to check locks repeatedly. Examples of other common compulsions include counting, repeating actions, requesting reassurances, ordering and arranging objects, and hoarding (Rasmussen & Tsuang, 1986; Rasmussen & Eisen, 1989).

Foa and Kozak (1991) noted that the DSM diagnostic criteria for OCD have been influenced by several traditional concepts—some explicitly stated, some tacit. These include the ideas that (1) obsessions elicit subjective feelings of distress or anxiety; (2) obsessions and compulsions can be either functionally related or independent of one another; (3) obsessions are cognitive events (e.g., thoughts, ideas, images) while compulsions are overt behaviors (e.g., washing, checking); and (4) individuals with OCD recognize that their OC symptoms are senseless. Recent findings have suggested that some of these traditional views may require reevaluation.

Obsessions and Compulsions: Nature and Relationship

The first three issues are interrelated in that they are all concerned with the definition and function of obsessions and compulsions. The

DSM-III-R reflects the view that obsessions are mental events and tacitly implies that they induce distress. One may surmise from the criteria that obsessions arouse discomfort because the person seeks to "ignore, suppress, or neutralize" them (DSM-III-R; p. 247). Compulsions are overt behaviors that are intentional and purposeful. In addition, compulsive behavior is clearly described as reducing obsession-related discomfort, indirectly suggesting that obsessions cause discomfort. Clarification of these issues is critical in that they bear on treatment strategies as well as diagnostic considerations.

The view that there is an anxiety-related functional relationship between obsessions and compulsions was proposed by Hodgson and Rachman (1972), and reiterated by Foa and colleagues (Foa, Steketee, & Ozarow, 1985; Kozak, Foa, & McCarthy, 1988). Empirical support for the notion that obsessions induce anxiety is found in studies showing that ruminative thoughts elicit greater heart rate elevation and skin conductance than do neutral thoughts (Boulougouris, Rabavilas, & Stefanis, 1977; Rabavilas & Boulougouris, 1974). In other studies, both in-vivo and imaginal exposure to contaminants elicited increased heart rate, self-reported anxiety (Hodgson & Rachman, 1972; Kozak, Foa, & Steketee, 1988), and skin conductance responding (Hornsveld, Kraaimaat, & van Dam-Baggen, 1979).

Studies of OC patients have also demonstrated that compulsive behavior serves the function of reducing anxiety. Hodgson and Rachman (1972), reported that the act of washing after exposure to contamination resulted in decreased heart rate and self-reported discomfort. Comparable findings have been reported with the performance of checking rituals (Carr, 1971; Roper & Rachman, 1976; Roper, Rachman, & Hodgson, 1973).

These data are consistent with the DSM-III-R criteria that imply a dynamic functional relationship between obsessions and compulsions. However, this appears to conflict with the concurrent idea presented in the DSM that compulsions may be independent of obsessions (i.e., "compulsions are . . . behaviors that are performed in response to an obsession *or* according to certain rules or in a stereotyped fashion" [italics ours] (p. 247).

Neutralizing Thoughts: Obsessions or Compulsions?

As noted, in the DSM-III-R, obsessions are described as mental events (e.g., thoughts, ideas, images) while compulsions are overt, observable behaviors (e.g., washing, checking, repeating actions). At the same time, the criteria for obsessions imply the existence of two types of mental events: unwanted, intrusive obsessions that the person attempts to ignore or suppress, and mental events that serve to neutralize the intrusive thoughts. This ambiguity is represented in obsession criterion A2: "the person attempts to ignore or suppress such thoughts or impulses or to neutralize them with some other *thought* or action" [italics ours] (p. 247). Thus some mental events seem to function as overt compulsions and can be referred to as cognitive rituals. However, in the description of compulsions, there is no mention of cognitive rituals nor of the idea that thoughts can reduce or prevent distress.

Clinical observations suggest that individuals with OCD frequently report having cognitive compulsions, either alone or with ritualistic actions. Common cognitive rituals include silent praying, counting or repeating certain words or phrases to oneself, and mental reviewing of past events or conversations. For example, a person who has the obsessive fear that thinking "unclean" thoughts will lead to terrible consequences (e.g., acting on aggressive impulses, selling one's soul to the devil) may neutralize such thoughts by mentally reciting set prayers or thinking "good" thoughts. A person who fears that the number 9 is unlucky may silently repeat the "lucky number" 4 to counteract the anxiety associated with seeing the number 9.

A DSM-IV workgroup has endeavored to clarify issues related to the OCD diagnostic criteria and the definition and diversity of component symptoms. In a multi-site field trial, involving structured interviews conducted at several OCD clinics, the extent to which obsessive-compulsives reported having cognitive compulsions was investigated. The results indicated the presence of mental compulsions in the majority of obsessive-compulsives: about 79% of the sample reported having both behavioral and mental compulsions (Foa & Kozak, 1992).

Clarification of the DSM criteria may lead clinicians to increased awareness of cognitive rituals and to more accurate diagnoses. It is possible that some individuals who are considered "pure obsessionals" (i.e., those who manifest only obsessions in the absence of overt compulsions) may actually counter their obsessional distress with cognitive rituals, and therefore should not be considered purely obsessional.

Do Obsessive-Compulsives Recognize Their Symptoms as Senseless?

Another view that influenced the DSM-III-R diagnostic criteria for OCD is that obsessive-compulsive individuals maintain insight and recognize the senselessness of their obsessions and compulsions. In some of the early reports of the disorder (Westphal, 1878), the thinking of obsessive-compulsives was described as irrational or insane. However, Janet (1908) noted that obsessions were experienced as foreign to the personality and absurd. The latter view has clearly influenced successive DSM descriptions of OCD, despite reports that some obsessive-compulsives do not recognize that their symptoms are senseless or unreasonable (Foa, 1979; Insel & Akiskal, 1986; Lelliott, Noshirvani, Basoglu, Marks, & Monteiro, 1988).

Insel and Akiskal (1986) and Lelliott et al. (1988) have suggested that the strength of the patient's belief in the senselessness of obsessive-compulsive symptoms may represent a continuum. Some sufferers readily admit that their symptoms are completely irrational; some are not convinced that their obsessions and/or compulsions are senseless. At the extreme end of the continuum are those who are convinced that their OCD symptoms are entirely sensible. Insel and Akiskal suggested that these individuals might best be described as having an "obsessive compulsive psychosis."

Commonly, the person's recognition of the senselessness of his or her symptoms varies across times and situations. For example, the person may recognize a compulsion to wash his or her hands 30 times as senseless when discussing it in a "safe situation" (e.g., the therapist's office), but not when distressed by an obsession or exposed to a contaminant. According to the DSM-III-R, recognition that the obsessions or compulsions are unreasonable is usually accompanied by a desire to resist (i.e., ignore, disregard, not engage in) them. Conversely, when the person does not demonstrate such recognition, there may be little or no resistance.

The question of whether obsessive-compulsives recognize the senselessness of their obsessive fears was explored in the DSM-IV field trial on obsessive-compulsive disorder. The results converged with the findings of the literature reviewed above: strength of belief in feared harm was broadly distributed in the OCD sample (Foa & Kozak, 1992). Among obsessive-compulsives concerned with disastrous consequences if they did not perform rituals, only 13% were completely convinced that their fear was senseless; at the other extreme, 4% firmly believed that some harm would ensue if they did not perform rituals. The remainder of the sample reported intermediate degrees of certainty about the senselessness of their fears.

ONSET, COURSE, AND FAMILIAL PATTERN OF OCD

Most studies find that slightly more than half of those suffering from OCD are female (Rasmussen & Tsuang, 1986). The average age of onset of the disorder ranges from late adolescence to early twenties, although it typically occurs earlier in males than females. In a sample of 250 OC patients, Rasmussen and Eisen (1990) reported that peak age of onset for males was 13 to 15 years (around puberty) and for females it was 20 to 24 years. The onset of obsessive-compulsive disorder is typically gradual and insidious, but acute onset has been reported in some cases. For many

OCD sufferers, over seven years lapse between age of onset of significant symptoms and age of first presentation for psychiatric treatment (Rasmussen & Tsuang, 1986). Frequently, OCD patients endure many years of substantial impairment in social and occupational functioning before seeking treatment.

The clinical course of OCD is most often chronic with waxing and waning symptom severity. Episodic and deteriorating courses have been observed in 2% and 10% of patients, respectively (Rasmussen & Eisen, 1989). Those with a deteriorating course were noted to have given up resisting OC symptoms and to manifest severe anxiety that did not habituate with flooding techniques.

Impairment due to OCD can be severe in both occupational and interpersonal spheres. Marital distress is common (Emmelkamp, de Haan, & Hoogduin, 1990), although it has been shown to improve following behavioral treatment for OCD (Riggs, Hiss, & Foa, 1991).

Genetic contributions to OCD have been evidenced by higher concordance of the disorder in monozygotic twins than in dizygotic twins, and by a high incidence of OCD in first degree relatives of individuals with the disorder (Pauls, Raymond, Hurst, et al., 1988; Swedo, Rapoport, Leonard, Lenane, & Cheslow, 1989). Rasmussen and Tsuang (1984) reviewed several studies and reported that of a total of 51 monozygotic twin pairs in which at least one twin had OCD, 63% were concordant for obsessive-compulsive symptoms. A study by Pauls et al. (1988), conducted with 100 OCD patients, indicated that up to 25% of first degree family members of OCD probands also manifested the disorder. An additional 17% had OC symptoms or features, but did not meet criteria for the disorder.

COMORBIDITY AND DIFFERENTIAL DIAGNOSIS

As frequently reported (Karno, Golding, Sorensen, & Burnam, 1988; Rasmussen & Tsuang, 1986; Tynes, White, & Steketee, 1990), OCD commonly co-occurs with other symptoms and complaints. Depression, anxiety, phobic avoidance, and excessive worry are common, making differential diagnosis an important and often difficult process.

Depression

Numerous investigators have reported a clear association between depression and OCD (Foa, Steketee, Kozak, & Dugger, 1987; Karno et al., 1988). Rasmussen and Eisen (1989) reported that almost 70% of patients with OCD have a lifetime history of major depression. In their reported sample of 100 OC patients, 30% had a coexisting major depression upon admission, which was usually viewed as secondary to the interference of OCD symptoms in patients' lives. Based on the ECA study, Karno et al. (1988) reported that onset of OCD frequently precedes that of depression, and that about 30% of individuals with OCD met criteria for major depressive episode. Rasmussen and Tsuang (1986) found that 80% of their sample of 44 OCD patients evidenced symptoms of depression, and that three-fourths of these were secondary to OCD.

The presence of depressive disorders with OCD is important in that such co-occurrence may have implications for treatment. Some studies have suggested that a severe depression may interfere with the efficacy of behavioral treatment of OCD (Foa, 1979; Foa, Grayson, Steketee, & Doppelt, 1983).

The co-occurrence of depression in OCD points the question of how to distinguish depression-induced rumination from the obsessions of OCD. Rumination about unpleasant life circumstances or problems is common and is considered a mood congruent aspect of depression rather than an obsession. Also, unlike the obsessions of OCD, this type of brooding is characterized neither by attempts to ignore or suppress the distressing thoughts nor by excessive anxiety (Rasmussen & Eisen, 1989).

Anxiety Disorders

The coincidence of obsessive-compulsive disorder with other anxiety disorders is high. Rasmussen and Tsuang (1986) reported that in a sample of 44 OC patients, lifetime incidence of simple phobia was 27%, social phobia was 18%, separation anxiety disorder was 18%, panic disorder was 14%, and agoraphobia was 9%. Using a sample of 468 individuals with a lifetime diagnosis of OCD, Karno et al. (1988) found that the co-occurrence of OCD and panic disorder was 13.8% and that of OCD and phobia was 46.5%.

The high rate of comorbidity with other anxiety disorders and anxiety symptoms can present diagnostic challenges. For example, generalized anxiety disorder (GAD) is characterized by excessive worry. Such worries are distinguished from obsessions in that worries are usually excessive concerns about real life circumstances, and are experienced by the person as appropriate concerns. Accordingly, excessive concern that one may develop serious financial problems and lose one's home would be considered a worry, rather than an obsession. In contrast, the content of obsessions is likely to be unrealistic, and to be experienced as inappropriate and inconsistent with one's values. For example, an unwanted idea about losing control and stabbing someone, in the absence of a history of poor impulse control, would be considered an obsession.

To the extent that it depends upon a clinician's judgment about whether the content of an intrusive idea is realistic, distinguishing between worries and obsessions might seem at times problematic. In practice, however, the rituals that are so commonly associated with obsessions leave them readily distinguishable from the worries of GAD that are not accompanied by rituals. Thus, the issue of distinguishing between OCD and GAD on the basis of the content of an intrusive idea would arise only in the cases where there were no compulsions. Although the conventional wisdom is that the incidence of "pure" obsessionals is low, estimates have ranged up to 25% (Welner, Reich, Robins, Fishman, & Van Doren, 1976). In the DSM-IV field trial for OCD, only about 2% of the OCD sample reported having obsessions without compulsions (Foa & Kozak, 1992).

Obsessions may occur as repeated thoughts about relatively low-probability, catastrophic events. These are typically events that *are* realistic and could possibly occur, but the individual focuses on, and magnifies, the minute risk of such occurrence. Examples of such exaggerations are fears of hitting a pedestrian while driving a car, or of developing cancer from exposure to household chemicals.

Individuals with contamination-related obsessions may appear similar to simple phobics in their symptoms. For example, people with either disorder may become terrified in the presence of dogs and avoid contact with dogs. However, there are at least two ways in which the OCD sufferer differs from the simple phobic. First, even if the feared object or situation is identical for both, the perceived threat or *reason* they fear it differs. Using the above example, dog phobics are typically afraid of being bitten. In contrast, an obsessive-compulsive patient typically fears dogs because they may carry diseases such as rabies or contaminants like feces. Secondly, because of the circumscribed nature of the fear (i.e., being bitten), simple phobics can successfully avoid or escape dogs and thereby reduce phobic distress. The threat perceived by a person with OCD is not eliminated by the removal of the dog because the contamination remains.

Since passive avoidance fails to reduce obsessional distress, the obsessive-compulsive person must actively ritualize in response to exposure to the feared situation (e.g., washing hands, checking for illness after contact with a dog). Nevertheless, people with OCD frequently display fearful avoidance of situations that evoke the obsessions, such as being around dirt, bathrooms, or other sources of contamination. For example, a person with obsessions about germs may avoid public toilets; a person with obsessions about hitting people with a car may avoid driving. In severe cases, activity may be so restricted by avoidance that the individual becomes housebound and appears agoraphobic.

Delusional Disorders

According to the DSM-III-R, recognition of the excessive or unreasonable nature of OC behavior may not be present in young children or "people whose obsessions have evolved into overvalued ideas" (p. 245).

Overvalued ideation is defined as an "almost unshakable" belief which can be acknowledged as potentially untrue only after extensive discussion. Their definitions notwithstanding, DSM-III-R does not provide formal guidelines for making reliable diagnostic distinctions between obsessions, overvalued ideas, and delusions. This can lead to diagnostic confusion because obsessive-compulsives evidence a continuum of strength of belief in the senselessness of their OC symptoms. The following case illustrates an obsessive-compulsive patient with impaired recognition of the senselessness of his obsessive fear.

Case 3

Chuck is a 28-year-old, white, single man. He sought treatment because his obsessive compulsive symptoms were interfering significantly with his educational progress. Pursuing a degree in nursing, Chuck was hindered by obsessive fear that he would fail to learn some critical piece of information that would be essential to his competence in future clinical practice. He was convinced that his deficient knowledge would lead to catastrophes such as patient death or disability, or even the death of whole groups of people by accidental poisoning. Other obsessions concerned fears of impregnating women via highly unlikely routes of transferring his sperm. For example, Chuck worried that if he masturbated in the shower and thoroughly cleaned the shower stall afterwards, some semen might remain on the walls or in some place that his female housemate might inadvertently touch. She would then get sperm on her hands and transfer it to her vagina, resulting in pregnancy. Chuck experienced many other obsessions that concerned fears of causing harm to others, such as spreading contaminants that would cause illness or death, and hitting someone with his car.

These obsessive fears led to extensive washing and checking compulsions. Chuck's handwashing and showering rituals occupied several hours per day. He avoided contact with very young, elderly, or sick people, which impeded his work in the hospital. His extensive checking for errors and perfectionistic, time-consuming study rituals occupied so much time that Chuck was unable to complete his course work or his required clinical practica in nursing school.

It became apparent through working with Chuck that he truly *believed* that his sperm could impregnate a woman via distal, nonsexual contact, despite assurance to the contrary by medical authority. Similarly, he was completely convinced that if he failed to acquire perfect mastery of all text and course work, it was highly likely that he would kill someone via negligence and incompetence.

This case clearly depicts an obsessive-compulsive patient who does not recognize the senselessness of his OC symptoms.

Individuals with OCD who express strong convictions about their OC beliefs (i.e., exhibit "overvalued ideation") may have obsessions that are of a delusional intensity. In this case example, Chuck not only believed that it was possible to impregnate a woman via the transfer of sperm on objects like shower curtains, but also that his knowledge of this was special and superior (i.e., other people were just wrong about it). Delusional disorder is characterized by persistent nonbizarre delusions involving situations that occur in real life, such as being followed or having a disease. Because most obsessive-compulsives have both obsessions and compulsions, obsessions of delusional intensity can usually be distinguished from the delusions of delusional disorder by the presence of associated compulsions.

Obsessions may be extremely bizarre, such as the idea that the person might accidentally seal him or herself into an envelope and get deposited into a letter box. Although obsessional fears that are strongly believed, or that have strikingly bizarre content, may occur in individuals with OCD, these individuals do not show other symptoms of thought disorder or psychosis, such as incoherence or marked loosening of associations, hallucinations, flat or grossly inappropriate affect, and thought insertion or projection, unless there is a coexisting psychotic disorder. It has been suggested that overvalued ideas are associated with poor response to behavioral treatment (Foa, 1979), but some investigators have been unable to document such a relationship (Lelliott & Marks, 1987; Lelliott et al., 1988). Thus, at present, the relationship between fixity of obsessive-compulsive beliefs and treatment outcome remains uncertain and merits further study.

Hypochondriasis

Hypochondriacal concerns are common in OCD, especially in individuals with illness- or disease-related obsessions (Rasmussen & Tsuang, 1986). Obsessive-compulsives with these concerns may exhibit somatic checking rituals and may repeatedly visit physicians to seek reassurance. Rasmussen and Eisen (1989) suggested that hypochondriacs with somatic obsessions and checking rituals should probably be diagnosed with OCD, but acknowledged that the differential diagnosis is often difficult.

In hypochondriasis, the individual has the unfounded belief that he or she has a disease and consults physicians for diagnoses and treatment. Illness-related obsessions of individuals with OCD are formally similar to those of individuals with hypochondriasis. If the symptoms consist only of preoccupation with the person's own health and excessive information-seeking about health and/or treatment, a diagnosis of hypochondriasis is most likely appropriate. If other obsessions and/or compulsions are present in addition to concerns for one's own health then a diagnosis of OCD is indicated. For example, the presence of obsessions about spreading illness to other people, or of rituals such as excessive hand-washing or checking, indicate a diagnosis of OCD.

A disorder which appears similar to hypochondriasis is body dysmorphic disorder (BDD). The essential feature of BDD is an obsessive preoccupation with an imagined physical defect in a person with essentially normal appearance. For example, a person may believe that his or her ears are hideously and abnormally large and should be surgically repaired, but to others the ears are unremarkable. Body dysmorphia is sometimes coupled with compulsive checking behavior. In the above example, the individual may feel compelled to ask everyone if his or her ears are too large.

If other obsessions or compulsions are present in a person with body dysmorphic disorder, a diagnosis of OCD may be indicated. In part on the basis of positive response to serotonergic drug treatment in 5 cases of BDD, Hollander, Liebowitz, Winchel, Klumker, and Klein (1989) suggested that this disorder may be closely related to OCD. More research is needed to investigate such a linkage.

Personality Disorders

The essential feature of obsessive-compulsive personality disorder (OCPD) is a "pervasive pattern of perfectionism and inflexibility" (DSM-III-R; p. 354), characterized by preoccupation with details, unreasonable insistence that others do things his or her way, excessive devotion to work, indecisiveness, overconscientiousness, restricted expression of affection, stinginess, and inability to discard worthless possessions. Tynes et al. (1990) noted that while the only criterion from this list that overlaps with a common OCD symptom is hoarding, the general traits of perfectionism and inflexibility do appear characteristic of many individuals with OCD.

Jenike and Baer (1990) argued that there is no evidence that OCD predisposes to OCPD or vice versa, nor that individuals with OCD are more likely to have OC personality disorder than any other Axis II disorder. Nonetheless, estimates of the co-occurrence of DSM-III-R diagnosed OCPD and OCD range from about 5% to 25% (Joffe, Swinson, & Regan, 1988; Jenike & Baer, 1990). Jenike and Baer attributed this variability in part to the inconsistent and subjective process of personality evaluation and lack of agreement among assessment devices. A traditional basis for the differential diagnosis has been whether the symptoms are "ego-dystonic" (e.g., experienced as unwanted, foreign) as in OCD or "ego-syntonic" (e.g., consistent with one's self-concept, valued) as in OCPD. Rasmussen and Eisen (1989) suggested that this distinction is insufficient and sometimes inaccurate. They noted the incidence of patients with severely impaired functioning due to OC symptoms who still maintain that their concerns and behaviors are important and/or reasonable.

There is empirical support to suggest that Axis II disorders are more likely to occur in individuals with OCD than in the general population. In their sample of 44 OCD patients, Rasmussen and Tsuang (1986) found that 29 (66%) exhibited at least one personality disorder: 55% met criteria of OC personality disorder, 9% met criteria for histrionic, 7% for schizoid, and 5% for dependent personality disorder.

Tic Disorders

Repetitive, stereotyped behavior is evident in both Tourette's Syndrome (TS) and tic disorder, but is distinguished from compulsive behavior in that it is generally involuntary and purposeless. Tourette's syndrome is characterized by both motor and vocal tics. A high incidence of OCD in individuals with TS has been documented, with estimates ranging from 36% to 63% (Leckman & Chittenden, 1990; Pauls, Towbin, Leckman, Zahner, & Cohen, 1986; Pitman, Green, Jenike, & Mesulam, 1987). The incidence of TS in OCD is lower, with estimates ranging between 5% and 7% (Rasmussen & Eisen, 1989). However, simple tics are frequently observed in those with OCD. Pauls (1989) reported that 20% to 30% of individuals with OCD admitted the presence of current or past tics.

Further evidence of a relationship between OCD and Tourette's syndrome comes from family studies. About 10% of first degree relatives of Tourette's syndrome probands had TS, about 20% had tic disorder, and about 20% had OCD (Pauls et al., 1986).

Eating and Impulse Control Disorders

Coincidence of OCD with eating disorders, such as anorexia nervosa and bulimia nervosa, has been noted. According to Kasvikis, Tsakiris, Marks, and Basoglu (1986), about 10% of females with OCD have had a history of anorexia nervosa. The coincidence of OCD with bulimia nervosa is more striking: between 33% and 66% of bulimics had a lifetime incidence of OCD (Hudson, Pope, Yurgelun-Todd, Jonas, & Frankenburg, 1987; Laessle, Kittl, Fichter, & Wittchen, 1987).

Over-eating and other problem behaviors such as gambling, substance abuse, trichotillomania (hair pulling), and kleptomania are often described as compulsive in nature. Most if not all of these disorders are characterized by a sense of compulsion to carry out an act that the person typically admits is unreasonable or self-destructive.

According to the DSM-III-R, what distinguishes such pathological behaviors from "true" compulsions is that rather than serving only to reduce tension, they elicit a subjective sense of pleasure or gratification. However, some investigators oppose a distinction made on this basis. Dar, Omer, and Griest (1992) suggested that OCD, bulimia, alcohol and substance abuse, some paraphilias, and impulse control disorders are all members of a compulsive spectrum. They argued that these disorders are elements of a compulsive spectrum for three reasons: they share a common phenomenological picture with specific emotional/motivational, cognitive, and behavioral aspects; all show response to the same treatments (pharmacologic and behavioral); and all are consistent with a single unified conceptualization or underlying mechanism.

CONCLUSION

In this chapter, we have reviewed the characteristics of OCD and described several cases that illustrate the range of symptoms that are manifested in this disorder. We have examined several traditional concepts that are present in the DSM-III-R diagnostic criteria for OCD and highlighted their shortcomings. The available data suggest that some of these traditional concepts are unsupported, and that certain aspects of the DSM-III-R diagnostic criteria could be improved.

We have concluded that the available research supports the DSM-III-R emphasis on a functional relationship between most obsessions and compulsions. The data also suggest that a minority of obsessions and compulsions are unrelated and this supports their independence. We have, however, challenged the traditional notion that obsessions are mental events and compulsions are overt behaviors; the available evidence is inconsistent with this idea. Finally, we argued that obsessive-compulsives show a broad range of recognition of the senselessness of their OC fears and that is important for the clinician to know that not all individuals with OCD view their symptoms as senseless.

In this chapter, we also discussed issues of comorbidity and differential diagnosis. The literature suggests extensive comorbidity of OCD and depression and other anxiety disorders. Hypochondriacal concerns, personality disorders (perhaps especially obsessive-compulsive personality disorder), tic disorders, and eating disorders also co-occur with OCD with significant frequency. We concluded the chapter with brief mention of the view that OCD is one of several disorders in a "compulsive spectrum" of pathology. The potential advantage of this view in advancing our knowledge of the etiology and treatment of OCD needs to be explored in future research.

REFERENCES

American Psychiatric Association. (1980). *Diagnostic and statistical manual of mental disorders,* (3rd ed.). Washington, DC: Author.

American Psychiatric Association. (1987). *Diagnostic and statistical manual of mental disorders,* (3rd ed., rev.). Washington, DC: Author.

Boulougouris, J. C., Rabavilas, A. D., & Stefanis, C. (1977). Psycho-physiological responses in obsessive-compulsive patients. *Behaviour Research and Therapy, 15,* 221–230.

Carr, A. T. (1971). Compulsive neurosis: Two psychophysiological studies. *Bulletin of the British Psychological Society, 24,* 256–257.

Dar, R., Omer, H., & Griest, J. H. (1992). Compulsive spectrum disorders. Submitted for publication.

Emmelkamp, P. M. G., de Haan, E., & Hoogduin, C. A. L. (1990). Marital adjustment and obsessive-compulsive disorder. *British Journal of Psychiatry, 156,* 55–60.

Foa, E. B. (1979). Failure in treating obsessive-compulsives. *Behaviour Research and Therapy, 16,* 391–399.

Foa, E. B., Grayson, J. B., Steketee, G., & Doppelt, H. G. (1983). Treatment of obsessive-compulsives: When do we fail? In E. B. Foa & P. M. G. Emmelkamp (Eds.), *Failures in behavior therapy.* New York: Wiley.

Foa, E. B., & Kozak, M. J. (1991). Diagnostic criteria for obsessive-compulsive disorder. *Hospital and Community Psychiatry, 42,* 679–684.

Foa, E. B., & Kozak, M. J. (1992). DSM-IV field trial: Obsessive-compulsive disorder. Unpublished manuscript.

Foa, E. B., Steketee, G. S., Kozak, M. J., & Dugger, D. (1987). Imipramine and placebo in the treatment of obsessive-compulsives: Their effect on depression and on obsessional symptoms. *Psychopharmacology Bulletin, 23,* 7–12.

Foa, E. B., Steketee, G. S., & Ozarow, B. (1985). Behavior therapy with obsessive-compulsives: From theory to treatment. In M. Mavissakalian (Ed.), *Obsessive-compulsive disorder: Psychological and pharmacological treatment.* New York: Plenum Press.

Freud, S. (1909/1957). Notes upon a case of obsessional neurosis. In S. Freud, *Collected papers* (Vol. 3). (pp. 291–383). London: Hogarth Press.

Hodgson, R. J., & Rachman, S. (1972). The effects of contamination and washing in obsessional patients. *Behaviour Research and Therapy, 10,* 111–117.

Hollander, E., Liebowitz, M. R., Winchel, R., Klumker, A., & Klein, D. F. (1989). Treatment of body dysmorphic disorder with serotonin re-uptake blockers. *American Journal of Psychiatry, 146,* 768–770.

Hornsveld, R. H. J., Kraaimaat, F. W., & van Dam-Baggen, R. M. J. (1979). Anxiety/discomfort and handwashing in obsessive-compulsive and psychiatric control patients. *Behaviour Research and Therapy, 17,* 223–228.

Hudson, J. I., Pope, H. G., Yurgelun-Todd, D., Jonas, J. M., & Frankenburg, F. R. (1987). A controlled study of lifetime prevalence of affective and other psychiatric disorders in bulimic outpatients. *American Journal of Psychiatry, 10,* 144, 1283–1287.

Insel, T. R., & Akiskal, H. (1986). Obsessive-compulsive disorder with psychotic features: A phenomenologic analysis. *American Journal of Psychiatry, 12,* 1527–1533.

Janet, P. (1908). *Les obsessions et la psychosthenie* (2nd Ed.). Paris: Bailliere.

Jenike, M. A., & Baer, L. (1990). *The relationship between obsessive-compulsive personality disorder and obsessive-compulsive disorder.* DSM-IV Position Paper.

Joffe, R. T., Swinson, R. P., & Regan, J. J. (1988). Personality features of obsessive-compulsive disorder. *American Journal of Psychiatry, 145,* 1127–1129.

Karno, M. G., Golding, J. M., Sorensen, S. B., & Burnam, A. (1988). The epidemiology of OCD in five U.S. communities. *Archives of General Psychiatry, 45,* 1094–1099.

Kasvikis, Y. G., Tsakiris, F., Marks, I. M., Basoglu, M. (1986). Past history of anorexia nervosa in women with obsessive-compulsive disorder. *International Journal of Eating Disorders, 5,* 1069–1075.

Kozak, M. J., Foa, E. B., & McCarthy, P. (1988). Obsessive-compulsive disorder. In C. G. Last & M. Hersen (Eds.), *Handbook of anxiety disorders,* pp. 87–107. New York: Pergamon Press.

Kozak, M. J., Foa, E. B., & Steketee, G. (1988). Process and outcome of exposure treatment with obsessive-compulsives: psychophysiological indicators of emotional processing. *Behavior Therapy, 19,* 157–169.

Laessle, R. G., Kittl, S., Fichter, M. M., Wittchen, U. H. (1987). Major affective disorder in anorexia nervosa and bulimia: A descriptive diagnostic study. *British Journal of Psychiatry, 151,* 785–789.

Leckman, J. F., & Chittenden, E. H. (1990). Gilles de La Tourette's syndrome and some forms of obsessive-compulsive disorder may share a common genetic diathesis. *L'Encephale, XVI,* 321–323.

Lelliott, P. T., & Marks, I. M. (1987). Management of obsessive-compulsive rituals associated with delusions, hallucinations, and depression: A case report. *Behavioural Psychotherapy, 15,* 77–87.

Lelliott, P. T., Noshirvani, H. F., Basoglu, M., Marks, I. M., & Monteiro, W. O. (1988). Obsessive-compulsive beliefs and treatment outcome. *Psychological Medicine, 18,* 697–702.

Maudsley, H. (1895). *The pathology of the mind.* London: Macmillan.

Pauls, D. L. (1989). *The inheritance and expression of obsessive-compulsive behaviors.* Proceedings of the American Psychiatric Association, San Francisco, CA.

Pauls, D. L., Raymond, C. L., & Hurst, C. R. (1988). *Transmission of obsessive-compulsive disorder and associated behaviors.* Proceedings of the 43rd Annual Meeting of the Society of Biological Psychiatry, Montreal, Canada.

Pauls, D. L., Towbin, K. E., Leckman, J. F., Zahner, G. E., & Cohen, D. J. (1986). Gilles de la Tourette's Syndrome and obsessive-compulsive disorder. *Archives of General Psychiatry, 43,* 1180–1182.

Pitman, R. K., Green, R. C., Jenike, M. A., & Mesulam, M. M. (1987). Clinical comparisons of Tourette's disorder and obsessive-compulsive disorder. *American Journal of Psychiatry, 144,* 1166–1171.

Rabavilas, A. D., & Boulougouris, J. C. (1974). Physiological accompaniments of ruminations, flooding and thought-stopping in obsessive patients. *Behavior Research and Therapy, 12,* 239–243.

Rasmussen, S. A., & Eisen, J. L. (1989). Clinical features and phenomenology of obsessive-compulsive disorder. *Psychiatric Annals, 19,* 67–73.

Rasmussen, S. A., & Eisen, J. L. (1990). Epidemiology of obsessive-compulsive disorder. *Journal of Clinical Psychiatry, 51,* 10–14.

Rasmussen, S. A., & Tsuang, M. T. (1984). The epidemiology of obsessive-compulsive disorder. *Journal of Clinical Psychiatry, 45,* 450–457.

Rasmussen, S. A., & Tsuang, M. T. (1986). Clinical characteristics and family history in DSM-III obsessive-compulsive disorder. *American Journal of Psychiatry, 1943,* 317–382.

Riggs, D. S., Hiss, H., & Foa, E. B. (1991). *Marital distress and the treatment of obsessive-compulsive disorder.* Unpublished manuscript.

Robins, L. N., Helzer, J. E., Weissman, M. M., Orvaschel, H., Gruenberg, E., Burke, J. D., & Regier, D. A. (1984). Lifetime prevalence of specific psychiatric disorders in three sites. *Archives of General Psychiatry, 41,* 949–958.

Roper, G., & Rachman, S. (1976). Obsessional-compulsive checking: Experimental replication and development. *Behaviour Research and Therapy, 14,* 25–32.

Roper, G., Rachman, S., & Hodgson, R. (1973). An experiment on obsessional checking. *Behaviour Research and Therapy, 11,* 271–277.

Swedo, S. E., Rapoport, J. L., Leonard, H., Lenane, M., & Cheslow, D. (1989). Obsessive-compulsive disorders in children and adolescents: Clinical phenomenology of 70 consecutive cases. *Archives of General Psychiatry, 46,* 335–345.

Tynes, L. L., White, K., & Steketee, G. S. (1990). Toward a new nosology of obsessive-compulsive disorder. *Comprehensive Psychiatry, 31,* 465–480.

Welner, A., Reich, T., Robins, E., Fishman, R., Van Doren, T. (1976). Obsessive-compulsive neurosis: record, follow-up, and family studies. *Comparative Psychiatry, 17,* 527–539.

Westphal, C. (1878). Zwangsvor stellungen. *Arch. Psychiat. Nervenkr., 8,* 734–750.

CHAPTER 11

Anxious and Phobic States in Childhood

KAREN L. LOMBARDI, PhD

Attempts to understand and to remediate states of acute psychological anxiety have motivated both clinical and conceptual investigations of human psychic functioning since the time of Freud. Disagreements in the field, both in the past and present, have taken the form of the nature-nurture controversy. That is, can the familial patterns observed in the expression of anxiety be best accounted for by theories of genomic transmission, or by theories which take into account the interpersonal field? And similarly, is anxiety instinctual in origin or object relational in origin? The way one thinks about these questions has very real implications, as it guides prognosis and treatment plans.

The study of phobic and anxious states in childhood, as they first emerge developmentally, puts us closer to the origins of psychic anxiety. The intent of this chapter is to make a contribution to the integration of empirical and clinical data with theoretical understanding of the meaning of phobic and anxious states.

CLINICAL SYNDROMES OF ANXIETY IN CHILDHOOD

The DSM-III categorizes three anxiety disorders as first evident in childhood or adolescence. The first, separation anxiety disorder, is characterized by excessive anxiety on separation from primary attachment figures or from the home. This anxiety may manifest itself through "shadowing," wherein the child follows the parent around the house as if he were the parent's own shadow, through clinging behavior, and through refusal to leave the house and/or the parent. Although the DSM-III distinguishes between what it considers true school phobia (fear of *school* itself and alone) and school refusal on the basis of anxiety at separation from the parent, school phobia is thought by many (Bowlby, 1973) to be a subset of separation anxiety. Associated features include somatic complaints, travel phobias, and preoccupations with death and dying.

Avoidant disorder is marked by a shrinking from contact with strangers and acquaintances to a degree that substantially interferes with social functioning. Such children are to be distinguished from those who are schizoid or depressively withdrawn, as they demonstrate a clear and intense desire for warmth and affection with family members and others (usually on a one-to-one basis) with whom they feel more familiar. The picture presented here is more one of pathological shyness than of withdrawal. When social anxiety becomes intense, some children may become temporarily inarticulate or even mute. Such children tend to experience a painful lack of self-confidence, are unassertive, and are incapacitated by the sorts of competition which children experience in normal school and social environments.

Last in the DSM-III categorization system is overanxious disorder of childhood, which is characterized by chronic anxious worrying about concerns or events that are not directly related to separation. Anxiety tends to center around concerns of not meeting the expectations of the self or of others; for example, worries about not doing well on examinations, about not meeting deadlines, about not doing chores, or about the perceived dangers inherent in various anticipated situations. Such children often have tendencies to perfectionism, obsessive self-doubt, and a pathological need for approval. This disorder may be difficult to distinguish from obsessive-compulsive neurosis, particularly in its obsessive aspects.

There are three other anxiety and phobic states which, according to DSM-III criteria, may first appear in childhood. The first, simple or specific phobia, are anxieties that focus on rather specific and encapsulated objects or situations. These may include fear of heights, claustrophobia, and animal phobias. Some researchers (Agras, Sylvester, & Oliveau, 1969; Gittelman, 1986; Orvaschel & Weissman, 1986) have found certain phobias to be typical of certain ages. For example, in early childhood, fears of doctors, injections, darkness, and strangers are common; these phobias decline sharply with age. In middle childhood through adolescence, fears of animals, heights, storms, enclosed places, and social situations predominate. Because simple phobias are not unusual in childhood, and often abate without treatment, this is a diagnosis that has more weight when it persists into adulthood.

Obsessive-compulsive neurosis may often begin in childhood. The obsessive preoccupations are experienced as invasive, unwanted thoughts, images, or impulses that cause the individual emotional discomfort. Compulsions, ritualized activities such as hand-washing, counting, or touching, are often paired with obsessions and may be experienced as attempts to control the unwanted thoughts and impulses. A clinical illustration of an obsessive-compulsive routine is a child who obsessively ruminates about the chances that a fire will break out in the furnace room of his house, and who is unable to sleep at night because he must continually touch the floor and the electrical sockets in his room to prevent an outbreak of fire. Psychotic thinking is absent; the child knows that his compulsion to touch the floor will not actually prevent fire, but he is driven to repeat the behavior in order to have some control over warding off his anxieties of impending danger.

It should be noted that post-traumatic stress disorder is also an anxiety disorder from which children suffer. Because of its special precipitating circumstances which are catastrophic (either natural or man-made) in nature, it requires special attention which is outside the purview of this paper.

ETIOLOGY OF PHOBIC AND ANXIOUS STATES IN CHILDHOOD

Why do children become pathologically anxious? The current empirical literature leads us in two directions on this question. Several recent studies (Berg, 1976; Moreau, Weissman, & Warner, 1989; Weissman, Leckman, Merikangas, Gammon, & Prusoff, 1984) and reviews of studies (Gittelman, 1986; Puig-Antich & Rabinovich, 1986) report relationships between anxiety disorders in children and anxiety or depressive disorders in their parents (particularly their mothers). It appears that depressive parents have significantly more children who develop anxiety disorders, including panic disorders (Moreau et al., 1989; Weissman et al., 1984). Parents with panic disorder have been reported to have three times the incidence of separation anxiety in their children (Weissman et al., 1984), while data from England indicate that agoraphobic mothers had significantly more school-phobic children than the general population (Berg, 1976).

Some researchers (Ballenger, Carek, Steele, & Cornish-McTighe, 1989; Moreau et al., 1989) have found that the constellation of symptoms that comprises panic attacks in adults can also exist in young children. Panic attacks occur without obvious external provocation, and are characterized by somatopsychic symptoms such as palpitations, choking or smothering sensations, derealization, paresthesias, trembling, sweating, and so on. These researchers have argued that what is diagnosed as separation anxiety may in fact be panic attack. The import of such an argument, though it may not be apparent from reading the literature, bears on both etiology and treatment of anxiety disorders in children. Those researchers and clinicians who work within the tradition of behavioral medicine tend to interpret familial patterns as genetic in origin, and to look toward pharmacological rather than psychological treatment. Other recent studies (Hayward, Killen, & Taylor, 1989), while confirming that panic attacks are not confined to adults, have demonstrated correlational relationships between young adolescents with panic attacks and depression, separation or divorce in their families of origin, and smoking cigarettes. The results of this study suggest that early loss or sensitivity to separation is an underlying factor in panic attacks, and that there is a relationship between this form of anxiety and depression.

In summary, the studies referred to in this paper present inconclusive evidence with regard to the etiology of childhood anxiety disorders. While recent data, both empirical and clinical, rather consistently suggest a relationship between childhood anxiety and parental anxiety and/ or depression, the inferences drawn by researchers tend to be split between those who implicate genetic factors on a physiochemical basis, and those who see the social and emotional history, and specifically a psychological sensitivity to separation, as the crucial factors. Correlational studies (the empirical studies referred to in this paper are correlational or small case studies) suggest relationships between variables studied; they do not prove etiology. So while one group might, on the basis of their data, argue for seeing children as having panic disorder rather than separation anxiety, it might just as well be argued that panic disorder in adults is anchored in an underlying separation anxiety.

I would like at this point to turn to ethological data to afford an additional perspective on some of the issues involved in the etiology of anxiety. It was once thought that anxiety was an altogether human phenomenon, born of internal conflict (Freud, 1905). We now have a multitude of evidence for the existence of separation anxiety in nonhuman primates. Observations of contact-seeking, exploration away from the primary caretaker, and physiological activation under stress in young primates all seem to argue against the internal conflict model as the only model for anxiety, and seem to validate attachment and relational models. Separation anxiety has been observed repeatedly and consistently in young primates removed from their mothers, or their social group (Harlow, 1958; Suomi, 1986). When returned to their sources of attachment, the more intensely expressed highly anxious state abates, but over the course of the next several days, weeks, or months, those subjects who suffered separation display much higher levels of anxious behavior than they did prior to separation. For example, primate infants will increase the frequency and intensity of contact-seeking behavior toward the mother, while ordinary exploratory and social play that would move them away from the mother will correspondingly decrease. Juvenile and adolescent primates will regress to clinging behaviors in relation to the mother, while those older will become agitated and disquieted. Suomi (1986) reports factors that increase anxiety in primates which are similar to what human attachment theorists would hypothesize: early or frequent separations from the mother; rearing by a neglectful or abusive mother; frequent changes in the composition of the primary social group; lack of stability in the social group's dominance hierarchy. These factors are readily translatable into the human environment, with the last two accounted for by frequent moves or changes within the family composition, and changes in the authority structure (or the person of authority) in the family.

As the primate subjects get older, developmental markers of anxiety change as the symptomatology changes. Where infant and "toddler" primates will become increasingly clingy, and juvenile primates will regress to a need for contact with the mother when that need had all but disappeared developmentally, older (adolescent and young adult) primates' primary symptoms are that of agitation, stereotyped behaviors, and a withdrawal from ordinary exploratory, playful, and sexual behaviors. These observations are particularly interesting in light of symptomatic expressions of human anxiety, providing some empirical support for the earlier stated view that panic disorders in adults (and adolescents, and occasional precocious children) are later, derivative expressions of an underlying separation anxiety.

Physiological studies of young monkeys (Suomi, 1981) indicate that those who are highly reactive to stress on a behavioral basis also tend to be highly reactive physiologically. High reactors tend to show vegetative signs of depression when subjected to significant separations from their mothers; low reactors tend to show the expected anxiety behaviors, but do not manifest depressive symptomatology. High and low reactive monkeys seems to be more or less related to each other; however, genomic differences can only be inferred. Regardless of whether or not the tendency to depressive symptomatology is genetically transmitted, it is important to emphasize that high reactors react only under conditions of stress, which are interpersonal in nature.

DEVELOPMENTAL ISSUES IN ANXIETY: PSYCHOANALYTIC PERSPECTIVES

Anxiety, in its various forms and phases of development, has occupied psychoanalytic thinking from its beginnings to the present. Various theoretical perspectives within psychoanalysis emphasize different types of anxiety. These types of anxiety—castration anxiety, signal anxiety, separation anxiety, stranger anxiety, depressive anxiety, and the anxiety of insecurity—will be discussed.

Castration Anxiety

The Freudians tend to emphasize castration anxiety, the fear of losing the penis, or the feelings of power and efficacy associated with it, because of attendant anxiety and guilt over one's own forbidden libidinal impulses. That is, it is what one wishes and desires, but what must be repressed because it is forbidden, which leads to anxiety states. Castration anxiety fits the internal conflict model of anxiety. Developmentally, castration anxiety would not be a predominant anxiety experience until four or five years of age, when superego structures and attendant functions of guilt and inhibition are in place in the child.

Signal Anxiety

Ego psychologists, and, more recently, Kohutians, tend to emphasize the importance of signal anxiety (also an original contribution of Freud), which stresses anxiety as a signal to the ego of impending danger from without. In this model (Freud, 1926), anxiety is not the expression of dammed up libido, but rather functions as a signal to the ego to respond adaptively to the threat of a traumatic situation. Adaptive responses might include inhibition of behavior on the part of an older child, or attracting the attention of a caretaker to relieve distress on the part of a younger child. Anxiety as the reaction of the ego to danger in these cases might be the danger of separation or loss of love. The young child is at risk when he is separated from the mother; therefore he develops expressions of anxiety as safety devices to secure reunion. Signal anxiety fits the theory of secondary drive. That is, the drive for attachment is secondary to the drive for pleasure; attachment results from cathecting the source of the physiological pleasure.

Self psychologists have extended the notion of signal anxiety to include the function of transmuting internalizations. Tolpin (1971) proposes that precursors of signal anxiety operate at much earlier ages than previously thought, and depend upon the capacity of the mother to mediate or attenuate anxiety experiences of the infant. She postulates that the mother's anxiety-relieving responses to the infant's distress are preserved as psychic structure, as long as the mother serves as an effective auxiliary ego until the child develops enough mental workings to soothe himself. If the mother-infant dyad does not work well together to relieve anxiety, beginning distress snowballs into unremitting pathological anxiety states, rather than ending in the more soothing adaptive functions of signal anxiety. Contact security, and the reliability of a good holding environment which the mother provides for the child, are what contribute to the child's ability ultimately to soothe himself and manage his own anxiety. Though object relational in intent, Tolpin's model is fundamentally an ego psychological model, as her assumptions rest on the notion that the child naturally has anxiety but not the ability to diminish it, and that the mother's function is to mediate or alleviate the anxiety through serving as an auxiliary ego.

Stranger Anxiety

A developmentally early appearing form of anxiety is called eight-month or stranger anxiety (Spitz, 1965). Stranger anxiety appears somewhere around the seventh, eighth, or ninth month, and is characterized by some expression of distress when encountered with a nonfamiliar person. Stranger anxiety may express itself through persistent crying and difficulty being soothed if the infant is left with a stranger, to crying, pulling away, or averting one's glance from an unpleasing stranger even when the baby remains in the mother's presence. These reactions, even when quite intense in their expression at eight months or so, tend to disappear soon after this phase is negotiated if things are well between the baby and his primary objects of attachment. Developmentally, the appearance of stranger anxiety is thought to mark the recognition of the unfamiliar. There is evidence, however, that babies have the cognitive capacity for *recognition* of the unfamiliar before this time, so perhaps stranger anxiety more accurately marks displeasure with certain instances of the unfamiliar. Many theorists view stranger anxiety as a turning point in the development of object relations, as it is thought to indicate the child's capacity to attach to a specific individual object and to mark the onset of anxiety about loss. In this way, it is seen as the earliest prototype of separation anxiety. The timing of the appearance of stranger anxiety—eight months plus or minus a month or two—coincides with what Klein (1946) calls the depressive position and what Stern (1985) calls the discovery of intersubjectivity, indicating that theorists and researchers coming from different perspectives recognize that something of developmental significance is occurring.

Sandler (1977) expands the concept of stranger anxiety to include not only anxiety around the loss of the object but loss of the continuity of the self. Sandler's view of development is that the child constructs representations of the object and of the self out of the subjective mother-child matrix, so that the child's self-representation gradually comes to be distinct from object representations. The process of this self-other differentiation, she believes, puts the child in a fragile state which requires a smoothly flowing dialogue between mother and child to alleviate the anxiety of loss. This dialogue may be interrupted in the face of the stranger's intrusion, creating anxiety in the child and a need for re-establishment of that dialogue, both with the mother as familiar object and with the self as one's old familiar self.

Depressive Anxiety

Depressive anxiety, a cornerstone of Kleinian developmental theory, occurs developmentally at about the same time as stranger anxiety. In

Kleinian theory (Klein, 1935; Segal, 1964), the depressive position corresponds to the infant's increasing ability to relate to the mother (and other primary objects of attachment) as a whole person, with an identity that comes to be recognized as separate from the infant's own. Good object experiences with the mother and bad object experiences with the mother begin to be integrated, so that the infant begins to experience himself as the same person who both loves and hates the mother. As the loved and hated aspects of the object come closer together, the result is an increased fear of loss, as one's own aggressive impulses are recognized as being directed against the loved object. Depressive anxiety and guilt arise out of the fear that the child's aggressive phantasies will destroy the object, and, through the mechanism of projection, the self as well. Anxiety in the depressive position, then, centers around feeling that one's own destructive impulses have destroyed or will destroy the loved and needed object. Klein sees experiences of depressive anxiety as beginning at around six to nine months, which corresponds with Mahler, Pine, and Bergman's (1975) "differentiation" phase, as well as with Spitz's observed stranger anxiety and Stern's discovery of intersubjectivity. Depressive anxiety is relational in nature, involving concern regarding the fate of those whom the child has destroyed in phantasy. The capacity for empathy and reparative gestures arise from the concerns of the depressive position.

The Anxiety of Insecurity

The "anxiety of insecurity" is modeled on ideas of Winnicott (1952) and Sullivan (1953), although it also relates to concepts developed by Fairbairn (1941; 1963) and Bowlby (1973). Sullivan views anxiety as an altogether interpersonal phenomenon, and traces the origins of anxiety not to endogenous needs, conflicts, or physical states within the infant, but to disturbances in the interpersonal field, wherein the primary caretaker(s) is herself disrupted by anxiety. Sullivan's theorem of anxiety contagion is that the tension of anxiety, when present in the (m)other, induces anxiety in the infant. Sullivan explicitly states his view that anxiety tensions are not physicochemical in origin; rather, anxiety is expressed in communal existence from one person to another, with reference to a personal environment. The relief of anxiety tension brings with it not satisfaction or gratification in the way in which Freud would have meant it, but a sense of interpersonal security. Sullivan sees what he calls need tensions—"physicochemical" needs such as hunger and thirst, as well as emotional needs such as the need for contact—as constructive sorts of tensions. Under ordinary circumstances, the infant expresses needs through crying, reaching out, and other forms of communication, which elicit a tender response from the caretaker, and all goes well. Under such circumstances, the tension of needs sets up an interpersonal process that fosters integrating tendencies in the child. The tension of anxiety, however, often leads to trouble, as the sorts of gestures the infant makes toward the mother to elicit soothing—crying or reaching out—is not met with tenderness, as the mother is already compromised by her own anxiety. Such circumstances lead to a snowballing of distress between parent and child, increasing anxiety and leading to disintegrative experiences. Sullivan regards the tension of anxiety as the early prototype for emotional disturbances of all sorts.

Winnicott's (1952) delineation of early appearing anxiety—what he calls anxiety associated with insecurity—is compatible with Sullivan's. The developmentally earliest form of anxiety, and the paradigm for later anxieties, is related to being insecurely held. Winnicott sees the earliest anxieties as object relational, not institutional or biological, in nature. Anxieties expressed in experiences of disintegration, depersonalization, and shifts from true to false self-organization are, in their pathologic forms, prevented by good-enough maternal care, which consists of a sufficiency of being held as well as the ability to fail in manageable and graduated ways.

Separation Anxiety

Discussion of separation anxiety is left for last not because it is the earliest appearing form of anxiety, but because of its importance to psychoanalytic and developmental theorists of many shades and colors. Although the cornerstones of Freudian theory are castration anxiety and related superego anxiety, Freud (1926) does state in his later work that anxiety is a response to the danger of object loss. Such theorists as Mahler et al. (1975) observe separation anxiety as a developmentally normal occurrence during the rapprochement struggle. The rapprochement subphase, which Mahler et al. place at around 18 months to around 24 months, is viewed as part of the young child's move towards psychological differentiation from the mother. These theorists describe the original state of the human being in early infancy as "normally autistic," without object ties. When the infant, in the second and third months begins to recognize the mother, it is within the context of a symbiotic orbit, wherein the infant does not make distinctions between self and others. Gradually, beginning at about four or five months, the infant begins to differentiate himself from others, which Mahler et al. characterize in terms of the struggle for psychological individuation. The rapprochement subphase is characterized by the progressive disengagement of the child from the mother as independence grows, as well as rather intense demandingness and need for contact as he begins to realize that the price paid for independence is some experience of loss of the mother.

Separation anxiety, here, is related to the child's developing sense of an independent self that is inevitably accompanied by an ensuing sense of loss of the mother (who, importantly, is in most cases not actually lost, but who, in this theory, is no longer experienced as of one and the same mind and being with the child. It should be further noted, parenthetically, that other theories of psychoanalytic child development—for example, Stern, 1985—disagree with the notion that development proceeds from symbiosis to separation-individuation).

Bowlby (1958, 1960, 1973), and the attachment theorists whose research derives from him (e.g., Ainsworth, Blehar, Waters, & Wall, 1978; Main, Kaplan, & Cassidy, 1985), postulate that anxiety is a primary response due to a rupture in the attachment to mother. Bowlby differs from the classical and ego psychological positions in psychoanalysis which hold that attachment to the mother is derivative of her function as a need gratifier. According to the classical position, the child does not experience true object love prior to the development of the superego and a full acceptance of the reality principle. It was thought that young (pre-Oedipal) children did not truly mourn for lost objects; rather, they experienced transient reactions to deprivation until a new need-gratifying object appeared. In this system, one good mother was interchangeable with another good mother. Bowlby was one of the first theorists to suggest that children as young as six months old do mourn at separation or loss of primary caretakers, because from the beginning the infant has the capacity for strong attachments. (It should be noted that from another perspective, Klein's (1937) theory of the depressive position and the child's reparative gestures towards the mother to ensure her well-being also presumes primary attachment experience. Although nominally a drive theorist, Klein's position was that object relations begin at the breast, from the moment of first contact.) Bowlby saw attachment as the basis for reconceptualizing all basic areas of classical psychoanalytic theory. All anxiety is related to separation from the mother or the mother figure; dependency and clinging is understood in terms of anxious attachment; anger is a response to separation; and psychic defenses are in the service of deactivating the need for attachment, particularly the thwarted or frustrated need for attachment.

A Revisionist Perspective

Of what importance is such a reconceptualization for the understanding of phobic and anxiety states in childhood? Childhood psychopathology would then be viewed primarily in terms of failure of attachment or of anxious attachment rather than in terms of the conflicts of various psychosexual stages. So we can, for example, speak of the anorexic, the obsessive-compulsive, the enuretic, the phobic child in terms of the dynamics that go on around issues of attachment. The quality of the original attachment between mother (or other caregiver) and child is what determines the negotiation of anxieties as they arise for the child. Children who are securely attached to their primary caregivers tend to manage early separations in adaptive ways. Bowlby describes typical responses to the event of significant separations from the primary caretaker in children from six months of age. Significant separations, according to Bowlby, are those of several days, and at least some of the data he reports concern separations under stressful situations—hospitalization of the mother, hospitalization of the child, and separation during wartime. The typical responses he observed consist of three phases. The first, called protest, lasts from a few hours to a week or more, and is characterized by observable distress on the part of the child and active efforts to recapture the mother; by crying, throwing himself about, or looking eagerly toward any sight or sound that might herald the return of the mother. The next phase, called despair, is marked by continued preoccupation on the part of the child with the missing person, but with a marked diminishment in activities meant to call her back. Hopelessness and depression have begun to set in. Children in this phase appear undemanding and withdrawn, which may be mistaken for having recovered from the loss. The third phase, detachment, seems like true recovery, for the child begins to take an active interest in what is going on around him, and will accept attention from others. However, children who reach this phase will turn away from the mother on reunion, acting as if they do not know her or care if she is there. The picture here is one of schizoid adjustment, with superficial sociability toward others, and little or no sociability toward the mother.

Children who have difficulties in the quality of the original tie to the mother have characteristic difficulties in the management of what appear to be more ordinary and momentary separations. The Strange Situation paradigm, (Ainsworth et al., 1978), which consists of a number of episodes of separation and reunion between infants or young children and their mothers, provides empirical confirmation of Bowlby's work. Based on the child's responses to the mother's comings and goings, children have been classified as securely attached, avoidant, and ambivalently or insecurely attached. Although such attachment styles do not necessarily lead to psychopathology, there is reasonable indication that children who are avoidant or insecurely attached are at higher risk for psychopathology (Rutter, 1987; Sroufe, 1988). Using Bowlby's paradigm, avoidant children would be more vulnerable to schizoid or depressive disorders, while anxiously attached (what Ainsworth calls ambivalent) children would be more vulnerable to anxiety disorders.

Anxiously attached children appear to be clingy, demanding "overdependent," and what some might call "spoiled." Some promoting conditions in childhood are early separations (both literal and figural) from primary maternal figures. Hospital stays of significant length of either parent or child, threats of abandonment for discipline purposes, acrimonious parental fights (which bring the risk, or the fantasy, that a parent might depart), parental depression or threats of suicide, or any similar situation which threatens the security of the child's tie to the parent, predisposes to anxious attachment.

There has been a tendency in the behavioral literature to underread Bowlby. Gittelman (1986), for example, comes to the conclusion that since clinicians report that children with school phobia and/or separation anxiety tend to come from close knit families, early separation does not contribute to the development of anxiety disorders in children. What threatens the security of the child's original tie to the mother is not simply literal physical separations, but words, affects, and attitudes that communicate the tenuousness of the tie. A mother, for example, who hugs her child close to her and cries as she rocks her, or a parent who says "You'll be the death of me" when the child fails to be compliant will, eventually, communicate to the child something of the tenuousness of their relationship. Where Bowlby stresses the threat to the integrity of the tie to the mother, Sullivan stresses the inducement of the mother's anxiety directly in the child, and Winnicott stresses the adequacy of the holding environment, all point to the development of security in the sense of relatedness which develops between child and primary caregiver(s). Anxiety states stand in contradistinction to the development of security.

School phobia may serve as a prime example of anxious attachment. School phobia consists of the child not only refusing to attend school, but expressing much anxiety when pressed to go. The anxiety may take the form of psychosomatic symptoms, or be more directly expressed by fearfulness, tearfulness, and clinging to the mother. Most often the family is intact, the child is well-behaved to the point of inhibition, and there have not been long or frequent physical separations. Parent-child relationships may be unusually close, perhaps to the point of suffocation. Bowlby (1973) describes four typical patterns of family interaction in phobic children. In what he calls type A, the mother, and sometimes the father, suffers from chronic anxiety and retains the child home as a companion. In type B, the child fears that something dreadful will happen to the mother or the father while he or she is away, and so stays home to prevent it. In type C, the child fears that something dreadful will happen to him while he is away. And in type D, the mother, and sometimes the father, fears something dreadful will happen to the child while away, and so keeps him at home. Each of these patterns, although differently motivated, are instances of close but intensely ambivalent relationships. The fears and anxieties that are transmitted between parent and child are unconscious in nature, and usually not experienced on a consciously aware level. Bowlby would apply the same clinical paradigm to agoraphobia, anxiety or panic attacks, phobias, obsessive anxieties, and other phobic and anxious states.

To summarize with clinical examples: A young girl of four, who has already spent a year in nursery school, has difficulty letting her mother out of her sight. When she does let her go, she tends to need to check back with her on a momentary basis, similar to how Mahler would describe the necessity to refuel during the rapprochement period. The child has become afraid of school and of her teacher, describing her as a mean witch. She has asked her mother to take her out of school, and not to send her to another school that has such a mean witch in it. The mother, who in no way resembles a mean witch herself, has complied with her daughter's request and sees some sense in it. She is very attentive to her daughter and worries excessively about her daughter's unhappiness. She has an older daughter who appears comfortable and reasonably happy, who is neither clingy with her mother nor reluctant to go to school. Is it genetic, the mother wonders, this tendency to cling and to be fearful and to be unhappy with oneself? Has her daughter somehow inherited this tendency, from some not-too-distant family member? The child, it turns out, is especially attuned to the problems in the parents' relationship to each other, which intensified just a year or two before. She is also especially attuned to the mother's depression, which on the surface the mother keeps in very good check. Projective testing reveals an inordinately precocious child who is so attuned to the nuances of interpersonal relationships that she is in danger of losing her own internal focus. Her anxiety sometimes keeps her at home while her mother is off at work, but often keeps her at home while her mother is home. When her mother is at home, it is the best between them, for then they are both momentarily free of the responsibilities of supporting others and can simply enjoy each others' company. The burdens that this child feels are not unlike the burdens that her mother feels. In the child's case, however, her anxiety about her own welfare is exceeded only by her anxiety about her mother's welfare. Unlike her mother, she cannot go out to work to support the family, but she can feel the anxiety of that burden as well as countless others, and she can express it through her discomfort about going to school, using her talents, and enjoying herself.

The little boy mentioned earlier who felt compelled to touch the floor to prevent a fire from raging was also especially empathic, sensitive to his mother's burdens about being left (emotionally) alone to raise four small children and his father's anxieties about making a sufficient living. His father's impatience with the fears of others further contributed to his need to contain his own anxieties and anger, a need that ultimately broke down despite vigorous compulsive attempts. Although not the exclusive domain of precociously empathic children, phobic and anxious states tend to manifest themselves in children who are especially sensitive to the fragile equilibrium of their parents.

REFERENCES

Agras, S., Sylvester, D., & Oliveau, D. (1969). The epidemiology of common fears and phobias. *Comprehensive Psychiatry, 10,* 151–156.

Ainsworth, M. D. S., Blehar, M., Waters, E., & Wall, S. (1978). *Patterns of attachment: A psychological study of the strange situation.* Hillsdale: Erlbaum.

Ballenger, J. C., Carek, D. J., Steele, J. J., & Cornish-McTighe, D. (1989). Three cases of panic disorder with agoraphobia in children. *American Journal of Psychiatry, 146,* 922–924.

Berg, I. (1976). School phobia in the children of agoraphobic women. *British Journal of Psychiatry, 128,* 86–89.

Bowlby, J. (1958). The nature of the child's tie to the mother. *International Journal of Psychoanalysis, 39,* 350–373.

Bowlby, J. (1960). Separation anxiety. *International Journal of Psychoanalysis, 41,* 89–113.

Bowlby, J. (1973). *Separation: Anxiety and anger.* New York: Basic Books.

Fairbairn, W. R. D. (1941). A revised psychopathology of the psychoses and psychoneuroses. In *Psychoanalytic studies of the personality.* London: Routledge, 1952.

Fairbairn, W. R. D. (1963). Synopsis of an object-relations theory of the personality. *International Journal of Psychoanalysis, 44,* 224–5.

Freud, S. (1905). Three essays on infantile sexuality. *The standard edition,* Vol. VII, London: Hogarth Press, 1959.

Freud, S. (1926). Inhibitions, symptoms, and anxiety. *The standard edition,* Vol. XX, London: Hogarth Press, 1959.

Gittelman, R. (1986). Childhood anxiety disorders: correlates and outcome. In R. Gittelman (Ed.), *Anxiety disorders of childhood.* New York: Guilford Press.

Harlow, H. F. (1958). The nature of love. *American Psychologist, 13,* 673–685.

Hayward, C., Killen, J. D., & Taylor, C. B. (1989). Panic attacks in young adolescents. *American Journal of Psychiatry, 146,* 1061–1062.

Klein, M. (1935). A contribution to the psychogenesis of manic-depressive states. In *Love, guilt, and reparation.* London: Hogarth Press, 1975.

Klein, M. (1937). Love, guilt, and reparation. In *Love, guilt, and reparation.* London: Hogarth Press, 1975.

Klein, M. (1946). Notes on some schizoid mechanisms. In *Envy and gratitude.* London: Hogarth Press, 1975.

Mahler, M. S., Pine, F., & Bergman, A. (1975). *The psychological birth of the human infant.* New York: Basic Books.

Main, M., Kaplan, N., & Cassidy, J. (1985). Security in infancy, childhood and adulthood: A move to the level of representation. *Monographs of the Society for Research in Child Development, 50,* 66–104.

Moreau, D. L., Weissman, M., & Warner, V. (1989). Panic disorder in children at high risk for depression. *American Journal of Psychiatry, 146,* 1059–1060.

Orvaschel, H. G., & Weissman, M. M., (1986). Epidemiology of anxiety disorders in children: A review. In R. Gittelman (Ed.), *Anxiety disorders of childhood*. New York: Guilford Press.

Puig-Antich, J., & Rabinovich, H. (1986). Relationship between affective and anxiety disorders in childhood. In R. Gittelman (Ed.), *Anxiety disorders of childhood*. New York: Guilford Press.

Rutter, M. (1987). Continuities and discontinuities from infancy. In J. Osofsky (Ed.), *Handbook of infant development*. New York: Wiley.

Sandler, A. M. (1977). Beyond eight-month anxiety. *International Journal of Psychoanalysis, 58,* 195–207.

Segal, H. (1964). *Introduction to the work of Melanie Klein.* New York: Basic Books.

Spitz, R. A. (1965). *The first year of life.* New York: International Universities Press.

Sroufe, L. A. (1988). The role of infant-caregiver attachment in development. In J. Belsky & T. Nezworski (Eds.), *Clinical implications of attachment.* Hillsdale: Erlbaum.

Stern, D. (1985). *The interpersonal world of the infant.* New York: Basic Books.

Sullivan, H. S. (1953). *The interpersonal theory of psychiatry.* New York: W. W. Norton.

Suomi, S. J. (1981). Genetic, maternal and environmental influences on social development in rhesus monkeys. In B. Chiarelli & R. Coruccini (Eds.), *Primate behavior and sociobiology.* Berlin: Springer-Verlag.

Suomi, S. J. (1986). Anxiety-like disorders in young nonhuman primates. In R. Gittelman (Ed.), *Anxiety disorders of childhood.* New York: Guilford Press.

Tolpin, M. (1971). On the beginnings of a cohesive self: An application of the concept of transmuting internalization to the study of the transitional object and signal anxiety. In *Psychoanalytic Study of the Child,* v. 26. New York: Quadrangle Books.

Weissman, M. M., Leckman, J. F., Merikangas, K. R., Gammon, G. D., & Prusoff, B. A. (1984). Depression and anxiety disorders in parents and children. *Archives of General Psychiatry, 41,* 845–852.

Winnicott, D. W. (1952). Anxiety associated with insecurity. In *Through pediatrics to psychoanalysis.* London: Hogarth Press, 1978.

CHAPTER 12

Anxiety in Old Age

ROBERT J. KASTENBAUM, PhD

Researchers have known for some time that introducing the term "old" has a marked and predictable attitudinal effect (Tuckman & Lorge, 1953; Kogan & Shelton, 1962). Consider, for example, the following sentence-stems:

Most people become anxious when . . .
Most young people become anxious when . . .
Most old people become anxious when . . .

The most salient finding from attitudinal research is that adult age is perceived as a powerful variable both by the general population and by professional service providers (Palmore, 1990). The specific attributions and expectations are secondary to the predisposition to utilize "old" as a basic discriminant category. This predisposition could introduce inadvertent bias into the examination of anxiety in old age. Simply by identifying old age as a separate domain we risk the perpetuation of age stereotypes. It might be useful, then, to begin by reminding ourselves that age is but one contributing factor to anxiety and related disorders. We will take five examples: gender, race, health, personality, and cohort. Each of these sources of influence interact with age and often provide more useful cues for assessment and management of anxiety than does age taken by itself.

SOME CONTRIBUTING FACTORS TO ANXIETY IN THE LATER ADULT YEARS

Gender

Many sources of anxiety in the later adult years are mediated by gender-related experiences. Survival is itself correlated with sex/gender: the differential survival gap favoring females increases with advancing adult age (Gee, 1989). This means that elderly females are more likely to face anxieties related to (a) caring for a terminally ill spouse, (b) grieving his death, and (c) adjusting to postmarital life over an extended period of time. Although fewer elderly men survive their wives, those who do tend to have more difficulty in sharing their grief and seeking social support (Stroebe & Stroebe, 1990).

Gender is also a significant factor in many other types of vulnerability to anxiety in the later adult years. Elderly women tend to have fewer economic resources than men (Torres-Gil, 1992) and, as a result, have more reason to be concerned about basics such as food, transportation, home repairs, heating and telephone bills. In turn, a precarious financial situation is likely to arouse anxieties about losing one's own home and therefore also losing the sense of independence that is so highly valued in our society.

Major gender differences also exist with respect to the sense of usefulness and social integration. Retirement from full-time, long-term occupational activity is still predominantly a challenge for men (although an indirect challenge, for their wives). It is more often the man who is faced with anxiety-arousing questions about personal identity, continued usefulness, and related issues. The much higher suicide rate for elderly men vis à vis women is seen by some researchers as an outcome of the male's greater loss of identity and perceived self-worth upon retirement (Canetto, 1992). Suicide and other self-destructive acts (e.g., drinking binges) may be panic responses to the perceived sudden loss of status and value. On the other hand, women are likely to face job discrimination at an even earlier age than men, especially for positions that are above the entry level or minimum wage category (Christy, 1990). Women tend to be penalized both by the "glass ceiling" obstacle to advancement in mid-career and by societal attitudes that consider females to lose their value more rapidly than men after young adulthood. Aging, then, seems to present somewhat different anxiety-arousing signals in the occupational realm according to one's gender.

Elderly women are more likely than men to experience a sense of personal powerlessness (Degelman, Owens, Reynolds, & Riggs, 1991). Therefore, aging females may become relatively more vulnerable to anxiety that is related to lack of efficacy and control. Aging tends to challenge the sense of empowerment for both men and women, but gender-linked differences could be as significant as the shared age-related effects.

Race

Hardships, deprivations, and unequal access to social resources show race-linked patterns from infancy onward. Differential risk factors can both reduce the chances of surviving into old age (Gee, 1989) and contribute to unfavorable economic and health status in old age. An elderly African-American, for example, may experience anxiety as the result of a lifetime of prejudice and discrimination, but also because of stress and deprivation in the immediate situation (Barresi, 1987).

As Jackson (1993) suggests, socioeconomic class may be the major determinant of the risk factors that have been found associated with race. People in the lower socioeconomic brackets are at greater risk for health and other problems whatever their race. Furthermore, it is not only the differential sources of anxiety that seem to be race-linked, but there is also a tendency to focus on middle-class whites in research, educational, and clinical contacts.

For example, an elderly African-American man of rural Southern origins was a candidate for independent living after several years in a New England geriatric facility. He was seen by a psychologist who recognized that some of Mr. S.'s concerns were identical with those of other (white) residents who had faced the same challenge. However, Mr. S. also had a more distinctive source of anxiety. He was alarmed at the prospect of stepping out of his life-long role as a compliant and subserviant individual. (This anxiety first came to light when he insisted on sitting in the back of the bus when he joined a number of other residents in an outing.) Mr. S. readily accepted help in preparing himself to cope with some of the specific tasks and problems he would be encountering in the community, but he became paralyzed with anxiety whenever he sensed that he might be crossing the line to the kind of independence and privilege he associated with whites. Mr. S.'s age itself had very little to do with this reaction, which was not seen among white residents of his age and older. It would have been a mistake to interpret this reaction as the anxiety of old age when it was the unfortunate residue of a lifetime of mistreatment.

Health

It is easier to describe an individual's functional status, than to ascribe this status confidently to "aging." Gerontologists have learned to be cautious in offering such interpretations because an observed deficit or impairment can arise from a variety of sources. The tremor in an old person's voice, for example, could well be a symptom of neurological disorder rather than a just-to-be-expected correlate of the aging process (Case, 1993). Another elderly person's psychomotor retardation and confusion could prove to be the result of overmedication. For example, it was common to see significant improvement in mental status within a few days after admission to the geriatric facility in which Mr. S. resided, simply because the aged men and women were liberated from the mind-dulling medication they had been receiving in nursing care facilities.

People with limited experience in gerontology and geriatrics are more likely to assume that problems experienced by elderly people are part and parcel of old age. Unfortunately, this assumption too often eventuates in a self-fulfilling prophecy. A medical problem that might well have responded to treatment becomes chronic and recalcitrant because of misplaced therapeutic nihilism. An anxiety reaction that has been precipitated by potentially identifiable events and amenable to intervention may be dismissed as "senile agitation." At its worst, this assumption becomes a justification for withholding competent assessment and treatment opportunities from elderly men and women.

Aging adults themselves often have difficulty in distinguishing between "normal" changes and acquired disorders—made all the more complicated by such lifestyle factors as repeated dieting, over or under exercising, careless use of prescription or nonprescription drugs, insomnia secondary to depression, and so forth. A well-trained geriatric diagnostician will also have difficulty at times in distinguishing more or less expected age changes from symptoms of illness or other disorder.

The person experiencing these changes may be at risk for increased anxiety either through misinterpretation or uncertainty. For example, Mrs. D., a woman in her late seventies, fractured her hip in a fall. Mrs. D. (uncharacteristically) became so anxious that hospital staff as well as family had difficulty in dealing with her. As it turned out, Mrs. D. had put together bits of information she had heard or read to conclude that she was suffering from bone cancer—a disease that had painfully ended her mother's life. The anxiety quickly subsided when Mrs. D. accepted the medical evaluation that she was free of cancer but did have a problem with osteoporosis. Other elderly men and women have brought themselves to a state of anxious exhaustion by trying to understand the nature of their problems.

From a pragmatic standpoint, it may not seem to make much difference whether an elderly person's physical problems are related primarily to intrinsic aging or to a genetic or acquired disorder. Painful is painful; fatigue is fatigue. However, it does make a difference if we look at the whole picture over a period of time. People tend to be less anxious when they have a coherent explanation for their difficulties and an active course of action that has some potential to provide relief. There is a need for caution in interpreting a presenting picture of impairment and distress as "just what one might expect in a person of that age." It was not long ago that anxiety and confusion on the part of an elderly patient was often dismissed as senile agitation. Today, geriatricians are more likely to explore the sources of expressed anxiety with an open mind. (This writer's father would not have enjoyed his 90th birthday had not an older physician taken "vague complaints" seriously and discovered a gall bladder on the verge of rupture.)

Personality

Stereotypes about "the old person" perhaps misrepresent reality most enormously with respect to personality. Attitudinal studies such as those cited earlier have found that elderly people as a class are regarded as rigid, past-oriented, judgmental, asexual, and so forth. These stereotypes are not supported by direct studies of personality in the later adult years. What we find instead is a great diversity of personality types or lifestyles (e.g., Costa & McRae, 1984; Kogan, 1990). Although gerontologists disagree with respect to specific approaches to personality (e.g., trait vs. contextual models), there is fairly strong consensus regarding the fact of diversity. It is commonly noted that people become more rather than less individualized as they move through years of unique experiences.

There is no need here to survey the many competing models of personality that continue to contend for the support of clinicians, educators, and researchers. Partisans of a particular theory or classification system can determine for themselves how well their favored approach works when applied to elderly adults. One does not have to abandon all that one has previously learned and invent entirely new models. For example, trait theorists who have focused on extraversion-introversion in young adult populations might well be proficient in identifying differential sources of anxiety and differential coping strategies in elderly adults based on this salient dimensions.

Similarly, clinicians who draw upon the psychoanalytic tradition will find many clues to understanding problems experienced in the later adult years. For example, a fashion buyer for a major department store was so valued for her skills that the organization asked her to continue to work past the usual retirement age. Some of her colleagues protested vigorously against keeping her on, however, pointing out that she was a constant source of tension and conflicts in her relationships with them. In this instance, a psychoanalytically-oriented counselor helped the elderly woman reconstruct a long-term pattern of developing masochistic and competitive relationships, the only type of relationships she could trust. (The "oppositional dualism" dynamics of this type of case are described by Panken, 1973, especially pp. 139 ff.)

The point here is not to endorse any particular personality theory, but simply to note that in approaching the anxiety disorders experienced by elderly adults, one can glean insights and leads from a variety of theories. It is probable that theories with a strong developmental component will be more useful. Although trait theories often are favored by mainstream personality researchers and provide convenient ways to describe and classify, we are likely to find more substantive value in theories that emphasize time, change, and context. As always, however, the skill of the particular clinician, researcher, or educator is a major variable in determining a theory's usefulness.

A central controversy in the study of personality across the adult years could have significant bearing on anxiety. This is the question of *continuity vs. change*. There is now fairly broad agreement that the personality patterns established earlier in life remain salient throughout the adult years, although modified to some extent through by experience and changed circumstances. And, as already noted, there is also agreement that a variety of personality types can be observed in the later adult years both because diversity is evident from the start and because people tend to become even more individuated through their distinctive life experiences. The question at issue is whether or not there is a transformation process that operates across the observed diversity and continuity. Is there something about "aging" that introduces systematic change within all the enduring personality types?

One possibility here may have particular relevance for understanding anxiety in the later adult years: the Jungian-flavored, cross-culturally-researched theory proposed by David Guttmann (1987; 1993). He suggests that there is a systematic change in *mastery styles* from youth through old age. This theory will be considered in a little more detail later in this chapter. What is important for the moment is the recognition that the personality characteristics of elderly people might be more complicated than previously supposed: a variety of lifestyles, each enduring with some modifications within its own frame of organization, but all perhaps being subjected to a general process of change.

Cohort

Why is this octogenarian so preoccupied with even very small financial matters and such a penny-pincher when there seems to be no need for being so? A "fancy" interpretation might dwell on biological changes with age and the hypothetical recrudescence of anal-retentive features. Most gerontologists, however, would probably go first with a simpler interpretation: This person's coming of age occurred during the Great Depression. He or she may have seen anxiety, confusion, anger, and deprivation on all sides. Perhaps he or she personally missed out on educational or career opportunities that never came around again. The possible influence of the Great Depression on personality and adaptation in the later years of life is one example of the role of cohort effects. What might be mistaken for the consequences of aging or the expression of a particular personality type might instead by more cogently understood as the response to sociohistorical circumstances encountered because of one's membership in a particular birth cohort.

Several other examples were implied earlier in this chapter. For example, expectations and opportunities for women have varied significantly from generation to generation in the course of this century. These differences encompass the entire range of life activities, from careers to community service, from political involvement to sexuality. In an intergenerational group meeting, one elderly widow observed that "I'll tell you what my sexual anxiety was—seriously. It was not wanting to hurt my husband's feelings by turning him down, but not wanting to get pregnant again. . . . Oh, well, listen! We didn't talk about those things like you do today, not even in the bedroom. Now couples talk about sex and birth control like they talk about what to have for supper! . . . Yes, I think it's better today, much better!" When a few minutes, the discussion turned to AIDS, the elderly widow somberly agreed that not all the changes were for the better.

Cohort effects are also strong and varied along the dimensions of race and ethnicity. Think, for example, of the differential expectations and opportunities experienced by elderly African-Americans in their youth—and compare this experience with the prospects that motivate and frustrate their grandchildren today. Specific historical events can also have differential impacts on people of varying cohorts. For example, the sudden rise in discrimination against Japanese-Americans during World War II resulted in heightened stress and, for some, significant loss. This experience took markedly different forms, however, for young and old. Senior adults had to cope with such feelings as surprise, anger, and disappointment that they would be treated as though disloyal to America, and the fear that all they had worked for over the years was now in jeopardy. However, they also had the resources of experience and maturity to call upon in coping with this crisis. By contrast, children also felt the sting of discrimination and the sense of stress and anxiety that enveloped their families—but they did not have a fully developed perspective within which to contain and cope with this situation. Therapists interested in ameliorating the anxiety of elderly Japanese-Americans would have had markedly different situations to deal with in the mid-1940s as compared with today: a person whose well-established life pattern had been disrupted and assailed by his or her host society, or a person who carries forward from childhood the memories of discrimination, trauma, and distrust.

It would be simplistic to proceed on the basis of a prototypical elderly person who has a particular kind of anxiety and a particular way of dealing with this anxiety. Gender, race, ethnicity, health, personality, and cohort membership all contribute to who this particular person is and how he or she attempts to cope with anxiety in the later years of life. Furthermore, these influences are interactive at all points in the total life course.

Mrs. P., for example, cannot be understood adequately in terms of her 87 years. We must take into account the role of the female as expected within first generation Polish-American culture and modified to some extent over the decades, a competitive personality that helped her to advance her own claims within a large family network, and a double-hip fracture that has severely restricted her mobility and independence in her old multilevel home. Moreover, we still would be ignorant of some of the most powerful influences and resources in her life if we did not take into account the ethnic neighborhood in which she resides—and the social and economic pressures that this traditional conclave is now facing itself. As it happened with Mrs. P., her intensified anxiety centered on an impending marriage that, to her way of thinking, would leave her in a socially isolated and less empowered position. She could cope with this and she could cope with that—but not with the threat of losing power within the family and neighborhood social structure.

OVERVIEW: GENERAL CHARACTERISTICS OF ANXIETY IN OLD AGE

It is helpful to identify several of the most salient age-related themes, contexts, and expressions of anxiety in the later adult years. As might be expected from the preceding discussion, these age-related phenomena are mediated by all the factors that contribute to making a particular individual that particular individual.

The following characteristics tend to be more common and salient among older adults:

1. *Anxiety frequently arises from realistic concerns.* Clinicians who are primed to recognize and treat neurotic disorders in younger adults have sometimes felt powerless as well as disoriented when first called upon to work with elders. Although neurotic men and women grow older and take their anxieties with them, there are also many people whose sense of security has been challenged by emergent circumstances. In such instances, it is neither accurate nor useful to see them as tilting with windmills of their own devising or merely stewing in long-term conflicts. They are facing genuine threats (or, at least, the plausible "threat of a threat") to their health, independence, self-esteem, and so forth.

There are many implications. For example, in a study of more than a thousand male veterans (aged 25 to 90), it was found that there were some men with high, moderate, and low levels of expressed anxiety at every age level (McRae, Bartone, & Costa, 1976). A provocative difference showed up when highly anxious men of various ages were compared with each other on their reporting of physical complaints. Young and middle-aged anxious men reported more physical symptoms than adjusted men of the same age. But anxious elderly men reported *fewer* physical symptoms than less anxious men of the same age.

The investigators then constructed a discrepancy index that compared the number of complaints reported by the men with the actual findings of very thorough medical examinations. The age-anxiety pattern again showed a reversal. Young and middle-aged men with high anxiety reported more illnesses than their physicians could find, but in old age, the less anxious men reported more illnesses. The anxious elderly men underestimated and underreported the actual hazards to their health, while anxious young men could afford to focus on symptoms because they did not truly think their lives were in danger. The adjusted elderly men seemed to be actively monitoring their own physical status in a realistic manner, while elevated anxiety in old age seems to interfere with attending to realistic health problems.

This is but one illustration of what one might discover when starting with the recognition that there are realistic emergent sources of anxiety in the later adult years, along with the perpetuation of neurotic conflicts. Furthermore, there can be a variety of interactions between realistic age-related concerns and pre-existing neurotic patterns. For example, the realistic threat of reduced financial circumstances can unmask or intensify earlier fears such as being exposed as a failure or "losing one's substance." An elderly woman living alone with some difficulty may be alarmed when a neighbor of the same age is admitted to a nursing home—an alarm that has one foot in reality and the other in a lifelong hypersensitivity to being unloved and abandoned.

2. *There is often a reduction in the resources available to cope with anxiety.* Many people deal with stress, threats, and conflicts by moving away from them, exhibiting avoidant behavior. A hassled teenager runs away from home, a quarreling lover drives off, a pressured employee quits his or her job. This strategy may have paid off many times, not necessarily by solving problems but by providing time outs and preventing more extreme behaviors. Elderly adults tend to have fewer opportunities to move away from sources of anxiety. Limitations on physical mobility and finances often reduce the ability to put distance between oneself and a frustrating or abusive situation. Furthermore, a complex web of mutual dependencies may keep people together in stressful and destructive relationships. Forced proximity, especially without the opportunity for respite, can intensify anxieties around privacy, empowerment, and a variety of other issues that mediate quality of life.

An extreme example came to public attention recently in Arizona when a 94-year-old man shot and killed two of his mobile home park neighbors. Other neighbors reported that the two victims were unpleasant people who had enjoyed tormenting the old man by playing music at a very high volume despite his continual protests. The old man himself was seen as a "crusty" fellow. Feeling that he could neither tolerate the abuse nor move away from it, he armed himself and shot them dead. Less extreme and violent, but also highly stressful, examples can be found in many geriatric facilities where elderly residents may be forced into close and regular contact with people they dislike or fear.

Within the family circle, a senior adult may feel stressed and outraged by the behavior of others, yet consider that he or she has no viable residential alternative. Mrs. L., a woman recovering from a stroke accepted her daughter's invitation to move in with her. From the older woman's standpoint, the situation soon became a living hell as "two bratty kids" did whatever they wanted, and she herself was treated like a child. Worst of all, her daughter, still legally married, would bring men home and disappear behind the bedroom door with them. Mrs. L. wept tears of anger at her perceived helplessness to do anything about the situation.

One does not have to assume that there is anything fundamentally different about the elderly person whose high level of anxiety has been provoked or maintained by constant exposure to stressful people and circumstances. Young people feel pretty much the same way when they can neither readily resolve nor escape from a problem.

3. *Normative transitions and uncertainties tend to keep people on an anxious footing.* Again, the basic phenomenon here is one that can be experienced by people of any age. We tend to feel most secure (least anxious) in familiar and stable situations, and when we can predict future developments and outcomes with a sense of confidence. The anxieties of adolescence have often been interpreted within the context of the transitions and uncertainties that tend to become salient as one attempts to establish an individual and adult identity. Although the particulars differ markedly, elderly adults also tend to find themselves in a transitional situation which, in this case, challenges the identity and security that had previously been achieved.

For example, people in their sixties face such normative transitions as:

- From career to retirement
- From relatively high to relatively low empowerment
- From marriage to widowhood
- From independent to assisted living.

Each of these transitions involves a set of more specific challenges and decisions. Anxiety may be even higher when these transitions are in prospect than when one is facing them directly. For example, the wife of a "workaholic" public agency administrator feared that her husband would go "looney-tunes—and take me with him" when forced to retire.

In her own words, "I made myself a nervous wreck worrying about becoming a nervous wreck!" As it turned out, however, the workaholic "sobered up" spontaneously after he drew his final paycheck and did not seem to miss either his previous busywork or authority. The couple felt less anxious "when retirement actually struck" than the wife had when anticipating the dreaded day.

Uncertainty tends to intensify apprehensions regarding health, independence, and survival. One cannot predict when significant problems will arise in these spheres. For example, people entering their seventh decades in good health could be continuing to enjoy independent living a decade later, or develop a serious ailment or impairment within a short time. Some people respond to this normative situational uncertainty with a perpetual bubbling of anxiety. Others, however, just stop scanning the future and take life day-by-day. An interesting study by Kulys and Tobin (1980) found that intellectually competent elderly adults who did not project their thoughts forward into the remote future were adapting this strategy of not burdening themselves with uncertainties. Those with low future concern were also less anxious and less hostile than those who were inclined to scan the temporal horizon for the disasters that might lie ahead.

To some extent, then, anxiety in later adult years can be conceptualized as part of a lifespan developmental story that has always featured developmental challenge, hazard, and opportunity. When society as well as the individual is changing, the sense of instability and unpredictability is exacerbated. For example, a middle-aged adult who expected this to be a settled and prosperous time of life may be more anxious than ever because his or her job is jeopardized by corporate failure or downsizing. This person now must cope not only with sources of anxiety that are more or less normative in middle adulthood but also with dislocations and dangers introduced by socioeconomic forces. Similarly, elderly adults today must cope not only with the universal sources of concern associated with advancing age, but also with technological change and the destabilizing effects of postmodernism on those who grew up with more traditional views of self and society (Kastenbaum, 1993). The ailing old woman who is being asked to complete baffling bureaucratic forms by a stranger at the admissions desk of a hospital is not just experiencing her own idiosyncratic anxiety, but the anxiety of a generation.

4. *Elderly people tend to be anxious about dying, not death.* The three themes already mentioned all converge here. Dying and death are realistic concerns in later adult years; one can no more escape from mortality than one can escape from one's own skin; and the process of departing from this life to the unknown is as universal and normative a transition as birth.

There is no firm evidence for the proposition that elderly men and women are more anxious about death than the general population. In fact, the available data suggest that younger adults have higher levels of everyday death anxiety than do healthy senior adults (Kastenbaum, 1987; 1992a). Peaks of death-related anxiety usually are seen only in elderly adults who are having a psychotic or trauma-evoked reaction, or as a fleeting reaction to an emergent situation (e.g., learning that one has cancer). Studies usually find that age itself explains relatively little about an individual's anxiety or other attitudes toward death.

Death-related anxiety is quite different, however, from fear or anxiety regarding death as such. For example, many people at any age have life concerns that are exacerbated by the prospect of death. An elderly woman who has lived for many years with a variety of painful and disabling conditions may be ready to see her life end, but anxious about who will look after her "old man." Another elderly person may be more concerned about what will become of the family estate when it falls into squabbling hands after his death. Would-be counselors or other service-providers will be more useful if they learn to distinguish between existential anxiety regarding death and the variety of life-oriented concerns that can perturb people who are nearing the end of their lives.

Dying is perhaps the most salient of all death-related issues. Anxiety in the last phase of life often arises from dread of prolonged suffering and helplessness, feeling burdensome on others, and draining the family's financial resources. Again, a distinction must be made between how a person copes with the problem once it is directly at hand, and the fears and apprehensions that one may have lived with when thinking about a final ordeal. Experience with hospice care (e.g., Mor, 1987) has found that many elderly adults cope very well with their terminal illness, or serve as effective caregivers for a dying spouse. With competent and caring support from others, including state-of-the-art symptom relief, elderly men and women often can remain comfortable and secure, still a valued part of their families, until their last breath. Anxiety-reduction approaches, then, can take two general forms: relieving apprehensions about the dying process in advance through emotional support and information-giving, and preventing or ameliorating suffering and isolation during the dying process by competent and sensitive care. Counselors or other caregivers who are themselves highly anxious about their own mortality may not be in a position to provide either of these services.

ASSESSMENT AND INTERVENTION: A FEW SPECIFICS

In conclusion, we will look briefly at a few selected topics that may be of interest for those conducting anxiety disorder assessment, intervention, or research in later life.

The Cognition-Anxiety Link

Many associations are found between cognition and anxiety at all age levels. This linkage may be especially salient among elderly adults. For example, memory lapses may induce anxiety that is out of proportion to the incidents themselves. Furthermore, the increasingly widespread awareness of Alzheimer's disease has so sensitized some middle-aged and elderly adults that they may interpret "garden variety" forgetfulness as a pathognomic sign of a progressive dementing disease. In helping people cope with this source of anxiety, one should not underestimate the difficulties involved in making accurate assessments of Alzheimer-type disorders early in their course, nor be unaware of the variety of other organic and functional explanations for memory lapses.

Withdrawal from activities and relationships may also be consequences of anxiety about one's ability to perform cognitive tasks. Elderly people may fear humiliation or failure because they no longer trust their ability to learn new names and other facts, process information rapidly and reliably, and retrieve knowledge from memory on demand. One or two adverse experiences may lead to a loss of self-confidence and start a cycle of withdrawal and depression. "Test anxiety" is a variation of this concern.

"Flights into senility" may occur when an elderly person feels unable to cope with change, stress, and threat. The apparent inability to *comprehend* reality proves at times to be a strategy intended to *protect* one from a hostile or overwhelming reality.

Loss of Efficacy, Control, and Confidence Are Primary Sources of Anxiety

Early in life one must often work to achieve efficacy, control, and confidence. "I can accomplish; I can manage; I can do" are self-judgments that are earned only after many attempts, some of which are miserable failures. Circumstances often compel elderly adults to ask themselves, "Can I still accomplish? Can I still manage? Can I still do?" Some older men and women seem to have an inexhaustible personal account to draw upon to maintain their confidence; others are more easily made to feel insecure when they encounter situations where their efficacy and control seems unequal to the task. Anybody might have a particular experience in which "the old touch" doesn't seem to work. It is when one starts to doubt his or her general ability to influence the world and exercise a reasonable amount of control that the danger of catastrophic anxiety arises.

The efficacy/control/confidence issue has its interpersonal and objective as well as its subjective side. One's success in continuing to live a confident and competent life may depend much on how others cooperate. A supportive "convoy" of friends and relations (Antonucci & Akiyama,

1993) can provide just enough help to make up for possible age-related decrements in efficacy and control. The loss of significant others and the indifference of strangers can lead to a series of disappointments and frustrations that contribute to a loss of self-confidence.

The objective side is now the subject of intensified study of lifespan developmentalists and gerontologists (e.g., Baltes & Baltes, 1986; Langer, 1989). Studies conducted in field situations (e.g., nursing homes), as well as the laboratory, are exploring the limits and potentialities for maintaining control over one's own life in the later adult years. It would be premature to draw conclusions either about the nature and extent of age-related decrements in control or the possibility of compensating for deficits. For now it may be enough to note that objective control and the sense of control both are gaining recognition as major factors in adjustment to the challenges of aging. Anxiety disorders should be less common, intense, and enduring among those elderly men and women who can continue to feel confidence in their ability to influence the world around them.

"Opening Up" Can Liberate Energy and Reduce Anxiety

Here is one of the more significant emergent areas in gerontology. The basic thesis is that people often must "plow under" some of their creative potential in order to fulfill their obligations in the family and the workplace. This chronic suppression of interests and talents may contribute to a vague sense of dissatisfaction. Despite health, financial stability, and supportive relationships, they feel somehow unfulfilled and thwarted. This might be termed the anxiety of the unfulfilled.

One specific theory has been offered by David Gutmann (1987), whose work was mentioned briefly earlier. His cross-cultural research seems to support Jung's conception that females and males each tend to suppress the other-gender side of their nature throughout the first half of their lives. The challenge of the second half of life, then, is to actualize the other side of our natures and, in general, open ourselves to the creative potentials that previously lay dormant. For men, this process involves moving from an active mastery to a symbolic mastery orientation; for women, the movement is in the opposite direction. Guttmann's theory also takes social change factors into account, especially the tendency of mass, high-tech societies to treat elders as useless rather than provide them with places of honor and respect. Maduro's (1974) research in Northern India has demonstrated that society can also encourage and support creativity in old age.

Academic studies of creativity (e.g., Simonton, 1991; Kastenbaum, 1992b), clinical reflections (e.g., Carlsen, 1991) and applied programs to encourage expressive activities (e.g., Goff & Torrance, 1991) are starting to make it clear that anxiety can be reduced and latent energies liberated when elderly men and women open themselves up to their creative potentials. This itself is not entirely an anxiety-free enterprise because risk-taking is inherent in all creative activity. There is the immense advantage, however, of feeling oneself to be the source of impulse, idea, and activity rather the pawn or victim of forces outside one's control.

CONCLUSION

It may be suggested in conclusion that although many elderly men and women experience anxiety (e.g., MacDonald & Schnur, 1987), this does not necessarily signify that anxiety disorders are rife. There are many realistic sources of concern in the later adult years, so the frequent sounding of the anxiety alarm can be an adaptive function that speaks well of the individual's situational awareness. Elderly people are survivors. They have many resources of skill, character, and experience that can continue to benefit themselves and others. Competent service-providers need not develop their own anxiety disorders in contemplating preventive and interventive activities.

REFERENCES

Antonucci, T. C., & Akiyama, H. (1993). Convoys of social relationships across the lifespan. In R. Kastenbaum (Ed.), *The encyclopedia of adult development.* Phoenix: Oryx Press.

Baltes, M. M., & Baltes, P. B. (Eds.). (1989). *The psychology of control and aging.* Hillsdale, NJ: Erlbaum.

Barresi, C. M. (1987). Ethnic aging and the life course. In D. E. Gelfand & C. M. Barresi (Eds.), *Ethnic dimensions of aging* (pp. 18–34). New York: Springer.

Bengtson, V. L., Reedy, M. N., & Gordon, C. (1985). Aging and self-conceptions: Personality processes and social contexts. In J. E. Birren & K. W. Schaie (Eds.), *Handbook of the psychology of aging.* 2nd ed. (pp. 544–593). New York: Van Nostrand Reinhold.

Canetto, S. (1992). Gender and suicide in the elderly. *Suicide & Life-Threatening Behavior, 22,* 80–97.

Carlsen, M. B. (1991). *Creative aging: A meaning-making perspective.* New York: W. W. Norton.

Case, J. L. (1993). The voice: From youth through adulthood. In R. Kastenbaum (Ed.), *The encyclopedia of adult development.* Phoenix: Oryx Press.

Christy, S. (1990). Women, work, and the work-place. In L. L. Lindsay (Ed.), *Gender roles: A sociological perspective.* (pp. 179–201). Engelwood Cliffs, NJ: Prentice-Hall.

Costa, P. T., Jr., & McCrae, R. R. (1984). Personality as a lifelong determinant of well being. In C. Z. Malatesta & C. E. Izard (Eds.), *Emotion in adult development.* (pp. 141–157). Beverly Hills: Sage.

Degelman, D., Owens, S. A. A., Reynolds, T., & Riggs, J. (1991). Age and gender differences in beliefs about personal power and injustice. *International Journal of Aging & Human Development, 33,* 101–112.

Gee, E. (1989). Mortality rate. In R. Kastenbaum & B. K. Kastenbaum (Eds.), (pp. 183–185). *Encyclopedia of death.* Phoenix: Oryx Press.

Goff, K., & Torrance, E. P. (1991). The Georgia studies of creative behavior: Venturing into studies of creativity in elders. *Generations, 14,* 53–55.

Gutmann, D. (1987). *Reclaimed powers.* New York: Basic Books.

Gutmann, D. (1993). Mastery types, development, and aging. In R. Kastenbaum (Ed.), *The encyclopedia of adult development.* Phoenix: Oryx Press.

Jackson, J. S. (1993). African American experiences through the adult years. In R. Kastenbaum (Ed.), *The encyclopedia of adult development.* Phoenix: Oryx Press.

Kastenbaum, R. (1987). Death-related anxiety. In L. Michelson & L. M. Ascher (Eds.), *Anxiety and stress disorders.* (pp. 425–441). New York: The Guilford Press.

Kastenbaum, R. (1992a). *The psychology of death.* Rev. ed. New York: Springer.

Kastenbaum, R. (1992b). The creative process: A lifespan approach. In T. Cole, D. D. Van Tassel, & R. Kastenbaum (Eds.), *Handbook of the humanities and aging.* (pp. 285–306). New York: Springer.

Kastenbaum, R. (1993). Encrusted elders: Arizona and the political spirit of postmodern aging. In T. Cole, A. Achenbaum, & R. Kastenbaum (Eds.), *Voices and contexts: Toward a critical gerontology.* (pp. 285–306). New York: Springer.

Kogan, N. (1990). Personality and aging. In J. E. Birren & K. W. Schaie (Eds.), *Handbook of the psychology of aging.* 3rd ed. (pp. 330–346). San Diego: Academic Press.

Kogan, N., & Shelton, F. C. (1962). Beliefs about "old people": A comparative study of older and younger samples. *J. Genet. Psychol., 100,* 93–111.

Kulys, R., & Tobin, S. (1980). Interpreting the lack of future concerns among the elderly. *International Journal of Aging and Human Development, 11,* 111–126.

Langer, E. J. (1989). *Mindfulness.* Reading, MA: Addison-Wesley.

MacDonald, M. L., & Schnur, R. E. (1987). Anxieties and American elders: Proposals for assessment and treatment. In L. Michelson & L. M. Ascher (Eds.), *Anxiety and stress disorders.* (pp. 395–424). New York: The Guilford Press.

McCrae, R. R., Bartone, P. T., & Costa, P. T., Jr. (1976). Age, personality, and self-reported health. *International Journal of Aging & Human Development, 6,* 49–58.

Mor, V. (1987). *Hospice care systems.* New York: Springer.

Palmore, E. B. (1990). *Ageism.* New York: Springer.

Panken, S. (1973). *The Joy of Suffering*. New York: Jason Aronson.

Simonton, D. K. (1991). Creative productivity through the adult years. *Generations, 14,* 13–16.

Stroebe, M. S., & Stroebe, W. (1989–1990). Who participates in bereavement research? A review and empirical study. *Omega, Journal of Death and Dying, 20,* 1–30.

Torres-Gil, F. M. (1992). *The new aging: Politics and change in America.* New York: Auburn House.

Tuckman, J., & Lorge, I. (1953). Attitudes toward old people. *Journal of Social Psychology, 37,* 249–260.

CHAPTER 13

Post-Traumatic Stress Disorder (PTSD): Its Biopsychobehavioral Aspects and Management

ERWIN RANDOLPH PARSON, PhD

PTSD, "a dark and dismal subject"

—*SIGMUND FREUD*

POPULARITY, CONTROVERSY, CLINICAL UTILITY, AND RATIONALE FOR THE DIAGNOSIS

Post-traumatic stress disorder (PTSD) (APA, 1987) is a complex psychiatric disorder, conceptualized in the present contribution as a *tripartite* clinical entity based upon an emerging body of clinical and empirical evidence. PTSD impacts the total self: its *biological*—central (CNS), peripheral sympathetic (SNS), and neuroendocrine systems; *psychological*—endopsychic processing of trauma elements, to include cognitive, affective and control devices; and *behavioral*—implied in abnormalities seen in disturbed interpersonal and social-ecologic transactions. The tripartite model used here intends to increase conceptual acumen, and to guide formulation, assessment, and interventions of greater efficacy with trauma victims who endured human-engineered, natural, and technological catastrophes.

PTSD has a controversal history: Some people believe that untoward events in life are to be overcome by sheer will and personal strength. When will and character do not suffice and the individual becomes overwhelmed then the causative factors are believed to have originated in childhood. Others held that an event can be so overwhelming that most people will succumb to it and break down. This controversy is still begin debated, though many issues have been resolved empirically. PTSD, as conceptualized in the DSM-III-R, is ahistorical and atheoretical: it's a disorder that relies neither on childhood etiology nor on a specific theory.

Post-traumatic stress disorder is a condition of great clinical and cultural interest; however, as Kardiner (1959) aptly pointed out, the disorder "alternates between being the urgent topic of the times and being completely and utterly neglected" (p. 242). He maintained that PTSD may be caused by war and "peacetime" traumatic experiences, which are too often "swallowed up in oblivion" (p. 245). But why recognize, study, assess, and treat PTSD, a psychiatric disorder that Freud himself referred to as "the dark and dismal subject"? With the explosion of violence around the world, and the increasing number of patients seeking assistance for traumatic stress syndromes, the topic continues to be one of importance.

PTSD is a major public health problem (Helzer, Robins, & McEnvoy, 1987; Kulka et al., 1988; Parson, 1990d). The public health threat derives from the brutalization of rape, the fastest growing crime in America; increase in child physical and sexual abuse; incest; aircraft accidents; railroad mishaps; natural disasters; drug-instigated violence and witnessing of terror, death, and annihilation by black and Hispanic children in urban neighborhoods (Parson, 1993), and other traumatizing events.

Though worldwide estimates of PTSD are unknown, there is evidence to suggest that the disorder is also a world health problem. Many people have been exposed to the ubiquity of human catastrophic misery and "global traumatic stress" (Parson, 1992) from mass violence and horrors of Cambodian genocide (Lee & Lu, 1989; Mollica, 1988); governmental sexual torture (Agger, 1989); political persecution and repression as in South Africa (Simpson, 1993); violent street and residential crime (Resnick, 1989); and children traumatized by Central American warfare (Arroyo & Eth, 1985), or by a school bus accident in Israel (Milgram, Toubiana, Klingman, Raviv, & Goldstein, 1988). Since 1980, "PTSD [has been regarded] as a diagnosis that spans national and cultural boundaries" (Weisaeth & Eitinger, 1992). But current world use is technically unofficial until the World Health Organization (WHO) adopts the diagnosis in its Tenth Edition of *International Classification of Diseases* (ICD) to be published in the near future. This would "promote systematic use of the term" (Weisaeth & Eitinger, 1992).

In addition, PTSD is probably the only disorder in contemporary nosological systems that features: (1) an etiological link to specific external-ecologic stimuli (e.g., floods, war, rape) as opposed to problematic childhood experiences with parental figures; (2) an intensity dimension of the etiologic agent; that is, extraordinary stressors (e.g., disasters) versus mundane stressors (e.g., financial losses, death of a loved one, family illness); (3) a latency (asymptomatic) period during which time a "meaningful" trauma-associated stimuli can trigger the full-blown psychiatric disorder (i.e., PTSD). The fact that an external stressor is both necessary and sufficient for PTSD and that childhood traumas are not necessary for the condition. This position has added fuel to the controversial nature of PTSD, as argued by Breslau and Davis (1987) and Horowitz (1983), who maintain that non-extraordinary stressors may be "traumatic" to certain individuals.

PTSD can occur at (1) any age or stage in the life cycle; (2) may not get better over time, but may become more debilitating and even irreversible with age. Treatment of PTSD requires an interdisciplinary model that integrates contributions from psychology, psychiatry, psychoanalysis, social welfare, psychiatric and nursing science, general medicine, rehabilitation medicine, military medicine, neurology, law enforcement, emergency rescue services—to name a few.

Despite this interdisciplinary appeal, PTSD is perhaps the clinical entity for which there is least consensus among the professional and scientific disciplines. Kardiner's (1969) 40 years of experience in the traumatic neuroses foreshadowed contemporary developments when he noted that, although "a vast store of data [was] available," it was "hard to find a province of psychiatry in which there is less discipline than this one [PTSD]." Noting the lack of consensus and continuity in the field, Kardiner also remarked that "There is practically no continuity to be found anywhere, and the literature can only be characterized as anarchic." He continued, "every author has his own frame of reference—lengthy bibliographies notwithstanding" (p. 245).

Boulanger (1990) has written about this "state of anarchy," and bring attention to sociocultural and structural problems that "institutionalize" this anarchic state of affairs, despite the long-recorded history of the concept of PTSD (Boulanger, 1985; Brende & Parson, 1986; Breuer & Freud, 1893/1895; Trimble, 1981).

Despite its controversial nature, PTSD continues to have great appeal to the mass media, the public, and the U.S. government. The mass appeal of PTSD is a cultural phenomenon with rational and irrational aspects. Popular talk shows highlight the irrational (unconscious) aspects as hosts and studio audiences create a popular culture of victims and victimization—the "televictims" (Parson, 1989, 1992). Talk shows thrive on the victim's dramatic revelations about trauma, victimization, and the most dramatic symptoms of PTSD. Thus, in many ways the popularity of PTSD may say as much about the post-traumatic sequelae in victims as it does about society itself.

PTSD is becoming a field of study in its own right. According to Figley (1988), the professional and scientific developments nationally and internationally over the past decade meet the essential criteria for a legitimate field of study. Greater understanding of PTSD may also contribute to early detection, recognition, and prevention of the development of chronic, maladaptive behavioral patterns, inhibitions, and symptomatology; and, at the same time, prevent intergenerational transmission of traumatopathology that also ruin the lives of victims' children.

This chapter presents a comprehensive understanding of psychological traumatization. It begins with an historical background to place contemporary concepts and findings in perspective, and then provides definitions, etiological models, course of the disorder, diagnosis, co-morbidity, and a flexible interconceptual model for treating PTSD, to include cognitive, behavioral, psychodynamic, and pharmacological approaches.

HISTORY OF TRAUMATIC NEUROSIS

The psychiatric nosological entity, post-traumatic stress disorder (PTSD), is a new term for an old condition with a long history. It was first listed in the third edition of DSM-III (APA, 1980), and is in the evolutionary line of several sociocultural and clinical entities used to describe post-traumatic reactions for decades.

In addition to war, the world has subjected its inhabitants to severe traumatic incidents throughout history, including bubonic plagues, volcanic eruptions, toxic gas seepage, typhoons, earthquakes, tidal waves, industrial accidents, and destructive hurricanes. Perhaps the earliest account of war is to be found in the writings of Herodotus, who wrote about the wars between the Greeks and the Persians.

Ellis (1984) discusses Homer's account of a "case of hysterical blindness" during the Battle of Marathon in 490 B.C. The valiant soldier, Epizelus, had been exposed to extreme levels of war stress: the blindness had occurred "though wounded in no part of his body . . . [and persisted] for the rest of his life" (p. 168). This soldier, like many contemporary combatants, had experienced "adaptive biopsychic responses" to avoid witnessing and participating in further devastation of human life, probably motivated by guilt-driven defenses and a need for punishment.

Daly (1983) reported on the traumatic experiences of Samuel Pepys during the Great Fire of London on September 2, 1666. As first-hand witness to horror, Pepys gazed at this formidable, raging inferno which became indelibly imprinted or internalized, and etched upon his memory. As a now permanent aspect of his psychological functioning, Pepys was flooded by vivid images in the daytime and, at night, traumatic dream imagery. Many people who witnessed the fire ended their personal torment by committing suicide. Pepys' symptoms reached criteria for post-traumatic stress disorder.

During the American Civil War, soldiers fell prey to the effects of war stress in large numbers, and were called nostalgics, suffering from "irritable heart" (Da Costa in Skerritt, 1919), while accidents caused by the explosion of machines and transportation systems during the Industrial Revolution produced "accident neurosis" (Kelly, 1981; Leader, 1961). A new litigious climate and suspicion about the legitimacy of victims' claims for compensation created the cynical medicolegal term "greenback neurosis" (Schroeder, 1961). The term "traumatic neurosis" was coined by Oppenheim and Thompson in 1800 (Trimble, 1981), and along with "shell shock" (Mott, 1919) and "traumatic war neurosis" (Brill, 1967) was used during World War I by psychoanalysts and the medical community.

Clinical and field studies of disastrous fires, floods, tragedies at sea, and other mishaps affecting large numbers of people, led to the inclusion of the term "gross stress reaction" in the first edition of the *Diagnostic and Statistical Manual of Mental Disorders* (DSM-I) in 1952. This condition was distinguished from neurosis and psychosis by its clinical course, transience, and reversibility. Having acknowledged that victims of overwhelming, catastrophic events may have no "apparent underlying mental disorders" (APA, 1968, p. 49), the editors of the DSM-II advanced the term "transient situational disturbances" in 1968, while ironically deleting "stress" from the new diagnostic category.

THE STRESS-RESPONSE SPECTRUM

Historically, war has always given impetus to concerns about posttraumatic syndromes. In 1980, the lingering effects of the Vietnam War led to the diagnosis of post-traumatic stress disorder being entered in the third edition of the *Diagnostic and Statistical Manual of Mental Disorders* (DSM-III). The term *stress* was originally used in engineering, architecture, and physics to describe the effects of an external force exerting pressure or physical strain upon an inanimate object, structure, or system. Later, stress had been generalized to mean forces exerting pressure on the human organism, leading to physical or mental ill health.

The stress spectrum consists of three-dimensional intensities of the stress response, which range from "instrumental stress" (positive) at the beginning, and "biopsychobehavioral stress" (mostly negative) at the toxic end of the spectrum. The intermediate level of stress is called "detrimental stress." Can each of these three stressor intensities produce PTSD? The issue of the stressor criterion for PTSD is still controversial (Breslau & Davis, 1987; Horowitz, 1983; Solomon & Canino, 1990).

Instrumental stress promotes vital bodily processes; it contributes to individual efficiency, concentration, and peak performance. It achieves positive outcomes congruent with the individual's sense of well-being. Detrimental or negative stress, on the other hand, is the stress that makes people physically and mentally ill, first described by Hans Selye in the 1930s, and first measured systematically by Holmes and Rache (1967) with the Social Readjustment Scale. Negative stress is characterized by tension, muscle stiffness, and soaring heart rate and blood pressure. These responses are linked to physical problems such as tension headaches, back pain, ulcers, smoking, drug and alcohol abuse, high blood pressure, heart attack and, in general, to problems between the nervous and immune systems.

The third kind of stress response is biopsychobehavioral stress (or biopsychic stress). It refers to the condition commonly called "psychological trauma," "stress response syndrome" (Horowitz, 1976), and PTSD (Horowitz, Wilmer, & Kaltreider, 1980) in the stress literature. The concept of biopsychobehavioral stress is a more comprehensive term capturing the pervasive disturbance in not only the psychological sphere, but also in biological and behavioral organizations of the total self.

PTSD AS A BIOPSYCHOBEHAVIORAL DISORDER

Clinical observation and advanced technology, knowledge, and measurement sophistication in the behavioral and social sciences, in laboratory physiological techniques, and in the neurosciences offer convincing evidence that PTSD is a multidimensional disorder, requiring biological, psychological, and behavioral approaches to conceptualization and intervention.

Phenomenology and Clinical Symptomatology

Biopsychic stress results in post-traumatic stress disorder. Phenomenologically, survivors of trauma experience a disturbance in the sense of self now weakened and rendered "unable to hold the pieces together." Multiple, intense and overwhelming stimuli stretch, strain, and ultimately overwhelm an otherwise integrated and well-functioning ego (Freud, 1920).

During the immediate moments after the trauma, the victim is caught up in a phenomenophysiological experience: the victim "experiences his or her life as being threatened and responds with fear, helplessness, and an accompanying physiological 'fight-flight' activation of pulse, blood pressure, perspiration, and muscle activity" (Brende & Parson, 1986). Intrusive ideas, emotions, and memories of the frightening event constantly remind victims that the structure of life before the event is perhaps gone forever, eclipsed by a new "reality principle" born of the new realization that "the mind is wax to receive impressions, but marble to retain them" (Shatan, 1982).

For whereas in the past the victim had a relatively stable identity, of-fering predictability and inner security, the victim now faces "automatic dyscontrol," which essentially undermines a sense of self, self-sameness, continuity, and personal sociohistory. The predictability of life has been eclipsed by a perpetual "fear of [psychic] breakdown" and related "primitive agonies" (Winnicott, 1970), as the emotional context of trauma continues to exert its disorganizing power. This "down under self experience" is a feeling of suffocation, of being stripped of control and of being buried alive.

Post-traumatic déjà vu is the sudden experience of having been over the same mental-experiential terrain at some time in the past. Victims' daytime experiences eclipses nighttime experiences, but altered con-scious mental states resemble dreams of trauma. Incursive phenomena (intrusive ideation, feelings, and memories) induce in victims the feeling of being under "intrapsychic seige," as illusions, hallucinations, and dis-sociative reenactments emerge as mediums for processing and mastering the trauma.

Pierre Janet spoke of how famous personalities "of olden days drew attention to the way in which certain happenings (that is, traumatic inci-dents) would leave indelible and distressing memories—memories to which the sufferer was continually returning, and by which he was tor-mented by day and night (Janet, 1925). Incursive ideation and memory remind the victim of the images and symbols of fear, anxiety, helpless-ness, loss of control, and of continuing threat—threat of the "return of the dissociated" (Parson, 1984).

Many victims are tainted by a traumatic history of destruction, viola-tion, annihilation, breakdown, and death. The victim, moreover, experi-ences what Kierkegaard has called "dread" and that "sickness unto death." As an unconscious design on mastering the trauma, reenactment takes many forms to include reliving terror, loss, violation, destruction, death-image and death anxiety. The victim may be preoccupied over the personal meaning of having come so close to "premature and unaccept-able dying" (Lifton, 1982, p. 1014).

Psychological Immunocompetence

On the person-environment level, the main problem of adaptation (Hart-mann, 1939; Kardiner & Ovesey, 1950) after psychological trauma is to stave off intrusion (Parson, 1985). In many cases, this is achieved through relentless internal battles to fight back or ward off "invading armies of noxious ideas and affects" which threaten to overrun the vic-tim's inner defenses and sense of safety and regulated control. This de-fensive-protective action is metaphorically akin to the immunologic system's function of discriminating between self and nonself (Calabrese, Kling, & Gold, 1987).

Psychological immunocompetence derives from the field of immunology, applied to the psychological domain. The victim's struggle here is to make the mind immune to tormenting thoughts, memories, and emotions. It may range from successful adaptive forms to failed, regressive destabilized forms. It refers to the person's capacity to protect existing homeostatically stable inner structures against regressive enfeeblement. Chronic failure to meet the "antigenic challenge" posed by intrusive symptoms of PTSD is a case of failed psychic immunocompetence which may often induce a sense of learned helplessness, generalized sense of failure, low self-esteem, narcissistic mortification, depression, and identity fragmentation. Additionally, failed immunologic mental controls leads to maladaptive or pathological behavioral forms as in psychic numbing and denial.

Since it is beyond the capacity of most human beings to endure the intense, intrusive-repetitive pangs of unrelieved anxiety for a long period of time, a desperate desire to end the torment emerges. This relief comes from numbing oneself to feelings, from denying that the traumatic event's intrinsic power to end one's life has meaningful relevance, or from avoiding ideas, people, places, or things that resemble the traumatic past. But for many victims or survivors, numbing brings dubious results, and so itself may become the problem. Intimacy, feelings of love, and sexual desire are adversely affected by this defensive-protective mental device.

Numbing is intrapsychically too close to the terror-generated paralysis associated with the original trauma-response. Moreover, it has the unconscious equivalents of additional trauma and death. This is in part because the unconscious now equates quiescence and sense of "stability" with the potential for "violent traumatic eruptions." After trauma, victims are no longer confident that another trauma will not reoccur—either "deployed within the mind" (as in intrusive thoughts and images) or coming from the social and physical environments.

To bolster psychic survival, some victims strangle spontaneous emotions and inner vitality, embark on a "wandering lifestyle," while "settling for dullness" (Lipkin, Blank, Parson, & Smith, 1982), and find themselves trapped in the sense of nothingness. Survivors of massive trauma may seek relief through other death-equivalents in their post-traumatic adaptations. For example, through chronic depressions and self-loathing, self-defeating behaviors, alcohol and drug abuse, and other addictions including sexual promiscuity.

Though avoidance and numbing used for short periods of time after the event offers the victim some reassurance of psychological survival, avoidance as a way of life is very detrimental over time. But since most forms of chronic avoidance are maladaptive and fail to bolster self-esteem and a stable sense of self, they are bound to soon fail because of intrinsic fragility of related defenses. When failures occur, intrusive breakthroughs occur, creating a new "round" of anxious arousal, irritability, anger, fears, and potential explosiveness.

In chronic forms of traumatic stress, the biphasic nature of PTSD—that is, of intrusion-reliving and numbing-denying—shapes a biopsychic flashpoint for post-traumatic burnout, as helplessness deepens and narcissistic rage rises (Parson, 1981). Post-traumatic burnout comes from the vicious cycle of intrusion and numbing, and often produces radical personality change in which ego processes are constricted and a coarctated adaptational lifestyle eclipses pre-traumatic adaptational forms. The unpredictable nature of the trauma and the "meaning-shattering" context it generated in its wake, induces the sense of an absence-of-meaning-in-life (Parson, 1986).

Therapy with victims achieves working through the trauma not only by exploration and analysis of trauma-associated memories or situational elements and associated shame and guilt, but also by addressing intrapsychic conflicts on the symbolic level of personal meaning. Early intervention with victims may prevent immediate trauma reactions from becoming chronic, leading to post-traumatic personality disorders. When left untreated, these problems develop into patterns of irritability, explosiveness, paranoid rage, and schizoid emotional isolation.

PTSD-generating stress may be experienced alone (as in rape, incest, some assaults) or in groups (as in natural and technological disasters like dangerous nuclear incidents in Chernobyl and Three Mile Island, or in the chemical disaster in Bhopal, India, or the American and Israeli school bus accidents). The disorder is said to be severer and longer lasting in the context of human-induced victimization (rape, sexual torture, other violent assaults) than in "Acts of God" disasters. Children and the elderly tend to be at higher risk for PTSD than younger adults due to biopsychological developmental vulnerabilities.

Victims with PTSD often suffer allied conditions like anxiety, depression, sporadic explosions of aggressive behavior, impulsive behavior, memory deficits, problems in concentrating, emotional lability, headaches, and vertigo. The disorder can occur at any stage of the life cycle: in children and adolescents (Doyle & Bauer, 1989; Eth & Pynoos, 1985; Parson, 1993; Terr, 1983a,b), and in adults, to include the senior years (Danieli, 1981; Kahana, Harel, & Kahana, 1988).

Victims with PTSD may suffer mild to severe impairment in some or most areas of their lives; for example, in interpersonal relationships, work, and in the capacity for regulated spontaneous behavior. Person-defeating behavior unconsciously aimed at self-punishment due to guilt may be present, as well as suicidal ideation, plan, and action; shame, substance abuse disorders, and exacerbated character reactions, may prove complicating factors. In cases of severe physical assault and accidents in which head injury has occurred, an organic mental disorder may be an accompanying diagnosis, as well as other conditions such as anxiety, depression, phobias, and post-traumatic character disorders.

The Diagnosis of Post-Traumatic Stress Disorder (PTSD)

While the basic descriptive symptom configurations remain the same between the DSM-III and the DSM-III-R (APA, 1980, 1987), changes are significant enough to warrant discussion. The revised (DSM-III-R) operational criteria for the diagnosis of PTSD appears in Table 13.1.

In general, DSM-III-R sharpened the diagnostic criteria in a number of areas; for example, (1) it provides greater clarity on the stressor; (2) it provides greater understanding of primary and secondary reactions and symptoms of the disorder; (3) it expands victim populations to include children; (4) it increases behavioral specificity for avoidance symptoms ("numbing was basically replaced by "avoidance"; (5) it specifies and clarifies symptoms of physiological reactivity; (6) it eliminates "survivor guilt"; and (7) it includes unconscious symbolic meaning associated with increased psychological distress and physiologic (autonomic) reactivity when encountering intrapsychic and environmental/sociologic reminders of the trauma.

The diagnosis of PTSD consists of five kinds of events and responses. These five criteria are: (1) the *stressor* (Criterion A), (2) *intrusive-reexperiencing* (Criterion B); *avoidance* (Criterion C), *arousal* (autonomic; Criterion D), and the *temporality* factor which requires that Criteria B, C, and D be present for at least a month. If the trauma-response occurs at least six months after the catastrophic event, "delayed onset" is entered as part of the diagnostic decision. Each Criterion is discussed in detail.

Requisite Stressor Toxicity: Threats to Self, Family, Home, and Community

The stressor criterion in DSM-III-R is more stringent than DSM-III, and achieves greater specifity in that it highlights threat or harm to self, family, home, community, as well as "eye-witness" exposure. Examples of stressors reaching criteria for PTSD are: serious threat to one's life or physical integrity; serious threat or harm to one's children, spouse; sudden destruction of one's home or community; or seeing another person who has recently been or is being, seriously injured or killed as a result of an accident or physical violence (APA, 1987).

TABLE 13.1.   Operational Criteria for Post-Traumatic Stress Disorder (DSM-III-R, 1987)

A. The victim/survivor has experienced an event that is outside the range of usual human experience and that would be markedly distressing to almost anyone, e.g., serious threat to one's life or physical integrity; serious threat or harm to one's children, spouse, or other close relatives and friends; sudden destruction of one's home or community; or seeing another person who has recently been, or is being, seriously injured or killed as the result of an accident or physical violence.

B. The traumatic event is persistently re-experienced in at least one of the following ways:

   (1) Recurrent and intrusive distressing recollections of the event (in young children, repetitive play in which themes or aspects of the trauma are expressed)

   (2) Recurrent distressing dreams of the event

   (3) Sudden acting or feeling as if the traumatic event were recurring (includes a sense of reliving the experience, illusions, hallucinations, and dissociative [flashback] episodes, even those that occur upon awakening or when intoxicated)

   (4) Intense psychological distress at exposure to events that symbolize or resemble an aspect of the traumatic event, including anniversaries of the trauma.

C. Persistent avoidance of stimuli associated with the trauma or numbing of general responsiveness (not present before the trauma), as indicated by at least three of the following:

   (1) Efforts to avoid thoughts or feelings associated with the trauma

   (2) Efforts to avoid activities or situations that arouse recollections of the trauma

   (3) Inability to recall an important aspect of the trauma (psychogenic amnesia)

   (4) Markedly diminished interest in significant activities (in young children, loss of recently acquired developmental skills such as toilet training or language skills)

   (5) Feeling of detachment or estrangement from others

   (6) Restricted range of affect, e.g., unable to have loving feelings

   (7) Sense of a foreshortened future, e.g., does not expect to have a career, marriage, or children, or a long life.

D. Persistent symptoms of increased arousal (not present before the trauma), as indicated by at least two of the following:

   (1) Difficulty falling or staying asleep

   (2) Irritability or outbursts of anger

   (3) Difficulty concentrating

   (4) Hypervigilance

   (5) Exaggerated startle response

   (6) Physiologic reactivity upon exposure to events that symbolize or resemble an aspect of the traumatic event (e.g., a woman who was raped in an elevator breaks out in a sweat when entering any elevator).

The trauma-response is a consequence of events (stressors) that overwhelm the biopsychological organization of the victim's personality by sudden, toxic stimuli. Recovery from traumatic disorganization and integration of personality fragmentation which attends PTSD, requires efficient endopsychic cognitive-affective processing of traumatic internal stimuli and information. However, when this process is obstructed (due to ego weakness and structural damage, maladaptive characterological defenses, or to a negative post-trauma socioecology), traumatic ego decline occurs.

Empirical studies and clinical theories on the etiology of PTSD have found that the best predictor of PTSD is exposure to an overwhelming event or stressor. These studies produced two explanatory etiological models. These are: the "historicogenic" theory of traumatogenesis (based on individual differences); and the "situogenic" theory (based on situational impact).

Freud's (Freud, Ferenczi, Abraham, Simmel, & Jones, 1921) view of the traumatic and war neuroses (or PTSD) was consistent with the historicogenic view on etiology which he had applied to all forms of neuroses. The psychoanalytic position expected people exposed to traumatic events, regardless of intensity and duration, to speedily rebound symptom-free to pre-exposure levels (referred to as the "stress evaporation" theory) (Borus, 1973a,b; Figley, 1978).

If symptoms persisted far beyond the traumatic occurrence ("residual stress" theory) (Figley, 1978), the conclusion was that premorbid vulnerability was operative. Psychoanalysis began with the study of psychological trauma, which Freud (Breuer & Freud, 1895/1955) first saw as a basic disturbance of memory, due to a breakdown of repressive barriers against inner dangers caused by the overstimulation of trauma.

Freud (1896/1962) held that all psychopathology was caused by an *actual* traumatic event. So convinced was he at first (Freud, 1896/1962) that external events (not internal fantasy) were the chief etiologic agent in trauma that he was led to state that "the ultimate cause of hysteria always is the sexual seduction of a child by an adult." He maintained this position on etiology for many years; however, this view was later changed in his *Introductory Lectures* (Freud, 1916–1917), and he argued that it was not real events (of seduction, genital stimulation, incest, or rape) that caused trauma, but rather the reality-distorting imaginal processes of the child related to Oedipal and primal scene-related dynamics.

The situogenic theory is implied in Abraham Kardiner's (1941) expanding view of etiology. He believed that a situation could be sufficiently overwhelming to overrun even the healthy personality. Shatan (1977) echoed this observation over three decades later through clinical studies of concentration camp survivors and Vietnam war veterans. He thus maintained that psychic structure may not be as immutable as we once believed.

In contrast to the psychoanalytic model is the behavioral paradigm on etiology. PTSD may be said to originate in a "traumatic mental imprinting," as implied in Pavlov's classical theory of trauma. He had found that repeated dosages of overwhelming excitation over time mobilized the organism's innate reflexive responses (or defensive reaction). He believed primary responses were then associatively linked to cues (conditioned stimuli) in the traumatizing environment. This association potentiates the conditioned stimuli to elicit the primary defensive responses by itself (conditioned response).

Borrowing from Stampfl and Levi's adaptation of Morwer's two-factor theory, Keane, Fairbank, Caddell, Zimering, and Bender (1985) explain the etiology and maintenance of PTSD for all trauma victims' groups. The authors advance the classical conditioning paradigm (in which a fear response is acquired through associative learning), while in operant conditioning (in which victims avoid classically conditioned anxiety-inducing cues) as essential constructs in understanding the immediate and long-term effects of PTSD. For example, a victim of a tidal wave or flood may experience the pangs of fear upon hearing or seeing thunder and lightning (associatively learned), and then employ avoidant behaviors (operant learning) to manage affective arousal (anxiety and fear).

Empirical studies have found both premorbid or vulnerability factors (historicogenic) and traumatic event-specific factors (situogenic) to be essential in predicting post-traumatic stress disorder. However, the empirical findings have been inconsistent. The most clinically useful view of research findings is that etiology is a complex, multidimensional factor. This is because a multiplicity of issues related to pre-trauma personality factors, current coping capacity, degree of exposure, nature of the post-trauma recuperative milieu, and the victim's personal meaning (mostly unconscious) of the event are all operative and interactive. Espousing this multifactorial view based upon extensive review of veterans studies on etiology, Foy, Carroll, and Donahue (1987) write: "The basic issue is: What are the relative contributions of premilitary adjustment, military adjustment, and combat exposure toward predicting PTSD?" (p. 24).

Disaster Stress

Fulfilling this criterion are also traumatizing stimuli like the Coconut Grove Supper Club fire (Adler, 1943; Lindemann, 1944); the Andrea Doria disaster (Friedman & Lin, 1957); Buffalo Creek Dam collapse (Titchener & Kapp, 1976); and the Beverly Hills Supper Club fire (Green, Grace, Titchener, & Lindy, 1983). Communal traumatic stressors found in technological disasters such as the Buffalo Creek Dam collapse can lead to a "loss of communality" and the related struggle for progress from "chaos to responsibility" (Erikson, 1976; Stern, 1976). Leopold and Dillon (1963) conducted a four-year follow up of 27 seamen who experienced a tragic accident involving a tanker-freighter collision in the Delaware River. The authors found that 70% of the survivors had significant post-traumatic psychiatric conditions. The South Australian bushfires reported by McFarlane (1984) is another example of requisite criterian for a PTSD stressor.

Hiroshima: A-Bomb Stress

Lifton (1967) found symptoms of the traumatic syndrome among survivors of the A-bomb in Hiroshima after World War II. The syndrome he identified included a sense of permanent contamination and helplessness, death imprint, the anticipation of intergenerational defilement of their offspring, and identification with the dead.

Traumatic Witnessing in Children

Etiologic factors in children succumbing to PTSD are basically the same as for adults (Parson, 1993; Eth & Pynoos, 1985; Terr, 1983a,b, 1989). Black, other minorities, and white indigent children are at risk for PTSD from both witnessing violence and being the object of it in the home, streets, parks, and other recreational locations in the communities. Numbed existence is a way of life for many inner city black and minority children of trauma. For example, recently in Baltimore a young man was shot at point-blank range, resulting in a large cavity in the victim's head. A number of black children living in the community had witnessed the shooting. Instead of responding with terror, fear, anxiety, tremulous withdrawing, or tearfully losing control over emotions, these children began playing a game using imaginary guns in their hands as they chantingly said, "Bang, bang; you're dead!"

They played gleefully as though nothing out of the ordinary had happened, as though they had been through such events before. The children appeared totally devoid of feelings for the victim. But the play was marked by agitation, and a quiet uneasiness, characterized as a "numbed furtive awareness." Through shooting imaginary guns, the children engaged in "traumatic reenactments-in-play," a repetitive-compulsive mechanism to aid endopsychic processing of the event, and master the internal, menacing representations of the trauma (Parson, 1993).

In addition to witnessing, studies on biopsychic trauma in children involve the stressors of physical abuse, sexual assault, and collective trauma through kidnapping (Terr, 1979). A four-year follow-up report on the 26 children buried in a vehicle in Chowchilla, California, showed a range of post-traumatic symptomatology, to include trauma-originating dreams, post-traumatic play, sense of vulnerability, and other emotional distress (Terr, 1983a,b).

Frederick (1985) found that 77% of children he studied with histories of surviving disasters, physical abuse, and molestation suffered from PTSD. He also found that in a sample of 300 children who were molested, PTSD was clearly manifested in the behavior of children over the age of six. Biopsychologically traumatized children suffer secondary conditions like sleep disturbance, disturbed attachment behavior, conduct disturbance, hyperactivity, concentration and attending deficits, cognitive and academic dysfunctions (e.g., learning disability and pseudoimbecility, pseudolearning disability), self-doubts, phobias, helplessness, depression, and low self-esteem.

Rape: Violent Transgression of the Self

Rape is perhaps the crime with the most damaging impact on the self organization of the victim. This is in part because the victim is "not only deprived of autonomy and control, experiencing manipulation and often injury to the envelope of the self, but also intrusion of inner space, the most sacred and private repository of the self" (Bard & Ellison, 1974). So overwhelming is this experience that empirical studies and clinical experience show that rape predicts the development of PTSD (Kilpatrick et al., 1989).

The rape trauma syndrome was first identified and described by Burgess and Holstrom (1974) in a two-phase recovery process (acute disorganization phase and long-term reorganization phase), characterized by three basic types of post-rape reactions: impact, somatic, and emotional responses. Katz and Mazur (1978) have also contributed to understanding and intervening with rape victims.

Rape victims often suffer a variety of biological, psychological, and behavioral symptoms to include physiological responses such as trembling, shaking, nausea, muscle tension, rapid breathing, feelings of shock, anxiety, physical pain and general discomfort, muscular tension, genitourinary symptoms, hyperarousal, anxiety, humiliation, shame, disrupted sexual patterns and dysfunctions of desire, a sense of personal contamination, and social stigma.

Victims also experience intense fear, rage-toward-self, blaming of self, guilt, guilt over sexual arousal, depression, suicidal ideation and action, rage-toward-men, need for revenge, accidental pregnancy, need to right the wrong, rage-toward-society, poor general social functioning.

Incest: The Ultimate Violation

Childhood sexual experiences with adults is particularly stressful and devastating to young victims. This stressor often occurs in the context of severely overt and covert dysfunctional family systems. Victims experience a shattering of normal fantasies of self-integrity and well-being.

They experience depression, sexual problems, prostitution, self-hate, and personality disturbances. The most deleterious and long-term effect on the incest victim is a devastated, damaged self-image—the sense of being unworthy and incompetent. Symptoms of PTSD often appear.

Sexual abuse is a profound assault on the child's evolving personality, which may result in disorders of the self and later vulnerability to psychiatric illness, such as schizophrenia, paranoid schizophrenia, bipolar illness, and other conditions, such as substance abuse disorders, eating disorders, multiple personality disorders, borderline personality disorders, and somatic disorders, eating disorders, anxiety disorders, and depressive disorders.

Stressor Dimensionalization

Traumatic events (such as combat and disasters) are often seen as unitary, undifferentiated occurrences; however, closer observation reveals they have multiple divergent features, each of which may produce its own brand of post-traumatic symptomatology. The dimensionalizing of the "stressor universe" of a generalized traumatizing environment has important implications for assessment and therapy (Table 13.2).

As Yehuda et al. (1992) note, "Differentiating subgroups of PTSD patients by type of stress exposure or symptom profile may explain why certain patients are amenable to some forms of therapeutic interventions, while other remain treatment refractory" (p. 333). Years earlier, Laufer (Laufer, Brett, & Gallops, 1985a) had written that "Allowing that there are multiple ways of responding to trauma, it is likely that different traumatic experiences will produce different types of symptom responses"

TABLE 13.2.   Stressors Intrinsic to Indochinese
Mass Violence

- Governmental torture and victimization
- Sexual torture and rape
- Brutal physical harm and injury
- Vicious attacks by bandits
- "Autogenocide" by Pol Pot
- Witnessing disembowelments
- Witnessing violent deaths of relatives and friends
- Wholesale loss and destruction of communality
- The Thai border camp experiences
- Kampuchean labor camp experiences
- Reeducation camps in Vietnam and other places
- Effects of war on civilian populations

(p. 539). Dimensionalizing occurs along the range of stressor intensity and stressor typology. Traumatic occurrences, then, are probably not undifferentiated events.

Dimensionalizing War Stress

The generalized traumatizing environment of war and natural disasters contain stressor specificities. In war, for example, there is the general exposure to fighting, killing enemy soldiers, being wounded, participating in and witnessing atrocities, and serving two or more tours. Each of these reach operational criteria for the diagnosis of PTSD.

Levels of Life-Threat

Scientific studies have shown that severity of the traumatic situation predicts the development of PTSD. Each level of life-threat was associated with specific aspects of post-traumatic symptomatology.

Violation of Inner Moral Agency

Laufer, Brett, et al. (1985a,b) investigated the relationship of combat, witnessing atrocities, and participation in atrocities to symptoms of PTSD. Findings showed combat was associated most strongly with intrusive imagery, secondly to hyperarousal, and thirdly to numbing, while participation was associated most strongly with cognitive disruption. Yehuda et al. (1992) also found combat and atrocity stressors to be related to intrusive symptoms.

Combat Job, Subjectivity, Injury, and Death

Table 13.3 shows the types of events that qualify as stressors for PTSD. Included are the experiences of a 25-year-old gunner in a B-24 during World War II. He had sought clinical assistance for depression, physical exhaustion, anxiety, suicidal thoughts, homicidal ideas, and intense intolerance for his dysfunctional state (Grinker & Speigel, 1945). Wilson noted a relationship between war zone roles and soldiers' subjective assessment of the stressor, and the specific traumatic stimuli. He reported that the stressor or "injury/death" strongly predicted all dimensions of PTSD: depression, physical symptoms, stigmatization, sensation-seeking, anger, intrusive imagery, and intimacy conflict (Wilson & Kraus, 1985).

Post-Traumatic Socioecology

What happens in the aftermath of trauma is also predictive of PTSD. For example, Wilson and Kraus (1985) found that the variable "psychological isolation" was the best predictor of PTSD. This factor involved feelings of isolation and rejection by family and community; and cynicism, distrust,

**TABLE 13.3.   Example of War-Related Stressors
Qualifying for DSM-III-R's Criterion A**

An Army Air Corps soldier during 27 months had experienced:
- Two crashes in the United States
- Two combat-related crashes in Europe
- Fired upon by a German battleship
- Shells screamed past his plane
- Flying at 27,000 feet, engines of bomber failed; plane fell
  25,000 feet before engines restarted
- Plane was hit on his 23rd mission
- He was knocked out of turret by explosion
- The co-pilot, the bombadier, and the radioman were killed.

and anger toward authority figures. Though positive social-supportive environments are facilitative of post-traumatic recovery (Figley, 1988; Lazarus & Folkman, 1984), negative socioecologic responses, such as absence of medical care in natural disasters, societal rejection and blaming of Vietnam veterans, and "second wound" infliction on rape victims by law enforcement officials, may aggravate the victim's problems, and significantly undermine recovery. Parson (1988a) has used the term, "sanctuarial traumatic stress" to highlight the self-experience of betrayal and narcissistic wounding due to unanticipated institutional neglect, insensitivity, and disrespect in settings victims expect succorance.

Dimensionalizing Holocaust Stress

Many of the survivors of the Holocaust developed post-traumatic symptomatology and character changes deeply rooted in the "psychotic culture" of the death camps (Danieli, 1981; Krystal, 1968; Wilson, Harel, & Kahana, 1988). Kuch and Cox's (1992) recent study of Holocaust survivors found that 46% of the sample had DSM-III-R PTSD.

Having observed that no recent scientific study had explored the full spectrum of symptoms among Jewish Holocaust survivors, Kuch and Cox reviewed the German files of 145 survivors and selected 124 for the study. In the sample, 63% had been in concentration camps, and 78% of their relatives were killed. The subjects were divided into three groups: those with concentration camp experience, a subgroup consisting of 20 Auschwitz survivors with tattooed identification numbers on their left forearms with numbers beginning with the letter "A" (a group with well-documented exposure to terror, violence, atrocities, and death), and a group with no concentration camp experience.

Dimensionalizing the stressor environment of the death camps revealed that tattooed Auschwitz survivors had significantly more symptoms and were three times more likely to have PTSD than survivors with no tattoos. Like findings with war veterans, this study's conclusion was that atrocity-exposed survivors were at greater risk for chronic PTSD.

Person Dimensionalization

Vulnerability to PTSD is a critical variable often neglected in the scientific and clinical literature (McFarlane, 1990; Parson, 1984, 1987). Person variables such as previctimization personality (motives, beliefs, values, ego strengths/coping capacities, and defensive-adaptive organization), genetic, developmental, chronic life stress, and family psychiatric history are essential to prediction and treatment outcome. This view integrates the historicogenic and situogenic perspectives. McFarlane's (1986) study of survivors of a communal disaster substantiates the role of vulnerability factors in assessment and treatment of PTSD.

Child, Adolescent, and Senior Vulnerability

The developmental phase of the victim is an important etiologic consideration. Children have been regarded as particularly vulnerable to extreme stress; for example, in Central American warfare (Arroyo & Eth, 1985), physical and sexual abuse (Green et al., 1983; Findelhor, 1984); and a school bus kidnapping event (Terr, 1983a,b). Adolescents are also vulnerable to traumatic stress (Eth & Pynoos, 1985). Van der Kolk's (1985) study found adolescence predicted PTSD among war veterans. Etiologic vulnerability is also found in individuals in their senior years, due chiefly to inflexible biopsychological adaptive mechanisms.

The Structure of Meaning: Role of Ethnocultural Factors

The etiologic role of individual meaning is essential in assessment and treatment. The role of race, ethnicity, and culture in the development and maintenance of PTSD (Allen, 1987; Brende & Parson, 1985; Laufer, Brett, & Gallops, 1984; Parson, 1985; Wilson, 1989). These shape the subjective appraisal and meaning of the trauma (Parson, 1985), and gives the event its particular traumatizing character (McFarlane, 1990; Parson, 1984; Ulman & Brothers, 1988). Parson (1984) thus theorized that a "structure of meaning" was the critical variable in post-traumatic developments in black veterans.

Emotional bonding, based on shared minority status with the Vietnamese, created chronic guilt in black and other minority soldiers who killed and harmed the Vietnamese. These experiences were later correlated with chronic post-war psychopathology (Brende & Parson, 1986; CDC, 1988; Green et al., 1990; Laufer et al., 1984; Laufer & Parson, 1985). Race and ethnocultural differences in rates of PTSD were observed by Kulka et al. (1988). Black and Hispanic veterans suffered the disorder at the rate of 20.6 and 27.9%, respectively, compared with 13.7% for veterans classified as "white/other."

Incursive Phenomena: States of Altered Consciousness

According to DSM-III-R, the victim experiences recurrent intrusive recollections of the event, such as distressing dreams, sudden behavior, and emotions as if the trauma were recurring. Incursive symptoms are also connected with intense psychological distress when the person is exposed to events that unconsciously symbolize or resemble an aspect of the trauma. DSM-III-R adds greater specificity here as well; for example, it includes illusions, hallucinations, and dissociative [flashbacks] episodes, during the waking state and intoxication, as well as anniversary reoccurrences of the trauma, and repetitive play behavior in young children.

Recurrent Distressing Ideation, Emotions, and Memories. Reexperiencing phenomena which are a cardinal feature of PTSD have greater salience than most other symptoms and disorder indicators. Clinical experiences show a number of stress ideation, emotions, and memories:

- Attacks of anxious arousal.
- Fear of losing control over impulses, affects, and drives.
- Fear over loss of bowel and bladder control.
- Fear that painful intrusive elements of the trauma will not cease.
- Fear that grief will result in ceaseless crying and uncontrollable emotional turbulence.
- Fear of total breakdown.
- Guilt over being alive.
- Guilt over specific behaviors enacted during event.
- Guilt over specific actions done during event.
- Concerns whether intrusive symptoms constitute condemnation to future life of punishment.
- Narcissistic rage reaction over inability to control intrusive thoughts (narcissistic mortification).
- Delayed awareness of the implications of the life threat.
- Anger/rage toward authorities, persons, and institutions blamed for the mishap.
- Guilt over presumed lost opportunity to effect a less tragic outcome.

Recurrent Distressing Dreams. Traumatic dreams and nightmares are "nocturnal torments" (Parson, 1986), a form of post-traumatic incursive (or reliving) experience. Traumatic dreams and nightmares are also central markers for PTSD. They are best described as "dreams of incomplete, unconsummated action," requiring endopsychic processing in order to gain mastery over the powerful, disorganizing affects. Mastery leads to adaptive trauma-completing devices. The impact of the traumatic onslaught renders inoperative the survivor's integrative actional systems. Kardiner (1959) saw traumatic dreams as "the most universal earmark of the traumatic syndrome. These often recurrent dreams of the failure to consummate successful actions are, in fact, the key to the actual trauma-topathology" (p. 249). Whereas Freud used dreamwork to discover meaning in the neurotic dream that he saw as the royal road to the unconscious, Parson (1986, 1988a) used traumawork to decipher the meaning, sequence, actions and inactions in traumatic dreams and saw these dreams as "the royal road to the traumatic events." Thus, these dreams may unfold into a vital guide toward resolution and adaptive control.

Symptoms, reactions, and themes pertaining to traumatic dreams are:

- Inability to complete an important action that would facilitate survival at the moment.
- Sense of being fettered and totally frozen by fear and catastrophic expectations.
- Pervasive sense of vulnerability due to threats of disintegrative or annihilation anxieties.
- Images of self as dead.
- Specific family member or friend "targeted" for violence in the dream.
- Self as victim of dangerous, menacing forces with tenacious intent to do harm.
- Attempts to escape from menacing pursuing force is foiled by feet growing roots into the ground.
- In combat, weapons that do not fire.
- In rape, the victim finds herself or himself unable to run from assailant or to a place of safety.

Extensive post-traumatic dreamwork analysis had led this author to classify nightmares or traumatic dreams on a continuum, from "experience-near" to "experience-distant." The dream continuum begins with relative simplicity (concrete, nonsymbolic) and progresses to utter complexity (mostly symbolic).

1. Frightening nocturnal imagery depicting all or most of the traumatic reality (most of dream tells what really happened).
2. Frightening nocturnal imagery that replicated some discrete and recognizable feature of the traumatic reality (dream tells what

really happened, but only partially; it also has images not directly related to the event).

3. Frightening nocturnal imagery that relate ambiguously to traumatic reality (dream tells of events which may or may not have occurred in reality).

4. Frightening nocturnal imagery with no recognizable associated feature to traumatic reality (dream tells of events and experiences that did not occur in relation to the trauma).

Wilmer (1982) has a similar classification of traumatic dreams he developed with Vietnam combat veterans. Brockway (1987) reported themes of helplessness in 78% of post-trauma dreams analyzed, and that 72% of recurrent nightmares were markedly reduced through specialized group therapy. Starker (1974, 1984) reported that persons with chronic nightmares were high on measures of anxiety-distraction, guilt-dysphoria, and guilt-fear of failure during the waking hours. Ross, Fall, Sullivan, Stanley, and Caroff (1989) view disturbed dreaming as the hallmark of PTSD.

Post-Traumatic Dissociation: Illusions, Hallucinations, and Flashbacks. The term "dissociation" was created by Pierre Janet, whose early work records the biopsychic mechanisms of post-traumatopathology (Ellenberger, 1970; Janet, 1925, 1919; van der Kolk, Brown, & van der Hart, 1989). Dissociation is a disjunctive biopsychic defense against walled off terror which results in discontinuities among the various aspects of self—memory, perceptual, sensory, affective, and somatic realities. Psychodynamically, this lack of coordinated functioning is related to a breakdown in normal synthetic-integrative ego functions. Dissociation reduces effective adaptation as it reinforces what Shatan (1985) calls a "traumatic sense of reality."

Freud (1936) saw traumatic neurosis as forming a dissociative split in the ego. In discussing dissociative mechanisms in PTSD, Parson (1981) notes that biopsychic trauma "forms an autonomous split-off mental organization . . . that participate in the . . . personality . . . in a non-integrated, non-ego coordinated fashion (hence, the split-off, dissociated phenomenon of flashbacks and other incursive, automatic ideas and feelings)" (p. 15).

Unlike the previous forms of reliving experiences mentioned above, dissociative symptoms (such as illusions, hallucinations, and flashbacks) in general have a much lower clinical and epidemiological incidence. Brende (1987) found that in a sample of hospitalized veterans 88% reported "flashback-related aggressive outbursts—feeling as if they were fighting for survival." Guilt, a very neglected topic in clinical writings and research, was associated with certain dissociative experiences like "blackouts" (p. 79).

Rose (1986) found that some rape victims dissociate during the victimizing experience by mentally hovering above the victim's body, while experiencing feelings of sorrow and anguish for the victim. Moreover, Burstein (1984) reported a flashback prevalence rate of 8 to 13% among victim/survivors of assault, motor vehicle or industrial accidents, while Brett and Mangine (1985) found that 24% of their sample reported dissociative episodes. Additionally, using a cutoff score of 30 on the Dissociative Experience Scale, Bremner et al. (1992) found that PTSD patients had scores that were almost double those of non-PTSD patients (27.7 versus 13.7).

Massive traumatic stress may lead to extreme forms of dissociation producing "traumatic identity splintering"—the etiologic roots of multiple personality disorder (MPD). Brende (1987) notes that patients with MPD are often diagnosed as suffering from PTSD and borderline syndromes, and notes that studies have reported as much as 97% of adult patients with MPD had suffered from childhood trauma.

Characteristics of post-traumatic dissociative phenomena are as follows:

- Inner sense of fragmentation—of things crumbling and falling apart.
- States of amnesic disorientation.
- Derealization.
- Feelings of depersonalization.
- "Double conscience" and "split personality" (Freud, 1936).
- Disturbance in the sense of self.
- Psychogenic fugues states.
- "Recurring hysteri-form twightlight" responses (Jaffe in Ulman and Brothers, 1988).
- Walled-off fear and rage.
- "Automatic ideas and feelings" (Parson, 1984).
- The "killer-self" versus the "victim-self" (Brende, 1983).

Increased Distress upon Exposure to Trauma-Symbolic Stimuli.
The power of unconscious "traumatized structures" induce distress in victims merely by encountering situations, objects, people, and atmospheric conditions. This response has been given more prominence in DSM-III-R than in the DSM-III. Table 13.4 presents a number of events that precipitate emergency distress in victims of trauma and war veterans. These precipitating stimuli come from cognitive, affective, somatic-sensory, and socioecologic areas of victim's experiences.

TABLE 13.4. Triggering Events Symbolizing Original Trauma in Victims

Class of Symbolizing Agent	Specific Triggering Agents	Biopsychic Responses of PTSD
Intrapsychic ideational and affective	Unconscious guilt, survivor guilt, grief, shame, and feelings of terror	Emotional agitation, depression, anxiety, suicidal ideation, withdrawal, and sense of "falling apart"
Cognitive circularity and memory	Anniversary dates: reliving traumatic distress on specific dates of the rape, disaster, war event	Emotional agitation, affective turbulence, suicidal feelings, depression, grief, rage, anxiety, separation anxiety
Loss and threats of separation	Death of relatives, children, and friends; serious illness; lost love; divorce	Withdrawal, grief, rage, suicidal thoughts and attempts (with and without executive plans)
Authority persons/ institutions	Sense of betrayal, "put down," humiliated, shamed, and forced to "surrender" to authority persons/institutions perceived as blameworthy for rape, disaster, or war	Reactivation of "fragging" impulses, homicidal impulses, need for revenge, and narcissistic mortification, absence of sexual desire
Somatopsychic flashbacks	Sensory activation: A rainy or hot day, smell of fuel, olfactory stimuli reminiscent of burnt human flesh for veterans, aspects of intimacy and sexual contact for some rape victims	Anxiety, agitation, physiological arousal, physiological reliving, fear and trepidation over "return of the dissociated"
Socioecologic	Sociocommunicational event: viewing "televictims" of rape on electronic media and while reading accounts of fellow victims of rape or disaster; return of hostages held in Iraq, war with Iraq, and "rumors of wars"	Murderous rage, need for revenge, homicidal, fratricidal (peers unaffected by the trauma and who appear uncaring or judgmental), and "androphobic" reactions

Cognitobehavioral Avoidance

Cognitive avoidance in survivors of Australian bushfires may be the best predictor of acute post-traumatic symptomatology (McFarlane, 1988). Avoidance symptoms differentiated experimental from control groups, identifying 63% of the Williams Pipeline disaster victims (sensitivity), while these symptoms was 100% absent in the controls (specificity).

Biopsychological defense against intrusive ideation, feelings, memories, and images are generally referred to as numbing or avoidance symptoms, which DSM-III-R describes these Criterion C symptoms as "persistent avoidance of stimuli associated with the trauma or numbing of general responsiveness" (APA, 1987). More stringent criteria than the DSM-III the III-R calls for three of seven possible statements to be true of the victim.

Biobehavioral Phenomena and Increased Arousal

This group of responses (Criterion D) are experienced as "persistent symptoms of increased arousal (not present before the trauma)" (APA, 1987), and are given greater emphasis in the revised version. Contemporary neuroscience and psychophysiological laboratory studies show alterations in the central nervous system, resulting in excessive sympathetic nervous system (SNS) arousal, and lowered efficiency in modulating hyperarousal, irritability, aggression, and chronic inner states of tension.

Disorders of Sleep.   The psychological aftermath of trauma is characterized by a "mutation of expectational structures." This means that the victim no longer has confidence in predictive reality. After trauma a new reality exists in the absence of a stable sense of self, without a sure identity. Erik Erikson (1968) noted that for trauma sufferers "the sense of sameness and continuity and the belief in one's social role were gone" (p. 67). In the absence of self-security after trauma, the victim finds it difficult to give up control, a self-commodity victims feel was stripped away from them by the traumatic experience. What victims want more than anything else is to increase control; going to sleep is the unconscious equivalent of the state of ultimate helplessness and evaporation of control, namely, death. Sleep anxiety, a nocturnal manifestation of "death anxiety" (Lifton, 1982) is a real problem for many victims.

As a possible hallmark of PTSD, dysfunctional REM sleep may be involved in the pathogenesis of PTSD, and this condition may be relatively specific to the disorder (Ross et al., 1989). Most victims of trauma, as a part of their clinical symptomatology, present sleep disturbance to clinicians. Generally, sleep disturbance is at least twice as high in trauma populations than in nontraumatized populations. Biological mechanisms operative in flashbacks and startle reactions may also be related to dream disturbances (Burstein, 1985; Ross et al., 1989).

Irritability and Outbursts of Aggression.   Kardiner (1941) spoke of irritability and explosive outbursts of aggression as essential features of PTSD. These responses are common among victims' post-trauma reactions. Wilkinson (1983) found anger in about 35% of victims of the Hyatt Regency Hotel mishap, while Horowitz, Wilner, and Alvarez (1980) report that 82% of a sample consisting of victims of violence, accidents, personal injuries, and serious illnesses suffered problems with anger and irritability.

Biopsychobehavioral Nature of PTSD

Brain functioning and behavior is emerging as a vital area for PTSD research as investigators seek knowledge from molecular to cellular to behavioral to the cognitive dimensions of the disorder. Highlighting the biopsychobehavioral properties of PTSD, Kardiner and Spiegel (1947) wrote that "the nucleus of the [traumatic] neurosis is a physioneurosis," and that the disorder was marked by irritability, outbursts of anger, difficulties in concentrating, sleep disturbances, an atypical dream life, fixation on the trauma, and exaggerated startle reactions (APA, 1987; Kardiner, 1941). It is now well-established empirically that PTSD is not a purely psychological disorder, sociocultural disorder, nor a purely biological one. PTSD incorporates these self-dimensions.

Psychoendocrinology of PTSD

Trauma causes long-term alterations and abnormalities in specific brain systems. New discoveries on neuroregulators are changing the way the brain is being understood. Instead of the usual cyberneticopsychic model of the brain as "dry" computer technology, a new model is emerging of the brain as a "wet" hormonal gland (Bergland, 1985; Burgess, Watson, Hoffman, & Wilson, 1988). The traditional physical and engineering sciences models are being expanded or replaced by models which can better describe "nonideal systems, such as turbulence, climatic change, wave motion that are almost chaotic or quasirandom" (Groves & Young, 1986, p. 18).

Empirical studies are increasing clinical understanding of nonlinear, nonideal, chaotic patterns that characterize PTSD dynamics. Psychoendocrinology of PTSD is the study of glands of internal secretion and their role in human physiology, psychology, and behavior. These studies investigate brain chemistry, the action of neurochemical transmitters and cell function, sleep abnormalities, and somatic therapies. Freud (1920) saw PTSD as primarily a psychological disorder, but was aware of the role biology played in "the symptomatic picture" which was marked by "motor symptoms," "strongly marked signs of subjective ailment," and a "comprehensive general enfeeblement . . ." (p. 04). Despite this awareness, Freud (1920/1955) was an adamant critic of neurologists and psychiatrists who treated PTSD with electrical methods.

Psychophysiological studies provide a bridge between biological and psychological perspectives. Generally, alterations in the central nervous system (CNS) and the sympathetic nervous system (SNS) undergird the pathology of PTSD. Traumatic events are experienced as a vicious onslaught upon the self, which mobilize basic bioreflexive (or phylogenetic) mechanisms. Brende and McCann's (1984) analysis of forms of traumatic regression concluded that trauma forces victims to re-experience "the archaic racial heritage" of humankind, "emanating from subcortical centers . . . involved in primitive aggression and sexuality [and] basic survival" (p. 61).

In laboratory studies with Vietnam war veterans and other survivors of extreme stress, findings have consistently found higher physiological reactivity in subjects with PTSD than in controls. When exposed to trauma cues (via visual, auditory, and imaginal modalities), veterans with PTSD showed consistently higher pathophysiological reactivity through excessive heart rate, respiration, pulse, anxiety, agitation, systolic blood pressure, temperature, and forehead muscle activity than veterans without PTSD (Blanchard, Kolb, Gerardi, Ryan, & Pallmeyer, 1986; Kolb, 1987; Pallmeyer, Blanchard, & Kolb, 1986; Pitman, Van der Kolk, Orr, & Greenberg, 1990).

Underlying these physiological responses to the sudden shock of threat-generated stress is the deployment of catecholamines, specifically, epinephrine, norepinephrine (NE), dopamine (DA), and serotonin (SE), which intensely stimulate and alter neuronal functions in the CNS. Autonomic arousal is mediated by the sympathetic-adrenal-medullary system via NE secretion. This adrenergic action not only supplies biochemical provisions for emergency, but it also ensures successful management of aversive external stimuli and internal cascading physiological changes to affect recovery to pretrauma levels of steady-state equilibrium through fight, flight, or catatonoid response. These are normally the chemicals of guaranteed resiliency and survival. However, there is a relative absence of speedy recovery and resiliency in PTSD. Thus, Van der Kolk (1988) correctly alludes to the absence of resiliency in PTSD when he writes that "In PTSD, autonomic arousal is no longer a preparation for, but a precipitant of emergency responses which bear little relationship to the nature of contemporary stimulus" (p. 275).

"Noradrenergic Burnout": Excessive Neuronal and Biochemical Responses

When victims encounter stressful events for long periods of time, the persistent secretion of neurotransmitters leads to a diminished supply of needed catecholamines, which are synthesized in the neuronal cells of the brain system. Chronic depletion of norepinephrine is due to overuse exceeding synthesis or production (Anisman & Zacharko, 1986; Van der Kolk, Greenberg, Boyd, & Krystal, 1985), which leads ultimately to norepinephrine ultrasensitivity in the CNS. Thus, subsequent to the original trauma, low amounts of norepinephrine can trigger a storm of autonomic reactivity even to minor stressful events.

Chronic noradrenergic hypersensitivity leads to noradrenergic burnout (Norbo), a state of gross decreased tolerance for arousal, which is accompanied by a decrease in motivation, in learning ability, and in memory functions, as anxiety, pain sensitivity, and defensive reactivity to novel stimuli increases, all to the detriment of adaptive recovery from trauma. Norbo is the biochemical or noradrenergic correlate to psycho-occupational burnout widely discussed and studied in recent years. Norbo underlies all forms of burnout experiences (Parson, 1981).

Studies on the locus coeruleus have shown how this brain system may be involved in PTSD. As the "brain trauma center," the locus coeruleus controls emergency functioning and is the site for integrated organization of memory, behavior, and autonomic arousal (Krystal, 1990). It is regulated by the ANS via noradrenergic innervations of the limbic system, cerebral cortex, cerebellum, and the hypothalalmus. Massive, prolonged noradrenergic activity during the trauma sets in motion a long-term biopsychic condition of "hyperpotentiated pathways [which] are reactivated at times of subsequent arousal" (Van der Kolk, 1988, p. 277). These potentiated pathways expand memory traces or tracts and accounts for intrusive thoughts, nightmares, flashbacks, and other incursive symptomatology.

Offering direct evidence of the sympathoadrenal "connection" in PTSD, McFall, Murburg, Ko, and Veith, (1990) found significantly higher levels of plasma epinephrine, pulse, blood pressure, and subjective distress than controls. Since neither NE nor cortisol measurements alone were sufficient to distinguish patients with PTSD from those without the disorder, Mason et al. (1988) combined measures from both adrenergic (norepinephrine [N]) and catecholaminergic (cortisol [C]) to form an N/C ratio. Results showed that increased levels in N/C ratio distinguished PTSD patients from those having other psychiatric diagnoses (with a diagnostic sensitivity was 78% and specificity of 94%). In a later study, Mason et al. (1990) noted unexpectedly low levels of cortisol (in comparison to high levels of norepinephrine) after exposure to traumatic laboratory stimuli. They believed that low levels of cortisol were a consequence of a suppression of arousal or what this writer calls a "biopsychic downregulation" of harmful cortisol-influenced arousal. This results in numbing and reduced responsiveness.

Ver Ellen and Van Kamen (1990) theorized about a "corticol-catecholamine dissociation" due to the relatively higher levels of NE and low urinary levels of 17-hydroxycorticosteroids (cortisol). Brende (1982, 1984) also theorized about dissociative processes as evidenced by cerebral lateralization. Mason et al. (1990) also measured serum testosterone at 2-week intervals during hospitalization of veteran patients. PTSD inpatients had higher levels of testosterone than patients with depression or bipolar illness. Another significant psychoendocrinological study by Kosten, Mason, Giller, & Ostroff (1987) found significantly higher 24-hour urinary excretion of norepinephrine and epinephrine than comparison groups of other psychiatric patients.

Experimental PTSD-Induction: Animal Models and Learned Helplessness

Animals exposed to inescapable shock is the experimental equivalent of biopsychic traumatization seen in patients with PTSD. Noted in these animals after shock were deficits in memory, motivation, a "basic giving up on life," conditioned fear response, depression, impairments in learning ability, immunosuppression resulting in genesis of tumor, and changes in multiple brain systems (Van der Kolk, 1988). Significant excretions of dopamine, norepinephrine, and opiates were found in parts of the brain along with changes in cortisol levels and the hypothalamic-pituitary-adrenal axis (HPA). When the animals are subjected to prolonged exposure to stress (shock) an eventual depletion of norepinephrine occurred (Anisman & Zacharko, 1986; Samson, Mirin, Hauser, Fendon, & Schildkraut, 1992; Seligman & Maier, 1967; Van der Kolk, 1987).

Centrally Mediated Endogenous Opiod Response

Studies on learned helplessness with animal models show a conditioned opiod release response after stressful experiences. Called "stress-induced analgesia" (SIA) (Van der Kolk, 1988), this reaction to trauma can be reversed by the opiod receptor site blocker Naloxone (Kelly, 1982). Van der Kolk, Pitman, and Orr (1989) and Pitman, Van der Kolk, Orr, and Greenberg (1990) have demonstrated SIA in human subjects with PTSD. Van der Kolk et al.'s study involved eight matched Vietnam veterans with PTSD and eight without PTSD who viewed the combat movie *Platoon*. Results showed that subjects with PTSD produced analgesia equivalent to an 8 mg injection of morphine.

Psychological Aspects of PTSD

Dynamico-Cognitive Aspects of Hypervigilance

Kardiner (1941) found that persons with traumatic stress response syndromes experience an "enduring vigilance for and sensitivity to environmental threat" (p. 8). These symptoms are associated with intense annihilation anxiety and paranoid fears, but especially with internal traumatic terror. This anxiety and fear are also motivated by conscious and unconscious stimuli that threaten a breakthrough of the "return of the dissociated." The lost sense of security motivates self-protective defenses that anticipate danger and attack from an environment that is no longer trusted to sustain the self with normal predictive security.

The term "pansuspicious orientation" highlights the victim's anticipation of ubiquitous dangers—internally, interpersonally, socially, and environmentally. Basically, paranoid aggression is associated with pervasive feelings of dread, terror, post-traumatic helplessness, and a sense of "self-under-seige." It is basically aggression without malice toward others; instead it is motivated to maintain an inner sense of equilibrium, and guard the self against situations that may prove traumatomimetic (retraumatizing). Pansuspicious perception is biased perception: it features an intrapsychic program that sees a moment's calm and tranquility with suspicion because of the belief that such moments are an "opportunistic facade" and a prelude to betrayal, humiliation, loss, or even annihilation.

Even ideas and spontaneous feelings are "suspect": they may suddenly turn against the self in any unguarded moment. The consequences of CNS dysregulation in PTSD poses yet another area of anticipatory catastrophe for the victim; namely, a threat from the somatic system. Such dysregulation undermines the normal capacity for biopsychic modulation and control of aggression, anxiety, and bodily tensions.

Replicating Foa, Feske, McCarthy, and Kozak's (1990) study in which she found Stroop interference for rape-related words with rape victims, McNally, Kaspi, Riemann, and Zeitlin (1990) studied combat veterans with and without PTSD, utilizing the modified Stroop task. Subjects were asked to name the colors of neutral words (e.g., input), positive words (e.g., love), obsessive-compulsive disorder (OCD) words (e.g., germs), and PTSD words (e.g., bodybags). Compared with the normal controls, the PTSD patients took significantly longer to color-name words reflective of PTSD, than color-naming other words (neutral, OCD, and positive words). The authors maintain that the delay or interference in color-naming was indication of intrusive cognitive activity.

In their victimization survey, Kilpatrick and Veronen (1984) found that among rape victims, 64% felt they would be injured or killed by the attack, while 96% felt scared, 96% were worried, 92% were terrified, and 88% expressed helplessness. At the three-year followup, 89% were still experiencing intrusive ideation and avoidance. In a sample of 102 victims of the Hyatt Regency Hotel skywalk collapse, Wilkinson (1983) found that 44% suffered concentration deficits while 27.4% of a sample of 102 subjects had memory problems.

Archibald and Tuddeham (1965) had reported on the cognitive deficits in World War II veterans during a 20-year followup: 75% complained of concentration difficulties, while 67% had memory deficits. In a study with survivors of a natural disaster, Madakasira and O'Brien (1987) reported that 82% of the sample suffered intrusive thoughts, 61% had memory problems, and 66% had concentration difficulties.

The self-experience of falling apart psychologically and somatically (due to significant noradrenergic upheavals) results in low self-esteem, a sense of unworthiness, powerlessness, and a profound post-traumatic sense of incompetence. Predominating in the psyche of victims are self-blame, guilt, shame, hostility, narcissistic rage, lack of confidence in self-management, in intimate relationships, childrearing, and career management. Neurophysiological pathology may produce a feeling of coldness, aloofness, feeling dead inside, "numbed awareness," and low tolerance for strong affect—intrapsychically, intrasomatically, and interpersonally.

Behavioral Abnormalities

Social dysfunctioning in areas of play and leisure, love and marriage, and work, appear to be more related to PTSD than to combat exposure itself (Solomon & Mikulincer, 1987). Incest victims often suffer eating disorders, substance abuse disorders, somatoform disorders, sexual dysfunctions and promiscuity, problematic human relationships, impulsivity, and suicidal behavior, while another study found burglary victims to be distrustful of other people, experience fear of being alone, and to have intense anxiety upon entering the house alone.

Distrust of people is particularly intense in human-engineered (as opposed to natural occurrences) traumatic sequelae in victims. The profound shattering of internal structures of humanity and attachment (best described by the British object relations theories) often leads to feelings of antipathy, hostility, and avoidance of others. Behavioral abnormalities marked by aggression are often observed in interaction with persons and institutions of authority, and, in many victims, the proclivity to create new victims to mirror their own internal image of helplessness and lack of self-efficacy in life.

Validity of the Diagnosis of PTSD

The search for validity strategies for PTSD is progressing at a rapid rate. This is in part due to the continuing controversy surrounding the diagnosis. Despite major clinical and scientific progress in understanding and delineating PTSD, some continue to view the disorder as the "illegitimate child in a family of nosological entities." Some have argued that PTSD does not have a unique set of symptoms separating it from other well-known psychiatric disorders, and that the stressor criterion is itself flawed (Breslau & Davis, 1987; Davidson, Lipper, Kilts, Mahorney, & Hammett, 1985; Goodwin & Guze, 1984; Solomon & Canino, 1990).

The primary challenge to PTSD validity is to: (1) determine if people with PTSD significantly differ from individuals without a psychiatric diagnosis; and (2) determine if victims with PTSD differ from persons with other psychiatric diagnoses. The two aspects of this challenge were fulfilled by a number of research scientists investigating key validational areas: PTSD instrumentation (use of psychometric and interview data), epidemiology of the disorder, and allied morbidity.

PTSD Instrumentation

To achieve validational power, it is important that assessment procedures incorporate a broad spectrum of cognitive, emotional, behavioral, and physiological indicators that comprehensively describes the individual. PTSD instrumentation features behavioral measures, cognitive measures, and psychophysiological measures (Malloy, Fairbank, & Keane, 1983) in a comprehensive, multimodal assessment system.

Structured interview formats and psychometric tests utilized to achieve validity are: (1) *The Jackson Structured Interview for PTSD* (Keane et al., 1985); (2) *The Structured Clinical Interview for DSM-III-R* (SCID) (Spitzer & Williams, 1985); (3) the *Schedule for Affective Disorders and Schizophrenia* (SADS) (Endicott & Spitzer, 1978); (4) *Diagnostic Interview Schedule* (DIS) (Robins, Helzer, Croughan, Williams, & Spitzer, 1981); (5) *The Vietnam Era Stress Inventory* (VESI) (Wilson & Kraus, 1985); (6) *The Keane MMPI PTSD Scale* (Hathaway & McKinley, 1967; Keane, Malloy, & Fairbanks, 1984; Lyons & Keane, 1992); (7) *Impact of Events Scale* (IES) (Horowitz, Wilner, & Alvarez, 1979); (8) *Beck Depression Inventory* (BDI) (Beck et al., 1967); (9) *State-Trait Anxiety Inventory* (STAI)(Spielberger et al., 1970; (10) *The Laufer-Parson Guilt Inventory* (L-PGI) (Laufer & Parson, 1985); and (11) *Traumatosalutogenesis Scale* (TSS) (Parson, 1990).

Studies using the above structured interview procedures and instruments have collected sufficient and consistent data to support the validity of the diagnosis of PTSD. Validity studies need to be broadened to accommodate the full range of traumatized populations, as well as a full range of positive posttrauma outcomes.

Epidemicity of Biopsychic Stress

The most significant study to date on the prevalence of PTSD is the National Vietnam Veterans Readjustment Study (NVVRS), a study that investigated the psychological effects of the War on the entire generation. It is the model par excellence for the study of PTSD since it used multiple measurements to increase sensitivity and diagnostic accuracy. In term of current cases of PTSD, NVVRS study found 15.2% among male veterans and 8.5% among women veterans. Other studies on the prevalence of PTSD reported: 25% among Special Forces veterans (Chemtob, Bauer, & Neller, 1990); 46% among POWs from Vietnam, 30% from Korea, and 19% among World War II veterans (Blake et al., 1990); 4.6% in survivors of disasters (Robins et al., 1986); and 21% in firefighters in Australia almost 30 months after the event (McFarlane, 1986).

Moving from estimating the prevalence of PTSD in specific target populations, other studies have focused on the epidemiology of trauma. Breslau, Davis, Andrecki, and Peteerson (1991) reported a frequency of traumatic experiences of 39% in a sample of 1,000 adults, while Kilpatrick and Resnick (1992) with a national probability sample of 1,500 women found current rates of PTSD to be 1 to 13% and lifetime (proportion of women meeting criteria for PTSD at any time in their lives) rates of 10 to 39%. In a recent study of the epidemiology of trauma, Norris (1992) investigated the frequency of 10 potentially traumatic events in a sample of 1,000 black, white, male and female adults, with a developmental range from young, middle-aged, and older adults.

Norris found that 69% of the sample had experienced at least one traumatic event during their lifetime, with lifetime exposure greater for whites and men and for blacks and women. Recent rates were highest for younger adults. Of the 1,000 subjects, over 200 had suffered a traumatic event during the past year. This is the first and only study to investigate the biopsychic stress in African American civilian populations. The 10 categories of traumatic events studied were robbery, physical assault, sexual assault, fire, Hurricane Hugo, other disaster, other hazard, tragic death, motor vehicle crash, and combat. Epidemiological studies contribute to the validational process by providing prevalence data on a variety of victim groups.

Allied Morbidity and Differential Diagnosis

Validity necessitates the establishment of critical boundary between multiple diagnostic categories of disorders. Psychological and psychoendocrinological studies show a number of common biological and phenomenological factors PTSD shares with many other diagnoses, particularly anxiety, depression, panic disorders, and substance abuse disorders (Behar, 1983; Birkhimer, DeVane, & Muniz, 1985; Green, Lindy, & Grace, 1985; Horowitz et al., 1980; Keane et al., 1988; Silver & Iacono, 1984). Among a sample of veterans, Sierles et al. (1983) found that 56% of veterans with PTSD had one additional psychiatric diagnosis, 20% two additional diagnoses, and 8% had three additional diagnoses. Clinical experience and empirical studies point to the necessity for differential diagnosis among such conditions as factious PTSD (Sparr & Pankratz, 1983), somatization disorder, schizophrenia, bipolar disorder, social phobia simple phobia, agoraphobia, adjustment disorder, malingering, and personality disorders like antisocial, borderline, and others.

Traumatic Personality Disorders

Pretraumatic personality factors (measured retrospectively) and co-PTSD personality disorders are essential factors in validation. Though

DSM-III-R Axis I diagnoses and syndromes are the subject of most valid-ity studies, Axis II personality disorders are equally important. No sys-tematic investigation of personality have been conducted to date, though some work has begun in this area with treatment samples (Funari, Piekarski, & Sherwood, 1991; Hyer, Woods, & Boudewyns, 1991) and theoretical development (Parson, 1982). Since personality configurations serve as a matrix for shaping responses, it is assumed that expression of post-traumatic stress are shaped by psychological steady-state internal structures of the personality. In addition to contributions from personal and social experiences, and biogenic factors, post-traumatic personal-ity disorders may add to the clinical picture the interaction of psychody-namics, biopsychological imprinting of associated catacholaminergic-cholinergic biphasic functions of alternation between agitation and arousal, and avoidance and depression.

Traumatosalutogenesis (TSS): The Strengthening Effects of Trauma

Epidemiological studies have been remiss in the blatant omission of posi-tive, facilitating sequelae of traumatic experiences. Validity studies would do well to incorporate the broadest possible universe of victims' responses, and this should include the positive outcomes generated by the event. The purely negative emphasis in mental health research may ham-per more realistic descriptions of acute and long-term adjustment in PTSD scientific studies. In validational studies, it is quite possible to find that victims endorse as many salutogenic items as pathology items on research questionnaires.

Over a decade ago, Wilson (1980) coined the term "psychosocial ac-celeration" to describe the growth-enhancing impact of trauma sur-vivors. In what might be called bifurcated functioning, this writer has also noted over the years that assessment and therapy with Vietnam vet-erans with PTSD showed trauma-derived strengths (e.g., in terms of in-sight, resilience, and "generativity prosocial tendencies.") in their overall functioning. Many demonstrated unusual insight and generativity wis-dom beyond their chronological age. Ursano (1981), in an early paper, found that Vietnam POW pilots had been strengthened in significant ways when pre- and postwar psychological, psychiatric, and medical measurements were analyzed.

Antonovsky and Bernstein (1988) are among the few professionals to address the issue of health-generated properties of trauma, and first used the term "salutogenesis" in this regard. (See also recent contributions by Lyons, 1991b.) Their awareness of the dearth of interest in this area led them to wonder, "Who studies the successful coper?" In one of his many clinical contributions Scurfield (1985) also wrote about the health-engendering outcomes of traumatic experiences. Noting the importance of a balanced view of the client, he recommended "Helping the client to fully experience both the negative and positive aspects of the trauma experience [since this] is critical to full integration of the trauma experience" (p. 247).

Brende and Parson (1986) describe the third and fourth recovery phase of the natural history of PTSD and noted that the survivor had grown from having a narrow perspective to "a larger perspective" on the trauma, from having a negative, destructive attitude to having a "positive and constructive" one, from being fixed on the past, to an openness to new possibility thinking about the future in which trauma is placed into "its proper perspective" and seen "as merely a past memory" (p. 218). Parson (1989) wrote of veterans giving up self-pity, self-destructiveness and distrust and becoming positive and prosocial in their orientation to self and community.

The Traumatosalutogenesis Scale (TSS) (Parson, 1990) is a move toward correcting the absence of a salutogenetic point of view in current research and therapy (Parson, 1990a). It points to the often ignored fact that the traumatic mishap is not all pain, loss, and breakdown, with absolutistic indelible images of annihilation and death. But it may also yield post-traumatic outcomes of value, with purchasing power toward a better future worthy of an esteemed status in the community. The term "traumatosalutogenesis" refers to trauma-facilitated health outcomes of practical and existential utility.

Without a traumatosalutogenic view in research and clinical practice, professionals will inevitably continue to inadvertently contribute to propagated images of victims as weak, helpless, and mentally deformed by the experience (Janoff-Bulman, 1992; Mazelan, 1982; Parson, 1988a, 1989, 1991). Traumatic suffering needs to be balanced by positive images that realistically portray the true essence of victims' lives. This writer's professional experience with victims is that trauma both weakens and strengthens people, and may accelerate personal growth.

Among the many valuable life-enhancing byproducts of traumatic suffering are an increase in the sense of competence and self-efficacy, an enhanced sense of one's true-self identity; increased courage to be, and a heightened sense of self-worth. Acquiring a special knowledge or insight into the dialectic of life and death, along with enhanced valuing of and sensitivity to people—in both intimate and non-intimate relationships— are also empowering post-trauma outcomes. Many survivors have a basic feeling of rejuvenation, an awareness of a personal resurrection, a second life, and a second chance to live with greater vitality and increased sense of meaning and purpose.

MANAGEMENT: POST-TRAUMATOTHERAPY OF BIOPSYCHIC STRESS

An imbalance exists at the present time in terms of what is known about victims' biopsychic problems and actual knowledge to ameliorate their suffering. To date, there are no large-scale, controlled outcome studies with traumatized populations. The biopsychobehavioral approach to conceptualization and assessment, discussed so far, also informs the treatment of PTSD. An intertheoretical model of treatment is probably the most realistic approach when intervening with victims of traumatic events (Table 13.5). This is because the victim's response involves multiple self-systems, so that no one theoretical model can suffice in addressing the wide array of disabilities (Crump, 1987; Parson, 1984, 1988a). The clinical and scientific necessity to integrate divergent schools of psychotherapy is gaining great momentum (Beitman, Goldfried, & Norcross, 1989). Presented here is a generic model of care for victims of biopsychic stress

TABLE 13.5. Fear-Based Countertransferential Avoidance in Post-Traumatherapy

Countertransferential Neutrality. Therapists with this kind of response tendency with trauma victims or survivors uses the technical-professional aspects of his or her role to avoid getting "too close." The dynamically-oriented may assume the "blank-screen" posture, while the behavior therapist may use an affectless, "technically correct" procedure with the victim.

Countertransferential Enmeshment. Here, the therapist's anxiety motivates counterphobic defenses. Because boundary regulation is lost, the therapist may show difficulty in separating personal issues from the legitimate therapeutic concerns of the patient. In "losing oneself" in the patent's traumatopathlogy, the therapist is reassured that he or she is well, and is no danger of being exposed to the incredible suffering the patient presents.

Countertransferential Distantiation. This is a particularly affectively "cold" response. The therapists unconscious fear is related to concerns of "being contaminated by the victim's experience. This "deep freeze" response undermines empathy, objective assessment of the survivor's problems, and impairs the chances for establishing a meaningful therapeutic alliance with the patient.

Countertransference Repugnance. In this response, the victim is "put down" by the therapist who unconsciously asks, "How could you have gotten yourself in such a mess. I would have known better to avoid the situation." This supercilious attention classes with the victim's need to be understood and receive support and acceptance.

or PTSD. The utility of the biopsychobehavioral perspective is in logically and pragmatic applications of meaningful procedures to the broad spectrum of problems, deficits, and conflicts in victims. The model is flexible: it may be applied to acute cases (phases 1 and 2), requiring days or weeks of care, or to chronic cases (phases 1 through 4).

Management of PTSD begins with a systematic collection of data on the victim's developmental history and premorbid functioning, and a chronologically ordered, sequentially specific detailing of the entire traumatic event. This detailing focuses on the time of the day, the day of the week, the month, and year; the people involved in the event—relatives, friends, strangers, helpers, or rescuers, authorities; the victim's evaluation of his or her performance during the event; and so on.

Second, management requires the administration of brief standardized tests (Lindy, 1988) to assess: (1) the degree of experienced stress (selection made for specific trauma or modified), (2) cognitive processing (e.g., Impact of Event Scale (IES) (Horowitz et al., 1979)); and (3) global severity index of overall psychopathology (e.g., Symptom Checklist-90 [SCL-90], Derogitis, 1977). The clinician may choose to administer parts of this battery during the course of the treatment to objectively monitor progressive and regressive changes in the areas of stress responses, cognitive processing of the trauma, and in global severity of the patient's psychopathology.

Third, management continues with a multiphasic interconceptual model of post-traumatotherapy. The model attempts to realistically address the multiplicity of variables and complexities of PTSD as discussed in this chapter so far. It spans comprehensively from addressing the victim's initial biopsychic disorganization and intrusive ideas and images, adrenergic hyperreactivity and associated affectivity of anxiety and fear of falling apart and of losing control, to working through the trauma to build "prophylactic structures of maturation" (to guard against future regressions).

Integrating multiple schools of psychotherapy, the model uses cognitive-phenomenological (to deal with pathology-sustaining beliefs and emotionality), behavioral (actional patterns), somatic (biophysiological aspects), psychodynamic (awareness and insight), and existential (to deal with meaning) techniques to meet the patient's spectrum of needs comprehensively over time. Thus, the model espouses reparative techniques that span from crisis to integration.

Called "post-traumatotherapy," the model consists of four phases geared to repair the massive damage to self processes, and to heal attachment dysfunctions, described in this chapter. These phases incorporate the usual psychotherapy stages of engagement, pattern search, change, and termination (Beitman et al., 1989). Psychotherapy is the major reparative modality, with somatic and social therapies playing vital, facilitative roles. The model is applied to addressing the needs of battered women (Kemp, Rawlings, & Green, 1991; West, Fernandez, Hillard, Schoof, & Parks, 1990); rape victims (Katz & Mazur, 1978); and other trauma populations. It incorporates the patient's situational stresses such as minority status (Penk & Allen, 1991), and divorce (Dreman et al., 1991). Action becomes the critical healing dimension of each phase. Thus three self-in-action dimensions are addressed in each phase: self-focus (e.g., cognitive processing of trauma elements, guilt, rage), self in relation to others, and self in relation to the social and physical environment.

POST-TRAUMATOTHERAPY: THE PHASES OF REPAIRING DYSFUNCTIONAL ATTACHMENT

Phase 1. Shielding: Stablizing Affectivity

During the immediate post-traumatic or post-emergency period the victim is caught up in the throes of powerful affectivity from central noradrenergic reactivity, and reactive cognitive responses which may escalate to dangerous levels and result in cognitive dissociation. The major task after a traumatic crisis (whether acute or chronic [occurring after a trigger]) is the immediate management of the state of post-traumatic affective stress response syndrome, which consists of intense anxiety, fear, guilt, shame, anger, outrage, depressive mood, narcissistic rage, and phobic reaction in the context of dissociative mechanisms.

Risks of cardiovascular damage and neuromuscular strain are significant for some victims during this phase. The goal, therefore, is to downregulate the influx of mental imagery and peripheral SNS reactivity and reverse varying degrees of biopsychic regression in the patient (Brende & McCann, 1987). At this point of engagement, the victim is in need of a cohesive system of holding and protection from stimuli referred to as "shielding." Shielding is achieved via: (1) the therapist's basic calmative and trust-engendering attitude; (2) psychopharmacotherapy; (3) cognitive and behavioral procedures; and (4) stress management.

Safe-Holding as Prerequisite for Post-Traumatic Reattaching

PTSD is also disorder of "dysattachment." Through the therapist's reassurance, safety, and shielding functions, the victim's inner world of turmoil, fear and threat of losing control abates, allowing attachment to reoccur. However, the therapist must be perceived as a safe, benevolent, reliable, competent, and idealizable (Kohut, 1977) person who knows how to handle the internalized anguish, fear, intense anxieties, aggression, and anticipated threats of breakdown in victimization. This is a form of psychobiological synchroniety, similar to Field's description of being "on the same wavelength."

Safe-holding is a therapeutic relationship factor: it relates to the therapist's capacity to shield the victim from further noxious stimulation as a material one shields and protects the young child who is being torn apart by primitive agonies. Self-holding and shielding are prerequisite for repairing broken bonds or dysattachment. The therapist is required "to go all out" for the patient (Little, 1957), while monitoring a variety of countertransference (CT) reactions (Parson, 1988a).

Psychopharmacotherapy

Drug therapy is an important dimension of the overall psychotherapeutic enterprise with PTSD patients especially in the beginning of the therapy. The success of psychotherapy with victims often depends on the rational use of specific drugs by sensitive, trauma-informed, and experienced psychiatrists (Yost, 1987). Pharmacologic therapy may help increase the patient's capacity to differentiate between external and internal and control cognitive dissociative trends so essential to learning in psychotherapy. Drugs may thus perform the very critical task of "biological preparation" for therapy and increase in personal well-being.

As noted before, PTSD has a stable biological profile which reflects changes in the SNS, neuroendocrine system, and sleep-dream cycle. Thus, during the immediate post-traumatic period, patients experience intrusive-repetitive symptoms and hyperarousal. Drug treatment and the therapist's reassuring and idealizing posture may alleviate the menacing subjective experience of "lost somatopsychic security."

As an arousal disorder characterized by a "hypoadrenocortical state" (Friedman, 1988; Kramer, Kinney, & Scharf, 1982), PTSD is marked by insomnia and disturbed sleep pattern for which drug therapy is particularly valuable for the patient. Psychopharmacological agents have been found to be particularly effective with specific intrusive-arousal symptomatology of PTSD. DSM-III-R's Criterion B and Criterion D are most responsive to medications, while numbing and avoidance symptoms are not as responsive, unless they are accompanied by depression (Friedman, 1988).

The multi-symptomatic nature of PTSD make selection of proper medication very difficult (Embry & Callahan, 1988). In acute cases, the physician is careful not to give medications before a clear picture emerges. In chronic cases, a careful evaluation for suicide and a physical examination are warranted since studies have shown that chronic PTSD is associated with significant medical complaints from deterioration in physical health.

Addressing Intrusive-Arousal Symptoms. Embry and Callahan (1988) found tricyclic antidepressants (TCAs) to be the best pharmacologic group of agents for PTSD treatment, second only to the combination of TCAs and neuroleptics (N) or benzodiazepine (BDZ). Though TCAs are routinely used in nontrauma contexts for dysphoric symptoms like anhedonia, concentration problems, and insomnia, Embry and Callahan (1988) found TCAs (chiefly Imipramine [Tofranil] and Doxepin [Sinequan] to alleviate flashbacks, recurrent dreams, anxiety, depression, sleep disturbance, feeling of detachment, and anhedonia. Other studies found that Amitriptyline (Elavil) was also helpful in reducing the adverse effects of nightmares, flashbacks, dysphoric mood, and insomnia (Falcon, Ryan, Chamberlain, & Curtis, 1985; Roth, 1988).

Burstein (1984) had also found Imipramine to ameliorate intrusive symptoms in victims of vehicular accidents, while Kolb, Burris, and Griffith (1984) found that the monoamine oxidase inhibitors (MAOIs) propranolol (Inderal) and clonidine (Catapres) useful in regulating outbursts of aggression, nightmares, hyperalertness, exaggerated startle response, insomnia, and arousal in war veterans with chronic PTSD.

Benzodiazepines like Diazepam (Valium) and Oxazepam (Serax) are useful for high levels of anxiety, while Alprazolam (Xanax) alleviates panic attacks, and Flurazepam (Dalmane) was helpful with insomnia (Friedman, 1981; Van der Kolk, 1983). Phenelzine (Nardil), a MAOI, features an antidepressant and antipanic effect. Anti-anxiety (or benzodiazepines) psychotropic agents marketed as hypnotics (sleep medications) are Triazolam (Halcion), Flurazepam (Dalmane), and Temazepam (Restoril) and are used with significant success in ameliorating this PTSD symptom. In addition to BDZs, the MAOI propranolol, and lithium carbonate are also used as hypnotic agents (Van der Kolk, 1983). Shalev and Rogel-Fuchs' (1992) study of the arousal phenomenon of auditory startle-reflex in PTSD patients found that clonazepam was helpful in the treatment of this symptom.

Autopharmaco-"Therapy." Alcohol and anti-anxiety agents, the benzodiazepines, are abused by many combat veterans who need to self-medicate for arousal symptomatology. Assessment of the history and current status of this practice is important to the treatment experience.

Teaching Pretherapy

Pretherapy informs the victim what he or she is to expect from the therapy, offering an opportunity for informed consent. Definitions of therapy, reasons for therapy, who seeks therapy, why, and possible risks are among the important issues to be explored in pretherapy. This procedure reduces anxiety over the unknowns of therapy, and prevents premature termination.

Cognitive Procedures

These procedures aid the anti-adrenergic effects of drug therapy by promoting opportunities for the successful cognitive processing of the event in an attempt to overcome cognitive distortions of PTSD and to cognitively organize and master the trauma. Horowitz's (1976) "crisis-oriented psychodynamic therapy" is founded on the premise that trauma causes information overload which overwhelms the victim's information-processing cognitive capacities. He recommends that when the patient is in the intrusive-repetitive mode the therapy focuses on developing controls from the external world, while the therapist serves as an extension of the patient that organizes information for the victim.

Additionally, rest and relaxation are important as well as reducing external demands upon the patient. If the patient is in the denial-numbing mode the therapy focuses on reducing the effects of these defenses. Other cognitive procedures used during this phase by this writer are: cognitive restructuring and other rational-emotive therapy techniques (Ellis, 1962) and educopsychological procedures to enhance information-processing through helping victims achieve a cognitive grasp of their trauma responses, and move toward a self-managed life style (Williams & Long, 1975).

Behavioral Procedures

Behavioral approaches assist the victim to manage memories of the trauma through the application of implosive therapy and imaginal flooding (Keane et al., 1985), systematic desensitization (Schindler, 1980), relaxation training (Bernstein & Borkovec, 1975; Parson, 1984), behavioral rehearsal (Fairbank & Keane, 1982), stress inoculation training (SIT) (Meichenbaum, 1974), and behavioral bibliotherapy (Marafioti, 1980; Parson, 1984). Kilpatrick and Resnick (1992) and Foa et al. (1991) used SIT, and cognitive-behavioral procedures and counseling for rape victims who showed fear, anxiety, tensions, and depression.

Stress Management and Biofeedback

Stress management consists of procedures aimed at increasing physiological regulation, inner tranquility and sense of competence over the subjective sense of losing control.

Social Skills and Communications Training

The ordinary tendency to isolation and to feeling misunderstood by family, friends, and work peers and supervisors is a very significant area requiring direct intervention. Communications skills are core elements in successful reintegration into family, work, and community.

The therapist's basic technical posture in phase 1 is characterized by active engagement and self-disclosing behavior.

Phase 2. Consolidation and Deepening of Trust

This phase presupposes that a significant reduction of the uncontrolled adrenergic eruptions of phase 1 (stabilization) has occurred. Building self-esteem, idealizability, and trust are key processes during this phase. Victims gradually learn to face self—to stay with trauma-induced feelings without backing off. Specific behavioral techniques are taught to assist the victim learn skills in relaxation, and self-management (Williams & Long, 1975). Cognitive approaches are geared to help some patients overcome black-white thinking (Alford, Mahone, & Fieldstein, 1988), and manage emotions associated with somatization disorder and overcome aspects of social stigma, especially among Vietnam veteran patients (Fleming, 1985).

As carryover from first phase of the natural history of PTSD, symptoms involving "the heart, stomach, urinary tract, genitals, muscles, nerves, and blood pressure" (Brende & Parson, 1986, p. 222) are present during this phase. Additionally, problematic phase 2 symptoms of emotional detachment and numbing, partial or full amnesias, and anhedonia (Brende & Parson, 1986) are essential focus for treatment. Responses are integrated into the treatment and are conducted within a context of therapeutic support, with a "suppressive-repressive" emphasis, which prepare the patient for the strenuous demands of phase 3.

The victim's cognitive and affective functioning are carefully monitored to determine the degree of numbing defenses utilized and the relative relation to intrusive ideation and related anxious arousal. Specific techniques are employed to build skills in becoming an effective partner in the therapeutic venture. The patient's concerns, guilt, and dynamics in relation to his or her children (Haley, 1987), family (Figley, 1988), work, career, and the future in terms of effectance (or sense of competence) are important issues during this phase in order to solidify the therapeutic relationship.

Deconditioning emotional responses to traumatic memories associated to PTSD such as Shapiro's (1989) eye movement desensitization is valuable during this phase. The therapist is always mindful of the need to keep all procedures connected to the patient's presenting traumatic complaints in the beginning of the therapy. Therapist's self-disclosure is very important in this phase to reduce isolation, offer continued reassurance, and increase self-esteem. A full evolution of PTSD patterns as well as search for characterological patterns emerge in this phase. Preparation for phase 3 is essential to secure to the overall treatment enterprise, and the therapist's posture is active with less self-disclosing information than previous phase.

Phase 3. Controlled Regression

This phase consists of psychologically returning to the "psychic site of the trauma." It presupposes the development of sufficient trust and the acquisition of new psychological structure and integration of the trauma to "permit" the anxiety-provoking regression. Systematic stress management skills and employment of these techniques prepare the patient for the journey back. The goal of this phase is abreaction, a prerequisite integration of the trauma. Therapeutic regressive or reexposure techniques may include hypnosis, yoga, implosive flooding therapy (Keane, Fairbank, Caddell, & Zimering, 1989) or the "helicopter ride therapy" devised for traumatized veterans (Scurfield, 1992). The therapist's total focus is on the patient's needs around regressive reliving of the event.

Phase 4. Integration and Completion

This phase utilizes psychodynamic procedures and techniques to further consolidate the victim's personality. Using chiefly the tool of interpretation, confrontation, and overt exploration of transference, the goal of the phase is personality change at deep levels. This may serve prophylactic functions against the eruptions of latent trauma elements which form the dissociated bedrock of the personality. If it is determined that the goal of the overall treatment can be enhanced by collateral therapeutic procedures or modalities (such as stress management, marital therapy, group therapy) arrangements are made with other therapists or agencies.

Healing the split-off aspects of self is a major objective of the overall treatment enterprise. These splits or disjunctive gaps are associated with the victim's sense of attachment to self and others. Attachment theory (Emde, 1982) sheds light on the profound rupturing of the sense of connectedness between the victim's self and the world. Healing and integration of necessity, therefore, calls for a "re-attaching" of severed strands of the self's fabric which connects it to life-sustaining forces in others and in the environment.

The phase ends with an existential focus through which the victim's meaning system is consolidated. Some victims may continue to require cognitive, behavior modification, and stress management procedures to retain the change and growth they had achieved in therapy. This can in part be determined through the administration of the post-traumatic assessment battery. Ultimately, for anchored change and transformation to occur, the survivor becomes socially engaged to achieve internal balance and establish equanimity and control. For psyche and soma "cannot fully integrate internally until [they] attain harmony communally" (Tien, 1987, p. 181).

SUMMARY AND CONCLUSION

Post-traumatic stress disorder (PTSD) is a nosological entity that appeared officially for the first time in the DSM-III (APA, 1980). The diagnosis requires five criteria: history of trauma and intrusive, avoidance, arousal, and a temporal factor. It is one of the most exciting areas of scientific inquiry and therapeutic work. Interests in the area grows daily, and the national and international organizations recently established the symposia, lectures, and professional, scientific, and popular publications in the area attest to the significance of PTSD in psychology, psychiatry, psychoanalysis, sociology, and law. It affects children, adolescents, young adults, middle-aged, and senior-aged individuals. It impacts all nations, and all racial and ethnic groups. Its devastating effects damage the victim's physiology, biology, cognition, and behavior.

PTSD appears to be a pressing public health problem, as drug-related violence, social violence, and family violence infest communities. As this ubiquitous pattern of violence flares up and engulfs people's lives, PTSD becomes an ever-increasing threat and reality. Though estimates of PTSD in some trauma populations have been reported (for example, Vietnam veterans [CDC], 1988; Weiss, Marmar, Schlenger, & Fairbank, 1992), prevalence rates in the general population are not known at the present time. However, Helzer et al. (1987) have reported the controversial rate of PTSD of 1 to 2% in the general population. Though this figure seems small it means that at least 2 to 5 million persons suffer from PTSD are in need of effective intervention strategies to prevent life cycle-long disabilities that attend this disorder.

Assessment and therapy in PTSD requires a wide ranging theoretical and practical information base. They thus call for an appreciation of basic physiological stress response processes, the employing of scientifically-based traumatic stress assessments (Keane et al., 1987; Lyons, 1991a; Malloy et al., 1983; Penk & Allen, 1990), and understanding the role culture and adapted character styles play in the expression and meaning of the trauma (Boehnlein, 1987; Parson, 1985a, 1992; Sherwood, 1990). The integration of multiple therapies such as psychotherapy (Lindy, 1988; Parson, 1984; Scurfield, 1985), sociotherapy (Parson, 1990b), drug therapy (Davidson, 1992), may provide the most efficacious treatment plan for victims of biopsychic stress.

Toward DSM-IV, ICD-10, and Beyond

Despite the progress in PTSD instrumentation and research and adequate levels of diagnostic accuracy, sensitivity, and specificity for PTSD, there exists to date no "gold standard" for diagnosing PTSD (Penk & Allen, 1991). Clinical experience and scientific studies have raised questions bearing on the taxonomic appropriateness since PTSD may have its own nosologic or taxonomic boundaries that separate it from other disorders. Perhaps some changes in current classification and descriptions based on clinical observation and scientific findings may increase diagnostic specificity.

Traumatic Stress Syndromes

Is PTSD an anxiety disorder? Anxiety is related to PTSD but is not a predominating factor or precondition for the disorder (APA, 1987). Unlike the anxiety in anxiety disorders (e.g., GAD, phobic disorder, obsessive-compulsive disorder), which are seen as irrational responses ("irrational anxiety"), anxiety responses in PTSD are connected to real events ("rational anxiety") which did actually occur. PTSD is probably not an anxiety disorder, and should therefore be reclassified to another nosological category such as "traumatic stress syndromes," with specific subcategorizations could conceivably contribute to achieving an increase in diagnostic accuracy by refining description, prediction, and explanatory formulations. Such reclassification could aid in the development of a common language among clinicians and scientists, and reduce the historical and contemporary chaos in the field (Boulanger, 1990).

Subcategorizations of PTSD

Green et al. (1985) maintain that problems dealing with etiology, natural course of the disorder, and diagnostic specificity are important issues to be grappled with in the field. Not all stressors are equal; not all stressors produce the same form or degree of long-term post-traumatic symptomatology. For example, human-engineered events leading to PTSD are more devastating to the victim than trauma caused by natural events. Thus, rape produces more distress and negative experiences than other crimes (Kilpatrick et al., 1989). War experiences are probably very different from torture experiences, and a victim of a technological disaster may differ from an incest trauma victim. As noted earlier, life-cycle stage or age at the time of trauma tend to have differential impact, with children and the elderly being most vulnerable. Additionally, prior trauma or family psychiatric history may be important variables in succumbing to PTSD and its maintenance into the chronic stage. The diagnostic scheme should allow for *nonpathological* traumatic stress responses.

Proposed here is a classification that takes these factors into account. The diagnosis of PTSD is accompanied by additional information bearing on etiology-vulnerability and coping. Stressor characteristics such as intensity, duration, and type of stressor are balanced with personal factors like vulnerability and coping. Thus the following sequence of data presentation is proposed: diagnosis (di), precipitating stimuli (ps), vulnerability (vu), and coping (co). A woman with PTSD who was raped and had a history of family psychiatric illness and good coping at the present time would be coded as: PTSD (di), rape (ps), FPI (vu), and + (co). A war veteran who killed in the war and was also wounded, with no psychiatric history, and currently has poor coping is recorded as: PTSD, war (specify stressor[s]), NFPI (no family psychiatric illness), and —. A child who witnessed parental murder with good adjustment, no mental illness in family, with moderate coping capacity would be: PTSD, witness, NFPI, child, and + −. Additionally, a woman who survived a tornado mishap where others died and reports mild, normal responses to trauma, but has a prior history of trauma (incest), and blames an authority for the mishap is recorded as PTSD/CNAMD ("Conditions Not Attributable to a Mental Disorder"), tornado—HE (human-engineered), prior trauma (pt) and +. This victim may be expected to go through later eruptions of post-traumatic symptoms due to both the impact of prior trauma and the human-induced nature of the trauma.

O'Donohue and Elliott (1992) have argued eloquently for a similar reclassification, while Green et al. (1985) had earlier advocated a specific focus on etiology, natural course of the disorder, and factors bearing on diagnostic accuracy in order to improve the assessment and diagnostic accuracy in the DSM-IV. Herman (1992) argues persuasively for the inclusion of DESNOS (Disorders of Extreme Stress Not Otherwise Specified) in DSM-IV for cases of "complex PTSD" characterized by prolonged, repeated trauma. As "a diagnosis that spans national and international boundaries," the World Health Organization's ICD-10 (International classification of diseases, 10th ed.) "will promote the systematic global use of the term" (Weisaeth & Eitinger, 1992, p. 1).

This chapter was written to offer the clinician a broad spectrum of issues in assessment and treatment of PTSD, and guide the research investigator to salient gaps in knowledge in which to direct effort in scientific study. It continues to be clear that much research needs to be done in every major area of PTSD in order to build on the present clinical and empirical foundations of this new emerging field.

REFERENCES

Adler, A. (1943). Neuropsychiatric complications in victims in Boston's Coconut Grove disaster. *Journal of the American Medical Association, 123,* 1098–1101.

Agger, I. (1989). Sexual torture of political prisoners: An overview. *Journal of Traumatic Stress, 2,* 305–318.

Alford, J., Mahone, C., & Fieldstein, E. (1988). Cognitive and behavioral sequalae of combat: Conceptualization and implications for treatment. *Journal of Traumatic Stress, 1,* 489–502.

Allen, I. M. (1987). Post-traumatic stress disorder among black Vietnam veterans. *Hospital and Community Psychiatry, 37,* 55–61.

American Psychiatric Association. (1968). *Diagnostic and statistical manual of mental disorders.* Washington, DC: Author.

American Psychiatric Association. (1980). *Diagnostic and statistical manual of mental disorders,* 3rd ed. (pp. 236–238). Washington, DC: Author.

American Psychiatric Association. (1987). *Diagnostic and statistical manual of mental disorders,* 3rd ed., rev. (pp. 247–250). Washington, DC: Author.

Andreason, N. C. (1980). Post-traumatic stress disorder. In H. Kaplan & B. Sadock, *Comprehensive textbook of psychiatry—IV.* (pp. 918–924). Baltimore: Williams & Wilkins.

Anisman, H., & Zacharko, R. (1986). Behavioral and neurochemical consequences associated with stressors. *Annals of the New York Academy of Sciences, 467,* 205–229.

Antonovsky, A. & Bernstein, J. (1988). Pathogenesis and salutogenesis in war and other crises. In N. Milgram (Ed.), *Stress and coping in time of war.* New York: Brunner/Mazel.

Archibald, H. & Tuddeham, R. (1965). Persistent stress reaction after combat. *Archives of General Psychiatry, 12,* 475–481.

Arroyo, W., & Eth, S. (1985). Children traumatized by Central American warfare. In S. Eth & R. Pynoos (Eds.), *Post-traumatic stress disorder in children.* (pp. 62–80). Washington, DC: American Psychiatric Press.

Bard, M., & Ellison, D. (1974). Crisis intervention and investigation of forcible rape. *Police Chief, 5,* 68–74.

Beck, A. T. (1967). Depression: Clinical, experimental, & theoretical aspects. London: Staples.

Behar, D. (1983). Confirmation of concurrent illnesses in post-traumatic stress disorder [Letter]. *American Journal of Psychiatry, 141,* 1310–1311.

Beitman, B., Goldfried, M., & Norcross, J. (1989). The movement toward integrating the psychotherapies: An overview. *American Journal of Psychiatry, 146,* 138–146.

Bergland, R. (1985). *The fabric of mind.* Ringwood: Pinquin Books of Australia.

Bernstein, A., & Borkovec, T. (1975). *Progressive relaxation training: A manual for the helping professions.* Champaign, IL: Research Press.

Birkhimer, L., DeVane, C., & Muniz, C. (1985). Post-traumatic stress disorder: Characteristics and pharmacological response in the veteran population. *Comprehensive Psychiatry, 26,* 304–310.

Blake, D., Keane, T., Wine, R., Mora, C., Taylor, K., & Lyons, J. (1990). Prevalence of PTSD symptoms in combat veterans seeking medical treatment. *Journal of Traumatic Stress, 3,* 15–27.

Blanchard, E., Kolb, L., Gerardi, R., Ryan, P., & Pallmeyer, T. (1986). Cardiac response to relevant stimuli as an adjunctive tool for diagnosing post-traumatic stress disorder in Vietnam veterans. *Behavior Therapy, 17,* 592–606.

Boehnlein, J. (1987). Culture and society in post-traumatic stress disorder: Implication for psychotherapy. *American Journal of Psychotherapy, 41,* 519–528.

Borus, J. (1973a). Incidence of maladjustment in Vietnam returnees. *Archives of General Psychiatry, 30,* 554–557.

Borus, J. (1973b). Reentry, II: "Making it" back in the states. *American Journal of Drug and Alcohol Abuse, 6,* 301–312.

Boulanger, G. (1985). Post-traumatic stress disorder: An old problem with a new name. In S. Sonnenberg, A. Blank, & J. Talbott (Eds.), *The trauma of war: Stress and recovery in Vietnam veterans.* (pp. 30–48). Washington, DC: American Psychiatric Press.

Boulanger, G. (1990). A state of anarchy and a call to arms: The research and treatment of post-traumatic stress disorder. *Journal of Contemporary Psychotherapy, 20,* 5–16.

Bremner, J., Southwick, S., Brett, E., Fontana, A., Rosenheck, R. & Charney, D. (1992). *American Journal of Psychiatry, 149,* 328–332.

Brende, J. O. (1982). Electrodermal responses in post-traumatic syndromes: A pilot study of cerebral hemisphere functioning in Vietnam veterans. *Journal of Nervous and Mental Disease, 170,* 352–361.

Brende, J. O. (1983). A psychodynamic view of character pathology in Vietnam combat veterans. *Bulletin of the Menninger Clinic, 47,* 193–216.

Brende, J. O. (1984). An educational-therapeutic group for drug and alcohol abusing combat veterans. *Journal of Contemporary Psychotherapy, 14,* 120–133.

Brende, J. O. (1987). Dissociative disorders in Vietnam combat veterans. *Journal of Contemporary Psychotherapy, 17,* 77–86.

Brende, J. O., & McCann, I. L. (1984). Regressive experiences in Vietnam veterans: Their relationship to war, post-traumatic symptoms and recovery. *Journal of Contemporary Psychotherapy, 14,* 57–75.

Brende, J. O., & McCann, L. (1987). Regressive experiences in Vietnam veterans: Their relationship to war, post-traumatic symptoms and recovery. In W. Quaytman (Ed.), *The Vietnam veteran: Studies in post-traumatic stress disorders.* New York: Human Sciences Press.

Brende, J. O., & Parson, E. R. (1986). *Vietnam veterans: The road to recovery,* p. 215. New York: Signet.

Breslau, N., & Davis, G. (1987). Post-traumatic stress disorder: The stressor criterion. *Journal of Nervous and Mental Disease, 175,* 255–264.

Breslau, N., Davis, C., Andrecki, P., & Peteerson, E. (1991). Traumatic events and post-traumatic stress disorder in an urban population of young adults. *Archives of General Psychiatry, 48,* 216–222.

Brett, E., & Mangine, B. (1985). Imagery and combat stress in Vietnam veterans. *Journal of Nervous and Mental Disease, 173,* 309–311.

Breuer, J., & Freud, S. (1895/1955). Studies in hysteria. In *Standard edition, 2.* London: Hogarth.

Brill, N. Q. (1967). Gross stress reaction, II: Traumatic war neurosis. In A.M. Freedman & H. I. Kaplan, (Eds.), *Comprehensive Textbook of Psychiatry.* (pp. 1031–1035). New York: Williams & Wilkens.

Brockway, S. (1987). Group treatment of combat nightmares in post-traumatic disorders. *Journal of Contemporary Psychotherapy, 17,* 27–284.

Burges, S., Watson, I., Hoffman, I. & Wilson, G. (1988). The neuropsychiatry of post-traumatic stress disorder. *British Journal of Psychiatry, 152,* 164–173.

Burgess, A., & Holstrom, L. (1974). Rape trauma syndrome. *American Journal of Psychiatry, 131,* 981–986.

Burstein, A. (1984). Treatment of post-traumatic stress disorder with imipramine. *Psychosomatics, 25,* 681–687.

Burstein, A. (1985). Post-traumatic flashback, dream disturbances, and mental imagery. *Journal of Clinical Psychiatry, 46,* 374–378.

Calabrese, J., Kling, M., & Gold, P. (1987). Alterations in immunocompetence during stress, bereavement, and depression: Focus on neuroendocrine regulation. *American Journal of Psychiatry, 144,* 1123–1134.

Center for Disease Control (1988). Health status of Vietnam veterans: I. Psychosical characteristics. *Journal of the American Medical Association, 259,* 2702–2707.

Chemtob, C., Bauer, G., & Neller, G. (1990). Post-traumatic stress disorder among Special Forces Vietnam veterans. *Military Medicine, 155,* 16–20.

Crump, L. D. (1987). Gestalt therapy in the treatment of Vietnam veterans experiencing PTSD symptomatology. In W. Quaytman (Ed.), *The Vietnam veterans: Studies in post-traumatic stress disorders.* New York: Human Sciences Press.

Daly, R. (1983). Samuel Pepys and post-traumatic stress disorder. *British Journal of Psychiatry, 143,* 64–68.

Danieli, Y. (1981). Countertransference in the treatment and study of Nazi Holocaust survivors and their children. *Victimology, 5,* 355–367.

Davidson, J. (1992). Drug therapy of post-traumatic stress disorder. *British Journal of Psychiatry, 160,* 309–314.

Davidson, J., Lipper, S., Kilts, C., Mahorney, S., & Hammett, E. (1985) Platelet MAO activity in post-traumatic stress disorder. *American Journal of Psychiatry, 142,* 1341–1344.

Derogitis, L. (1977). *R. Version. Manual (SCL-90).* Baltimore: Johns Hopkins University.

Dobbs, D., & Wilson, W. Observations on persistence of war neurosis. *Diseases of the Nervous System, 21,* 40–46.

Doyle, J., & Bauer, S. (1989). Post-traumatic stress disorder in children: Its identification and treatment in a residential setting for emotionally disturbed youth. *Journal of Traumatic Stress, 2,* 275–288.

Ellenberger, H. (1970). *The discovery of the unconscious: The history and evolution of dynamic psychiatry.* New York: Basic Books.

Ellis, A. (1962). *Reason and emotion in psychotherapy.* New York: Lyle Stuart.

Ellis, P. S. (1984). The origins of war neuroses. *Journal of the Royal Navy Medical Service, 70,* 168–177.

Embry, C., & Callahan, B. (1988). Effective psychopharmacotherapy for post-traumatic stress disorder. *VA Practitioner,* 57–66.

Emde, R. (1982). *The development of attachment and affiliative systems.* New York: Plenum.

Endicott, J. & Spitzer, R. (1978). A diagnostic interview: Schedule for affective disorders and schizophrenia. *Archives of General Psychiatry, 35,* 837–844.

Erickson, E. (1968). *Identity, youth and crisis.* New York: Norton.

Erickson, K. (1976). Loss of communality at Buffalo Creek. *American Journal of Psychiatry,* 302–305.

Eth, S., & Pynoos, R. (1985). *Post-traumatic stress disorder in children.* Washington, DC: American Psychiatric Press.

Fairbank, J., and Keane, T. (1982). Flooding for combat-related stress disorders: Assessment of anxiety reduction across traumatic disorders. *Behavior Therapy, 13,* 499–570.

Falcon, S., Ryan, C., Chamberlain, K., & Curtis, G. (1985). Tricyclics: Possible treatment for post-traumatic stress disorder, *Comprehensive Psychiatry, 46,* 385–389.

Ferenczi, S., Abraham, K., Simmel, E., & Jones, E. (1921). *Psychoanalysis and the war neurosis.* New York: International Psychoanalytic Press.

Field, T. (1985). Attachment as psychobiological attunement: Being on the same wavelength. In M. Reite & T. Fields (Eds.), *The psychobiology of attachment and separation.* Orlando: Academic Press.

Figley, C. R. (1978). *Stress disorders among Vietnam veterans.* New York: Brunner/Mazel.

Figley, C. R. (1988). Toward a field of traumatic stress. *Journal of Traumatic Stress, 1,* 3–16.

Findelhor, D. (1984). *Child sexual abuse: New theory and research.* New York: Free Press.

Fleming, R. (1985). Post-Vietnam syndrome: Neurosis or sociosis? *Psychiatry, 48,* 122–139.

Foa, E., Feske, U., McCarthy, P., & Kozak, M. (1990). *Processing of threat-related information in rape victims.* Unpublished manuscript.

Foa, E., Rothbaum, B., Riggs, D., & Murdock, B. (1991). Treatment of post-traumatic stress disorder in rape victims: A comparison between cognitive-behavioral procedures and counseling. *Journal of Consulting and Clinical Psychology, 59,* 715–723.

Foy, D., Carroll, M., & Donahue, C. (1987). Etiological factors in the development of post-traumatic stress disorder in clinical samples of Vietnam combat veterans, *Journal of Clinical Psychology, 43,* 17–27.

Frederick, C. (1985). Children traumatized by catastrophic situations. In R. Pynoos & S. Eth (Eds.), *Post-traumatic stress disorder,* (pp. 82–96). Washington, DC: American Psychiatric Press.

Freud, S. (1894/1962). The Neuro-psychosis of defense. *Standard edition, 3,* pp. 45–61. London: Hogarth.

Freud, S. (1896/1962). Further remarks on the neuro-psychosis of defense— Aetiology of hysteria. In *Standard edition, 3.* (pp. 182–185). London: Hogarth.

Freud, S. (1900). The interpretation of dreams. In *Standard edition,* 4 and 5. London: Hogarth.

Freud, S. (1916–1917). Introductory lectures on psycho-analysis. In *Standard edition,* 15 and 16. London: Hogarth.

Freud, S., (1920). Beyond the pleasure principle. In *Standard edition, 18,* pp. 3–64. London: Hogarth.

Freud, S. (1920/1955). Appendix—Memorandum on the electrical treatment of war neurotics. In *Standard edition, 17.* (pp. 211–216). London: Hogarth.

Freud, S. (1936). A disturbance of memory on the Acropolis. In *Standard edition, 22.* (pp. 239–248). London: Hogarth.

Freud, S., Ferenczi, S., Abraham, K., Simmel, E., & Jones, E. (1921). *Psychoanalysis and the war neuroses.* Vienna: International Psychoanalytical Press.

Friedman, M. (1981). Post-Vietnam syndrome: Recognition and management. *Psychosomatics, 22,* 931–943.

Friedman, M. (1988). Toward rational pharmacotherapy for PTSD. *American Journal of Psychiatry, 145,* 281–285.

Friedman, P., & Lin, L. (1957). Some psychiatric notes on the Andrea Doria disaster. *American Journal of Psychiatry, 114,* 426–432.

Funari, D., Piekarski, A., & Sherwood, R. (1991). Treatment outcomes of Vietnam veterans with post-traumatic stress disorder. *Psychological Reports, 68,* 571–578.

Goodwin, D. & Guze, S. (1984). Psychiatric diagnosis. New York: Oxford University Press.

Green, B., Grace, M., Titchener, J., & Lindy, J. (1983). Levels of functioning impairments following a civilian disaster: The Beverly Hills Supper Club fire. *Journal of Consulting and Clinical Psychology, 51,* 573–580.

Green, B., Lindy, J., & Grace, M. (1985). Post-traumatic stress disorder: Toward DSM-IV. *Journal of Nervous and Mental Disease, 173,* 406–411.

Green, B., Lindy, J., Grace, M., Gleser, G., Korol, M., & Winget, C. (1990). Buffalo Creek survivors in the second decade: Stability of stress symptoms. *American Journal of Orthopsychiatry, 60,* 43–54.

Grinker, R., & Speigel, J. (1945). *Men under stress.* New York: McGraw-Hill.

Groves, P., & Young, S. (1986). Neurons, networks, and behavior: An introduction. In L. Judd & P. Groves (Eds.), *Psychobiological foundations of clinical psychology.* New York:

Haley, S. (1987). The Vietnam veteran and his preschool child: Child rearing as a delayed stress in combat veterans. In W. Quaytman (Ed.), *The Vietnam veteran: Studies in post-traumatic stress disorders.* (pp. 112–119). New York: Human Sciences Press.

Hartmann, H. (1939). *Ego Psychology & the Problem of Adaptation,* pp. 276–292. New York: International Universities Press.

Hathaway, S. & McKinley, J. (1951). Minnesota Multiphasic Personality Inventory: Manual for Administration & Scoring. Minneapolis, MN: University of Minnesota.

Helzer, J., Robins, L., & McEnvoy, L. (1987). Post-traumatic stress disorder in the general population: Findings of the epidemiological catchement area survey. *New England Journal of Medicine, 317,* 1630–1634.

Herman, J. (1992). Complex PTSD: A syndrome in survivors of prolonged and repeated trauma. *Journal of Traumatic Stress, 5,* 377–391.

Holmes, T., & Rache, R. (1967). The social readjustment scale. *Journal of Psychosomatic Research, 11,* 213–218.

Horowitz, M. (1976). *Stress response syndromes,* 2nd ed. Northvale, NJ: Aronson.

Horowitz, M. (1983). Post-traumatic stress disorder. *Behavioral Science and Law, 1,* 9–20.

Horowitz, M., Wilner, N., & Alvarez, W. (1979). Impact of events scale: A measure of subjective strength. *Psychosomatic Medicine, 41,* 209–218.

Horowitz, M., Wilner, N., & Kaltreider, N. (1980). Signs and symptoms of post-traumatic stress disorder. *Archives of General Psychiatry, 37,* 85–92.

Hyer, L., Woods, M., & Boudewyns, P. (1991). A three-tier evaluation of PTSD among Vietnam combat veterans. *Journal of Traumatic Stress, 2,* 165–194.

Janet, P. (1889). *L'automatisme psychologique: Essai de psychologie expérimentale sur les formes inférieures de l'activité humaine.* Paris: Felix Alcan.

Janet, P. (1925). *Psychological healing,* vols. 1, 2, p. 589. New York: Macmillan (original version: Les medications psychologiques, vols. 1–3. Paris Felix Alcan, 1919).

Janoff-Bulman, R. (1992). *Shattered Assumptions: A new psychology of trauma.* New York: The Free Press.

Kahana, B., Harel, Z., & Kahana, E. (1988). Predictors of psychological well-being among survivors of the Holocaust. In J. P. Wilson, Z. Harel, & B. Kahana (Eds.), *Human adaptation to extreme stress: From the Holocaust to Vietnam.* (pp. 171–192). New York: Plenum.

Kardiner, A. (1941). *The traumatic neuroses of war.* New York: Hoeber.

Kardiner, A. (1959). Traumatic neurosis of war. In S. Arieti (Ed.), *American handbook of psychiatry, Vol. 1.* New York: Basic Books.

Kardiner, A. (1969). Traumatic neurosis of war. In S. Arieti (Ed.), *American handbook of psychiatry.* New York: Basic Books.

Kardiner, A., & Ovesey, L. (1950). *The mark of oppression.* Cleveland: World Publishing Company.

Kardiner, A., & Spiegel, H. (1947). *War stress and neurotic illness.* New York: Hoeber.

Katz, S., & Mazur, M. (1978). Understanding the rape victim: A synthesis of research findings. New York: Wiley Interscience.

Keane, T., Caddell, J., & Taylor, K. (1988). Mississippi scale for combat-related PTSD: Three Studies in Reliability and Viability.

Keane, T., Fairbank, J., Caddell, J., & Zimering, R. (1989). Implosive (flooding) therapy reduces symptoms of PTSD in Vietnam veterans. *Behavior Therapy, 20,* 245–260.

Keane, T., Fairbank, J., Caddell, R., Zimering, & Bender, M. (1985). A behavioral approach to assessing and treating post-traumatic stress disorder in Vietnam veterans. In C. R. Figley (Ed.), *Trauma and its wake: The study and treatment of post-traumatic stress disorder.* New York: Brunner/Mazel.

Keane, T., Malloy, P., & Fairbanks, J. (1984). Empirical development of an MMPI subscale for the assessment of combat-related post-traumatic stress disorder. *Journal of Consulting and Clinical Psychology, 52,* 888–891.

Keane, T., Wolfe, J., & Taylor, K. (1987). Post-traumatic stress disorder: Evidence for diagnostic validity and methods of psychological assessment. *Journal of Clinical Psychology, 43,* 132–43.

Kelly, D. (1982). The role of endorphins in stress-induced analgesia. *Annals of New York Academy of Sciences, 398,* 260–271.

Kelly, R. (1981). Post-traumatic syndrome. *Journal of the Royal Society of Medicine, 74,* 243–245.

Kemp. A., Rawlings, E., & Green, B. (1991). Post-traumatic stress disorder (PTSD) in battered women: A shelter sample. *Journal of Traumatic Stress, 4,* 137–148.

Kilpatrick, D., & Resnick, H. (1992). PTSD associated with exposure to criminal victimization in clinical and community populations. In J. Davidson and E. Foa (Eds.), *Post-traumatic stress disorder in review: Recent research and future directions.* (pp. 200–235). Washington, DC: American Psychiatric Press.

Kilpatrick, D., Saunders, B., & Amick-McMullen, R. (1989). Victim and crime factors associated with the development of crime-related post-traumatic stress disorder. *Behavior Therapy, 20,* 199–214.

Kilpatrick, D., & Veronen, L. (1984). Treatment of fear and anxiety in victim of rape. Final report, NIMH grant No. HMH29602.

Kilpatrick, D., Veronen, L., & Best, C. (1985). Factors predicting psychological distress in rape victims. In C. Figley (Ed.), *Trauma and its wake.* (pp. 113–141). New York: Brunner/Mazel.

Kohut, H. (1977). *The restoration of the self.* New York: International Universities Press.

Kolb, L. (1987). Neuropsychological hypothesis explaining post-traumatic stress disorder. *American Journal of Psychiatry, 144,* 989–995.

Kolb, L., Burris, B., & Griffith, S. (1984). Propranolol and clonidine in treatment of chronic post-traumatic stress disorders of war. In B. van der Kolk

(Ed.), *Post-traumatic stress disorder: Psychological and biological sequelae.* Washington, DC: American Psychiatric Press.

Kosten, T., Mason, J., Giller, E., & Ostroff, R. (1987). Sustained urinary norepinephrine elevation in post-traumatic stress disorder. *Psychoneuroendocrinology, 12,* 13–20.

Kramer, M., Kinney, L., & Scharf, M. (1982). Sleep in delayed stress victims. *Sleep Research, 11,* 113.

Krystal, H. (1968). *Massive psychic trauma.* New York: International Universities Press.

Krystal, J. (1990). Animal models for post-traumatic stress disorder: In E. Giller (Ed.), *Biological assessment and treatment of PTSD.* Washington, DC: American Psychiatric Press.

Kuch, K., & Cox, B. (1992). Symptoms of PTSD in 124 survivors of the Holocaust. *American Journal of Psychiatry, 149,* 337–340.

Kulka, R., Schlenger, W., Fairbank, J., Hough, B., Jordan, B., Marmar, C., & Weiss, D. (1988). *National Vietnam veterans readjustment study (NVVRS): Descriptional current status, and initial PTSD prevalence rates.* Washington, DC: Department of Veterans Affairs.

Laufer, R., Brett, E., & Gallops, M. (1984). Post-traumatic stress disorder (PTSD) recommended: PTSD among Vietnam veterans. In B. van der Kolb (Ed.), *Post-traumatic stress disorder: Psychological and biological seguelae.* (pp. 60–79). Washington, DC: American Psychiatric Press.

Laufer, R., Brett, E., & Gallops, M. (1985a). Dimensions of post-traumatic stress disorder among Vietnam veterans. *Journal of Nervous and Mental Disease, 173,* 538–545.

Laufer, R., Brett, E., & Gallops, M. (1985b). Symptom patterns associated with post-traumatic stress disorder among Vietnam veterans exposed to war trauma. *American Journal of Psychiatry, 142,* 1304–1311.

Laufer, R., & Parson, E. R. (1985). *The Laufer-Parson Guilt Inventory.* New York: International Policy Research Institute.

Lazarus, R., & Folkman, S. (1982). *Stress, appraisal, and coping.* New York: Springer.

Leader, J. (1961). Accident neurosis. *British Medical Journal, 1,* 1018–1919.

Lee, E., & Lu, F. (1989). Assessment & treatment of Asian-American survivors of mass violence, *Journal of Traumatic Stress, 2,* 93-120.

Leopold, R., & Dillon, H. (1963). Psychoanatomy of a disaster: A long-term study of post-traumatic neuroses in survivors of a marine explosion. *American Journal of Psychiatry, 119,* 913–921.

Lifton, R. J. (1967). Death in life: Survivors of Hiroshima. New York: Simon & Schuster.

Lifton, R. J. (1982). The psychology of the survivor and the death imprint. *Psychiatric Annals, 12,* 1011–1020.

Lindemann, E. (1944). Symptomatology and management of acute grief. *American Journal of Psychiatry, 101,* 141–148.

Lindy, J. (1988). *Vietnam: A casebook.* New York: Brunner/Mazel.

Lipkin, J. O., Blank, A., Parson, E. R., & Smith, J. R. (1982). Vietnam veterans and post-traumatic stress disorder. *Hospital and Community Psychiatry, 33,* 908–912.

Little, M. (1957). The analyst's total response to his patient's needs. *International Journal of Psychoanalysis, 38,* 240–254.

Lyons, J. (1991a). Issues in assessing the effects of trauma: Introduction. *Journal of Traumatic Stress, 4,* 3–6.

Lyons, J. (1991b). Strategies for assessing the potential for positive adjustment following trauma. *Journal of Traumatic Stress, 4,* 93–112.

Lyons, J., & Keane, T. (1992). Keane PTSD Scale: MMPI and MMPI-2 update. *Journal of Traumatic Stress, 5,* 111–118.

Madakasira, S., & O'Brien, K. (1987). Acute post-traumatic stress disorder in victims of a natural disaster. *Journal of Nervous and Mental Disease, 175,* 286–290.

Malloy, P., Fairbank, J., & Keane, T. (1983). Validation of a multimethod of assessment of post-traumatic stress disorders in Vietnam veterans. *Journal of Consulting and Clinical Psychology, 51,* 488–494.

Mason, J., Giller, E., Kosten, T., & Ostroff, R. (1988). Elevation of urinary epinephrine/cortisol ratio in post-traumatic stress disorder. *Journal of Nervous and Mental Disease, 176,* 498–502.

Mason, J., Kosten, S., Southwick, S. & Gillen, E. (1990). The use of psychoendocrine strategies in post-traumatic stress disorder. *Journal of Applied Social Psychology, 20,* 1822–1846.

Mazelan, P. (1982). Stereotypes and perceptions of the victims of rape. *Victimology, 5,* 121–132.

McFall, M., Murburg, M., Ko, G., & Veith, R. (1990). Autonomic responses to stress in Vietnam combat veterans with post-traumatic stress disorder. *Biological Psychiatry, 27,* 1165–1175.

McFarlane, A. (1984). The Ash Wednesday bushfires in South Australia. *Medical Journal of Australia, 141,* 286–291.

McFarlane, A. (1986). Post-traumatic morbidity of a disaster. *Journal of Nervous and Mental Disease, 174,* 4–14.

McFarlane, A. (1988). The longitudinal course of post-traumatic morbidity. *Journal of Nervous and Mental Disease, 176,* 30–40.

McFarlane, A. (1990). Etiology of post-traumatic stress disorder. In M. Wolf and A. Mosnaim (Eds.), *Post-traumatic stress disorder: Etiology, phenomenology, and treatment.* Washington, DC: American Psychiatric Press.

McNally, R., Kaspi, S., Riemann, B., & Zeitlin, S. (1990). Selective processing of threat cues in post-traumatic stress disorder. *Journal of Abnormal Psychology, 99,* 398–402.

Meichenbaum, D. (1974). *Cognitive behavior modification.* Morristown, NJ: General Learning Press.

Milgram, S., Toubiana, Y., Klingman, A., Raviv, A., & Goldstein, I. (1988). Situational exposure and personal loss in children's acute and chronic stress reactions to a school bus disaster. *Journal of Traumatic Stress, 1,* 339–352.

Mollica, R. (1988). The trauma story: The psychiatric care of refugee survivors of violence and torture. In F. Ochberg (Ed.), *Post-traumatic therapy and victims of violence.* (pp. 295-314). New York: Brunner/Mazel.

Mott, F. W. (1919). *War neurosis and shell shock.* London: Hadden & Stoughton.

Norris, F. H. (1992). Epidemiology of trauma: Frequency and impact of different potentially traumatic events on different demographic groups. *Journal of Consulting and Clinical Psychology, 60,* 409–418.

O'Donohue, R. & Elliott, A. (1992). The current status of PTSD as a diagnostic category: Problems and proposals. *Journal of Traumatic Stress, 5,* 421–439.

Pallmeyer, T., Blanchard, E., & Kolb, L. (1986). The psycho-physiology of combat-induced post-traumatic stress disorder in Vietnam veterans. *Behavior Research and Therapy, 24,* 645–652.

Parson, E. R. (1982). *PTSD and personality: Post-traumatic borderline and post-traumatic paranoid personality disorders.* National Conference of the Society for Traumatic Stress Studies.

Parson, E. R. (1984). The reparation of the self: Clinical and theoretical dimensions in the treatment of Vietnam combat veterans. *Journal of Contemporary Psychotherapy, 14,* 4–54.

Parson, E. R. (1985). The intercultural setting: Encountering black Vietnam veterans. In S. Sonnenberg, A. Blank, & J. Talbott, (Eds.), *The trauma of war: Stress and recovery in Vietnam veterans.* Washington, DC: American Psychiatric Association.

Parson, E. R. (1986). Life after death: Vietnam veteran's struggle for meaning and recovery. *Death Studies, 10,* 11–26.

Parson, E. R. (1987). Transference and post-traumatic stress: Combat veterans' transference to the Veterans Administration Medical Center. *The Journal of the American Academy of Psychoanalysis, 14,* 349–375.

Parson, E. R. (1988a). Post-traumatic self disorders (PTsfD). In J. Wilson, Z. Harel, & B. Kahana (Eds.), *Human adaptation to extreme stress: From the Holocaust to Vietnam.* New York: Plenum.

Parson, E. R. (1988b). *The transtheoretical perspective: Multiple theories at work in the treatment of PTSD.* Presented at the annual conference of the Society for Traumatic Stress Studies.

Parson, E. R. (1989). Future looks good: Vietnam veterans find hope in past. *Joiner Center Newsletter,* Vol. 3, No. 1, pp. 3, 7.

Parson, E. R. (1990a). *Traumatosalutogenesis scale (TSS).* New York: Parson Psychological Consulting Service.

Parson, E. R. (1990b). Post-traumatic psychocultural therapy (PTpsyCT): Integration of trauma and shattering social labels of the self. *Journal of Contemporary Psychotherapy, 20,* 237–258.

Parson, E. R. (1990c). *Victims: Image and reality.* Presented at the miniconvention on the effects of media on human behavior at the Annual Meeting of the American Psychological Association, Boston, MA, August 1990.

Parson, E. R. (1990d). *The psychobiology of traumatic stress: Public health crisis, epidemicity, and prevention of post-traumatic stress disorder.* Invited address at the Annual American Public Health Association Convention in New York City on October 3.

Parson, E. R. (1991). The American psyche in hiding: Behavioral science and stigmatization. *Voices—The Art and Science of Psychotherapy, 27,* 121–127.

Parson, E. R. (1992). Post-traumatic ethnotherapy (P-TET): Issues in assessment and intervention in aspects of global traumatic stress. In M. B. Williams & J. Sommers (Eds.), *Handbook of post-traumatic therapy.* Westport, CT: Greenwood.

Parson, E. R. (1993). Children of community trauma: Inner city violence, images of the media, and therapists' perception and response. In J. P. Wilson & J. Lindy, (Eds.), *Countertransference in the treatment of post-traumatic stress disorder.* New York: Guilford Press.

Pavlov, I-P (1927/1960). Conditioned reflexes: An investigation of the psychology activity of the cerebral cortex. G. V. Anrep (Ed./Trans.). New York: Dover.

Peebles, M. (1989). Post-traumatic stress disorder: A historical perspective on diagnosis and treatment. *Bulletin of the Menninger Clinic, 53,* 274–286.

Penk, W., & Allen, I. (1991). Clinical assessment of post-traumatic stress disorder (PTSD) among American minorities who served in Vietnam. *Journal of Traumatic Stress, 4,* 41–67.

Pitman, R., Van der Kolk, B., Orr, S., & Greenberg, M. (1990). Naloxone-reversible analgesic response to combat-related stimuli in post-traumatic stress disorder. *Archives of General Psychiatry, 47,* 541–544.

Resnick, H. (1989). Victims and crime factors associated to the development of crime-related post-traumatic stress disorder. *Behavior Therapy, 20,* 199–214.

Robins, L., Fischbach, R., Smith, E., Cottler, L., Solomon, S., & Goldring, E. (1986). Impact of disaster on previously assessed mental health. In J. Shore (Ed.), *Disaster stress studies: New methods and findings* (pp. 22–48). Washington, DC: American Psychiatric Press.

Robins, L., Helzer, J., Croughan, J., Williams, J., & Spitzer, R. (1981). *NIMH Diagnostic Interview Schedule, Version 3.* Rockville, MD: National Institute of Mental Health, Public Health Service.

Rose, D. (1986). "Worse than death": Psychodynamics of rape victims and the need for psychotherapy. *American Journal of Psychiatry, 143,* 817–824.

Ross, R., Fall, W., Sullivan, K., Stanley, N., & Caroff, S. (1989). Sleep disturbance as the hallmark of post-traumatic stress disorder. *American Journal of Psychiatry, 146,* 697–707.

Roth, W. (1988). The role of medication in post-traumatic therapy. In F. Ochberg (Ed.), *Post-traumatic therapy and victims of violence.* New York: Brunner/Mazel.

Samson, J., Mirin, S., Hauser, S., Fendon, B., & Schildkraut, J. (1992). Learned helplessness and urinary MHPG levels of unipolar depression.

Schindler, F. (1980). Treatment by systematic desensitization of a recurring nightmare of a real life trauma. *Journal of Behavior Therapy and Experimental Psychology, 11*, 53–54.

Schroeder, O. C. (1961). The Medicolegal forum: Traumatic neurosis. *Post-Graduate Medicine, 29*, A48–59.

Scurfield, R. (1985). Post-trauma stress assessment and treatment: Overview and formulations. In C. R. Figley (Ed.), *Trauma and its wake*. New York: Brunner/Mazel.

Scurfield, R. (1992). An evaluation of the impact of "Helicopter ride therapy" for in-patient Vietnam veterans with war-related PTSD. *Military Medicine, 157*, 67–73.

Seligman, M., & Maier, F. (1967). Failure to escape traumatic shock. *Journal of Experimental Psychology, 74*, 1–9.

Shalev, A., & Rogel-Fuchs, Y. (1992). Auditory startle reflex in post-traumatic stress disorder patients treated with Clonazepam. *Israeli Journal of Psychiatry and Related Sciences, 29*, 1–6.

Shapiro, F. (1989). Efficacy of the eye movement desensitization procedure in the treatment of traumatic memories. *Journal of Traumatic Stress, 2*, 199–224.

Shatan, C. (1977). Bogus manhood, bogus honor: Surrender and transfiguration in the United States marine corps. *Psychoanalytic Review, 64*, 585–610.

Shatan, C. (1982). The tattered ego of survivors. *Psychiatric Annals, 12*, 1031–1038.

Shatan, C. (1985). Have you hugged a Vietnam veteran today? The basic wound of catastrophic stress. In W. Kelly, (Ed.), *Post-traumatic stress disorder and the War veteran patient*. New York: Brunner/Mazel.

Sherwood, R. (1990). Adapted character styles of Vietnam veterans with post-traumatic stress disorder. *Psychological Reports, 66*, 623–631.

Sierles, F., Chen, J., & McFarland, R. (1985). Post-traumatic stress disorder and current psychiatric illness: A preliminary report. *American Journal of Psychiatry, 140*, 1177–1179.

Sierles, F., Chen, J., MacFarland, R., & Taylor, M. (1983). Post-traumatic stress disorder and concurrent psychiatric illness: A preliminary report. *American Journal of Psychiatry, 140*, 1177–1179.

Silver, S. & Iacono, C. (1984). Factor analytic support for DSM III's post-traumatic stress disorders. *Journal of Clinical Psychology, 40*, 5–14.

Simpson, M. (1993). Traumatic stress and the bruising of the soul: The effects of torture and coercive interrogation. In J. Wilson & B. Raphael (Eds.), *International Handbook of Traumatic Stress Syndromes* (pp. 667-684). New York: Plenum.

Skerritt, P. (1919). Anxiety and the heart: A historical review. *Psychological Medicine 13*, 17–25.

Solomon, S., & Canino, G. (1990). The appropriateness of DSM-III-R criteria for post-traumatic stress disorder. *Comprehensive Psychiatry, 31,* 227–237.

Solomon, Z., & Mikulincer, M. (1987). Combat stress reactions, post-traumatic stress disorder, and social adjustment. *Journal of Nervous and Mental Disease, 175,* 277–285.

Sparr, L., & Pankratz, L. (1983). Factitious post-traumatic stress disorder. *American Journal of Psychiatry, 140,* 1016–1019.

Spitzer, R., & Williams, J. B. (1985). *Structured clinical interview for DSM, patient version.* New York: Biometric Research Department, New York State Psychiatric Institute Patient version.

Stern, G. (1976). From chaos to responsibility. *American Journal of Psychiatry, 133,* 300–301.

Terr, L. (1979). Children of Chowchilla: Study of psychic trauma. *The Psychoanalytic Study of the Child, 34,* 547–623.

Terr, L. (1983a). Chowchilla revisited: The effects of psychic trauma four years after a bus kidnapping. *American Journal of Psychiatry, 140,* 1543–1550.

Terr, L. (1983b). Life attitudes, dreams, and psychic trauma in a group of "normal" children. *Journal of the American Academy of Child Psychiatry, 22,* 221–230.

Terr, L. (1989). Treating psychic trauma in children: A preliminary discussion. *Journal of Traumatic Stress, 2,* 3–20.

Tien, S. (1987). The Phases of renewal: Steps to integration of self in psychotherapy. *Journal of Contemporary Psychotherapy, 19,* 171–182.

Titchener, J., & Kapp, F. (1976). Family character change at Buffalo Creek. *American Journal of Psychiatry, 133,* 295–299.

Trimble, M. (1981). *Post-traumatic neurosis.* New York: Wiley.

Ulman, R., & Brothers, D. (1988). *The shattered self: A psychoanalytic study of trauma.* Hillsdale, NJ: Analytic Press.

Ursano, R. (1981). The Vietnam era prisoner of war: Precaptivity personality and the development of psychiatric illness. *American Journal of Psychiatry, 138,* 315–318.

Van der Kolk, B. (1983). Psychopharmacological issues in post-traumatic stress disorder. *Hospital and Community Psychiatry, 34,* 683–691.

Van der Kolk, B. (1985). Adolescent vulnerability to post-traumatic stress. *Psychiatry, 20,* 365–370.

Van der Kolk, B. (1987). *Psychological trauma.* Washington, DC: American Psychiatric Press.

Van der Kolk, B. (1988). The trauma spectrum: The interaction of biological and social events in the genesis of the trauma response. *Journal of Traumatic Stress, 1,* 273–290.

Van der Kolk, B., Brown, P., & Van der Hart, O. (1989). Pierre Janet on post-traumatic stress. *Journal of Traumatic Stress, 2,* 365–378.

Van der Kolk, B., Pitman, R., and Orr, S. (1989). Endogeneous opiods, stress-induced analgesia and post-traumatic stress disorder. *Psychopharmacology Bulletin, 25,* 108–112.

Ver Ellen, P., & Van Kamen, D. P. (1990). The biological fundings in post-traumatic stress disorder: A review. *Journal of Applied Social Psychology, 20,* 1789–1871.

Weidner, G., & Griffitt, W. (1983). Rape: A sexual stigma? *Journal of Personality, 51,* 152–166.

Weisaeth, L., & Eitinger, L. (1992). Research on PTSD and other post-traumatic reactions: European literature (Part II). *PTSD Research Quarterly, 3,* 1–8.

Weiss, D., Marmar, C., Schlenger, W., and Fairbank, J. (1992) The prevalence of lifetime and partial PTSD in Vietnam veterans. *Journal of Traumatic Stress, 5,* 365–376.

West, C., Fernandez, A., Hillard, J., Schoof, M., & Parks, J. (1990). Psychiatric disorders of abused women at a shelter. *Psychiatric Quarterly, 61,* 295–301.

Wilkinson, C. (1983). Aftermath of a disaster: The collapse of the Hyatt Regency Hotel skywalks. *American Journal of Psychiatry, 140,* 1134–1139.

Williams, R., & Long, J. (1975). *Toward a self-managed life style.* Boston: Houghton-Mifflin.   Wilmer, H. (1982). Post-traumatic stress disorder. *Psychiatric Annals, 12,* 995–1006.

Wilson, J. P. (1980). Conflict, stress, and growth: The effects of war on psychosocial development among Vietnam veterans. In C. R. Rigley & S. Leventman (Eds.), Strangers at home (123-154).

Wilson, J., Harel, Z., & Kahana, B. (Eds.) (1988). *Human adaptation to extreme stress: From Holocaust to Vietnam.* New York: Plenum.

Wilson, J., & Kraus, G. (1985). Predicting post-traumatic stress disorders among Vietnam veterans. In W. Kelly (Ed.), *Post-traumatic stress disorder and the war veteran patient.* New York: Brunner/Mazel.

Wilson, J. P. (1988). Treating the Vietnam veteran. In F. Ochberg (Ed.), *Post-traumatic therapy and victims of violence.* New York: Brunner/Mazel.

Wilson, J. P. (1989). *Trauma, transformation, and healing: An integrative approach to theory, research, and post-traumatic therapy.* New York: Brunner/Mazel.

Winnicott, D. W. (1970). Fear of breakdown. *International Review of Psychoanalysis, 1,* 103–107.

Yehuda, R., Southwick, S., Giller, E., Ma, X., & Mason, J. (1992). Urinary catecholamine excretion and severity of PTSD symptoms in Vietnam combat veterans. *Journal of Nervous and Mental Disease, 180,* 321–325.

Yost, J. (1987). The psychopharmacological management of post-traumatic stress disorder (PTSD) in Vietnam veterans and in civilian situations. In T. Williams (Ed.), *Post-traumatic stress disorders: An handbook for clinicians.* Cincinnati, OH: Disabled American Veterans National Headquarters.

PART THREE

Diagnostic and Treatment Methods

CHAPTER 14

Diagnostic Methods and Issues

ROGER D. DAVIS, MS, and THEODORE MILLON, PhD

Scores of instruments are available to diagnose and assess anxiety. More are published each year, so that no one can be acquainted with all of them—new and old instruments; instruments that are empirically derived; instruments that claim a theoretical basis; instruments that assess a particular content domain well; instruments that measure many domains of content; instruments that look good, but have little validational evidence; instruments that possess a substantial research base, but were constructed in the looser nosologic climate of a bygone day—and these are just a few of the possibilities that come to mind.

When confronted with so many alternatives, a database is needed, a list of like kinds of things, systematically arranged, information regarding each systematically presented, together with a set of guidelines for making a selection intelligently. Unfortunately, no database such as this could be confined to a single chapter. Consequently, only the more widely used interview techniques, self-report measures, and clinician rating scales will be considered here. Instruments specific to various anxiety disorders are presented in tabular form near the end of the chapter. Despite this caution, we hope this chapter will be sufficient to inform the clinician or researcher about what exists in the way of anxiety instruments and point him or her in the direction of original sources.

CLASSIFICATION ISSUES: A CONTEXT FOR DIAGNOSIS AND ASSESSMENT

Before reviewing diagnostic methods and instrumentation, it would be wise to examine certain assumptions that justify their use and interpretation. What is a taxonomy of mental disorders and why is it needed?

A taxonomy is a way of grouping together like kinds of things (Millon, 1991). Essentially, a taxonomy reflects the belief that the items classified fall into more or less discrete categories. In psychopathology, taxonomies are usually referred to as nosologies. When explicitly articulated, groups and their clinical attributes form a diagnostic system. The presence or absence of such attributes can then be systematically inquired in order to determine group membership, a procedure known as differential diagnosis. The Diagnostic and Statistical Manual (DSM) consists of categories of psychopathology sanctioned by the American Psychiatric Association (e.g., DSM-III-R, 1987), of which the anxiety disorders constitute one particular species.

A nosology serves certain functional ends. From a research perspective, it provides a means of organizing the dynamic body of knowledge that undergirds a science, allowing the history of substantive questions to be probed and gaps in scientific knowledge to be discerned. From a clinical perspective, a nosology provides a means of organizing clinical phenomena. By abstracting across presentations, a nosology formalizes certain clinical commonalties, relieving the clinician of the burden of dealing with each patient sui generis. At a minimum, persons within a taxon should be more alike than those selected across taxons. The converse is trivial, but also true. Patients from different groups should be more diverse than patients selected within the same group. Similarity-dissimilarity, then, is ultimately the organizing principle on which a nosology is constructed.

Unfortunately, similarity is a fuzzy notion. Exactly how, in what way, are persons who receive the same diagnosis alike? Two levels of similarity must be distinguished, manifest and latent. Patients whose psychopathologies are similar at a manifest level give presentations that look alike. In an empirical nosology, these patients are classified together. The latent level, however, deals with genotypic similarity. Taxons are formed on the basis of theoretical or etiologic commonalties. Patients possessing such commonalties are classified together, regardless of how the pathology is manifest.

Which kind of similarity forms the better basis for a nosology? Table 14.1 presents possible agreements and disagreements between latent and manifest similarity for two patients.

As can be seen in the table, for any two patients, four possibilities exist. First, going clockwise, two presentations that appear similar, may be similar. In this case, etiologically identical pathways have produced manifestly similar results. Second, two presentations that appear similar, may be different. Here diverse etiologic pathways have produced manifestly similar results difficult to tease apart. Third, two presentations that appear different, may be different. In this case, different manifest characteristics legitimately depict the output from different etiologic pathways. Fourth, two presentations that appear different, may be similar. Here the interaction of identical pathology with individual differences produces diverse presentations.

TABLE 14.1.   Matches and Mismatches for Latent and Manifest Levels of Similarity

| | | Similar at a Latent Level? | |
		Yes	No
Similar at a Manifest Level?	Yes	I. Things that appear similar, are in fact similar.	II. Things that appear similar are in fact different. (Nosologically problematic)
	No	IV. Things that appear different are in fact similar. (Nosologically problematic)	III. Things that appear different are in fact different.

Table 14.1 resembles other tables used to present the logic of diagnostic efficiency statistics—true positives, false negatives, and so on (e.g., Baldessarini, Finklestein, & Arana, 1983). Whereas the latter compares the apparent or obtained diagnosis with the so-called "true" diagnosis for a single subject, illustrating the diagnostic dilemma associated with imperfect predictors in ignorance of the "true" state of nature, Table 14.1 represents the nosologic dilemma, whereby multiple taxons must be established for multiple subjects, the "true" taxonic membership of each being unknown.

We have been speaking as if both manifest and latent levels were known and knowable. In fact, only a manifest level is ever observed. Latent structures and functions, traits and taxons, are, by definition, inferred. Nosologically, this presents tremendous difficulties for psychopathology, the implication being that the pursuit of patterns of covariation among imperfect predictors will lead us, in the second quadrant, to establish one taxon where two, or perhaps many, are needed, and, in the fourth quadrant, to establish two, or perhaps several, taxons where only one in fact exists.

Such is the "bet" of pure empiricism: That things which look alike, are alike, and conversely, that things which do not resemble each other, are in fact different. That no cases of mismatched manifest and latent similarity exist. Since the "true" state of nature remains unknown, it is impossible to determine how often these mismatches actually occur. Perhaps they occur only a few times in the entire DSM, and perhaps the current nosology is rife with them. In any case, since diagnostic labels ideally represent a shorthand means of communicating a theory about the patient's pathology, one wonders about the worth of the current diagnostic agenda.

From the standpoint of what is required of a science, this empirical approach to the anxiety disorders is deficient in at least two ways. First, the current nosology lacks any integrative theoretical schema to explain why the psychopathology of anxiety takes the form of these particular disorders rather than others. Second, lack of an undergirding theoretical schema retards the progress of research attempting to illuminate specific

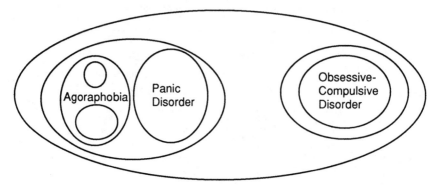

Figure 14.1. A pseudotopographic set diagram illustrating the level of abstraction problem in empirical taxonomies. Smaller circles represent fewer patients, more severe pathology, and the presence of additional clinical attributes. How many taxons are there? One? Three? Or more?

mechanisms of particular disorders. Indeed, given the logic of Table 14.1, it can be seen that empirical methods alone are an insufficient basis on which to determine either the nature or the number of anxiety disorders.

The "number" side of this "nature-number" dilemma is intimately related to another contentious problem, the level of abstraction at which a nosology should be articulated. Are more or fewer taxons generally desirable? Pragmatically, the taxons represented must ensure adequate coverage. Scientifically, however, it does not appear possible to constrain the number of taxons that constitute a taxonomy on empirical grounds alone (see Figure 14.1). Cluster analytic methods exemplify this problem. As Blashfield (1980) notes, no sure method exists for solving the "number of clusters" problem. Yet, "Why does nature express itself in these taxons rather than others?" is a legitimate, if not fundamental, scientific question.

As with nature and nurture, nature and number seem to be intimately connected. Within the anxiety disorders, such a relationship can perhaps be seen in the transition from DSM-II to DSM-III. Frances, Widiger, and Fyer (1990, p. 43), commenting on the issue of "splitting" versus "lumping" and its influence on comorbidity, described the DSM-III-R as a "splitter's dream and a lumper's nightmare" (p. 43). As these authors noted,

A possible example of the splitting issue is the distinction among the DSM-III anxiety disorders of panic disorder, agoraphobia, and generalized anxiety disorder (GAD). Panic Disorder was included in DSM-III in large part because of Klein's research demonstrating that imipramine blocks recurrent panic attacks but has no apparent effect on associated anxiety or nonassociated phobic anxiety. GAD was created to cover the domain of DSM-II anxiety neurosis not covered by panic. There is now considerable interest in assessing the comorbidity of panic disorder with a variety of syndromes, including GAD. Data supporting the validity of the panic disorder diagnosis are extensive, and the diagnosis provides valid and useful information. However, much of the research on the comorbidity of panic and agoraphobia may be due to their mapping a common, overlapping domain of psychopathology. (p. 43)

Apparently, patients are not compelled to hug the taxonic high ground when presenting their clinical pictures. Nonprototypal and overlapping cases illustrate that many patients are quite at home in the taxonic "borderlands" as well.

Even more taxonomically distressing, nature-number issues are not confined to a single branch of the nosologic hierarchy. The relationship between anxiety and depression has long been a contentious issue. Many researchers have approached this problem by examining the relationship between anxiety and depression inventories. Dobson (1985), found that for 16 studies reviewed, anxiety-anxiety, depression-depression, and anxiety-depression scale correlations were all significant, ranging from .61 to .69. Clark and Watson (1991) examined approximately 400 self-report and clinician-rated studies using mood, symptom, and syndrome measures. Disappointing convergent and discriminant validity patterns were again found for most instruments, which, together with factorial evidence, led these authors to argue that "Anxiety and depressed syndromes share a significant nonspecific component that encompasses general affective distress and other common symptoms, whereas these syndromes are distinguished by physiological hyperarousal (specific to anxiety) versus the absence of positive affect (specific to depression) (p. 331)." A mixed mood disorder, which these authors advocate adding to the nosology, would be represented by symptoms concerned with the absence of positive affectivity (e.g., apathy, hopelessness) and those related to an approximately equal level of negative affectivity. On other fronts, Maser and Cloninger (1990) offer an edited book that authoritatively and comprehensively treats the comorbidity of mood and anxiety disorders from a wide variety of perspectives.

Our purpose is not to propose a solution to the taxonomic quandaries that concern the anxiety disorders. Nevertheless, much can be learned by comparing ideals and actualities. To place the above issues in highest relief, we contrast the current diagnostic agenda with an "ideal" nosology: In a mature clinical science, theory, nosology, instrumentation, and intervention form a conceptually unified whole (Millon, 1990). The critical element that lends this structure cohesiveness is that its undergirding concepts posses systematic import (Hempel, 1965), that is, that these concepts are more or less invariably associated with a large number of other characteristics relevant to prediction in the subject domain. This explanatory and heuristic power suggests a nonarbitrary taxonomic organization within which major nosolgic categories can be grouped and differentiated. Because such a nosology makes theoretical and etiological statements about category members, the assignment of persons to groups is an explanatory rather than merely descriptive affair, illuminating mechanisms of pathology and suggesting intervention strategies.

The current nosology is not yet at a mature, theoretically-driven stage. The current state of psychopathologic nosology and diagnosis resembles that of medicine a century ago. Concepts remain overwhelmingly descriptive. Yet, by definition, a clinical science must be applied to individual cases. How can the individual case be approached in a scientific, rather than descriptive, fashion? In short, the professional must "bootstrap" within a single subject, that is, develop a theory or theories of the individual and the individual's pathology which, in an iterative process of inference and hypothesis testing, unify available data and resist falsification sufficiently to justify their use in the construction of intervention strategies. Such theoretical development requires instrumentation.

THE TRIPLE RESPONSE MODEL:
A CONTENT × METHOD APPROACH

Whether one is dealing with taxonomic matters or with individual cases, the utility of a theory is a function of both its simplicity and scope. The former is simply the number of theoretical constructs required to account for the phenomena of the subject domain. An evaluation of the latter, however, assumes that the range of things to be explained is known in advance. In the hard sciences, such as physics, the extent of the subject domain is easily discernable, in part because these constructs are assumed to possess some form of physical existence. As one moves from harder to more weakly organized sciences, however, linear causal models give way to feedback (and possibly feedforward) processes that appear to operate not only horizontally, within a given "level" of organization, whether psychological, biological, or physical, but vertically, across organizational levels as well. As a result, psychological concepts are more often multireferential constructs that "float" above the level of data and resist unequivocal quantification by any one particular measurement technique.

It has proven difficult to say exactly what anxiety is, and to distinguish it from what are merely its correlates. Perhaps anxiety is primarily the result of unconscious conflicts striving for expression, of an inability to escape from situations in which one experiences a lack of self-efficacy, of overgeneralization of the anxiety response, of ruminative thoughts, of irrational primary and secondary appraisal, or of daily hassles coupled with neuroendocrine imbalances, and so on. More likely, however, anxiety is as often the result of some or all of these as it is of any one. In lieu of a comprehensive theory of anxiety pathology, we could at least ask for some way of ordering the constellation of causes and correlates that have been associated with the construct.

The triple-response concept represents such an approach, an approach which addresses the multireferential nature of the anxiety construct by grouping clinical phenomena into several distinct content areas. As explained by Eiffert and Wilson (1991), Lang (1968) introduced the triple-response model for emotional behaviors, arguing that emotional behaviors are mediated by partially independent brain centers. These centers control three systems or modalities: motor, physiological, and verbal-cognitive. The motor component consists of observable aspects of the pathology, such as the degree of avoidance or rate of panic attacks. The physiological modality consists of muscle tension, heart rate, respiration, perspiration, hormonal fluctuations, and other somatic aspects of the pathology. The verbal-cognitive modality consists of verbal reports of anxiety or fear, as well as thoughts that occur before or during such episodes as panic attacks, compulsive rituals, and so on.

Whether the division of the organism into content areas is more pedagogic or substantive, as Lang (1968) apparently believed, the triple response concept has had a number of beneficial effects on anxiety research (Eiffert & Wilson, 1991). Theoretically, it has been helpful in suggesting connections between the behavioral, physiological, and cognitive modalities across a variety of emotional problems and disorders. Methodologically, it has led to the use of multiple assessment instruments within and across methods and modalities. Clinically, it has pointed to the multireferential nature of the anxiety construct and consequent need for comprehensive assessment, and thereby led to a greater integration of assessment and treatment through consideration of each construct domain in the formulation of intervention strategies.

However, Eiffert and Wilson (1991) also argue that what is measured, the various content areas of the triple response paradigm, has often been confounded with the way of measuring it, that is, method of assessment. These authors recommend a "matrix model" to clearly distinguish method and content, and the division of the "verbal-cognitive-subjective" mode into a cognitive mode concerned with such things as information processing and cognitive styles, and an affective mode concerned with the phenomenology or subjective report of various mood states (see Table 14.2). Unfortunately, many of the cells in the matrix require some kind of special equipment, a certain kind of expertise, or an extended period of time to implement, any of which may not be readily available to clinicians.

TABLE 14.2.   Content × Methods-of-Assessment Matrix

Content Area Assessed	Method of Assessment		Instrument or Apparatus
	Self-Report Verbal or Nonverbal	Observation	
Motoric	Mobility inventory, daily activity log	BAT	Pedometer, activity meter
Physiological	Body sensations questionnaire	Perspiring, blushing	GSR, EMG
Cognitive	Attributional style questionnaire	Response latency	STROOP test
Affective	Adjective checklists, mood visual analog scale	Facial expression	Not available

Source: Adapted from Eifert & Wilson (1991).

Although the content by methods-of-assessment matrix does not offer a theory of the anxiety disorders, it does argue for the insufficiency of any single method for measuring the four content areas. Given the influence of method variance (Campbell & Fiske, 1959), such a model suggests an interesting empirical critique of the DSM anxiety disorders and their associated clinical interviews. Although the DSM anxiety disorders criteria do get at verbal, cognitive, physiological, and affective criteria (though not consistently), they rely almost exclusively on the self-report method (though perhaps elicited by interview) for differential diagnostic purposes. To the extent that the patterns of covariation or comorbidity that suggested and shaped current diagnostic boundaries are artifactually influenced by method variance, the current constellation of anxiety disorders is specific to the self-report method. If variance across methods was taken into account, might diagnostic boundaries shift radically? Might entirely new taxons reveal their existence?

CATEGORICAL APPROACHES TO ANXIETY: STRUCTURED AND SEMI-STRUCTURED INTERVIEWS

Although a number of other formulations are possible, clinical conditions have traditionally been thought of categorically. Categorical systems provide a single label for a constellation of clinical attributes that ideally covary with such tenacity that they seem to characterize a discrete diagnostic entity. Thus categorical systems restore unity to the patient's pathology (Millon, 1991) and often suggest aspects of pathology that might otherwise have gone unobserved.

Eight anxiety disorders are recognized in the DSM-III-R: Panic Disorder with and without agoraphobia, agoraphobia without history of panic disorder, social phobia, simple phobia, obsessive compulsive disorder, post-traumatic stress disorder, generalized anxiety disorder, and anxiety disorder not otherwise specified. DSM-IV will likely include another, hybrid category, anxious depression. Descriptions and diagnostic and differential diagnostic criteria for these disorders can be found in the DSM, as can associated features, age at onset, course, impairment, complications, predisposing factors, prevalence, sex ratio, and familial pattern, when such information exists and is believed to be reliable.

Historically, clinical interviews have consisted mainly of a comparatively nondirective history-taking and mental status examination (Wiens, 1990). In the early days of psychopathology, such informality was not problematic: The elements of clinical science—theory, taxonomy, instrumentation, and intervention—were largely unintegrated. Prior to the introduction of psychotropic medication, interventions were often the same, regardless of diagnosis. In such cases, diagnostic errors were meaningless.

Psychiatric diagnoses have also been notoriously unreliable (e.g., Matarazzo, 1990). This served as a considerable barrier to the development of psychopathology as an integrated science. To the extent that each clinician serves as his own criterion, clinical judgment is no better than opinion. Clinically, such a state of affairs communicates nothing about a patient's disorder and is worthless as a basis for intervention. Experimentally, unreliable diagnosis limits group homogeneity, introducing noise into research designs.

This began to change with the introduction of DSM-III and the explicit formulation of diagnostic criteria, from which diagnostic interviews could be developed. Structured and semi-structured interviews increase diagnostic reliability by providing the interviewer with a highly formalized set of questions. These questions internalize diagnostic criteria and standardize the encounter between interviewer and client. Generally, the degree of formality required depends upon the level of expertise of the interviewer. Structured interviews are usually intended to be administered by trained laypersons and therefore tend to be more highly rigorous. Semi-structured interviews, in contrast, rely more heavily on the clinical judgement of the professional and can afford to be more open-ended.

Structured interviews have largely accomplished their intended purpose. The introduction of reliable structured interviews and the adoption of modern diagnostic models, beginning with DSM-III with its multiaxial taxonomy, polythetic categories, and field trials, together with the subsequent explosion of psychiatric research, have together produced a clinical science whose elements are now more coupled. Far from being irrelevant, diagnostic errors now often result in wasted time by clinicians and patients, wasted money by patients and third-party payers, mismedication, and possibility of legal entanglements. Arriving at a correct (or at least consensual) diagnosis is more important than ever before. To this end, the purpose of the modern clinical interview is to obtain a detailed history and statement of current symptoms which can serve as a competent basis for diagnosis and intervention.

Schedule for Affective Disorders and Schizophrenia (SADS)

The SADS (Endicott & Spitzer, 1978) was designed to make diagnoses in accordance with the Research Diagnostic Criteria (RDC; Spitzer, Endicott, & Robins, 1978). Since its inception, the SADS has grown into a family of instruments that includes the regular form, a lifetime form (SADS-L), a follow-up or change form (SADS-C), and more recently, a lifetime anxiety version (SADS-LA). The SADS-LA (Fyer, Endicott, Mannuzza, & Klein, 1985) was developed from the SADS-L explicitly for the investigation of anxiety disorders, including separation anxiety disorder and adjustment disorder with anxious mood. All diagnoses covered in the lifetime version, such as major depression and substance use, frequently comorbid with the anxiety disorders, are also included. RDC, DSM-III, and DSM-III-R diagnoses can be generated.

One notable feature of this instrument is its lifetime sequential approach to assessment (Mannuzza, Fyer, Klein, & Endicott, 1986). Rather than simply ask whether the particular symptoms of a given disorder have ever been present, the SADS-LA seeks to provide a comprehensive portrait of the onset of symptoms, syndromes, and a variety of life events ranging from marriage, to career change, to the death of a child. These are recorded on a Life Chart Digital Coding Form. The eventual result is a computer-generated Life Chart, effectively a history of all relevant psychopathology, and its beginning and ending in relation to prominent life events. As a result, a great variety of investigations can be supported, for example, lifetime as well as cross-sectional comorbidity, and the sequencing of symptoms and life events in the development of disorder, for a variety of diagnostic criteria.

Test-retest reliability for the SAD-LA appears strong. An investigation by Mannuzza, Fyer, Martin, et al. (1989) using highly trained interviewers showed lifetime kappas ranging from .60 for general anxiety disorder to .90 for agoraphobia. Simple phobia showed poorer reliability, which the authors attribute to imprecision of the DSM-III-R impairment and distress criterion for this disorder. Agreement was generally better for current episodes rather than past ones, especially for obsessive-compulsive disorder (.91 vs. .58) and social phobia (.68 vs. .33). No significant reliability differences were found between RDC and DSM-III-R criteria for any disorder. One limitation of the interview is its somewhat lengthy administration time, one and one-half to two and one-half hours.

The Structured Clinical Interview for the DSM-III-R—Patient Version (SCID-P)

The SCID-P (Spitzer, Williams, & Gibbon, 1988) is a semi-structured interview designed for use by trained clinicians and mental health professionals with psychiatric patients. Nonpatient (SCID-NP) and Axis II (SCID-II) versions are also available. While the entire SCID can be administered at intake, modules for each major diagnostic group are provided, allowing the clinician to "confirm and document a suspected DSM-III-R diagnosis" (Spitzer, Williams, Gibbon, & First, 1990, p. 1). Moreover, the authors encourage the adaptation of the inverview for specific purposes. Thus, a familiar or favored interview technique or scale can be synthesized with the advantages of a structured interview, and customized for particular studies.

Eleven modules make up the SCID-P, including an Overview Module and the Summary Score Sheet. During the overview, the interviewer records basic demographic information such as age, sex, education, and work history. Treatment history and a description of the current illness are also elicited. The authors note that upon completing the overview, the interviewer should possess sufficient information to justify a "tentative differential diagnosis." Current and lifetime diagnoses are generated, with the exception of, in the anxiety module, generalized anxiety disorder. These diagnoses are then recorded on the Summary Score Sheet, current diagnoses as present or absent, lifetime diagnoses as present, absent, or subthreshold. Administration time generally runs 60 to 90 minutes. The SCID-P is sufficient to meet the needs of most clinicians or researchers, but it does not (nor is it intended to) characterize the subject's psychopathology as richly as the Life Chart of the SADS-LA. Other versions of the SCID available include the SCID-UP, developed for the detailed study of Panic and Generalized Anxiety Disorders, and the SCID-NP-V for posttraumatic stress disorder.

Anxiety Disorders Interview Schedule—Revised (ADIS-R)

Di Nardo, O'Brien, Barlow, Waddell, and Blanchard (1983, p. 1070) state that the ADIS was developed "for three major purposes: to permit differential diagnosis among the DSM-III anxiety disorder categories, to provide sufficient information to rule out psychosis, substance abuse, and major affective disorders, and to provide data beyond basic information required for establishing diagnostic criteria." The Hamilton Anxiety Scale and Hamilton Depression Scale are embedded in the interview by content area. Since the goal of the interview is the comprehensive description of anxiety pathology, skip-outs are infrequent.

Di Nardo and Barlow (1990) reported ADIS kappa coefficients of .905 for social phobia, .854 for agoraphobia with panic, .825 for obsessive-compulsive disorder, .651 for panic disorder, .571 for generalized anxiety disorder, and .558 for simple phobia. Blanchard, Gerardi, Kolb, and Barlow (1986) reported a kappa of .857 for the presence or absence of PTSD using "expert opinion" as the criterion diagnosis.

Critique of the Categorical Approach and Diagnostic Interviews

Although diagnostic interviews have greatly improved the reliability of diagnosis, a number of problems remain. Reliability is no substitute for validity. Diagnostic categories should reflect some underlying reality. Whether the current scheme of anxiety disorders accomplishes this goal is by no means certain. The standardized format of interview techniques imbues diagnostic categories with a measurement precision one would expect only from taxons which indeed exist. As we have seen, however, manifest similarity can mask genotypic heterogeneity. The reliability of diagnostic interviews promotes the masquerade of such "composite" taxons as singular disorders.

At a practical level, questions remain about the internal structure of the interviews themselves. Although interdiagnostician reliability at the diagnostic level may be fairly high, reliability at the symptom level has less often been examined. Since a polythetic model requires an individual meet only a subset of diagnostic criteria, the interrater reliability of the diagnosis itself is surely greater than the reliability of individual interview questions intended to assess specific symptoms or content areas. Yet a reliable symptom picture is exactly what is needed to inform personalized intervention strategies.

DIMENSIONAL MEASURES: SELF REPORT

Many self-report instruments are available. Those which deal with anxiety as a unidimensional construct mainly include items associated with generalized anxiety and panic attacks. For the most part, these instruments were constructed prior to DSM-III, before the DSM-II category anxiety neurosis was split into generalized anxiety disorder, panic, and agoraphobia. Such instruments might be called syndrome measures, because they assess anxiety as it cuts across many different disorders. Items related to obsessional or compulsive content and phobias are fewer, when present. Consequently, the specificity of these scales to any one anxiety disorder is probably limited.

The Beck Anxiety Inventory (BAI)

The BDI (Beck, Ward, Mendelson, Mock, & Erbaugh, 1961; Beck & Steer, 1987) is a well-known and extensively used instrument (for a review, see Beck, Steer, & Garbin, 1988). The BAI (Beck, Epstein, Brown, & Steer, 1988) is a more recent development and has not yet been well researched. The authors state that "The BAI was developed to address the need for an instrument that would reliably discriminate anxiety from depression while displaying convergent validity" (p. 893).

The scale consists of 21 items, each scored 0 (Not at all) to 3 (Severely—I could barely stand it) according to the degree the respondent has been "bothered" by the particular symptom within the past week. The final score ranges from 0 to 63. A factor analysis reported by the authors yielded two factors: (1) somatic symptoms and (2) subjective anxiety and panic symptoms. The scale is weighted toward the first factor. The authors report high internal consistency (alpha = .92) and a BAI-BDI correlation of only .48.

State-Trait Anxiety Inventory (STAI)

One can distinguish between an enduring tendency to feel or behave in a particular way, and the way one feels now, that is, between traits and states, a distinction which underlies the STAI (Spielberger & Rickman, 1990). The STAI is composed of two scales, A-Trait and A-State, each 20 items long. The A-Trait scale regards frequency. Subjects are requested to report how they generally feel. The A-State scale regards intensity. Subjects are instructed to report how they currently feel. The STAI was originally published as Form X in 1970. This was revised in 1983 to address such problems as response biases and discriminant validity in relation to depression. A children's version is also available.

Validity information concerning the STAI comes not only from "experimental" evidence (state-anxiety manipulating paradigms, such as test taking or relaxation training), but from an examination of its psychometric characteristics as well. The internal consistency of both the trait and state scales is high, approximately .90. Test-retest reliability of the A-trait scale is also high, while test-retest reliability of the A-state scale is much lower over long intervals. That these psychometric characteristics conform to such theoretical expectations speaks well of the scale.

Spielberger has recently applied the trait-state distinction in another inventory, the State-Trait Anger Expression Inventory (STAXI; Spielberger, 1988). The STAXI yields measures of State-Anger, Trait-Anger, and Anger Expression. The latter concerns whether anger is expressed (Anger-Out) or suppressed (Anger-In), a distinction no doubt having important behavioral health and psychodynamic implications.

Minnesota Multiphasic Personality Inventory–2

The MMPI, originally published in 1943, has long been a staple for mental health professionals. Unfortunately, construction by the empirical keying approach, which neglects content and internal consistency concerns, rendered interpretation of individual scales problematic, ultimately resulting in the use of two- and three-point codes profiles and a variety of MMPI "cookbooks."

In 1989, the MMPI-2 was published with the addition of fifteen content scales, developed using "multi-stage, multi-method procedures that combined rational and statistical methods" (Butcher, Graham, Williams, & Ben-Porath, 1990, p. 26). These can be interpreted instead of or in addition to the heterogeneous clinical scales. The content scales include the ANX (23 items) anxiety scale, the OBS obsessiveness (16 items) scale, the FRS (23 items) fears scale, and the DEP (33 items) depression scale. Regarding the ANX and OBS scales the authors state:

> High scorers on ANX report general symptoms of anxiety including tension, somatic problems (i.e., heart pounding and shortness of breath), sleep difficulties, worries, and poor concentration. They fear losing their minds, find life a strain, and have difficulty making decisions. They appear to be aware of these symptoms and problems, and admit to having them.
>
> High scorers on OBS have tremendous difficulty making decisions and are likely to ruminate excessively about issues and problems, causing others to become impatient. Having to make changes distresses them, and they may report some compulsive behaviors like counting or saving unimportant things. They are excessive worriers who frequently become overwhelmed by their own thoughts. (p. 36)

Although the content scales are relatively new, scale descriptions and reliability statistics are promising. Butcher et al. (1990) report internal consistencies ranging from .82 to .90 for the ANX scale, .78 to .84 for the OBS scale, and .71 to .84 for the FRS scale, for male and female subjects from psychiatric, alcoholic, and military samples. As might be expected, the ANX and OBS scales show moderate intercorrelation, .66 and .72 for males and females respectively. Much of this can be explained as item overlap. Two shared items heavily influence the correlation due to the relative shortness of the OBS scale. Without these items the correlation drops to .44 and .52 for males and females, respectively.

Millon Clinical Multiaxial Inventory–II (MCMI-II)

Compared to the MMPI, the MCMI (Millon, 1987) is a short (less than 200 items) instrument intended to coordinate with the multiaxial format of the DSM. The personality scales of the MCMI are grounded in a three-polarity metapsychology derived from evolutionary theory (Millon, 1990). The MCMI-II contains several subscales intended to screen for typical Axis I disorders, such as anxiety, dysthymia, and alcohol dependence. Millon (1987) reported a sensitivity of .69 and a positive predictive power of .74 for the anxiety scale.

Symptom Checklist–90–R

The SCL-90-R (Derogatis, 1977) is "a multidimensional self-report symptom inventory designed to measure symptomatic psychological distress" (Derogatis, 1982, p. 277). Ninety items are rated from "Not at all" to "Extremely" on a 5-point scale in relation to symptom severity. From these 90 items, nine primary clinical-rational symptom dimensions are formed: somatization (12 items), obsessive-compulsive (10 items), interpersonal sensitivity (9 items), depression (13 items), anxiety (10 items), hostility (6 items), phobic anxiety (7 items), paranoid ideation (6 items), and psychoticism (10 items). In addition, three global severity indexes are derived, a global severity index (GSI), a positive symptom total (PST), and a positive symptom distress index (PSDI). The global indexes provide different ways of looking at the severity of symptoms in conjunction with the number of symptoms. The PST is simply the number of symptoms reported. The PSDI, however, is described as "a pure intensity measure, adjusted for the number of symptoms present" (Derogatis, 1982, p. 278), while the GSI reflects both the intensity of distress and number of reported symptoms. Norms for psychiatric outpatients, inpatients, nonpatient adolescents, and nonpatient normals are available for both sexes. Symptoms are generally assessed during the past week, however, the time frame is flexible for research purposes. Administration time runs 15 to 20 minutes, and a microcomputer scoring program is available.

Although the SCL-90-R is a popular and widely used instrument, some researchers have questioned its internal structure. Wetzler (1989) noted that while Derogatis, Lipman, Covi, and Rickels (1972) and Prusoff and Klerman (1974) reported that the SCL-90 clearly discriminated depressed and anxious patients, later studies (e.g., Angst & Dobler-Mikola, 1985; Clark & Friedman, 1983) failed to confirm this finding. Other researchers have questioned the independence and composition of its scales. Cyr, McKenna-Foley, and Peacock (1985) opened a literature review of the factor structure of the SCL-90-R and related variants by stating that "Many studies provide evidence of the poor item consistency among factors across studies, the low frequency of factor replication based on postulated dimensions, and questionable factorial constancy across various criteria for the several forms of the Symptom Checklist." These authors advised using the SCL-90-R as a measure of general distress only.

Profile of Mood States (POMS)

The POMS (McNair, Lorr, & Droppleman, 1971) is a 65-item affect adjective checklist developed through factor analytic research with both psychiatric patients and normals. Six primary mood dimensions are assessed: tension-anxiety, depression-dejection, confusion-bewilderment, anger-hostility, vigor-activity, and fatigue-inertia. Each item is rated on a five-point scale from "Not at all" to "Extremely." The time frame of the instrument is "the past week including today." College and outpatient norms for males and females are provided.

Moods are by definition more time-limited than are symptoms and traits. Reliabilities therefore are constrained by the transient nature of the construct. One month test-retest correlations of from .61 to .69 (McNair & Lorr, 1964) and 20-day correlations (McNair et al., 1971) of from .65 to .74 have been reported. Internal consistencies for the POMS dimensions range from acceptable, .74, to high, .92. The POMS anxiety and depression scales, though moderately intercorrelated, appear to possess higher convergent and discriminant validities than the Multiple Affect Adjective Checklist anxiety and depression measures, in part because each item is scaled rather than simply checked (Clark & Watson, 1991).

DIMENSIONAL MEASURES: CLINICIAN RATINGS

Numerous clinician-rated instruments are available to assess anxiety. Two will be considered here, the Hamilton Anxiety Rating Scale (HRSA) and the Zung Anxiety Scale (ZAS).

The Hamilton Rating Scale for Anxiety (HRSA)

Hamilton introduced the HRSA in 1959 to assess the severity of clinical anxiety in patients diagnoses as suffering from anxiety neurosis.

Apparently, several slightly different versions of the original scale are in use. Generally, the HRSA consists of approximately 90 symptoms of anxiety grouped rationally under 13 to 15 categories, including anxious mood, tension, fears, insomnia, cognitive symptoms, depressed mood, somatic symptoms (muscular), somatic symptoms (sensory), cardiovascular symptoms, respiratory symptoms, gastrointestinal symptoms, genitourinary symptoms, autonomic symptoms, and behavior-at-interview. These items are scored 0 (not present) to 4 (very severe) depending on severity in the last one week, and then totaled to obtain a global severity rating. Sheehan and Harnett-Sheehan (1990, p. 91) notes that "scores above 18 are usually considered abnormal."

Hamilton (1959) reported a correlation of .89 between independent ratings of the same interview. Two orthogonal factors, a general severity factor, and a bipolar psychic vs. somatic factor were also reported. Maier, Buller, Philipp, and Heuser (1988) found joint-rater interview reliabilities of .74, .73, and .70 for the total score, the psychic factor, and the somatic factor, respectively.

Since its publication, the HRSA has become one of the most widely used rating scales for anxiety. Nearly every study regarding the effectiveness of potential anxiolytics includes it. Both Hamilton scales are included on the ADIS. Nevertheless, the HRSA has its limitations. The HRSA is not intended to be used with patients whose anxiety is associated with other psychiatric disorders. Although the HRSA covers a wide variety of symptoms, these were grouped into variables on rational grounds, so that there is no guarantee that such groupings in fact form natural clusters. The reliability of some items (respiratory symptoms, behavior at interview, and autonomic symptoms) appears low, less than .30 (Maier et al., 1988), and it is unclear how enduring severe symptoms and severe symptoms of brief duration (e.g., panic attacks) should be weighted when appraising the patient's condition. Nor is the HRSA especially useful for the differential diagnosis of anxiety disorders. No obsessional or panic-specific items are included. In a patient sample studied by Di Nardo and Barlow (1990), no significant difference between HRSA scores for panic disorder, generalized anxiety disorder, agoraphobia, and obsessive-compulsive disorder were found.

A number of investigators have taken up the task of refining the HRSA. Snaith, Baugh, Clayden, Husain, and Sipple (1982) recently developed the Clinical Anxiety Scale (CAS) from an item analysis of the HRSA. The CAS consists of six variables scored on a five-point scale. Exact scoring instructions are given. The authors state (p. 520) that the CAS is largely confined to "psychic anxiety and tension in the somatic musculature."

The Zung Inventories

Zung (1971) developed the Self-Rating Anxiety Scale (SAS) and the clinician-rated Anxiety Status Inventory (ASI). Both are 20-item instruments based on DSM-II description of anxiety neurosis and other anxiety symptoms described by authoritative psychiatry texts of the time. Five items assess affective symptoms; fifteen assess somatic complaints. The ASI deals with the severity of each symptom, while the SAS deals with the frequency of each symptom.

ASI items are scored 1 to 4. Clinicians are encouraged to use all available information in assigning severity values, including intensity ("How bad was it?"), duration ("How long did it last?"), and frequency ("How much of the time did you feel that way?") (Zung, 1971, p. 373). These are assumed to co-vary so that, for example, a "2" corresponds to

"Mild in intensity or duration, present some of the time in frequency." An Interview Guide is presented in order to facilitate administration and coverage, however, the clinician is allowed to ask additional questions and probe for details. The time frame is arbitrarily limited to one week.

Each SAS item corresponds to a similar item in the ASI. Items are again scored 1 to 4, from "None or a little of the time" to "Most or all of the time," and the time frame is again set at one week. Five items are scored opposite to the other fifteen to discourage response biases.

Little data is available regarding the reliability and validity of the ASI and SAS. Zung (1971) reported correlations between the ASI and SAS of .66, but only .30 between the SAS and TMAS and .33 between the ASI and TMAS. Within an anxiety disordered group the ASI-SAS correlation rose to .74. Split-half correlations of .83 (ASI) and .71 (SAS) were reported. Jegede (1977) studied the characteristics of the SAS in a group of normals and a group of Nigerian outpatients. Alpha's of .69 for the normal group and .81 for the patients were reported. Item 17 ("My hands are usually dry and warm") was negatively correlated with the remaining items in both samples, suggesting that scale performance might be improved by deleting this item.

DISORDER SPECIFIC SCALES AND DIAGNOSTIC EFFICIENCY STATISTICS

Anxiety is what is common to the anxiety disorders. Logically, then, unidimensional scales of anxiety should possess only limited specificity with regard to the disorders themselves. Fortunately, given the development of many scales specific to the anxiety disorders and aspects of these disorders, the possibility of using these comparatively short scales in place of reliable, but tedious, structured interviews becomes an issue of great clinical import. The anxiety disorders are considered in detail elsewhere in this text. Nevertheless, Tables 14.4 through 14.7 list instruments relevant to the anxiety disorders.

What are diagnostic efficiency statistics and in what ways are scores on disorder specific scales diagnostic? Adoption of the polythetic model in DSM-III approached a paradigm shift in the conception of mental disorders. By this model, no single criterion is necessary or sufficient for the diagnosis of disorder. Instead, only some number of diagnostic criteria must be met, say four or five. The polythetic model recognizes the natural heterogeneity among patients which exists even within a single diagnostic taxon. In terms of the medical model of mental illness, which finds its greatest applicability in the Axis I disorders, we might say that, ideally, this heterogeneity derives from the interaction of individual differences and an underlying disease entity or process, so that variability is a natural characteristic in the manifestation of pathology.

Since all clinical attributes are to some extent the result of a disease by individual differences interaction, that is, fallible rather than unequivocal predictors, the probability of possessing the disorder given any one predictor or set of predictors becomes of interest. Indeed, this is the diagnostician's dilemma: What is the positive predictive power (PPP), the probability of disorder, given the symptom or clinical picture? Presumably, when a certain number of critical predictors or symptoms are present, the probability of disorder is deemed sufficiently high to justify intervention, and a diagnosis is made. Although the positive predictive power of diverse sets of diagnostic criteria taken, say, four at a time, need not be equal (Widiger, Hurt, Frances, Clarkin, & Gilmore, 1984), such is the justification of diagnostic thresholds.

Positive predictive power is part of a larger family of diagnostic efficiency statistics which includes sensitivity, specificity, and negative predictive power (NPP). Sensitivity is the proportion of all patients who possess the symptom of interest, while specificity is equal to the proportion of patients without the disorder who do not possess the symptom of interest. Negative predictive power is the proportion of patients without the symptom of interest, and without the disorder. These statistics are easily summarized in tabular form (see Table 14.3).

Unfortunately, diagnostic efficiency statistics often sometimes seem to work counterintuitively or at odds with one another. For example, it is quite possible for sensitivity to be low, yet PPP, high. This occurs when very few patients with a given disorder possess a particular symptom, but when they do, it is an extremely good predictor. Moreover, optimal diagnostic cutting scores vary with the prevalence (base) rate of a disorder (see especially Baldessarini et al., 1983). When base rates across clinical settings are substantially different from development conditions, optimal

TABLE 14.3.   Diagnostic Efficiency Statistics

Diagnosis Given the Symptom:	True (or Criterion) Diagnosis	
	Possess Disorder	Lack Disorder
Positive	True-Positives (a)	False-Positives (b)
Negative	False-Negatives (c)	True-Negatives (d)
Total	Total with Disorder (a + c)	Total without Disorder (b + d)

Base rate = $(a + c)/(a + c + b + d)$
Sensitivity = $a/(a + c)$
Specificity = $d/(b + d)$
Positive predictive power = $a/(a + b)$
Negative predictive power = $d/(c + d)$

TABLE 14.4.   Instruments for Use with Post-Traumatic Stress Disorder

Clinician-Administered PTSD Scale—Form 1	Blake et al. (1990)
Crime-Related Post-Traumatic Stress Scale (within SCL-90-R)	Saunders, Arata, & Kilpatrick (1990)
Impact of Events Scale	Horowitz, Wilner, & Alverez (1979)
Incident Report Interview	Kilpatrick et al. (1987)
Keane MMPI Subscale	Keane, Malloy, & Fairbank (1984)
Mississippi Scale for Combat Related PTSD	Keane, Cadell, & Taylor (1988)
Mississippi Scale for Combat Related PTSD (Short Form)	Hyer, Davis, Boudewyns, & Woods (1991)
Penn Inventory for PTSD	Hammerburg (1992)
The PTSD Interview	Watson et al. (1991)
Rape Aftermath Symptom Test	Kilpatrick (1988)
Sexual Experiences Survey	Koss & Gidycz (1985)
Vietnam Stress Inventory	Wilson & Krauss (1984)

cutting scores can vary widely. Although some authors have considered this factor when providing instrument validation data (e.g., Keane, Caddell, & Taylor, 1988), on the whole such information is lacking.

We will not examine the all of the vissitudes of diagnostic efficiency statistics here (see Baldessarini et al., 1983; Meehl & Rosen, 1955;

TABLE 14.5.   Instruments for Use with Agoraphobia and Panic Disorder

Agoraphobia Scale	Ost (1990)
Agoraphobic Cognitions Questionnaire	Chambless, Caputo, Bright, & Gallagher (1984)
Anxiety Sensitivity Index	Reiss, Peterson, Gursky, & McNally (1986)
Body Sensations Questionnaire	Chambless et al. (1984)
Dyadic Adjustment Scale	Spainer (1979)
Fear Survey Schedule (FSS-III)	Wolpe & Lang (1964)
Fear Questionnaire	Marks & Mathews (1979)
Locke-Wallace Marital Adjustment Scale	Locke & Wallace (1959)
Marital Satisfaction Inventory	Synder, Wills, & Keiser (1981)
Mobility Inventory	Chambless, Caputo, Jasin, Gracely, & Williams (1985)
Panic Attack Questionnaire	Norton, Dorward, & Cox (1986)
Panic Attack Symptom Questionnaire	Clum, Broyles, Borden, & Watkins (1990)
Panic Attack Cognitions Questionnaire	Clum et al. (1990)
Sheehan Panic Attack and Anticipatory Anxiety Scale	Sheehan (1983)

TABLE 14.6. Instruments for Use with Obsessive-Compulsive Disorder

Compulsive Activity Checklist	Marks, Hallam, Connolly, & Philpott (1977)
Hamburg Obsession/Compulsion Inventory-Short Form	Klepsch, Zaworka, Hand, Lunenschloss, & Jauernig (1991)
Leyton Obsessional Inventory (Card Sort)	Cooper (1970)
Leyton Obsessional Inventory (Paper & Pencil)	Kazarian, Evans, & Lefave (1977)
Lynfield Obsessional Compulsive Questionnaire	Allen (1977)
Maudsley Obsessional-Compulsive Questionnaire	Hodgson & Rachman (1977)
Padua Inventory	Sanavio (1988)
Yale-Brown Obsessive Compulsive Scale	Goodman et al. (1989a,b)

Widiger et al., 1984), but only note that some of these can be grasped intuitively if connected to the level-of-abstraction issue. Consider Figure 14.2. For polemical purposes, assume that, as in the earlier example, agoraphobia and panic disorder indeed map a common domain of psychopathology, and that, as shown, agoraphobia contains two smaller

TABLE 14.7. Instruments for Use with Social Phobia

Embarrassibility Scale	Modigliani (1968)
Fear of Negative Evaluation Scale	Watson & Friend (1969)
Fear of Negative Evaluation Scale (Brief Version)	Leary (1983a)
Fear Questionnaire	Marks & Mathews (1979)
Fear Survey Schedule (FSS-III)	Wolpe & Lang (1964)
Interaction Anxiousness Scale	Leary (1983b)
Shyness Scale	Cheek & Buss (1981)
Situation Questionnaire	Rehm & Marston (1968)
Social Anxiety History Questionnaire	Turner, Beidel, Dancu, & Keys (1986)
Social Anxiety Questionnaire	Arkowitz, Lichtenstein, McGovern, & Hines (1975)
Social Anxiety Inventory	Richardson & Tasto (1976)
Social Avoidance and Distress Scale	Watson & Friend (1969)
Social Interaction Self-Statement Test	Glass, Merluzzi, Biever, & Larsen (1982)
Social Performance Survey Schedule	Lowe & Cautela (1978)
Social Phobia and Anxiety Inventory	Beidel, Turner, Stanley, & Dancu (1989)
Social Reticence Scale (SRS)	Jones & Russell (1982)
SRS—Revised	Jones, Briggs, & Smith (1986)
Social Situations Questionnaire	Bryant & Trower (1974)
Stanford Shyness Survey	Zimbardo (1977)
Survey of Heterosexual Interactions	Twentyman & McFall (1975)

Source: Glass & Arnkoff (1989), brief review of most of these instruments.

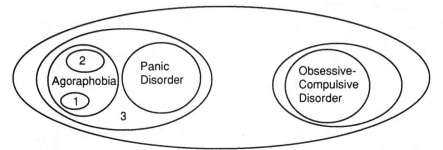

Figure 14.2. A pseudotopographic set diagram for illustrating the relationship between sensitivity and positive predictive power. Smaller circles are assumed to represent fewer patients, severe pathology, and the presence of additional clinical attributes. Attribute 1 possesses high PPP for agoraphobia, but poor sensitivity. Attribute 3 possesses high sensitivity, but poor PPP due to a large number of false positives.

"sub-taxons," and that they have as their nearest neighbor obsessive-compulsive disorder. Assume further that all those within a set also possess the given attribute. Attribute 1 represents the case of low sensitivity and high PPP. In regard to attribute 2, more patients possess the symptom, which also predicts disorder. Thus attribute 2 possesses moderate sensitivity and high PPP. For agoraphobia, attribute 3 possesses high sensitivity, in that all those with agoraphobia also possess attribute 3. Unfortunately, attribute 3 is also common to panic disorder, which, on the basis of this attribute alone, leads to a large number of false positives and thus possesses poor differential diagnostic positive predictive power relative to either agoraphobia or panic disorder. Nevertheless, the attribute holds high differential power relative to obsessive-compulsive disorder.

SUMMARY

The current scheme of anxiety disorders is essentially an empirical creation, lacking an undergirding theoretical schema. Disputes concerning the nature and number of the disorders themselves continue both within (e.g., the validity of GAD) and across (e.g., relationship between anxiety and depression) branches of the diagnostic hierarchy. Fortunately, a means exists of organizing both the clinical phenomena related to anxiety and methods for its investigation through the content by methods-of-assessment matrix. Beyond suggesting the possibility of new nosologic taxons, the use of multimethod approaches across a variety of content areas should be quite helpful in developing a unified theory of the patient's pathology.

Several diagnostic interviews have proven highly reliable, but to revisit theoretical shortcomings, reliability is no substitute for validity, that is, for a theoretical basis. Numerous dimensional measures of anxiety exist, in both clinician-rated and self-report formats. However, anxiety is what is common to the anxiety disorders. Logically, then, a unidimensional anxiety scale can possess only limited differential diagnostic utility. That is not to say that such scales are useless, only that they will probably not be sufficient to answer which anxiety disorders are present, to what degree, and in what way.

Fortunately, the specification and refinement of diagnostic criteria in DSM-III and later editions, together with the development of structured interviews, have led to the emergence of a variety of scales intended to assess specific anxiety disorders. The Mobility Inventory (Chambless, Caputo, Jasin, Gracely, & Williams, 1985), for example, is intended to assess self-reported agoraphobic avoidance. Since these scales are much more tightly focused than, say, the HRSA, they should be particularly helpful in suggesting the presence or absence of symptoms, illuminating areas of intervention, and measuring therapeutic progress. While an exclusively empirical approach to psychopathology cannot be recommended, in general these scales should offer a considerable improvement in predictive power and specificity over unidimensional anxiety scales, and should be invaluable in determining the future directions of this area both clinically and experimentally.

REFERENCES

Allen, J. J. (1977). The measurement of obsessionality: First validation studies of the Lynfield obsessional/compulsive questionnaire. *Journal of International Medical Research, 5(5),* 12–15.

American Psychiatric Association. (1987). *Diagnostic and statistical manual of mental disorders* (3rd ed. rev.). Washington, DC: Author.

Angst, J., & Dobler-Mikola, A. (1985). The Zurich study: VI. A continuum from depression to anxiety disorders? *European Archives of Psychiatry and Neurological Science, 235,* 179–186.

Arkowitz, H., Lichtenstein, K., McGovern, K., & Hines, P. (1975). Behavioral assessment of social competence in males. *Behavior Therapy, 6,* 3–13.

Baldessarini, R. J., Finklestein, S., & Arana, G. W. (1983). The predictive power of diagnostic tests and the effect of prevalence of illness. *Archives of General Psychiatry, 40,* 569–573.

Beck, A. T., Epstein, N., Brown, G., & Steer, R. A. (1988). An inventory for measuring clinical anxiety: Psychometric properties. *Journal of Consulting and Clinical Psychology, 56,* 893–897.

Beck, A. T., & Steer, R. A. (1987). *Manual for the revised Beck Depression Inventory.* San Antonio, TX: The Psychological Corporation.

Beck, A. T., Steer, R. A., & Garbin, M. G. (1988). Psychometric properties of the Beck Depression Inventory: Twenty-five years of evaluation. *Clinical Psychology Review, 8,* 77–100.

Beck, A. T., Ward, C. H., Mendelson, M., Mock, J., & Erbaugh, J. (1961). An inventory for measuring depression. *Archives of General Psychiatry, 4,* 561–571.

Beidel, D. C., Turner, S. M., Stanley, M. A., & Dancu, A. V. (1989). The Social Phobia and Anxiety Inventory: Concurrent and external validity. *Behavior Therapy, 20,* 417–427.

Blake, D. D., Weathers, F. W., Nagy, L. M., Kaloupek, D. G., Klauminzer, G., Charney, R., & Keane, T. M. (1990). A clinician rating scale for assessing current and lifetime PTSD: The CAPS-1. *The Behavior Therapist, 13,* 187–188.

Blanchard, E. B., Gerardi, R. J., Kolb, L. C., & Barlow, D. H. (1986). The utility of the Anxiety Disorders Interview Schedule (ADIS) in the diagnosis of Post-Traumatic Stress Disorder (PTSD) in Vietnam veterans. *Behaviour Research and Therapy, 24,* 577–580.

Blashfield, R. K. (1980). Propositions regarding the use of cluster analysis in clinical research. *Journal of Consulting and Clinical Psychology, 48,* 456–459.

Bryant, B., & Trower, P. E. (1974). Social difficulty in a student sample. *British Journal of Educational Psychology, 44,* 13–21.

Butcher, J. N., Graham, J. R., Williams, C. L., & Ben-Porath, Y. S. (1990). *Development and Use of the MMPI-2 Content Scales.* Minneapolis: University of Minnesota Press.

Campbell, D. T., & Fiske, D. W. (1959). Convergent and discriminant validation by the multitrait-multimethod matrix. *Psychological Bulletin, 56,* 81–105.

Chambless. D. L., Caputo, C., Bright, P., & Gallagher, R. (1984). Assessment of fear in agoraphobics: The Body Sensations Questionnaire and the Agoraphobic Cognitions Questionnaire. *Journal of Consulting and Clinical Psychology, 62,* 1090–1097.

Chambless, D. L., Caputo, G. C., Jasin, S. E., Gracely, E. J., & Williams, C. (1985). The Mobility Inventory for Agoraphobia. *Behaviour Research and Therapy, 23,* 35–44.

Cheek, J. M., & Buss, A. H. (1981). Shyness and sociability. *Journal of Personality and Social Psychology, 41,* 330–339.

Clark, A., & Friedman, M. J. (1983). Factor structure and discriminant validity of the SCL-90 in a veteran psychiatric population. *Journal of Personality Assessment, 47,* 396–404.

Clark, L. A., & Watson, D. (1991). Tripartite model of anxiety and depression: Psychometric evidence and taxonomic implications. *Journal of Abnormal Psychology, 100,* 316–336.

Clum, G. A., Broyles, S., Borden, J., & Watkins, P. L. (1990). Validity and reliability of the Panic Attack Symptoms and Cognitions Questionnaire. *Journal of Psychopathology and Behavioral Assessment, 12,* 233–247.

Cooper, J. E. (1970). The Leyton Obsessional Inventory. *Psychological Medicine, 1,* 48–64.

Cyr, J. J., McKenna-Foley, J. M., & Peacock, E. (1985). Factor structure of the SCL-90-R: Is there one? *Journal of Personality Assessment, 49*, 571–578.

Derogatis, L. R. (1977). *SCL-90-R administration, scoring, and procedures manual*, vol. 1. Baltimore: Clinical Psychometric Research.

Derogatis, L. R. (1982). Self-report measures of stress. In L. Goldberger & S. Breznitz (Eds.), *Handbook of stress: Theoretical and clinical aspects* (pp. 270–294 New York: The Free Press).

Derogatis, L. R., Lipman, R. S., Covi, L., & Rickels, K. (1972). Factorial invariance of symptom dimensions in anxious and depressive neuroses. *Archives of General Psychiatry, 27*, 659–665.

Di Nardo, P. A., & Barlow, D. H. (1990). Syndrome and symptom co-occurrence in the anxiety disorders, In J. D. Maser & C. R. Cloninger (Eds.), *Comorbidity of Mood and Anxiety Disorders* (pp. 205–230). Washington, DC: American Psychiatric Press.

Di Nardo, P. A., O'Brien, G. T., Barlow, D. H., Waddell, M. T., & Blanchard, E. B. (1983). Reliability of DSM-III anxiety disorder categories using a new structured interview. *Archives of General Psychiatry, 40*, 1070–1074.

Dobson, K. S. (1985). The relationship between anxiety and depression. *Clinical Psychology Review, 5*, 307–324.

Eifert, G., & Wilson, P. H. (1991). The triple response approach to assessment: A conceptual and methodological reappraisal. *Behaviour Research and Therapy, 29*, 283–292.

Endicott, J., & Spitzer, R. L. (1978). A diagnostic interview: The Schedule for Affective Disorders and Schizophrenia. *Archives of General Psychiatry, 27*, 678–687.

Fyer, A. J., Endicott, J., Mannuzza, S., & Klein, D. F. (1985). *Schedule for Affective Disorders and Schizophrenia-Lifetime Version* (modified for the study of anxiety disorders). New York: Anxiety Disorders Clinic, New York State Psychiatric Institute.

Frances, A., Widiger, T., & Flyer, M. R. (1990). The influence of classification methods on comorbidity. In J. D. Maser & C. R. Cloninger (Eds.), *Comorbidity of Mood and Anxiety Disorders* (pp. 41–60). Washington, DC: American Psychiatric Press.

Glass, C. R., & Arnkoff, D. B. (1989). Behavioral assessment of social anxiety and social phobia. *Clinical Psychology Review, 9*, 75–90.

Glass, C. R., Merluzzi, T. V., Biever, J. L., & Larsen, K. H. (1982). Cognitive assessment of social anxiety: Development and validation of a self-statement questionnaire. *Cognitive Therapy and Research, 6*, 37–55.

Goodman, W. K., Price, L. H., Rasmussen, S. A., Mazure, C., Fleischmann, R. L., Hill, C. L., Heninger, G. R., & Charney, D. S. (1989a). The Yale-Brown Obsessive-Compulsive Scale: I. Development, use, and reliability. *Archives of General Psychiatry, 46*, 1006–1011.

Goodman, W. K., Price, L. H., Rasmussen, S. A., Mazure, C., Delgado, P., Heninger, G. R., & Charney, D. S. (1989b). The Yale-Brown Obsessive-Compulsive Scale: II. Validity. *Archives of General Psychiatry, 46*, 1012–1016.

Hamilton, M. (1959). The assessment of anxiety states by rating. *British Journal of Medical Psychology, 32,* 50–55.

Hammerburg, M. (1992). Penn Inventory for Posttraumatic Stress Disorder: Psychometric properties. *Psychological Assessment, 4,* 67–76.

Hempel, C. G. (1965). *Aspects of scientific explanation.* New York: Free Press.

Hodgson, R. J., & Rachman, S. (1977). Obsessional-compulsive complaints. *Behaviour Research and Therapy, 15,* 389–395.

Horowitz, M., Wilner, N., & Alverez, W. (1979). Impact of Events Scale: A measure of subjective distress. *Psychosomatic Medicine, 41,* 209–218.

Hyer, L., Davis, H., Boudewyns, P. A., & Woods, M. G. (1991). A short form of the Mississippi Scale for Combat-Related PTSD. *Journal of Clinical Psychology, 47,* 510–518.

Jegede, R. O. (1977). Psychometric attributes of the Self-Rating Anxiety Scale. *Psychological Reports, 40,* 303–306.

Jones, W. H., Briggs, S. R., & Smith, T. G. (1986). Shyness: Conceptualization and measurement. *Journal of Personality and Social Psychology, 51,* 629–639.

Jones, W. H., & Russell, D. (1982). The Social Reticence Scale: An objective measure of shyness. *Journal of Personality Assessment, 46,* 629–631.

Kazarian, S. S., Evans, D. R., & Lefave, K. (1977). Modification and factorial analysis of the Leyton Obsessional Inventory. *Journal of Clinical Psychology, 33,* 422–425.

Keane, T. M., Cadell, J. M., Taylor, K. L. (1988). Mississippi Scale for Combat-Related Posttraumatic Stress Disorder: Three studies in reliability and validity. *Journal of Consulting and Clinical Psychology, 56,* 85–90.

Keane, T. M., Malloy, P. F., & Fairbank, J. A. (1984). Empirical development of an MMPI subscale for the assessment of combat-related posttraumatic stress disorder. *Journal of Consulting and Clinical Psychology, 52,* 888–891.

Kilpatrick, D. G. (1988). Rape Aftermath Symptom Test. In M. Herson & A. S. Bellack (Eds.), *Dictionary of Behavioral Assessment Techniques* (pp. 366–367). New York: Pergamon Press.

Kilpatrick, D. G., Veronen, L. J., Saunders, B. E., Best, C. L., Amick-McMullen, A., & Paduhovich, J. (1987). *The psychological impact of crime: A study of randomly surveyed crime victims.* (Final Report, Grant No. 84–IJ-CX-0039). Washington, DC: National Institute of Justice.

Klepsch, R., Zaworka, W., Hand, I., Lunenschloss, K., & Jauernig, G. (1991). Derivation and validation of the Hamburg Obsession/Compulsion Inventory—Short Form (HOCI-S): First results. *Psychological Assessment: A Journal of Consulting and Clinical Psychology, 3,* 196–201.

Koss, M. P., & Gidycz, C. A. (1985). Sexual Experiences Survey: Reliability and Validity. *Journal of Consulting and Clinical Psychology, 53,* 422–423.

Lang, P. J. (1968). Fear reduction and fear behavior: Problems in treating a construct. In J. M. Schlien (Ed.), *Research in psychotherapy* (Vol. III.) (pp. 90–102). Washington, DC: APA.

Leary, M. R. (1983a). A brief version of the Fear of Negative Evaluation Scale. *Personality and Social Psychology Bulletin, 9,* 371–376.

Leary, M. R. (1983b). Social anxiousness: The construct and its measurement. *Journal of Personality Assessment, 47,* 66–75.

Locke, H. J., & Wallace, K. M. (1959). Marital-adjustment and prediction tests: Their reliability and validity. *Marriage and Family Living, 21,* 251–255.

Lowe, M. R., & Cautela, J. R. (1978). A self-report measure of social skill. *Behavior Therapy, 9,* 535–544.

Maier, W., Buller, R., Philipp, M., & Heuser, I. (1988). The Hamilton Anxiety Scale: Reliability, validity, and sensitivity to change in anxiety and depressive disorders. *Journal of Affective Disorders, 14,* 61–68.

Mannuzza, S., Fyer, A., Klein, D., and Endicott, J. (1986). Schedule for Affective Disorders and Schizophrenia-Lifetime Version modified for the study of anxiety disorders (SAD-LA): Rationale and conceptual development. *Journal of Psychiatric Research, 20,* 317–325.

Mannuzza, S., Fyer, A. J., Martin, L. Y., Gallops, M. S., Endicott, J., Gorman, J., Liebowitz, M. R., & Klein, D. F. (1989). Reliability of anxiety assessment: I. Diagnostic agreement. *Archives of General Psychiatry, 46,* 1093–1101.

Marks, I. M., & Mathews, A. M. (1979). Brief standard self-rating for phobic patients. *Behaviour Research and Therapy, 17,* 263–267.

Marks, I., Hallam, R., Connolly, S., & Philpott, R. (1977). *Nursing in behavioural psychotherapy: An advanced clinical role for nurses.* London and Tonbridge: Whitefriars Press.

Maser, J. D., & Cloninger, C. R. (Eds.), (1990). *Comorbidity of Mood and Anxiety Disorders.* Washington, DC: American Psychiatric Press.

Matarazzo, J. D. (1990). Psychological assessment versus psychological testing: Validation from Binet to the school, clinic, and courtroom. *American Psychologist, 45,* 999–1017.

McNair, D. M., & Lorr, M. (1964). An analysis of mood in neurotics. *Journal of Abnormal and Social Psychology, 69,* 620–627.

McNair, D. M., Lorr, M., & Droppleman, L. F. (1971). Profile of Mood States. San Diego: EdiTS/Educational and Industrial Testing Service.

Meehl, P. E., & Rosen, A. (1955). Antecedent probability and the efficiency of psychometric signs, patterns, or cutting scores. *Psychological Bulletin, 52,* 194–216.

Millon, T. (1987). *Manual for the Millon Clinical Multiaxial Inventory–II.* Minneapolis: National Computer Systems.

Millon, T. (1990). *Toward a new personology.* New York: Wiley.

Millon, T. (1991). Classification in psychopathology: Rationale, alternatives, and standards. *Journal of Abnormal Psychology, 100,* 245–261.

Modigliani, A. (1968). Embarrassment and embarrassibility. *Sociometry, 31,* 313–326.

Norton, G. R., Dorward, J., & Cox, B. J. (1986). Factors associated with panic attacks in nonclinical subjects. *Behavior Therapy, 17,* 239–252.

Öst, L-G. (1990). The Agoraphobia Scale: An evaluation of its reliability and validity. *Behaviour Research and Therapy, 28,* 323–329.

Prusoff, B., & Klerman, G. L. (1974). Differentiating depressed from anxious neurotic outpatients: Use of discriminant function analysis for separation of neurotic affective states. *Archives of General Psychiatry, 30,* 302–309.

Rehm, L. P., & Marston, A. R. (1968). Reduction of social anxiety through modification of self-reinforcement. *Journal of Consulting and Clinical Psychology, 32,* 565–574.

Reiss, S., Peterson, R. A., Gursky, D. M., & McNally, R. J. (1986). Anxiety sensitivity, anxiety frequency, and the prediction of fearfulness. *Behaviour Research and Therapy, 24,* 1–8.

Sanavio, E. (1988). Obsessions and compulsions: The Padua Inventory. *Behaviour Research and Therapy, 26,* 169–177.

Saunders, B. E., Arata, C. M., & Kilpatrick, D. G. (1990). Development of a Crime-Related Post-Traumatic Stress Disorder scale for women within the Symptom Checklist-90-Revised. *Journal of Traumatic Stress, 3,* 439–448.

Sheehan, D. V. (1983). *The anxiety disease.* New York: Scribner's.

Sheehan, D. V., & Harnett-Sheehan, K. (1990). Psychometric Assessment of Anxiety Disorders. In N. Sartorius, V. Andreoli, G. Cassano, L. Eisenberg, P. Kielholz, P. Pancheri, & G. Racagni (Eds.), *Anxiety: Psychobiological and clinical perspectives* (pp. 85–100). New York: Hemisphere.

Snaith, R. P., Baugh, S. J., Clayden, A. D., Husain, A., & Sipple, M. A. (1982). The Clinical Anxiety Scale: An instrument derived from the Hamilton Anxiety Scale. *British Journal of Psychiatry, 141,* 518–523.

Spanier, G. B. (1979). The measurement of marital quality. *Journal of Sex and Marital Therapy, 5,* 288–300.

Spielberger, C. D. (1988). *State-Trait Anger Expression Inventory manual.* Odessa, FL: Psychological Assessment Resources.

Spielberger, C. D., & Rickman, R. L. (1990). Assessment of state and trait anxiety. In N. Sartorius, V. Andreoli, G. Cassano, L. Eisenberg, P. Kielholz, P. Pancheri, & G. Racagni (Eds.), *Anxiety: Psychobiological and clinical perspectives* (pp. 69–84). New York: Hemisphere.

Spitzer, R. L., Endicott, J., and Robins, E. (1978). Research Diagnostic Criteria: Rationale and reliability. *Archives of General Psychiatry, 35,* 773–782.

Spitzer, R. L., Williams, J. B. W., & Gibbon, M. (1988). *Structured Clinical Interview for DSM-III-R.* New York: Biometric Research Department, New York State Psychiatric Institute.

Spitzer, R. L., Williams, J. B. W., Gibbon, M., & First, M. B. (1990). *User's guide for the Structured Clinical Interview for DSM-III-R.* Washington, DC: American Psychiatric Press.

Synder, D. K., Wills, R. M., & Keiser, T. W. (1981). Empirical validation of the Marital Satisfaction Inventory: An actuarial approach. *Journal of Consulting and Clinical Psychology, 49,* 262–268.

Turner, S. M., Beidel, D. C., Dancu, C. V., & Keys, D. J. (1986). Psychopathology of social phobia and comparison to avoidant personality disorder. *Journal of Abnormal Psychology, 95,* 389–394.

Twentyman, C. T., McFall, R. M. (1975). Behavioral training of social skills in shy males. *Journal of Consulting and Clinical Psychology, 43,* 384–395.

Watson, C. G., Juba, M. P., Manifold, V., Kucala, T., & Anderson, P. E. D. (1991). The PTSD interview: Rationale, description, reliability, and concurrent validity of a DSM-III-based technique. *Journal of Clinical Psychology, 47,* 179–188.

Watson, D., & Friend, R. (1969). Measurement of social-evaluative anxiety. *Journal of Consulting and Clinical Psychology, 47,* 525–535.

Widiger, T. A., Hurt, S. W., Frances, A. F., Clarkin, J. F., & Gilmore, M. (1984). Diagnostic efficiency and DSM-III. *Archives of General Psychiatry, 41,* 1005–1012.

Wiens, A. N. (1990). Structured clinical interviews for adults. In G. Goldstein & M. Herson (Eds.), *Handbook of Psychological Assessment* (2nd ed.). (pp. 324–341). New York: Pergamon.

Wilson, C. G., & Krauss, G. E. (1984, September). *The Vietnam Era Stress Inventory: A scale to measure war stress and Post-traumatic Stress Disorder among Vietnam veterans.* Paper presented at the 3rd National Conference on Post-traumatic Stress Disorder, Baltimore.

Wolpe, J., & Lang, P. J. (1964). A fear survey schedule for use in behavior therapy. *Behavior Research and Therapy, 2,* 27–30.

Zimbardo, P. G. (1977). *Shyness: What it is and what to do about it.* Reading, MA: Addison-Wesley.

Zung, W. W. K. (1971). A rating instrument for anxiety disorders. *Psychosomatics, 12,* 371–379.

CHAPTER 15

Pharmacotherapy of Anxiety Disorders

EDWARD K. SILBERMAN, MD

Over the past two decades, research interest in the pharmacologic treatment of anxiety disorders has grown enormously. Research and theorizing about the biological bases of anxiety disorders have developed in parallel with pharmacologic studies. Adrenergic hyperactivity has been suggested as an important factor in mediating panic disorder (PD), post-traumatic stress disorder (PTSD), and social phobia (SP); dysfunction in serotonergic systems has been seen as important in obsessive-compulsive disorder (OCD), and regulation of the GABAergic system has been the focus of theorizing about generalized anxiety disorder (GAD). Other biological theories have dealt with disordered respiratory physiology in PD, and dysfunction of endogenous opioid systems in PTSD.

While there is not yet any definitive evidence in favor of a biological etiology for any anxiety disorder, it is clear that these conditions are usually highly responsive to medication. This chapter summarizes current knowledge about the use and efficacy of psychotropic medications in GAD, PD, PTSD, OCD, SP, and agoraphobia.

GENERALIZED ANXIETY DISORDER

Benzodiazepines

Benzodiazepines have been the most widely used treatment for generalized anxiety over the past two decades, having almost completely replaced barbiturates and meprobamate. The majority of controlled comparisons have demonstrated greater anxiolytic efficacy of benzodiazepines than barbiturates, and to a lesser extent, meprobamate (Shader & Greenblatt, 1974). However, the major advantages of benzodiazepines are their much greater margin of safety, their ability to control anxiety without excessive sedation, and their generally (although not invariably) milder withdrawal effects.

Rates of effectiveness of benzodiazepines have been difficult to specify exactly. Rickels (1978) found an overall response rate of about 75%, which may be compared to the 30% average placebo response described by Shader and Greenblatt (1974). However, both drug and placebo responses have varied widely across studies.

Variability of benzodiazepine response is due both to methodological differences and to the heterogeneity of patients treated for generalized anxiety. A great many nonpharmacologic factors have been found to affect patients' acute response to benzodiazepines (Rickels 1978). Better response has been found in women, those who are employed, those who have higher socioeconomic status, those who see their problems as emotional (rather than due to physical disease), and those who expect medication to help them. Patients with severe anxiety, especially if it is of acute duration, those without concurrent physical illness, and those who have responded well to prior anxiolytic treatment or had no prior treatment, tend to respond best. Physicians' warmth and optimism about the treatment have been found to enhance both medication and placebo responses (Rickels et al. 1970), while ongoing unfavorable life events during treatment diminish response. The lesson of these findings is that patient's social and psychological problems, and the attention the doctor pays to them, may affect the course of generalized anxiety as much as the way in which medication is prescribed.

While patients with generalized anxiety often present with a mixture of symptoms, benzodiazepines do not address them all equally. Rickels (1978) found that drug-placebo differences are due mainly to improvement on HSCL anxiety and somatization factors, with relatively little contribution from depression, obsessive-compulsive, or interpersonal sensitivity factors.

Parameters of dosing and response vary widely among patients. Published studies have generally used the equivalent of 10 to 40 mg diazepam daily, most often in three divided doses. Marked response can often be seen during the first week of treatment, and may even occur within a few days. While patients may continue to improve through the first several weeks of treatment, response generally plateaus by the end of the fourth week (Rickels, Schweizer, Csanolosi, Case, & Chung, 1988). Downing and Rickels (1985) found that patients who responded to diazepam most robustly during the first week of treatment showed the best outcome after six weeks.

Very little systematic work has been done on long-term treatment with these medications. Many clinicians have been reluctant to prescribe benzodiazepines chronically for fear that patients would habituate to the therapeutic effects, require escalating doses, remain tied to the medication due to withdrawal symptoms, or even develop addictive behaviors that did not exist previously. The few systematic studies of long-term benzodiazepine used to date have not supported these concerns.

While transient withdrawal syndromes on cessation of benzodiazepines are common, Rickels and colleagues (Rickels, Case, Downing, & Winokur, 1983) found that patients taking such medications for longer than eight months were more likely to experience clinically significant withdrawals. Withdrawal effects are more pronounced with abrupt than with gradual withdrawal, and with short-acting rather than long-acting drugs. However, a significant number of patients will have difficulty remaining off medication due to withdrawal effects, even with long-acting benzodiazepines and gradual tapering.

Studies comparing benzodiazepines have found no consistent evidence that some are more efficacious than others. Therapeutic choices are therefore made on the basis of the drug's profile of potency, half-life, and degree of sedation. Patients vary widely in the dose of benzodiazepines they require and tolerate. A typical dosing recommendation would be to start at 2 mg t.i.d. of diazepam, 5 to 10 mg t.i.d. of chlordiazepoxide, or 0.5 mg t.i.d. of alprazolam, and titrate doses upward as necessary, to a maximum dose of 40 mg daily diazepam equivalent.

Tricyclic Antidepressants

The older literature comparing doxepin to benzodiazepines suggested a possible role for this tricylcic in anxious patients with or without some degree of concurrent depression. More recently, amitriptyline, desipramine, and imipramine have been compared to placebo and/or benzodiazepines in double-blind studies, most but not all of which have found them superior for treatment of generalized anxiety. It is difficult to know how to interpret these results, since only two of the studies (Kahn et al., 1986; Hoehn-Saric, McLeod, & Zimmerli, 1988) used current, specific diagnostic classifications, or attempted to factor out the effects of depression or panic-type anxiety on medication response. It is not clear whether the efficacy of tricyclics is due to their well-known antidepressant or antipanic effects, or to alleviation of generalized anxiety itself.

In their double-blind study, Kahn et al. compared 150 to 200 mg daily of imipramine with 60 to 80 mg chlordiazepoxide over an eight-week period. They analyzed separately patients who were primarily anxious, those who were primarily depressed, and those who had anxiety of the panic type. In the primarily anxious group, whether or not there were panic attacks, chlordiazepoxide was more effective than imipramine in improving sleep and anxiety early in the trial, while imipramine was superior to chlordiazepoxide in treating depression and anxiety later in the trial. This study, therefore, suggests a direct effect of imipramine on generalized anxiety.

In the only study to date using DSM-III criteria, Hoehn-Saric et al. (1988) compared imipramine and alprazolam in patients who met criteria for GAD, but not major depression. After a six-week trial, imipramine was superior in alleviating psychological symptoms of anxiety, obsessive-compulsive symptoms, interpersonal sensitivity, paranoia, and depression, while alprazolam was better in alleviating somatic symptoms of anxiety.

In most studies, tricyclics have shown increasing advantages over benzodiazepines as the four- to eight-week study periods progress. This may be due to the general tendency of tricyclic side effects to diminish, and therapeutic effects to increase over the first several weeks of treatment. On average, controlled studies have reported a 42% dropout rate on tricyclics, which seems somewhat higher than the 26% average benzodiazepine rate, but probably not much different from the 35% dropout on placebo.

Buspirone

Buspirone, a drug of the azapirone class with serotonergic inhibitory effects, is the first approved new medication type for generalized anxiety since the advent of benzodiazepines. Clinical interest in buspirone stems from its very different side effect profile from benzodiazepine anxiolytics. It does not tend to cause fatigue or sedation, does not interfere with psychomotor performance, does not interact with CNS depressants, such as alcohol, and does not produce a withdrawal syndrome when abruptly withdrawn. Like benzodiazepines, buspirone has a very high margin of safety; unlike them, it appears to have no anticonvulsant, muscle-relaxant, or euphoriant effects.

Buspirone has been compared to diazepam, clorazepate, alprazolam, lorazepam, and oxazepam, as well as to placebo in many double-blind trials. These trials have consistently demonstrated its superiority to placebo, and overall equivalence to benzodiazepines (Rickels, 1990). Doses in these studies have typically ranged from 15 to 40 mg daily, given on a t.i.d. schedule. While some studies have found clinically significant anxiolytic effects of buspirone after one week of treatment, its efficacy generally lags behind that of benzodiazepines for the first two to four weeks.

Common side effects of buspirone include nausea, dizziness, headache, or, paradoxically, symptoms related to increased arousal and tension, especially early in treatment. These side effects seem to be less well tolerated than those of benzodiazepines, since many investigators have reported a higher dropout rate on buspirone in clinical studies, especially among those patients who have previously received benzodiazepine treatment. Patients who have come to expect a rapid onset of action from benzodiazepines may have a particularly hard time tolerating the slower onset of buspirone, although a physiologic explanation for the poorer results in this subgroup has not been ruled out.

Most studies of buspirone have been no longer than four to six weeks. However, Rickels and colleagues (Rickels & Schweizer, 1990) have conducted a six-month maintenance study on a group of patients who were then followed for up to 40 months. At the end of six months, efficacy of buspirone was equivalent to that of clorazepate, with no evidence of loss of efficacy of either drug over time. Upon double-blind withdrawal of medications, withdrawal and rebound symptoms were evident in clorazepate, but not in buspirone users. At both six and 40 months of follow-up, patients on buspirone were significantly less likely to have moderate or severe anxiety, or to be using anxiolytics, than those who had taken clorazepate. These data suggest that buspirone may produce longer lasting effects than benzodiazepines, a possibility that will have to be confirmed in future studies.

Other Agents

Because of their ability to decrease adrenergic activity, beta-adrenergic blocking agents have been viewed as potential anxiolytics. Hayes and Schulz (1987) recently reviewed the results of double-blind studies of beta blockers for generalized anxiety, eight using propranolol and five using other agents. The authors concluded that while beta-blockers tend to be more effective than placebo, they are usually less effective than benzodiazepines. While earlier workers suggested that beta-blockers might be more effective in alleviating the somatic rather than psychological aspects of anxiety, this has not been confirmed in more recent work (Meibach, Donner, Wilson, Ishiki, & Dager, 1987).

Since their introduction, phenothiazines have been known to have anxiolytic properties in nonpsychotic as well as psychotic patients. This has been demonstrated in several controlled studies comparing neuroleptics to placebo (Mendels et al., 1986). However, there have been no controlled studies comparing neuroleptics to other anxiolytics in nonpsychotic patients. Since the risks of both acute and chronic extrapyramidal side effects are obvious liabilities of neuroleptics, their use could not be recommended without data suggesting specific indications or advantages over more commonly used anxiolytics.

PANIC DISORDER AND AGORAPHOBIA

Tricyclic Antidepressants

Imipramine is the drug most systematically studied for treatment of panic and agoraphobia. Of 13 studies in which imipramine has been compared to placebo under double-blind conditions, 10 have clearly demonstrated the drug's efficacy. Imipramine's antipanic effects have been found to be separate and independent from its antidepressant effects. Some investigators have found primary antipanic and secondary anti-avoidant effects while others have found the reverse.

The efficacy of imipramine without concurrent behavioral therapy has been somewhat less convincingly demonstrated than the benefit of adding imipramine to such therapies. While simple exposure instructions may be effective as adjuncts to medication, patients who are encouraged to continue avoiding phobic situations seem not to do well on medication.

The average dose of imipramine reported in controlled studies is about 160 mg daily, which is comparable to the usual minimum antidepressant dose in nongeriatric adults. There is evidence that patients at times respond more poorly at doses substantially above or below this level (Ballenger et al., 1984). Furthermore, some patients seem to get good therapeutic responses at very small doses, at times as low as 10 or 15 mg daily (Jobson et al., 1978). There have been few studies of blood levels in relation to therapeutic effects, and the results of those have been inconsistent.

The range of response rates in published reports is 60 to 80%, with a mean of about 78% substantially improved on medication. Most, though not all of these rates, have been measured in terms of efficacy of antipanic effects. By comparison, the range of reported placebo responses is 33 to 72%, with a mean of 51%. Thus, a great many potentially medication-responsive patients may do equally well on placebo (Mavissakalian, 1987).

Time of onset of antipanic action is generally two to four weeks. However, some authors have reported continued improvement as far as five or six months into treatment, so that maximum benefit may require a fairly lengthy trial (Zitrin et al., 1983). A major factor effecting time of onset is the difficulty in getting patients up to a therapeutic dose because of poorly tolerated side effects. In addition to the usual anticholinergic and hypotensive effects, panic patients appear to be especially prone to "amphetamine-like" effects of imipramine, including feelings of increased anxiety, energy, tension, restlessness, or shakiness, with or without concomitant palpitations, diaphoresis, tremulousness, and sleep disturbance.

There is general agreement that substantial numbers of patients will relapse when taken off medication, but there is little systematic data available. Published reports cite relapse rates of 20 to 50% following medication withdrawal, but the studies vary as to length of follow-up and amount of concurrent behavior therapy.

At present, the literature offers few predictors of imipramine response. Long duration of illness, increased severity, prominent depressive symptoms, relative lack of panic attacks, and predominance of simple phobia have all been associated with poorer outcome (Sheehan et al., 1980; Mavissakalian & Michelson, 1986). Recently, personality pathology has been associated with poorer global outcome, but not with antipanic effects of medication.

There is no reason to think that imipramine is unique in its antipanic efficacy among cyclic antidepressants. Controlled studies have demonstrated similar efficacy of clomipramine and zimelidine, and uncontrolled trials and anecdotal reports have suggested the efficacy of desipramine, amitriptyline, and nortriptyline. Clinical experience confirms the utility of these and other cyclic antidepressants in treating panic attacks.

Monoamine Oxidase Inhibitors

The antipanic effect of MAO inhibitors has been less thoroughly studied than that of imipramine and other cyclic antidepressants. The literature contains six controlled studies (five dealing with phenelzine) and a number of uncontrolled clinical trials. Methodological inadequacies notwithstanding, all published reports have found some type of anxiolytic effect for MAOIs, with an average response rate of about 80%. A study by Sheehan et al. (1980) provides the only controlled comparison of phenelzine and imipramine, showing a trend toward superiority of the former drug on most measures of improvement. The range of target symptoms affected by MAO inhibitors is very similar to those of cyclic antidepressants.

Doses of phenelzine have been reported in the range of 30 to 90 mg daily, but most studies have not used more than 45 mg, which may be under the optimal level. There is, as yet, no published data on the relationship of platelet MAO activity to therapeutic effect.

Time of improvement ranges from three to eight weeks of treatment, with a mean of about four weeks. About 20% of patients fail to complete treatment across studies, suggesting that MAOIs may be somewhat better tolerated by panic-agoraphobic patients than cyclic antidepressants.

At present there is little guidance for predicting which patients will respond to MAOIs, or which drug within the class may be most effective. Level of depression, personality pathology, and duration of illness have been associated with poorer outcome in some, but not all studies.

Fluoxetine

In addition to its antidepressant and antiobsessional effects, fluoxetine appears to be an effective antipanic agent in a few reports published to date. Schneier et al. (1990) reviewed the charts of 25 patients who had received open trails of fluoxetine for panic disorder, and found improvement in 76%. The dose range was 2.5 to 80 mg daily, and the dropout rate was 16%. The authors noted that many patients needed to start on as little as 2.5 mg daily, with no more than weekly increments, in order to tolerate the treatment. The main difficulty is the early side effects which may include jitteriness, agitation, decreased sleep, and gastrointestinal disturbance. On the other hand, anticholinergic effects and weight gain are generally absent with fluoxetine.

Benzodiazepines

Although Klein (1964) suggested in early reports that benzodiazepine-type anxiolytics were ineffective for panic attacks, interest in possible antipanic properties of these medications has revived considerably in the past decade. The major focus of attention has been on the triazolobenzodiazepine, alprazolam (Ballenger et al., 1988) although this compound is not unique among benzodiazepines in its antipanic effects.

Of 10 controlled studies of alprazolam in panic disorder all have shown the effectiveness of the drug, with a mean response rate of about 72% compared to a placebo response ranging from 14 to 63%. Alprazolam has been found to reduce both spontaneous and situational panic attacks, as well as anticipatory anxiety.

Daily doses of alprazolam have ranged from 1 to 10 milligrams, with a mean of 3.7 mg. Although carefully designed studies of dose response have not been done, some authors have suggested that 40% or more of patients may need 4 to 10 milligrams daily for a good response. Alexander and Alexander (1986) obtained good antipanic effects at a mean dose of 2.2 mg, but needed an average of 3.9 mg for substantial improvement of phobic avoidance.

Alprazolam appears to be both faster in onset and better tolerated than antidepressants. Virtually all reports have described a clinically significant response in one week or less, although continued improvement has been found after six or seven weeks of treatment. Alprazolam is the only antipanic drug so far studied for which the placebo dropout rate (28% in three studies) exceeds the dropout on active drug (12% in six studies).

The most common concerns about alprazolam and other benzodiazepines are the possibility of habituation to therapeutic effects, and the risk of rebound/withdrawal syndromes when the dose is lowered. While many patients may require an increase over their initial therapeutic dose early in treatment, follow-up studies of up to four years have demonstrated that doses of benzodiazepines tend to remain stable or decrease over time (Davidson et al., 1990). Thus, there is little evidence that patients become habituated to therapeutic effects, or escalate dosage inappropriately.

Recent controlled studies of benzodiazepines other than alprazolam, including diazepam, lorazepam, and clonazepam, suggest that they too are effective antipanic agents. Clonazepam, a high-potency benzodi-azepine with a half life of 18 to 54 hours (as compared to 8 to 14 hours for alprazolam) has received particular attention because its longer half-life mitigates interdose rebound/withdrawal effects and attendant antici-patory anxiety. Herman et al., (1987) found that most patients were able to use a twice daily dosing schedule on clonazepam, whereas they had required four or more daily doses when taking alprazolam.

POST-TRAUMATIC STRESS DISORDER

Monoamine Oxidase Inhibitors

Because of their history of use in patients with highly anxious depres-sions, MAO inhibitors have been logical choices for treatment trials in PTSD. While many anecdotal reports and uncontrolled trials have been published, there have been only two controlled studies of MAOIs to date. Outcomes in these reports have been quite variable. In the controlled studies, Frank, Kosten, Giller, and Dan (1988) found that 64% of patients improved on phenelzine compared to only 27% on placebo, while Shes-tatzky, Greenberg, and Lerner (1988) found no significant difference be-tween phenelzine and placebo, although a trend favored the former. In two open trials, the overall response rate averaged about 78% showing at least moderate improvement. The number of patients in these studies is quite small, ranging from 10 in the smallest study to 34 in the largest.

Improved sleep, decreased nightmares, and decreased intrusive day-time recollections have been the most commonly reported benefits among patients who improve on MAO inhibitors. Most authors have re-ported decreased flashbacks as well, although some have noted that flashbacks may worsen on these medications. Thus, when they are effec-tive, MAO inhibitors appear to ameliorate some of the core symptoms of PTSD independent of their effect on depression and anxiety. These latter symptoms have been reported to improve markedly by some authors and relatively little by others. Avoidance of thoughts, feelings, activities, or situations associated with the trauma is unlikely to be affected by MAO inhibitors in these reports. A number of authors comment on the positive interaction between these medications and psychotherapy.

Medication doses range from 30 to 90 mg daily; only two investigators measured platelet MAO levels, both at greater than 80% inhibition, and both reporting positive results. While some reports describe almost im-mediate improvement in some patients, others suggest a need to treat for at least six to eight weeks to attain maximum improvement. In most pub-lished reports, patients have been followed for no more than a few months, and there are as yet no systematic long-term studies of PTSD patients on MAO inhibitors.

It is not clear from the currently available literature why treatment response is so variable, nor have any predictors of response yet emerged. The group reporting the poorest therapeutic response to MAO inhibitors (as well as to other antidepressants) describes a patient population with much lower rates of substance abuse and antisocial behaviors than most published studies. It is not apparent why this should predispose to poor medication response, however.

Tricyclic Antidepressant

The status of our knowledge about tricyclic antidepressants for PTSD, and the general pattern of results with these medications are quite comparable to those with MAO inhibitors. The literature contains three controlled, double-blind studies of tricyclics, five open studies or systematic chart reviews, and a number of unsystematic or anecdotal reports. While all studies reported evidence of improvement on tricyclics, the proportion of patients improved has been quite variable, and the improvement is frequently of modest degree. Among the controlled studies, improvement rates (along various dimensions) range from 27 to 75%, while placebo responses range from 11 to 27% (Frank et al., 1988; Reist et al., 1989; Davidson et al., 1990). Among uncontrolled studies in which improvement rates are reported, from 68 to 100% of patients were reported to be better on some dimension after tricyclic treatment.

The response profile with tricyclics has been quite similar to that with MAO inhibitors. Insomnia, nightmares, intrusive recollections, hypervigilence, and autonomic arousal generally improve, while affective blunting and avoidance generally do not. The relationship between improvement in PTSD core symptoms and improvement in depression or anxiety has been quite variable. Reported doses of tricyclics have been comparable to antidepressant doses, ranging from 50 to 350 mg daily (imipramine equivalents), and averaging in the 150 to 300 mg range. Blood levels have been reported to correlate with improvement in depression in one study using desipramine (mean level 107.3 mg/ml, Reist et al., 1989), but to be unrelated to response in another which employed amitriptyline (Davidson et al., 1990). Length of treatment has ranged from three to eight weeks. While some investigators have described almost immediate improvement, others have found a lag time, with significantly greater response at eight than at four weeks. In the only long-term follow-up of PTSD patients on tricyclics, 9 of 12 Cambodian refugees were symptomatically improved after 12 months on dimensions of sleep and hypervigilence, but only 5 no longer met criteria for the disorder.

Among the tricyclics used for PTSD have been amitriptyline, imipramine, desipramine, and doxepin. In the only direct, double-blind, controlled comparison of antidepressants, imipramine and phenelzine were both significantly better than placebo, although phenelzine appeared slightly more effective in relieving core symptoms of nightmares, flash-backs, and intrusive memories (Frank et al., 1988). Some authors have suggested that amitriptyline may be more effective than other tricyclics (possibly because of its sedating effects), but there have been no system-atic tests of this impression. As with MAO inhibitors, consistent predic-tors of tricyclic response are lacking as yet.

Fluoxetine

Recent reports of cases and open trials have suggested that the potent serotonergic reuptake inhibitor, fluoxetine, may be especially useful in treating PTSD. Fluoxetine used in 20 to 80 mg daily doses has been re-ported to alleviate not only hyperarousal and re-experiencing, but also avoidance, which is generally resistant to other pharmacotherapy. In one open trial (McDougle, Southwick, Charney, & St. James, 1991), 65% of patients responded to fluoxetine with a 50% or more drop in symptoms after four to eight weeks of treatment. The drug has also been reported to produce relief of insomnia, nightmares, and flashbacks within 48 to 72 hours in chronic PTSD sufferers when used in conjunction with low doses of tricyclic antidepressants.

Benzodiazepines

There is little systematically collected data about use of benzodiazepines, and what exists is not very encouraging. Many of the reports about anti-depressant use describe patients who had been on benzodiazepines for many years with little benefit prior to antidepressant therapy. Feldman (1987) conducted a chart review of 20 outpatient Veterans Administra-tion hospital patients who had been taking alprazolam for from 1 to 12 months. Doses ranged form 0.5 to 6 mg daily. Sixteen of the 20 patients were reported to be improved, particularly in sleep parameters, mood, and anxiety and arousal levels. By contrast, Braun et al. (1987) found no significant difference between alprazolam and placebo in a double-blind, crossover study of 16 patients. Doses of alprazolam ranged up to 6 mg daily, and each leg of the trial lasted five weeks. There was some ten-dency for alprazolam to have mild anxiolytic effects in this study, but no effects on core PTSD symptoms.

In addition to questionable efficacy, there may be special problems with the use of benzodiazepines in PTSD patients. In one study, attempts to withdraw patients from alprazolam produced severe rebound symp-toms even though the dose was tapered very gradually. Prior heavy use of alcohol in this group may sensitize patients to benzodiazepine with-drawal in the same way that prior use of benzodiazepines themselves has been hypothesized to do.

Lithium

Lithium's mood stabilizing properties make it a plausible treatment for PTSD. No controlled studies have yet been done to test this hypothesis, but clinical evidence is somewhat positive. Kitchner and Greenstein (1985) presented a series of five PTSD patients who were treated with lithium. Doses ranging from 300 to 600 mg daily (producing blood levels in the 0.2 to 0.4 meq range) decreased rage, anxiety, nightmares, depression, and alcohol abuse. Patients were also found to make better use of psychotherapy on lithium than they had previously. These impressions were supported by van der Kolk (1987), who reported that 14 of 22 patients tried on lithium had decreased signs of autonomic hyperarousal, as well as decreased alcohol abuse. Systematic studies will be needed to confirm these preliminary results.

Carbamazepine

A kindling hypothesis of PTSD would suggest trials of carbamazepine and other mood stablizer/anticonvulsants for the disorder. Lipper et al. (1986) reported an open trial of 10 patients who received a mean dose of 666 mg daily for five weeks (mean blood level 8.2 g/ml). Seven of the 10 were substantially improved in symptoms related to intrusive memories, but not in avoidant behaviors, depression, or anxiety. Wolf, Alan, and Mosnaim (1988) describe a group of 10 patients openly treated with 800 to 1200 mg carbamazepine as being globally improved, but give no further details of the treatment or types of response.

Other Medications

A variety of other strategies have been reported sporadically in the literature. Blockers of alpha and beta adrenergic activity have been used with some success. Neuroleptics have generally not been advocated for PTSD because the risks of such drugs would be unacceptable for treating a nonpsychotic syndrome. However, some authors recommend their use acutely for sedating effects in patients who are agitated and difficult to control by other means.

OBSESSIVE-COMPULSIVE DISORDER

Clomipramine

Clomipramine is the best studied medication for treatment of OCD, with close to two dozen reports of controlled trials now in the literature. The salient early questions about clomipramine in OCD were whether it is really more effective than other tricylcic antidepressants, and whether its efficacy is due to a true antiobsessional, rather than antidepressant action. The weight of current evidence is positive in both regards.

Clomipramine has been found superior to placebo in about two-thirds of the double-blind studies done to date, and all of those that are methodologically adequate (Clomipramine Collaborative Study Group, 1991). The overall rate of clinically meaningful response to clomipramine (variously defined) is about 70%, compared to placebo responses which are generally under 20%. Out of eight studies in which clomipramine has been blindly evaluated against other tricyclics or MAO inhibitors, six have clearly favored clomipramine, one has been equivocal, and one has found no difference between either active drug and placebo.

The anti-obsessional effect of clomipramine is separate and independent from its antidepressant effect, and occurs in obsessive-compulsive patients with little or no concurrent depression (Katz & DeVeaugh-Geiss, 1990). While investigators have generally found that both depressive and obsessive-compulsive symptoms are alleviated by effective pharmacotherapy, the weight of current opinion is that the depression lifts secondarily to the relief of burdensome obsessive-compulsive symptoms.

The mean maximum daily dose of clomipramine in controlled studies is about 250 mg, and the mean daily dose is 174 mg. Although formal dose response studies have not been done, those studies using markedly lower doses have tended to show poorer results. Stern, Marks, Mawson, and Luscombe (1980) have found that plasma levels in the range of 100 to 250 ng/ml of clomipramine are associated with better response than levels outside that range after 10 weeks of treatment. At the same time, levels of the metabolite desmethylclomipramine in the range 230 to 550 ng/ml were associated with better antidepressant, but not antiobsessional response.

Other authors have reported better anti-obsessional response in patients with clomipramine levels above 200 ng/ml. These reports suggest that low doses and blood levels may be important factors in medication nonresponsiveness.

There is general agreement that robust anti-obsessional response takes longer than antidepressant responses in patients suffering from primary depression. Length of controlled trials has ranged from 4 to 36 weeks, with a mean of about 11 weeks. Most studies have not found significant drug effects before 5 to 10 weeks, and several authors have noted that patients often continue to improve for the first several months of treatment. As with other anxiety disorders, however, there may be considerable interindividual variability in response times, since some investigators have reported significant medication effects after as little as one to two weeks.

In general, obsessional thoughts and compulsive rituals respond about equally well to clomipramine treatment. Case reports have suggested that atypical variants such as hair pulling (trichotillomania), obsessional religious scrupulosity, bowel and other somatic obsessions, intrusive musical material, and depersonalization may respond to clomipramine as well as classic obsessive-compulsive symptoms (Swedo et al., 1989).

No consistent predictors of clomipramine response in OCD have yet been identified. Age, sex, duration of illness, baseline severity of obsessive-compulsive or depressive symptoms, predominance of obsessions versus compulsions, bizarreness of ideation, ability of the patient to resist ritualizing, and Axis II comorbidity have not been found to relate to outcome. However Jenike, Baer, Minichiello, Schwartz, and Carr (1986) have reported poorer outcomes in OCD patients with schizotypal personality disorder which, as part of the schizophrenia spectrum, may represent a special case.

While medication tends to produce global improvement, it is generally of moderate degree. Controlled studies average 42% symptom reduction with clomipramine (compared with 5% on placebo and about 15% on less serotonergic antidepressants) which represents a substantial improvement in patients' ability to cope with their symptoms, but not a complete remission of the disorder. Thus, 50% or more of patients may be expected to continue to meet criteria for OCD after medication treatment.

Patients have been followed on clomipramine for over two years and have been found to maintain their therapeutic benefits. However, when medication is withdrawn, relapse is common, ranging above 80% by some estimates (Pato, Zoher-Kadouch, Zohar, & Murphy, 1988). At the same time, patients may often be well maintained on less than their maximum acute dose.

Other Serotonergic Agents

A variety of relatively newer selective serotonergic agents, including fluoxetine, sertraline, and fluvoxamine, are promising additions to clomipramine for treatment of OCD. At present, the most widely used of these is fluoxetine, which has been reported effective in case reports, several open trials, and one controlled study (Pigott et al., 1990). Higher doses of this drug have been used for OCD than for depression, with systematic trials generally using a maximum of 80 mg daily. Authors report a 50 to 65% decline in severity of obsessions, compulsions, and depressive symptoms over the first two months of treatment, with a more shallow slope of improvement thereafter. As with clomipramine, fluoxetine response does not appear to depend upon the presence of clinically significant depression. In the one blind comparison of fluoxetine and clomipramine to date, the two drugs were found essentially equivalent in therapeutic efficacy.

However, patients reported fewer side effects on fluoxetine than on clomipramine in this study.

Sertraline is another serotonergic reuptake blocker that has recently become commercially available in the United States. It has been tested in two double-blind studies with OCD patients, one of which showed it to be significantly more effective, and the other found it to be no different from placebo. While serotonergic agents appear to be the most useful medications for OCD presently available, it remains for future studies to determine the range and possible differences in therapeutic efficacies among these drugs.

Non-Serotonergic Agents

Most of the literature on drugs other than specific serotonergic agents for OCD consists of case reports and uncontrolled studies, which do not suggest robust therapeutic efficacy. Furthermore, many investigators note that patients in controlled studies of serotonergic agents have often had unsuccessful trials of other antidepressant or anxiolytic medications. However, the literature does provide indications that such medications may be useful in individual cases, or for specific indications. Cyclic antidepressants and MAO inhibitors have been reported helpful in isolated cases of OCD, especially in patients who have other types of anxiety symptoms, such as panic attacks, in addition to obsessions and compulsions (Foa, Steketee, Kozak, & Dugger, 1987; Jenike, Surman, Cassem, Zusky, & Anderson, 1983). Anxiolytic medications may also be beneficial in such patients, although there are case reports of OCD patients who have no other types of anxiety symptoms responding well to alprazolam or clonazepam in the usual anxiolytic doses. Buspirone, a nonbenzodiazepine anxiolytic with proven efficacy for generalized anxiety, has been reported to alleviate OCD symptoms in some cases, although reports are conflicting.

Other medications may be helpful in special subgroups of patients with obsessive-compulsive symptoms. Carbamazepine has been reported helpful in patients with a history of overt seizures, and lithium may alleviate obsessive-compulsive symptoms in patients with bipolar disorder.

Strategies for Treatment-Resistant OCD

A variety of augmentation strategies have been suggested for increasing therapeutic response in treatment resistant OCD patients. None have been tested in controlled studies, but the most promising appears to be adding a second serotonergic agent to one of the first-line drugs.

Probably the best studied combination to date is buspirone added to fluoxetine. In two open trials (Jenike, Baer, & Bottolph, 1991; Markovitz,

Stagno, & Calabrese, 1990), buspirone in 30 to 60 mg doses was added in patients who had had a well-established, but partial response to fluoxetine, resulting in additional improvement after 4 to 8 weeks. However, controlled studies of buspirone in combination with clomipramine or fluoxetine have not demonstrated any benefit of dual therapy (Pigott et al., 1992).

Other case reports have described further improvement after trazodone was added to fluoxetine therapy, or fluoxetine was added to clomipramine therapy. Methodological shortcomings make these reports difficult to evaluate. Similar issues cloud reports of improvement after the addition of lithium to clomipramine or other tricyclic antidepressants. Among the other strategies reported helpful in resistant cases have been l-tryptophan, triiodothyronine, and clonidine added to first-line medications, or intravenous clomipramine in patients who have not responded to oral dosing, but there is little systematically collected data on these methods as yet. Controlled studies of lithium or thyroid hormone added to serotonergic drugs have not demonstrated any benefit over monotherapy to date (McDougle, Price, Goodman, Charney, & Heninger, 1991; Pigott et al., 1991). Addition of fenfluramine, a serotonin releasing agent, has been reported in several cases in which patients responded to clomipramine, fluoxetine, or fluvoxamine, but could not tolerate the therapeutic dose. The addition of 20 to 40 mg of fenfluramine allowed the patients to maintain therapeutic benefits on lower doses of antidepressant than with monotherapy.

A special case of treatment resistance may be OCD patients who also meet criteria for schizotypal personality disorder. In one study of patients who had not responded to fluvoxamine therapy the addition of pimozide 6.5 mg or thioridazine, 75 to 100 mg daily resulted in improvement in 88% of patients who had tic spectrum disorders or schizotypal personality, but only 22% of those who did not (McDougle et al., 1990).

SOCIAL PHOBIA

Monoamine Oxidase Inhibitors

A great deal of current interest centers around the use of monoamine oxidase inhibitors in treatment of social phobia. These medications had been reported successful in treating mixed groups of patients with social phobias and agoraphobia, but early reports did not distinguish drug responsivity between the two. Studies of atypical depression have also found MAO inhibitors to be effective in dealing with interpersonal hypersensitivity. Such results suggested that MAO inhibitors might be effective in social phobia (Liebowitz, Gorman, Fyer, & Klein, 1985).

This hypothesis has been recently tested in two open trials and two controlled studies. In open trials, 72% of a total of 43 patients, many of whom had done poorly on beta-blockers or tricyclic antidepressants responded well to phenelzine or tranylcypromine. Six of the patients did best at doses of no more than 45 mg phenelzine daily.

Controlled studies of MAO inhibitors have partially confirmed earlier impressions. Liebowitz et al. (1988) conducted a double-blind, eight-week comparison of phenelzine (mean daily dose 72 mg), atenolol, and placebo. They found that phenelzine was superior to both comparison groups on a broad range of measures related to social phobia after four or more weeks of treatment. While 64% of phenelzine-treated patients were considered responders, only 36% of atenolol and 31% of placebo-treated patients were so judged. While the authors state that "atenolol is effective for patients with discrete performance anxiety, but not generalized social anxiety . . . [and] phenelzine appears effective for generalized social anxiety but not for discrete performance anxiety," they do not present data to support this impression.

These results were only partially confirmed by Gelernter et al. (1991) who compared exposure instructions plus phenelzine, alprazolam, or placebo to formal cognitive therapy with no medication in a 12-week, double-blind trial. For phenelzine patients, 60% compared to 28% of alprazolam, 20% of placebo, and 24% of cognitive therapy patients were judged to be responders. However, only two items out of the seven assessment scales used showed significant superiority of phenelzine, or indeed significant differences between conditions at all. At two months follow-up, phenelzine patients tended to maintain their gains better than patients in the other conditions. It is possible that the lower average dose of phenelzine in this study (55 mg daily) contributed to the somewhat equivocal therapeutic superiority.

Beta-Adrenergic Blockers

Reports of acute treatment of performance anxiety with beta-blockers suggested possible efficacy of these drugs in social phobia. An open trial of 10 patients with diagnosed social phobia (Gorman, Liebowitz, Fyer, Campeas, & Klein, 1985) supported this conclusion. They found that atenolol, given in 50 to 100 mg daily doses for six weeks resulted in some improvement in 90% of their patients, and marked improvement in 50%. In this study, efficacy was equivalent for patients with specific, versus generalized social phobias.

Two controlled studies have failed to find robust therapeutic effects of beta-blockers, however. Falloon, Lloyd, and Harpin (1981) conducted a study of 16 patients undergoing behavioral therapy plus either propranolol (160 to 320 mg daily) or placebo. While all patients improved, there was no added benefit of medication over the four-week trial. The more recent study by Liebowitz and colleagues using atenolol (50 to 100 mg daily) similarly failed to demonstrate superiority of the drug over placebo. While beta-blockers may benefit patients with social or performance anxiety therefore, it is not clear whether they confer added benefit over education and exposure instructions.

Benzodiazepines

Three open trials provide evidence that benzodiazepines may be helpful to patients with social phobia. Reich and Yates (1988) using alprazolam (mean daily dose 2.9 mg), and Munjack, Baltazar, Bohn, Cabe, and Appleton (1990) and Reiter, Pollack, Rosenbaum, and Cohen (1990) using clonazepam (dose range 0.75 to 6 mg daily) reported clinically significant improvement in 60 to 80% of those treated. Patients improved on most measures within two weeks, but dimensions such as fear of negative evaluation and social avoidance, which may require practice and social relearning appeared to improve more slowly. Patients with both generalized and specific social anxiety have been reported to improve in these studies. The one controlled study of benzodiazepines to date, as mentioned above, found that patients improved on alprazolam, but not to a greater degree than those receiving cognitive therapy or simple exposure instructions with no medication. Thus, as with beta-blockers, the specific contribution, if any, of benzodiazepines to treatment of social phobia is not yet clear.

Other Medications

While patients undergoing treatment trials for social phobia often report previous lack of response to tricyclic antidepressants, no systematic studies of these drugs have yet been in such patients. Anecdotal reports suggest that tricyclics may be helpful in socially phobic patients with mitral valve prolapse, and this may be true of others as well.

Isolated reports of other treatments have recently appeared in the literature. In one case, a patient with social phobia who had not responded to alprazolam, propranolol, or phenelzine, improved rapidly when given clonidine 0.1 mg twice daily. Munjack et al. (1991) reported on an 8-week open trial of buspirone in 16 patient (maximum dose 60 mg daily). Over one-third of patients dropped out before completion of the study, but 80% of completers benefited to a moderate or marked degree. When corrected for the number of statistical tests performed, however, the degree of improvement was no longer significant. Further trials with these medications will be needed before any conclusions can be drawn.

REFERENCES

Alexander, P. L., & Alexander, D. D. (1986). Alprazolam treatment for panic disorder. *Journal of Clinical Psychiatry, 47,* 301–304.

Ballenger, J. L., Burrows, C. D., DuPont, P. L., Lasser, I. M., Noyes, R., Pecknold, J. D., Refkin, A., & Swinson, R. P. (1988). Alprazolam in panic disorder and agoraphobia. Results from a multicenter trial. I. Efficacy in short-term treatment. *Archives of General Psychiatry, 45,* 413–422.

Braun, P., Greenberg, A., Dasberg, H., & Lerer, B. (1987). Core symptoms of posttraumatic stress disorder unimproved by alprazolam treatment. *Journal of Clinical Psychiatry, 51,* 236–238.

Clomipramine Collaborative Study Group (1991). Clomipramine in the treatment of patients with obsessive-compulsive disorder. *Archives of General Psychiatry, 48,* 720–738.

Davidson, J., Kudler, H., Smith, R., Mahoney, S. L., Lipper, S., Hammett, L., Saunders, W. B., & Cavenar, J. O. (1990). Treatments of posttraumatic stress disorder with amitriptyline and placebo. *Archives of General Psychiatry, 47,* 259–266.

Downing, R. W., & Rickels, K. (1985). Early treatment response in anxious outpatients treated with diazepam. *Acta Psychiatria Scandinavica, 72,* 522–528.

Falloon, I. R. H., Lloyd, G. G., & Harpin, R. E. (1981). The treatment of social phobia. Real life rehearsal with nonprofessional therapists. *Journal of Nervous and Mental Disease, 169,* 180–184.

Feldman, T. B. (1987). Alprazolam in the treatment of post-traumatic stress disorder. *Journal of Clinical Psychiatry, 48,* 216–217.

Foa, E., Steketee, G., Kozak, M., & Dugger, D. (1987). Effects of imipramine on depression and obsessive-compulsive symptoms. *Psychiatry Research, 21,* 123–136.

Frank, J. B., Kosten, T. R., Giller, E. L., & Dan, E. (1988). A randomized clinical trial of phenelzine and imipramine for post-traumatic stress disorder. *American Journal of Psychiatry, 145,* 1289–1291.

Gelernter, C. S., Uhde, T. W., Cimbolic, P., Arnkoff, D. B., Vittone, B. J., Tancer, M. E., & Bartko, J. J. (1991). Cognitive-behavioral and pharmacologic treatments of social phobia. A controlled study. *Archives of General Psychiatry, 48,* 938–945.

Gorman, J. M., Liebowitz, M. R., Fyer, A. J., Campeas, R., & Klein, D. F. (1985). Treatment of social phobia with atenolol. *Journal of Clinical Psychopharmacology, 5,* 298–301.

Hayes, P. E., & Schulz, S. C. (1987). Beta-blockers in anxiety disorders. *Journal of Affective Disorders, 13,* 119–130.

Herman, J. B., Rosenbaum, J. F., & Brotman, A. W. (1987). The alprazolam to clonazepam switch for the treatment of panic disorder. *Journal of Clinical Psychiatry, 7,* 175–178.

Hoehn-Saric, R., McLeod, D. R., & Zimmerli, W. D. (1988). Differential effects of alprazolam and imipramine in generalized anxiety disorder: Somatic versus psychic symptoms. *Journal of Clinical Psychiatry, 49,* 293–301.

Jenike, M., Baer, L., & Bottolph, L. (1991). Buspirone augmentation of fluoxetine in patients with obsessive-compulsive disorder. *Journal of Clinical Psychiatry, 52,* 13–14.

Jenike, M., Baer, L., Minichiello, W., Schwartz, C., & Carr, R. (1986). Concomitant obsessive-compulsive disorder and schizotypal personality disorder. *American Journal of Psychiatry, 143,* 530–532.

Jenike, M. A., Surman, O. S., Cassem, N. H., Zusky, P., & Anderson, W. M. (1983). Monoamine oxidase inhibitors in obsessive-compulsive disorder. *Journal of Clinical Psychiatry, 44,* 131–132.

Jobson, K., Linnoile, M., Gillan, J., & Sullivan, J. L. (1978). A successful treatment of severe anxiety attacks with tricyclic antidepressants: A potential mechanism of action. *American Journal of Psychiatry, 135,* 863–874.

Kahn, R. J., McNair, D. M., Lipman, R. S., Covi, L., Rickels, K., Downing, R., Fisher, S., & Frankenthaler, L. M. (1986). Imipramine and chlordiazepoxide in depressive and anxiety disorders. II. Efficacy in outpatients. *Archives of General Psychiatry, 43,* 79–85.

Katz, R. J., & DeVeaugh-Geiss, J. (1990). The antiobsessional effects of clomipramine do not require concomitant affective disorder. *Psychiatry Research, 31,* 121–129.

Kitchner, L., & Greenstein, R. (1985). Low dose lithium carbonate in the treatment of post-traumatic stress disorder: Brief communication. *Military Medicine, 150,* 378–381.

Klein, D. F. (1964). Delineation of two drug-responsive anxiety syndromes. *Psychopharmacologia, 5,* 347–408.

Liebowitz, M. R., Gorman, J. M., Fyer, A. J., Campeas, R., Levin, A. P., Sandberg, D., Hollander, E., Papp, L., & Goetz, D. (1988). Pharmacotherapy of Social Phobia: An interim report of a placebo-controlled comparison of phenelzine and atenolol. *Journal of Clinical Psychiatry, 49,* 252–257.

Liebowitz, M. R., Gorman, J. M., Fyer, A. J., & Klein, D. F. (1985). Social Phobia Review of a neglected anxiety disorder. *Archives of General Psychiatry, 47,* 729–736.

Lipper, S., Davidson, J. T., Grady, T., Edinger, J., Hammet, E., Mahorney, S. L., & Cavenar, J. O. (1986). Preliminary study of carbamazepine in post-traumatic stress disorder. *Psychosomatics, 27,* 849–854.

Markovitz, P. J., Stagno, S. J., & Calabrese, J. (1990). Buspirone augmentation of fluoxetine in obsessive-compulsive disorder. *American Journal of Psychiatry, 147,* 798–800.

Mavissakalian, M. (1987). The placebo effect in agoraphobia. *Journal of Nervous and Mental Disease, 175,* 358–361.

Mavissakalian, M. & Michelson, L. (1988). Agoraphobia: Relative and combined effectiveness of therapist-assisted in vivo exposure. *Journal of Clinical Psychiatry, 47,* 117–122.

McDougle, C. J., Goodman, W. K., Price, L. H., Delgado, P. L., Krystal, J. M., Charney, D. S., & Heninger, G. R. (1990). Neuroleptic addition in fluoxamine-refractory obsessive-compulsive disorder. *American Journal of Psychiatry, 147,* 552–554.

McDougle, C. J., Price, L. H., Goodman, W. K., Charney, D. S., & Heninger, G. R. (1991). A controlled trial of lithium augmentation in fluoxamine-refractory obsessive-compulsive disorder: Lack of efficacy. *Journal of Clinical Psychpharmacology, 11,* 175–184.

McDougle, C. J., Southwick, S. M., Charney, D. S., & St. James, R. L. (1991). An open trial of fluoxetine in the treatment of posttraumatic stress disorder. *Journal of Clinical Psychopharmacology, 11,* 325–326.

Meibach, R., Donner, D., Wilson, L., Ishiki, D., & Dager, S. (1987). Comparative efficacy of propranolol, chlordiazepoxide, and placebo in the treatment of anxiety: A double-blind trial. *Journal of Clinical Psychiatry, 48,* 355–358.

Mendels, J., Krajewski, T. F., Hoffer, V., Taylor, R. J., Seconde, S., Schless, A., Sebastian, J. A., Semchyshyn, G., Durr, M. J., Melmed, A. S., & Whyte, A. (1986). Effective short-term treatment of generalized anxiety disorder with trifluoperazine. *Journal of Clinical Psychiatry, 47,* 170–174.

Munjack, D. J., Baltazar, P. L., Bohn, P. B., Cabe, D. D., & Appleton, A. A. (1990). Clonazepam in the treatment of social phobia: a pilot study. *Journal of Clinical Psychiatry, 51* (5 supplement), 25–40.

Munjack, D. J., Brons, J., Baltazar, P. L., Brown, R., Leonard, M., Nagy, R., Koek, R., Crocker, B., & Schafer, S. (1991). A pilot study of buspirone in the treatment of social phobia. *Journal of Anxiety Disorders, 5,* 87–98.

Pato, M. T., Zoher-Kadouch, R., Zohar, J., & Murphy, D. L. (1988). Return of symptoms after discontinuation of clomipramine in patients with obsessive-compulsive disorder. *American Journal of Psychiatry, 145,* 1521–1525.

Pigott, T. A., L'Heureux, F., Hill, J. L., Hihari, L., Bernstein, S. E., Murphy, D. L. (1992). A double-blind study of adjuvant buspirone hydrochloride in clomipramine-treated OCD patients. *Journal of Clinical Psychopharmacology, 12,* 11–18.

Pigott, T. A., Pato, J. T., Bernstein, S. E., Grover, G. N., Hill, J. L., Tolliver, T. J., & Murphy, D. L. (1990). Controlled comparisons of clomipramine and fluoxetine in the treatment of obsessive-compulsive disorder. Behavioral and biological results. *Archives of General Psychiatry, 47,* 926–932.

Pigott, T. A., Pato, M. T., L'Heureux, F., Hill, J. L., Grover, G. N., Bernstein, S. E., Murphy, D. L. (1991). A controlled comparison of adjuvant lithium carbonate or thyroid hormone in clomipramine-treated patients with obsessive-compulsive disorder. *Journal of Clinical Psychopharmacology, 11,* 242–248.

Reich, J., & Yates, W. (1988). A pilot study of treatment of social phobia with alprazolam. *American Journal of Psychiatry, 145,* 540–544.

Reist, C., Kauffman, C. D., Haier, R. J., Sangdahl, C., De Met, E. M., Chicz-De Met, A., & Nelson, J. N. (1989). A controlled trial of desipramine in 18 men with posttraumatic stress disorder. *American Journal of Psychiatry, 146,* 513–516.

Reiter, S. R., Pollack, M. H., Rosenbaum, J. F., & Cohen, L. S. (1990). Clonazepam for the treatment of social phobia. *Journal of Clinical Psychiatry, 51,* 470–472.

Rickels, K. (1978). Use of antianxiety agents in anxious outpatients. *Psychopharmacology, 58,* 1–17.

Rickels, K. (1990). Buspirone in clinical practice. *Journal of Clinical Psychiatry, 51* (9 supplement) 51–54.

Rickels, K., Case, G., Downing, R. W., & Winokur, A. (1983). Long-term diazepam therapy and clinical outcome. *Journal of the American Medical Association, 250,* 767–771.

Rickels, K., Lipman, R., Park, L. C., Covi, L., Uhlenhuth, E. H., & Mock, J. E. (1970). Drug, doctor warmth, and clinical setting in the symptomatic response to minor tranquilizers. *Psychopharmacologia, 20,* 128–152.

Rickels, K., & Schweizer, E. (1990). The clinical course and long-term management of generalized anxiety disorder. *Journal of Clinical Psychopharmacology, 10,* 1015–1105.

Rickels, K., Schweizer, E., Csanalosi, I., Case, E., & Chung, H. (1988). Long-term treatment of anxiety and risk of withdrawal. Prospective comparison of clorazepate and buspirone. *Archives of General Psychiatry, 45,* 444–450.

Schneier, F. R., Liebowitz, M. R., Davies, S. O., Fairbanks, J., Hollander, E., Campeas, R., & Klein, D. F. (1990). Fluoxetine in panic disorder. *Journal of Clinical Psychopharmacology, 10,* 119–121.

Shader, R. I., & Greenblatt, D. J. (1974). *Benzodiazepines in Clinical Practice.* New York: Raven Press.

Sheehan, D. V., Ballenger, J., & Jacobson, G. (1980). Treatment of endogenous anxiety with phobia, hysterical, and hypochondriacal symptoms. *Archives of General Psychiatry, 37,* 51–59.

Shestatzky, M., Greenberg, D., & Lerner, B. (1988). A controlled trial of phenelzine in posttraumatic stress disorder. *Psychiatry Research, 24,* 149–155.

Stern, R. S., Marks, I. M., Mawson, D., & Luscombe, D. K. (1980). Clomipramine and exposure for compulsive rituals: II plasma levels, side effect, and outcome. *British Journal of Psychiatry, 136,* 161–166.

Swedo, S. E., Leonard, H. L., Rapoport, J., Lenane, M., Goldberger, E., & Cheslow, D. L. (1989). A double-blind comparison of clomipramine and desipramine in the treatment of trichotillomania (hair pulling). *New England Journal of Medicine, 321,* 497–501.

van der Kolk, B. A. (1987). The drug treatment of post-traumatic stress disorder. *Journal of Affective Disorders, 13,* 203–213.

Wolf, M. E., Alan, A., & Mosnaim, A. (1988). Post-traumatic stress disorder in Vietnam veterans. Clinical and EEG findings: Possible therapeutic effects of carbamazepine. *Biological Psychiatry, 23,* 642–644.

Zitrin, C. M., Klein, D. F., Woerier, M. G., & Ross, D. C. (1983). Treatment of phobias I: Comparison of impramine hydrochloride and placebo. *Archives of General Psychiatry, 40,* 125–38.

CHAPTER 16

Psychoanalysis and Related Methods

JONATHAN M. JACKSON, PhD

In all psychoanalytic psychotherapies, far from being an isolated target of diagnostic concern and treatment, or simply a troubling symptom to be controlled, anxiety functions as an invaluable assistant to patient and therapist in their task of identifying areas for exploration and understanding. Moreover, despite their differences, all psychoanalytic approaches treat the presence of anxiety as an indication of a problem with self-regulation.

While the DSM-III-R defines anxiety in terms of intensity and duration of signs and symptoms, psychoanalytic models assert the centrality of the role anxiety in personality development and psychopathology, but with importantly different emphases. Four of the most widely practiced and published models—classical Freudian, interpersonal, object relations, and self-psychological—will be discussed with regard to the role of anxiety and its treatment in clinical practice. Space limitations necessitate emphasizing some authors and schools of thought over others, but a wide sampling is nevertheless included.

CLASSICAL APPROACHES TO ANXIETY

I will begin with the classical Freudian view, since subsequent psychoanalytic developments treat Freud's work as a point of departure. Starting with the classical approach, it is necessary to present the theory of the unconscious origins and causes of anxiety, because classical psychoanalysis is a depth therapy that does not aim for symptom amelioration directly, but rather aims to address the unconscious determinants of symptoms. In fact, this is true of most psychoanalytic theory and practice, and this point will be developed throughout this chapter. As Beck (Beck & Emery, 1985) stated:

> Anxiety . . . is not the pathological process in so-called anxiety disorders any more than pain or fever constitute the pathological process in an

injury or an infection. We should not allow nature's mechanism for dramatizing the feeling of anxiety to mislead us into believing that this most salient subjective experience plays the central role in the so-called anxiety disorders. (p. 14)

Thus, anxiety in current psychoanalytic approaches is to be investigated for its underlying dynamic causes, and not directly alleviated per se. In practice, then, anxiety becomes the *starting point* for a psychoanalytic inquiry. That is why, for example, in the initial interview we typically look for the trigger to the present disturbance or, as it is usually called, the precipitating event. Without this information concerning the point around which anxiety surfaced, the therapist may often feel dislocated, at a loss to know how to proceed. Freud himself treated anxiety as only a starting point for treatment. To Freud, anxiety was both a striking and a common feature of everyday human life, familiar to normal and neurotic individuals alike. More importantly, anxiety in psychoanalysis became the central vantage point for arriving at a full and deep understanding of mental life. For these reasons, anxiety was one of the first problems for which Freud suggested an explanation.

Toxic Theory of Anxiety and Clinical Practice

Even though the experience of anxiety is common to all, the unrealistic and irrational nature of anxiety set it apart from fear. After describing anxiety's morbid manifestations, Freud turned to the problem of alleviating anxiety in neurotic individuals. In his earliest formulations, Freud (1895/1963) asserted that neurotic anxiety, seen most typically in its phobic or free floating forms, resulted from unemployed libido. Anxiety came from unexpressed sexual urges.* This principle constitutes what has been termed Freud's *primary* (Fischer, 1970) or *toxic theory* of the causes of anxiety. The theory derives its name from the so-called toxic effects of sexual urges which, when unable to find discharge or suitable gratification, are instead transformed into the noxious experience of anxiety which in turn disrupts the functioning of the psychic system. The cause of ungratified sexual urges were thought to be many, including trauma, repression, and unhealthy sexual practices such as coitus interruptus or abstinence.

In the case of trauma, such as sexual seduction in childhood, the relatively immature ego of the child is unable to master the sudden and

---

*The term *urge* will generally be used in place of the terms instinct or drive. The author believes it conveys Freud's idea of the subjective experience of the pressure of the drive and some of the biological sense of the term instinct, but in more everyday experiential terms. See G. Klein's (1970) article, "Freud's two theories of sexuality" for an interesting discussion of this problem.

immense activation of conscious and unconscious urges and associated fantasies that typically result. This inability, combined with societal injunctions against disclosing sexual trauma and its sequelae, leaves the child in a state of excessively high excitation without the ability or opportunities necessary to relieve it. The traumatic nature of childhood experiences inhere in the helplessness of the child to relieve in any appreciable way or mitigate against their effects.

Repression, on the other hand, contributed to the build up of anxiety in a different way. Freud (1917/1963) stated, "Repression corresponds to an attempt at flight by the ego from libido which is felt as a danger" (p. 410). In repression, a defense of the ego against threatening urges, the ideational component of the urge (the wish) is banished to the unconscious. Since, however, the affective (or, in Freud's biological terms, energic) component of the sexual urge cannot be similarly done away with, it is transformed into anxiety.

The idea Freud had developed, and which formed the theoretical basis for his toxic theory of anxiety, is that sexual energies could never be quieted. If denied expression over a prolonged period of time, sexual urges would accumulate until they eventually created a toxic psychophysiological environment, the result of inhibitory practices that blocked the psychic system from its usual method (discharge) for regulating internal tensions and excitations. The inner toxic environment was experienced subjectively as anxiety. Freud's theory of psychopathology was thus, at this early stage, heavily influenced by this biological model of the human psyche. The idea of mental treatment for the neuroses had not yet gained acceptance. Treatments for anxiety states at this stage in Freud's clinical practice were most typically electrotherapy, drugs, baths, massage, suggestion, and hypnosis. Hypnosis captured Freud's attention, and he used it extensively to suggest symptom abatement to his patients and to bring about *abreaction,* an opening up of blocked pathways allowing the free flow of previously dammed up psychic tensions.

Abreaction is viewed today as an elementary form of treatment for anxiety. Aspects of this approach constitute the essential starting point for therapy of some anxiety disorders such as those resulting from posttraumatic stress disorder (PTSD) of war or combat experience, sexual or physical abuse, and other stressors (e.g., sudden loss of a loved one due to divorce or illness, and personal illness which exceeds the individual's usual capacity to handle problems of everyday life). To illustrate how abreaction in clinical practice works, consider the case of PTSD. Hendin and Haas (1988) explain how repetitive dreams of combat trauma constitute an attempt to be prepared after the original traumatic events. Repetition in dream experience may dissipate traumatic anxiety because, unlike the original trauma where the individual was unprepared and thus overwhelmed by horror and fright, this time the individual exerts a degree of control over the experience by recreating it himself, under conditions of safety. Psychotherapy of the PTSD patient usually entails vivid re-experiencing of trauma in waking life, so that as in dreams, previously blocked affect is released, undoing the anxiogenic effects of the original trauma. In therapy, the ego is assisted so that the overwhelming conditions (such as helplessness) which prevailed at the time of the original trauma are mitigated. In the psychoanalytic treatment of adult survivors of childhood sexual abuse, re-experiencing the hated and feared intensity of the original trauma either through abreaction or in the transference relationship, is also deemed necessary. Re-experiencing trauma in one form or another is a precondition for eventual healing of the various fractures and dissociations that evolved to deal with the original traumatic events (Davies & Frawley, 1992; Shengold, 1989).

The technique of free association also borrows from toxic theory. In free association, a patient is instructed to say everything that comes to mind no matter how seemingly trivial. This is based on the idea that the repression of wishes that threaten the ego has been at work and needs to be countermanded. The permissiveness of the psychoanalytic treatment situation is meant to correct the repressive attitudes and practices of the ego, and instead to allow the unblocked flow of ideas previously barred from consciousness.

As discussed, the toxic theory of anxiety informs psychoanalytic methods for working with patients suffering anxiety from repressed traumatic experience in adult life and earlier in childhood. In addition, aspects of toxic theory lie behind treatment approaches to inhibitions in sex and at work. In general, it could be said that any time a clinician helps an individual to find appropriate expression of previously inhibited conscious and unconscious fantasies and associated urges, that clinician is employing toxic theory to allow the patient a more fully employed libido and its resultant, lessened anxiety. For Freud, full employment of libido in love and work was the best insurance against the occurrence of severe anxiety (Freud, 1926/1963).

Signal Theory of Anxiety and Clinical Practice

In his later work, Freud (1926/1963) developed what has come to be called the *signal theory of anxiety*. Put simply, if in the toxic theory "anxiety is the consequence of repression," in signal theory the direction of causality is reversed and "repression is the consequence of anxiety" (Eagle & Wolitzky, 1988, p. 122).* Freud (1926/1963) theorized that the

---

*As Eagle and Wolitzky (1988) point out, signal theory did not replace toxic theory, it merely added to it. In most of Freud's clinical work, he relied on both theories simultaneously.

ego was capable of manifesting a small but noticeable amount of anxiety which was not primarily reflective of pathology but rather which functioned to warn or signal the individual that a danger situation was imminent. As mentioned earlier, for Freud a danger situation was traumatic in that it threatened an individual with helplessness in the face of strongly activated libidinal urges. These urges were dangerous both because they exceeded the ego's capacity for expression and because they placed the individual in a conflictual situation. The conflict was typically one where an individual, because of past experience, feared abandonment, loss of love, castration, or guilt as a result of acting on certain urges. Thus, whereas toxic anxiety ensues from negative experiences already suffered, signal anxiety serves to warn the individual about negative experience anticipated in the future; and whereas toxic anxiety originated somewhere in the body (i.e., the seminal vesicles or the subcortex), signal anxiety is a product of the mind, originating in the ego.

The development of the signal theory of anxiety came at the same time that Freud expanded the role of the ego in his structural theory of the mind. Whereas toxic theory was concerned with the fate of libidinal urges, signal theory focused instead on the reasons and methods by which the ego kept certain wishes and urges from awareness. The signal function of the ego explained the deployment of ego defense mechanisms in the following way. With the onset of signal anxiety, the ego would employ a variety of defenses, principally repression, which would insure that the forbidden and feared wish remained out of awareness with no possibility of becoming enacted. In this way, anxiety resulting from anticipated danger situations was usually controlled. The signal theory opened the door to the analysis of anxiety, and not merely to the unblocking of its negative effects via abreaction. Now anxiety could be viewed as an adaptive affect, not merely one that reflected a pathological process. Psychoanalysis could now view anxiety as a guide-post, an alarm concerning an impending danger situation such as separation from mother, loss of body contents and bodily harm, or death itself. Following the eruption of anxiety back through the train of free associations to its incipient moment became a method of uncovering unconscious conflict. For example, if in the course of a psychotherapy session, a patient became quiet, conciliatory, or vague, it could be viewed as a defensive response to an anticipated danger situation. Seen this way, the cause of anxiety and the various ways in which it is defended against in the therapeutic arena (i.e., defense and resistance), takes center stage, promising to point the way to unconscious terrain.

The promotion of insight through interpretation of unconscious conflicts and unconscious origins of anxiety is the primary goal and method, respectively, of psychoanalysis. An anxious response of a patient, for example, may, upon inquiry, turn out to be based on anticipated reprisals from significant people in the environment. Take the case of a young man who is prevented by anxiety from asking his boss for a raise. At suitable opportunities, he stammers or becomes vague. Signal anxiety is at work, prompting defensive avoidance of the danger situation. But just what is the danger. This young man may unconsciously expect that his request will be viewed as a wish to challenge, to engage in a competition with his boss, and as a result he may fear disapproval or loss of his job as a punishment. Interpretation of the unconscious source of his anxiety and his unrealistically harsh superego might help him manage his wish for a raise both by distinguishing it from urges rooted in the vagaries of father-son competitiveness, and by focusing on realistic tactics and opportunities for securing a higher salary.

This model of conflict between, on the one hand, unconscious urges and prohibitions of the superego and between unconscious urges and the capacity of the ego to construct suitable outlets for these urges, makes fundamental the role of anxiety in psychoanalytic treatment. Anxiety is painful and as such it helps to motivate inquiry into its causes. In a sense, anxiety is the play maker, the force that instigates the therapeutic work.

Ironically, in the psychoanalytic method, the absence of anxiety is maladaptive because it does not serve the clinical process, and it can suggest the presence of a defeatist attitude or large scale withdrawal. Schacht, Henry, and Strupp (1988) point out that it may be necessary in some instances to actually stimulate anxiety in psychoanalytic patients to motivate and facilitate the inquiry in unconscious conflicts. A clinical vignette highlights this issue.

> A 14-year-old girl presented for treatment at a psychoanalytic treatment center saying her mother thought it was a good idea for her to talk to someone. Following this opening, she added that her mother had difficulty with her, and that in talking she hoped to learn something about herself.

In spite of the girl's reasonableness and apparent willingness to enter treatment, she had no emotionally compelling answer to the question about why treatment was being sought now. She had recently participated in two quasi-treatment experiences at her school, but represented these more as passtimes or educational modules than a needed remedy to pressing personal difficulties. The therapist confronted the blandness of the girl's presentation and uncovered a pattern of giving up in the guise of passive conformance to external demands. She feared her own independent desires would be expressed in the form of rebellious hostility, and be received with counterhostility by her mother.

Thus, classical psychoanalytic methods emphasize not only the importance of reducing anxiety of traumatic proportions through expressive release, but also the utility of anxiety insofar as it may help shed light on an individual's struggle with particular unconscious urges. Psychoanalysis views anxiety as a basic condition of human nature. We have primitive and animalistic urges that must be held in check for the sake of preserving the social order. Although anxiety may be inevitable, a sine qua non of existence, its causes can be discerned and our ability to alleviate it is increased. The essence of psychoanalysis as a therapy is its use of the patient's attempt to recreate or reinstate a situation in the analytic relationship which is similar to that in which anxiety used to occur. With the aid of insight and reason, the patient and analyst try to find new solutions that promise an improvement over the old. This contribution and lasting legacy of classical psychoanalysis is basic to all subsequent approaches.

INTERPERSONAL APPROACHES TO TREATMENT OF ANXIETY

Freud's work on the signal theory of anxiety was published late in his career. Perhaps as a result, signal theory never fully supplanted toxic theory. It functioned as an add-on rather than a basic floor plan. A fuller understanding and appreciation for the centrality of anxiety in mental functioning was thus turned over to Freud's followers, the interpersonalists.

Among them, Harry Stack Sullivan (1953, 1956) is generally viewed as the earliest theoretician and clinician to have offered a collection of relatively complete seminal works. Although not as vast or comprehensive as Freud's works, Sullivan's do nevertheless provide a stimulating alternative to the classical view of anxiety. In addition the writings of Horney (1937, 1950), Fromm-Reichman (1950, 1955), and more recently Levenson (1983, 1987, 1991) and Greenberg and Mitchell (1983) offer varied emphases and additions to Sullivan's. This section will be limited by space to Sullivan. The reader can consult the works of other interpersonalists, starting with Greenberg and Mitchell (1983) who locate Sullivan and others along a spectrum of what they term *relational theorists*.

The role of anxiety in interpersonal psychoanalysis is at least as important as it is in the classical approach. Sullivan's objective in clinical work was to trace patterns of interpersonal processes that unfolded throughout the developmental stages. In doing so, there were two fundamental concerns to keep in mind: (1) an individual's pursuit of satisfaction of bodily needs, and (2) pursuit of security concerning avoidance of anxiety. Unfortunately, the two aims sometimes collided, creating conflict.

A logical positivist, Sullivan emphasized the importance of what could be directly observed, meaning what the patient said about his relationships with others and what he did in his relationship with the analyst.

Sullivan believed that emotional difficulties resulted from poorly observed and, hence, poorly understood experience. Sullivan (1956) felt that no one had severe difficulties in living if he had a very good idea of what was happening to him. Self-awareness and social comprehension were necessary in order to successfully integrate with other people and get on with satisfaction of basic needs.

Interfering with self-awareness and social comprehension was what Sullivan called "selective inattention," scrupulous avoidance of vital aspect of social interactions. The cause of selective inattention was theorized to be anxiety. There are different degrees of being anxious, but Sullivan spoke mainly of two points in the continuum. One which concerned him very little was mild anxiety, an everyday occurrence for most people. The other which occupied a significant degree of Sullivan's theoretical concern, was sudden, severe, disruptive anxiety that is akin to terror or dread and that occurs for the most part during infancy and in severe pathological states. The individual who has experienced severe anxiety is anxious primarily about being anxious per se, and not primarily about castration or guilt as in classical theory. Sullivan believed that all of us, but pathological individuals in particular, spend considerable amounts of time in our own lives reducing anxiety we already have and in avoiding more of the same.

In Sullivan's theory, anxiety originates not from internally experienced excitation or undischarged libido, but rather from the vagaries of mother-infant relatedness. Because of a strong, innate, empathic link between them, mother and child communicate unpleasurable states of anxiety and pleasurable states of satisfaction back and forth between them. Good feelings in the mother allow her to maintain her attentiveness and positive attitude toward her child and simultaneously afford the child a sense of emotional security or well-being. Anxiety in the mother breaks her attunement to her child, but more importantly, her anxiety is immediately and directly transmitted to the child in the form of a disruptive experience. If the anxiety is strong enough, dread and intense insecurity ensue. From this, Sullivan pointed out, the child learns about the same as he would from a sharp blow to the head. What actually occurs is that in the interest of maintaining security, the child learns, starting in infancy, to avoid or inattend anything that might make the mothering one anxious. For his own sake, the child learns to identify anxiety states in himself and significant others, to direct behavior, and to conceptualize himself and others as bad (arousing anxiety) or good (not arousing anxiety) in accordance with the overarching goal of minimizing anxiety and preserving interpersonal security.

The interactive strategies or, as Sullivan calls them, "security operations," that an individual evolves to avoid experiencing anxiety and to preserve security is known as the self-system. The self-system is comprised of personifications called the "good me," "the bad me," and the "not me." Not surprisingly, these personifications result from reflected appraisals from significant others and are organized according to the individual's degree of success or failure in minimizing anxiety in others.

The "not me" refers to dissociated aspects of experience that would bring with them overwhelmingly intense anxiety. The individual is normally able to keep "not me" experiences out of awareness, exceptions including dreams and psychotic states. The "good me" experiences are associated with a reduction in anxiety in the self and in the mother, and thereby promote integration and security. "Bad me" experiences increase anxiety and are associated with parental disapproval or "forbidding gestures," as Sullivan called them, and a reduction in the sense of personal security.

Thus, anxiety in the interpersonal model is caused in childhood by the mothering one, and not by internal states of unrelieved tension. Defenses are not against awareness of unconscious sources of anxiety, but against causing anxiety in other persons. The self system is indispensable as an organizer of experience and as a regulator of the dangers of anxiety. As Eagle and Wolitzky (1988) point out, the self system functions not unlike signal anxiety in that it can warn the individual of circumstances that could result in anxiety in the individual or in a significant other.

To this point in our discussion of anxiety in interpersonal theory, there has been no explicit depiction of the self system's regulation of anxiety as pathological in any way. In fact, the self system is necessary for social relations. In the process, however, of serving the individual's need for emotional security, the efficiency of the self system often becomes a limitation. Security operations become automatic and entrenched because by their nature they restrict awareness through limiting the free flow of attention. New information that might allow an individual some understanding of, for example, the circumstances governing his experience of anxiety or his expectation of causing anxiety in others is never attended. To attend to such information might leave an individual more vulnerable to the very anxiety he is trying to ward off. To illustrate, consider the following:

A child's mother is made anxious every time she approaches her for intimacy and closeness. The mother conveys her anxiety in the form of tightened facial expressions, physical distancing, and remarks about her daughter's infantilism. The child learns to deny her need for closeness around her mother and anyone else in a position to offer it (e.g., teachers, nurses, counselors, lovers). To facilitate her denial of her need for closeness, she assumes an aloof and uncaring demeanor, and so converts to coldness anyone's offer of closeness.

This situation often results in a schizoid adaptation in which an individual repeatedly eschews warmth in interpersonal settings, saving herself anticipated anxiety and coldness from others. In the process, such an individual reflexively and repeatedly fails to attain a degree of intimacy and closeness necessary to feel satisfaction with another person. Because of the noxious effects of anxiety, it must be avoided at almost all costs. The good me functions at a considerable emotional cost. Sullivan (1953, 1956) fashioned therapeutic techniques that followed from his understanding of how and why the self system evolved in the first place. The techniques emphasized the importance of the therapist establishing and maintaining a climate of security in the therapy sessions, so that patients might be afforded freedom from their habitual security operations. If interpersonal growth is to occur, patients will need to integrate new information about themselves and others, and this learning cannot occur in the presence of heightened interpersonal anxiety or vigilant security operations that limit awareness about oneself and others.

Perhaps most central to interpersonal analytic techniques is the concept of the detailed inquiry (Sullivan, 1953). It is a form of psychoanalytic inquiry that involves pursuing data, inquiring meticulously into the details and events of the patient's present and past experience in an effort to widen the scope of awareness. This therapeutic strategy revolves around understanding the patient's experience and how he has obscured it. The data pursued are not those concerning infantile urges, but those that concern the dual task of maintaining relationships while avoiding anxiety that could jeopardize security. In interpersonal analysis, the therapist attempts to gradually dislodge the patient from the comfort of his entrenched security operations by asking often discomfiting questions and making observations that bring the patient's awareness to previously inattended data. Many patients habitually talk with such coherence, consistency, and closure that decentering them via questions is not easily accomplished. Consider the following example:

A young married man reports fear over having an anxiety attack and losing control of his feelings. He recently had an anxiety attack at a public arena and had to be escorted home by his wife. He also has irritable bowel syndrome with bouts of diarrhea and is afraid to take some trips away from home. He described intense worry over the preceding weekend about a planned trip to a nearby suburb. When asked where he was going and who he was going to see, he snapped back, "I don't see what that's got to do with anything!"

A moment of anxiety had clearly been reached, evidenced by his forceful rebuke. As the inquiry focused on details he previously inattended, anxiety erupted forcefully, clouding the emerging focus of awareness.

Later discussions revealed he was planning to visit his wife's family and was ashamed of the extent to which he feels pampered, adored, and even infantalized by them, and he expected the analyst to belittle him for his indulgence.

In this instance as in most, detailed inquiry entails a cost, the *creation* of a certain amount of anxiety, but it also promises the benefit of increased interpersonal awareness and competence. Remember that Sullivan believed the patient was socially maladapted because he did not know what was happening to him and around him. The individual needed to increase awareness of himself and others in order to respond adequately to them. Recall the example of the isolated woman who sees only rejection, only social cues that conform to the aims of her self system. She suffers from not seeing openness and warmth in others where it exists, and from engendering aloofness in others. She does not see her own aloofness because this would expose her anew to the possibility and attendant anxieties that come into play in human intimacy. As Levenson (1987) points out, the purpose of the detailed inquiry is the search for the truth inherent in appearances, not the search for truth behind or hidden by appearances. The classical psychoanalytic model proceeds on the assumption that the truth is being disguised by the ego because it is threatening in some way, whereas interpersonalists assume truth is there all along, if only an individual can be free from anxiety and notice it.

Sullivan was not very interested in transference, because it was not useful to him. Freudians place great stock in the patient's re-experiencing unconscious conflicts in the analytic relationship, as a means for studying conditions under which anxiety first emerged. The interpersonalists view transference as a sign of excessive interpersonal anxiety and a potential mire. Sullivan wanted to keep anxiety to a minimum in the analytic relationship to allow for more accurate perception of self and others.

OBJECT RELATION APPROACHES

While in this country, Sullivan was writing and teaching the importance of anxiety experienced in early mother-child interactions and in later peer relations, object relations theorists in England such as Fairbairn (1952) and Guntrip (1968) were developing their own ideas about early experience and personality development.. Object relations theory rejects the central classical Freudian idea about libido. These theorists posited an entirely different libido, one that was foremost object seeking, and not pleasure seeking as was Freud's. This basic shift in theoretical orientation lead to an emphasis on the need for attachment per se, and a corresponding de-emphasis on the need to gratify and regulate sexual and aggressive urges. If, in classical theory, the object is a means to the goal of instinctual gratification, then in object relations theory the instinctual urge is a means to the goal of establishing and maintaining a relationship with another person. Urges are seen as nature's way of assisting people to find others and form lasting attachments.

In discussing the nature of anxiety as proposed by object relations theorists, it is important to keep in mind their view that the earliest experiences of the human infant are characterized by complete dependency. As Winnicott (1960) said, "There is no such thing as an infant, only an infant and its mother" (p. 39). The infant's method of relating to others is through primary identification. Thus, without the other, the infant has no self-experience, no feeling of substance, continuity, or durability. Loss of the object is tantamount to loss of the self. This, then, is the basic anxiety in object relations theory, the experienced threat of loss of the primary object and subsequent loss of the self.* Fairbairn felt that in an ideal society, children should be allowed greater periods of dependence than is customary, and that if permitted to outgrow their dependence according to their own timetable, they would not develop pathological defenses against the feared loss of dependency. Conflicts arise between the desire to maintain infantile dependence and the desire to mature and attain a less extreme and more differentiated form of dependence. Evidently, Fairbairn believed in the idea of mature dependence, allowing that throughout life one would need to maintain some dependent relationships, and that psychological health could be measured by an individual's success in this area throughout the life cycle.

Having once suffered the anxiety of a premature loss of infantile dependence, the individual is motivated to organize certain defensive positions against suffering its reoccurrence. The basic defense according to Fairbairn and Guntrip is the schizoid condition, wherein part of the personality becomes organized around a retreat from relationships with others and becomes attached to internal objects instead. Internal objects are shut off from the outside world and as such offer no opportunities for personality growth or change. What they do offer, however, is protection from potentially depriving or frustrating real objects. This trade off is what is referred to as "the schizoid compromise." The schizoid condition also offers protection for external objects that may come into a person's life. Because of his self-isolation, the schizoid individual need not fear overwhelming others with the intensity of his needs or hurting others with anger over frustration of these needs. Unconscious attachment to internal objects is a source of stability in personality organization for everyone. The problem for schizoid people is that their anxiety

*Although in this presentation primary object loss is viewed as the core anxiety, it is important to keep in mind that experiences of persecution and engulfment by the object are also posited as basic anxieties in object relations theory. These anxieties are reflected in defensive organization of the personality just as object loss is.

over both object loss and over destroying the object out of intense need or anger is so great, that they cling relatively exclusively to internal objects and afford themselves little or no chance for involvement with new external objects.

Schizoid individuals use the analytic setting and the analyst to re-enact early experience by relating to the analyst as if he or she were a remnant of early unsatisfying experiences with caregivers. If this continues unchecked, the present becomes a replay of the past and the future is predetermined. Life is static, still, empty, lacking vitality. Ogden (1989) likened the schizoid's experience to that of an infant suffering merycism, where the same food is swallowed, regurgitated, and reswallowed again and again. The food is thus depleted of all nutritive value, yet it fills the infant's mouth and stomach.

The reason the schizoid compromise is maintained takes us back to the problem of anxiety. There are two feared resultants to resolving the schizoid's pathological adaptation to object relating. They both harken back to the issue of dependency. The schizoid individual dreads new experience that may be conferred by external objects because it threatens to undo the stable, albeit unfulfilling, attachments to internal objects. This threat brings dependency upon an unknown, untested, untried external object (the analyst in the treatment setting). The other fear is that the schizoid's love is destructive, owning to the object's frailty or the intensity of the individual's needs. If these fears are confirmed, the schizoid individual again is faced with an intolerable outcome—aloneness and objectlessness.

Consider the following example:

> A 27-year-old single woman came for treatment reporting difficulty getting over her unreliable former boyfriend. Her father was a cocaine addict whose involvement with her was intense but sporadic. She has been counseled by her family to be sensible and to forget the boyfriend, to try and find a better, more reliable man the next time. She complains that this sort of advice, although well intended, goes only to her head and not to her heart, and this is a schism she actively maintains. For example, to the analyst's suggestions that they work on bridging her two modes of experiencing, she rejoins that she's been told that before and it does not help the feeling in her heart which she cannot forsake.

She is attached to an exciting but abandoning internal object derived from frustrating but powerfully effecting interactions with her charismatic but unreliable father. Her actual experience with her boyfriend reinforced her attachment to an intense internal object. She will hear none of her analyst's appeals to her intellect because she experiences these words as an effort to lure her away from what she calls "her heart," a shorthand metaphor for her compelling internal object world. To this unconscious domain the patient stubbornly and tenaciously clings despite conscious and visible suffering of unfulfilled needs for intimate relations.

In the clinical arena, the analyst offers himself as a new object for identification, thereby reactivating the schizoid patient's primary anxieties. The analyst's unwillingness to conform to the patient's projections (i.e., insistence or preconception of how relationships are structured) confronts the patient with the problem of new experience with a relatively unknown external object. In an effort to ward off the impact of new experience, the patient may display contempt and haughtiness with or without withdrawal. Interpretations help mitigate the anxiety of a new relationship by offering a commentary or a guidebook, so to speak, for new territory. Unlike classical analysts who stress the value of timely interpretations, object relations therapists emphasize the psychoanalytic relationship in and of itself as a vehicle of cure, insofar as it offers the patient new experience. The relationship as the locus of developmental and therapeutic personality growth is key. Interpretations of unconscious fantasies may help the patient understand the nature of basic anxieties over leaving the familial structure of the internal object world, but an attachment to the analyst as a new object, different from internal objects, is indispensable in helping the patient experience the potential for new, less absolute, more differentiated forms of dependency.

SELF PSYCHOLOGICAL APPROACHES

Heinz Kohut's (1971, 1977, 1984) theories of the nature and treatment of anxiety depart radically from Freudian theory, and hold much in common with object relations. For Kohut, the central anxiety is over experiences of disintegration or what he termed loss of the cohesive self. In its extreme, this experience is a loss of a sense of humanness, a feeling of being totally bereft of needed emotional connectedness with others. Unlike classical theory, what is feared is not unmanageable libido, but the threatened breakup of the self.

The cohesive self ordinarily obtains from early experiences of what Kohut called mirroring and idealization. Accordingly, individuals require in the course of normal development, extended periods during which nascent feelings of grandiosity are mirrored or supportively reflected by the parents. In addition, individuals require opportunities to idealize caregivers' traits of, for example, power, strength, or mastery. In everyday terms, the grandiose self of the child may be mirrored in the mother's proud smile; the idealized traits of the parent depicted in the image of the father's repair of a broken toy. Owing usually to inadequate empathy on the part of the parents (but also resulting from constitutional factors of the child), insufficient or unreliable provision of vital emotional experiences or mirroring and idealization can leave an individual with an enfeebled self vulnerable to anxiety over disintegration.

To illustrate this point, consider the different emphases classical and self-psychological approaches place on oedipal anxieties.

Kohut believed that the experience of castration anxiety, normally present in the oedipal phase, is not necessarily traumatic for the child. Given a sufficient degree of empathic involvement from the parents, a child could accrue feelings of pride and vigor from successful mastery of oedipal rivalry. The parents could admire the child for the adult he or she will become, and actively assist him or her in appropriate steps toward that goal. If, however, the parents are deficient in offering empathy, the child may remain fearful and angry at the parent, beyond a phase-appropriate time period. Left alone with these feelings, anxiety over disintegration will mount and defenses such as anger and withdrawal are erected to manage it.

The relationship of the individual to an empathically mirroring or idealizable other was termed a self-selfobject relationship (Kohut, 1977). By use of this terminology, Kohut aimed to develop a psychology emphasizing an individual's need for different kinds of empathic relationships at various developmental stages. So, for example, one and two year olds may need selfobjects for mirroring, just as adults may need the self-selfobject relationship of twinship (Kohut, 1977) to provide a sense of cohesion through connectedness to a like or similar other. Just as Fairbairn and other object relations clinicians believed forms of dependency should be accommodated in adult life, so did Kohut believe that the need for selfobjects persisted throughout the life cycle, and that mental health depended on availability and freedom to utilize a wide range of these relationships.

The need for selfobjects resolves directly around the problem of anxiety over the lack of a cohesive self. The more available empathic objects are early in life, the more cohesive the self and the more able the individual is to manage anxiety. Self-psychological treatment methods focus on provision of needed empathic relationships with the therapist. Should a patient, for example, require mirroring to support an activated but weak grandiose self-structure, the therapist will provide it. Since any therapists's capacity for empathic involvement is by no means absolute, however, breaks in empathy ultimately occur, leaving a patient vulnerable to disintegration experiences of varying degree and kind. These are typically manifested clinically as drops in self-esteem (e.g., shame reactions), feelings of discontinuity (e.g., depersonalization, disorientation), or intense range reactions. The therapist's role at such junctures is to identify his empathic failure, provide understanding to the patient about the anxiety-producing effects of the failure, and in so doing to restore an experience of empathic attunement. In this way, a sense of cohesiveness is restored. Most importantly, two other therapeutic gains are realized. For one, the patient may evolve a sense of himself as relatively durable and strong insofar as he recovers from anxiety over his rage. Providing anxiety is not too extreme, it can be suffered and relieved. This is strengthening and growth promoting for the grandiose self. Secondly, the patient forms an amended view of his therapist as someone who is imperfect but nevertheless available. The selfobject is tarnished, but its shine is restored. Repeated nontraumatic experiences of anxiety over loss of the grandiose self or idealizable others are therapeutic because the patient learns to depend less absolutely on self-objects who are tolerated as less than perfect. Ultimately, the patients learns to find self-objects in his life that take the place of the analyst.

Self-psychology's similarity to object relations is underscored by the fact that in both treatment methods, the evolving relationship with the therapist is crucial as a method for encountering anxiety and for creating new experience. In both models, relationships are primary, and not secondary to the more primary problem of libidinal regulation. Most centrally for this chapter, both methods see anxiety resulting from the loss of primary or essential objects and subsequent loss of the sense of self. This stands in contrast to the classical method where anxiety stems from conflicts over sexual or aggressive libidinal urges that are forbidden by societal norms.

CONCLUSION

There are large differences in the understanding and treatment applied by different psychoanalytic schools to the problem of anxiety. These differences have been clearly outlined recently by Greenberg and Mitchell (1983) in their distinction between the drive/structure and the relational/structure models. Classical theory adheres to the former model, while interpersonal, object relations and self-psychology fall under the latter. Regarding treatment, the centrality of the patient's struggle to maintain a relationship to the analyst and to others is obviously given more weight in the relational/structure models.

What all of these treatment approaches hold in common include a view that, as Beck (Beck & Emory, 1985) argued, anxiety is not the pathological process to be treated per se in anxiety disorders. Instead, it is an indicator of unseen disturbances that must be unearthed. Whether the metapsychology of a particular approach predicates blocked libido, inattended experience, object loss, or loss of self-cohesion as the basis for anxiety, all schools nevertheless view anxiety as a symptom and not as an illness in itself. As a symptom making its appearance in the analytic encounter, it is an invitation to psychoanalytic inquiry and understanding in the context of a containing and reparative relationship.

REFERENCES

Balint, M. (1979). *The basic fault: therapeutic aspects of regression.* (pp. 159–172). New York: Brunner/Mazel.

Beck, A. T., & Emery, G. (1985). *Anxiety disorders and phobia: A cognitive perspective.* (p. 14). New York: Basic Books.

Davies, J. M., & Frawley, M. G. (1992). Dissociative processes in the psychoanalytically oriented treatment of adult survivors of childhood sexual abuse. *Psychoanalytic Dialogues, 2*, 5–76.

Eagle, M., & Wolitzky, D. L. (1988). Psychodynamics. In C. G. Last & M. Hersen (Eds.), *Handbook of anxiety disorders.* (pp. 251–277). New York: Pergamon.

Fairbairn, W. R. D. (1952). *Psychoanalytic studies of the personality.* (pp. 3–58). London: Tavistock.

Fischer, W. F. (1970). *Theories of anxiety.* (pp. 1–18). New York: Harper & Row.

Freud, S. (1895/1963). On the grounds for detaching a particular syndrome from neurosthenia under the description "anxiety neurosis." In J. Strackey (Ed. and Trans.), *The standard edition of the complete psychological works of Sigmund Freud,* (Vol. 3, pp. 87–117). London: Hogarth Press. (Original work published 1895).

Freud, S. (1917/1963). Introductory lectures on psychoanalysis. In J. Strackey (Ed. and Trans.), *The standard edition of the complete psychological of Sigmund Freud,* (Vol. 16, pp. 392–411). London: Hogarth Press. (Original work published 1917).

Freud, S. (1926/1963). Inhibitions, symptoms and anxiety. In J. Strackey (Ed. and Trans.), *The standard edition of the complete psychological works of Sigmund Freud,* Vol. 20, pp. 77–175). London: Hogarth Press. (Original work published 1926).

Fromm-Reichman, F. (1950). *Principles of intensive psychotherapy.* (pp. 45–188). Chicago: Chicago University Press.

Fromm-Reichman, F. (1955). Psychiatric aspects of anxiety. In C.M. Thompson, M. Mazur, & E. Wittenberg (Eds.), *An outline of psychoanalysis.* (pp. 113–133). New York: Modern Library.

Greenberg, J. R., & Mitchell, S. A. (1983). *Object relations in psychoanalytic theory.* Cambridge, MA: Harvard University Press.

Guntrip, H. (1968). *Schizoid phenomena, object relations and the self.* New York: International Universities Press.

Hendin, H., & Haas, A. P. (1988). Post-traumatic stress disorder. In C. G. Last & M. Hersen (Eds.), *Handbook of anxiety disorders.* (pp. 127–142). New York: Pergamon Press.

Horney, K. (1937). *The neurotic personality of our time.* New York: Norton.

Horney, K. (1950). *Neurosis and human growth.* New York: Norton.

Klein, G. S. (1970). Freud's two theories of sexuality. In L. Breger (Ed.), *Clinical-cognitive psychology: Models and integrations.* (pp. 136–181). New Jersey: Prentice Hall.

Kohut, H. (1971). *Analysis of the self.* New York: International Universities Press.

Kohut, H. (1977). *Restoration of the self.* New York: International Universities Press.

Kohut, H. (1984). *How analysis cures.* New York: International Universities Press.

Levenson, E. (1983). *The ambiguity of change.* New York: Basic Books.

Levenson, E. (1987). The interpersonal model. In A. Rothstein (Ed.), *Models of the mind: their relationship to clinical work.* (pp. 49–67). Connecticut: International Universities Press.

Levenson, E. (1991). *The purloined self.* New York: Contemporary Psychoanalysis Books.

Ogden, T. (1989). *The primitive edge of experience.* (pp. 9–46). New Jersey: Jason Aronson.

Schacht, T. E., Henry, W. P., & Strupp, H. H. (1988). Psychotherapy. In G. G. Last & M. Hersen (Eds.), *Handbook of anxiety of disorders.* (pp. 317–337). New York: Pergamon.

Shengold, L. S. (1989). *Soul murder.* New Haven, CT: Yale University Press.

Sullivan, H. S. (1953). *The interpersonal theory of psychiatry.* (pp. 158–171). New York: Norton.

Sullivan, H. S. (1956). *Clinical studies in psychiatry.* (pp. 3–11, 38–60). New York: Norton.

Winnicott, D. W. (1960). The theory of the parent-infant relationship. (pp. 37–55). In D. W. Winnicott, *The maturational processes and the facilitating environment.* New York: International Universities Press, 1965.

CHAPTER 17

Behavioral Therapies

K. ELAINE WILLIAMS, PhD, and DIANNE L. CHAMBLESS, PhD

Behavioral therapy for anxiety disorders offers advantages for both therapist and client. Behavioral techniques are research-based. Thus, as both therapist and client consider using a behavioral intervention, they have some assurance of the effectiveness of the treatment approach. Also, except for the most extreme cases, these interventions involve short-term therapy. Given the constraints on treatment length imposed by managed care and the increasingly limited resources of publicly funded mental health clinics, the availability of an effective, brief treatment is a real plus.

EXPOSURE THERAPY

Exposure therapy is the treatment of choice for most phobias and obsessive-compulsive disorder (OCD). Also, it may be useful in the treatment of post-traumatic stress disorder (PTSD; Foa, Rothbaum, Riggs, & Murdock, 1991; Keane, Fairbank, Caddell, & Zimering, 1989). Exposure therapy consists of exposing the client to exactly those stimuli he or she fears. It is an extremely effective approach, which may be flexibly applied to a variety of feared situations.

Treatment Parameters

Imaginal vs. In Vivo Exposure

In general, direct exposure to the feared stimuli is more effective. However, imaginal exposure has a strong place in the treatment of anxiety disorders. It is a useful tool when it is not practical to arrange for *in vivo* exposure. For example, it would be quite expensive for a person who fears flying to purchase multiple airplane tickets to use for *in vivo* exposure to

Preparation of this chapter was supported in part by National Institute of Mental Health Grant R01-MH44190 to Gail Steketee and Dianne Chambless.

flying. A more economical approach would be for the therapist to provide several sessions of imaginal exposure to be followed by an actual airplane flight. In addition, imaginal exposure often affords the only means to provide exposure treatment for individuals with PTSD.

Imaginal exposure also has a key role in the treatment of OCD (Foa, Steketee, Turner, & Fischer, 1980). In many of these cases, it is important that the client be exposed not only to the feared stimulus, but also to the anticipated consequences of dealing with the stimulus. Frequently, imaginal flooding is the only ethical and practical means of providing such exposure. For example, an OCD checker may fear that leaving the house without checking to be sure that all electrical appliances are switched off will result in fire. In such a case, *in vivo* exposure and response prevention would be used to help the client leave home without checking. Imaginal exposure would be used to facilitate habituation to excessive guilt for having behaved negligently and allowing the house to be destroyed.

Therapist-Assisted vs. Independent Practice

In vivo exposure is a time-consuming undertaking. For this reason, therapists may consider implementing exposure via homework assignments. There are indications from research in the treatment of agoraphobia and OCD that successful exposure may be accomplished with a minimum of therapist time (Emmelkamp, van Linden van den Heuvell, Ruphan, & Sanderman, 1989; Ghosh & Marks, 1987). However in clinical practice, therapists may anticipate treating more severely avoidant clients whose initial level of motivation is not optimal. In such cases, exposure treatment will probably be more successful if the therapist accompanies the client during the exposure exercises. The client should also complete exposure homework between therapist-assisted sessions.

Frequency of Sessions

Early in the history of exposure treatment, it appeared that clients benefited more from intensive scheduling of sessions (Foa, Jameson, Turner, & Payne, 1980). In a typical protocol, the phobic client would undergo ten exposure sessions, conducted daily except for weekends. Results of recent studies, however, (Chambless, 1990; Emmelkamp et al., 1989) indicate that more gradual spacing (typically, twice weekly) of sessions is just as effective. Therefore, it would seem that, depending on scheduling constraints, either approach may be considered.

Conducting in Vivo Exposure

Prior to undertaking exposure, the therapist will want to meet with the client several times to assess the nature and extent of the fears and the ways in which they interfere with daily functioning. It is helpful if the therapist and client work together to establish a hierarchy of feared situations that will be used for exposure. It is often useful to instruct the client in the use of Wolpe's (1973, p. 120) Subjective Units of Discomfort Scale (SUDS), where 0 represents the complete absence of anxiety and 100 signifies the most extreme terror. Exposure typically begins with a situation to which the client assigns a SUDS score of 50 and progresses systematically to items in the 100 range. However, if there is an activity that would make a major difference in the client's quality of life, the clinician may consider using that situation earlier than indicated by the hierarchy in order to boost the client's morale.

A hierarchy for a client having panic disorder with agoraphobia might consist of visiting a large shopping mall accompanied (50 SUDS), driving on residential streets alone (55 SUDS), entering a shopping mall alone (60 SUDS), driving on city streets alone (70 SUDS), driving on expressways accompanied (85 SUDS), and driving on expressways alone (100 SUDS). If this case involves a mother who desperately wants to be able to pick her child up from school, the therapist should consider starting with having her drive on neighborhood streets alone, then gradually progress to entering shopping malls alone and driving on expressways alone.

Therapist and client should allow at least 90 minutes per exposure session, as it is important for the anxiety to attenuate before the client leaves the situation. A client fearful of expressway driving, for example, might start with driving just one exit length repeatedly until habituation occurs. Then, the increments in distances traveled on expressways would be increased and, again, practiced until habituation occurs. The client should be instructed to focus on the stimuli associated with the situation. For exposure to be maximally effective, the client needs to remain mentally aware of the stimuli confronted.

Sometimes clients have a habit of breathing rapidly when made anxious by their phobic stimuli. They may experience symptoms of hyperventilation syndrome (e.g., heart palpitations, dizziness, and dissociation) that compound their anxiety and interfere with habituation. These clients should usually be instructed in respiratory control. An exception to the rule would be some panic-disordered clients who respond fearfully to interoceptive cues. For these clients, the therapist may need to repeatedly guide them in hyperventilating for several minutes at a time to permit habituation to the feared body sensations to occur.

The therapist providing therapist-assisted exposure needs to be flexible about his or her role during treatment sessions. In some situations, the therapist needs to be very actively involved. For example, Ost, Salkovskis, and Hellstrom (1991) view therapist's modeling of target behaviors (e.g., touching animals in the case of an animal phobic) as an integral part of the treatment of simple phobias. Therapist modeling is also helpful for work with obsessive-compulsives who have contamination fears and who may be encouraged to touch a particularly distressing object by the therapist's example. Otherwise, the therapist should concentrate on encouraging the client to undertake the exposure, finding ways to break the exposure down into smaller steps if necessary, and reinforcing the client for following through. In some cases, however, the therapist will need to initiate the exposure session for the client, then fade him or herself out of the picture at a key point, and return at a set time. Examples are work with agoraphobics who fear going places alone and obsessive-compulsive checkers who are relatively calm about not checking if another responsible adult is present.

Conducting Imaginal Exposure

Setting the Stage

Before embarking on imaginal exposure, the therapist must consider the physical setting where exposure will take place, scene construction, and the client's ability to imagine phobic stimuli with the attendant affect.

The basic setting for imaginal exposure is a quiet room, prior arrangements to prevent interruptions, and a soft recliner or sofa for the client. A session or two should be scheduled for the purpose of obtaining information regarding the hierarchy of fears, the specific fear stimuli, and the sensory cues that the client associates with the feared situations. For example, in planning imaginal exposure for a checker with the obsession that he or she is killing pedestrians when driving, the therapist will want to know how the interior of the car feels and looks to the client and if there are any odors associated with it. The therapist will also need detailed information about the routes the client typically drives. Do these paths involve city driving with brick buildings and pedestrian crosswalks? Or does the route consist of interstate highways with construction workers walking along the shoulders?

Sample Imaginal Exposure Scene

"You are now in your car driving on a country road. Notice the blue vinyl of the car seats. You hear the vinyl squeak as you shift the way you are sitting. You have your hands around the blue plastic steering wheel. It feels cool in your hand. You feel the pressure of your foot against the gas pedal. You are on the road, surrounded by nothing but wide open blue skies and the colorful trees lining the road.

"Oh no! As you look up, you see an orange sign on your right. As you get closer, you can make the black letters out against the orange sign, 'Caution. Road work ahead.' Your heart is beating faster. Now you see the big orange and white striped barrels. Beyond them are piles and piles of brown earth, rusty orange bulldozers, and several men. You want to turn back, to be as far away as possible from them. You are fighting the impulse to flee the scene because you are trying so hard to follow your therapist's instructions to face your fears.

"You are forcing yourself to drive by the road workers. You are looking at them now. You see them in their yellow hard hats. They are all wearing blue denim pants, work boots, and flannel shirts. Some are holding shovels in their hands. There seems to be a ditch just beyond where they are standing. You feel sick. Why do they have to stand so close to the highway?

"The dread is washing over you. You feel *sure* that you hit the one with the black hair sticking out of the hard hat. You are almost certain that you heard the crash of the metal of your car hitting his shovel. You felt the thud of the car hitting his body. You are thinking, 'No, it didn't happen, I've gone through this image a thousand times. It has never happened.' You force yourself to drive on. You want desperately to look back, to make sure everything is all right. But your therapist has instructed you to totally give up checking. But this seems so real.

"You pull onto the shoulder of the highway. Did it happen or not? The wish to know is overpowering. You push aside your therapist's instructions. You are now looking in your rear view mirror. You see a swarm of yellow hard hats gathered together looking down into the ditch. You feel sicker. This really could be real. You step out onto the road shoulder and walk to the gathering of men. Their angry faces are turned toward you.

"As you get closer, you can see into the ditch. You see the limp body in the ditch. Your stomach flip flops. Your legs feel like lead. You want with all your being for him to be alive. You *have* to know. You jump in the ditch and grab his wrist. No, no pulse. You see the trickle of red blood coming from his mouth. You put your palm under his nose. No breath. His chest is not rising. His brown eyes are open, with a fixed, blank stare. Now, the doubt is gone. You know for sure that you have killed a man. Your negligence caused this. You were out of control. Your worst fear finally happened."

This session should continue with variants of the last part of this scene being repeated until habituation occurs. Imaginal exposure sessions are usually lengthy, often 90 minutes to 2 hours, in order to permit habituation. For homework exposure, the client is given a tape of the scene to be listened to daily.

RESPONSE PREVENTION

Response prevention is an important component of treatment for OCD. It consists of blocking the performance of the compulsive rituals. While exposure is the treatment of choice for OCD, it must be used in tandem with response prevention for maximum efficacy (Foa, Steketee, & Milby, 1980). The performance of rituals has a powerful reinforcement value in

OCD. If the purpose of rituals is conceptualized as reducing anxiety aroused by obsessive material, it is clear that their continued performance would interfere with the natural habituation that usually occurs with exposure therapy.

Behavior therapists have implemented response prevention both in extremely strict and in more graduated ways. In the early days of behavior treatment for OCD, the rituals were immediately and completely blocked. For example, a person with a washing compulsion would be limited to one 10-minute shower per week and absolutely no handwashing. A checker would similarly be prohibited from carrying out checking of any sort. Treatment was often conducted in a psychiatric hospital where staff closely monitored compliance with response prevention.

Exposure and response prevention are now frequently conducted on an outpatient basis, and response prevention instructions parallel the level of exposure the client is undergoing. For example, the exposure hierarchy for someone who washes due to AIDS fears might consist of doorknobs, shopping cart handles, and handrails at the low end; public restrooms, physician and dental offices at the moderate level; and AIDS clinics and blood at the high end. The response prevention protocol for such a client would typically consist of limiting showering to once every two days and eliminating handwashing. However, allowances for handwashing might be made if the client came in contact with a contaminant at a level on the exposure hierarchy that had not yet been reached. For example, a client who was dealing with low level contaminants in the hierarchy but then visited a public restroom, would be allowed a 5-second handwash, provided he or she immediately touched public handrails or doorknobs to recontaminate with low level stimuli.

Not all clients with OCD are capable of adhering to response prevention guidelines on their own. This treatment is extremely stressful and requires a great deal of motivation. If treatment is being conducted on an outpatient basis, it is often helpful if the client has a relative or friend who can supervise compliance with response prevention. However, clients for whom the rituals are ego-syntonic, who are under an inordinate amount of stress from other sources, or whose OCD is exceptionally severe, may need to have their intervention take place in a hospital where response prevention can be more closely supervised.

PROGRESSIVE RELAXATION

In the 1920s, Edmund Jacobson, a physiologist, published his observations that deep muscle relaxation was an effective treatment for various anxiety disorders (Jacobson, 1974). Since then, behaviorally oriented clinicians have adopted variations of progressive muscle relaxation into their repertoires. Although relaxation alone has been found beneficial in the treatment of some anxiety disorders, it seems to be even more helpful when incorporated into a multicomponent intervention, such as systematic desensitization, applied relaxation, or anxiety management training. Procedures for progressive relaxation will be discussed in this section, followed by presentations of these multicomponent treatments.

One commonly used method of relaxation training was developed by Bernstein and Borkovec (1973). It consists of training the client to attend to, tense, and relax, what are initially treated as 16 separate muscle groups of the body. Once the client has mastered this step, the muscle groups are reorganized, at first into 7 groups, then into 4 groups. The client ultimately learns to quickly identify and release any sign of muscular tension throughout his or her body, as a whole.

Preparations

As was the case with imaginal exposure, an appropriate setting is important for effective relaxation training to occur. The therapist should use a quiet room with dim lights. A soft recliner, designed to completely support one's body, should be provided for the client. He or she should be advised beforehand to wear comfortable, loose-fitting clothing. Glasses, watches, and shoes should be removed before the training begins.

First Phase: 16 Muscle Groups

Relaxation training begins with the therapist and client agreeing upon a signal the therapist may use to indicate when tensing and relaxing should take place. The therapist then instructs the client to close his or her eyes and to tense the dominant hand and forearm by making a fist at the signal. The therapist waits for 5 to 7 seconds to pass before signaling for the tension to be released. During this interim, the therapist calls attention to the feeling of tension. Bernstein and Borkovec (1973) suggest that the therapist make a brief comment such as, "Feel the muscles pull, notice what it is like to feel tension in these muscles as they pull and remain hard and tight" (p. 26). Upon giving the signal to relax, the therapist similarly directs the client's attention to the sensation of releasing the tension, to the contrast between tension and relaxation. The process of tensing and relaxing the dominant hand and forearm is then repeated.

Each muscle group receives at least two cycles of tensing and relaxing. The therapist proceeds to the next muscle group once he or she is confident that complete relaxation of the previous one has taken place. Each of the following 16 muscle groups are attended to in this way:

1. Dominant hand and forearm
2. Dominant biceps

3. Nondominant hand and forearm
4. Nondominant biceps
5. Forehead
6. Upper cheek and nose
7. Lower cheek and jaws
8. Neck and throat
9. Chest, shoulders and upper back
10. Abdomen or stomach
11. Dominant thigh
12. Dominant calf
13. Dominant foot
14. Nondominant thigh
15. Nondominant calf
16. Nondominant foot

After this entire network of muscle groups has been relaxed, the therapist conducts a review to ensure that the client has been able to relax the entire system. The client is asked to signal if there is even a little tension anywhere, and problem areas receive additional tensing and relaxing. The client leaves each session with the homework assignment to repeat this process twice per day.

Second Phase: 7 Muscle Groups

Once the client has mastered deep relaxation by focusing on each of the above 16 muscle groups, the therapist initiates relaxation training with the following 7 muscle groups:

1. Dominant arm and hand
2. Nondominant arm and hand
3. Facial group
4. Neck and throat
5. Chest, shoulders, upper back, and abdomen
6. Dominant leg and foot
7. Nondominant leg and foot

Third Phase: 4 Muscle Groups

When the client can reliably accomplish deep relaxation using 7 muscle groups, training with just these 4 muscle groups is begun:

1. Both arms and hands
2. Face and neck
3. Chest, shoulders, back, and abdomen
4. Both legs and feet

Final Touches

Once the client has mastered progressive relaxation, the next step is graduation to relaxation through recall. The client is instructed to notice any existing feelings of tension, to remember how those areas felt when relaxed, and to relax them.

After relaxation through recall has been practiced several times, the client is trained in differential relaxation. The client is instructed to go about his or her day noticing which muscles are unnecessarily tense, given the tasks being performed. For example, sitting at a desk requires a certain amount of muscle tension in the neck, back, and abdomen. However the facial muscles, arms, hands, legs, and feet could be completely relaxed. The client is advised to practice releasing the unnecessary tension from these muscle groups. Homework is assigned to practice differential relaxation while engaged in differing activities, some requiring more muscle tension and movement than others.

Relaxation Induced Anxiety

Some chronically anxious clients are not initially amenable to treatment via relaxation training. These are people for whom the process of relaxing induces heightened anxiety or even panic attacks (Heide & Brokovec, 1984). It is speculated that, for them, the process of releasing muscular tension is associated with a frightening loss of control. An appropriate intervention for such clients is graduated exposure to relaxation, with emphasis on their control over how fully and when they relax.

SYSTEMATIC DESENSITIZATION

Systematic desensitization, a combination of relaxation and mild, graduated exposure, has long been used as an intervention for phobias (Wolpe, 1973) and more recently has become one of the treatments for PTSD (Bowen & Lambert, 1985).

Systematic desensitization was once thought to be based on the principle of reciprocal inhibition. That is, the experience of anxiety was thought to be inhibited by the experience of a competing response, such as relaxation. However, it is probably more likely that systematic desensitization works by (a) enhancing imagery, enabling the client to process anxious stimuli more completely, and (b) reducing arousal to allow more rapid habituation.

As with other forms of exposure treatment, desensitization may be conducted imaginally or *in vivo*. However, if imaginal treatment is provided, the client usually receives homework instructions to conduct *in vivo* desensitization to stimuli that have been dealt with imaginally in the office sessions.

Procedures

In implementing systematic desensitization therapy, the first several sessions are devoted to training the client in progressive relaxation and to constructing the hierarchy of anxiety-inducing material to be used for desensitization. Once the client is able to relax quickly and deeply, sessions are used for desensitization.

Desensitization conducted imaginally begins with the client in a relaxed state. Starting with material very low on the hierarchy, the therapist introduces anxiety-arousing material. The therapist briefly describes a scene intended to generate slight anxiety and instructs the client to really be in the situation. The therapist lets the client stay with the image for 5 to 7 seconds, then gives instructions to turn off the scene and asks for the level of SUDS generated by the image. The client is instructed to resume relaxation, and, after allowing 20 to 30 seconds for him or her to do so, the therapist either returns to the first scene or introduces the next one. The therapist moves on to the next scene in the hierarchy, only after the previous scene elicits 0 SUDS. Some scenes will, therefore, be presented only once, whereas others may need 10 repetitions paired with relaxation.

Case Example

This hypothetical case example involves systematic desensitization of a young woman presenting with social phobia, specifically fear of public speaking. As is typical with many speech phobics, this young woman expects her audience to be critical of her. It is especially difficult for her to write or otherwise perform a task in front of others because she fears that her hands will tremble and cause her to fumble.

Hierarchy

The following is an abbreviated version of a hierarchy for this speech phobic:

1. Making a 5-minute speech to a group of three people whom she knows; she is sitting; faces are friendly.
2. Making a 5-minute speech to a group of three people whom she knows; she is standing behind a podium; faces are friendly.
3. Making a 5-minute speech to a group of 10 people whom she knows; she is standing behind a podium; faces are friendly.
4. Making a 10-minute speech to a group of 10 people whom she knows; she is standing behind a podium; faces are friendly.
5. Making a 10-minute speech to a group of 10 people whom she knows; she is standing, no podium; faces are friendly.
6. Making a 10-minute speech to a group of 10 strangers; she is standing, no podium; faces are friendly.
7. Making a 10-minute speech to a group of 10 strangers; she is standing, no podium; faces are neutral.
8. Making a 10-minute speech to a group of 10 strangers; she is standing, no podium; faces are bored.
9. Making a 10-minute speech to a group of 10 strangers; she is standing, no podium, faces are critical.
10. In addition to 9, she must write a brief outline on the chalkboard in front of the audience.
11. In addition to 9, she must write an extensive outline on the chalkboard in front of the audience.
12. While she is writing the extensive outline in front of the critical audience, her hand trembles.
13. While she is writing the outline in front of the critical audience, her hand trembles, causing the chalk to break.

Desensitization

This client would first receive instruction in progressive relaxation until she was able to relax through recall. Information for hierarchy construction would be simultaneously gathered.

In the first desensitization session, the client would be given instructions regarding the finger signal to acknowledge scene induction and regarding the use of SUDS. She would then be allowed 5 minutes in which to completely relax.

The therapist would introduce the first image, "You are seated with your three acquaintances in front of you. You are speaking from your notes. As you look at your audience of three, you see them smiling. See them now." The client would raise her left index finger to indicate that she had the image. After 7 seconds, the therapist would ask for a SUDS report, then advise the client to focus on relaxing. If the SUDS score were any higher than 0 the therapist would repeat the image, ask for a second SUDS report, and reintroduce relaxation. The therapist would present the second scene on the hierarchy only after a SUDS score of 0 was attained.

The same strategy would be used as therapist and client worked their way up the entire hierarchy. This intervention would probably require a course of ten 45-minute desensitization sessions. The client would also be instructed to engage in graded *in vivo* desensitization to the situations in her hierarchy. For example, she could make use of opportunities at her place of work to present reports to co-workers, gradually inviting an increasingly larger number of them to sit in on her presentations.

APPLIED RELAXATION AND ANXIETY MANAGEMENT TRAINING

Applied relaxation (AR) and anxiety management training (AMT) are different terms used to describe very similar treatment processes. Like systematic desensitization, AR and AMT involve a combination of exposure and relaxation training. Unlike systematic desensitization, they stress the use of relaxation as an active coping mechanism. Their purpose is not to extinguish anxiety directly, but to give the client a sense of empowerment in dealing with anxiety. Anxiety is thought to fade secondarily to the client's increased confidence in his or her coping ability.

AR or AMT is the recommended treatment for generalized anxiety disorder (Butler, Cullington, Hibbert, Klimes, & Gelder, 1987; Suinn, 1990; Tarrier & Main, 1986). These procedures are also helpful in the treatment of some simple phobias (Ost, Lindahl, Sterner, & Jerremalm, 1984), panic (Ost, 1988), and social phobia (Jerremalm, Jansson, & Ost, 1986).

There are several variations in the way in which different professionals conduct what they call either AR or AMT. Ost (1987) recommends that the following be included in the AR treatment package:

1. Rationale that applied relaxation is a skill, requiring practice, the goals of which are to be able to relax quickly and to counteract anxiety in any situation.
2. Training in identifying early anxiety signals
3. Progressive relaxation
4. Relaxation through release-only: The client no longer alternates between tension and release, but relaxes the muscle groups directly.
5. Cue-controlled relaxation: Relaxation is conditioned to exhaling.

6. Differential relaxation
7. Rapid relaxation: Using neutral cues in nonstressful situations, the client learns to relax within 20 to 30 seconds.
8. Application training: This involves several sessions, each devoted to exposure to a variety of anxiety-inducing stimuli. The presentation of each stimulus is much briefer (10 to 15 minutes) than it would be if pure exposure therapy were being conducted and much longer than in the case of systematic desensitization. The client is encouraged to relax before approaching each stimulus, to identify the first physiological symptoms of anxiety experienced upon confronting the stimulus, and to control the anxiety through relaxation.

Treatment Variations

In addition to muscle relaxation, Suinn (1990) emphasizes the use of relaxing imagery as a coping strategy. In Suinn's (1990) version of AMT, clients first receive training in both muscle relaxation and the development of imagery. They are then guided in using muscle relaxation and relaxing imagery as ways of dealing with anxiety-inducing images ranked on a hierarchy of increasing difficulty. As therapy progresses, the length of exposure to the anxiety scenes and their intensity increase, enabling the client to build confidence that he or she can cope with situations high on the hierarchy. Once the client becomes proficient in coping with anxiety induced imaginally, he or she is assigned homework to practice anxiety management strategies in anxiety-inducing *in vivo* situations.

Yet another variant of coping interventions involves the use of cognitive strategies. Although AR and AMT are usually considered purely behavioral techniques, some clinicians (e.g., Butler et al., 1987) instruct their clients to use self-talk strategies to cope with distressing thoughts.

Caveat

Workshops in anxiety or stress management have become popular offerings in public mental health clinics and college counseling centers. Typically, these workshops involve a 1 to 3 session format in which the participants are instructed in the basic coping strategies. Although such training may be helpful for the average person wishing to expand his or her repertoire of coping skills, these workshops do not constitute adequate treatment for anxiety-disordered clients. People dealing with anxiety of clinical proportions often need a great deal of guidance in mastering relaxation techniques and in learning to cope with anxiety-inducing stimuli. If they fail to benefit from participation in a brief workshop, they may unnecessarily lose faith in themselves, behavioral techniques, or both.

SOCIAL SKILLS TRAINING

Although exposure therapy and applied relaxation have been found helpful in the treatment of social anxiety, behavioral therapists treating this disorder should also be aware of the utility of social skills training (SST). SST used alone has demonstrated efficacy in treating social phobia (Stravynski, Marks, & Yule, 1982), and clinicians may wish to combine it with another treatment approach, such as exposure.

When used in the treatment of social phobia, SST's purpose is to increase the client's sense of social competency, thereby decreasing the feelings of awkwardness and embarrassment that contribute to social anxiety. Additionally, the person who learns to put his or her best foot forward is more likely to experience positive results when interacting with others. Interactions then become less aversive and, thereby, less anxiety-inducing.

It is essential that, prior to initiating SST, the therapist carefully evaluate the nature of the client's social skill deficits. Information is best gathered not only through interviewing the client, but also by observing him or her in various social situations. If SST is provided in a group setting, a ready-made social microcosm is available in which to observe each client. For SST conducted individually, the therapist may need to engage some confederates to arrange social situations in which to observe the client.

Deficits commonly displayed by socially anxious people include failure to maintain eye contact, failure to initiate conversation with others, an excessively soft voice, withdrawn body posture, and constricted affect. The therapist will need to observe the client for these and other socially inappropriate behaviors and to identify what type of situation is most likely to elicit them. Does the client interact smoothly when in a same-sex group, but clam up and look down when in the presence of the opposite sex? Does his or her voice fall and facial expression freeze only when in a public-speaking situation? The therapist needs such specific information to arrange suitable situations in which behavioral practice will take place.

Once the skill deficits are identified, the therapist acts as a coach, instructing the client in corrective behaviors, modeling them, setting up situations in which the client can practice appropriate behaviors, and giving specific feedback and reinforcement. The client may find it extremely informative if the practice sessions are videotaped and the tapes used for feedback purposes. Formal role-plays directed by the therapist are useful for beginning skill practice. A less structured situation, such as engaging in open-ended conversation with a confederate, is an intermediate step to be used before sending the client out to engage in totally unstructured real world practice. Ideally, the client will have met several real-life challenges before the conclusion of treatment. He or she then has the opportunity to refine the progress by consulting with the therapist about the outside interactions, what could have been done differently, and to practice those behaviors in the therapeutic setting.

Case Example

A young man, currently in treatment at our program, reported severe anxiety when interaction with others was required of him. His behavior reflected the extreme discomfort he experienced in these situations. When first observed walking down the hall, his shoulders were hunched forward, and his eyes were downcast. He continued to avoid eye contact as he met the interviewer, and his affect was flat. His responses even to open-ended questions were brief, and he introduced little information on his own. His voice was barely audible. His demeanor was so striking that the interviewer's first diagnostic impression was schizotypal personality disorder. This proved to be false; this client was eager for the social relationships he was unable to form.

As the interview progressed, it became clear that social anxiety and social skill deficits were interfering with his functioning. He was unemployed and hunting for a job. He found it extremely difficult to deal with the people in personnel departments and employment agencies. He also wanted to return to college, but was discouraged at the prospect because when he last attended school he was lonely and did not know how to make friends, male or female. It was also evident to the interviewer that this young man's withdrawn behavior would not enhance his chances of gaining employment or making friends.

Individually conducted SST is now underway for this client. Because gaining employment is so important to him, both for monetary and self-esteem reasons, SST began with role-plays in which he made job inquiries of the therapist who played a personnel officer. This young man quickly learned to display appropriate verbal behavior. He answered questions fully and posed his own well-developed questions to the therapist role-playing an employment interviewer. However, voice quality, affect, eye contact, and body posture were more resistant to change. SST is now focused on modifying these behaviors through the use of therapist feedback and modeling. He is also practicing his newly developing skills by making several real job inquiries each week and reviewing this process with the therapist.

It is expected that the focus of SST for this client will soon shift to peer relationships. Through the use of role-plays with confederates, the client will practice participating in conversations while maintaining appropriate voice quality, smiling, looking others in the eye, and keeping his posture upright. Because interacting with other men is easier for him, the confederates will initially be men, but will eventually be replaced by women. Although these peer role-plays will be highly structured by the therapist at first, the client will gradually be given responsibility for determining their scope and direction.

CONCLUSION

We hope that this chapter will have familiarized its readers with the behavioral interventions used for anxiety disorders. However, it does not provide adequate preparation for using these techniques clinically. Anxiety-disordered clients can be quite fragile, and some of these interventions are powerful. Used inappropriately, behavioral therapy may be ineffective or even harmful. Treatment of PTSD provides a case in point. Although Foa et al. (1991) and Keane et al. (1989) indicate that imaginal exposure is helpful for PTSD, there have been clinical reports of Vietnam veterans with PTSD growing worse with this treatment. It is clear that behavioral therapy needs to be expertly conducted. Clinicians interested in using behavioral techniques should obtain specialized training and initially work under the supervision of an experienced behavioral therapist. The following resources are provided for those interested in learning more about behavioral therapy for anxiety disorders.

SUGGESTIONS FOR FURTHER READING

Barlow, D. H., & Cerney, J. A. (1988). *Psychological treatment of panic.* New York: Guilford.

Bernstein, D. A., & Borkovec, T. D. (1973). *Progressive relaxation training.* Champaign, IL: Research Press.

Goldfried, M. R., & Davison, G. C. (1976). *Clinical behavior therapy.* New York: Holt, Rinehart & Winston.

Goldstein, A., & Foa, E. B. (Eds.). (1980). *Handbook of behavioral interventions.* New York: John Wiley & Sons.

Kelly, J. A. (1982). *Social skills training.* New York: Springer.

Mathews, A. M., Gelder, M. G., & Johnston, D. W. (1981). *Agoraphobia: Nature and treatment.* New York: Guilford.

Steketee, G. S. (in press). *Obsessive-compulsive disorder.* New York: Guilford.

Suinn, R. M. (1990). *Anxiety management training.* New York: Plenum.

Turner, S. M., & Beidel, D. C. (1988). *Treating obsessive-compulsive disorder.* New York: Pergamon.

Wolpe, J. (1991). *The practice of behavior therapy* (4th ed.). New York: Pergamon.

TRAINING RESOURCES

Anxiety Disorders Association of America (ADAA), 6000 Executive Blvd., Suite 200, Rockville, MD 20852. ADAA sponsors an annual conference, usually in April. It includes workshops and seminars led by anxiety disorder specialists, some of whom work from a behavioral orientation.

Association for the Advancement of Behavior Therapy (AABT), 15 West 36th St., New York, NY 10018. AABT's annual conference is usually held in November. It also includes workshops and conferences, many of which focus on anxiety disorders, led by behavioral specialists.

REFERENCES

Bernstein, D. A., & Borkovec, T. D. (1973). *Progressive relaxation training.* Champaign IL: Research Press.

Bowen, G. R., & Lambert, J. A. (1985). Systematic desensitization therapy with post-traumatic stress disorder cases. In C. R. Figley (Ed.), *Trauma and its wake: Vol. II: Traumatic stress theory, research and intervention* (pp. 280–291). New York: Brunner/Mazel.

Butler, G., Cullington, A., Hibbert, G., Klimes, I., & Gelder, M. (1987). Anxiety management for persistent generalised anxiety. *British Journal of Psychiatry. 151,* 535–542.

Chambless, D. L. (1990). Spacing of exposure sessions in treatment of agoraphobia and simple phobia. *Behavior Therapy, 21,* 217–260.

Emmelkamp, P. M. G., van Linden van den Heuvell, C., Ruphan, M., & Sanderman, R. (1989). Home-based treatment of obsessive-compulsive patients: Intersession interval and therapist involvement. *Behaviour Research and Therapy, 27,* 89–94.

Foa, E. B., Jameson, J. S., Turner, R. M., & Payne, L. L. (1980). Massed vs. spaced exposure sessions in the treatment of agoraphobia. *Behaviour Research and Therapy, 18,* 333–338.

Foa, E. B., Rothbaum, B. O., Riggs, D. S., & Murdock, T. B. (1991). Treatment of posttraumatic stress disorder in rape victims: A comparison between cognitive-behavioral procedures and counseling. *Journal of Consulting and Clinical Psychology, 59,* 715–723.

Foa, E. B., Steketee, G., & Milby, J. B. (1980). Differential effects of exposure and response prevention in obsessive-compulsive washers. *Journal of Consulting and Clinical Psychology, 48,* 71–79.

Foa, E. B., Steketee, G., Turner, R. M., & Fischer, S. C. (1980). Effects of imaginal exposure to feared disasters in obsessive-compulsive checkers. *Behaviour Research and Therapy, 18,* 449–455.

Ghosh, A., & Marks, I. M. (1987). Self-treatment of agoraphobia by exposure. *Behavior Therapy, 18,* 3–16.

Heide, F. J., & Borkovec (1984). Relaxation-induced anxiety: Mechanisms and theoretical implications. *Behaviour Research and Therapy, 22,* 1–12.

Jacobson, E. (1974). *Progressive relaxation.* Chicago: The University of Chicago Press.

Jerremalm, A., Jansson, L., & Ost, L-G. (1986). Cognitive and physiological reactivity and the effects of different behavioral methods in the treatment of social phobia. *Behaviour Research and Therapy, 24,* 171–180.

Keane, T. M., Fairbank, J. A., Caddell, J. M., & Zimering, R. T. (1989). Implosive (flooding) therapy reduces symptoms of PTSD in Vietnam combat veterans. *Behavior Therapy, 20,* 245–260.

Ost, L-G. (1987). Applied relaxation: Description of a coping technique and review of controlled studies. *Behaviour Research and Therapy, 25,* 397–409.

Ost, L-G. (1988). Applied relaxation vs. progressive relaxation in the treatment of panic disorder. *Behaviour Research and Therapy, 26,* 13–22.

Ost, L-G., Lindahl, I-L., Sterner, U., & Jerremalm, A. (1984). Exposure *in vivo* vs. applied relaxation in the treatment of blood phobia. *Behaviour Research and Therapy, 22,* 205–216.

Ost, L-G., Salkovskis, P. M., & Hellstrom, K. (1991). One-session therapist-directed exposure vs. self-exposure in the treatment of spider phobia. *Behavior Therapy, 22,* 407–422.

Stravynski, A., Marks, I., & Yule, W. (1982). Social skills problems in neurotic outpatients: Social skills training with and without cognitive modification. *Archives of General Psychiatry, 39,* 1378–1385.

Suinn, R. M. (1990). *Anxiety management training.* New York: Plenum.

Tarrier, N., & Main, C. J. (1986). Applied relaxation training for generalised anxiety and panic attacks: The efficacy of a learnt coping strategy on subjective reports. *British Journal of Psychiatry, 149,* 330–336.

Wolpe, J. (1973). *The practice of behavior therapy* (2nd ed.). New York: Pergamon.

CHAPTER 18

Cognitive Therapy of Anxiety Disorders

CORY F. NEWMAN, PhD

The cognitive model of psychopathology and psychotherapy developed by Beck and his collaborators (e.g., Beck, Emery, & Greenberg, 1985; Beck, Freeman, & Associates, 1990; Beck, Rush, Shaw, & Emery, 1979) posits that an individual's affective state is highly influenced by the manner in which the individual perceives and structures his or her experiences. According to this model, patients who suffer from anxiety disorders tend to misperceive particular stimuli and/or life situations as being far more threatening or dangerous than they actually are. Further, such patients compound their problems by underestimating their abilities to cope with these stimuli and situations, thus causing a reduction in self-esteem.

This chapter will focus on the cognitive therapy of three main types of anxiety disorders: (1) generalized anxiety disorder (GAD), which is typified by numerous excessive worries in everyday life coupled with a wide range of physical symptoms; (2) phobic disorders (nonpanic), which are characterized by exaggerated and intense fears of discrete, innocuous stimuli or situations; and (3) panic disorder (with or without agoraphobia), in which patients experience a sudden escalation of fear that seems to come "out of the blue," along with extreme changes in somatic sensations (e.g., rapid heart rate, hyperventilation, dizziness) and a desire to avoid many activities that the patients associate with the onset of attacks.

There are marked similarities between the types of physical symptoms that accompany each of these three classes of anxiety disorders. The most basic similarity is that they all represent increased sympathetic nervous system activity—the "fight, flight, or freeze" reactions that humans evince in response to the perception of danger and risk. In fact, there is considerable overlap between both the symptomatology and treatment of each of these three classes of anxiety disorders, and many patients meet diagnostic criteria for more than one anxiety disorder. However, there are some important distinctions between the aforementioned anxiety disorders that have implications for case conceptualization and treatment

(Clark, 1989), which will be reflected in the case studies reviewed later in this chapter.

The treatment of anxiety disorders often is complicated by collateral problems, such as depression (Barlow, 1988), personality disorders (e.g., avoidant personality disorder and dependent personality disorder) (Sanderson & Beck, 1991), abuse of drugs, alcohol, or prescription anxiolytics as a form of self-medication (Bibb & Chambless, 1986), and strained marital and family relationships (Butler, 1989). The case studies will address these additional problems as well.

COGNITIVE THERAPY: BASIC ELEMENTS

Cognitive therapy attempts to treat anxiety disorders by teaching patients to identify, test, and modify the thoughts and beliefs that accompany their excessive alarm reactions, as well as the avoidance behaviors that perpetuate their faulty appraisals and responses. In similar fashion to cognitive therapy for depressive disorders (Beck et al., 1979; Newman & Beck, 1990), cognitive therapy for anxiety disorders is a collaborative process of investigation, reality testing, and problem solving between therapist and patient. The therapists do not forcefully exhort patients to change their views, nor do they denigrate the patients' thinking styles. Rather, the therapists show respect for their patients, try to accurately understand how the patients have come to develop their problems, and proceed to teach them a set of durable skills that will help them to think more objectively, flexibly, and constructively.

Cognitive therapy is a structured and highly active form of treatment. Anxious patients who report that they often feel "scattered" or "out of control" benefit from therapy sessions in which agendas are set, goals are defined, priorities are established, and problems are concretized. Therapists and patients share the responsibility for the work of therapy, with therapists being willing to respond to direct questions with direct answers, but also using Socratic questioning in order to help patients gradually learn to recognize and solve problems for themselves. Further, the implementation of between-session homework assignments helps patients to translate their new hypotheses and goals into actual behaviors that increase self-esteem, reduce anxieties, fears, and avoidance, and improve the patients' quality of life.

GENERALIZED ANXIETY DISORDER—COGNITIVE CASE PROFILE

The cognitive model of GAD (Beck et al., 1985) proposes that individuals who experience chronic, compelling, and pervasive anxieties maintain beliefs that make them prone to interpret numerous situations as posing risk and threat (Clark, 1988). These beliefs (also called underlying assumptions) often center around themes of personal acceptability, personal adequacy, and control. More specifically, the generally anxious patient may believe that the failure to perform a given task perfectly means that he or she is defective and incompetent. Similarly, such a patient may assume that by making a slight social error he or she will be humiliated, vilified, and cast aside by acquaintances, friends, and loved ones. Further, these patients frequently demonstrate a fear of "what might happen?" if they neglect to take rigorous measures to guarantee favorable outcomes. By holding such beliefs, patients place themselves under excessive and continual pressure to succeed and ward off trouble. These individuals are identifiable in everyday life as people who seem never to relax, who continually feel "keyed up" or "on edge," and who are dubbed as "worry warts" by others in their lives.

For example, Roy is a successful, 47-year-old attorney who seems to have a rather secure and rewarding life. He earns a healthy salary, is well respected by the local legal community as an expert litigator, serves as an officer on the boards of a number of civic organizations, owns a beautiful home, and has a loving wife and two daughters. Nevertheless, Roy sought therapy, as he felt that he was going to "collapse under the strain." When the therapist helped Roy to assess the breadth and depth of his professional and personal activities, it became clear that he was carrying a tremendous burden of responsibilities, the likes of which would be stressful for anyone. These factors alone did not distinguish Roy as suffering from GAD. Instead, it was his *beliefs* about needing to prove himself at every turn that fueled his anxieties and his quest to take part in more and more challenging activities.

To highlight this patient's anxiogenic cognitive style, Roy viewed each trail in which he litigated as "make or break" for his career. Although all the objective evidence suggested that his glowing reputation was secure in the minds of his colleagues and family, Roy believed that "I'm only as good as my last case." Such an outlook led to his overpreparing for his court dates to the point of exhaustion. His anxiety steadily built as each trial drew near, whereupon he would typically utilize his "nervous energy" to put on a tour de force performance that would all but assure a favorable outcome for his clients. Thus, he came to believe that "I have to get myself worked up into a frenzy in order to succeed. If I'm relaxed, I will fail. If I fail, my career will be ruined." Such an absolutistic chain of beliefs dictated that he must never *test* this way of thinking. In Roy's mind, if he so much as attempted to take his wife's advice to "relax a bit" he was certain that the result would be professional disaster. Thus, he silently avoided allowing himself to get some rest and recreation, a tactic that supported the maintenance of his negative beliefs.

Roy's anxiety-producing beliefs didn't stop here, as he also frequently worried about maintaining his financial standing. He reported to his therapist that he often lay awake at night wondering how he would continue to make payments on his very expensive home, cars, country club memberships, daughters' college tuitions, and travel plans if his earnings were to decrease from their current level. Such financial obligations might be daunting to anyone, but Roy's belief system compounded the problem. Specifically, he felt driven to win the love and approval of as many people as possible, and he believed that only a high-profile mixture of affluence and generosity would assure this outcome. Therefore, he actually sought out new financial burdens that he thought would accomplish his goal of social popularity, including the purchasing of a boat and making huge donations to charitable organizations. His erroneous assumption that he would be valued less as a person if he cut back on his expenses fed into his constant worries about money. By the time he sought treatment, Roy was convinced that he no longer could cope with the demands of his life.

SIMPLE AND SOCIAL PHOBIAS—COGNITIVE CASE PROFILE

Phobias are chronic, exaggerated fears of particular stimuli or situations that are in fact not dangerous (Butler, 1989). Patients who suffer from phobias are so impaired by their fears that they experience disruptions in important aspects of their everyday lives. An example is a patient who is so afraid of elevators that she turns down a very attractive job offer solely on the basis of the fact that her office would be on the 30th floor of a high-rise building, thus necessitating the daily use of an elevator.

A *simple* phobia involves a single, specific feared object or situation (e.g., bridges, snakes, sight of blood). Patients who are diagnosed with simple phobias generally do not demonstrate fearfulness as long as they can avoid coming into contact with, or thinking about, their phobic situations. A *social* phobia involves abnormally strong concerns about interpersonal interactions and evaluations. Patients with social phobias usually evidence more pervasive anxiety and fearfulness than simple phobics, as it is considerably more difficult to avoid people than to avoid discrete situations such as heights or snakes.

Social phobics may fear particular aspects of social discourse more than others, such as public speaking or dating. Regardless of the overt elements of social interactions that the patients fear, the underlying concerns are consistent across this diagnostic class of patients. These include expectations of being socially inept and/or experiencing derision and rejection from others. Many social phobics, by virtue of their social avoidance, lock themselves into self-defeating vicious cycles. They so fear botching their chances to win the support, approval, acceptance, and praise of others that they either isolate themselves (thus perpetuating their loneliness and depriving them of opportunities to gain experience in the social realm), or reveal their anxieties by acting awkwardly (thus causing embarrassment and fulfilling their negative prophecies). Some social phobics demonstrate no appreciably noticeable behaviors that would suggest ineptitude in dealing with other people, yet such patients nevertheless assume that they are coming across poorly and that others do not enjoy their company.

"Leslie," a 22-year-old college senior, demonstrated both simple and social phobias. Her simple phobias were specific fears of going to dental and medical appointments. These fears were of such intensity that she had had no check-ups in over four years. One of the reasons for Leslie's entering therapy was her ongoing embarrassment in postponing dental appointments.

The patient's social phobia was especially pronounced in the area of public speaking. Although she was quite secure and adept in having one-on-one conversations with close friends, she generally remained quiet when in the presence of a group of people. Her worst fears concerned having to speak in class. Leslie, as a senior, was taking two advanced level seminars that strongly emphasized the importance of class participation, thus putting her in "peril" of having to answer questions before her professor and classmates on a moment's notice. She had attempted to circumvent this problem by privately asking her professors not to call on her in class, but both instructors agreed to this arrangement only on a temporary basis. Thus, Leslie entered therapy as a "last resort before I have to drop the classes."

Although Leslie's simple and social phobias seemed unrelated on the surface, the patient maintained two underlying beliefs that tied together the two types of fears. Specifically, Leslie believed that, "I cannot tolerate discomfort without becoming a nervous wreck," and "If I become a nervous wreck in front of others they will think I'm crazy and they will reject me." Although the kind of discomfort that Leslie presumed she would experience as a medical or dental patient was physical, while her expected classroom discomfort was psychological, Leslie anticipated that both of these types of experiences would cause her to "become a nervous wreck" in front of others. She envisioned becoming tongue-tied in class, resulting in her screaming in frustration and having to flee from the class. Similarly, she imagined that she would dissolve into tears if her physician recommended a blood test or her dentist suggested that she would have to drill a tooth. Leslie was certain that she would "create a scene," the likes of which would prevent her from ever showing her face to these people again.

PANIC DISORDER AND AGORAPHOBIA—COGNITIVE CASE PROFILE

The cognitive model of panic disorder (Beck & Greenberg, 1988; Clark, 1988; Ehlers, 1991; Greenberg, 1989; Salkovskis & Clark, 1991) holds that individuals produce the onset of attacks by tending to make catastrophic interpretations about a wide range of physical sensations and mental states that they may experience. Exacerbating this habit is the panic patient's hypervigilance to (and dread of) normal changes that take place in the body and mind. The most common misinterpretations that panic patients make include the following:

1. Believing that a rapid heart rate and chest tightness are indicative of an impending coronary and sudden death
2. Viewing difficulty in breathing as leading to asphyxiation
3. Interpreting mental phenomena such as memory flashbacks, déjà vu, senses of unreality and depersonalization, and disruption of attention span as precursors to insanity
4. Expecting that the discomfort associated with a number of symptoms (e.g., dizziness, cardiopulmonary distress, abdominal pain, feeling detached from one's surroundings) will become so intolerable as to cause the patient to "lose control," resulting in a number of dreaded consequences, such as social humiliation (e.g., screaming, fainting, losing control of one's bowels) or committing terrible acts (hurting oneself or loved ones).

Two key factors seem to perpetuate the panic patients' extreme fears: (1) a patient having a panic attack is in such a state of alarm that he or she unwittingly activates the sympathetic nervous system even further. The resultant rush of adrenaline in the bloodstream exacerbates the very symptoms that the patient fears in the first place, thus "confirming" that the symptoms are out of control. (2) Panic patients often avoid situations that the associate with the attacks (e.g., staying away from places that are deemed "unsafe," such as cars, shopping malls, theaters, and any place from which escape will be difficult in the event of emergency), and/or engage in fear-driven rituals (e.g., going to the emergency room of a nearby hospital) at the onset of attacks, thus depriving such patients of ever realizing that their symptoms are not dangerous (Salkovskis, 1988).

For example, an individual may have had a hundred panic attacks in his lifetime, each time fearing that he was having a heart attack. In spite of the fact that no heart attack ever actually occurred, the patient's fear does not extinguish because he believes that his ritualistic actions in response to the attacks (e.g., calling his wife, taking a pill, going to the hospital, escaping from the room) save his life each time. In this way, the patient's thinking style maintains the fear, even in the repeated absence of the feared outcome.

The avoidance that is described above is a prime factor in the development of the agoraphobic component of the disorder (Chambless & Goldstein, 1982). Patients often begin to steer clear of any and all situations that they associate with the likelihood of experiencing a panic attack. Some patients accomplish this goal subtly, such as by making advance plans to obtain theater tickets that will be on an aisle or deliberately sitting in the last pew at church, so that an easy exit can be made if an attack seems imminent. In more severe cases, however, the patient may refuse to venture outside of a very restricted "safe zone" (the definition of which is entirely a product of the patient's beliefs), which sometimes entails remaining completely housebound. Common beliefs that agoraphobic patients maintain include:

1. If I venture outside of my safe zone, I will be bereft of necessary assistance should I have an attack.
2. I cannot cope with anything new and unfamiliar.
3. I need to plan easy escape routes lest I become trapped in a situation in which everyone will discover my mental illness.
4. If I go into a situation in which I previously had a panic attack, I will surely have another attack.
5. Avoiding situations that cause my panic attacks is the best way to eliminate my panic attacks.
6. If I can't avoid situations that cause my panic attacks, I can rely on a "safe person" to take care of me.
7. If I can't rely on a "safe person" to take care of me, I have no choice but to rely on my medications or alcohol.

"Penny" is a 35-year-old single woman who suffers from both panic disorder and agoraphobia. Although she successfully meets the demands of her high-level, white-collar job without suffering appreciable anxiety, she has great difficulty in coping with traveling moderate distances or staying at home alone. Thus, when her roommate got married and moved out, Penny felt compelled to ask her boyfriend to move in with her in order to make her feel safe from panic attacks, even though she had no intention of making the relationship more serious. Unfortunately, the boyfriend took the invitation to move in as a sign that Penny was looking to get married, and he began to talk about plans for their future. Penny felt trapped; on the one hand she believed that she needed her boyfriend in order to help her to cope with her anxiety, but to keep him close by meant that she would have to abandon her dreams of becoming involved with another man with whom she had fallen in love.

Further complicating Penny's dilemma was the fact that she felt very guilty for "using" her boyfriend in this way. This feeling in and of itself often triggered panic attacks, characterized by heart palpitations and breathing difficulties that were so severe that she thought she was going to suffocate. Ironically, the boyfriend was well-schooled in coming to Penny's aid when she would experience these symptoms, thus becoming both her source of comfort and guilt at the same time.

"Tim," the man with whom Penny was in love, lived approximately 30 miles from her home. Interestingly, Penny claimed that she was unable to travel more than 25 miles from her home without suffering the onset of high anxiety and panic attacks. After two months of therapy, she was able to identify for the first time a very telling automatic thought that would cross her mind whenever she drove close to her limit of 25 miles—namely, "If I drive any further, I might be tempted to go to Tim's house." This thought was accompanied by momentary images of making love to Tim, and she would begin to feel sexually aroused. Both the feelings of guilt and physiological arousal that Penny experienced as a result of these thoughts and images brought on panic attacks, thus effectively dissuading her from considering the possibility that she could drive long distances. In essence, Penny was caught between a figurative sense of suffocation in her relationship with her boyfriend, and actual breathing difficulties brought on by thoughts of becoming involved with Tim. Although Penny could plainly see the interpersonal factors that were feeding her anxiety, panic, and agoraphobia, she continued to believe that any given panic attack could lead to her death by asphyxiation. As a result, she continued to be hypervigilant to changes in her breathing, and avoided all situations in which she believed she might have a panic attack. She remained with her boyfriend and grew increasingly frustrated and anxious.

COGNITIVE CONCEPTUALIZATION AND THERAPY: TECHNIQUES AND STRATEGIES FOR ASSESSMENT AND TREATMENT

As noted, the assessment and treatment of GAD, simple and social phobias, and panic (with or without agoraphobia) entail some basic similarities. In each of these types of anxiety disorders, the cognitive therapist strives to do the following:

1. Assess the patients' thoughts that precede, accompany, and follow typical situations where anxieties, fears, panic, and avoidance occur.
2. Assess the patients' core beliefs that underlie their automatic thoughts about themselves (and their disorders), their lives, and their futures.
3. Review the patients' life experiences that fostered such maladaptive core beliefs.
4. Elucidate the current life factors that seem to maintain the patients' problematic thoughts, emotions, and behaviors.

Note: Taken together, these four points comprise a case conceptualization (cf. Persons, 1989).

5. Establish a warm, collaborative, trusting therapeutic relationship as an important part of the process of change.
6. Teach patients to become more objective evaluators of themselves and their life situations. For example, describe to patients the common cognitive distortions of all-or-none thinking, overgeneralizing, fortune-telling, mind-reading, catastrophizing, and other biased processes outlined in Beck et al. (1979) and Burns (1980); then, train patients to respond with alternative, more adaptive responses.
7. Instruct patients in the skills of active problem-solving (Nezu, Nezu, & Perri, 1989) in order to build hope, increase self-efficacy, foster independence, and make meaningful, lasting changes in patients' lives.
8. Help patients to become aware of their most salient areas of vulnerability, so as to prepare for scenarios that might otherwise precipitate relapse.

This section of the chapter will focus first on the treatment of GAD, reviewing many of the strategies and techniques that are pertinent to *all* of the anxiety disorders. Then, as attention turns to the treatment of phobias, more emphasis will be placed on the behavioral aspects of treatment that are so important when patients habitually avoid feared situations. Finally, the case description of panic disorder with agoraphobia will review the highly specific techniques of interoceptive exposure (panic induction), breathing control, and recognition of emotions that are so important with this population (Barlow, 1988; Salkovskis & Clark, 1991). Taken as a whole, the three case studies will explicate many of the key ingredients of cognitive assessment and cognitive therapy for the full range of anxiety disorders.

Assessment and Treatment of GAD: Roy

Roy presented himself as an assertive, gregarious, "take charge" person. He was articulate, speaking with great animation about a recent high-profile case that he won for his firm, and about an upcoming amateur golf tournament that he aspired to win. The therapist began the process of facilitating a positive therapeutic relationship with Roy by giving him appropriate positive feedback for his stories of success, while also showing some sympathy for "all the pressures that you must have to face on a regular basis."

Roy stated that, "I am where I am today [a successful person] because I always go to the limit of my endurance. People have always been able to depend on me, knowing that I can get the job done. I can't go backwards now. I've worked too hard to reach this point to start slacking off."

Over the course of a number of sessions, the therapist was able to demonstrate to Roy that his *beliefs* (e.g., those noted above) played at least as big a role in his anxiety as his actual life demands. Roy's statements revealed that he ascribed all his success in life to his frenetic pace. He gave little credit to his natural abilities, and saw any let-up as an invitation to disaster. Further, it was clear that he highly valued others' being able to depend on him (as he believed that this made him a likable person), and he viewed any diminution in his daily demands as tantamount to "slacking off." Roy's over devotion to work at the expense of his health and personal life, along with his stubbornness, over attention to details, certainty that his points of view were correct, and need to be in control indicated an obsessive-compulsive personality disorder (OCPD) in addition to his GAD diagnosis. By recognizing this aspect of Roy's personality, the therapist was able to formulate methods that would help the patient to change, yet still allow Roy to maintain a much-valued feeling of independence and control.

In order to appeal to Roy's sense of autonomy and in order to minimize resistance (e.g., to the therapists' attempts to get Roy to relax and enjoy life at a slightly slower pace), the therapist taught Roy a number of standard cognitive therapy skills that he could apply on his own. For example, Roy was given the "challenge" (Roy could not resist a challenge!) to take mental inventory of his thoughts at times of high stress. This kind of cognitive self-monitoring is a key ingredient of cognitive therapy, as it teaches patients to recognize how their internal dialogues contribute to their emotional and behavioral reactions.

Roy also was given the task of charting his activities, in order to evaluate where he was "pushing the limit" too far, even by his standards. The therapist was able to motivate Roy to engage in this task by using Socratic questioning in the following manner:

T: Roy, you've told me that you believe that you must maintain your current level of activities in order to succeed. Is that right?

R: Basically.

T: Does your current level of demands fatigue you and place a great strain on you?

R: Yes, of course. That's what we've been talking about.

T: OK then. How *efficient* are you, as an attorney, as a golfer, as a family man, and as an active leader in the community when you're fatigued and wrung out from worrying?

R: Not as efficient as I'd like, but I still get the job done.

T: Roy, believe me, I know that you are capable of accomplishing some extraordinary things. I have a lot of respect and admiration for you, but, do you remember what you said when you entered therapy? Something about a "collapse" being imminent?

R: (Nods.) I felt like an engine about to overheat and break down.

T: That's a great analogy. You've been a super-charged, high-performance engine for a long time. What kind of engine *care* have you been doing in order to keep it from breaking down?

R: Not much. My doctor thinks I'm a candidate for a coronary.

T: And then how efficient will you be?

R: I guess I've got to let the engine recoup once in a while.

T: You said it.

Following this, Roy was willing to keep tabs on, and then eliminate, some of his lower priority activities.

Another important facet of his treatment was Roy's learning how his beliefs fed into his need to over achieve. By taking a close look at Roy's personal history as well as his current thoughts, the therapist and patient were able to ascertain how Roy actually perceived threat and danger if he *didn't* over extend himself in everything he was doing. Earlier in life, his father had demanded perfection from Roy, and fostered an all-or-nothing mentality by ignoring him when Roy would be a "disappointment," and praising him to the sky when he would make him "proud to be your father." The message was clear—"You'll be loved if you are the best. Anything less than that and you will be inadequate and a disappointment." In the present, Roy lived out this credo by going to great lengths to be the best—not just out of a need to succeed—but as a way to avoid deprivation of love and nurturance. This realization opened the therapeutic door for Roy to attempt new ways of *thinking* (e.g., "I can turn this case over to my colleagues and still be held in high esteem by the firm. Meanwhile I'll have a little more time to relax!" and "I can perform my job at 95% efficiency and still win the lion's share of my cases. 100% isn't always necessary, and it's best that I pace myself at times.") and *acting* (e.g., clearing an entire morning off of his Wednesday schedule in order to swim or play a *leisurely* game of golf with his wife). Roy's therapeutic improvement showed itself not only in his subjective sense of well-being, but also in his decreased blood pressure.

Assessment and Treatment of Phobias: Leslie

Leslie entered therapy hoping that she could rid herself of her fears of public speaking, as well as her trepidation of seeing her physician and dentist. Unfortunately, it had not occurred to her that part of her treatment might entail directly confronting her fears. The therapist explained to the patient that exposure to the feared situations was an important part of the treatment package (cf. Butler, 1985), and assured her that he would do everything he could to teach her a set of skills that would help her to get through the "ordeals" in such a way that she would find the feared situations progressively more tolerable. In the end, a critical achievement would be Leslie's increased self-confidence as a result of her in vivo practice.

The therapist's simply discussing this aspect of treatment brought forth a flood of tears from the patient. He asked Leslie what was going through her mind that made her so upset, whereupon Leslie replied, "I can't do it. I just can't do it." The therapist asked Leslie why she believed so strongly that she was incapable of dealing directly with feared situations. The patient explained that she had been a fearful person all her life. She added that most of her mother's side of the family suffered from anxieties and phobias as well. She concluded that her "cowardice was inborn," therefore it was inevitable that she would always feel incapacitated by fears. She said, "I'm just like my mother, my grandmother and my uncle . . . we can't tolerate anything uncomfortable. We're all pathetic. I'm ashamed of my family, and I'm ashamed of myself."

The therapist acknowledged that there seemed to be a hereditary component to her disorder. He also silently realized that Leslie's phobias probably were part of an avoidant personality disorder, a common diagnosis in people who have such long histories of fears and avoidance (indeed, she met diagnostic criteria for the disorder, as per the DSM-III-R, APA, 1987). However, he began to question Leslie's conclusions in an attempt to have her rethink some of her suppositions. Some of the questions that the therapist asked Leslie to ponder were:

- Do you have *all* your mother's genes? What role does your father play in your genetic make-up? How fearful is *he?*
- How much of your fearfulness and lack of self-worth was *learned?*

- What are some memorable experiences that you've had in your life where you *learned* to fear things?
- What are some *differences* between you and your mother? Did she go to college like you? Did she get along well with friends on a one-to-one basis the way that you do?

Leslie was intrigued by these questions. She admitted that her father seemed "normal" in that he wasn't fazed by very much. Also, she noted that, unlike herself, her mother never went to college, as the mother was afraid of dealing with all the social and scholastic demands. The therapist asked Leslie what she could conclude from this, and the patient said, "I guess I'm not as hopeless as my mother after all. It just seems that way sometimes because certain things frighten me."

With this incremental increase in hope, Leslie was willing to start working on her self-image, as well as her exaggerated senses of risk and danger in speaking in class. An important tool to be used in this process was the Daily Thought Record (DTR) (Figure 18.1). The standard format of the DTR presents patients with five columns in which they write about:

1. Problematic situations,
2. Concomitant emotions,
3. Dysfunctional automatic thoughts,
4. Adaptive alternative thoughts, and
5. The outcome of the DTR exercise (in terms of resultant emotions and residual belief in the dysfunctional automatic thoughts).

The DTR is a powerful part of therapy if patients persevere in practicing its use on a regular basis. The most critical sections of the DTR are the third and fourth columns—"automatic thoughts," and "adaptive responses." In column three, patients ask themselves what they are thinking during their times of emotional distress. This helps to concretize the problem, to demystify the emotions that seem to arise out of nowhere, and to start the process of the patients' beginning to open their minds to more constructive ways of viewing their situations. Such adaptive (or "rational") thinking, which is recorded in column four, often leads to decreased anxiety and improved problem-solving skills and self-esteem.

In order to facilitate the process of discovering adaptive responses, the therapist instructed Leslie to ask herself the following four questions in response to her automatic thoughts:

1. What is the *evidence* that supports or refutes my automatic thoughts and beliefs?

Situation	Emotion(s)	Automatic Thought(s)	Adaptive Response	Outcome
I asked Dr. Gilbert (after class) if he could refrain from asking me questions in class due to my problems with public speaking. He seemed impatient and told me I would have to participate in class-room discussions in order to pass the course.	Embarrassed Scared Helpless	1. He thinks I'm an idiot, that I'm pathetic.	1. I'm mindreading here. I don't know how he really views me. He *did* give me good feedback on my paper.	Still somewhat scared and embarrassed
		2. I'll never be able to speak up in class. I'm hopeless.	2. I'm fortune-telling here. I don't know what the future will bring. Maybe therapy will help me to get over my fears.	Much less helpless
		3. I'm a failure.	3. This is personalizing and overgeneralizing. Failing at one task does not make me a failure as a person.	
		4. I'll die if Dr. Gilbert calls on me in class.	4. This is catastrophizing. I won't die. I'll feel embarrassed, but this isn't the end of the world.	
		5. I should just drop the course.	5. This is avoidance. I refuse to interrupt my education because I'm scared! I want to graduate on time! That's more important than avoiding anxiety.	
		6. I should quit school altogether.	6. I've been through 3 years of college and I have a 3.0 GPA. I've earned the right to graduate and to be proud. I will *not* quit.	

Figure 18.1. Leslie's Daily Thought Record (DTR) regarding speaking in class.

For example, when Leslie predicted that her mind would go blank if she tried to answer a question in class, she was asked to review her scholastic history in order to judge how well she had done in similar situations in the past. Leslie noted that she was inexperienced in answering questions on the spot in class, but there had *never* been an episode when her mind went blank and when she had to leave the class out of embarrassment.

2. What are some other ways that I can view this situation?

Leslie believed that her fears of social evaluation would cause her to make a fool of herself in class, and that she would be so embarrassed that she'd run out of the room screaming. However, there were many other plausible ways to view the situation. First, Leslie's anxiety might be barely noticeable to others, and though she might struggle to answer the questions, she might very well succeed in answering correctly. Second, even if she didn't know how to answer the professor's questions, the other students might be sympathetic, rather than hostile and rejecting. Third, even if the other students chuckled at Leslie's answer, they might forget about the matter in a few minutes, and still remain on friendly terms with her. Fourth, if Leslie were to try to participate more actively in class discussions, she conceivably could *improve* her performance, thus resulting in better grades and increased self-confidence.

3. Realistically, what is the worst case scenario, and how would it ultimately affect my life?

Though Leslie visualized academic and social catastrophe, the actual worst case scenario was less noxious. When the patient pondered this question, she realized that the worst that could happen would be that she would fail to answer the question, and that she would blush and feel embarrassed. While this would make her feel uneasy, it would not portend failure and loneliness for the rest of her life.

4. What active steps can I take to solve this problem?

Since many clinically anxious patients spend more time and energy worrying about problems than trying to do something about them, this question becomes quite useful in turning their attention to the issue of problem solving. The therapist taught Leslie to recognize when she was catastrophizing, and to use this as her cue to "shift into problem-solving mode." In the present example, Leslie dealt actively with her concerns by increasing her study time, practicing answering questions in role-play exercises with both the therapist and her boyfriend, and by making a small foray into the area of speaking in class by *asking* questions. Later, she would agree to begin to *answer* questions by volunteering to comment on the topics in which she had the most knowledge. This graded-hierarchy was a vital part of her treatment, as it helped her to tolerate increments of social discomfort a little at a time.

As Leslie began to utilize the four questions outlined above, she agreed to compose a hierarchy of feared social situations that she would tackle step by step. She practiced her use of the four questions in order to prepare mentally for the exercise, and then experimented with the new behaviors (e.g., asking questions in class). Her anxiety persisted at first, but she was pleasantly surprised by the positive results of her attempts to confront her feared situations directly. These positive outcomes instilled a more optimistic view of herself and her abilities, and her avoidance decreased further.

At present, Leslie's social phobia has markedly diminished, and she continues to work in cognitive therapy in order to deal with her simple phobias of going to see the dentist and physician. The same principles of adaptive responding (through the use of the DTR and the four questions) and behavioral experiments are being utilized in these areas of concern as well.

Assessment and Treatment of Panic Disorder: Penny

Penny's responses to the Panic Beliefs Questionnaire (Greenberg, 1989) indicated that she strongly believed that:

1. She was especially vulnerable to panic attacks if she were alone.
2. Intense emotions were dangerous and needed to be avoided.
3. It was important to be vigilant in monitoring her bodily sensations (see Figure 18.2).

In spite of the fact that this patient was a successful businesswoman (and therefore seemed to be quite independent), she met DSM-III-R (APA, 1987) criteria for the diagnosis of dependent personality disorder (DPD). Further complicating the clinical picture were the patient's problematic over-reliance on her medication, as well as her discord, ambivalence, and guilt in her relationship with her boyfriend.

A review of the etiology of Penny's panic attacks revealed that they began approximately four years earlier, ten months after her mother died suddenly of a severe asthma attack. The patient had been extremely close to her mother, who had served as the patient's best friend, confidante, and guidance counselor. At the time of the mother's death, Penny alternated between a catatonic-like state of shock, and fits of anxiety and rage. Her physician sedated her heavily on large doses of Xanax, which

Panic Belief Questionnaire

NAME: _____Penny_____   DATE: _____October 27_____

Please rate how strongly you believe each statement on a scale from 1–6, as follows:

1 = Totally Disagree   3 = Disagree Slightly   5 = Agree Very Much
2 = Disagree Very Much   4 = Agree Slightly   6 = Totally Agree

__5__ 1. Having a bad panic attack in a situation means I will definitely have one there again.

__3__ 2. Having panic attacks means I'm weak, defective or inferior.

__5__ 3. If people see me having a panic attack, they'll lose respect for me.

__5__ 4. I'll have disabling panic attacks for the rest of my life.

__4__ 5. Exerting myself physically during a panic attack could cause me to have a heart attack and die.

__4__ 6. If I have panic attacks, it means there's something terribly wrong with me.

__4__ 7. I'm only safe if I can control every situation I'm in.

__5__ 8. I'll never be able to forget about panic attacks and enjoy myself.

__4__ 9. If I have to wait in line or sit still, there's a good chance I'll lose control, scream, faint, or start crying.

__3__ 10. There's something wrong with me that the doctors haven't found yet.

__5__ 11. I must be watchful or something terrible will happen.

__3__ 12. If I lose my fear of panic attacks, I might overlook other symptoms that are dangerous.

__3__ 13. If my children (or others close to me) see me having panic attacks, they'll become fearful and insecure.

__*6__ 14. I have to keep checking how my body is reacting or I might have a panic attack.

__2__ 15. Crying too much could cause a heart attack.

__4__ 16. I have to escape the situation when I start having symptoms or something terrible could happen.

__4__ 17. There's only so much anxiety my heart can take.

__4__ 18. There's only so much anxiety my nervous system can take.

__5__ 19. Anxiety can lead to loss of control and doing something awful or embarrassing.

__*6__ 20. My emotions (anxiety, anger, sadness, or loneliness) could become so strong I wouldn't be able to tolerate them.

__3__ 21. Panicking while driving or while stuck in traffic is likely to cause an accident.

__5__ 22. A panic attack can give me a heart attack.

__*6__ 23. A panic attack can kill me.

__4__ 24. A panic attack can drive me insane.

__2__ 25. A little anxiety means I'll be as bad as I was at my worst.

__*6__ 26. I could experience terrible emotion that never ends.

__*6__ 27. Expressing anger is likely to lead to losing control or provoking a fight.

__5__ 28. I could lose control of my anxiety and become trapped in my own mind.

__4__ 29. It could be dangerous to carry on my usual activities during a panic attack.

__*6__ 30. I must be near my companion to be protected from panic.

Figure 18.2 Penny's panic beliefs at intake. (Note the importance of the asterisked beliefs.)

were effective in helping Penny to function socially and vocationally in the months following the tragedy.

Ten months after her mother's death, Penny decided to go off the medication all at once and, as a consequence, experienced numerous, intense panic attacks. She immediately resumed use of the anxiolytic medication, and continued to do so for four years. At the same time, she began a friendship with a man at work who seemed very nurturing. Although she didn't love him, Penny believed that she needed someone to take care of her as her mother always had.

In the years to come, Penny settled into a "comfortable" routine with the boyfriend. She believed she needed him in order to prevent her panic attacks from ruining her life, yet she was vaguely aware that the relationship had no future. This realization increased her anxiety and panic attacks to the point where even high dosages of Xanax (e.g., 4 mg/day) were insufficient treatment. At this time, she sought help at the Center for Cognitive Therapy.

It was noted that Penny's most salient catastrophic fear was that her panic attacks would make her suffocate and die. This fear clearly was tied to the fact that her mother asphyxiated as the result of a severe asthma attack. Therefore, Penny was extremely aware of any changes in her breathing patterns, to the point that she would begin to worry if her rate of breathing changed even in reaction to natural and innocuous physical activity. The therapist initially hypothesized that this was one of the reasons that Penny had panic attacks during sexual encounters with her boyfriend. Later, both the therapist and patient would come to realize that Penny's feelings of guilt played a significant role as well.

The therapist asked Penny to keep records of her panic attacks on a panic log (see Figure 18.3). This device helps to spot patterns that pertain to the disorder, including the role of various stressful situations, catastrophic thoughts that typically occur, medications on which the patient relies, and behavioral consequences of the attacks. Penny's panic logs indicated that her attacks had a number of interesting things in common:

1. They occurred in association with extreme interpersonal situations—loneliness at one extreme and sexual feelings or activity at the other extreme.

2. Her agoraphobic symptoms were recent phenomena, and her "safe" distance was just a little shy of the distance she would have to travel in order to spend the night at the home of the man she truly loved, Tim.

3. Each panic attack involved symptoms of hyperventilation, and concomitant fears of sudden death.

Name: _____ Penny _____ Date: _____ November 3–9

Instructions: Please record all instances of panic over the past week. A panic attack is defined as a sudden rush of anxiety in which the symptoms build up quickly. These panic attacks are accompanied by fear or apprehension and at least four symptoms.

Weekly Panic Log

Date, Time, and Duration of Panic Attack	Situation in Which Panic Attack Occurred and Severity of the Panic Attack (1–10)	Description of Panic Attack Symptoms and Sensations Experienced	Interpretaions of Sensations and Accompanying Thoughts and Images	Was This a Full-Blown Attack (Yes/No) If No, Explain Why	Your Response to Panic Attack What Did You Do? (Specify any medication taken and dosage in mgs.)
1. Monday 7:00 PM 40 minutes	Eating dinner alone at home. Feeling scared and lonely. 9	Dizziness. Fainting. Rapid breathing. Heaviness in chest. Choking. Fear of dying.	Afraid I would faint and stop breathing. Nobody would be there to save me.	Yes	I called my boyfriend and asked him to leave work.
2. Friday 8:00 PM An hour	Driving to the office party at Mary's place. 10	Rapid breathing. Choking. Heart palpitations.	I can't drive anymore. I have to stop. I can't cope with seeing Tim at the party.	Yes	I took 1 mg tablet Xanax and went to the party.
3. Saturday 2:00 PM An hour	In the car with my boyfriend. I feel trapped with him. 10	Choking. Sweating. Fear of losing control.	I'm a bad person for wanting to end this relationship. He's so good to me. I feel so guilty.	Yes	I took 1 mg tablet Xanax and tried to sleep, but I was crying.
4. Sunday 10:00 PM	Watching the movie "Terms of Endearment" at home.	Fear of dying. Heart palpitations. Rapid breathing. Fainting.	Why did my mother die? I loved her so much. I'll probably die the same way.	Yes	I cried and talked it out with my boyfriend. He understands my feelings about Mom.

Figure 18.3. Penny's panic log.

4. Each attack was "cured" by the presence of another person, including her boyfriend. The use of Xanax was the next best choice if nobody was nearby.

5. Feelings of anger and guilt also typically preceded Penny's attacks.

These data were invaluable in devising a strategy for treatment. The therapist chose a two-pronged approach that is commonly used in the treatment of panic disorder. One main strategy dealt with the phenomenology of the acute panic attack itself—examining the thoughts, beliefs, emotions, behaviors, and physiological changes that took place before, during, and after the attacks. The goal of this strategy was to modify these aspects of the patient's functioning in order to de-escalate the catastrophic misinterpretations, fears, and physiological arousal.

The second strategy involved examining the patient's entire life situation for broader issues that needed to be addressed. As panic patients often avoid recognizing or dealing with strong emotions *other* than fear (Chambless & Goldstein, 1982), this approach attempted to focus Penny's attention on the issues that the panic attacks often disguised.

Consistent with the first strategy, the therapist taught Penny the role that hyperventilation (Clark, Salkovskis, & Chalkley, 1985; Salkovskis & Clark, 1991) and hypersensitivity to bodily sensations (Ehlers, 1991) played in her panic attacks. Specifically, by worrying about changes in her breathing (e.g., breathing too hard, or feeling constricted and asthmatic) Penny over activated her sympathetic nervous system, which exacerbated the breathing problem by pumping adrenalin into her system so that hyperventilation increased. The resultant symptoms, including dizziness and breathlessness, mimicked oxygen *debt,* thus inducing Penny to try to breath harder. The therapist explained that this reaction was in direct opposition to the body's natural tendency to return to homeostasis— in this case by *reducing* respiration in order to achieve the appropriate balance of oxygen and carbon dioxide in the bloodstream. The result was Penny's subjective sense that she was unable to breathe freely, thus spurring more of her catastrophic misinterpretations about asphyxiating as did her mother. In reality, Penny was in no danger.

The therapist utilized many of the techniques that have been described previously in the cases of Roy and Leslie, but added an important technique that is specifically geared to the panic patient. This technique involves the deliberate induction of a panic attack in session via overbreathing (Beck & Greenberg, 1988; Salkovskis & Clark, 1989). Here, the patient is instructed to breathe deeply and quickly for up to two minutes, while the therapist provides coaching and support (Note: The therapist obtains permission from the patient's primary care physician before undertaking this procedure). In many cases, this exercise precipitates symptoms that mimic panic symptoms. When the breathing trial is over, the therapist asks the patient:

1. What are your thoughts right now?

   This question often elicits the kinds of "hot cognitions" that shed light on the reasons behind the patient's fears.

2. How similar is this experience to an actual panic attack?

   In most cases, patients rate the overbreathing exercise to be highly reminiscent of a full-blown panic attack.

3. What can you conclude about the role of hyperventilation in these panic symptoms?

   Most patients will come to see that overbreathing is a major physiological factor in the onset and exacerbation of the attacks. Although they may argue that they do not breath in such an exaggerated fashion in everyday life, the therapist can point out that while the real-life process is a bit more prolonged and gradual than in the present exercise, the cumulative result is very similar.

4. How do you feel right now?

   Most patients report feeling "recovered" from the effects of this exercise (e.g., breathlessness, dizziness, heart palpitations, nausea) within a minute after normal breathing is restored. This is usually in sharp contrast to their typical experiences with panic, when their catastrophic thinking fuels the attack for a more prolonged period. When the therapist provides distraction in the form of questions, the patients often feel better quite quickly. This serves as an important in vivo learning experience that teaches the patients that they can "turn off" the symptoms by "turning off" the concomitant worries.

5. What does this experience teach you about the degree of control that you have over your panic attacks?

   After taking part in a panic induction exercise, patients come to see that their attacks are more under their control than they had realized. They can deliberately induce the attacks via overbreathing, and they can facilitate their diminution by distracting themselves from their catastrophic worries.

Penny responded very well to the panic induction, as well as the concomitant techniques of *distraction* (e.g., focus attention on a task, or a pleasant memory, or an adaptive cognitive response) and *breathing control* (learning to breathe slowly and gradually in response to anxiety and panic, so as to restore the oxygen/carbon dioxide balance in the bloodstream and therefore reduce the symptoms.)

The therapist also helped Penny to deal with her issues of unresolved grief over her mother's death, as well as her guilt and sexual frustration over her inability to end an over-dependent relationship with a man she didn't want to marry, while she was forfeiting a potential relationship with a man that she *did* want to marry.

Penny had never allowed herself to speak or think at any length or depth about her mother's death. She had used the comforting effects of Xanax and her boyfriend to avoid the issue altogether. Now, however, she wanted to terminate her relationship with her boyfriend, but reacted to these desires with extreme guilt, as well as a sense of doom in that she would have to relinquish her "safe" person. Now, Penny reasoned, if things did not work out with Tim, she would be left to deal with her grief, loneliness, and fears on her own.

Much therapeutic work was done in clarifying the patient's goals for her future. She realized that in order to achieve her life's objectives she would have to: (1) leave her boyfriend, (2) travel more freely, (3) decrease or eliminate her Xanax use, (4) deal with her grief over her mother, and (5) take a chance on a new relationship. Topics that had long been avoided were now being discussed. These issues were very anxiety-arousing for Penny, but she no longer avoided discussing them, as she had learned some powerful tools for coping with the onset of panic attacks.

At this time, she has taken some major steps in changing her life, including: (1) ending her relationship with her boyfriend (resulting in her living alone, a situation with which she has coped beautifully); (2) spending more time with the friends whom she had previously neglected in favor of her boyfriend, (3) taking things very slowly with Tim, so as not to foster dependency once again; (4) significantly cutting back on her overuse of Xanax, to the point where she now uses the medication only on an as-needed basis; and, (5) talking more freely about her mother's death with the therapist and with her closest friends, which makes her feel melancholy, but far less anxious about her own breathing patterns.

OUTCOME STUDIES

There is a growing body of literature that collectively supports the efficacy of the methods that have been outlined in this chapter (e.g., Brown, Beck, Greenberg, Newman, et al., 1991; Butler, Fennel, Robson, & Gelder, 1991; Clark et al., 1985; Newman, Beck, Beck, Tran, & Brown, 1990; Sanderson & Beck, 1991; Sokol, Beck, Greenberg, Wright, & Berchick, 1989).

The Butler et al. (1991) study demonstrated that patients receiving cognitive-behavioral interventions benefited from treatment in terms of diminished anxieties *as well as decreased dysphoria,* thus suggesting that the approach may be successful in treating patients who meet criteria for both an affective disorder and an anxiety disorder.

Sanderson & Beck's (1991) data stand out in that they indicate the efficacy of cognitive therapy for GAD in a natural population, *including those patients who were diagnosed as having at least one concomitant personality disorder* (although the progress of the personality disordered patients was less pronounced than the progress of the nonpersonality disorder group).

The Newman et al. (1990) findings are striking in that the patients demonstrated marked reductions in panic frequency, general anxiety, and depressed affect across the board at termination and at one-year follow-up, *including those patients who tapered off their anxiolytic medications while in cognitive therapy* (over half of the medicated sample succeeded in becoming medication-free by the end of therapy). The importance of these findings cannot be understated, as anxiety disorder patients who use medications such as benzodiazepines often have great difficulty with physiological dependence, tolerance effects, and rebound anxiety and panic upon withdrawal (Rickels, Schweizer, Case, & Greenblatt, 1990).

The data of Brown et al. (1991) provide further support for the cognitive model of panic. The Panic Belief Questionnaire (Greenberg, 1989), having been found to be psychometrically sound, discriminated those patients who responded extremely well to cognitive therapy from those whose progress was less complete. Specifically, the patients who benefited the most endorsed fewer dysfunctional beliefs about panic (e.g., "A panic attack can give me a heart attack."). Those patients who were most successful in modifying their beliefs about panic evinced the most significant and complete recovery from the disorder.

REFERENCES

American Psychiatric Association (1987). *Diagnostic and statistical manual of mental disorders.* (3rd ed., rev.). Washington, DC: Author.

Barlow, D. H. (1988). *Anxiety and its disorders: The nature and treatment of anxiety and panic.* New York: Guilford.

Beck, A. T., Emery, G., & Greenberg, R. L. (1985). *Anxiety disorders and phobias: A cognitive perspective.* New York: Basic Books.

Beck, A. T., Freeman, A., & Associates (1990). *Cognitive therapy of personality disorders.* New York: Guilford.

Beck, A. T., & Greenberg, R. L. (1988). Cognitive therapy of panic disorder. In A. J. Frances & R. E. Hales (Eds.), *American Psychiatric Press Review of Psychiatry* (Vol. 7). (pp. 571–583). Washington, DC: Author.

Beck, A. T., Rush, A. J., Shaw, B. F., & Emery, G. (1979). *Cognitive therapy of depression.* New York: Guilford.

Bibb, J. L., & Chambless, D. L. (1986). Alcohol use and abuse among diagnosed agoraphobics. *Behaviour Research and Therapy, 24,* 49–58.

Brown, G. K., Beck, A. T., Greenberg, R. L., Newman, C. F., Beck, J. S., Tran, G. Q., Clark, D. A., Reilly, N. A., & Betz, F. (1991). *The role of beliefs in the cognitive treatment of panic disorder.* Presented at the Annual Convention of the Association for the Advancement of Behavior Therapy, New York.

Burns, D. D. (1980). *Feeling good: The new mood therapy.* New York: William Morrow.

Butler, G. (1985). Exposure as a treatment for social phobia: Some instructive difficulties. *Behaviour Research and Therapy, 23,* 651–657.

Butler, G. (1989). Phobic disorders. In K. Hawton, P. M. Salkovskis, J. Kirk, & D. M. Clark (Eds.), *Cognitive behaviour therapy for psychiatric problems.* New York: Oxford University Press.

Butler, G., Fennel, M., Robson, P., & Gelder, M. (1991). Comparison of behavior therapy and cognitive behavior therapy in the treatment of generalized anxiety disorder. *Journal of Consulting and Clinical Psychology, 59,* 167–175.

Chambless, D., & Goldstein, A. (Eds.), (1982). *Agoraphobia: Multiple perspectives on theory and treatment.* New York: Wiley.

Clark, D. M. (1988). A cognitive model of panic attacks. In S. Rachman & J. D. Maser (Eds.), *Panic: Psychological perspectives* (pp. 71–89). Hillsdale, NJ: Erlbaum.

Clark, D. M. (1989). Anxiety states: Panic and generalized anxiety. In K. Hawton, P. M. Salkovskis, J. Kirk, & D. M. Clark (Eds.), *Cognitive behaviour therapy for psychiatric problems.* New York: Oxford University Press.

Clark, D. M., Salkovskis, P. M., & Chalkley, A. J. (1985). Respiratory control as a treatment for panic attacks. *Journal of Behavioral Therapy and Experimental Psychiatry, 16,* 23–30.

Ehlers, A. (1991). Cognitive factors in panic attacks: Symptom probability and sensitivity. *Journal of Cognitive Psychotherapy: An International Quarterly, 5*(3), 157–174.

Greenberg, R. L. (1989). Panic disorder and agoraphobia. In J. M. G. Williams & A. T. Beck (Eds.), *Cognitive therapy in clinical practice: An illustrative casebook* (pp. 25–49). London: Routledge & Kegan Paul.

Newman, C. F., & Beck, A. T. (1990). Cognitive therapy of the affective disorders. In B. Wolman & G. Stricker (Eds.), *Depressive disorders: Facts, theories, and treatment methods.* New York: Wiley.

Newman, C. F., Beck, J. S., Beck, A. T., Tran, G. Q., & Brown, G. K. (1990). *Efficacy of cognitive therapy in reducing panic attacks and medication.* Presented at the Annual Meeting of the Association for the Advancement of Behavior Therapy. San Francisco.

Nezu, A. M., Nezu, C. M., & Perri, M. G. (1989). *Problem-solving therapy for depression: Theory, research, and clinical guidelines.* New York: Wiley.

Persons, J. B. (1989). *Cognitive therapy in practice: A case formulation approach.* New York: Norton.

Rickels, K., Schweizer, E., Case, G., & Greenblatt, D. J. (1990). Long-term therapeutic use of benzodiazepines: I. Effects of abrupt discontinuation. *Archives of General Psychiatry, 47,* 899–907.

Salkovskis, P. M. (1988). Phenomemology, assessment and the cognitive model of panic. In S. Rachman & J. D. Maser (Eds.), *Panic: Psychological perspectives* (pp. 11–136). Hillsdale, NJ: Erlbaum.

Salkovskis, P. M., & Clark, D. M. (1989). Affective responses to hyperventilation: A test of the cognitive model of panic. *Behaviour Research and Therapy, 28,* 51–61.

Salkovskis, P. M., & Clark, D. M. (1991). Cognitive therapy for panic attacks. *Journal of Cognitive Psychotherapy: An International Quarterly, 5*(3), 215–226.

Sanderson, W. C., & Beck, A. T. (1991). *Cognitive therapy of Generalized Anxiety Disorder: A naturalistic study.* Presented at the Annual Meeting of the Association for the Advancement of Behavior Therapy, New York.

Sokol, L., Beck, A. T., Greenberg, R. L., Wright, F. D., & Berchick, R. J. (1989). Cognitive therapy of panic disorder: A pharmacological alternative. *Journal of Nervous and Mental Disease, 177,* 711–716.

CHAPTER 19

Interactional Psychotherapy of Anxiety Disorders

BENJAMIN B. WOLMAN, PhD

Fear is a reaction to danger. Fear is related to a low estimate of one's own power as compared to a high estimate of the power of the threatening situation. A change in the balance of power puts an end to fear. Anxiety is not a fear, it is a *prolonged feeling of helplessness and hopelessness.* Anxiety-ridden people expect an impending doom and are afraid to take initiative. They tend to be irritable, are withdrawn, and avoid close social relationships. The change of balance of power does not put an end to anxiety. Anxiety may or may not be related to danger (Barlow, 1988).

Zinbarg, Barlow, Brown, and Hertz (1992) in their review of anxiety disorders, wrote that "despite enormous strides, development of effective psychological treatments of anxiety has not by and large, been guided by theories about the nature of anxiety" (p. 243). However, the present volume describes several psychological treatment methods based on distinct theoretical systems. This chapter introduces a treatment method based on the *interactional theory* (Wolman, 1982).

One of the underlying ideas of interactional psychotherapy is that the treatment of mental disorders is basically a process of *emotional reeducation* as suggested by Alexander and French (1946). People I see in my practice are mature and reasonably well-adjusted adults who function rationally in *some* areas of life, but they have retained some childlike and irrational attitudes and emotions. Some of my patients are physicians, lawyers, and business executives who have done well in their careers, but they have badly mismanaged their personal lives (Wolman, 1973).

There are three phases in interactional therapy: (1) the analytic phase, (2) the search for identity, and (3) self-realization (Wolman, 1984).

THE ANALYTIC PHASE

In this phase, the patient acquires a good sense of reality, emotional balance, and social adjustment. The sense of reality is a necessary prerequisite for any adjustment to life and any chance of finding oneself in life. People who distort reality, who have exaggerated notions of themselves and of the world, or who underestimate themselves or overestimate obstacles can hardly, if ever, live a successful life.

Emotional balance includes four factors. First, the emotional reaction must be appropriate to the situation. We react with sorrow to defeat and with joy to success. Disturbed people react in a paradoxical way, enjoying their defeat and finding success unacceptable. Second, well-balanced emotionality is also proportionate. Disturbed individuals overreact or underreact to success and failure. Manic patients, for instance, can be ecstatic about small successes that don't warrant much joy, while in depressed moods, they experience deep sorrow not related to the real situation. The third factor in emotional balance is the ability to control and express emotions. Infants and disturbed people are unable to control their emotions and react in a way that will serve their purpose and help them in attaining their goals. The fourth factor in emotional balance is adjustability. No matter how deep the sorrow is or how great the joy, life goes on and one cannot live in the past. Neurotics live in the past. Well-adjusted adults never deny the past but instead go ahead in life, being aware of the fact that there is just one road in life, and that road ultimately leads to death. This road must be followed with maximum wisdom and maximum courage.

The third achievement in the analytic phase should be social adjustment. People who have undergone psychotherapy should be able to develop a meaningful relationship with one or more individuals, and to form with others a rational give-and-take relationship that would not hurt them and would prevent them from being hurt by them.

THE SEARCH FOR IDENTITY

The analytic phase clears up past difficulties and enables the individual to think clearly and to act in a realistic way, but it does not solve the problem of direction in life. What patients are going to do with themselves, what life should mean to them, what the goals in their lives are—these are the problems dealt with in the second phase of interactional psychotherapy, which is called the search for identity.

Quite often, toward the end of the first phase, patients feel an abundance of energy; they feel that so much more could be done with their newly acquired energy that has been liberated from inner conflicts. They crave self-realization and fulfillment, and they search for meaning and purpose.

SELF-REALIZATION

The third phase of interactional psychotherapy should enable individuals to decide where they are going to direct their energy, and how they are going to utilize their intellectual and emotional resources. In this phase, patients should find the meaning of their lives.

No human being can always achieve or always do something that pleases him and others. No human being can always be successful. No human being can reach the sun and stars every day, but to have goals and to go in the right direction gives meaning to one's life. Not to have achieved, but *achieving;* not arriving at the inn, but walking toward the inn; not resting on one's laurels, but moving toward those laurels and putting one's talents to the most constructive use.

INSIGHT AND GUIDANCE

Interactional psychotherapy with anxious people who intentionally albeit unconsciously fail in stage performance, exams, tests, job interviews, public appearances, and intimate encounters should be conducted on two levels. The first task of the therapist is to unravel the hidden motivation of the self-defeating person. One cannot solve a problem unless one understands it and actively participates in its resolution (Langs, 1976).

The insight gained in therapy should help to substitute the feelings of inadequacy and helplessness by a realistic appraisal of one's abilities and potential risks. Seeing things as they are and learning to face problems by adequate assessment and mobilization of one's resources enhances one's self-confidence and self-esteem (Craske & Barlow, 1991).

But insight is not enough; one must reinforce the insight by action. Avoidance of dangers does not enhance one's courage. One must force oneself, within reason, to do things one is afraid of. Every effort contributes to one's self-respect, and every victory paves the road for a next and a bigger victory. A combination of *insight* with a *conscious effort* is likely to produce best results (Bandura, 1986).

Interactional psychotherapy is a process of constructive interaction. In most cases, the therapist must offer positive guidance and encourage the patients' conscious efforts and productive activities. If individuals are faced with a threat that their house may be burglarized, they may sit and wait for the burglars to come; but if they put heavy locks on the doors and install an alarm system that connects their apartment with the police, their productive action increases their morale and reduces their feelings of helplessness. Doing things in a purposeful way requires a great deal of self-discipline and it counteracts anxiety and disinhibition. Goal-directed behavior counteracts regression into infantile dependency, because the individuals take their fate in their own hands and do not wait for someone to take care of them. Productive activity leads to an increase in their belief in themselves and reduces their anxiety.

Productive action has a priceless value in cities war-torn by revolution or destroyed by a flood or earthquake. Productive action can produce miracles in group morale. When people, instead of hiding in their houses or shelters, begin to do something to improve their situation, whether by digging trenches against possible attacks by the enemy; by joining the firemen, civil defense units, or medical corps; or any kind of productive action, their actions reduce their anxiety. Giving people productive tasks that can counteract the danger improves their morale, increases their ability to withstand stress, reduces anxiety, and is an important contribution to their mental health.

No one can stand alone, and the more allies, associates, and friends one possesses, the better are the chances for survival. To belong to a group and to interact with other people increases one's feeling of security and reduces anxiety. Loneliness is one of the main sources of anxiety. Lonely people often fear that their enemies will overcome them and no one will come to their aid; the feeling of anxiety is greatly increased by being isolated from other individuals.

In childhood, the attitude of parents, their acceptance and protection, gives the child a feeling of security. The feeling of security is the feeling that one is strong enough to cope with whatever dangers may occur, and this feeling may be fostered by parental attitudes. Karen Horney (1950) was right when she stated that people can renounce their security.

PRINCIPLES OF GUIDANCE

1. Admit to yourself that you are facing a challenge that requires a mobilization of your resources and, most probably, of the total personality.
2. Don't take challenges lightly. Prepare yourself thoroughly. It is better to be overcautious than undercautious. A solid preparation increases the chances for success and reduces the feelings of helplessness and depression (Wolman & Stricker, 1990).

3. Don't assume that you must always be successful. No one can win all the time, especially in competitive tasks where other people may have an edge.

4. You may lose several skirmishes and still win the war; a lost battle is not necessarily the end of the war.

5. The worst fear is the fear of fear. Before taking a chance, you need to clearly analyze the stakes. Testing reality counteracts anxiety. Can you lose what you don't have yet? There might be another chance and other opportunities.

6. You may suffer several defeats, but you should not allow yourself to lose self-respect. You must act in a way so that you could say to yourself: I did everything possible; I have never given up.

The treatment of anxiety in states of emergency should follow the following principles:

1. A *realistic appraisal* of your resources and of the external threats. Such an appraisal reduces anxiety and enables you and the group to seek realistic ways of coping with problems.

2. Directing your reaction of anger *against* external threat. Anger tends to mobilize your resources and increases your power and your estimate of your own power.

3. *Productive* action. Inaction increases anxiety and feelings of guilt. Goal-directed action aimed at reducing the danger (building shelters, erecting fortifications, having air-raid alerts, etc.) reduces the feeling of guilt, increases self-discipline, counteracts the realistic threats, and improves the morale of the group.

4. *Strengthening* of intragroup ties. The feeling of power is increased by having allies, whereas loneliness reduces it. Thus, cementing group unity and fostering interpersonal relations among the members of the group substantially enhances its combat efficiency and morale.

Here is an example of a case. A patient of mine, Dr. H., who applied for a teaching position in sociology, expressed profound anxiety: "I made a mistake. I feel panicky. I don't know what to do," he said. "Who needs it? What for? I applied for a teaching position—I worry they may reject me and I worry they may accept me. I am sure I'll make a fool of myself. The students will find out my ignorance and I will be exposed. Either way, I feel hostile. I better withdraw my application." Dr. H. had received his Ph.D. with distinction. He was a gifted young man, highly qualified in his field. His former professors wrote glowing letters of recommendation, and he had a good chance to be appointed to the faculty of the university.

"Let's check all this against reality," I said. "We can't predict the future, but we can explore the possibilities. Should they turn you down, still there will be no reason for despair. There are more than 50 schools of higher learning in the metropolitan area. If you were the dean, you too would have probably chosen the best qualified candidate. If you are the best one, they will hire you; they may, however, hire someone who is a better-qualified candidate. Should they turn you down, it is not rejection; one cannot lose what one has not got, and you will apply to other schools. If they hire you, you will have several months ahead of you to prepare yourself. You can't predict the future, but you can do your best to prepare yourself for what could be reasonably expected. There are no assurances for either success or failure, but a realistic appraisal of a situation improves the chances for success."

REFERENCES

Alexander, F., & French, T. (1946). *Psychoanalytic therapy*. New York: Ronald Press.

Bandura, A. (1986). *Social foundations of thought and action*. Englewood Cliffs, NJ: Prentice-Hall.

Barlow, D. H. (1988). *Anxiety and its disorders: The nature and treatment of anxiety and panic*. New York: Guilford.

Craske, M., & Barlow, D. H. (1991). *Mastery of your anxiety and worry*. New York: Graywind.

Horney, K. (1950). *Neurosis and human growth*. New York: W. W. Norton.

Langs, R. (1976). *The therapists interaction*. New York: Aronson.

Wolman, B. B. (1973). *Victims of success: Emotional problems of executives*. New York: Quadrangle, New York Times Books.

Wolman, B. B. (1982). Interactional theory. In B. B. Wolman (Ed.), *Handbook of developmental psychology*. Englewood Cliffs, NJ: Prentice-Hall.

Wolman, B. B. (1984). *Interactional psychotherapy*. New York: Van Nostrand Reinhold.

Wolman, B. B., & Stricker, G. (Eds.), (1990). *Depressive disorders: Facts, theories and treatment methods*. New York: Wiley.

Zinbarg, R. E., Barlow, D. H., Brown, T. A., & Hertz, R. M. (1992). Cognitive-Behavioral approaches to the nature and treatment of anxiety disorders. In *Annual Review of Psychology*, Vol. 43, pp. 235–267.

CHAPTER 20

Anxiety and Family Therapy

MICHAEL D. ZENTMAN, PhD

Systemic family therapy, the most prevalent model of family treatment today, views the individual as an integral component of a unit of organization—the family. Systems theory postulates that a person cannot be viewed, nor treated, out of the context in which that person is embedded. This context, the family, may be the nuclear family (one generation) or the extended family (three or more generations). Regardless of whether the focus is the nuclear or extended family, the pathology experienced by an individual is viewed as a manifestation of some level of dysfunction in the family system. The identified patient (IP), the individual that the family is presenting for treatment, is expressing the family's conflict through the metaphor of a symptom. The IP may be viewed as the weak link in the system, the family member who is most vulnerable to stress and, therefore, most likely to develop the symptom. Or one might see the IP as the individual who is most attuned and sensitive to the dysfunction in the system and capable of expressing it in order to facilitate resolution. In either case, the individual's symptoms reflect a family dysfunction rather than an intrapsychic phenomenon. Anxiety, traditionally viewed as an internal psychological process signaling danger, can be examined in the context of the family system.

Nathan Ackerman (1954) was the first clinician to report the treatment of whole families on an ongoing basis. In his effort to clarify the nature of family dynamics and their influence on an individual's psychological functioning, he described the family as a, "conveyor belt for anxiety and conflict. . ." (p. viii). He observed the "contagion of mental illness" that affects all family members with such intensity that no one family member can be immune to its destructive effects. Ackerman observed a process in families in which anxiety shifted erratically from one person to another or from one family pair to another. Although unaware of the impact of his observations on the final direction taken by family theory, his interactive formulations anticipated the current systemic conceptualization of family dynamics.

Like most of the pioneers in family therapy, Ackerman was trained psychoanalytically. This is apparent in theoretical formulations that continuously weave together psychoanalytic concepts and family relational observations in an effort to formulate a separate theory of family treatment. A radical shift took place when Don D. Jackson (1957), also psychoanalytically trained, abandoned the prevailing view of individual psychopathology in favor of the revolutionary belief that pathology did not exist in the individual, but only within relationships. To Jackson, emotional dysfunction and symptomology could be traced to family interaction and pathogenic relationship patterns. The patient was seen as the individual who manifested the covert pathology of the family. Jackson referred to this member of the family as the identified patient, since the actual patient was the family as a whole. Treatment entailed the use of strategic interventions aimed at altering patterns of interaction within the family. Jackson's total rejection of psychoanalytic constructs in favor of observable family interaction was to have a profound effect on the evolving field of family therapy.

As a result of Jackson's view that family theory and psychoanalytic theory were antithetical, a polarization occurred in the family therapy movement. As noted by Samuel Slipp, Watzlawick, Beavin, and Jackson (1967) saw psychoanalysis as discontinuous with systems theory because of its reliance on energy concepts rather than information and transactional patterns to explain motivation and behavior. Jackson and his colleagues erroneously believed that all schools of psychoanalysis subscribed to drive theory when, in fact, much of psychoanalysis had moved beyond this conceptualization to include relationships and issues of adaptation. "The intrapsychic level is not a closed system, . . . but interacts with and determines the interactional level." (Slipp, 1984, p. 34). But the polarization had already taken place. Two models of family systems theory were evolving. One adhered to Jackson's original premise that all psychopathology can be understood within the context of information exchange or transactional patterns. The other incorporated the concept of the family as a system with the traditional view of the individuals as separate entities possessing an inner life affecting both themselves and the family as a whole.

A TRANSACTIONAL/INFORMATION MODEL

Some of the leading theorists subscribing to the transactional/information model include Salvador Minuchin, Jay Haley, John Weakland, Mara Selvini Palazzoli, and Paul Watzlawick. They rely exclusively on patterns of interaction between family members: behavioral, cognitive, or both. Since dysfunctional processes occur in the relational field, between family members rather than within individuals, affective experience is relevant only to the extent that it manifests itself in dyadic interchanges. Anxiety, as an intrapsychic process, is not applicable to these models of family therapy unless it becomes an observable event between two or more people.

Minuchin (personal communication, February 1992) when asked what is the place of anxiety in Structural Family Therapy, replied, "I do not think structural people recognize anxiety." This is true particularly in structural work where transactional patterns of behavior are the medium through which dysfunctional family organization is expressed. While anxiety can be a target symptom in treatment, it does not have a place in the theory of these models of family therapy.

AN INDIVIDUAL/RELATIONAL MODEL

Several theorists approach the family systemically without excluding individual intrapsychic processes including Murray Bowen, James Framo, Ivan Boszormenyi-Nagy, and Carl Whitaker. This list is not comprehensive and in this chapter only Bowen's work will be examined in detail. What they all share is the basic belief that an individual, in addition to being influenced by the push and pull of the family, has an inner life that affects and is affected by the system. Boszormenyi-Nagy considers internalization of objects as a key determinant in his theory on patterns of loyalty (Boszormenyi-Nagy & Spark, 1984, p. 25). Whitaker is constantly living and working in his own and the family's unconscious and primary process. Bowen refers to the need for an, "analysis of deeper intrapsychic problems" in the latter stages of treatment (1990, p. 114). While these theorists are fully committed to the belief that all emotional processes are intimately linked to the family system, they also recognize the existence and importance of the individual's inner experience.

The focus of the remainder of this chapter will be on the work of Murray Bowen, including an overview of Bowen theory, a detailed examination of his theory of anxiety and its place in the family system, followed by treatment considerations. Bowen theory assumes that an understanding of human behavior includes the study of the individual and the relational system. For Bowen, the individual can be understood within the context of two interacting variables: the degree of differentiation of self and the degree of chronic anxiety. Kerr and Bowen (1988) define differentiation as, "the ability to be in emotional contact with others yet still autonomous in one's emotional functioning" (p. 145). This definition refers to a person's capacity to be involved with others in meaningful relationships without experiencing a loss of self; to the person's capacity to manage individuality and togetherness within a relationship system.

Bowen considered individuality and togetherness to be the primary forces that influence the operation of the family emotional system. Individuality is demonstrated in a person's capacity to be distinct; to feel, think, and act for oneself without concern about whether others feel, think, and act in the same way. The responsibility for happiness, comfort, and well-being is one's own. Other people are not blamed for one's shortcomings or failures. Bowen called this the "I" position (Bowen, 1990). Togetherness, or the "we" position, reflects an individual's striving to act, think, and feel like others and have others act, think, and feel like themselves. It defines family members' shared beliefs, attitudes, and philosophies. When a person is in the "we" position, there is a tendency to feel responsible for the experiences of others and hold others to be responsible for one's own feelings, thoughts, and actions. The degree of differentiation of self is a function of the balance between the forces of individuality and the forces of togetherness. Higher levels of differentiation typically accompany a greater capacity for individuality, while lower levels of differentiation correlate with an intolerance for individuality and an excessive need for togetherness. In more practical terms, individuality and togetherness refers to the amount of "life energy" (Kerr & Bowen, 1988) each person invests in a relationship and the amount they direct to their lives separate from the relationship. A state of balance exists and a relationship can develop when each person invests a comparable amount of "life energy" and retains a corresponding amount to direct their own lives. As an outgrowth of this process, people with similar levels of differentiation are drawn to each other and the two people can coexist in a state of relative harmony, with neither feeling too little or too much involvement.

Bowen proposed a scale of differentiation that outlines the qualities of individuals within four ranges of functioning. Before discussing the profiles, a distinction must be made between a person's "basic" and "functional" level of differentiation. Basic level refers to an individual's actual degree of differentiation based on overall assessment of functioning in family relationships, job performance, social relationships, and physical and psychological health over the course of one's lifetime. It can be conceptualized as a person's actual level of differentiation unaffected by external stimuli, not dependent on the relationship process. Functional differentiation is a measure of an individual's current level of functioning and is dependent on the relationship process. It can either be higher or lower than basic level depending upon several factors. People with low levels of basic differentiation will appear higher or lower on the scale under various conditions. As long as environmental, social, economic, and relational stress is low, they can function quite well. Capacity to adjust is enhanced by available supports. When stress is high, functional level diminishes. A person can also appear to function higher on the scale of differentiation in a relationship in which the partner underfunctions. The effect on the partner, however, is a lower level of functional differentiation. Bowen's scale (Bowen, 1990, p. 366) refers to basic differentiation and is divided into four groups:

1. *Low level of differentiation—0 to 25:* These people live in a feeling-dominated world in which it is impossible to distinguish feeling from fact. They are totally relationship bound and lack a cohesive sense of self separate from others. For this reason, their relationships are usually conflictual and difficult to maintain. They experience high levels of chronic anxiety and strive, above all, to find comfort either in extremely dependent relationships or through some other means such as drugs or religious dogma. Since they cannot effectively differentiate between feelings and thoughts, they are almost totally governed by emotional reactivity to external events. Incapable of making decisions for themselves, their thoughts and actions are usually derived from opinions of others. Responses range from automatic compliance to extreme oppositionalism.

2. *Moderate level of differentiation—25 to 50:* People in this range have poorly defined selves, but have the capacity to begin to distinguish between feeling and thought. They continue to be overly influenced by emotional processes and, lacking in beliefs and convictions of their own, are prone to conform to prevailing ideologies. They typically seek outside authorities, such as religion, cultural values, philosophy, rules, the law and politics to define and support their own viewpoints. In the mid-range, 35 to 40, people are sufficiently adaptive and do not manifest the extreme impairment evident in people on the lower end of the scale. Yet they remain highly reactive to emotional stimuli and are sensitized to emotional disharmony. Self-esteem is dependent on others and much energy is invested in the goal of pleasing others in an ongoing effort to receive praise and approval. These people have a well-developed pseudo-self based on adaptation to external beliefs, attitudes, and philosophies. It is created by emotional pressure and can be modified by emotional pressure. Nevertheless, it provides the individual with an ability to reduce anxiety and enhance emotional and physical functioning. Although it lacks the foundation of a solid self, it can effectively provide stability in the person's life. People in the 40 to 50 range have a better developed solid self and are less likely to be severely impaired and more likely to recover completely from the effects of stress.

3. *Moderate to good level of differentiation—50 to 75:* In this range, the capacity to think independently is sufficiently developed to

allow the individual to function autonomously without being dominated by the emotional system. People are freer to make choices of their own, unrestrained by attitudes and opinions of others. There is less chronic anxiety and less emotional reactivity. This enables the person to move freely between emotional closeness and self-directed activity.

4. *High level of differentiation—75 to 100:* Individuals in this range are sure of their beliefs and convictions without the need to be dogmatic and rigid. They can listen to another point of view and modify their own if necessary. This person can listen without reacting and can communicate without antagonizing. Functioning is not affected by praise or criticism and expectations of self and others are realistic. Levels of chronic anxiety are low and most stress is tolerated without becoming symptomatic. For Bowen, the upper ranges of this level are, for the most part, hypothetical.

Level of differentiation determines a person's capacity to adapt to stress and reflects the amount of chronic anxiety experienced in a relationship system. The lower the differentiation, the greater the chronic anxiety. Kerr and Bowen (1988, p. 113) define chronic anxiety as a "process of actions and reactions that, once triggered, quickly provides its own momentum and becomes largely independent of the initial triggering stimuli." In fact, the individual responds to the disturbance in the balance of the relationship, rather than to the triggering event itself. When the relationship is relied on to provide for all of one's social, emotional, and psychological needs, a condition of hypersensitivity is created to the slightest threat to the relationship. A state of chronic anxiety results from the constant fear of change or loss. The level of chronic anxiety is a function of the person's level of basic differentiation. Kerr and Bowen (1988) offer an explanation for why chronic anxiety increases as differentiation decreases. Since differentiation reflects the extent of one's emotional separation from family of origin, the less differentiated, the greater the anxiety about living independently and becoming a responsible adult. People in the 0 to 25 range of differentiation have achieved minimal separation and are continuously overwhelmed with anxiety. With little access to the intellectual system, anxiety escalates and runs rampant. Those individuals in the 25 to 50 range experience a less intense version of chronic anxiety than people lower on the scale. The anxiety most often takes the form of worry, uncertainty, rumination, anticipating the worst, fear of disapproval, concerns over one's inadequacy, and feeling overloaded with responsibility. Well-differentiated people do not depend on others to provide affirmation nor are they inordinately responsible for the psychological well being of others, which leaves them feeling fairly calm and relatively free of chronic anxiety.

The management of chronic anxiety is a complex process that occurs within relationships and within the individual. A relationship develops when two people with similar levels of differentiation find each other. They bring into the relationship an amount of chronic anxiety related to the degree of their struggle to function independently. Initially a good deal of relief from the anxiety will be experienced as each person focuses on the other and provides mutual approval and reinforcement. With low and moderately differentiated couples, neither enters the relationship with a complete sense of self and they compensate each other for the missing ingredients. Together they are a whole person. This initial period of bliss, however, is not likely to last. With reduced individual functioning, each person's well-being and freedom from anxiety hinges on the relationship. Any perceived threat to its balance will threaten harmony and unleash their anxiety.

As differentiation decreases, couples become highly reactive when faced with anxiety. They do not have the capacity to problem solve in a thoughtful manner and must resort to one of several methods to bind the anxiety: adaptation, distancing, conflict, and triangulation. Through the process of adaptation, one or both people accomodate to the relationship with the goal of restoring harmony. When each one accomodates, they give up some individuality to temporarily reduce the threat to togetherness. The price they pay is a further reduction in separateness and decreased flexibility of the relational system. The temporary gain of reduced anxiety is offset by the increased risk of further deterioration of the relationship. When only one person accomodates and sacrifices personal functioning to preserve harmony, they conform to the perceived wishes of the other. In the process, they lose self to the relationship while their partner gains self. This will be reflected in levels of functional differentiation. The one who adapts will underfunction while the other will overfunction.

The creation of distance provides people with emotional insulation from each other. As distance increases, anxiety decreases. While this is an effective strategy to manage chronic anxiety in a relationship, the price is a loss of emotional closeness. Conflict, while creating the appearance of distancing, is actually a more complex process in which the intensity of interaction provides emotional contact while the anger facilitates emotional distance. The basis of the conflict is each person's attempt to control how the other person thinks and acts while simultaneously resisting the attempts of the other to do the same. In other words, they both push for more togetherness while tenaciously holding on to individuality. The anxiety is absorbed in the ongoing conflict. Since it is the process rather than the content of the conflict that is important, the relationship, if sufficiently undifferentiated, will remain chronically embattled.

Triangulation is a process whereby the anxiety generated within a two-person relationship is diluted by the addition of a third party. Anxiety is reduced in the following way (Bowen, 1990, p. 478), "As tension mounts in a two-person system, it is usual for one to be more uncomfortable than the other, and for the uncomfortable one to 'triangle in' a third person by telling the second person a story about the triangled one. This relieves the tension between the first two and shifts the tension between the second and third." The original two people, the 'insiders' of the initial relationship, pull in the third person, the 'outsider,' who now becomes an 'insider' thereby reducing the intensity between the first two. Triangles are repetitive and become very predictable with each family member filling their role as "anxiety generator," "anxiety amplifier," and "anxiety dampener," (Kerr & Bowen, 1988, p. 142). The "generator" sets the emotional tone, gets nervous about a problem, and is often accused of upsetting people. Due to an inability to remain calm, the "amplifier" adds to the problem by exaggerating its urgency and paves the way for the "dampener" to introduce emotional distance in order to control reactivity. While in the short run this will maintain a degree of calm, in the long run, the process of triangulation is perpetuated since no one in the triangle assumes responsibility for their own anxiety. A commonly encountered triangle in clinical practice is father-mother-child. Tension between the couple, in which the father is usually the detached, uninvolved "outsider," is detoured through the child who develops an intense relationship with mother; either conflictual or overly intimate. Mother and child are now the "insiders" and the original dyad, the marital couple, are no longer faced with the intolerable tension.

Although relationships are the most effective anxiety-binders, individuals have other alternatives. People with low levels of differentiation are highly reactive to others and can reduce their anxiety through avoidance of relationships. However, since undifferentiated people also have great emotional need for others, becoming a loner is rarely the preferred option. Substance abuse (including alcohol, tranquilizers, and illegal drugs) is a popular anxiety-binder. The drug not only anesthetizes the user, but also provides the family with a controversial subject to focus on while overlooking more stressful emotional issues. Overeating and undereating serve similar functions for the individual as well as the family. Somatization and hypervigilence to bodily functions are also effective ways to insulate oneself from anxiety. The list is endless and can include overachievement, underachievement, over-spending, gambling, compulsive collecting, perpetual pursuit of academic degrees, and a host of personality characteristics such as pessimism, idealization, indecisiveness, impulsiveness, passivity, aggressiveness, and procrastination. Any action or trait that helps the person avoid conflict or creates a false sense of security will provide insulation from the experience of chronic anxiety in relationship systems.

This discussion of treatment will not focus on anxiety as a target symptom, but rather on the reduction of chronic anxiety as it relates to levels of basic differentiation. As level of differentiation increases, chronic anxiety decreases. Kerr and Bowen (1988, p. 79) state it succinctly, "Focus on self, an awareness of the emotional process in the family, and the ability not to be governed by anxiety and emotional reactivity are all components of a long-term effort to increase one's level of differentiation." The positive outcome of any treatment that results in a change in the individual's personality or character structure, whether the technique is psychoanalytic or systemic, will include an increase in level of basic differentiation. Bowen (Carter & McGoldrick, 1989) used the term "coaching" to describe the treatment process in family of origin work. He directed his therapeutic efforts to that portion of the family that was most motivated and capable of change. This usually meant seeing one or both parents, but rarely the identified patient who is least likely to derive direct benefit from the coaching process (Bowen, 1990). This clinical philosophy is based on Bowen's belief that when one person in a triangle can reduce emotional reactivity while remaining in emotional contact with the other two people, the tension in the triangle, as a whole, will subside. When the central triangle in a family has been altered, other family triangles are automatically modified without the involvement of other family members in treatment. Based on this theory, coaching usually involves therapeutic work aimed at elevating the level of differentiation of one person that will reduce the chronic anxiety of that individual as well as the level of chronic anxiety in the family.

Coaching consists of working with an individual to emotionally separate from family of origin by examining multigenerational dynamics, the individual's place in the system and strategies to normalize relationship patterns and respond appropriately to emotionally toxic issues. It is important to distinguish emotional separation from physical separation. Physical separation, in the form of avoidance of contact or cut-offs [extreme disengagement and distance to the point of no involvement] are merely methods to bind anxiety through distancing. It does not facilitate growth. In fact, coaching attempts to reverse patterns of cutoffs, enmeshment [extreme emotional overinvolvement] and triangles (Carter & McGoldrick, 1989). These dysfunctional patterns of interaction are replaced by increased sharing of self with decreased reactivity. Carter and McGoldrick (1989) outline four stages in coaching: (1) *Detriangling,* which involves the capacity to remain in emotional contact with one's parents without reacting to the traditional demands of the triangle, such as over affiliation with one parent and distancing from the other.

(2) *Person-to-person contact*—in which opportunities are created for individual sharing and exchange with family members in order to move from extreme distance or closeness to genuine intimacy. (3) *Reversals* are prescriptions to behave in the opposite fashion of the family's expectation and thereby facilitate new behavior and alternate patterns of interaction. This might include responding with humor rather than anger and defensiveness, or being playful instead of serious. And finally, (4) *Reconnecting*—establishing or enhancing nuclear or extended-family relationships in order to expand relationship options and become more involved in the larger system, including family history.

Since emotional reactivity undermines emotional autonomy, improving one's level of differentiation and reducing chronic anxiety requires a person to develop more awareness of and control over emotional reactivity. Kerr and Bowen (1988, p. 111) consider treatment to be based on "an intellectual decision to engage people and situations one prefers to avoid and a decision to tolerate the anxiety associated with not doing things one normally does to reduce anxiety in oneself in those situations." It is a slow and arduous process that usually takes several years to accomplish. But the benefits are significant; for the individual in treatment, for their nuclear and extended families, and for future generations that will have the opportunity to develop greater autonomy and independence.

REFERENCES

Ackerman, N. W. (1958). *The psychodynamics of family life.* p. viii. New York: Basic Books.

Boszormenyi-Nagy, I., & Spark, G. M. (1984). *Invisible Loyalties* (3rd ed.). p. 25. New York: Brunner/Mazel.

Bowen, M. (1990). *Family therapy in clinical practice* (4th ed.). p. 114, 366, 478. New York: Aronson.

Carter, B., & McGoldrick, M. (1989). *The changing family life cycle* (2nd ed.). Lexington, MA: Allyn and Bacon.

Jackson, D. D. (1957). The question of family homeostasis. *Psychiatric Quarterly (Suppl.) 31,* 79–90.

Kerr, M. E., & Bowen, M. (1988). *Family Evaluation.* New York: Norton.

Minuchin, S. Personal communication. February 1992.

Slipp, S. (1984). *Object relations—a dynamic bridge between individual and family treatment.* p. 34. New York: Aronson.

Watzlawick, P., Beavin, J. H., & Jackson, D. D. (1967). *Pragmatics of human communications.* New York: Norton.

Whitaker, C. Personal communication.

CHAPTER 21

Group Psychotherapy

MAX ROSENBAUM, PhD

There are many methods of attitudinal change. Some people are influenced by religious healing or religious conversion. Some respond to placebo, while others have succumbed to forms of brainwashing. Jerome Frank (1961) has written about these approaches in great detail, but psychotherapy remains the most effective method of attitudinal change (Strupp, 1973). Group psychotherapy, which harnesses the talents of both patients and the trained group leader, tremendously reinforces the effects of individual psychotherapy.

Today, the practicing professional and the patient in need of psychotherapy find that there is pressure to expedite the process of psychotherapy—to achieve the "quick fix." The pressure comes largely from insurance companies who are pushing the concept of "cost containment" or "managed health care" with a strong emphasis upon biological treatment for psychological problems. As we move toward the real possibility of government rationing of all types of health care, there is pressure to emphasize short-term interventions as a form of psychotherapy. Indeed, some practitioners emphasize that all psychotherapy should be short-term with patients returning through their lifetimes for additional psychotherapy as needed. There is the real possibility that psychotherapists, under the mandate of "curing" emotional problems in 10 or 20 visits, will begin to create a new diagnostic procedure that is wedded to economics rather than the real needs of people in distress.

There are many self-help organizations. For the most part, they effectively relieve the isolation and loneliness that so many emotionally distressed people feel. The patient and professional psychotherapist may ignore the "political agenda" that many self-help groups (which describe themselves as group psychotherapy) proselytize. For example, a self-help group that is devoted to the radical feminist view will obscure or ignore the underlying pathology that is part of the patient's psychic distress. People in distress may be encouraged to look for simplistic solutions to complex problems. As mentioned earlier, the current push to pharmacological intervention may relieve the manifest symptoms but will not resolve intrapsychic distress or problems of relating interpersonally.

This chapter concentrates on the group treatment of anxiety disorders. The current Diagnostic and Statistical Manual of Mental Disorders III (DSM-III-R, rev.) lists six categories of anxiety disorders. These are panic disorder (PD) with or without agoraphobia, obsessive-compulsive disorder (OCD), post-traumatic stress disorder (PTSD), generalized anxiety disorder (GAD), social phobia (SP), and simple phobia. The recommended approaches are education, psychotherapy (psychodynamic), behavior therapy, cognitive therapy, and pharmacological approaches.

The emphasis in this chapter will be upon psychodynamic intervention. There will be some attention given to the rationale and wisdom of combining pharmacological approaches with group psychotherapy approaches.

Therapists who work psychodynamically often differ radically in their ways of working with anxious patients. This is related to their perception of the origins and meaning of anxious behavior. But all psychotherapists agree on the fundamental significance of anxiety in psychopathology. Anxiety is viewed as some type of threat to the self-image. The more traditionally trained psychotherapists define affects as a combination of ideas and experiences of pleasure or unpleasantness. When the affect of unpleasantness becomes combined with an anticipation of danger or disaster, the emotional response is labeled anxiety. If the anxiety continues over prolonged periods, it often leads to depression. The traditionally trained psychotherapist looks for childhood origins as an approach to resolving the disabling effects of anxiety.

There are many different aspects of anxiety. The anxieties of failing in one's responsibility is different from situational anxiety (often referred to as a phobic response). Anxiety about losing one's marital partner is different from anxiety about losing control over one's behavior.

Freud's early model of intervention was based on biology and the physical sciences, related to his early background as a neurologist. He moved on to an awareness of the patient's inner world and to the psychic realities of the inner world. Freud at the outset conceptualized all anxiety as being caused by repression—the libido is blocked or repressed and this converts into anxiety.

As Freud continued his work, he realized that anxiety *caused* repression. This led him to explore the sources of anxiety and to probe more deeply into the realm of psychic conflict. He moved from his example of mechanical blockage to the concept of psychological conflict. He also came to realize that aggression plays a large part in both guilt and anxiety.

In Europe, neurosurgeons who follow a biological approach have used radical interventions for patients who have had many years of incapacitating anxiety disorders (Mindus & Nyman, 1991). This brain operation, known as capsulotomy, appears to be a very drastic intervention and the jury is still out as to the long-term results of this type of intervention. There has been some degree of immediate relief.

Many psychotherapists who work with groups are strongly influenced by Harry Stack Sullivan (1940, 1953a, 1953b), an American psychoanalyst who postulated a view of anxiety based on the idea that it is interpersonal in nature. He stated that anxiety is induced or "caught" from people who were or are significant figures in a person's world. Sullivan stated that three sets of needs had to be met for each person and depending on how these needs were met, anxiety would result—the degree of anxiety related to the unfulfilled need. The basic set of needs according to Sullivan consisted of the biological (satisfaction/fear), interpersonal security (anxiety), and interpersonal intimacy (love/loneliness). The psychotherapists who agreed with Sullivan, such as Erich Fromm (1955), Rollo May (1967), and Frieda Fromm-Reichmann (1950) expanded on Sullivan's view of anxiety. They stressed the need for personal fulfillment—personal expansion and self-knowledge. People who feel unfulfilled often express feelings of anxiety or loneliness. Fromm-Reichmann (1950) went so far as to state that "psychological death" is the end result of people who have not fulfilled themselves and have lived with constant dread.

The other need, personal orientation, a freedom from chaos, has been stressed by Erich Fromm in his writings (1947). He stressed the individual's need for some "rootedness." If this does not occur, people live life in a state of apprehension that leads in turn to what has been called chronic anxiety. Karen Horney also stressed the interpersonal aspects of anxiety (1939).

Current approaches to treatment of anxiety that emphasize psychodynamic inquiry are based on the work of object relations theorists (Guntrip, 1973; Winnicott, 1963) and practitioners who follow the self-psychology approach of Kohut (1971). Each theoretical school emphasizes an approach to anxiety that consists of containing the anxiety, reassuring the patient and ultimately precluding further disabling anxiety reactions.

In Latin America, as well as some European countries, group therapists often use techniques that follow the theoretical constructs of Bion (1959) who was strongly influenced by Melanie Klein and her concepts of personality development. Bion described all groups as shifting back and forth in certain regressive patterns. Bion called this the *basic assumption* (dependency, fight-flight, pairing) and *work* groups. He elaborated upon the complex intertwining between these two forms of group process as the group leader studied any segment of group interaction. A *basic assumption* group may be seen as a group of children who want immediate satisfaction of their needs or what they believe to be their needs.

The *work group* requires concentration and organization to be fully productive and this is where the group leader is very important. Another concept that Bion used is *valency,* referring to the patient's willingness to join with the group in the *basic assumption* (dependency, fight-flight, pairing) (Rioch, 1970). What Bion was postulating was a vision of the human being. In this respect, like all seminal thinkers, he had a vision of humankind.

Current research indicates that some people are more vulnerable to stress than others. Research that utilizes positron emission tomography (PET) indicates different levels of energy use in the limbic system of the brain leads to a panic disorder associated with fear and anxiety. It appears that some people are born with a genetic predisposition, which may effect the chemical system of the brain, so that they find difficulty in coping with stress and the chaos of everyday life. These are people often referred to as "high strung." There is controversy over whether or not stress experiences in childhood or adolescence may sensitize the brain's system so that these people are susceptible to generalized anxiety—a persistent nagging feeling that something is wrong. This feeling often escalates into panic attacks.

The current physiological research leads back to childhood and the impact upon the individual. A combination of drugs and psychosocial approaches appears to be effective with 80 to 90% of people who come for treatment. The approach must be tailored to the individual. While it is wise to be consistent as to the approach one will use with a patient, it is equally important to recognize that options are available.

The psychotherapist must recognize the physical symptoms that accompany anxiety: shortness of breath, faintness or dizziness, rapid heart rate or palpitations, nausea and stomach pain, trembling or excessive sweating, a feeling of unreality, numbness or tingling of extremities, chest pains and finally the most frightening—fear of "going crazy" or total loss of control. Freud's daughter, Anna Freud (1966) differentiated between anxiety and fear. *Fear* is related to an individual's response or attitude to *real* dangers that threaten one from the outside. *Anxiety* is a reaction to *internal* threats that come from one's psyche. *Anxieties* may develop into phobic behavior. *Fears* do not.

Experienced group psychotherapists do *not* ignore options of psychotherapy. Years of experience have indicated the enormous impact that group psychotherapy has when it is practiced by *experienced* group leaders.

The history of group psychotherapy goes back to the beginning of recorded time, since every religious movement that reaches groups of people might be described as group psychotherapy. This chapter is concerned with systematic approaches using the group method to relieve emotional problems, specifically anxiety reactions.

Joseph Hersey Pratt, an internist who practiced in Boston, Massachusetts, is considered to be the founder of contemporary group psychotherapy (1953). He began his work in 1905, working with tubercular patients who were discouraged and disheartened—in short, despairing and anxious. Most of Pratt's patients were of limited educational background and were victims of social disdain, since tuberculosis was considered a social disease. In many ways, the psychological climate was quite similar to what AIDS patients experience today.

As Pratt lectured, inspired, and cautioned his group of patients, he found that the spirit of camaraderie overcame whatever religious, ethnic, or racial differences existed among the tubercular patients. His work confirmed the writings of the French psychiatrists, Dejerine and Gauckler (1913) who wrote at the beginning of the 20th century that psychotherapy consisted mainly of the beneficial influence of one individual upon another. Another pioneer in group psychotherapy, Trigant Burrow (1927) was excited about the use of group approaches to emotional problems. His work was not greeted with great enthusiasm by Freud, to put it mildly. Freud viewed Burrow's work as an effort "to change the world." So Burrow worked in isolation as did Moreno (1946), the founder of psychodrama, a group psychotherapy approach that utilized a theatre method to resolve emotional problems. The various group approaches have been covered by this author (Rosenbaum, 1976) elsewhere, but it is important to know that whatever approach is used, group psychotherapy remains an effective way of treating people who are disabled because of anxiety.

Whatever labels are used in describing a group psychotherapy intervention: transactional analysis, psychodrama, interactional, interpersonal—there are basic principles at work when patients meet in a group led by a trained professional.

The group treatment of people who are anxiety-ridden may range from a repressive-inspirational approach with the emphasis on support and reassurance, to a regressive-reconstructive approach, where the emphasis is to elicit information about the original traumas that have led to the current problems.

A group that is largely repressive-inspirational in nature will be formed in the belief that the group members have a common problem. The emphasis will be upon support. The group leader will be directive and actively controlling since group members are perceived as "not knowing." The hope is that group members, once they have learned how to handle the overt problem, will no longer need to meet with one another. The group leader will be active, directive, inspirational, and advice-giving. The emphasis will be on current reality. Approaches that are cognitive (intellectual), behavioral, and educative represent the repressive-inspirational aspect of psychotherapy. If a group is composed of post-coronary patients who are anxiety-ridden about future life, support and reassurance are stressed. The group may be considered homogeneous in nature. The goal is to help with the transient anxiety. If male group members are concerned about their sexual activity, reassurance is appropriate as well as information and direction. If the ostensible anxiety about sexual activity masks a long-term anxiety about sexual impotence and fears of relating to women, the goals moves toward regressive-reconstructive group psychotherapy where the treatment is directed toward personality change. The woman who has had a mastectomy and is deeply anxious and troubled about her sexual attractiveness may be a suitable candidate for a short-term therapy group that is oriented toward reassurance. But if her mastectomy caps a long-term dissatisfaction with her body as well as her personality, her anxiety is of a more profound nature, and she is best served by becoming part of a long-term group that is totally heterogeneous, as is the outside world, and includes men and women and every variety of race, culture, and social class, as well as any emotional disturbance. This lends itself to a "talking" type of group psychotherapy. In this kind of group, members mature and leave the group and new members are introduced. Like life, the group never ends. Symbolically there are births—members entering the group—and deaths—actual or those who become discouraged about group psychotherapy and leave.

The group leader promotes the expression of affect in this type of group psychotherapy and encourages the re-enactment of past historical events, especially intrafamilial relationships. This is all related to behavior in the therapy group. Dreams, as well as fantasies and delusions, are brought to the group where they are discussed and explored. The immediate interaction of group members is analyzed as well as the personality mechanisms at work in the interaction. The group leader helps clarify the compulsive mechanisms at work and points to their recurrent nature. This is intensive group psychotherapy.

Most of the current controversies that relate to the use of group psychotherapy are concerned with the emphasis that some group therapists place upon the "group as a whole." In this approach, there is minimal attention given to the individual and intrapsychic exploration, and much emphasis is placed upon the curative value of the group and individual participation in the group. Alexander Wolf (1949), an early worker in the field of group psychotherapy, stressed that working with a group replaces the ideal of the single *parent-psychotherapist.* Instead of the omniscient ego ideal of the individual psychotherapist, the patient is presented with a group "with whose common aims he must align himself." The group precludes the evasion of social reality, which may exist in the one-to-one relationship of individual treatment. According to Wolf, "participation in the group helps to destroy the false antithesis of the individual versus the mass by helping the patient to become aware that his fulfillment can only be realized in a social or interpersonal setting." Yet in spite of the fact that Wolf apparently recognizes the importance of the "corrective emotional experience" (Alexander & French, 1946), which includes a corrective social experience, he and others who agree with him remain hostile to a group therapy approach that stresses group dynamics. He asks, "How do group dynamics achieve a healing objective?" (Wolf & Schwartz, 1962). In his most recent work (Wolf & Kutash, 1991), he remains antagonistic to the emphasis upon group dynamics in the "group as a whole" approach. He has attempted to work toward an egalitarian ideal in group therapy. His goal was the diminution of his own leadership role. He aimed for the distribution of authority, power, and leadership among his group of patients. He stressed that the *group qua group* cannot become the means by which its members resolve *intraphysic* difficulty. He stressed that he does not treat a group, but rather the individual in interaction with other individuals.

Wolf's approach is in marked contrast to group therapists such as Yalom (1985), a practitioner and researcher, who stresses *interaction* rather than the *intrapsychic*. Wolf's emphasis upon the individual within the group approach ignores the possibility that the group therapist's interpretation of the psychodynamics of the individual patient (or the transference at work) may encourage a certain degree of passivity on the part of group members as the group leader is seen as most expert. This "passivity" may be seen as a phase the group goes through until group members move toward autonomy.

The most quoted writer in group psychotherapy (Yalom, 1985) is fully wedded to an interactional approach to work with groups. He supports the ideas of concurrent group and individual therapy, the use of co-therapists (Roller & Nelson, 1991), the use of videotape (Berger, 1978), and a written summary that is shared with the patients.

Gill and Brenman (1948) stressed that the therapist's understanding of "emotional intercommunications" is central to psychotherapy. They noted that sound movies or other technical aids (long before the advent of video and other technical devices) could not replace the psychotherapist's hypotheses, predictions, and goals about the course of treatment. These "may prove the central methodological tool in clinical research." Their comments remain relevant today. Rosenbaum (1978) has set forth the issues of privacy and privileged communication that are involved if videotape techniques are used as part of group psychotherapy.

In the early editions of Yalom's book, the concept of transference was largely ignored in his approach, but in time, Yalom finally elaborated upon this important aspect of all psychotherapy. Yet he continues to ignore the aspects of countertransference—the therapist's response to the patient based upon unresolved problems of the therapist, having little or nothing to do with the patient. The essential difference between the analytic group psychotherapist and the group therapist who stresses an interactional approach is the emphasis placed upon countertransference as part of the healing process. Yalom has come to the position that ". . . cure is an illusion . . . the passing years have taught us that psychotherapy affects growth or change. . . ." It is just possible that therapists are beginning to be more thoughtful about issues such as responsibility, mortality, and the consequences of our own behavior—issues that have been avoided all too frequently. Rosenbaum (1982) has stressed in his own writings, that patients must be confronted with the ethical issues involved in living. This does *not* mean that a psychotherapist is to be a moralist, a task best left to the clergy. But there are ethical issues involved in all of life's decisions, and this is a proper area for group discussion, without the issues becoming politicized.

One group psychotherapy approach that has experienced a renaissance, especially in Europe and South America, is Moreno's technique of psychodrama, which is a form of group psychotherapy. Moreno's approach is action-oriented and his students have attempted to change patterns of social relatedness. Modifications of his technique include sociodrama, role playing, sociometry, and axiodrama. Moreno described psychodrama (1946; 1957) as using five instruments:

1. *The stage* which represents an extension of life beyond the reality of life. The stage is circular and may be equated with the aspiration levels of an individual moving from one circle of life to another.
2. *The patient* who is requested to be himself or herself on stage and to share private thoughts, to act freely, and *not* to perform.
3. *The director* who analyzes, interprets, and integrates the perceptions of the audience. The director keeps the action moving and maintains rapport with the audience—an integral part of the group process. The director may attack, criticize, or engage in humorous repartee with the patient.
4. *The auxiliary egos* who are a staff of people who serve as therapeutic actors, extensions of the director who portray real or imagined people in the patient's life.
5. *The audience* which has a double purpose. It serves first as a sounding board. Since it is a heterogeneous group, the audience is spontaneous in its responses. The patient, immobilized by anxiety, is helped by the accepting and understanding audience who confirms for the patient that all of us have been anxious to some degree. Secondly, the anxious patient also helps the audience as the patient reenacts the collective problems of audience members.

Moreno believed strongly in the importance of group participation. He stated that he had rediscovered the therapeutic aspects of the Greek drama and its effects upon mental catharsis. He stated, ". . . the psyche which originally came from the group, after a process of reconversion on the stage—personified by an actor (THE PATIENT)—returns to the group—in the form of psychodrama . . ." (1946).

Whatever theoretic format the group therapist follows, whether psychodynamic or behavioral, the most important aspect is the group therapist's capacity to cope with the manifest anxiety of the patient. We are clearly in the area of countertransference. Experience has indicated that the matching of the patient and the therapist is central to the therapeutic process. The psychotherapist who makes first contact with the anxiety-ridden patient serves as the transition point to the group. It is the patient's trust or distrust of this individual that will make therapy, at least at the outset, feasible or a failure.

Every patient, when the idea of a group is suggested, views the therapist as rejecting the one-to-one relationship. While the patient may not overtly express the feeling of being rejected, the therapist must be aware of this and believe strongly that the group experience is helpful and central to the patient's recovery and change. The patient will often believe that the group experience is second class in nature and experience the idea of group therapy as abandonment. The anxious patient often feels that his or her suffering is not significant enough to warrant the valued one-to-one relationship. It is possible that the patient has experienced a paucity of one-to-one experiences in early life and needs prolonged preparation before the idea of a group is brought to the fore. The anxiety-ridden patient is often dismissed as being attention-seeking or crying "wolf" much too often. But the pain and fear is real and the symptoms *are* disabling.

The psychotherapist is easily caught up in the symptomatology of the anxious patient and may rush to pharmacological intervention, but this type of intervention is only indicated when the anxiety is so paralyzing that it interferes with systematic psychological work in the group. Karasu (1982) has pointed out that medication is indicated for a "state" and psychotherapy is preferred when there is a "trait disorder" that has been long lasting. Group psychotherapists who are firmly wedded to a psychoanalytic tradition often express the opinion that therapy will be "contaminated" if medication is proposed, except in very critical situations. But current experience indicates that patients who are encouraged to discuss their medications openly as part of the group process will profit from an ancillary method of helping them cope with disabling anxiety. A more important problem is whether the group therapist should be the person who prescribes the medication. Does this influence the course of treatment and lead to too much dependency on the patient's part? The danger is that group psychotherapists may rush to the use of medication for patients as a way of coping with the therapist's anxiety about the patient's anxiety.

Group psychotherapy continues to be an effective method of treating patients who present anxiety problems that are disabling. It is critical that the therapist be aware of his or her need to be overprotective and directive. Anxiety-ridden patients need careful preparation for the group, otherwise the group becomes a life-long "crutch" and no substantial internal psychic change has occurred. Life-long dependency characterizes many of the self-help groups. Yet, there may be individuals who are so vulnerable through the years that they need the support of a subculture. But this is *not* group psychotherapy where the group is led by a professionally trained therapist.

Unlike Yalom, this writer believes that people are capable of dramatic change. The use of the word "cure" leads us into a blind alley. It makes more sense to use the word "change" which means becoming "something different." The word "help" means aid or support. Much of "change" in the patient depends upon the motivation and skill of the group psychotherapist. As research continues in the field of psychotherapy, we will find answers as to why some patients complete a process of group psychotherapy so successfully and others fail to achieve any significant growth. My own surmise is that the differential diagnosis is of critical importance. All too often, patients are "swept" into groups. Most important is the careful matching of the therapist and the patient and what earlier writers have called a "therapeutic alliance" (Zetzel, 1956) or a "working alliance" (Greenson, 1967). This is especially true with the anxiety-disabled patient who feels immobilized. The support, reassurance, and encouragement to explore, all of which exist in an effective group, bodes well for the patients who are diagnosed as suffering from anxiety disorders.

REFERENCES

Alexander, F., & French, T. M. (1946). *Psychoanalytic therapy.* New York: Ronald Press.

Berger, M. M. (1978). *Videotape techniques in psychiatric training and treatment* (rev. ed.). New York: Brunner/Mazel.

Bion, W. R. (1959). *Experiences in groups.* New York: Basic Books.

Burrow, T. (1927). The group method of analysis. *Psychoanalytic Review, 14,* 268–280.

Dejerine, J., & Gauckler, E. (1913). *The psychoneuroses and their treatment.* Philadelphia: Lippincott.

Frank, J. D. (1961). *Persuasion and healing.* Baltimore: Johns Hopkins University Press.

Freud, A. (1966). The ego and the mechanisms of defense. In *The writings of Anna Freud* (vol. 2). New York: International Universities Press.

Fromm, E. (1947). *Man for himself.* New York: Rinehart.

Fromm, E. (1955). *The sane society.* New York: Henry Holt.

Fromm-Reichmann, F. (1950). *Principles of intensive psychotherapy.* Chicago: University of Chicago Press.

Gill, M. M., & Brenman, M. (1948). Research in psychotherapy: Roundtable 194. *American Journal of Orthopsychiatry, 18,* 100–110.

Greenson, R. (1967). *The technique and practice of psychoanalysis.* New York: Hallmark Press.

Guntrip, H. (1973). *Psychoanalytic theory, therapy, and the self.* New York: Basic Books.

Horney, K. (1939). *New ways in psychoanalysis.* New York: Norton.

Karasu, T. B. (1982). Psychotherapy and pharmacotherapy: Toward an integrative model. *American Journal of Psychiatry, 138,* 1102–1113.

Kohut, H. (1971). *The analysis of the self.* New York: International Universities Press.

May, R. (1967). *Psychology and the human dilemma.* New York: Van Nostrand Reinhold.

Mindus, P., & Nyman, H. (1991). Normalization of personality characteristics in patients with incapacitating anxiety disorders after capsulotomy. *Acta Psychiatrica Scandinavia, 83,* 283–291.

Moreno, J. L. (1946). Psychodrama and group therapy. *Sociometry, 9,* 249–253.

Moreno, J. L. (1957). *The first book on group psychotherapy.* New York: Beacon House.

Pratt, J. H. (1953). The use of Dejerine's methods in the treatment of common neurosis by group psychotherapy. *Bulletin of the New England Medical Center, 15,* 1–9.

Rioch, M. J. (1970). The work of Wilfred Bion on groups. *Psychiatry, 33,* 56–66.

Roller, B., & Nelson, V. (1991). *The art of co-therapy.* New York: Guilford Press.

Rosenbaum, M. (1976). Group psychotherapies. In B. B. Wolman (Ed.), *The therapist's handbook* (Chapter 7). New York: Van Nostrand Reinhold.

Rosenbaum, M. (1978). The issues of privacy and privileged communication. In M. M. Berger (Ed.), *Videotape techniques in psychiatric training and treatment* (Chapter 26). New York: Brunner/Mazel.

Rosenbaum, M. (1982). *Ethics and values in psychotherapy.* New York: Free Press.

Strupp, H. H. (1973). *Psychotherapy: Clinical research and theoretical issues.* New York: Aronson.

Sullivan, H. S. (1940). Conceptions of modern psychiatry. *Psychiatry, 3,* 1–117.

Sullivan, H. S. (1953a). *Conceptions of modern psychiatry* (2nd ed.). New York: Norton.

Sullivan, H. S. (1953b). *The interpersonal theory of psychiatry.* New York: Norton.

Winnicott, D. W. (1963). *The maturation processes and the facilitating environment.* New York: International Universities Press.

Wolf, A. (1949). The psychoanalysis of groups. *American Journal of Psychotherapy, 3,* 16–50.

Wolf, A., & Kutash, I. (1991). *Psychotherapy of the submerged personality.* New York: Aronson.

Wolf, A., & Schwartz, E. K. (1962). *Psychoanalysis in groups.* New York: Grune & Stratton.

Yalom, I. D. (1985). *The theory and practice of group psychotherapy* (3rd ed.). New York: Basic Books.

Zetzel, E. R. (1956). An approach to the relation between concept and content in psychoanalytic theory. *The Psychoanalytic Study of the Child, 11,* 99–121.

Author Index

Subject Index